THE ENCYCLOPEDIA OF CHRISTIANITY

VOLUME III

GENERAL EDITOR
Philip E. Hughes

COORDINATING EDITOR
George R. Jaffray

ASSOCIATE EDITORS:
Morton H. Smith
Gordon H. Clark
J. Barton Payne
Charles Pfeiffer
C. Gregg Singer
Allan A. MacRae

GRAMMARIAN:
Carol Dykstra

MANAGING EDITOR
Jay Green

TYPOGRAPHER
Earl Powell

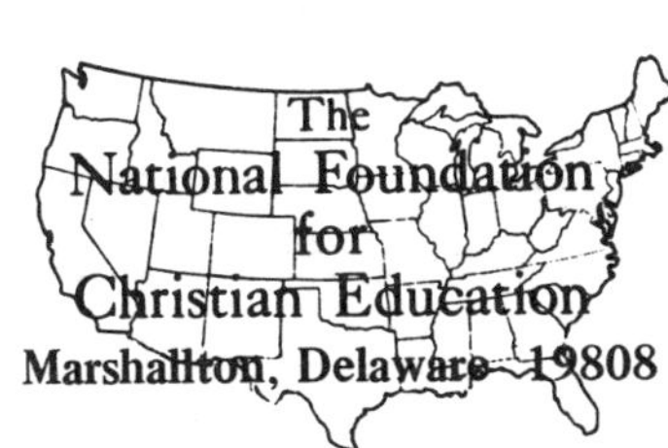

List of Contributors

Aalders, J.G., D.D.
Acworth, Richard, M.A. D-es-L (Sorbonne)
Adams, Jay E., S.T.M., Ph.D.
Andersen, Francis I., M.A., M.Sc., B.D., Ph.D.
Aune, David E., M.A., Ph.D.
Bales, James D., M.A., Ph.D.
Barkley, Alexander, M.A., B.D.
Bird, Herbert S., Th.M.
Blair, Hugh J., B.D.
Bodey, Richard A., A.B., M.Div.
Boland, Michael, M.A.
Broomall, Wick, A.M., Th.M.
Brown, Colin, B.D., Ph.D.
Bruce, F.F., M.A., D.D.
Buis, Harry, A.B., Th.M.
Cadier, Jean, D-em-Th.
Clark, Gordon H., Ph.D., D.D.
Cameron, William J., A.M., B.D.
Cohen, Gary G., B.S., Th.D.
Collins, G.N.M., B.D.
Courthial, Pierre, B.A., L.Th.
Dean, Lloyd F., M.A., Th.D.
DeKlerk, Peter J.S.
DeJong, Peter Y., S.T.M., Ph.D.
Douglas, J.D., M.A., S.T.M., Ph.D.
Duffield, Gervase E., M.A.
Duggan, Paul, B.A., B.D.
Ehlert, Arnold D. M.S.L.S., Th.D.
Ellison. H.L., B.A., B.D.
Emerson, D.N., LL.B., B.D., Ph.D.
Feenstra, Y., Th.D.
Foster, Lewis, A.M., S.T.M., Ph.D.
Franz, Harold J., A.M.
Freeman, David F., Th.M., Ph.D.
Freeman, David Hugh, M.A., Ph.D.
Freundt, Albert H., Jr., M.Div.
Gispen, W.H., Litt. Sem.M., Th.D.
Goddard, Burton L., S.T.M., Th.D., S.M.
Green, Jay P.
Grier, William Jr., B.A.
Harris, R. Laird, A.M., Th.M., Ph.D.
Harrison, R.K., Ph.D., D.D.
Hills, Edward F., Th.D.
Holliday, J.F., B.A., D.D.
Hughes, Philip E., M.A., D. Littl., Th.D.
Huttar, Charles A., A.M., Ph.D.
Jaffray, G.R., Jr., B.S., M.Div., M.A.
Jewett, Paul K., Th.M., Ph.D.
Kistemaker, Simon, A.B., Th.D.
Klassen, Peter J., M.A., Ph.D.
Knudsen, Robert D., Th.M., S.T.M., Ph.D.
Kuiper, R.B., A.M., B.D.
Leith, T.H., A.M.
Lovelace, Richard, B.A., Th.D.
Malefyt, Calvin S., Th.B., Ph.D.
Miller, R. Strang, B.A., LL.M., B.D.
Miller, Ward S.
Morris, Leon, M.Sc., M.Th., Ph.D.
Mulder, H., Th.D.
Murray, John, M.A., Th.M.
Nauta, D., Th.D.
Nederhood, Joel, A.B., Th.D.
Nicholas, Elmer H., B.D., M.A.
Nicole, J.M., M.A., S.T.M.
Packer, James I., M.A., Ph.D.
Payne, J. Barton, M.A., Th.D.
Pfeiffer, Charles F., S.T.M., Ph.D.
Praamsma, Louis, Th.D.
Reid, W. Stanford, Th.M., Ph.D.
Renwick, Alexander, A.M., Litt.D., D.D.
Ridderbos, Herman, D.Th.
Robinson, D.W.B., M.A., B.D.
Rodgers, John H., Jr., B.S., Th.D.
Rookmaaker, H.R., Ph.D.
Rowdon, Harold H., B.A., Ph.D.
Runia, K., Th.D.
Rushdoony, Rousas, M.A., B.D.
Sanderson, John, A.M., S.T.M., D.D.
Schulze, E.P.
Shepherd, Norman, B.A., Th.M.
Singer, C. Gregg, A.M., Ph.D.
Skilton, John H., Ph.D. Th. B.
Smith, Morton H., B.A., Drs, Th.D.
Spires, T. Grady, S.T.M.
Sproul, Robert C., B.A., B.D., Drs.
Thornbury, John, B.A.
Thorne, Charles Greenwood, Jr., A.M., B.Phil., M.Litt.
Tiller, John, M.A.
VanGroningen, Gerard, M.A., M.Th., Ph.D.
Vos, Johannes G., A.B., Th.M.
Wallis, Wilber B., M.A., S.T.M., Ph.D.
Wells, David F., Th.M., Ph.D.
Whitcomb, John C., Jr., A.B., Th.D.
Wood, Leon J., Th.M., Ph.D.
Woudstra, Sierd, A.B., Th.M.
Wright, J. Stafford, M.A.
Young, Edward J., Th.M., Ph.D.
Young, William, B.A., B.Litt., Th.D.

ABBREVIATIONS

I. Books of the Bible

Old Testament (OT)

Gen.
Ex.
Lev.
Num.
Deut.
Josh.
Judges
Ruth
I and II Sam.
I and II Kings
I and II Chron.
Ezra
Neh.
Esther
Job
Ps. (Pss.)
Prov.
Eccles.
Song of S.
Isa.
Jer.
Lam.
Ezek.
Dan.
Hos.
Joel
Amos
Obad.
Jonah
Micah
Nahum
Hab.
Zeph.
Hag.
Zech.
Mal.

New Testament (NT)

Mt.
Mark
Luke
John
Acts
Rom.
I and II Cor.
Gal.
Eph.
Phil.
Col.
I and II Thess.
I and II Tim.
Titus
Philemon
Heb.
Jas.
I and II Pet.
I, II, and III John
Jude
Rev.

II. Books of the Apocrypha

I and *II Esd.*
Tob.
Jth.
Ad. to Esther
Sir.
Ecclus.
Bar.
Sus.
Song of 3 Ch.
Bel and Dragon
Pr. of Man.
I and *II Macc.*
Wisd. of Sol.

III. Versions of the Bible

AT — American Translation
ARV — American Standard Revised Version
ARVm — American Standard Revised Version, margin
AV — Authorized Version (King James Bible)
BV — Berkeley Version
DV — Douay Version (RC)
ERV — English Revised Version
ERVm — English Revised Version, margin
EV — English Version(s) of the Bible
MKJV — Modern King James Version
NEB — New English Bible
RV — Revised Version
RVm — Revised Version, margin
RSV — Revised Standard Version
Vulg. — Vulgate
LXX — Septuagint
MT — Massoretic text
Syr. — Syriac

IV. Publications

AARAB — *Annales de l'Académie royale d'archéologie de Belgique*, Brussels.
AAS — *Acta Apostolicae Sedis*, Rome.
AASOR — *Annual of the American Schools of Oriental Research*, New Haven.
ABR — *Australian Biblical Review*, Melbourne.
ACO — *Acta Conciliorum Oecumenicorum*, Strasbourg.
ACW — *Ancient Christian Writers*, London.
ADAJ — *Annual of the Department of Antiquities of Jordan*, Jerusalem.
AER — *American Ecclesiastical Review*, Washington, D.C.
AFO — *Archiv für Orientforschung*, Graz.
AHR — *American Historical Review*, New York.
AJA — *American Journal of Archaeology*, Baltimore.
AJPh — *American Journal of Philology*, Baltimore.
AJSLL — *American Journal of Semitic Languages and Literatures*, Chicago.
AJTh — *American Journal of Theology*, Chicago.
AKKR — *Archiv für katholisches Kirchenrecht*, Mainz.
ALBO — *Analecta Lovaniensia Biblica et Orientalia*, Louvain.
Alf — H. Alford, *Greek New Testament*.
ALKG — *Archiv für Litteratur- und Kirchengeschichte des Mittelalters*, Freiburg.
AnalBoll — *Analecta Bollandiana*, Brussels.
ANET — J. B. Pritchard (ed.), *Ancient Near Eastern Texts Relating to the OT*, Princeton.
Ang — Angelos, *Archiv für neutestamentliche Zeitgeschichte und Kulturkunde*, Leipzig.
AOr — *Acta Orientalia*, Leiden.
ARG — *Archiv für reformationsgeschichte*, Gütersloh.
Arndt-G — W. F. Arndt and F. W. Gingrich, *A Greek-English Lexicon of the New Testament*, Chicago.
ARW — *Archiv für Religionswissenschaft*, Leipzig.
ASBoll — *Acta Sanctorum Bollandiana*, Brussels.
ATR — *Anglican Theological Review*, Evanston.
AuC — *Antike und Christentum*, Münster.

BA — *Biblical Archaeologist,* New Haven.
BASOR — *Bulletin of the American Schools of Oriental Research,* New Haven.
Bauer, Wb — W. Bauer, *Wörterbuch zum Neuen Testament*^{4}, Giessen.
BDASI — *Bulletin of the Department of Antiquities of the State of Israel,* Jerusalem.
BDB — Brown, Driver and Briggs, *Hebrew and English Lexicon of the Old Testament.*
Beng — J. Bengel, *Gnomon of the New Testament,* Edinburgh.
BFChrTh — *Beiträge zur Förderung christlicher Theologie,* Gütersloh.
BHG — *Bibliotheca Hagiographica Graeca*^{2}, Brussels.
BHL — *Bibliotheca Hagiographica Latina,* Brussels.
BHO — *Bibliotheca Hagiographica Orientalis,* Brussels.
BIES — *Bulletin of the Israel Exploration Society,* Jerusalem.
BiOr — *Bibliotheca Orientalis,* Leiden.
BiTrans — *Bible Translator,* Amsterdam.
BJPES — *Bulletin of the Jewish Palestine Exploration Society,* Jerusalem.
BJRL — *Bulletin of the John Rylands Library,* Manchester.
BK — *Bibel und Kirche,* Stuttgart-Bad Cannstatt.
BMQ — *British Museum Quarterly,* London.
BQ — *Baptist Quarterly,* Philadelphia.
BQR — *Baptist Quarterly Review,* Philadelphia.
BR — *Biblical Research,* Chicago.
BS — *Bibliotheca Sacra,* Dallas.
BSOAS — *Bulletin of the School of Oriental and African Studies,* London.
BTAM — *Bulletin de théologie ancienne et médiévale,* Louvain.
BW — *Biblical World,* Chicago.
BZ — *Biblische Zeitschrift,* Basel.
BZF — *Biblische Zeitfragen,* Zürich.
CAH — *Cambridge Ancient History,* Cambridge.
CBQ — *Catholic Biblical Quarterly,* Washington, D.C.
CE — *Catholic Encyclopaedia,* New York.
CGT — *Cambridge Greek Testament,* Cambridge.
CH — *Church History,* New York.
Charles, APOT — R. H. Charles (ed.), *Apocrypha and Pseudepigrapha of the Old Testament,* Oxford.
CHJ — *Cambridge Historical Journal,* Cambridge.
ChQR — *Church Quarterly Review,* London.
CHR — *Catholic Historical Review,* Washington, D.C.
ChrE — *Christelijke Encyclopedie,* Kampen.
CIG — *Corpus Inscriptionum Graecarum,* Berlin.
CIJ — *Corpus Inscriptionum Judaicarum,* Paris.
CIL — *Corpus Inscriptionum Latinarum,* Berlin.
CIS — *Corpus Inscriptionum Semiticarum,* Paris.
CivCatt — *La Civiltà Cattolica,* Rome.
CJTh — *Canadian Journal of Theology,* Toronto.
CMH — *Cambridge Medieval History,* Cambridge.
CModH — *Cambridge Modern History,* Cambridge.
CQ — *Crozer Quarterly,* Chester (Pa.).
CR — *Corpus Reformatorum,* Berlin.
CSCO — *Corpus Scriptorum Christianorum Orientalium,* Paris.
CSEL — *Corpus Scriptorum Ecclesiasticorum Latinorum,* Vienna.
CSHByz — *Corpus Scriptorum Historiae Byzantinae,* Bonn.
CTM — *Concordia Theological Monthly,* St. Louis.
DAB — *Dictionary of American Biography,* New York.
DACL — *Dictionnaire d'archéologie chrétienne et de liturgie,* Paris.
DB — *Dictionnaire de la Bible,* Paris.
DCA — *Dictionary of Christian Antiquities,* London.
DCB — *Dictionary of Christian Biography,* London.
DDC — *Dictionnaire de droit canonique,* Paris.
DEB — *Deutsche-Evangelische Blätter,* Berlin.
DECH — *Dictionary of English Church History,* Oxford.
DHGE — *Dictionnaire d'histoire et de géographie ecclésiastiques,* Paris.
DNB — *Dictionary of National Biography,* London.
DomSt — *Dominican Studies,* Oxford.
DSp — *Dictionnaire de spiritualité,* Paris.
DThC — *Dictionnaire de théologie catholique,* Paris.
DTT — *Dansk Teologisk Tiddskrift,* Copenhagen.
DubR — *Dublin Review,* London.
EB — *Encyclopaedia Biblica,* London.
EC — *Enciclopedia Cattolica,* Rome.
EHR — *English Historical Review,* London.
EJ — *Encyclopaedia Judaica,* Berlin.
EK — *Evangelisches Kirchenlexikon,* Göttingen.
EL — *Ephemerides Liturgicae,* Rome.
EncBrit — *Encyclopaedia Britannica,* London.
EO — *Échos d'orient,* Paris.
EQ — *Evangelical Quarterly,* London.

ER — *Ecumenical Review,* Geneva.
EstBi — *Estudios Bíblicos,* Madrid.
ET — *Expository Times,* Edinburgh.
ETL — *Ephemerides Theologicae Lovanienses,* Louvain.
EvTh — *Evangelische Theologie,* Munich.
Exp — *Expositor,* London.
ExpB — *Expositor's Bible,* London.
ExpGT — *Expositor's Greek Testament,* London.
FF — *Forschungen und Fortschritte,* Berlin.
FRLANT — *Forschungen zur Religion und Literatur des Alten und Neuen Testament,* Göttingen.
GCS — *Die griechischen christlichen Schriftsteller,* Berlin.
Gressmann, *Bilder* — H. Gressmann, *Altorientalische Bilder zum Alten Testament*^{2}, Tübingen.
Gressmann, *Texte* — H. Gressmann, *Altorientalische Texte zum Alten Testament*^{2}, Tübingen.
GThT — *Gereformeerd Theologisch Tijdschrift,* Kampen.
Harnack, *DG* — A. v. Harnack, *Lehrbuch der Dogmengeschichte*^{4}, Freiburg.
HAT — *Handbuch zum Alten Testament,* Tübingen.
HDAC — *Hastings' Dictionary of the Apostolic Church,* New York.
HDB — *Hastings' Dictionary of the Bible,* New York.
HDCG — *Hastings' Dictionary of Christ and the Gospels,* New York.
Hefele — K. J. v. Hefele, *Konziliengeschichte*^{2}, Freiburg i.B.
Hefele-Leclercq — *Histoire des conciles d'après les documents originaux,* Paris.
HERE — *Hastings' Encyclopaedia of Religion and Ethics,* New York.
HJ — *Hibbert Journal,* London.
HJb — *Historisches Jahrbuch,* Munich.
HNT — *Handbuch zum Neuen Testament,* Tübingen.
HTR — *Harvard Theological Review,* Cambridge.
HUCA — *Hebrew Union College Annual,* Cincinnati.
IB — *Interpreter's Bible,* New York.
IBD — *Imperial Bible Dictionary,* London.
ICC — *International Critical Commentary,* Edinburgh.
IEJ — *Israel Exploration Journal,* Jerusalem.
IJA — *International Journal of the Apocrypha,* London.
IKZ — *Internationale kirchliche Zeitschrift,* Bern.
Int — *Interpretation,* Richmond.
IRM — *International Review of Missions,* London.
IrThQ — *Irish Theological Quarterly,* Maynooth.
ISBE — *International Standard Bible Encyclopedia,* Chicago.
JA — *Journal asiatique,* Paris.
JAOS — *Journal of the American Oriental Society,* New Haven.
JASA — *Journal of the American Scientific Affiliation,* W. Lafayette (Ind.)
JbDTh — *Jahrbücher für deutsche Theologie,* Bonn.
JBL — *Journal of Biblical Literature,* Philadelphia.
JbGJJ — *Jahrbuch für die Geschichte der Juden und des Judenthums,* Leipzig.
JbPrTh — *Jahrbücher für protestantische Theologie,* Leipzig.
JBR — *Journal of Bible and Religion,* Boston.
JE — *Jewish Encyclopedia,* New York.
JEA — *Journal of Egyptian Archaeology,* London.
JEH — *Journal of Ecclesiastical History,* London.
JHS — *Journal of Hellenic Studies,* London.
JJGL — *Jahrbuch für jüdische Geschichte und Literatur,* Berlin.
JJLPh — *Journal of Jewish Lore and Philosophy,* Cincinnati
JJS — *Journal of Jewish Studies,* Cambridge.
JNES — *Journal of Near Eastern Studies,* Chicago.
JPOS — *Journal of the Palestinian Oriental Society,* Jerusalem.
JPS — *Jewish Publication Society.*
JQR — *Jewish Quarterly Review,* Philadelphia.
JR — *Journal of Religion,* Chicago.
JSOR — *Journal of the Society of Oriental Research,* Chicago.
JSS — *Journal of Semitic Studies,* Manchester.
JTS — *Journal of Theological Studies,* Oxford.
JTVI — *Journal of the Transactions of the Victoria Institute,* London.
JZWL — *Jüdische Zeitschrift für Wissenschaft und Leben,* Breslau.
KB — Koehler-Baumgartner, *Lexicon in Vet. Testam.*
KD — Keil and Delitzsch, *Commentary on the Old Testament.*
KV — *Korte Verklaring der Heilige Schrift,* Kampen.
KZ — *Kirchliche Zeitfragen,* Zürich.
LACTh — *Library of Anglo-Catholic Theology,* Oxford.
Loeb — *Loeb Classical Library,* Cambridge.
LThK — *Lexikon für Theologie und Kirche.*
MAH — *Mélanges d'archéologie et d'histoire,* Paris.
ME — *Mennonite Encyclopedia,* Scottdale.
MGH — *Monumenta Germaniae Historica,* Berlin.
MGWJ — *Monatsschrift für Geschichte und Wissenschaft des Judentums,* Dresden.
MIOG — *Mitteilungen des Instituts für österreichische Geschichtsforschung,* Vienna.

MM — Moulton-Milligan, *Vocabulary of the Greek Testament.*
MoyA — *Le moyen âge,* Paris.
MPG — J. P. Migne, *Patrologia Graeca.*
MPL — J. P. Migne, *Patrologia Latina.*
MQR — *Mennonite Quarterly Review,* Goshen, Ind.
MSt — McClintock-Strong, *Cyclopaedia of Biblical, Theological and Ecclesiastical Literature.*
MThZ — *Münchner theologische Zeitschrift,* Munich.
NedThT — *Nederlands Theologisch Tijdschrift,* Wageningen.
NGG — *Nachrichten von der Gesellschaft der Wissenschaften zu Göttingen,* Göttingen.
NJbDTh — *Neue Jahrbücher für deutsche Theologie,* Bonn.
NKZ — *Neue kirchliche Zeitschrift,* Leipzig.
NRTh — *Nouvelle revue théologique,* Louvain.
NSHERK — *New Schaff-Herzog Encyclopedia of Religious Knowledge,* Grand Rapids.
NSNU — *Nuntius Sodalicii Neotestamentici Upsaliensis,* Uppsala.
NT — *Novum Testamentum,* Leiden.
NTS — *New Testament Studies,* Cambridge.
NZM — *Neue Zeitschrift für Missionswissenschaft,* Schoeneck-Beckenried.
OC — *Oriens Christianus,* Leipzig.
OCD — *Oxford Classical Dictionary,* Oxford.
OCP — *Orientalia Christiana Periodica,* Rome.
ODCC — *Oxford Dictionary of the Christian Church,* Oxford.
OLZ — *Orientalische Literaturzeitung,* Wiesbaden.
OS — *Oudtestamentische Studiën,* Leiden.
PAOS — *Proceedings of the American Oriental Society,* Chicago.
PBA — *Proceedings of the British Academy,* London.
PEF — *Palestine Exploration Fund, Memoirs,* London.
PEFQSt — *Palestine Exploration Fund, Quarterly Statement,* London.
PEQ — *Palestine Exploration Quarterly,* London.
PSBA — *Proceedings of the Society of Biblical Archaeology,* London.
PTR — *Princeton Theological Review,* Princeton.
PW — *Realencyclopädie der klassischen Altertumswissenschaft,* Stuttgart.
QDAP — *Quarterly of the Department of Antiquities in Palestine,* Oxford.
RA — *Revue archéologique,* Paris.
RAC — *Reallexikon für Antike und Christentum,* Münster.
RB — *Revue biblique,* Jerusalem.
RBAB — *Revue des bibliothèques et des archives de la Belgique,* Brussels.
RBen — *Revue bénédictine,* Maredsous.
RCHL — *Revue critique d'histoire et de littérature,* Paris.
RE[3] — *Realencyclopädie für protestantische Theologie und Kirche*[3], Leipzig.
RechScRel — *Recherches de science religieuse,* Paris.
RechThAM — *Recherches de théologie ancienne et médiévale,* Louvain.
REJ — *Revue des études juives,* Paris.
RevExp — *Review and Expositor,* Louisville.
RevQ — *Revue de Qumran,* Paris.
RevS — *Revue sémitique,* Paris.
RGG — *Die Religion in Geschichte und Gegenwart,* Tübingen.
RH — *Revue historique,* Paris.
RHE — *Revue d'histoire ecclésiastique,* Louvain.
RHLR — *Revue d'histoire et de littérature religieuses,* Paris.
RHPR — *Revue d'histoire et de philosophie religieuses,* Strasbourg.
RHR — *Revue de l'histoire des religions,* Paris.
RicRel — *Ricerche religiose,* Rome.
RLV — *Reallexikon der Vorgeschichte,* Berlin.
ROC — *Revue de l'orient chrétien,* Paris.
RQH — *Revue des questions historiques,* Paris.
RScR — *Revue des sciences religieuses,* Strasbourg.
RSPhTh — *Revue des sciences philosophiques et théologiques,* Le Saulchoir.
RThPh — *Revue de théologie et de philosophie,* Lausanne.
RTR — *Reformed Theological Review,* Hawthorn/Melbourne.
SBE — *Semana Bíblica Española,* Madrid.
SC — *Sources chrétiennes,* Paris.
ScE — *Sciences ecclésiastiques,* Montreal.
SchwThZ — *Schweizerische theologische Zeitschrift,* Zürich.
Schürer[4] — E. Schürer, *Geschichte des jüdischen Volkes*[4], Leipzig.
SHERK — *Schaff-Herzog Encyclopaedia of Religious Knowledge,* New York.
SJT — *Scottish Journal of Theology,* Edinburgh.
SK — *Studien und Kritiken,* Hamburg.
ST — *Studi e Testi,* Rome.
Str-B — (H. L. Strack and) P. Billerbeck, *Kommentar zum Neuen Testament aus Talmud und Midrasch,* Munich.
STT — *Svensk teologisk Tidskrift,* Lund.
StudCath — *Studia Catholica,* Nijmegen.
StudOr — *Studia Orientalia,* Helsinki.
StudPatr — *Studia Patristica,* Cambridge.
StudTh — *Studia Theologica,* Lund.

SvEA — *Svensk Exegetisk Arsbok*, Uppsala.
SymbBU — *Symbolae Biblicae Upsalienses*, Uppsala.
SymbO — *Symbolae Osloenses*, Oslo.
ThGl — *Theologie und Glaube*, Paderborn.
ThJ — *Theologischer Jahresbericht*, Leipzig.
ThLbl — *Theologisches Literaturblatt*, Leipzig.
ThLZ — *Theologische Literaturzeitung*, Leipzig.
ThPrQs — *Theologisch-praktische Quartalschrift*, Linz.
ThQ — *Theologische Quartalschrift*, Tübingen.
ThR — *Theologische Revue*, Münster.
ThS — *Theological Studies*, *Woodstock* (Md.).
ThStKr — *Theologische Studien und Kritiken*, Gotha.
ThT — *Theologisch Tijdschrift*, Leiden.
ThZ — *Theologische Zeitschrift*, Basel.
TR — *Theologische Rundschau*, Tübingen.
TSBA — *Transactions of the Society of Biblical Archaeology*, London.
TSt — *Texts and Studies*, Cambridge.
TT — *Theology Today*.
TU — *Texte und Untersuchungen zur Geschichte der altchristlichen Literatur*, Leipzig.
TWNT — *Theologisches Wörterbuch zum Neuen Testament*, Stuttgart.
VC — *Vigiliae Christianae*, Amsterdam.
VD — *Verbum Domini*, Rome.
VF — *Verkündigung und Forschung*, Munich.
VT — *Vetus Testamentum*, Leiden.
WDB — Davis-Gehman, *Westminster Dictionary of the Bible*, Philadelphia.
WH — Westcott-Hort, *Text of the Greek New Testament*.
WO — *Die Welt des Orients*, Göttingen.
WThJ — *Westminster Theological Journal*, Philadelphia.
WZKM — *Wiener Zeitschrift für die Kunde des Morgenlandes*, Vienna.
Zahn, *Einl* — T. Zahn-*Einleitung in der Neuen Testament*[3], Leipzig.
Zahn, *Forsch* — T. Zahn-*Forschungen zur Geschichte des neutestamentlichen Kanons*, Leipzig.
Zahn, *GK* — T. Zahn-*Geschichte des neutestamentlichen Kanons*, Leipzig.
ZAW — *Zeitschrift für die alttestamentliche Wissenschaft*, Berlin.
ZCK — *Zeitschrift für christliche Kunst*, Düsseldorf.
ZDMG — *Zeitschrift der deutschen Morgenländischen Gesellschaft*, Wiesbaden.
ZDPV — *Zeitschrift der deutschen Palästina-Vereins*, Leipzig.
ZHTh — *Zeitschrift für die historische Theologie*, Hamburg/Gotha/Leipzig.
ZK — *Zeitschrift für Keilschriftforschung*, Leipzig.
ZKG — *Zeitschrift für Kirchengeschichte*, Gotha/Stuttgart.
ZKTh — *Zeitschrift für katholische Theologie*, Innsbruck.
ZNW — *Zeitschrift für die neutestamentliche Wissenschaft*, Berlin.
ZRG — *Zeitschrift für Religions- und Geistesgeschichte*, Erlangen.
ZSem — *Zeitschrift für Semitistik*, Leipzig.
ZSK — *Zeitschrift für Schweizer Kirchengeschichte*, Zürich.
ZSystTh — *Zeitschrift für systematische Theologie*, Göttingen.
ZThK — *Zeitschrift für Theologie und Kirche*, Tübingen.
ZWTh — *Zeitschrift für wissenschaftliche Theologie*, Leipzig.

CILICIA, former name of the area on the SE coast of Asia Minor adjoining Syria. In the ninth century B.C. the E part of it was occupied by the Hittites. In later times the two main sections into which the country geographically falls were called Cilicia Tracheia and Cilicia Pedias. The former, lying to the W, is mountainous and rugged. It was the home of wild tribes and for long a haunt of brigands and pirates. With the exception of Acts 27:4, however, all the NT references are to the E part, Cilicia Pedias, which was low lying and fertile. Goat's-hair cloth, from which tents were made, was exported from it (Acts 19:3). Under Roman rule, from 104 B.C. onward, Cilicia was at first associated with Phrygia; but in 23 B.C. it was united with Syria (cf. Acts 15:23, 24; Gal. 1:21). In 51 B.C. Cicero was governor of the province, which had a considerable Jewish population (Acts 6:9). Tarsus, the chief city and the birthplace of Paul, was situated on the River Cnidus. Paul spent much time there after his conversion (Acts 9:30; 11:25) and, perhaps, founded the churches which he afterwards visited (Acts 15:41). Tarsus stood at the end of the trade route through the Cilician Gates which he followed in the Second Missionary Journey.

CIRCUMCELLIONS. The circumcellions were an extremist group of North African peasants led by Axido and Fasir in A.D. 340. During the period of great agrarian and political unrest in North Africa these militant peasants waged guerilla attacks on Roman Catholics who accepted monetary and property grants from Constantine. The Roman Catholics gave these fanatics the name "circumcellions" (Latin: those who surround dwellings) because their mode of attack was to surround a Catholic complex while attacking it. They called themselves the "Agonistici" or the "soldiers of Christ." These extremists sought to purify the church from worldliness. They later joined the Donatist movement in North Africa.

See also DONATISTS.

ROBERT C. SPROUL

CIRCUMCISION. The first Biblical mention of circumcision is found in Genesis 17:10 in connection with God's covenant with Abraham. Circumcision was to be a sign of the covenant to be the God of Abraham and his descendants. All the males, both descendants and slaves, were to be circumcised. Male children were to be circumcised on the eighth day, and the child who was not circumcised was cut off from his people, having broken the covenant.

The Philistines and various other surrounding peoples are scorned as uncircumcised (Judges 14:3; Elam, Ezek. 32:24; Meshech, Tubal, Ezek. 32:26; Sidon, Ezek. 32:30; and others, Jer. 9:26). Actually, circumcision was practiced widely in antiquity as is shown by certain representations both in Mesopotamia and in Egypt. However, the Egyptian pictures of the operation show it performed in adulthood, probably at puberty as is done among the Arabs today. There does not seem to be any ancient evidence for infant circumcision outside of the Bible. It may be suggested that this was one reason God chose the rite of infant circumcision for

Israel. Puberty circumcision is sometimes associated with marriage rites and licentiousness. Infant circumcision in Israel would preclude the temptation to emulate one's neighbors in this regard.

The meaning of circumcision in the OT was not merely a sign of descent from Abraham. It was a sign of a national and spiritual covenant. For this reason the Israelite was exhorted to circumcise his heart (Deut. 18:16; Jer. 4:4; cf. Deut. 30:6).

There are more references to circumcision in the NT than in the Old. Paul makes a point that Abraham was not saved by circumcision, because he was saved first and received circumcision later as a seal of the righteousness of faith (Rom. 4:9-11). Indeed, he says that circumcision which is merely of the flesh is not circumcision (Rom. 2:28-29); it is actually mutilation (Phil. 3:2-3). The outward ordinance of circumcision is therefore classed as part of the OT ceremonial law, not required for Gentiles (Acts 15:24) and done away in Christ (Gal. 6:15).

R. Laird Harris

CIRCUMINCESSION. The term was employed by Sherlock (*Vindication of the Trinity*) as a translation of περιχώρησις (*perichōrēsis*), the term used to designate the Nicene conception of the mutual inhabitation of the Persons of the Trinity, connoting, in the words of Dr. Shedd, "an unceasing and eternal *movement* in the Godhead, whereby each Person coinheres in the others and the others in each." This conception safeguards the unity of the divine essence while maintaining the distinction of the Persons. Bishop Bull referred to Origen as believing that the Persons have no divided or separate existence (as three men have) but are "intimately united and conjoined one with another" and said "to exist in each other and to pervade and permeate one another by an ineffable περιχώρησις which the Schoolmen call *inhabitation*." From this *inhabitation* Petavius asserts that a *numerical* Unity must necessarily be inferred. A fine exposition of this theme, based on John 14:10, is contained in Athanasius' third oration against the Arians. The term is also employed by John of Damascus for the interchange of divine and human attributes in the Person of Christ.

Bibliography:

Athanasius, *Orations Against the Arians* (London, n.d.).

W. G. T. Shedd, *A History of Christian Doctrine*, I, 348 (New York, 1863).

D. Waterland, *Works*, II, 202 f. (Oxford, 1843).

William Young

CISTERCIAN ORDER, an order of monks founded by Robert of Molêsme in 1908. It was established at Cîteaux, on property donated by the Duke of Burgundy, for the purpose of reinvigorating Benedictine monasticism. Robert hoped that by strict maintenance of corporate as well as individual poverty the order would provide an example and stimulus to monastic reform. Under the leadership of Abbot Stephen Harding, daughter houses were established, the most important being Clairvaux in Champagne, of which Bernard of Clairvaux (*q.v*). became abbot in 1115. Granted papal approval in 1100, the first Chapter General of the order met in 1116 to draw up a constitution. Owing to its reputation for sanctity, the order quickly became very wealthy. This increase in wealth led, as in other monastic orders, to a spiritual decline. Between 1342 and 1790 the order experienced many ups and downs accompanied by a division into two groups, the Common Observance and the Strict Observance. As a result of the French Revolution the order almost disappeared, but in 1892 it was again reunified as "The Order of Reformed Cistercians of our Lady of La Trappe." In 1898 it returned to Cîteaux, and the old title was restored. It has 68 monasteries with some 4,800 members in 16 different countries.

W. STANFORD REID

CISTERNS AND WELLS. In Biblical times a cistern comprised a subterranean reservoir used for storing water collected from rainfall or from a spring. Cisterns only became popular in Palestine *c.* 1200 B.C., when the use of lime plaster to seal up the porous limestone became common. Cisterns were particularly valuable in the Palestinian dry season (May-September), and apart from their utility were status-symbols (Isa. 36:16). They were usually pear-shaped, and had a small opening at the top which could be covered over to prevent accidents or contamination. Cisterns were also used for storing grain, and some were large enough to be used as prisons (Gen. 37:2; Jer. 38:6). The Qumran community utilized several large cisterns.

By contrast with the limestone-sealed cisterns, the cylindrical shaft of a well collected water from percolation through its sides. Ancient wells varied greatly in depth and shape, depending upon the soil and the water-level. Wells were important for nomadic communities, supplying water for families and flocks alike (Gen. 29:2).

BIBLIOGRAPHY:

N. Glueck, *Rivers in the Desert* (1959), p. 94.

CITIES OF THE PLAIN. The term "Cities of the Plain" (Gen. 13:12; 19:29) refers to five cities located near the Dead Sea, viz., Sodom, Gomorrah, Admah, Zeboiim, and Bela (or Zoar). The term rendered "plain" is, literally, "circle" or "circuit."

Location

There has been much scholarly debate concerning the location of the Cities of the Plain, with opinions divided between a N and a S locale. Those who suggest a site N of the Dead Sea point out: (1) From the vicinity of Bethel, Abraham is said to have seen all the Plain of the Jordan (Gen. 13:8-12). The S area could not be seen from Bethel. (2) Moses from Mt. Nebo is said to have seen "the plain, the valley of Jericho, the city of palm trees, unto Zoar" (Deut. 34:3). The S end of the Dead Sea is not visible from Nebo. (3) After traveling southward through the area E of the Dead Sea, Chedorlaomer and his allies turned westward S of the Dead Sea, and then northward to Hazezontamar (En-gedi). It would be presumed that they continued their journey northward to meet the king of Sodom and his allies (Gen. 14:5-9).

There are, on the other hand, sound reasons for locating the Cities of the Plain S of the Dead Sea, and most contemporary scholars locate them there. Arguing for this viewpoint is the fact that: (1) Persistent traditions locate Zoar S of the Dead Sea. Josephus stated that the Dead Sea extended 580 stadia from Jericho to Zoar (*Wars*, IV, viii, 4), and Eusebius in his *Onomasticon* locates it in the same area (*Onom.*, 261). In medieval times Lot was honored by pilgrimages made to a monastery on a hill near Zoar which early became a Christian center with an episcopal seat dependent on Petra. At the time of the Crusades Zoar was an important stop on the journey from Elath to Jerusalem. (2) The traditional site of Sodom, *Jebel Usdum*, is SW of the Dead Sea. (3) Gen. 14:10 speaks of "slime pits" in the region of the battle. This may be a reference to the petroleum wells which are found S of the Dead Sea. The district is full of bitumen and asphalt.

The infamous Cities of the Plain appear to have been located in the area now submerged by water S of the peninsula known as *el-lisan* (the tongue) which projects from the E shore of the Dead Sea. The means used for their destruction could have been an earthquake accompanied by explosions, the ignition of natural gas, and a general conflagration.

The wickedness of Sodom was such that not even ten righteous persons could be found there (Gen. 13:13; 18:32).

Judgment

The sins of the city included sexual perversions (Gen. 19: 4-9; Jude 7), pride (Ezek. 16:48-50), and shameless arrogance (Isa. 3:9). The divine judgment upon Sodom and Gomorrah served as a reminder to future generations that God would not let sin go unpunished (Deut. 29:23; Isa. 1:9-10; Jer. 49:18; Amos 4:11; Mt. 10:15; 11:24; Rom. 9:29; II Pet. 2:6).

Before the judgment upon Sodom and Gomorrah, the Cities of the Plain were well populated and were located in a fertile district. Archaeological evidence indicates that the area was abandoned shortly after 2000 B.C. It is a hot, barren territory today, at least partially submerged under the Dead Sea. In classical and NT times ruins were still visible, not yet being covered with water (cf. Tacitus, *Histories*, V, vii).

BIBLIOGRAPHY:

W. F. Albright, "The Archaeological Results of an Expedition to Moab and the Dead Sea," *BASOR* 14 (1924), 2-12.

F. G. Clapp, "The Site of Sodom and Gomorrah," *AJA* 40 (1936), 323-344.

N. Glueck, *Rivers in the Desert* (New York, 1959).

J. P. Harland, "Sodom and Gomorrah: The Location of the Cities of the Plain," *BA* 5 (1942), 17-32.

J. P. Harland, "Sodom and Gomorrah: The Destruction of the Cities of the Plain," *BA* 6 (1943), 41-54.

CHARLES F. PFEIFFER

CITIZENSHIP. The essential points may be set forth under the following heads: (1) Membership in the Hebrew

I. Hebrew Citizenship

family, long before it became a nation at Sinai, was based primarily on physical descent from Abraham (Gen. 12:1-3). All Jews traced their ancestry back to him (Isa. 51:2; Mt. 3:9; John 8:33; Acts 13:26); by such ancestry they became citizens of "the commonwealth of Israel" (Eph. 2:12). (2) This citizenship was openly acknowledged and sealed in the rite of circumcision, which was divinely instituted in Abraham's time (Gen. 17:9-14; Rom. 4:9-12). Noncircumcision debarred a person from citizenship in "the holy city" (Isa. 52:1; cf. Ezek. 44:7,9). Neither Moses (Ex. 4:24-26) nor the Israelites (Josh. 5:2-9) were true representatives of their nation without this rite of God's covenant. (3) Citizenship in Israel consisted also in faithful obedience to all the ordinances and ceremonies instituted by God at Sinai. To refuse compliance with God's law meant that the disobedient person was to be "cut off" from Israel's commonwealth. The references listed here indicate the nature of the sin involved and the greatness of the penalty inflicted: Gen. 17:14; Ex.12:15; 30:33; 31:14; Lev. 7:20-27; 17:4,9,14; 18:29; 19:8; 20:17 f.; 22:3,29; Num. 9:13; 15:30 f.; 19:13,20. (4) Citizenship in Israel's commonwealth was conferred on those non-Israelites who voluntarily submitted to the rite of circumcision and faithfully complied with the ceremonial legislation enacted at Sinai (Ex. 12:49; Num. 9:14; 15:15 f., 29). Certain persons and nations—particularly eunuchs, bastards, Ammonites, and Moabites (Deut. 23:1-5)—were excluded absolutely from full rights of citizenship in Israel; others—Edomites and Egyptians—were excluded only until certain restrictions had been fulfilled (Deut. 21:7 f.). The nations of Canaan were excluded absolutely, lest, by intermarriage and treaties, they corrupt the purity of Israel's seed and religion (Ex. 23:31-33; 34:12-17; Deut. 7:1-6; Ezra 9:1-15; Neh. 9:2; 13:1). (5) Citizenship in Israel never meant participation in official functions (voting, office-holding, etc.) found in modern democracies.

Israel's government was ideally a theocracy. This meant that all the functions of government were controlled by divine legislation which the people could not change. The priesthood belonged to one tribe and family (Num. 17-18); the kingship likewise belonged to one tribe and family (Gen. 49:10; II Sam. 7:1-29). To rebel against either institution meant rebellion against God (I Sam. 13:8-14; I Kings 12:16-33). (6) The blessings of citizenship in Israel's commonwealth were largely spiritual in nature. These blessings—eight in number—are succinctly summarized by Paul in Rom. 9:4 f. But such blessings could be enjoyed fully only by absolute obedience to God (Deut. 7:7-26). (7) Finally, every believing Israelite realized that the outward signs of citizenship—circumcision and ceremonial sacrifice—represented spiritual realities that transcended the physical signs (Deut. 30:6; Jer. 4:4; Ps. 51:16 f.; 107:22; Rom. 2:28 f.; Phil. 3:3). Thus the believing Israelite came to realize that there was a spiritual Israel within the physical Israel. Such a person knew, by the eye of faith, that he was a pilgrim in this present world (Gen. 23:4; 47:9; Ps. 39:12; Heb. 11:13); he could look beyond earthly citizenship to heavenly citizenship in "a city . . . whose builder and maker is God" (Heb. 11:10; 12:22; 13:14).

Interest in this phase of our subject is largely enhanced by the fact that the Apostle Paul not only was a Roman citizen, but also wisely used his citizenship on several important occasions. Circumstances concerning Paul's acquisition of this right and privilege are unknown except for Paul's lone statement (Acts 22:28). However, this right of citizenship in the Roman Empire secured for Paul proper treatment when he was unjustly imprisoned (Acts 16:37), freedom from unlawful castigation (Acts 22:25), and the right to appeal his case to Caesar (Acts 25:11; cf. II Tim. 4:15 f.). These uses of his citizenship represent the basic rights and privileges of Roman citizenship.

II. Roman Citizenship

Two points here will summarize large areas of relevant material: (1) On the one hand, the NT clearly recognizes the fact that the Christian is a citizen in this present world. Christ explicitly affirmed the citizen's duty to the state, including the payment of taxes (Mt. 22:17-21); Paul, both by teaching (Rom. 13:1-7; Titus 3:1; cf. I Pet. 2:13 f.) and by example (Acts 16:37; 22:25; 25:11), enunciated the basic principles, both positive and negative, of the Christian's relationship to the state. (2) On the other hand, the NT, like its OT counterpart, reiterates the truth that Christians are, basically, "strangers and pilgrims" in the present world (I Pet. 2:11); even now, whether Jews or Gentiles, they have become "fellow citizens with the saints, and of the household of God" (Eph. 2:19). Furthermore, "our citizenship is in heaven" (Phil. 3:20, marg), where we are enrolled as citizens in "the city of the living God" (Heb. 12:22 f.). Like Abraham and the ancient worthies, we also look "for a city . . . whose builder and maker is God" (Heb. 11:10; 13:14).

III. Christian Citizenship

Bibliography:

E. R. Bernard, "Citizenship," *HDB* I (1898), 444-445.

O. Cullmann, *The State in the New Testament* (New York, 1956).

W. Durant, *Caesar and Christ* (New York, 1944), 25-27, 193-194, 394-395.

P. Fairbairn (ed.), "Citizenship," *IBD* (London, 1866), 336-337.

W. M. Ramsay, *St. Paul the Traveller and the Roman Citizen* (London, 1895), 30 f., 225.

R. Stob, *Christianity and Classical Civilization* (Grand Rapids, 1950). Copious bibliography.

A. Souter, "Citizenship," *HDAC* I (1916), 212-213.

Wick Broomall

CITY. The city is an important and basic concept in Scripture. Although the first city formally mentioned is Enoch, built by Cain (Gen. 4:17), the Garden of Eden was apparently created as the City of God. The Garden is shown in Revelation 21 and 22 as the heart of the New Jerusalem, with the tree of life and the river of the water of life contained therein. The purpose of Eden was the human community of God serving God and in communion with God. St. Augustine quite accurately saw history as the development of two rival forces, the Kingdom or City of God, and the Kingdom or City of Man.

Physically, a city in antiquity was a walled community, whereas a dwelling area without walls was a village (Lev. 25:29-31; I Sam. 6:18; Ezek. 38:11).

In ancient civilizations cities were considered to be religious communities. At the center of a city was an altar; and the city, with all the villages and tributary cities around it, was the religious abode of the god of the city and his people. Coulanges could thus write, "Every city was a sanctuary; every city might be called holy."

Citizenship was, therefore, wholly a religious fact, as was the census. The numbering of the people was a religious act, to be undertaken only by the priests, since it was the people of the god who were being numbered, not the people of the magistrates.

Citizenship rested squarely on atonement. Only those who accepted the atonement offered by the god of a city could be citizens thereof. The Roman citizen thus was required to partake in the annual rite of lustration, a purificatory ceremony. Lustration was necessary as the preliminary to entering the sanctuary and as the means of removing bloodguiltiness. Because all the citizens had a common religion, they had thus a common atonement and a common law. As Coulanges noted, "Law was nothing more than one phase of religion. Where there was no common religion, there was no common law."

A city was thus a theological concept, and out of the theologies of the various city-states there flowed political and legal theories in conformity with the basic theology. The rebellion and Fall of man was thus a rebellion against the authority of the first government, that of God. Denying the religion of Eden, man was cast out and excluded from Eden by the "flaming sword" of the cherubim (Gen. 3:24), which, to ancient man, meant clearly that that city had been walled against its enemies. St. Augustine noted that "to this founder of the holy city the citizens of the earthly city prefer their own gods, not knowing that He is the God of gods."

The medieval city was clearly a Christian community, with the church at its center and atonement basic to citizenship. The Puritan villages of New England, as well as the villages of England and Europe, long maintained the centrality of the church. The settlement of the whole United States tended to follow a religious pattern. According to Gaustad, "in approximately one-half of the counties of the nation, a single religious body accounts for at least 50% of all the membership in the county." In other words, various church (and national) groups tended to colonize a particular area. Within a large metropolitan center, the same colonization in terms of religion and racial homogeneity tends to occur when not interfered with by the state.

The twentieth century has seen what Hilfer has called "the revolt from the village," in actuality a revolt from the ancient concept of community to a new humanistic one. Lewis Mumford, in *The City in History*, has stated:

> When cities were first founded, an old Egyptian scribe tells us, the mission of the founder was to "put the gods in their shrines." The task of the coming city is not essentially different: its mission is to put the highest con-

cern of man at the center of all his activities.

> We must now conceive the city not primarily as a place of business or government, but as an essential organ for expressing and actualizing the new human personality—that of "One World Man."

The rise of the humanistic city saw the centers of civil government and the centers of commerce or of finance competing for centrality and primacy in the city. The church was moved to the side as no longer basic. Man's unity was no longer seen in faith in the triune God and His salvation, but rather man's unity was in his own saving work.

The modern city has thus no less a theological basis than had the ancient city; the modern city is indeed close to the ancient city in its pagan theology. The theology of the modern city is humanism; man is the true god of the city, and the chief end of the city is to glorify man and make possible his perpetual happiness. The crisis of the twentieth century city is thus a theological crisis: the thesis or faith of the modern city is being put to a critical test and is clearly failing. Mumford has called for a revival of faith in autonomous man as the key to the city's rejuvenation or regeneration. On the technical side, the development of the modern city has been remarkable. The technology of the city has seen vast wealth and ingenuity brought to bear on the problems of the city. Ironically, however, the more that modern concepts of design, as those of the Bauhaus, have been applied to the city, the more radical has been the depersonalization of man.

St. Augustine spoke of "the civil theology" of Rome. The civil theology of the modern city is spelled out in the hopes of modern sociology and in the modern theater. The purpose of the city is in every age to unite men in a common faith and worship. The civil theology of the modern city is humanism, which has been unable to unite man, because with every man his own god (Gen. 3:5), the consequences of the Fall are enthroned, disunity cultivated, and mankind reduced to anarchistic and atomistic dimensions. The modern city enjoys, in technology, the best forms of communication the world has yet seen, and yet it has a major spiritual problem of a lack of communication between man and man, of "alienation." The progression of the civil theology of humanism has thus been marked by the radical fragmentation of society into warring factions and into social atomism.

The theology of the city in terms of Scripture is that the goal of history is the community of Christ, the Kingdom of God, the New Jerusalem. All the nations shall be subordinated to the sovereign law-word of God the King (Rev. 21:24). Man, called originally to exercise dominion under God and to subdue the earth under Him (Gen. 1:26-28), fell from this calling and found all his work cursed because of his rebellion (Gen. 3:17-19). Restored into the image of God by the atoning work of Jesus Christ, man is restored into his original calling to subdue the earth and exercise dominion over it. In God's Kingdom, the curse of work is removed, and God's servants serve Him with joy and fulfilment (Rev. 22:3). The City of God is presented symbolically as foursquare, of equal length, breadth, and height, i.e., a perfect cube. The cube was an ancient symbol of perfection. Thus, the perfection of man, sought by the secular city outside of God, can be found only in Jesus Christ and in His true community.

Bibliography:

Augustine, *The City of God.*

F. Coulanges, *The Ancient City* (1864) (New York, 1956).

W. von Eckardt, "The Bauhaus," in *Horizon,* vol. IV, no. 2, Nov. 1961, pp. 58-75.

Freising, Otto, Bishop of, *The Two Cities, A Chronicle of Universal History to the Year 1146 A.D.* (New York, 1928).

H. J. Gans, *The Urban Villagers* (New York, 1962).

E. S. Gaustad, *Historical Atlas of Religion in America* (New York, 1962).
A. C. Hilfer, *The Revolt From the Village, 1915–1930* (Chapel Hill, N. C., 1969).
B. McKelvey, *The Urbanization of America, 1860–1915* (New Brunswick, N. J., 1963).
B. McKelvey, *The Emergence of Metropolitan America, 1915–1966* (New Brunswick, N. J., 1968).
R. E. Moreau, *The Departed Village* (London, 1968).
L. Mumford, *The City in History, Its Origins, Its Transformation, and Its Prospects* (New York, 1961).
L. Mumford, *The Urban Prospect* (New York, 1956).
S. C. Powell, *Puritan Village* (New York, 1965).
G. Scott, *The Architecture of Humanism* (New York, 1954).

ROUSAS JOHN RUSHDOONY

CLAPHAM SECT, an informal circle of wealthy and influential evangelicals chiefly within the Church of England around 1790-1830. The group centered in and around the parish church at Clapham, then a village near London, where John Venn (1759-1813) was rector from 1792 to 1813, and around the spacious library of the banker Henry Thornton (1760-1815). The members of this circle gave themselves to prayer, Bible study, and benevolent causes. Most of them were laymen, and several were members of Parliament. Prominent members included William Wilberforce (1759-1833), the parliamentary statesman; Charles Grant (1746-1832), Chairman of the East India Company; Lord Teignmouth (1751-1834), the Governor General of India; James Stephen (1758-1832), Under-Secretary for the Colonies; Granville Sharp (1735-1813), a classical scholar and philanthropist; Thomas Clarkson (1760-1846), an Abolitionist leader; Zachary Macaulay (1768-1838), editor of the *Christian Observer* from 1802 to 1816 and the Governor of a model colony for freed slaves in Sierra Leone; and the writer Hannah More (1745-1833). This fellowship of devolt, evangelical statesmen, writers, and philanthropists felt it a Christian duty to act as stewards of their time, energies, affluence, and position to advance the cause of evangelical missions and social reforms. They were constrained to apply the Christian faith to all areas of public and personal life. They were engaged in such humanitarian schemes and movements as the extension of Sunday Schools, the struggle for the abolition of the slave trade, and the establishment of many agencies, such as the British and Foreign Bible Society, the Proclamation Society, and the Society for Bettering the Conditions and Increasing the Comforts of the Poor. Their influence in Parliament and on public opinion was far out of proportion to their numbers, injecting a moral leaven into the conscience of the whole British empire.

BIBLIOGRAPHY:

G. R. Balleine, *History of the Evangelical Party in the Church of England* (New York, 1909).
J. W. Bready, *England: Before and After Wesley* (London, 1938).
F. K. Brown, *Fathers of the Victorians* (New York, 1961).
L. E. Elliott-Binns, *The Evangelical Movement in the English Church* (London, 1928).
T. C. Hall, *The Social Meaning of Modern Religious Movements in England* (New York, 1900).
M. M. Hennell, *John Vann and the Clapham Sect* (London, 1958).
E. M. Howse, *Saints in Politics* (Toronto, 1952).
J. H. Overton, *The English Church in the Nineteenth Century, 1800-1833* (London, 1894).
G. W. E. Russell, *Short History of the Evangelical Movement* (London, 1915).
J. Stephen, *Essays in Ecclesiastical Biography* (London, 1883).

ALBERT H. FREUNDT, JR.

CLARKE, Adam (1762?-1832), Methodist theologian. Born in Northern Ireland, his local school education was, through John Wesley's influence, supplemented in England at Kingswood School, Bristol. Having become a Methodist in 1778, Clarke was appointed a circuit preacher in Wiltshire in 1782, later traveling the British Isles as his preaching fame grew. From 1805 he lived chiefly in London, and was thrice president of the Methodist conference. Holder of an Aberdeen LL.D., his scholarship was impressive, encompassing classics, patristics, oriental languages and literature, geology, natural science, and even a side-glance at the occult. Clarke's greatest achievement was an eight-volume Bible commentary (1810-26). Theologically orthodox as a rule, Clarke nevertheless denied Christ's eternal Sonship while maintaining His Divinity; held that Judas repented and was saved; and rejected Calvin's view of predestination. Selected to edit Rymer's *Foedera*, bad health forced him to relinquish the task at volume two. Clarke's miscellaneous works in 13 volumes were printed in 1836.

JAMES DIXON DOUGLAS

CLARKE, John (1609-1676), one of the founders of Rhode Island. Born near London and trained as a physician, he left England in 1637 for Boston. Following a dispute with the Puritans, Clarke and other colonists were driven out, and bought from the Indians an island they called Rhodes. In April 1639 he was one of those who settled Newport, where he practiced medicine, participated in local government, and became also pastor of the Baptist church. Having collaborated with Roger Williams in the famous Code of Laws, Clarke's unifying zeal was illustrated in his accompanying Williams to England in 1651 to seek a new charter. Williams went home after three years, but Clarke remained as sole agent for the colony until 1663, when he secured from Charles II the royal charter that determined Rhode Island law till 1842. He reassumed his pastorate at Newport and was three times elected deputy governor of the colony.

JAMES DIXON DOUGLAS

CLARK(E), Samuel (1599-1683), Puritan minister and biographer. Born at Wolston, Warwickshire, and educated under Thomas Hooker at Emmanuel College, Cambridge, Clarke was ordained in 1622. After being inhibited from his lectureship in Coventry by Bishop Morton on account of his Nonconformity, he was presented by Lord Brooke, a good friend of Puritan clergy, with the rectory of "drunken Alcester," in 1633. His friend Richard Baxter heard the guns of Edgehill while preaching for him there in 1642. Soon after, despairing of the disorder produced in his area by the war, he moved to London and ministered at St. Bennet Fink. He was one of 57 ministers who signed a protest against Charles I's execution, and in 1653 he helped to draw up a manifesto from the London clergy against the lay-preaching practiced by Independents. He was a member of the Savoy Conference. Upon ejection in 1662, this "moderate Nonconformist," as Baxter calls him, settled at Isleworth, where he communicated regularly with his parish church.

Clarke was the leading Puritan biographer, gathering together from many sources several hundred edifying lives of Reformers, Puritans, clerical and lay, and other heroes of the faith. These he published in five books: *The Marrow of Ecclesiastical Historie* (1650), *A General Martyrologie* (1651), *A Martyrologie . . . of . . . the Church of England* (1652), *A Collection of the Lives of Ten Eminent Divines . . .* (1662), *The Lives of Sundry Eminent Persons in This Later Age* (1683). Clarke did more than any other to stir up, canalize, and satisfy the Puritan interest in spiritual biography.

BIBLIOGRAPHY:

S. Clarke, *The Lives . . .* (1683), s.v.
W. Haller, *The Rise of Puritanism* (New York, 1938), 102-114.
A. G. Matthews (ed.), *Calamy Revised* (London, 1934), s.v.

S. Palmer, *Nonconformists' Memorial* (London; 2nd ed., 1803), I, 97-101.
L. Stephen, *DNB*, s.v.

JAMES I. PACKER

CLARK(E), Samuel (1626-1701), Puritan theologian and commentator, the son of Samuel Clark(e) (1599-1683). Born at Shotwick, Cheshire, he was educated at Pembroke Hall, Cambridge, of which he became fellow in 1644. In 1651, however, he was deprived of his fellowship for refusing to take the "engagement" of fidelity to the Commonwealth. At the Restoration in 1660, he became rector of Grendon Underwood, Buckinghamshire, but was almost immediately ejected under the Act of Uniformity. He then settled in High Wycombe and gathered an Independent congregation there. His theology was broadly Baxterian, as appears from his *Scripture-Justification*, published in 1698, though written almost twenty years before. His most considerable achievement was his *Annotations* on the Bible (NT, 1683; whole Bible, 1690), which won the praise of, among others, Owen, Baxter, Whitefield, and Doddridge. Clarke also wrote *A Survey of the Bible* (1693), a supplement to the foregoing, and published two books defending the Divine authority of the vowel-points of the Hebrew OT. (For a review of the 17th-century debate on this matter, see J. Bowman, "A Forgotten Controversy," in *EQ* [Jan. 1948], 46-68.)

BIBLIOGRAPHY:

S. Clarke, *Peace the End of the Upright* (funeral sermon, by Clarke's son, 1701).
A. Gordon, *DNB*, s.v.
A. G. Matthews (ed.), *Calamy Revised*, (London, 1934), s.v.

JAMES I. PACKER

CLARKSON, David (1622-1686), Puritan theologian. Born at Bradford, Yorkshire, he studied at Clare Hall, Cambridge, becoming a fellow and tutor in 1645. Tillotson, the future archbishop, was among his pupils. In 1651 he became rector of Mortlake, Surrey. After being ejected in 1662, he lived in retirement and study until, in 1682, he was made co-pastor with John Owen of the latter's congregation in Bury Street, London. The next year Owen died, and Clarkson preached his funeral sermon. He was then sole pastor of the church until his own death.

He wrote a number of distinguished controversial works. Against Romanism, he wrote *The Practical Divinity of the Papists Discovered to Be Destructive of Christianity and Men's Souls* (1672). Against diocesan episcopacy advocated by Stillingfleet, he wrote *No Evidence for Diocesan Churches . . . in the Primitive Times* (1681); a defense of this work, the next year; and the posthumous *Primitive Episcopacy* (1688), which successfully shows that in Scripture and the church of the first three centuries a bishop was no more than a pastor of a local congregation. His posthumous *Discourse Concerning Liturgies* (1689) shows similarly that the imposing of liturgies was not a primitive practice.

Most of his sermons were published posthumously, hence their occasional unevenness and perfunctoriness. Generally, Clarkson's style is clear and unaffected, rather bare and chilly, but vigorous and earnestly evangelical. His theology is starkly Calvinistic, but his sermons center upon the main themes of the Gospel: sin, the mediation of Christ, justification, faith, and repentance. Baxter commended him for "solid judgment, healing moderate principles, acquaintance with the Fathers, great ministerial abilities, and a godly upright life" (*Reliquiae Baxterianae*, 1696, iii, 97).

BIBLIOGRAPHY:

J. Blackburn, "Memoir," *Select Works* (London, 1846).
D. Clarkson, *Practical Works* (Edinburgh, 1964).
A. Gordon, *DNB*, s.v.

JAMES I. PACKER

CLARKSON, Thomas (1760-1840), proponent of antislavery reform among the English evangelicals. Born in Wisbeach, England, Clarkson graduated from St. John's College, Cambridge in 1783, and shortly entered the competition for a prize Latin dissertation on the subject, "Whether it is right to make slaves of others against their will." We see Clarkson was profoundly moved by the injustices his research disclosed, and his anguish of conscience soon led him to exchange his intended vocation as a minister for a career as propagandist for the antislavery cause. His successful prize essay, published in 1786, immediately introduced Clarkson into the circle of reformers, mostly Quakers and evangelical churchmen who were currently leaders in antislavery sentiment. In the course of continued research on the issue during 1786-88, Clarkson enlisted the interest of a number of persons who were later to be of key significance in the antislavery struggle, among them Hannah More, William Wilberforce (whom Clarkson introduced to the converted slave trader, John Newton), and William Pitt; and in 1788 Wilberforce and Pitt began their long battle in Parliament against slavery. In 1788 and 1789 Clarkson published new essays demonstrating that the slave trade was not only morally unjust but economically impractical, and that it should be abolished rather than simply regulated. After a visit to France in 1789, where he obtained the sympathy if not the commitment of La Fayette and Mirabeau, Clarkson travelled ceaselessly in England, simultaneously gathering firsthand testimonies of the evils of slavery and promoting the growth of the opposition movement.

By 1794 his own inheritance had been spent in support of this cause, and his health was broken by the strains of travel and the severe opposition directed at the reformers by vested interests. He was forced to spend almost a decade in retirement, supported by a subscription obtained by Wilberforce. By 1805 he had recovered enough to make a second tour, and contributed some of the impetus that led to the passage in 1807 of the bill abolishing the slave trade. After publishing a history of the abolition movement thus far, in 1808 Clarkson continued to press for the suspension of the practice of slaveholding within the British Empire. In 1823 Clarkson and Wilberforce became vice-presidents of the English Anti-Slavery Society, which in 1833 secured passage of the Emancipation Bill, freeing 800,000 slaves with a compensation of £20,000,000 paid to their owners by the British government. After this point Clarkson continued to write in retirement until his death in 1840, his rest and reputation disturbed only by the controversy initiated by the publication of the life of Wilberforce by his sons, which asserted that Clarkson had unduly magnified his own role in the abolition movement.

Among Clarkson's writings, the antislavery works are valuable for their incisive development of lines of argument pioneered by the Quakers Anthony Benezet and John Woolman, and for their contemporary documentation, deep moral sentiment, and practical persuasiveness. Clarkson does not deal effectively with the theological problems involved in the Biblical permission and regulation of slavery, but he does meet and rebut the argument from the curse of Ham. Reasoning from a contractual theory of government, he holds that all men are free by nature and must be so to be accountable at the Final Judgment, and urges that the Golden Rule implicitly negates the practice of slavery. He notes that the crimes of slaves are incited by inhumane owners and governments, and that the supposed natural inferiority of slaves is a product of their oppressed condition.

Among Clarkson's other works, several deal with the religion of the Friends, which he had found so impressive in its testimony against slavery, and toward which he was drawn throughout his life, although he never joined the Society. Clarkson's *Portraiture of Quakerism* (1806) is a fascinating description of the current evolution of the movement in England and also reveals a certain looseness in Clarkson's connection with the evangelical cause. The work praises the practical moralism of Quakers, defends their behavioral distinctives, and minimizes the importance of the doctrines of the Trinity and justification by faith. RICHARD LOVELACE

CLASSIS, a name used in several Reformed churches for the ecclesiastical assembly of neighboring churches, or for the district in which these churches are to be found. About the same assembly is indicated by the Presbyterian term *presbytery.* However, whereas the congregation in a presbytery is represented only by an elder (the minister being not a member of the local church but a permanent member of the presbytery), a classis is composed of delegates of the local church, usually the minister and an elder. As an assembly, it has no permanent character, being dissolved after each meeting. This shows that the power of the church resides primarily in the governing body, the consistory of the local church. Higher assemblies, however, are not merely advisory; within limits their decisions are binding. Above the level of classis is the synod. This is made up of representatives from each classis rather than each local church. Presbyterian polity is much the same except that the presbytery has greater authority in relation to the local church, and the synod is more advisory. The origins of the classis are to be found in the meetings (coetus) of ministers and elders of the Protestant churches in England which consisted of continental exiles, during the reign of Edward VI; and in the meetings (colloques) of neighboring ministers in France in the same period. In the Netherlands the classis is mentioned for the first time in the Articles of Wesel (1568), and it received its proper place in the Church Order of Dort (1618-19) in these words: "The classical meetings shall consist of neighboring churches that respectively delegate, with proper credentials, a minister and an elder to meet at such a time and place as was determined by the previous classical meeting. Such meetings shall be held once in three months, unless great distances render this inadvisable."

BIBLIOGRAPHY:

H. Bouwman, *Gereformeerd Kerkrecht* (Kampen, 1934), II, 124-187.

H. E. von Hoffman, *Das Kirchenverfassungsrecht der Niederl. Reformierten* (Leipzig, 1902).

L. PRAAMSMA

CLAUDE, Jean (1619-1687), French Protestant minister. Born at Sauvetat-du-Dropt near Agen, Claude studied at Montauban and was ordained in 1645. After a pastorate at Saint-Affrique, he was called to Nîmes in 1654, to Montauban in 1662, and finally to Charenton in 1666. It was at Charenton that the Protestants of Paris met for worship, the building having a seating capacity of at least three or four thousand.

Claude engaged in controversy with the Jansenists, who were attracting to Romanism the famous Marshal Turenne. But his most important controversy was with Bossuet, at that time the leading RC theologian in France. Turenne's niece, Mlle de Duras, who was thinking of turning to Romanism, called for a public debate between the two theologians in 1678. Bossuet later confessed that Claude had made him tremble before the hearers. Nevertheless, Mlle de Duras became a Roman Catholic and Bossuet seemed to triumph.

The situation of the Huguenots was becoming more and more difficult under King Louis XIV's pressure. In a treatise (1681) Claude pleaded against the permission granted to children at the age of seven to transfer from the Reformed to the RC faith without their parents' approval. When the Edict of Nantes was revoked in 1685, Claude was one of the first to flee. An order personally signed by the king obliged him to leave Paris within 24 hours. He went to Holland, where he published his *Complaint of the Cruel Treatment of the Protestants in France*. Death overtook him shortly after at The Hague.

BIBLIOGRAPHY:

R. de la Devise, *Claude, Abrégé de sa vie* (Amsterdam, 1687).
E. E. Haag, *La France Protestante*, vol. IV (Paris, 2nd ed., 1883), 449-474.
T. Jackson, *The Life of Monsieur Claude*, A Library of Christian Biography, vol. X (1837).

J. NICOLE

CLAUDIA, a Christian woman at Rome who joined Paul in sending greetings to Timothy (II Tim. 4:21). There is no conflict with II Tim. 4:11, where Paul says that of his fellow workers and travelling companions only Luke remained with him, since Claudia and the others were ordinary church members and not evangelists. Though nothing further is known of her, the name probably indicates a connection with the imperial palace (see Phil. 4:22). Tradition has identified her as the mother, or, less likely, the wife of Linus, but later scholars have sought to identify her as the daughter of a British ruler and wife of Pudens. Questions of chronology, the separation of the names, Pudens and Claudia, in II Tim. 4:21, and the frequency of the occurrence of these names in Roman times make such speculation useless.

BIBLIOGRAPHY:

J. B. Lightfoot, *The Apostolic Fathers, Clement of Rome* (London, 1890), vol. I, part I.
T. Williams, *Claudia and Pudens* (Llandovery, 1848).

NORMAN SHEPHERD

CLAUDIUS CAESAR (10 B.C.-A.D. 54), fourth emperor of the Roman Empire, who began his rule in A.D. 41. Though feeble in body and lacking in intellectual vigor, he appears to have ruled with comparative success. This may have been due in part to the delegation of more power to subordinates who governed well. He was the first successor of Augustus to be deified. A number of references in ancient authorities show that famines were unusually prevalent during his reign. Gaius, his predecessor, had failed to regulate the grain supply properly, and the consequences of his mismanagement embarrassed Claudius (*Dio*, lix, 17, 2). However, he adopted rigorous measures; yet, according to Tacitus, the situation became so critical that at one time his life was in danger (*Ann.*, xii, 43). The famine mentioned by Luke (Acts 2:28) seems to have been at its height in Palestine about A.D. 46. Claudius was not anti-Semitic in his general policy. On his accession he restored certain privileges of which Gaius had deprived the Jews. Later, however, he forbade them to hold meetings (*Dio*, lx, 66), and in A.D. 49 he banished them from Rome (Acts 18:2; *Suet., Claudius*, xxv). Suetonius mentions disturbances caused by "Chrestus" as the reason for their expulsion. This may indicate some anti-Christian activity among the Jews.

BIBLIOGRAPHY:

P. V. M. Benecke, *HDB* (1898), s.v.
CAH, Cambridge, X (1934), 500 f.
J. M. Hutchison, *ISBE* (1915), s.v.
V. M. Scramuzza, "The Policy of the Early Roman Emperors Towards Judaism," *The Beginnings of Christianity* (London, 1933), 295-296.
A. Souter, *HDAC*[1] (1915), s.v.

WILLIAM J. CAMERON

CLAUDIUS LYSIAS, tribune of the cohort stationed at Jerusalem when the Jews seized Paul (Acts 21:27). He probably bought his Roman citizenship, as his gentile name suggests, in the reign of Claudius (Acts 22:28; 23:26; *Dio Cassius*, lx, 17, 5 f.). He took Paul into custody and bound him, assuming too hastily that he was a notorious leader of banditti (Acts 21:38; Josephus, *Wars*, 11, 13, 5). On discovering his mistake, however, he honored the Valerian and Porcian laws, which protected uncondemned Roman citizens. The next day he convened the Sanhedrin to investigate the incident, but when a heated dispute developed he withdrew Paul (Acts 23:10). He ultimately sent him under escort to Caesarea to save him from conspirators (Acts 23:23 f.). The inconsistency in his letter favors its genuineness (Acts 23:28). On the whole, he acquitted himself competently and honorably.

BIBLIOGRAPHY:

P. V. M. Benecke, *HDB* (1898), s.v.

T. R. S. Broughton, "The Roman Army," *The Beginnings of Christianity* (London, 1933), Pt. I, V, 427 f.

WILLIAM J. CAMERON

CLAUDIUS OF TURIN (d. 835), bishop of Turin. Nothing is known of his early life except that he was Spanish by birth. Later, in Aquitaine, he was master of the royal schools and acquired considerable fame as a Biblical commentator at the court of King Louis, third son of Charlemagne known as Louis the Pious. Shortly after Louis became joint-emperor, he promoted Claudius to the see of Turin in Italy (*c.* 817). Claudius soon showed himself possessed of reforming tendencies which were centuries ahead of his time, carrying them out fearlessly. He showed little regard for papal authority, but because of an unusual set of political circumstances, which made Pope Eugenius unwilling to assert himself against Louis, Claudius continued unrebuked by ecclesiastical superiors. Thus there ensued an extraordinary campaign of iconoclasm—of all places in a ninth-century Italian city. The bishop removed all images and pictures, condemned the use of the crucifix and many other symbols, and spoke out strongly against pilgrimages and the intercession of saints. This was not the limit of his views, however. He held that Peter's apostolic office ceased with Peter, that the power of the keys passed to the whole episcopacy, and that the bishop of Rome could legitimately claim apostolic power only insofar as he lived an apostolic life.

All this went very much further than the mildly reforming elements of the Council of Frankfort (794), which condemned the worship of ikons. Needless to say, his views were regarded by many as heretical and were refuted—though not too convincingly—by Theodemir, abbot of a monastery near Nîmes in France; by the Scotsman Dungal, one of the most learned theologians of the time; and by Jonas, bishop of Orléans. Yet even Theodemir himself admits that the majority of the great W prelates were on the whole inclined to support the reforming measures put forward by Claudius, to whom images were idols and to whom the worship of the cross signified nothing less than godlessness. Agobard, archbishop of Lyons, published a famous treatise in his defense. Claudius' learning was prodigious and his Bible commentaries displayed an unusually wide knowledge and grasp of the works of Augustine.

Buried for centuries in the valleys of the Piedmontese Alps, many of his opinions gradually reappeared in the course of recent centuries. Some of the older writers of the Waldensian Church of Italy have claimed him as their founder.

Most of his writings are still only in

ms. Those which have been published are represented in *MPL*.

BIBLIOGRAPHY:
MPL, CIV, 615-928.
E. J. Martin, *A History of the Iconoclastic Controversy* (1930), especially 262-66.

JAMES D. DOUGLAS

CLEMENT (Lat., "mild"), an active Christian in the church at Philippi (Phil. 4:3). Origen identifies him with Clement of Rome (*In Ioannem* 1:29) as does Eusebius (3:4). This, however, seems highly improbable. Chronology is against it, the name was common, and Clement of Rome appears never to have left the capital.

CLEMENT OF ALEXANDRIA (*c.* 150-*c.* 215), early church theologian. Titus Flavius Clemens, Clement of Alexandria, stands at the beginning of a new era in the course of Christianity. The church in Alexandria emerges in a clear picture from the considerable writings of Clement. Opposition to gnosticism and other heretical sects reaches a new height; the seeds of a system of theology are sown; Christian teaching is presented to meet the most cultured and educated of the pagans on their own ground. Clement was the head of the Christian catechetical school, situated in the shade of the famous Museum of Alexandria. Pagan and Jewish circles had already made Alexandria famous for allegorical interpretation, and Christian writings had since reflected the method (e.g., the *Epistle of Barnabas*). Clement developed it one stage further. Origen, Clement's pupil and successor, systematized allegorical interpretation its furthest extent, and in Origen is found much of Clement's influence and significance. Another deep interest of Clement was to present philosophy as Christian thought, parallel to God's revelation, rather than opposing it.

Life

Clement was the son of well-to-do parents. He was probably born at Athens (*Epiphanius* 32, 6) and began his education there. After his conversion to Christianity he travelled from place to place seeking the best in Christian instruction. After travelling to Greece, S Italy, Syria, and Palestine, he finally settled in Alexandria, where he studied under Pantaenus, the earliest known head of the catechetical school (d. *c.* 200). Clement succeeded his teacher and did his writing during the reign of Septimius Severus (193-211). During the persecutions of 202 and 203, he left Egypt and took refuge in Cappadocia with his pupil Alexander, later bishop of Jerusalem. He seems to have lived out his remaining years in Cappadocia.

Writings

Clement attempted to set forth Christian teaching using a conventional form of profane literature. His famous trilogy, the *Protrepticus*, the *Paedagogus*, and the *Stromata*, is written with each part geared for different readers. The *Protrepticus* (*Exhortation*) is an apology designed to convince the unconverted of the folly of pagan beliefs and show them the soul-satisfying truths of the "new song" in the Logos become flesh in Jesus Christ. Its purpose was to bring men to a decision, using a form of *protreptikoi* already employed by Aristotle, Epicurus, Poseidonius, and others. The *Paedagogus* (the *Instructor*) is a continuation, but now addresses the reader as a Christian and ready for ethical instruction. Here the problems of daily life in Alexandria are confronted. No total withdrawal from the cultural life of the time is advocated, but a severance from debauchery and vices must be maintained with the support of a new Christian spirit. The *Stromata* (the *Miscellanies*), adapted for the instruction of the mature Christian, treats primarily the problem of the Christian's regard for secular learning and Greek philosophy. Clement maintained that just as the law was a schoolmaster to lead the Hebrews to Christ, so philosophy was a preparation for the Greeks. Refutation against the gnostics and the presentation of true Gnosis are other major goals of the work.

Another extant writing of Clement, *Who Is the Rich Man That Is Saved?*, is a sermon on the text of Mark 10:17-31. Clement is concerned with assuring wealthy listeners that the meaning of the passage is not that they must give away all that they own in order to be saved, but that they must relinquish the passion for wealth.

Eclogae Propheticae (*Selections from the Prophetic Sayings*) and *Excerpta ex Theodoto* (*Epitomes from the Writings of Theodotus* and the so-called *Eastern Teaching of the Time of Valentinus*) were intended to follow the *Stromata*. They are evidently notes taken from the gnostic writings of a Valentinian named Theodotus, and the preliminary study notes made by Clement.

Other non-extant writings are—*The Hypotyposeis* (*Outlines* or *Sketches*), a commentary of allegorical interpretation on selected passages of the OT and NT (including the *Epistle of Barnabas* and the *Apocalypse of Peter*); *On the Pasch, Ecclesiastical Canon* or *Against the Judaizers, On Providence, Exhortation to Endurance* or *To the Recently Baptized, Discourses on Fasting* and *On Slander, On the Prophet Amos*, and various letters.

The major early sources concerning Clement are Eusebius, *Eccl. Hist.* 5,11; 6,6; 11,13; Jerome, *Catal.* 38; and Photius, *Cod.* 109-111.

Clement's weak points were (1) the unnecessary, degrading details concerning the licentious sects, (2) the use of allegory leading to extremely subjective conclusions, (3) the acceptance of a certain gnostic glorifying of knowledge above faith and love, and (4) the lack of a truly systematic presentation of his material. His strong points include (1) making Christ, the Logos, as center of all, (2) upholding the Scriptures as the supreme revelation, (3) giving reliable testimony concerning gnosticism, and (4) supplying a wealth of philosophical quotations and an appreciation for the potential role of education and culture in the Christian life.

Bibliography:

B. Altaner, *Patrologie* (Freiburg, 5th ed., 1958).

O. Bardenhewer, *Geschichte der altkirchlichen Literatur* (Freiburg, 2nd ed., 1914), II, 15-62.

C. Bigg, *The Christian Platonists of Alexandria* (Oxford, 1886), 36-114.

W. Boussett, *Jüdisch-christlicher Schulbetrieb in Alexandria und Rom* (Göttingen, 1915), 155-271.

G. W. Butterworth, *Clement of Alexandria* (London, 1919).

G. W. Butterworth, "Clement of Alexandria and Art," *VTS* 17(1916), 68-76.

R. P. Casey, "Clement of Alexandria and the Beginnings of Christian Platonism," *HTR* 18(1925), 39-101.

R. P. Casey, *The Excerpta ex Theodoto of Clement of Alexandria* (London, 1934).

L. Fruechtel, "Clemens Alexandrinus," *RAC* III (1957), 182-88.

F. J. A. Hort and J. B. Mayor, *Clement of Alexandria, Miscellanies, Book VII* (London, 1902).

E. Molland, "Clement of Alexandria on the Origin of Greek Philosophy," *Symb O* 25 (1936), 57-85.

E. Molland, *The Conception of the Gospel in the Alexandrian Theology* (Oslo, 1938).

J. Munck, *Untersuchungen über Klemens von Alexandrien* (Stuttgart, 1933).

J. E. L. Oulton, H. Chadwick, *Alexandrian Christianity* (Philadelphia, 1954), 15-165.

J. Patrick, *Clement of Alexandria* (Edinburgh, 1914).

J. Quasten, *Patrology* (Westminster, Maryland, 1953), II, 1-36.

A. Roberts, J. Donaldson, eds., *The Ante-Nicene Fathers* (Grand Rapids, Mich., 1951), II, 165-629.

O. Staehlin, *Die griechischen christlichen Schriftsteller der ersten drei Jahrhunderte* (Berlin, 1905-9), 1-3; 12(2nd ed., 1939); 15(2nd ed., 1939); 17(1909); 39, Index (1934-36).

R. B. Tollinton, *Clement of Alexandria* (London, 1914).

R. B. Tollinton, *Alexandrine Teaching on the Universe* (New York, 1932).

Lewis Foster

CLEMENT OF ROME, a leader in the church at Rome during the closing decades of the first century. He was the author of an epistle from the church at Rome to the church at Corinth known as *I Clement*, included among the writings of the Apostolic Fathers. A second epistle (*II Clement*), actually a middle-second-century sermon rather than a letter, mistakenly attributed to Clement, is also included in the same collection. Although he occupies an imposing role in later traditions, the historical figure of Clement has become lost from sight, and apart from his one authentic epistle, only his name is preserved.

Most earlier references to Clement in Christian literature also include remarks concerning his epistle to Corinth. About

I Clement

A.D. 170 Bishop Dionysius of Corinth assured the bishop of Rome, Soter, that they in Corinth would read his letter in their services even as they did "that which was formerly sent to us through Clement" (Eusebius, *Hist. eccl.* 4, 23, 11). The writing of Clement's epistle has been dated about A.D. 96 because of his introductory statement concerning "the sudden and repeated misfortune and calamities which have befallen us" (*I Cl.* 1,1). This has been interpreted as referring to the persecutions of Domitian which ceased at his death in 96, which allowed the writing of this epistle. Other allusions point also to the last decade in the first century establishing *I Clement* as the earliest datable Christian writing outside the NT. The occasion for writing the letter was a dispute which had arisen in the church at Corinth because, as Clement described it, "a few rash and self-willed persons have made [unholy sedition] blaze up to such a frenzy that your name, venerable and famous, and worthy as it is of all men's love, has been much slandered" (*I Cl.* 1,1). There had been an attempt to replace the older, respected presbyters with young men. Clement maintained that the rebellion resulted from jealousy (*I Cl.* 3, 2 ff.) and had brought discouragement, rejection, and grief upon others (*I Cl.* 46, 9) to the extent that outsiders were aware of the Christians' plight and the Lord's name was dishonored (*I Cl.* 47, 7). Clement urged that first repentance (*I Cl.* 7, 4 ff.) and obedience (*I Cl.* 9, 2 ff.) must come. Proper humility (*I Cl.* 16, 1 ff.) was necessary, and a respect for prescribed order and rank must be acknowledged and observed (*I Cl.* 21, 6; 41, 1). Prayer and forgiveness must follow (*I Cl.* 48, 1; 51, 1), and a willingness to sacrifice so that good may be gained for many (*I Cl.* 51, 2; 54, 2 ff.).

The study of Clement's epistle provides a sample of major subjects of continuing interest concerning the early church. For example, material is given for historical problems surrounding the death of Peter and Paul. In church order, Clement clearly uses the term presbyters (elders) as synonymous with bishops and reflects no monarchial episcopate at Rome as early as this period. The exact position occupied by Clement is not certain. Later sources refer to him as bishop but give contradictory testimony as to the order of succession. Irenaeus (*Adv. Haer.* 3, 3, 3) and Eusebius (*Hist. eccl.* 3, 4, 9) list Clement as third in the line at Rome, after Linus and Anacletus. Tertullian (*De Praescr.* 32), however, makes him the immediate successor of Peter, but the Liberian catalogue also puts him after Linus. Some doctrinal works referring to *I Clement* emphasize a difference between faith and works as found in Paul and in Clement, but the contrast is more in context than in conclusion. Literary study has been applied to the problem of Clement's heritage, whether it was Jewish or Hellenistic, but it has failed to offer a conclusive answer. A rather extensive prayer at the end of the epistle (*I Cl.* 59, 4-61, 3) and an alleged use of the

"Sanctus" (*I Cl.* 34) are referred to in liturgical studies, but these are not sufficient to determine a fixed wording for Roman liturgy at the end of the first century. Clement's use of the OT and NT are important in studying the canon. Almost 30 percent of Clement's epistle can be cited as coming from the OT (59 formally introduced citations), whereas only two formally introduced quotations come from NT writings (*I Cl.* 13, 2; 46, 8). Nevertheless, Paul is cited by name but without quotation (*I Cl.* 47, 5) and positive knowledge and use of NT Epistles and Gospels is evident. Though he did not grant less authority to apostolic writings than to the OT, Clement did not quote their writings in the same way that he quoted the ancient prophets. Indeed, as Irenaeus pictures Clement of Rome, "He had seen the apostles and associated with them, and still had their preaching sounding in his ears, and their tradition before his eyes" (*Adv. Haer.* 3, 3, 3).

The textual witness of *I Clement* is exceptionally early and broad. A Greek majuscule (5th-century Alexandrinus) and a Greek minuscule (11th-century Hierosolymitanus), and versions from E and W (12th-century Syriac, Cantabrigensis; 4th-century Coptic, Berlin, and 7th-century Coptic, Strassburg; and 11th-century Latin, Florinesis) provide the sources.

Spurious Works

The pseudo-Clementine literature seems to have had its beginning in the third century, when a Judaistic enthusiast of the church in Syria supplied a biography for Clement of Rome. This was written not from an interest in Clement as much as a desire to associate him with Peter. Writings exist in two forms: the *Twenty Homilies* contain mainly the missionary sermons of Peter, and the *Ten Books of Recognitions*, which tell of the tragic separation of Clements family and Peter's role in bringing them together again. Also from Syria in the third century, a zealous ascetic sent out instructions to virgins, unmarried persons or ascetics, whether men or women. From the continuity of the writing it seems that this was a single work in the beginning but soon was divided to form two epistles. The name of Clement was attached to these two letters. A fourth-century work which sought to enlist the name of Clement in its support was the *Apostolic Constitutions*, which claimed apostolic authorship, but bore the name of Clement of Rome in the title as the one through whom this manual of discipline, worship, and doctrine was compiled. In the same century a spurious correspondence of Clement with James, the Lord's brother, and the *Martyrium Clementis* by Symeon Metaphrastis were added, as well as revisions and additions to the older materials. In the ninth century, pseudo-Isidore used the name of Clement in presenting the spurious epistle of Clement to James plus another second epistle (both in Latin). This originated no earlier than the fifth century, and then three more were added, raising the number to five Latin letters of Clement. These are known as the False Decretals.

See CLEMENTINE LITERATURE; DECRETALS, FALSE.

BIBLIOGRAPHY:

B. Altaner, *Patrologie* (Freiburg, 5th ed., 1958).

K. Bihlmeyer, *Die apostolischen Väter* (Tübingen, 1924), Part I.

C. Eggenberger, *Die Quellen der politischen Ethik des I. Klemensbriefes* (Zürich, 1951).

J. Fischer, *Die apostolischen Väter* (Muenchen, 1956).

L. Foster, *Clement of Rome and His Literary Sources* (Diss., Harvard, 1958).

O. Gebhardt, A. Harnack, and Th. Zahn, *Patrum Apostolicorum Opera* (2nd ed., Lipsiae, 1875; ed. minor 2nd ed., 1920).

A. Harnack, *Einführung in die alte Kirchengeschichte* (Leipzig, 1929).

A. M. Javierre, *La primera «diadochè» de la patrística y los «ellogimoi andres» de Clem. R.* (Torino, 1958).

J. Klevinghaus, *Die theologische Stellung der*

apostolischen Väter zur alttestamentlichen Offenbarung (Gütersloh, 1948).
R. Knopf, *Die Lehre der zwölf Apostel, Die zwei Clemensbriefe* (Tübingen, 1920).
K. Lake, *The Apostolic Fathers* (Cambridge, 1945), I.
K. Lieang, *Het Begrip Deemoed in I Clemens* (Utrecht, 1951).
J. B. Lightfoot, *The Apostolic Fathers: Clement of Rome* (London, 1890), Part I, 2 vols.
Ch. Mohrmann, "Les Origines de la Latinate Chrétienne à Rome," *VC* 3(1949), 67-106; 163-82.
J. Quasten, *Patrology* (Utrecht, 1950), I.
C. C. Richardson, *Early Christian Fathers* (London, 1953).
L. Sanders, *L'Hellenisme de Saint Clement de Rome et le Paulinisme* (Louvain, 1943).
A. Stuiber, "Clemens Romanus I," *RAC* III (1957), 188-97.
W. C. van Unnik, "Is I Clement 20 Purely Stoic?," *VC* 4(1950), 181-92.
W. C. van Unnik, "I Clement 34 and the Sanctus," *VC* 5(1951), 204-48.
W. Wrede, *Untersuchungen zum ersten Klemensbriefe* (Göttingen, 1891).

LEWIS FOSTER

CLEMENTINE LITERATURE. The designation "Clementine" has reference to that corpus of writings from the postapostolic age which pseudonymously bear the name of Clement of Rome. Hence they are often referred to as *pseudo*-Clementine writings. This corpus includes such works as the Second Epistle of Clement, the Apostolic Constitutions, two Epistles to Virgins, the Clementine Homilies and Recognitions, and the Apocalypse of St. Peter. The writings are important in presenting clear insights into the drift of Hellenistic Judaism. The Clementine Literature grew out of an early Ebionite background which promoted a rigid sect of Judaizers. After coming under the influence of Hellenistic philosophy, a syncretistic form of Jewish-Christian gnosticism emerged. The views of this variety of gnosticism are polemically set forth in the Clementine Literature.

These writings lay heavy stress on rigorous piety and asceticism. Also, great importance is attached to the series of confrontations between Peter and Simon Magus. This debate has been considered crucial by F. C. Baur and the Tübingen school as it allegedly depicts a conflict between Petrinism and Paulinism. Paul is represented under the concealed guise of Simon Magus, as an apostate from the Mosaic faith and a type of anti-Christ.

H. J. Schoeps has attached great importance to the Clementine Literature with specific reference to the authenticity of Paul's apostleship. He maintains that the Clementines not only reflect a third-century climate of Jewish gnosticism but incorporate early Jewish challenges to Paul's authority. The polemic of Peter concerning revelation is connected to the Pauline apostleship question. Peter sets forth the primacy of direct communication in the waking state over against the visions and dreams of Paul. Paul's "subjective" revelations are deemed unreliable. The Clementine Literature reflects a thoroughly gnostic Christology, with Christ being viewed as an Eon. (See EON.)

Clement of Rome is the genuine author of an Epistle to the Corinthians. This letter is authenticated by the writings of Irenaeus and Eusebius.

BIBLIOGRAPHY:

H. J. Schoeps, *Paul* (Philadelphia, 1961).
H. J. Schoeps, *Jewish Christianity* (Philadelphia, 1969).

ROBERT C. SPROUL

CLEOPAS (short form of Gr. *Cleopatros*), one of the two disciples who went to Emmaus on the day of our Lord's resurrection. He may have been Luke's authority for the narrative (Luke 24:18). Zahn, Creed, and others identify him with Cleophas (John 19:25), but the evidence is insufficient for certainty.

CLEOPHAS, CLOPAS, probably the husband of one of the women at the cross (John 19:25). The form *Cleophas* is not supported by any Greek authority and is also not found in the Latin Codex Amiatinus. According to Hegesippus, Clopas was a brother of Joseph, the husband of the mother of Jesus, and was the father of Symeon, ultimately head of the church at Jerusalem. His identification with Alphaeus (Mt. 10:3) remains uncertain.

CLERGY, a term used of regular members of the ministry of the church as distinct from the laity. The word is derived from the Greek *klēros, klērikos.* Of the different terms used to designate clergy, the word *bishop* is derived from the Greek *episcopos* (I Tim. 3:1 ff.; Titus 1:2 ff.; Acts 20:28) and *priest* from the Greek *presbyteros* ("elder"). Usage is what it is, but we can note the historical confusion in the usage of the words resulting from the hierarchical development in the church. A word designating an office and institution in Israel *distinct from priesthood* has come to be used to designate the religious specialist we know as *priest. Deacon* is derived from the Greek *diaconos* ("minister"). The origin of the office is generally assumed to be found in Acts 6.

The varying conceptions of the Christian ministry seem to be closely akin to one's conception of the church. Here there are, broadly, two possible conceptions: naturalistic and supernaturalistic. The latter has the significant subdivisions of evangelical and sacerdotal. The naturalistic conception of the church would find the equivalent of its ministry in the religious specialists of ethnic societies, the *shaman* and the *priest.* The supernaturalistic and evangelical view of the origin of the church has fairly consistently resisted the sacerdotal principle, but it is significant that wherever the evangelical principle is obscured the tendency is toward a sacerdotal conception.

The sacerdotal conception of the ministry is most plausible when the priesthood of ancient Israel is conceived of sacerdotally. Philip Schaff says, "Those who condemn, in principle, all hierarchy, sacerdotalism, and ceremonialism, should remember that God himself appointed the priesthood and ceremonies in the Mosaic dispensation. . . ." (*History of the Christian Church,* II, 123). Sacerdotalism in the Christian church is symptomatic of a failure to rise to the conception of the Epistle to the Hebrews, which vigorously asserts the evangelical principle in all ages of the church and plainly teaches that the old priestly order of Levi has been superseded by the priestly order of Melchizedek, which is limited to the one person of Christ.

As Schaff points out (*ibid.*), the development of a special priesthood in the Christian church followed the supposed analogy of the Levitical priesthood: the latter's three ranks "naturally furnished an analogy for the ministry of bishop, priest, and deacon, and came to be regarded as typical of it." The obvious fallacy is the admitted fact that bishops and elders (presbyters, priests) are equivalent terms in the NT. However, aside from matters of organization, there is the separate question of the conception of the ministry: Is it an evangelical ministry, or is it a sacerdotalism, which is viewed as the channel of salvation? Protestantism, with some inconsistencies, has held to the former alternative.

The simple NT provision for leadership by elders obviously stems from a similar practice in ancient Israel (Num. 11:16 ff.), since there is no record of the origin of the office in the NT. The inference is that a well-known, workable scheme was adapted to new conditions.

The office of deacon also has its analogy, not in a specially priestly context in Israel, but in men like Joshua, who is called Moses' minister (Ex. 24:13), and Elisha, who ministered to Elijah (I Kings

19:21). Even Moses is significantly referred to as a minister in the house of God, of which Christ is the Lord and Head (Heb. 3:1-6; Num. 12:7; I Tim. 3:15).

The gradual development of hierarchical and sacerdotal schemes can be traced in Schaff (*op. cit.*, II and III). His conclusion may be taken as an adequate summary of the whole process: "The idea and institution of a special priesthood, distinct from the body of the people, with the accompanying notion of sacrifice and altar, passed imperceptibly from Jewish and heathen reminiscences and analogies into the Christian Church" (*ibid.*).

Bibliography:

A. Bertholet, "Priesthood," *Encyclopedia of Social Sciences*, Vol. 12.

J. Calvin, *Institutes of the Christian Religion*, IV, iii-vii.

A. Fliche, "Religious Institutions, Roman Catholic," *Encyclopedia of Social Sciences*, Vol. 13. Full Bibliography.

E. Hatch, *The Organization of the Early Christian Churches* (Bampton Lectures, 1880).

C. Hodge, *The Church and Its Polity* (London, 1879).

J. B. Lightfoot, *Saint Paul's Epistle to the Philippians*: Dissertation I, "The Christian Ministry."

T. M. Lindsay, *The Church and the Ministry in the Early Centuries* (London, 1902).

L. Morris, "Clergy," "Minister," "Ministry," *Baker's Dictionary of Theology*.

R. S. Paul, *Ministry* (Grand Rapids, 1965).

P. Schaff, *History of the Christian Church*, Vol. II, Chap. iv; Vol. III, Chap. v.

Wilber B. Wallis

CLERICUS, Johannes (Leclerc, Jean) (1657-1736), Arminian theologian. Leclerc was a descendant of a Huguenot family which had fled to Geneva. His father, Étienne Leclerc (d. 1676), was a professor of Greek; his mother, Susanna Galatin, was a native of Geneva. Already as a student in the gymnasium he gave evidence of great ability. In 1763 he began his studies at the university: philosophy under the Cartesian Chouet, originally from Saumur; Hebrew under his uncle J. Galatin; and after 1676, theology under F. Turretinus, Mestrezat, and Tronchin. At this time he felt drawn to the theology of Saumur. In 1680, as tutor of a boy from Grenoble, he attended Saumur himself, where he became acquainted with the writings of Episcopius and began a correspondence with Philippus van Limborch, Remonstrant professor in Amsterdam. At about this time Leclerc's first publication appeared, dealing with the Trinity, incarnation, and original sin. As a result of this work, he was accused of Sabellianism and Socinianism, partly because of his superficial treatment of the subject matter. In 1682 Leclerc left for London, where he sought contact with the Walloon Church. When it was evident that he had no chance of success in this, he proceeded to the Netherlands. In Amsterdam he joined with the Remonstrants, for whom he conducted the French services. In 1684, through the influence of Limborch, he was appointed to a professorship in classical literature, Hebrew, and philosophy, to which church history was added in 1712. A stroke in 1728 forced his resignation in 1733.

Leclerc was of service in publication of the works of Erasmus (Leiden, 1703-1706), which still is the only complete edition in existence, and in the publication of older works, e.g., those of Cotelier and Hugo Grotius. Leclerc became famous in Europe through the publication of a periodical that first appeared in 1686 under the title *Bibliothèque universelle et historique*, and which continued until 1727, its name later being slightly revised. The periodical contained critiques of many books. Leclerc opposed the Mosaic origin of the Pentateuch and had critical views about the inspiration of the Holy Scriptures, especially in connection with such books as Job, Proverbs, Ecclesiastes, and Song of Solomon. He published a Latin translation of the OT with a commentary (1700-1735). Leclerc was more a literary figure than a theologian. He strove after a practical Christianity devoid of superficiality and in which human reason assumed an important place. He was a defender of Locke's empiricism, had contacts with the Cambridge Platonists (*q.v.*), opposed Spinoza, and followed Malebranche. Leclerc can be viewed as a forerunner of the French Encyclopaedists. Strangely, however, he was an opponent of Pierre Bayle. Their relationship was one of mutual enmity. Leclerc maintained correspondence with numerous scholars.

BIBLIOGRAPHY:

A. Barnes, *Jean Leclerc (1657-1736) et la République des Lettres* (Paris, 1938).

Biographisch Woordenboek van Protestantsche Godgeleerfen in Nederland, II, 83-104.

R. L. Colie, *Light and Enlightenment* (Cambridge, 1957).

T. Dokkum, in *Nieuw Nederlandsch Biografisch Woordenboek* (1918), IV, column 430-434.

E. Haase, *Isaac Papin à l'époque de la Révocation.* Trois lettres inédites (to Jean Leclerc of Amsterdam), in: *Bulletin de la Société du Protest. français* (1952) IC, 94-122.

J. Roth, *Le "Traité de l'Inspiration" de Jean Leclerc*, in: *Rev. d'Histoiae et de philosophie religieuses* XXXVI (1956), 50-60.

P. Vernière, *Spinoza et la pensée français avant la Révolution* I (Paris, 1954), 72-81.

J. J. Wetstein, *Oratio funebris in obitum viri Joannis Clerici*, 22 Febr. 1736, in: *Archief voor kerkelijke geschiedenis inzonderheid van Nederland* IV (1833), 91-115.

D. NAUTA

CLERMONT, COUNCIL OF (1095), chief of several church councils held at Clermont-Ferrard in central France. It was summoned by the French pope Urban II and attended by 200 bishops. It was the occasion of the proclamation by Urban of the First Crusade. The "Truce of God" was confirmed, and the archbishop of Tours was given jurisdiction over Brittany. Thirty-two canons were passed, many of them lasting in effect. It was declared that the pilgrimage to liberate Jerusalem would supply the place of every other penance. This relaxed the discipline of the church and adversely affected morality. Other canons forbade the elevation of laymen to bishoprics and the purchase of benefices for personal gain. Lay grants of benefices (investiture) were forbidden. Meat was not to be eaten during Lent. Ordinations were to be at the ember seasons only. All communicants were to receive "corpus et sanguinem similiter" (i.e., in both kinds).

CLOPPENBURG, Johannes (1592-1652), Dutch Reformed theologian. A native of Amsterdam, Cloppenburg studied at Leiden, where he became a friend of Voetius. He felt closely drawn to Gomarus, under whom he studied Hebrew and other subjects. When Vorstius was then appointed to succeed Arminius, Cloppenburg opposed him in an anonymous writing (1610). In 1612 he attended the University of Franeker, and afterwards remained for various lengths of time at numerous other European academies, e.g., at Heidelberg, Basel (where he stayed for a year and had close contacts with Buxtorf), Geneva, and in France. Upon his return to the Netherlands, he became pastor at Aalburg in 1616; then in 1618 at Heusden near his friend Voetius; in 1621 at Amsterdam; and, when he had left this city after a dispute about the authority of the government in ecclesiastical matters, at Brielle in 1629. In 1640 he was appointed professor at the University of Harderwijk. Then he succeeded Vedelius at Franeker, where he presented his inaugural oration on May 18, 1644, and where he became a colleague of Cocceius.

In his writings Cloppenburg opposed the anabaptists, Remonstrants, and Socinians. In 1637, at the request of the Synod of S Holland, he published a treatise about usury and interest. In it he approved the establishment by the government of lending banks. The question of usury led to a written dispute with Salmasius. At Harderwijk he disputed with his colleague A. Densing, professor of medicine, regarding the relation of faith and knowledge. Cloppenburg opposed the idea of a world-soul which Densing accepted. He also feared that Densing's theories might have dangerous consequences, since they were reminiscent of the heresies of Nestorius and Origen. Every theological faculty was engaged in this dispute, and several writings were devoted to it. Although Densing was not accused of theological heresy, his acceptance of a world-soul and other ideas of his were suspect, and most debaters supported Cloppenburg. In this battle Cloppenburg represented the scholastic views of Thomas, who followed Aristotle, while Densing was more of a Platonist. Cloppenburg was a forerunner of the federal theology of Cocceius and supported the natural law tendencies of Melanchthon. He made the distinction between *paresis* and *aphesis*, which can also be found in the thinking of Cocceius.

The writings of Cloppenburg were published in 1684 at Amsterdam in two volumes by his grandson Johannes A. Marck, professor at Leiden (*Theologica Opera Omnia*).

BIBLIOGRAPHY:

Biographisch Woordenboek van Protestantsche Godgeleerden in Nederland II, 106-122.

W. B. S. Boeles, *Frieslands Hoogeschool en het Rijks Athenaeum te Franeker* II (Leeuwarden, 1889), 184-190.

H. Bouman, *Geschiedenis van de voormalige Geldersche Hoogeschool en hare hoogleraren* (Utrecht, 1844-47), 2 vols.

J. A. Cramer, *De Theologische Faculteit te Utrecht ten tijde van Voetius* (Utrecht, 1932).

A. A. M. de Haan, *Het Wijsgerig onderwijs te Harderwijk 1599-1811* (Harderwijk, 1960).

A. C. Duker, *Gisbertus Voetius* (Leiden, 1897-1904), 2 vols.

W. P. C. Knuttel, *Acta der Particuliere Synoden van Zuid Holland* ('s Gravenhage, 1908-1909).

D. Nauta, *Samuel Maresius* (Amsterdam, 1935).

O. Ritschl, *Dogmengeschichte des Protestantismus* III (Goettingen, 1926), 425-427, 441, 444.

G. Schrenk, *Gottesreich und Bund ins aelteren Protestantismus vornehmlich by Joh. Coccejus* (Guetersloh, 1923).

C. Sepp, *Het Godgeleerd onderwijs in Nederland gedurende de 16de en 17de eeuw* II (Leiden, 1874).

G. Voetius, *Politica ecclesiastica* IV (1676), 274.

D. NAUTA

CLOUD. The Hebrews were well aware that rain came from the clouds (Gen. 9:13, 14; Eccles. 11:3) which hold the waters that are above the firmament, or expanse, of the atmosphere (Gen. 1:7). The use of the term "windows of heaven" is simple metaphor (Gen. 7:11; II Kings 7:2; Mal. 3:10).

Israel normally experienced rain from October to April, and sunshine from May to September. Clouds build up from the Mediterranean (I Kings 18:44; Luke 12:54). After heavy winter rains the season closes with lighter rains that help the ripening grain (Deut. 11:14). From time to time clouds of dust sweep in from the southern deserts; these are "clouds without water" (Prov. 25:14; Jude 12).

Like other natural phenomena, clouds are used metaphorically to teach deeper truths. A light morning cloud, soon dissolved, symbolizes insincere devotion (Hos. 6:4), transitory prosperity (Job 30:15), and even life itself (Job 7:9). It pictures God's dissolving of our cloud of sin (Isa. 44:22). The ungenerous man is the cloud that does not fall as rain (Prov. 25:14), and so is the man who is swept along without being of any use to mankind (Jude 12). Returning clouds are like the worries of old age, which cannot be swept away as easily as in youth (Eccles. 12:2). Clouds that hide the sun symbolize the hiding of the mystery of God's Person (Ps. 97:2). When God rides on the clouds, He brings a storm of judgment or vindication (Isa. 19:1; cf. Ps. 18:9-15).

There are two special cloud manifestations. God led the people out of Egypt with a pillar of cloud (Ex. 13:21). This cloud rose from ground level, since later it moved behind the people and blocked the view of the Egyptians (Ex. 14:19, 20). The presence of God was manifested in a luminous cloud in the tabernacle and temple (Ex. 40:34-38; I Kings 8:10, 11). The Jews subsequently referred to this as the Shekinah, or Dwelling (of God). It is probable, though not certain, that the cloud at the Transfiguration (Mt. 17:5) and the Ascension (Acts 1:9) was the same cloud of the divine presence. Clouds are a feature of the Second Coming (Mt. 26:64; Luke 21:27; I Thess. 4:17; Rev. 1:7) and link Jesus Christ with what is said of the Son of man in Dan. 7:13. Either they are clouds of glory, or Christ is seen as Jehovah who rides on the clouds.

J. S. WRIGHT

CNIDUS, "age," in NT times a small free Roman city located on a peninsula at the SW tip of Asia Minor. It was the last point of land in Asia Minor passed by ships following the difficult and circuitous route to Rome from the E made necessary by prevailing westerly winds. In spite of unfavorable conditions, the ship on which Paul traveled did not make use of the fine harbor at Cnidus to await better conditions, lest the loss of time in the advanced season of the year would make sailing altogether impossible (Acts 27:7).

COAL, a translation of the OT גַּחֶלֶת (*gacheleth*) and פֶּחָם (*pechām*), the former meaning a live coal (II Sam. 14:7; Isa. 44:19) and often conjoined with "burning" or "fire" for emphasis (Prov. 6:28), and the latter meaning charcoal or quenched coals. Also the translation of ἄνθραξ (*anthrax*) or ἀνθρακία, "a live coal" (John 18:18; Rom. 12:20). The rendering of רִצְפָּה (*ritzpah*) in Isa. 6:6 should be a hot stone, and of רֶשֶׁף (*resheph*) in Song of S. 8:6 and Hab. 3:5 should be flames.

Mineral coal is probably not referred to, but rather charcoals made by charring wood stacked around a central fire, or in some cases wood embers. There is no evidence that the sparse and poor soft coals found today in local sandstones were used in the Biblical period.

THOMAS H. LEITH

COCCEIUS, Johannes (1603-1669), or **Johann Coch,** Reformed linguist and theologian, father of federal theology in Holland. Born in Bremen, Cocceius showed his great talents for the study of languages in his youth. He made Greek verses, translated a part of one of the apocrypha in Hebrew, and studied Islam. His teachers were, among others, the moderate Calvinists Martinius and Crocius, who had been members of the famous Synod of Dort. In 1625 he continued his studies in Hamburg, and in 1626 he departed for Franeker in the Netherlands, where he attended the theological lectures of Amesius and Maccovius. He was especially delighted with the lectures of the famous Orientalist Amama. In 1630 he succeeded Martinius in Bremen as professor in Biblical philology, and in his inaugural address he attacked scholastic philosophy and dogmatics. In 1636 he returned to Franeker, where he lectured on Oriental languages and, starting in 1643, on the exegesis of the OT and NT. In 1648 he edited his important exposition of federal theology: *Summa doctrinae de foedere et testamento Dei explicata.* Two years later he departed for Leiden. There he became involved in several theological disputes. The first one concerned the significance of the sabbath, which his colleague Heidanus had declared had only a ceremonial, not a moral meaning for the NT church. Cocceius supported him by applying the principles of federal theology to this problem, but he was opposed by several theologians, who were convinced that his views would promote an increasing tendency of profanation of the Lord's day. Another problem arose after the appearance of his commentary on Romans, in which he distinguished beween the manner of forgiveness of sins in the OT and in the NT. This distinction was also a consequence of his federal theology. He claimed that in the OT dispensation the Lord had overlooked (ἄφεσις) sin and that in the NT He took away (πάρεσις) sin. The leading dogmaticians Voetius and Maresius were strongly opposed to this distinction and they accused Cocceius of heterodoxy. After his death his *Collected Works* were published in Amsterdam (1673-1675).

The theology of Cocceius has been characterized by one word, *anti-scholastic* (A. van de Flier, *Dissertatio de Joanne Coccejo antischolastico*, 1859); but, although his dogmatic system reacted against scholastic tendencies in Calvinistic orthodoxy, Cocceius himself was not free from the faults which he found in the dogmatic works of his time. Through his *federal theology*, he wanted to avoid all speculations about and deductions from God's eternal decrees and to develop only the historical way of salvation in which these decrees were realized. This historical way was, according to Cocceius, a way of several covenantal dispensations that succeeded each other in such a manner that the new one meant the abrogation of the preceding one. The first dispensation was that of the covenant of works, established with Adam in Paradise. Then followed the covenant of grace with Moses, to be distinguished in three parts: before, during, and after the promulgation of the law. The third dispensation was that of the new covenant in Christ. This covenant was manifested in the history of the church in seven periods. In spite of his purpose to aim at a pure Biblical theology, Cocceius could realize his own system only by using some artificial means every now and then. In his exegesis of the OT he often resorted to an unconvincing allegorical interpretation, and his disciples often went further than their master in their manipulations of the text. Cocceius' conception of the sabbath and his idea of a twofold forgiveness of sins broke the unity of the OT and NT, and the more liberal-minded members of the Dutch Reformed Church made use of his point of view to defend a life view out of harmony with strict Calvinistic principles. A long struggle followed. Not until 18th-century toleration was introduced in Holland was this conflict over. In spite of his good intentions, Cocceius had become a precursor of the false views of the Enlightenment, especially by his critical attitude toward the doctrine of the church. His greatest merits are to be found in his linguistic studies; his Hebrew lexicon was reprinted in several editions until the end of the 18th century.

Bibliography:

H. Bavinck, *Gereformeerde Dogmatiek*[4] (Kampen, 1930), I, 160.

J. Cocceius, *Collected Works* (Amsterdam, 1673-5), 8 vols.

A. van de Flier, *Dissertatio de Joanne Coccejo antischolastico* (1859).

E. Hirsch, *Gesch. der neueren evangelischen Theologie* (1949), I, 237 ff.

A. Ritschl, *Geschichte des Pietismus in der reformirten Kirche* (1880), I, 130-152.

G. Schrenk, *Gottesreich und Bund im älteren Protestantismus, vornehmlich bei Joh. C.* (Gütersloh, 1923).

C. Sepp, *Het godgeleerd onderwys ir. Nederland gedurende de 16e en 17 eeuw* (Leiden, 1874), II, 60 ff.

L. Praamsma

CODEX, an ancient manuscript in book form. The codex form began to appear in the second century and eventually displaced the roll. In its simplest form a codex is made by folding a sheet twice the width required in the middle to form a quire of two leaves or four pages. A number of quires are then sewn together to make the book. Or, as many sheets as are thought necessary for the whole book may be placed on top of one another and folded into one huge quire (one such is known with 59 sheets or 118 leaves!). Ten or twelves leaves, however, prove to be most convenient. The codex was especially popular among Christians. Doubtless they found it useful for looking up proof texts and it was a convenience to have, say, the four Gospels in a single book (which was not possible with a roll).

LEON MORRIS

COELE-SYRIA. The name actually means "hollow Syria," and refers primarily to the long valley that extends between the Lebanon and Anti-Lebanons. Through this valley flow two important rivers: one in a northerly direction, the Orontes, the other in a southerly direction, the Leontes. The watershed of these rivers lies by the city of Baalbek, which was named Heliopolis by the Greeks. Later the name Coele-Syria came to refer to a larger and more extensive territory, which included the whole of Phoenicia and Palestine. We find it used in this way by the Jewish writer Flavius Josephus, among others. The name Coele-Syria is mentioned more than once in the books of the Maccabees, and here too it is used in a wider sense than simply for the valley described above (see I Macc. 10:69; II Macc. 3:5; 4:4; 8:8).

J. G. AALDERS

COKE, Thomas (1747-1814), Methodist bishop. A Welsh-born Oxford graduate, Coke was dismissed from his Anglican curacy for Methodist sympathies. Becoming a Methodist preacher in 1778, he urged the Methodists to undertake foreign missions, joined John Wesley in ordaining Methodist ministers for America, and himself went to Baltimore in 1784 as superintendent—a title the 1787 American conference changed to that of bishop in America, an enactment of which Wesley disapproved. Coke's outspoken opposition to slavery aroused hostility. He vainly proposed an Anglican-Methodist union in America (1792) and England (1799), and the establishment of bishops in English Methodism. Though he was twice president of the Methodist conference in England, he later unsuccessfully asked Lord Liverpool, prime minister, to appoint him a bishop of the Church of England in India. He died on the voyage to that country. Coke wrote a three-volume *History of the West Indies* (1808-11), and collaborated with Henry Moore in an inadequately researched *Life of the Rev. John Wesley* (1792).

JAMES DIXON DOUGLAS

COLERIDGE, Samuel Taylor (1772-1834), poet, thinker, and literary critic. The son of an Anglican clergyman, in Devonshire, Coleridge was educated at Christ's Hospital as a charity pupil. He entered Jesus College in Cambridge in 1791, but ran away because of debts and despondency.

After a brief military enlistment, from which his brothers extricated him, he returned briefly to Cambridge in 1794. Here he met Southey and took up the plan for a utopian Pantisocracy in Pennsylvania. The next year he married Sarah Fricker. After an unpromising book of juvenile poems (1796), some newspaper writing, and ten issues of *The Watchman*, he settled at Nether Stowey. There, surrounded by natural beauty, supported by friends, and associating with Wordsworth, he produced his best poems. His contributions to the *Lyrical Ballads* (1798) dealt with the supernatural. During much of the 1790's (from Cambridge years) Coleridge was a Unitarian. He filled a Unitarian pulpit for about a year but gradually reverted to more orthodox beliefs. Though restless and variable, he remained relatively orthodox and Trinitarian for the rest of his life.

Using an annuity from the Wedgwood brothers, Coleridge went to Germany with the Wordsworths for a year of study (1797-1798), through which he obtained a knowledge of Kant and which proved especially important in the development of his thought. During the Napoleonic era that followed his period of greatest poetic activity (1797-1803), he continued to move about, lectured at intervals, and wrote much. He neglected his family as the opium habit gained control over him, and his health deteriorated. From 1816-1834 he resided at the home of a Dr. Gilman in Higate.

An unsystematic thinker, Coleridge was nevertheless an acute and memorable literary critic who opened new horizons in the study of Shakespeare and under German influence exhibited a depth of aesthetic insight and subtlety not previously achieved in England. In philosophic and religious areas the chief influence outside of the Bible was probably Kant, and Coleridge endeavored to reconcile the dualistic contrarieties of Christian orthodoxy with the monastic simplicities of a transcendental neo-Platonic mysticism. He displayed great brilliance in metaphysics, but his impulsiveness and lack of system make his thought difficult to describe concisely.

BIBLIOGRAPHY:

S. A. Brooke, *Theology in the English Poets* (London, 1880).

E. Chambers, *Samuel Taylor Coleridge* (Oxford, 1938).

E. Blunden and E. L. Griggs (eds.), *Coleridge: Studies by Several Hands* (Toronto, 1934).

J. Colmer, *Coleridge, Critic of Society* (Oxford, 1959).

A. C. Dunstan, "The German Influence on Coleridge," *Modern Language Review* XVII (1922), 272-281 and XVII (1923), 183-201.

E. L. Griggs (ed.), *Unpublished Letters of Samuel Taylor Coleridge* (New Haven, 1933), 2 vols.

E. L. Griggs (ed.), *Wordsworth and Coleridge Studies* (Princeton, 1939).

E. L. Griggs (ed.), *Collected Letters of Samuel Taylor Coleridge* (Oxford, 1956-1959), 4 vols.

J. L. Haney, *The German Influence on Coleridge* (Philadelphia, 1902).

F. J. C. Hearnshaw, "Coleridge the Conservative," *The Nineteenth Century and After*, CXVI (1934), 104-113.

J. H. Muirhead, *Coleridge as Philosopher* (New York, 1954).

I. A. Richards, *Coleridge on Imagination* (New York, 1934).

H. Richter, "Die Philosophische Weltanschaung von S. T. Coleridge und ihr Verhaltnis sur deutschen Philosophie," *Anglia*, Bd. XLIV: N.F.B. 32 (1920), 261-290, 297-324.

R. J. White, *The Political Thought of S. T. Coleridge* (Toronto, 1938).

WARD S. MILLER

COLES, Elisha (1605?-1688), a lay Puritan divine. Coles was born in Northamptonshire and was in business for a time in London. In 1651, when John Owen was Vice-Chancellor of Oxford University, Coles appears there as a deputy registrar, and in 1657 he became steward of Magdalen College through the favor of the president, Thomas Goodwin. When, at the Restoration, the university passed out of Puritan control, Coles left Oxford and spent the rest of his working life as a clerk in the East India Company.

Coles's fame rests on *A Practical Discourse of God's Sovereignty* (1675), a work often reprinted during the next two centuries. C. H. Spurgeon reissued it in 1866 and kept it in print during his lifetime. Commendatory epistles from Owen and Goodwin prefaced the third edition. Although Coles knew no Latin or Greek and worked only from the English Bible, his book is an extremely acute, exact, and accurate exposition and defense of the classical Reformed view of the absolute sovereignty of God and His acts in which it finds expression —unconditional election, efficacious redemption, effectual calling, and final preservation. The running polemic against Arminian objections and alternative constructions is skilfully and cogently handled, and the practical bearing of each truth is very well thought out.

JAMES I. PACKER

COLET, John (1466-1519), dean of St. Paul's Cathedral (1505-1519) and founder of St. Paul's School (1510). The son of Sir Henry Colet, who was twice Lord Mayor of London, he studied at Oxford and visited Italy (1494-1496). He reacted against scholasticism based on Aristotelian premises and was influenced by Platonism, especially that of pseudo-Dionysius. An enthusiastic student of Latin literature, he set himself to learning Greek at the age of fifty. His lectures at Oxford on St. Paul's Epistles (1497) stressed the importance of historical context and literal meaning, though he did not repudiate the "fourfold sense" of Scripture and employed allegorical interpretation. His view of justification appears Reformed, but by "faith" he understands "faith and works." He accepted transubstantiation, the seven sacraments, and the authority of the pope. He deplored, however, abuses such as the corruption of the clergy and the prevalence of superstitious practices. These he denounced in his sermon before Convocation in February, 1512; and as dean of St. Paul's he strove, without success, to remove them. He founded St. Paul's School as an institution where especially Greek and Latin might be taught in a Christian environment. He was the friend of Erasmus and Sir Thomas More.

BIBLIOGRAPHY:

J. Colet, *Works.* For full details see E. W. Hunt, *Dean Colet and His Theology* (London, 1956), 131-133.

D. Erasmus, *The Lives of Jehan Vitrier and John Colet,* ed. J. H. Lupton (London, 1883).

E. W. Hunt, *Dean Colet and His Theology* (London, 1956).

S. Knight, *The Life of Dr. John Colet* (London, 1724; Oxford, 1823).

S. L. Lee, "Colet, John," *DNB* (1887), XI, 321-328.

J. H. Lupton, *The Influence of Dean Colet upon the Reformation of the English Church* (London, 1893).

J. H. Lupton, *A Life of John Colet* (London, 1887; 1909).

J. A. R. Marriott, *The Life of John Colet* (London, 1933).

F. Seebohm, *The Oxford Reformers* (London, 1867; rev. ed. 1869).

H. H. ROWDON

COL-HOZEH, "all seeing," a person mentioned in Neh. 3:15 in connection with his son Shallun, who is listed as having repaired the Fountain Gate after the return from exile. If the Col-Hozeh mentioned in Neh. 11:5 refers to the same person he also had a son named Baruch.

COLIGNY, Count Gaspard de (1519-1572), lord of Chatillon, Admiral of France, one of the greatest figures of Protestantism in France. While very young, Coligny chose the military profession and distinguished himself by his courage. Taken prisoner during the siege of Saint-Quentin in 1557, he read the Bible during his captivity and took his stand for the Reformation. His faith and his strictness made him the acknowledged head of the Protestant party. In 1562, after the massacre of Vassy, in which the troops of the Duke of Guise killed or wounded several hundred Protestants during a worship service, Coligny took charge of the Huguenot troops upon the courageous insistence of his wife, Charlotte de Laval, and at the side of the Prince of Condé. In 1563 the Duke of Guise was assassinated by Poltrot de Méré, and Coligny was accused of having organized the conspiracy. He always denied it, but the sons of the Duke of Guise vowed a mortal hatred toward him. Few persons have been vilified as much as Coligny. In particular, he was called a traitor for having given up the port of Le Havre to Queen Elizabeth of England by the Treaty of Hampton Court in 1562. This was a slander. Coligny had no part in this treaty, which, as a matter of fact, left Le Havre in the hands of Elizabeth only as a temporary pledge. In 1568, Coligny lost his heroic companion, Charlotte de Laval. One year before his death he married Jacqueline d'Entremont. In 1569, in spite of the defeat at Jarnac, during which the Prince of Condé died, Coligny rallied his troops and made a daring trek through France, from Poitou in the S all the way to Paris. Alarmed, the court signed the treaty of Saint Germain in 1570. The fortune of Coligny changed, and he became the advisor of King Charles IX, who called him "his father." Two factions contended for the mind of the king: Coligny on the one hand and, on the other, the Guise family, supported by the queen mother (Catherine de Medici) and the Duke of Anjou, who was the king's brother and the future Henry III. This second faction decided to do away with Coligny. In August of 1572, an assassin, Maurevert, posted at a window, fired a musket at him. But Coligny had bent over to adjust his shoes, and he was only hit on the arm. Catherine de Medici and Henry of Anjou were enraged at the failure and wrested from Charles IX the decision for a general massacre of the Protestants. This took place during the night of August 24, the night of Saint Bartholomew. The first victim was Coligny. Attacked in his home by henchmen of the Guise family, he was killed by a valet from Bohemia, named Besme. His body was thrown out of the window into the courtyard below, where his enemy, the Duke of Guise, kicked it. Coligny's head was cut off and carried to the king, and his corpse was exposed to view on the gallows of Montfaucon. During this time the slaughter continued, and the Seine was red with blood. Coligny remains the loftiest figure of the Protestant noblemen of the period. JEAN CADIER

COLLAR, used only twice in the AV and as the translation of two Hebrew words. It is said of Job (Job 30:18) that his garment was so disfigured that it bound him about like the collar (*peh*, lit. mouth) of his coat. The apparent meaning is that because of the terrible disease Job's body was so emaciated that his garment was no longer properly fitting but merely hung about him. In Judges 8:26 the AV uses "collars" as the translation for the Hebrew *netiphoth*, which were a kind of ornaments. The ARV and RSV translate *pendants*. The same Hebrew word is found in Isa. 3:19, where the AV translates *chains* and the ARV and the RSV *pendants*.

COLLECT, Latin "collecta," Gallic Latin "collectio," a compact form-prayer. The original meaning was possibly the gathering of people for worship, and then the gathering of their prayers into a comprehensive and compact petition (*colliger orationem*). Hence the collect became "the closing act of a stereotyped devotional form" at an early date (K. D. Mackenzie). Old Gallican rites show how the collect evolved. A litany discussed by Duchesne had a "collectio post precem." Some claim that the collect owes its origin to Leo I, bishop of Rome (d. 461).

Collects in the Reformed churches are chiefly those of the Book of Common Prayer (Anglican). They are for the days and seasons of the liturgical year, are also used in the Holy Communion service, and in Morning and Evening Prayer. In origin they are divided into the pre-Reformation collects (those included for the First Prayer Book of 1549) and those introduced into the revised Prayer Book of 1662. Two-thirds of the whole are pre-Reformation collects derived from the Leonine Sacramentary of the sixth century, from the Gelasian Sacramentary of the eighth century, or from the Sarum liturgical books.

A collect consists of 1) an invocation, 2) a petition, and 3) a pleading of Christ's Name or God's Glory. The thought and often the language is Biblical. This is a characteristic especially of the more recently composed ones.

Reformation collects are those for Advent I and II, Christmas, Circumcision, Quinquagesima, Ash Wednesday, Lent I, Easter I and II, the collects commemorating the Apostles, and All Saints' Day. Notable among the six provided in 1662 are the ones for Advent III and Epiphany VI, reminding us of Christ's Glorious Appearing.

COLLEGIANTS, proponents, in Holland during the 17th and 18th centuries, of meetings taking the place of regular church services. These gatherings, called "colleges," were organized on the basis of the general priesthood of believers for the purpose of mutual edification by means of Bible study and private testimony or free prophecy.

The participants in these "colleges" were found among the Dissenters, especially among the anabaptists and Remonstrants. Around 1645 a general movement having this spirit came into being. This movement allied itself with an already existing group which had a similar character, the "Rijnsburgers." The "Rijnsburgers" were Remonstrants from the vicinity of Leiden who had held meetings, initially at Warmond and after 1622 at Rijnsburg, under the leadership of a former elder, Gijsbert van der Codde. The meetings were organized on the basis of the idea of free prophecy. Baptism by immersion was also practiced. Rijnsburg continued to remain a center in the later development of the movement; adherents from the whole country assembled there twice a year. The Collegiants were characterized by an undogmatic piety, an adherence to ideas of natural law, the striving for moral reform in society, a strong degree of tolerance, and often by mysticism and chiliasm. They were similar to the Seekers of England. Most of their adherents were found among the well-to-do. Well-known collegiants were Adam Boreel, the poet Joachim Oudaen, Koenraad van Beuningen (mayor of Amsterdam), the physician Galenus Abrahamsz. de Haan (leader of the Flemish Anabaptists), and the lawyer Adr. Paets from Rotterdam. The last meeting, held at Rijnsburg in 1801, marked the end of the movement.

Bibliography:

C. B. Hylkema, *Reformateurs*. Geschiedkundige Studien over de godsdienstige bewegingen uit de nadagen onzer gouden eeuw, (Haarlem, 1900, 1902), 2 vols.

J. Lindeboom, *Stiefkinderen van het Christendom* ('s Gravenhage, 1929), 339-346.

C. W. Roldanus, *Coenraad van Beuningen, Staatsman en Libertijn* ('s Gravenhage, 1931).

C. W. Roldanus, *Zeventiende-eeuwsche geestesbloei* (Amsterdam, 1938), 88-109.

J. C. Van Slee, *De Rijnsburger Collegianten* (Haarlem, 1895).

D. Nauta

COLLINGES, John (1623-1690), Puritan theologian. Born at Boxted, Essex, Collinges went to school at Dedham, where he heard John Rogers and Matthew Newcomen. After graduating at Emmanuel College, Cambridge, he was ordained in 1645 and became family chaplain to the Wyncoll family at Bures. In 1646 he moved to Norwich, where he spent the rest of his life, ministering first at St. Saviour's and, from 1653 until his ejection in 1662, at St. Stephen's. At Norwich he lived with the family of Sir John Hobart, giving a weekly lecture and repeating one of the day's sermons each Sunday evening in their private chapel. He was a member of the Savoy Conference and anxiously sought an accommodation between opposing parties. In his early ministry he engaged freely in controversies, attacking lay preaching and pleading for more stringent church discipline, but after 1658 he abandoned polemics. He was one of Baxter's "meer Nonconformists," patient and pacific.

His major works, *Discourses Concerning the Actual Providence of God* (1678) and *Intercourses of Divine Love between Christ and His Church*, an exposition of the first two chapters of the Song of Solomon (1676), reveal a powerful, lofty, well-drilled mind, deeply exercised in contemplation of the revealed ways of God in providence and grace. His skill as an expositor was considerable, as seen in his contributions to Pool's *Annotations* (which include Jeremiah, the four Gospels, the Corinthian and Galatian Epistles, and Revelation). In 1675 he published a quaint tract, *The Weaver's Pocket Book, or Weaving Spiritualised*, in imitation of Flavel's *Husbandry Spiritualised*, for the benefit of the weavers of Norwich.

BIBLIOGRAPHY:
R. Bayne, *DNB*, s.v.
A. G. Matthews (ed.), *Calamy Revised* (London, 1934), s.v.

JAMES I. PACKER

COLONY, from the Latin *colonia*, which means literally "country estate." Anyone who worked on such an estate or who became its owner was a *colonus*, i.e., "farmer," "countryman." In later times this word received a more general meaning and was applied to persons who willingly or through force had left their fatherland and had settled in another place. In the new land they retained the customs and practices, and often the language, of the land of their origin. Generally speaking they remained bound to their fatherland. At that time a colony came to mean a transplanting of people.

Apparently the Phoenicians were the first people mentioned in history who in this sense had colonies outside their own territory. They established small trading stations at various places on the shores of the Mediterranean Sea, through which they maintained intensive commercial traffic. They also established themselves at places where gold, silver, tin, and copper were found. The Greeks also saw the great importance of similar settlements and established many of them. The colonies of the Romans were of a somewhat different nature. They were primarily military strongholds to keep subdued and occupied areas under control.

In the Bible, we read of a Roman colony. Philippi is mentioned as ". . . a city of Macedonia, the first of the district, a *Roman* colony . . ." (Acts 16:12 ARV). After the battle at Philippi in 42 B.C., in which Cassius and Brutus were defeated by Octavian and Mark Anthony, Roman colonists were settled there. Their number was increased when Octavian, in 31 B.C., defeated Mark Anthony at Actium. At that time, the city received the so-called *ius Italicum*, a law code like the one the Roman citizens enjoyed in Italy. This law included, among other things, freedom from land taxes such as the people of conquered areas had to pay.

A rather large number of demobilized soldiers were settled in Philippi. After their victories in the E, these men were required to settle in the area which they had conquered. The city government was organized in accordance with that of Rome. The city magistrate had the rank of *praetor*. In public he was accompanied by lictors who bore the *fascis* as insignia of his authority, and whose duty it was to clear the way for him (Acts 16:20).

BIBLIOGRAPHY:
H. Mulder, *Paulus' Kruistocht*, 1951, chap. 2.

H. MULDER

COLORS IN THE BIBLE. The writers of the Bible are impressed with the majesty and order of nature but have little to say about natural color, apart from the green of trees and vegetation (e.g., Gen. 1:30; Deut. 12:2). Christ, however, certainly appreciated the colorful beauty of the flowers (Mt. 6:28, 29).

The Hebrews used colors in daily life, but did not distinguish shades as we do today.

White. The color of joy (Eccles. 9:8), but especially of purity. Christ's clothes shone white at the Transfiguration (Mt. 17:2). Heavenly beings wear white (John 20:12; Rev. 4:4). God's people are washed white (Ps. 51:7; Isa. 1:18) and receive white robes (Rev. 7:9-14).

Black. We use this of sin, but this is not a Biblical use. However, darkness frequently is applied to sin in OT and NT. Black is used of horses (Zech. 6:2), hair (Lev. 13:37), scorched faces (Lam. 4:8), and the sky (Isa. 50:3).

Red. As the color of blood it symbolizes conquest and is used of the Lord (Isa. 63:2) and of the Satanic red dragon (Rev. 12:3). Skins dyed red covered the tabernacle (Ex. 35:7). This may have been a reminder of the continual need of blood in approaching the Lord.

Crimson and *scarlet* may represent similar colors. The color was obtained from an insect (*Coccus ilicis*). It made a bright and magnificent display, and was used for the tabernacle hangings (Ex. 25:4) and for rich clothes (II Sam. 1:24). Because of its ability to stain so permanently this was used to represent sin (Isa. 1:18).

Purple. The color of a dye extracted from a shellfish (*Murex*), and practically a monopoly of the Phoenicians. As a color of magnificence it was used in the tabernacle (Ex. 25:4) and by royalty and officials (Judges 8:26; Dan. 5:7). Purple and scarlet are linked in several places (e.g., Rev. 17:4). Since the Phoenician purple is nearer a fiery red than is modern artist's purple, Christ's robe could be described as scarlet (Mt. 27:28) or as purple (Mark 15:17; John 19:2).

Blue. Also from a shellfish (*Helix ianthina*), and associated with purple and scarlet. It was used in the tabernacle (Ex. 25 ff.; Num. 4) and temple (II Chron. 2). Ezek. 27:24 speaks of blue clothes. It is not mentioned in NT.

Vermilion. Used twice, of painted walls (Jer. 22:14) and painted idols (Ezek. 23:14. Cf. Wisd. of Sol. 13:14).

Yellow. Used only of hair in leprosy (Lev. 13:30 f.) and of gold (Ps. 68:13). "Golden" and "silver" are not used to denote color, but substance.

J. S. WRIGHT

COLOSSAE, a city lying in SW Phrygia in the valley of the river Lycus, about ten miles from Laodicea. Located on an ancient thoroughfare from Ephesus to the E, it was an important center in both the Lydian period and the later Pergamene kingdom. In Roman times the road to Pergamum was relocated to the W, and Colossae then became second in importance to Laodicea. The now-uninhabited site was identified in 1835 and found to contain the remains of an acropolis, a theater, and other structures. Inscriptions from the site reflect its importance in the Imperial period, when it was a center for textile manufacturing.

The Gospel reached Colossae while Paul was preaching at Ephesus (Acts 19:10), though Paul's epistle to the church there apparently preceded his visit (Col. 1:4; 2:1). The population was an amalgam of Greek, Jewish, and Phrygian elements, providing fertile soil for the speculative heresy condemned by Paul.

BIBLIOGRAPHY:

D. Magie, *Roman Rule in Asia Minor* (1950), pp. 126-7, 985-6.

COLOSSIANS, The Epistle to the. The letter to the Colossians names Paul and Timothy as coauthors (1:1), although such passages as 1:23 and 4:18 together with the frequent use of the pronoun "I" (1:24, 25, 29; 2:1, 4, 5; 4:8, 13), make it clear that Paul is the primary author of this short letter. Nevertheless, the occasional use of first person plural pronouns and verb forms reveals that Paul is consciously sharing his apostolic responsibility with his companions generally and Timothy in particular (1:3, 8, 9; 2:28). Since Paul dictated the letter (in 4:18 he draws attention to the fact that he is actually writing the concluding greeting himself), Timothy most likely served as his secretary.

I. Authorship and Authenticity

The canonical status of Colossians has never been seriously doubted. Standing in the shadow of the enormous popularity of Ephesians, it is not quoted or alluded to in I Clement, II Clement, or the Shepherd of Hermas. Colossians was apparently included in the collection of Pauline letters known to Ignatius of Antioch (died *c.* A.D. 117). The phrase "steadfast faith" from Col. 1:23 is found in Ign. Eph. 10:2, "things visible and invisible" from 1:16-20 in Trall. 5:2 and Smyrn. 6:1. Ignatius' greetings to the Trallian church in "apostolic fashion" (Trall. inscr.) clearly alludes to Col. 1:19-20, 27. Similarly, Polycarp of Smyrna, who wrote to the Philippian church *c.* A.D. 120, was also acquainted with a collection of Pauline letters (including the pastoral epistles), and probably derived the phrase "steadfast in the faith" used in Polyc. Phil. 10:1 from Col. 1:23. Colossians is listed in all of the extant canonical lists of NT writings.

The earliest external attestation of the Pauline authorship of Colossians is the letter to the Ephesians (*q.v.*), which is dependent literarily on Colossians. Those who regard Ephesians as an authentic Pauline letter view it as an elaboration and expansion of themes and emphases already expressed in the Colossian letter. Those who reject the authenticity of Ephesians (this view usually dates the letter *c.* A.D. 80-90) must regard it as the earliest attestation of the Pauline authorship of Colossians. The next clear attestation of authenticity is made by Marcion of Sinope (who arrived in Rome *c.* A.D. 137), since he included the letter in his canon of ten Pauline letters. Other early affirmations of Pauline authorship are found in Irenaeus (*Adv. haer.* 3, 14, 1), *c.* A.D. 180, and the Muratorian Canon, *c.* A.D. 170-90, after which the letter is frequently quoted and clearly attributed to Paul.

The Pauline authorship of Colossians was unquestioned until the middle of the nineteenth century, when G. Mayerhoff (*Der Brief an die Kolosser*, 1838) rejected the authenticity of Colossians on the basis of (1) vocabulary, (2) style, (3) theology, and (4) literary dependence on Ephesians (he accepted the authenticity of Ephesians). Mayerhoff was followed by F. C. Bauer and the "new Tübingen school," Hitzig, Hilgenfeld, Pfleiderer, and many others. By the middle of the twentieth century, serious doubts about the authenticity of Colossians remained largely confined to German NT scholarship (R. Bultmann, E. Käsemann, G. Bornkamm, E. Schweizer, E. Fuchs, H. J. Schoeps), whereas French and Anglo-American scholars generally could find no serious obstacles in the way of regarding the letter as authentically Pauline.

Although Mayerhoff's last argument regarding literary dependence on Ephesians can safely be disregarded since most scholars regard Ephesians as dependent on Colossians, we must consider the remaining three arguments which Mayerhoff and his spiritual successors have levelled against the letter's authenticity.

1. *Vocabulary.* It has been argued that the presence of 33 *hapax legomena* (that is, words found only once in the entire Greek New Testament) in Colossians places the authenticity of the letter in question (Holtzmann). Colossians has a total word count of 1,577 with a vocabulary of 431 words. The ratio of vocabulary to total number of words is therefore 36.5% The 33 *hapax legomena* of Colossians constitute 13% of its vocabulary. If we compare Colossians with Paul's letter to the Philippians, universally regarded as authentically Pauline, the statistical results are remarkably similar. Philippians has a total word count of 1,624 with a vocabulary of 448 words. The ratio of vocabulary to total word count is therefore 36.2%. The 41 *hapax legomena* of Philippians constitute 10.9% of its vocabulary. In view of the remarkably similar ratios between total word count, vocabulary, and unique words, no valid grounds can be adduced on the basis of the vocabulary of Colossians for rejecting its authenticity.

A negative approach in the denial of Pauline authorship is also made in the various writings of those who charge that such characteristically Pauline terms as "law," "salvation," "righteousness," "justification," and "revelation" are absent from the letter. This argument from silence is extremely precarious unless we are prepared to regard each and every Pauline letter as an exhaustive index to his theological thought. Since the subject matter of most of the Pauline letters (and therefore the vocabulary) has been called forth by the particular situation and needs of the communities with which the apostle corresponded, such a supposition would be patently absurd. If Colossians were in fact a pseudonymous letter produced by an admirer of Paul, one would certainly expect the would-be forger to have included those terms which are so characteristic of other Pauline letters. The argument from vocabulary is a very inconclusive and shaky basis for rejecting the authenticity of Paul's letter to the Colossians.

2. *Style.* E. Percy (*Die Probleme der Kolosser-und Epheserbrief*, 1946) has shown that the allegedly non-Pauline stylistic characteristics of Colossians are largely confined to the liturgical or hymn section (1:10-24) and the sections dealing with heretical teachings (2:4-23). In these sections Paul may well have borrowed phraseology as well as vocabulary from early Christian liturgical tradition as well as from the false teachers' own descriptions of their "philosophy." Positive stylistic features peculiar to Paul are found in the letter (one example is the pleonastic use of *kai* after *dia touto* in 1:9, cf. Rom. 13:6, I Thess. 3:5). In general, it should be noted that questions of authenticity cannot be decided on the basis of style when the document in question is of insufficient length (as in the case of Colossians).

3. *Theology.* Although the main basis of F. C. Bauer's rejection of Pauline authorship of Colossians was the presence of what he considered an anti-gnostic polemic which presupposed a second-century setting, recent research on the question of gnosticism and the New Testament has pulled the rug out from under this line of criticism. The proto-gnostic character of Paul's Corinthian opponents, for example, has been demonstrated by J. Schniewind and W. Schmithals. Several scholars (O. Cullmann, H. J. Schoeps, G. Quispel, R. M. Grant) have pointed out that the Dead Sea Scrolls, discovered in the years following 1947, reveal a variety of heterodox Judaism with gnosticizing tendencies which flourished in the century and a half prior to the destruction of Jerusalem in A.D. 70. Since some important constituent elements of second-century gnosticism were present in the religious

environment of early Christianity, the proto-gnostic characteristics of the Colossian heresy cannot be the basis for rejecting Pauline authorship.

Another theological argument for rejecting the authenticity of Colossians is the presence of what Ernst Käsemann has called the "eschatological reservation" (*eschatologische Vorbestehung*) in the genuine letters of Paul. According to Käsemann, when Paul speaks of the believer's dying and rising with Christ, he never uses the verb *egeirein* ("to rise") in the past tense (cf. Rom. 6:5, 8; 8:11; I Cor. 6:14; II Cor. 4:14). In both Colossians and Ephesians, however, the verb *sunegeirein* ("to rise with") is applied to the experience of believers in the past tense (Col. 2:12; 3:1; Eph. 2:6). By using this "eschatological reservation," it is argued, Paul does not fall into the hands of his proto-gnostic opponents who regard the resurrection as an event belonging only to the past (cf. II Tim. 2:18). This objection loses its force when it is realized that this heretical teaching is not a feature of the Colossian heresy, thereby making it unnecessary for Paul to articulate his doctrine of dying and rising with Christ with great care. Moreover, in the Colossian and Ephesian passages the reference is not primarily eschatological but rather retrospective to the significance of baptism (cf. Rom. 6:1 ff.). The theological arguments against the authenticity of Colossians have no firm basis in fact, and cannot be linked with the equally specious arguments from vocabulary and style to refute the Pauline authorship of this letter.

II. Date and Place of Origin

Since Paul was in prison when he wrote Colossians and its companion letter Philemon (Col. 4:3, 10, 18; Philemon 1, 13, 23), the problem of determining the date and place of origin of the letter is dependent on whether or not the particular imprisonment reflected in these two letters can be determined with any accuracy. Although the Acts of the Apostles records only three imprisonments of Paul (at Philippi, Acts 16:11-40; at Caesarea, Acts 21:27–26:32; and at Rome, Acts 28:11-30), Paul himself refers to "many imprisonments" (II Cor. 11:23, written between the Philippian and the Caesarean imprisonments). In addition to the Caesarean and Roman imprisonments, therefore, modern scholars have hypothecated an Ephesian imprisonment also. The hypothesis that Colossians and Philemon were written during an Ephesian imprisonment seems unlikely since Luke, mentioned in Col. 4:14 and Philemon 24, was not with Paul during his lengthy stay in Ephesus if he is the author of the "we" passages in Acts which constitute a travel diary (cf. Acts 16:10-17; 20:5-15; 21:1-18; 27:1–28:16). Then, too, Mark, who is mentioned as a companion in Col. 4:10 and Philemon 24, did not accompany Paul during his second missionary journey, when the Ephesian imprisonment is supposed to have taken place (cf. Acts 15:36-41). Since Aristarchus, mentioned as a fellow prisoner of Paul in Col. 4:10 and Philemon 24, is referred to in Acts 27:2 as one of those who sailed with Paul from Caesarea to Rome, either the Caesarean or the Roman imprisonment provides the appropriate background for the origin of Colossians and Philemon. The Caesarean hypothesis would necessitate dating the letters *c.* A.D. 55-57, whereas the Roman hypothesis would place them *c.* A.D. 58-60.

III. Destination and Purpose

Colossae, a moderately sized Hellenistic city in southwest Asia Minor which possessed a thriving textile industry, was the home of a flourishing Christian community of Gentile converts who had been evangelized by Epaphras, an associate of Paul (1:7; 4:12). After learning of the activities of heretical teachers, Paul felt obliged to write to the community, which he had never personally visited (2:1), with the object of convincing them that the ceremonial, cultic, and ascetic practices with which they had burdened themselves were inconsistent with the gospel originally received through Epaphras. He sought to achieve this aim by both emphasizing the errors of these false teachers and stressing the cosmic superiority and pre-eminence of Christ.

The tantalizingly brief references to the character of the Colossian heresy seem to link it with a gnosticizing tendency within heterodox Judaism. The focal passage in which the basic constituent elements of the heretical teaching are delineated is Col. 2:16-18, where five major elements may be distinguished: (1) ascetic requirements (2: 16a; cf. vs. 21), (2) ceremonial and calendar observances (2:16b), (3) self-abasement or excessive humility (2: 18a), (4) worship of angelic beings (2:18b; cf. 1:16, 19; 2:9), and (5) an inordinate emphasis on visions (2:18c). Some scholars, emphasizing the gnostic character of the heresy, have added the fact that the false teachers apparently claimed to possess a higher knowledge or "philosophy" (2:4, 8, 18). This characteristic is of little value, however, since it could as well be used to characterize the proclamation of the gospel by Paul (cf. 2:2-3).

The great importance attached to the ascetic and calendar observances such as food and drink, festivals, new moons, and sabbaths (2:16-17), can be accounted for by hypothecating the influence of Jewish heterodoxy. When Paul observes that these elements are a shadow of that which is to come (2:17), he implies that these observances are an illegitimate cultic anticipation of the conditions of heavenly existence. Since the present appropriation of eschatological salvation is mediated only through Jesus Christ, these ascetic and ritual observances are totally irrelevant for the believer.

The three closely connected elements mentioned in Col. 2:18, self-abasement, worship of angels, and an over-emphasis on visions, are also found in two other Jewish Christian documents, the Revelation of St. John (19:10; 22:8) and the Ascension of Isaiah (7:21). In these passages the seer (John or pseudo-Isaiah) is the recipient of a heavenly vision. When confronted with the angelic being whose duty it is to explain the meaning of the vision to the seer, the seer immediately reacts by worshipping the angel. This reaction is immediately rebuffed by the messenger. Among the Colossians, these elements had apparently lost their Christocentric significance and had become ends in themselves, and therein lay the error. The basis for the worship of angelic beings among the Colossians was apparently the supposition (characteristic of Ebionite Christianity) that Christ was just one angelic being among many. In order to refute this heretical belief, Paul emphasizes the cosmic superiority of Christ and his pre-eminence over all creation including supernatural beings (1:15-20; 3:11). Although Josephus reports that the Essenes were proficient in knowing the names of the angels (*Wars* 2. 141; his statements have been corroborated by the discovery of the so-called Angelic Liturgy among the Dead Sea Scrolls), there is no evidence that they actually worshipped angelic beings. The Essenes did believe that angels were present during times of worship (1 QS 11:7 f.; 1 QH 3:21 f.; 4:24 f.; 6:12 f.; 1 QSb 4), a belief apparently shared by Paul (I Cor. 11:10). In early para-Christianity, the worship of angels was advocated by Simon Magus, the Samaritan heretic with strong ties to Jewish Christianity (Tertullian *De praescr. haer.* 33: "Simoniae autem magiae disciplina angelis serviens"). It must be concluded that important elements of the Colossian heresy were of heterodox Jewish origin, and that these elements in combination with Christian teachings threatened to destroy the faith of the Colossian community.

Since the Pauline epistles are actual (though not "private") letters rather than artistic compositions cast into the letter-form, they are difficult to analyze structurally. Like other Pauline letters, the Colossian letter contains the basic components of the popular Hellenistic letter-form: the epistolary introduction (a salutation with the names of sender and recipient, a prayer, and a thanksgiving), the body of the letter, and a conclusion consisting of greetings and best wishes. In conformity with this general pattern, Colossians contains a salutation (1:1-2), a prayer (1:3-8), a thanksgiving (1:9 ff.), and a concluding section containing greetings and miscellaneous messages (4:7-18).

IV. Analysis of Contents

As the first Christian letter writer, Paul had a powerful and influential effect on all subsequent use of this literary form in early Christianity through his effective and creative use of this medium of communication. A substitute for oral communication, the Pauline letters consist of a mélange of sermonic and homiletical materials, ethical exhortations, hymnic and confessional materials, prophetic utterances, and evangelistic proclamation. It is the miscellaneous character of the contents of the Pauline letters which makes their satisfactory literary analysis so difficult.

Customarily, the Colossian letter has been regarded as having a natural division into two nearly equal sections, the first doctrinal (1:1–3:4), the second practical (3:5–4:18). This traditional analysis of the content of the letter is unsatisfactory for a number of reasons: (1) each section of the letter analyzed in this way contains a mixture of doctrinal and practical emphases; (2) to partition the letter in such a manner is to make an artificial distinction between doctrine and practice, belief and life, which cannot be supported from Pauline literature; (3) such a bifurcation of the letter utilizes a principle of analysis not found elsewhere in the epistolary literature of Paul or other early Christian authors.

The proper analysis of the movement of Pauline thought in the Colossian letter must be based on the formal and thematic development of the ideas which the apostle wished to communicate to the Colossian community. A careful analysis of the letter reveals that the flow of Paul's thought is formally structured or controlled by a chiastic thought pattern. This characteristically Semitic way of structuring oral and literary discourse was apparently the natural or unconscious way in which Paul arranged the material he wished to communicate. The analysis of the letter will be more in conformity with Paul's own mind if we view the composition as consisting of a series of closely related panels or sections defined by the formal criterion of the chiastic pattern. The following analysis attempts to transcend the artificiality involved in the more traditional outlines of the Colossian letter.

Paul has inserted the distinctive content of the letter to the Colossians into the framework provided by the traditional Hellenistic letter form. This content can be formally arranged in five sections, each of which exhibits the chiastic structure a/b/a or a/b/c/b/a:

I. Salutation (1:1-2)
II. The Essence of the Gospel: the Cosmic Superiority of Christ (1:3-23)
III. Paul the Minister of the Gospel (1:24–2:5)
IV. The Heretical Teachings as the Antithesis of the Gospel (2:6-19)
V. Implications of the Gospel for Christian Living (2:20–3:4)

VI. The New Life in Contrast to the Old (3:5-17)
VII. Miscellaneous Exhortations (3:18–4:6)
VIII. Miscellaneous Messages and Concluding Greeting (4:7-18)

The epistolary introduction to Colossians, consisting in the salutation (1:1-2), the prayer (1:3-8), and the thanksgiving (1:9 ff.), constitutes a section whose length cannot precisely be determined by ordinary methods of analysis. The thanksgiving which begins in 1:9 blends almost imperceptibly with the hymn quoted or composed by Paul in 1:15-20. On formal grounds alone, 1:3-23 constitutes the first major section of the letter, since it is bracketed by references to the "Gospel which you have heard" (1:5, 23) and to the "faith" (1:4, 23) of the Colossian Christians. Paul renders thanksgiving to God for the faith of the community (1:3-8) and is concerned that the Colossians are thankful for the redemption and forgiveness which they have received through Christ (1:9-14). The ground of salvation is the person and work of Christ (1:15-20), who has made the reconciliation of man to God possible through His death (1:21-22). The chiastic pattern evident in this section is a/b/c/b/a: (a) the themes of "faith" and "Gospel" (1:3-8) are followed by (b) the saving result of faith (1:9-14), followed by (c) the central emphasis of the section: the Christological ground of faith and life (1:15-20), followed by (b) the saving result of faith (1:21-22), and (a) repetition of the themes "faith" and Gospel."

In the next section, 1:24–2:5, Paul expresses the personal dimension of his concern for the faith of the Colossians, using his own vocation as a proclaimer of the Gospel as a transition. Bracketing the section with the theme of "rejoicing" (1:24; 2:5), Paul defines the gospel in terms of a "mystery" hidden for ages but now made fully known (1:25-27; 2:2-3). Central to the section is the emphasis on Paul's labor and concern in proclaiming the message of salvation through Christ among the Gentiles (1:28–2:1). As in the previous section, the chiastic pattern a/b/c/b/a is in evidence: (a) Paul rejoices that he may suffer for the Colossians (1:24), (b) the proclamation of God's "mystery" has occasioned this suffering (1:25-27), (c) Paul and his associates labor to proclaim this message and to foster and nourish the faith of all (1:28–2:1), (b) he wishes them to have full knowledge of God's "mystery" of Christ (2:2-3), and (a) he rejoices in the firmness of their faith. Through the expressions of personal concern for all who receive the Gospel, Paul makes it clear that his present interest in the faith of the Colossians is not unusual or inordinate, but rather characteristic of his apostolic ministry.

Colossians 2:6-19 constitutes the next section, in which Paul deals explicitly with the basic purpose of the letter—the refutation of the Colossian heresy, which consisted in the belief that certain ceremonial, cultic, and ascetic practices were absolutely crucial for Christian faith and life. Paul has already laid the groundwork in 1:15-20 for refuting this heresy by stressing the Christological nature of the Gospel. In the section immediately preceding 2:6-19, he has anticipated the antiheretical polemic by warning against those who come with "beguiling speech" (2:4). Col. 2:6-7 constitutes a transitional passage emphasizing the fact that faith in Jesus Christ (elaborated in 1:3-23) ought to determine the present existence of Christians (anticipating the discussion in 2:20–3:4 and 3:4-17). In this section, 2:6-19, as well as in the two following sections, we find that interweaving of doctrine and life so characteristic of Pauline theology. In 2:8, Paul characterizes the false teaching of the deceitful teachers as being "according to the elemental spirits of the universe," which is in antithesis to Christ. The specific characteristics of the false teaching which is antithetical to the Gospel are elaborated in 2:16-19. At the core of this section stands 2:9-15, in which Paul states that these ceremonial, cultic, and ascetic practices have been superseded by spiritual circumcision (old conditions no longer apply to Christians) and spiritual resurrection (a radically new situation is in effect), and so prepares for the "put off"–"put on" emphases of 3:5-17. This passage also moves in a chiastic pattern: (a) the description of the basic anti-Christological nature of the heresy (2:8), followed by (b) the Christological implications of Christian living (2:9-15), then back again to (a) an elaboration of the basic characteristics of the heresy (2:16-19).

In Col. 2:20–3:4, Paul elaborates on the implications of spiritual circumcision and spiritual resurrection with Christ for Christian living. Since spiritual circumcision, or the cessation of life lived "according to the flesh," is a reality for believers (2:20a), Paul draws out the implications of this truth by showing that ceremonial and ascetic regulations have no possible value or relevance for the new life in Christ (2:20b-23). In 3:1-4, he stresses the fact that spiritual resurrection with Christ is the basis for the believer's ability to live a godly life. Once again the chiastic pattern is exhibited in this section: (b) the Christological implications of Christian living (2:20a) is followed by (a) an elaboration of the cultic and ascetic regulations which are irrelevant for believers (2:20b-23), and then in (b) Paul moves back to an emphasis on the Christological basis for new life in Christ (3:1-4).

Colossians 3:5-17, closely related to the previous two sections, begins with a catalogue of those vices which are completely antithetical to Christian living (3:5-9a), having already observed that cultic and ascetic practices have proved impotent in dealing with sins of the flesh (2:23). Paul then moves again to the basis or ground of Christian faith which enables believers to "put off" these vices, and that is the appropriation of the new nature available in Christ (3:9b-11). The antithesis of the sins or "earthly things" listed in the vice catalogue is then stated in the form of a catalogue of Christian virtues, of which love is the basic and supreme quality (3:12-17). Here again the chiastic pattern is evident: (a) the catalogue of specific vices (3:5-9a) is followed by (b) the possibility of appropriating the new nature in Christ (3:9b-11), followed by (a) the virtue catalogue in antithesis to the vice catalogue (3:12-17). Col. 3:17, like 2:6-7, is a focal passage which underlines the Christocentric nature of the Christian life, thereby concluding the distinctive content of the letter with a short, succinct utterance.

The sequence of miscellaneous household duties (*Haustafeln*) and exhortations in 3:18–4:6 does not deal with the specific occasion for which Colossians was written, but rather constitutes a general section prior to the conclusion of the letter (4:7-18), in which Paul relates personal information regarding himself and his companions in prison. In 4:18 he concludes the letter with a greeting written with his own hand.

BIBLIOGRAPHY:

T. K. Abbott, *A Critical and Exegetical Commentary on the Epistles to the Ephesians and the Colossians* (1899).

F. W. Beare, "The Epistle to the Colossians: Introduction and Exegesis," *The Interpreter's Bible*, Vol. XI (1953).

F. F. Bruce, *The Epistle to the Colossians* (1958).

M. Dibelius, *Die Kolosser-, Epheser- und Philemonbriefe* (1927).

E. Lohmeyer, *Der Kolosser- und der Philemonbriefe* (1957).

E. Percy, *Die Probleme der Kolosser- und Epheserbriefe* (1946).

D. E. H. Whiteley, *The Theology of St. Paul* (1964).

DAVID E. AUNE

COLT, a word in the AV referring to an ass's colt except in Gen. 32:15, where it is used for that of the camel. In Zech. 9:9 it is prophesied that the Messiah would come "riding on an ass and on an ass's colt, the son of the she-asses." In their account of the fulfillment of this prophecy Mark (11:7), Luke (19:35), and John (12:14) mention only the colt, but Matthew (21:7) speaks also of its mother. There is no need, however, to adopt the view of the rationalistic critics who accuse Matthew of introducing this second beast out of misunderstanding of Hebrew parallelism. The dam might have been taken along in order to induce the young animal to follow. Similarly, Matthew's statement that Jesus "sat upon them" need not be taken to mean that Jesus sat on both animals simultaneously or first on one and then on the other. The word *them* probably refers to the garments which the disciples laid upon the colt.

COLUMBA (*c.* 521-597), great apostle to the Scots. Born of royal descent at Gartan, Donegal, Ireland, he studied principally under Finnian, "a doctor of wisdom and tutor of saints" at Clonard. He learned early the Celtic art of copying and superbly illuminating mss of the Bible, and he presented a copy of the Scriptures to each church he founded. The artistic beauty of the Book of Kells and the Book of Durrow, still extant, proves to us the high culture of the epoch in Irish monasteries.

Many great monasteries and churches were founded by Columba in Ireland. He was ordained a presbyter and remained such to the end, even when an abbot. Columba had a hot temper, and it gave way to gusts of passion. He was litigious, and in a dispute with Diarmid, the High King, he led his clan (the O'Neills) against him and was completely victorious at Culdremhne, where 3,000 were slain. He became penitent and sailed from Derry with 12 companions, resolved to save, through Christ, as many souls as the number of slain in the battle. He founded his monastery on the small island of Iona (in the Hebrides) in 563. It quickly became renowned for its learning, piety, and evangelical zeal. It was, however, completely destroyed by the Norsemen later in 825.

In 565 Columba visited the Pictish king, Brude, near Inverness, Scotland, with two cultured Pictish friends, Comgall and Kenneth. Brude was deeply impressed and opened his land to the Gospel. Columba was scholarly, impressive, eloquent, and lovable. His work for Scotland was vast.

BIBLIOGRAPHY:

Adamnan (7th century), *Life of St. Columba,* trans. by W. Reeves (Edinburgh, 1874).

Bede (8th century), *Eccles. Hist. of England,* trans. and notes by A. M. Sellar (London, 1912).

J. A. Duke, *The Columban Church* (Oxford, 1931).

J. Heron, *The Celtic Church in Ireland* (London, 1898), 219-252.

A. B. Scott, *Pictish Nation and Church* (Edinburgh, 1918).

W. D. Simpson, *The Historical St. Columba* (Aberdeen, 1927).

G. T. Stokes, *Ireland and the Celtic Church* (London, 1886; ed. by Lawlor, 1907).

COMENIUS, Johannes Amos (1592-1673), "that incomparable Moravian" (C. Mather's *Magnalia Christi Americana,* II, IV, 10), member and bishop of the Unity of Brethren. Born in Moravia, he studied under J. H. Alsted at Herborn (1611-12) and David Pareus at Heidelberg (1613-14). Moravian piety and Reformed intellectualism joined in him in giving rise to a vision of the aims and methods of education from which much is still to be learned. Comenius' educational masterpiece, *The Great Didactic,* directs man to his chief end, eternal happiness with God, and, taking account both of man's innate God-given capacities and the importance of his providentially ordered experience, devises means not yet outmoded for the imparting of knowledge. In his later years of exile, Comenius envisaged an ambitious ideal of Pansophy, comprising the classification and the proper definition of all things. The content of this encyclopedic system was to be obtained inductively, its arrangement determined by rational laws and the whole directed by Scripture, the ultimate source of knowledge. With the encouragement of the English philanthropist Samuel Hartlib, the outcome of Comenius' vision in England was the founding not of a Pansophic College but of the Royal Society.

Comenius' writings include 154 larger works, three volumes of correspondence, and 49 smaller works. Pietism is eloquently expressed in his descriptions of the labyrinth of the world and the paradise of the heart. Patriotism and ecumenicity join with pathos in *The Bequest of the Unity of Brethren.* Commending the Swiss Reformed Church for love of discipline, he admonishes her "to more simplicity and less speculation; also to a more discreet discussion concerning God and His most profound mysteries" (*Bequest*, XVII).

See ALSTED, JOHANN HEINRICH; PIETISM.

BIBLIOGRAPHY:

J. A. Comenius, *The Bequest of the Unity of Brethren,* trans. by M. Spinka (Chicago, 1940).

J. A. Comenius, *The Labyrinth of the World and the Paradise of the Heart,* trans. by F. Lutzow (London, 1905).

J. A. Comenius, *Naturall Philosophie Reformed by Divine Light: or a Synopsis of Physicks* (London, 1651).

J. A. Comenius, *Opera Didactica Omnia* (Amsterdam, 1657; includes the *Great Didactic* of 1633-8), 4 vols.

M. W. Keatinge, *Comenius* (New York and London, 1931; selections from the *Great Didactic*).

J. V. Klima (ed.), *Jan Amos Komensky* (Prague, 1947).

J. Needham (ed.), *The Teacher of Nations* (1942).

M. Spinka, *John Amos Comenius, That Incomparable Moravian* (Chicago, 1943).

J. F. Young, *Comenius in England* (1932).

WILLIAM YOUNG

COMFORT. The basic NT term for comfort is *paraclesis*, and the classical passage concerning the subject is II Cor. 1:3-7. Here Paul calls God the Source of "every sort of comfort" (vs. 3) that is needed to meet "every kind of tribulation" (vs. 4). Neither Paul nor the Corinthians could escape the trouble and suffering of Christ (vss. 5-7), since "a slave is not greater than his master" (John 15:20). But as they shared in His sufferings they also were privileged to enter into His comfort, which Paul declares he found to be both readily available and adequate. Comfort is opposed to suffering (vss. 5-7; cf. also Luke 16:25) and sorrow (II Cor. 2:7). Comfort always comes from another, who literally is "called to the side of," or, in our idiom, is "asked to stand behind" the one needing comfort. Comfort comes ultimately from the Holy Spirit (Acts 9:31), who is called "another Comforter," of the same kind as the Son (John 14:16, 17). The word *paraclete,* translated "comforter" in the King James Version, probably ought to be translated "counselor" or (particularly in John's writings) "advocate." But nevertheless, the idea of comfort is not lost in these translations since one of the principal functions of a counselor or advocate is to provide such assistance to another in his time of need as will set his mind at ease.

JAY E. ADAMS

COMMANDMENTS, TEN

I. Origin
II. Division
III. Content
IV. Biblical Usage
V. Ecclesiastical Usage

Scripture emphasizes the divine origin of the Ten Commandments. After thunderings and lightning flashed from Sinai, and after warning had been given to the people stressing the sacredness of the occasion, God Himself spoke to the people, orally delivering to them the Ten Commandments (Ex. 20). Then Moses drew near to God to receive further instructions, including a number of explanations of the individual commandments. Later, Moses was again invited to meet God on Sinai and he was given "two tables of testimony, tables of stone, written with the finger of God" (Ex. 31:18b).

I. Origin

This origin of the Ten Commandments is significantly found in the context of the covenant that God made with Israel at Sinai. God had graciously entered into covenant with Israel and the primary response of Israel was to be the keeping of the Ten Commandments. In fact, sometimes the commandments are called the covenant (I Kings 8:21) or the tables of the covenant (Deut. 9:15). This covenantal context is also stressed by the introductory statement, in which God describes Himself in terms of what He has done for Israel. When Moses broke the stone tablets, God gave him another set, which was then placed in the ark of the covenant at the command of God (Ex. 25:16).

Scripture says specifically that there are *ten* commandments (Ex. 34:28; Deut. 4:13; 10:4). However, nowhere does it enumerate the commandments. The result is that various religious traditions have enumerated them differently. Orthodox Judaism considers the introductory statement of vs. 2 as the first commandment. It then combines the commandment against polytheism in vs. 3 with the commandment against image worship in vs. 4 to form the second commandment. Augustine combined vss. 3 and 4 as the first commandment and then divided what most Protestants consider the tenth commandment, taking the version given in Deut. 5 making "desiring thy neighbour's wife" the ninth commandment and "coveting thy neighbour's house, etc.," the tenth commandment. The RC Church followed this enumeration, and in doing so dropped out the commandment against image worship. The Lutheran Church, following Luther himself, continued with the RC enumeration except that it made the ninth commandment "Thou shalt not covet thy neighbour's house" and took the remainder of vs. 17 as the tenth commandment.

II. Division

Josephus and Philo, representing the Judaism of the days of the NT, made the command against polytheism (vs. 3) the first commandment, the command against image worship (vs. 4) the second commandment, and then made vs. 16 against false witness the ninth commandment and vs. 17 against covetousness the tenth commandment. However, Philo switched the order of commandments six and seven. Origen and the Greek Catholics followed the same order as Josephus. Calvin also followed this order, thus fixing it as that followed by Reformed churches and and most other Protestants.

Another difference of division arises from the question concerning which of the commandments were on each of the tablets. Jews believe that there were five commandments on each table. However, since the tablets were written on both sides, this is not as even an arrangement as it would seem at first sight. Also, as the first five commandments are much longer than the last five, this would place much more writing on the first table than on the second, although this argument would not hold if the commandments were originally brief statements, as some scholars hold. Augustine considered the first table to include the first three commandments according to his enumeration, placing the commandment to honor father and mother as the first one on the second table. Calvin places the first four commandments according to his enumeration on the first table and therefore also begins the second table with the commandment about honoring parents. This division then places duties toward God on the first table and those toward man on the second, coinciding with Jesus' summary in the two great commandments.

Following the usual Protestant enumeration, we consider briefly the significance of the individual commandments:

III. Content

1. "Thou shalt have no other gods before me." This commandment demands absolute loyalty to God alone. False gods are not to be worshipped in addition to the one true God. Critics who insist that this commandment only requires monolatry (acceptance of the existence of many gods but the worship of only one of these many gods) rather than monotheism are influenced by an evolutionary conception which precludes from their minds the existence of monotheism at an early date.

2. "Thou shalt not make unto thee any graven image, or any likeness of any thing that is in heaven above, or that is in the earth beneath, or that is in the water under the earth: Thou shalt not bow down thyself to them nor serve them: for I the Lord thy God am a jealous God, visiting the iniquity of the fathers upon the children unto the third and fourth generation of them that hate me; and showing mercy unto thousands of them that love me, and keep my commandments." This command is not an absolute prohibition against all sculpture and painting, since in the explicit instructions on the construction of the tabernacle and its furnishings there are instances of such work being commanded by God. Another instance is God's command to make the brazen serpent (Num. 21:18). The command denounces the worship of objects representing some false god or mistakenly trying to represent the one true God. God is Spirit, and any attempt to represent Him visually cannot but distort our views of Him. God's jealousy must not be compared to sinful human jealousy, but is an expression of His great love, which recognizes that man harms himself seriously by false representations of God. Such false worship cannot but harm the worshipper himself and inescapably extend such harm to his children and his children's children. God's mercy is much greater than His wrath, for it extends to the thousandth generation of those who obediently worship Him aright (Deut. 7:9).

3. "Thou shalt not take the name of the Lord thy God in vain: for the Lord will not hold him guiltless that taketh his name in vain." In the days when the Bible was written, anyone's name was very closely associated with the person himself. "In vain" is used in the sense of lightly. This commandment thus forbids perjury, cursing, and using the name of God in worship without thinking of the significance of what one is saying. The positive side of the commandment is a great reverence for God and for any mention of His name. The commandment includes a reminder of the seriousness of the breaking of this law, which, with the others, was punished with the death penalty in the OT.

4. "Remember the sabbath day, to keep it holy. Six days shalt thou labour, and do all thy work: but the seventh day is the sabbath of the Lord thy God: in it thou shalt not do any work, thou, nor thy son, thy daughter, thy manservant, nor thy maidservant, nor thy cattle, nor thy stranger that is within thy gates: for in six days the Lord made heaven and earth, the sea, and all that in them is, and rested on the seventh day: wherefore the Lord blessed the sabbath day, and hallowed it." Sabbath means literally "rest." This rest day is to be "holy," that is, dedicated to God. The inclusion

of servants, animals, and aliens is a humane provision. The pattern of the rhythm of work and rest is founded in creation itself. This commandment has proven to be most controversial. Some have insisted that it must be the seventh day and no other upon which one is to rest to fulfill the demands of the commandment. Others have questioned that this commandment applies to Christians at all, seeing it as a ceremonial law rather than a moral law. The question of whether or not the creation days were literal 24-hour periods is also related to this commandment.

5. "Honor thy father and thy mother: that thy days may be long upon the land which the Lord thy God giveth thee." This commandment requires that children respect and obey their parents. In a sense it is related to the commandments concerning duty to God, since the parents are to exercise their God-given authority. Application of the commandment has often been extended to others in authority. The promise attached can be applied either to the individual or to the nation, with the latter being of primary application in the original context. A country where there is a strong family life will endure, whereas the nation that becomes inwardly decadent because of the breakdown of the family will collapse.

6. "Thou shalt not kill." This refers to murder, for OT precepts include instructions to kill animals, orders to participate in wars, and commands to inflict capital punishment for murder and for other serious offenses. It stresses the sacredness of human life created in the image of God.

7. "Thou shalt not commit adultery." Although strictly speaking this refers to having sexual relations with a married person, in its broadest scope it prohibits all sexual relations outside the marriage bond and therefore acts as a safeguard to marriage.

8. "Thou shalt not steal." This stresses the sacredness of property rights. It prohibits not only direct robbery but also all false methods for obtaining that which belongs to another.

9. "Thou shalt not bear false witness against thy neighbour." Although primary reference may be to testimony in a court of law, the commandment requires that care be taken to safeguard the reputation of one's fellow man. Thus it condemns all lying, insinuations, gossip and lack of care for another's good name.

10. "Thou shalt not covet thy neighbour's house, thou shalt not covet thy neighbour's wife, nor his manservant, nor his maidservant, nor his ox, nor his ass, nor anything that is thy neighbour's." This commandment reaches beyond actions to attitudes and motives. Our fellow man's possessions are not to be anxiously desired, lest this lead to adultery or theft. Even where such outward action does not occur, covetousness leads to the loss of the inner peace that God's people should have as they rejoice in what God has given to them rather than be dissatisfied as they note what He has given to others.

IV. Biblical Usage

As has been previously noted, considerable reference is made to many of the individual commandments in the remainder of the Mosaic legislation. A number of passages consist of comments on and amplifications of these commandments. The outstanding reference is the complete quotation of the commandments with minor changes in the sermon of Moses in Deuteronomy 5. Many minor differences, as well as several significant ones, exist between the two versions of the commandments. Some critics say that the original version consisted of brief statements and that both Exodus 20 and Deuteronomy 5 represent later expanded versions. Holding a high view of inspiration would point to the Exodus passage as being the original and account for the differences in Deuteronomy as the result of a free quotation by Moses as a part of his sermonizing. Scholars list twenty points of difference between the two versions, thirteen of which are additions that Deuteronomy makes to the Exodus version. However, seven of these additions are only the use of a connecting "and." Two of the additions are the words "as the Lord thy God hath commanded thee" to the sabbath command and the one on honoring parents. This is the kind of addition which could well be expected in sermonizing. In Deuteronomy the description of the animals that are to benefit from the sabbath rest is expanded. In the commandment on honoring parents the description of the promised blessings for obedience is expanded. There are three minor differences also in the wording of the second commandment.

The greatest difference is in the sabbath command. The verb "remember" is used in Exodus, but "keep" is used in Deuteronomy. The reason given for such sabbath observance is entirely different. Whereas in Exodus the reason given is the creative pattern, in Deuteronomy this is omitted. Instead, the idea of servants being included in the rest day is stressed, and the reason given for sabbath observance is the memory of their days of servitude and the mighty deliverance that God had wrought on their behalf.

A final difference to be noted is in the tenth commandment. In Exodus the order is "covet thy neighbour's house" and then "covet thy neighbour's wife, etc.," whereas in Deuteronomy we find "desire thy neighbour's wife" and then "covet thy neighbour's house, etc."

The "ten commandments" are referred to specifically in Exodus 34, where Moses is commanded to write them on a second set of tablets after having broken the first set, in the sermon of Moses in Deuteronomy 4:13, and again in Deuteronomy 10:4, where Moses called to remembrance how he had received them. In these three instances the translation is literally the "ten words."

Jesus referred specifically to several of the Ten Commandments in the Sermon on the Mount when He said, "Ye have heard that it was said by them of old time, Thou shalt not kill" (Mt. 5:21a), and when He said, "Ye have heard that it was said by them of old time, Thou shalt not commit adultery" (Mt. 5:27). In both instances, Jesus did not abrogate the commandment but insisted that they must be kept not only in letter but also in spirit, that thoughts and attitudes may violate the law as well as actions.

Jesus also mentioned several of the Ten Commandments specifically when approached by the rich young ruler. Jesus said to him, "If thou wilt enter into life, keep the commandments" (Mt. 19:17). When the young man asked to which commandments Jesus was referring, He replied by listing commandments six, seven, eight, nine, and four, and added, "Thou shalt love thy neighbour as thyself." That the exact order was not significant is evident from the fact that Luke and Mark list them as seven, six, eight, nine, and four, and in Mark the words "Defraud not" are inserted after the ninth commandment.

Jesus had considerable controversy with the Pharisees over the proper observance of the sabbath commandment. He rejected their negative legalism, but did not reject the commandment itself, for He said, "The sabbath was made for man," thereby not only approving of the principle of a rest day each week but affirming it as of universal validity rather than limited to Jewish ceremony.

Paul also made specific reference to several of the commandments. He stated that the tenth commandment had a particular role in his own religious experience. He was able to keep the other commandments, which he felt were satisfied by outward behavior, but the tenth commandment had made him aware of his inability to control his inner attitudes. "I had not known lust, except the law had said, Thou shalt not covet" (Rom. 7:7b).

Paul saw the law of love to one's neighbor as comprehending the later commandments, which he listed as seven, six, eight, nine, and ten (Rom. 13:9). Writing to the Ephesians, he made reference to the fifth commandment and applied the appended promise to the individual by saying, "Honour thy father and mother (which is the first commandment with promise) that it may be well with thee, and thou mayest live long on the earth."

V. Ecclesiastical Usage

Down through the centuries the RC Church used its interpretation of the Ten Commandments as part of its guidelines for its ethical teachings. When the Reformers examined critically all of the teachings of the RC Church they also reevaluated the relation of the Christian to the Ten Commandments. Although Luther believed that the Ten Commandments were addressed specifically to the Jews, he saw them as being largely in agreement with the natural law which Paul said was written on the hearts of all men, and therefore to that extent applicable to all men. In practice, Luther made considerable use of the Ten Commandments. He dealt with them in his treatise, *On Good Works*, wrote two hymns about them, preached expository series of sermons based on them, and gave their explanation a prominent place in both his catechisms.

Calvin said that the natural law contained elements of obscurity and therefore God gave us more exact knowledge through the written commandments. Calvin was emphatic in stating that the Ten Commandments are meant for Christians. He said that although they were abrogated as far as having the power to terrify the conscience, they were not abrogated in that they still teach the Christian what he should do and should not do. In his *Institutes*, Calvin laid down principles for the proper exposition of the Ten Commandments and then proceeded to expound them at length.

Significantly, the Heidelberg Catechism placed its exposition of the Ten Commandments in its third section as a description of how, through obedience, men are to show God gratitude for their salvation. The Westminster Catechism likewise gave the Ten Commandments a prominent place. It affirms: "This law, after his fall, continued to be a perfect rule of righteousness; and, as such, was delivered by God upon Mount Sinai in ten commandments, and written in two tables; the first four commandments contain our duty toward God, and the other six our duty to man. . . . The moral law doth for ever bind all, as well justified persons as others, to the obedience thereof; . . . Neither doth Christ in the gospel any way dissolve, but much strengthen this obligation." Where these standards are upheld, the Ten Commandments have a prominent place within the church.

In recent years various groups have deemphasized or eliminated the use of the Ten Commandments by Christians. Dispensationalists have emphasized that Christians are under grace and not under law. They insist that the law be used only for conviction of sin in evangelism but not as a means of Christian growth, and as a means of knowing more about the lawgiver. The situational ethicists, with their new morality, have eliminated all law from Christian ethics. In their view all law stirs up antagonism and must be replaced by an attitude of "love."

Bibliography:

J. Calvin, *Institutes of the Christian Religion*, II, viii.

R. H. Charles, *The Decalogue* (Edinburgh, 1926).
R. W. Dale, *The Ten Commandments* (New York, 1870).
H. J. Flowers, *The Permanent Value of the Ten Commandments* (London, 1927).
C. H. Gordon, "The Ten Commandments," *Christianity Today*, 8 (1964), 625-628.
H. G. G. Herklots, *The Ten Commandments and Modern Man* (London, 1958).
I. Klein, *The Ten Commandments in a Changing World* (New York, 1944).
H. J. Kuiper, ed., *Sermons on the Ten Commandments* (Grand Rapids, 1959).
J. V. McGee, "Ten Commandments in the Age of Grace," *BS*, Oct. 1958, 115:348-356.
G. C. Morgan, *The Ten Commandments* (London, 1901).
S. Mowinckel, *Le decalogue* (Paris, 1927).
O. Thelemann, *An Aid to the Heidelberg Catechism* (Grand Rapids, 1959), 332-405.
Ursinus, *Commentary on the Heidelberg Catechism* (Grand Rapids, 1954), 488-618.
J. K. Van Baalen, *The Heritage of the Fathers* (Grand Rapids, 1948), 390-566.

HARRY BUIS

COMMERCE. By 2000 B.C. trading ships sailed from the Persian Gulf to India, from the Red Sea to East Africa, and from Egypt and Phoenicia to Spain and probably to Britain and Scandinavia. By land a flourishing trade route ran along the Fertile Crescent from the Persian Gulf to Egypt (see, e.g., Geoffrey Bibby, *Four Thousand Years Ago*, London, 1962).

Abraham's family may have been traders in Ur, since Abraham had much silver and gold (Gen. 13:2), but the Hebrews did little trading until Solomon took advantage of the position of Palestine and traded extensively with Egypt and Asia Minor, probably exacting tolls also. He built large ships to sail from Ezion-Geber on the Gulf of Akaba, probably to India (I Kings 9:26-28; 10: 22-29). Foreign trade declined after Solomon. Tyre and Sidon continued to be the chief exporters and importers (Ezek. 27), and their merchants were visiting Jerusalem regularly as late as the time of Nehemiah (Neh. 13:16-22). The term "Canaanite" is used several times as the equivalent of travelling salesman and may be translated "merchant" (Prov. 31:24; Zeph. 1:11; Zech. 14:21).

Within the kingdoms of Judah and Israel there was normal buying and selling (Amos 8:5). Trade pacts allowed dealers to set up shops in neighboring capitals (I Kings 20:34). During the exile many Jews prospered in Babylonia and Persia, and records of a banking firm in Nippur, named Murashu (465-405 B.C.), contain many Jewish names.

In NT times all major trade was in Roman hands, and this is reflected in the description of Babylon (Rev. 18), which uses language from the description of Tyre in Ezekiel 27. There are allusions to trade in the Letter to Laodicea (Rev. 3:17, 18); and Lydia, a dealer in purple goods from Thyatira, is in Macedonia when Paul meets her (Acts 16:14).

Traders were expected to belong to their own guild or union (Acts 19:24, 25), and, since these guilds met for banquets in the temple of their patron god or goddess, Christian traders were often in great difficulties (cf. Rev. 13: 17; I Cor. 8:10).

J. S. WRIGHT

COMMISSION, THE GREAT. This title describes Christ's final commission to His disciples, as distinct from temporary commissions while He was on earth (e.g., Mt. 10:5 ff.). During the period between His resurrection and ascension He prepared His followers for their Gospel preaching. The following are the main elements in the commission:

(1) The empowering gift of the Spirit, first promised in the Upper Room (John 20:22; Luke 24:49) and reasserted before the ascension (Acts 1: 5, 8).

(2) The supreme authority of the One who commissions (Mt. 28:18).

(3) The fundamental nature of the

Gospel, involving the eternal alternatives of forgiveness or remaining in sin (John 20:21-23; Luke 24:47-49).

(4) On the human side there is the need for repentance (Luke 24:47) and obedience (Mt. 28:20).

(5) Baptism seals the contract, and is to be (literally) *into* the Name of the Trinity, i.e., it submerges into a new relationship with Father, Son, and Spirit (Mt. 28:19).

(6) All peoples are to hear the Gospel (Mt. 28:19), but the order of initial preaching is to Jews, Samaritans, and then Gentiles (Acts 1:8).

(7) Christ promises to be with His disciples always.

(8) The longer ending of Mark's Gospel includes the charge to go to all the world, to preach, and to baptize. Although faith and baptism are mentioned together, faith is mentioned twice and baptism once (Mark 16:16). Promises of casting out demons, healing, speaking with tongues, and being unaffected by snakebite were fulfilled in Acts, and no doubt there were occasions when Christians were unharmed by poison.

J. S. WRIGHT

COMMON GRACE. The term *common grace* is used in different senses in different theologies. Wesleyan Arminiansm teaches that, although man is by nature totally depraved, God bestows on every individual at birth sufficient grace to receive Christ in faith of his free volition. Because such grace is said to be bestowed on all, it is denominated "common." It is further contended that he who exercises that grace by believing in Christ is in consequence born again. The Reformed position, on the other hand, insists that only he who by the grace of the Holy Spirit has been born again is capable of saving faith. Therefore it rejects the Wesleyan Arminian concept of common grace and employs that term in a radically different sense. It distinguishes sharply between common grace and special or particular grace and ascribes renewing quality only to the latter.

Scripture teaches unmistakably that God bestows His saving grace only upon the elect, but it teaches just as clearly that He manifests an attitude of favor to all men. The Psalmist sang: "The Lord is gracious and full of compassion; slow to anger, and of great mercy. The Lord is good to all" (Ps. 145:8, 9). In Jesus' command to His disciples, "Love your enemies . . . that ye may be the children of your Father which is in heaven" (Mt. 5:44, 45), the love of God for His enemies is undeniably implicit. God's universal love is basic to the doctrine of common grace.

God's Favor to All

Scripture ascribes to the goodness of God the blessings of nature granted to all. Immediately after the Deluge God promised that the earth would not again be destroyed by a flood but that, so long as the earth remained, seedtime and harvest, cold and heat, summer and winter, day and night would not cease (Gen. 8:21, 22). Paul told the people of pagan Lystra and Derbe that God never left Himself without witness but did good, giving rain and fruitful seasons, and thus filling men's hearts with food and gladness (Acts 14:17). And in the Sermon on the Mount Jesus stated that God in love causes the sun to shine on the evil and the good, and rain to descend on the just and the unjust (Mt. 5:45).

When man fell into sin, God permitted him to retain certain vestiges of the Divine image in which he had been created. Prominent among those vestiges is a "sensus Deitatis." According to Romans 1:19-21, the heathen have some knowledge of God. In his *Institutes of the Christian Religion* Calvin insisted that "a sense of Deity is inscribed on every heart," even on the hearts of those

Vestiges of God's Image

who "seem to differ least from the lower animals" (I, iii, 1). Nor did God deprive man at his Fall of the precious gift of reason. It continued to be exercised by the offspring of ungodly Cain as well as by the descendants of godly Seth. In fact, in the early history of mankind the former excelled in the arts and sciences (Gen. 4:20-22). Calvin said: "In reading profane authors, the admirable light of truth displayed in them should remind us that the human mind, however much fallen and perverted from its original integrity, is still adorned and invested with admirable gifts from the Creator. If we reflect that the Spirit of God is the only fountain of truth, we will be careful, as we should avoid offering insult to him, not to reject or contemn truth wherever it appears." Referring to pagan lawgivers, philosophers, rhetoricians, physicians, and mathematicians, he declared: "We cannot read the writings of the ancients on these subjects without the highest admiration" (*Inst.*, II, ii, 15). Fallen man also continues to be a moral being; that is to say, he has a sense of right and wrong, a conscience which tells him it is right to do the right, wrong to do the wrong. The Gentiles "show the work of the law written in their hearts, their conscience also bearing witness, and their thoughts the mean while accusing or else excusing one another" (Rom. 2:15).

By no means does the fact of man's retention of vestiges of the Divine image detract from his total depravity. His Fall resulted in the complete loss of true knowledge of God, righteousness, and holiness (Eph. 4:24; Col. 3:10). The Apostle Paul charged the heathen with suppressing the truth by their wickedness (Rom. 1:18, RSV) and changing the truth of God into a lie (Rom. 1:25); and of both Jew and gentile he said: "There is none righteous, no, not one. . . . There is none that seeketh after God. . . . There is no fear of God before their eyes" (Rom. 3:10, 11, 18). Hence Calvin, having lauded the wisdom imparted by the Holy Spirit to the pagans of antiquity, went on to say: "Still, though seeing, they saw not. Their discernment was not such as to direct them to the truth, far less to enable them to attain it, but resembled that of the bewildered traveller who sees the flash of lightning glance far and wide for a moment, and then vanish into the darkness of the night, before he can advance a single step. So far is such assistance from enabling him to find the right path. Besides, how many monstrous falsehoods intermingle with those minute particles of truth scattered up and down in their writings as if by chance. . . . To the great truths, what God is in himself, and what he is in relation to us, human reason makes not the least approach" (*Inst.*, II, ii, 18). The Canons of Dort having granted that there remain in fallen man "the glimmerings of natural light, whereby he retains some knowledge of God, of natural things, and of the difference between good and evil, and shows some regard for virtue and for good outward behavior," go on to assert: "But so far is this light of nature from being sufficient to bring him to a saving knowledge of God and to true conversion that he is incapable of using it aright even in things natural and civil. Nay further, this light, such as it is, man in various ways renders wholly polluted, and hinders in unrighteousness, by doing which he becomes inexcusable before God" (III-IV, 4).

Restraint of Sin

God graciously restrains sin both in the individual and in the race. That truth is plainly implicit in the divine assertion, "My Spirit shall not always strive with man" (Gen. 6:3). With reference to Sarah, Abraham's wife, God said to Abimelech, king of Gerar: "I also withheld thee from sinning against me: therefore suffered I thee not to touch her" (Gen. 20:

6). And Scripture teaches that human government was ordained by God for the punishment of evil as well as the encouragement of that which is good (Rom. 13:1-4). Were it not for the Divine restraint of evil, human intercourse on this sin-ridden earth would be utterly chaotic. Since there is Divine restraint, a more or less orderly society occurs.

Encouragement to Good

Scripture teaches not only that God holds sin in check in the lives of the unregenerate; it ascribes to them the exercise of love and the doing of good. Said Jesus to His disciples: "If ye love them which love you, what thank have ye? for sinners also love those that love them. And if ye do good to them which do good to you, what thank have ye? for sinners also do even the same" (Luke 6:32, 33). Here it becomes necessary to distinguish between "love" and "love," "good" and "good." Elsewhere, Scripture says of the unregenerate: "There is none that doeth good, no, not one" (Rom. 3:12); and they are described as "haters of God" and "hating one another" (Rom. 1:30; Tit. 3:3). Only those who are born again are capable of "spiritual" good; that is to say, good motivated by love for God or that love for men which springs from love for God. The Heidelberg Catechism defines good works as "those which are done from true faith, according to the law of God, and to his glory" (Answer 91). Such works only the regenerate can perform. Yet, by virtue of the common grace of God others can and do perform good that may be denominated "civic" or "natural." But, though there is an outward conformance to precepts of God, there is something essentially lacking in them. Of such good the Westminster Confession of Faith says: "Works done by unregenerate men, although for the matter of them they may be things which God commands, and of good use both to themselves and others; yet, because they proceed not from a heart purified by faith; nor are done in a right manner, according to the Word; nor to a right end, the glory of God; they are therefore sinful and cannot please God, or make a man meet to receive grace from God. And yet their neglect of them is more sinful, and displeasing to God" (XVI, 7).

Sincere Offer of the Gospel

A most significant aspect of the doctrine of common grace is what Reformed theology designates "the universal and sincere offer of the Gospel." On the basis of Scripture, Reformed theology holds that from eternity God elected certain persons to eternal life and decreed that the others would because of their sins perish everlastingly. The latter phase of divine predestination is variously described as "preterition," "rejection," or "reprobation." Also on the basis of Scripture Reformed theology holds that "as many as are called by the Gospel are unfeignedly called. For God has most earnestly and truly declared in his Word what is acceptable to him; namely, that all who are called should come unto him" (Canons of Dort, III-IV, 8). Yet such passages as Ezek. 18:23; 33:11; Mt. 11:28; 23:37; and II Pet. 3:9 teach unmistakably that God not only promises eternal life to sinners in the case that they repent and believe, but most cordially invites all who hear the Gospel proclaimed to repent and believe in order that they may be saved. The last-named passage says in so many words that God is "not willing that any should perish, but that all should come to repentance." Thus Divine reprobation and the Divine offer of the Gospel admittedly constitute a paradox. Human reason has proved unable to harmonize them fully with each other. Here, as indeed everywhere, Reformed theology subjects human logic to the Divine *logos*. Commenting on Ezek. 18:23, Calvin said: "God desires nothing more earnestly than that those who are perishing and rushing to destruction should return into the way of safety. . . . If any one should object, 'then there is no election of God, by which he has predestinated a fixed number to salvation,' the answer is at hand: the prophet does not here speak of God's secret counsel, but only recalls miserable men from despair, that they may apprehend the hope of pardon, and repent, and embrace the offered salvation. If any one again objects, 'this is making God act with duplicity,' the answer is ready: that God always wishes the same thing though by different ways and in a manner inscrutable to us. Although, therefore, God's will is simple, yet great variety is involved in it, as far as our senses are concerned. Besides, it is not surprising that our eyes should be blinded by intense light, so that we cannot certainly judge how God wishes all to be saved, and yet has devoted all the reprobate to eternal destruction and wishes them to perish" (Calvin's Commentaries *in loco*).

Contrast with Saving Grace

Common grace as described in the foregoing paragraphs differs essentially from particular or saving grace. No amount of common grace will save a sinner from sin and death. Yet common and saving grace are closely related. They may be said to be interdependent. Saving grace presupposes common grace. For example, a covenant of nature, which God established with Noah and his descendants, guaranteed the continuity of the human race (Gen. 8:21–9:17). With that covenant as a background, God subsequently established a covenant of grace with Abraham and his seed, and in so doing guaranteed the continuity of the church (Gen. 12:1-3; 17:1-7). Had there been no human race, there could have been no church. In another example it may also be asserted without hesitation that because of His elect God frequently bestows blessings on men in general. For the sake of ten righteous persons God would have spared wicked Sodom and Gomorrah (Gen. 18:32). Jesus' saying, "Ye are the salt of the earth" (Mt. 5:13) indicates that God for the present bears with this sinful world because of the presence in it of His children as a preservative. The tribulation that will come to pass toward the end of time will be shortened for the elect's sake (Mt. 24: 22). Whether it is *solely* for the sake of His chosen people that God dispenses the blessings of common grace to mankind is definitely another matter. So sweeping an assertion would be unwarranted.

Historical Survey

Although the doctrine of common grace is found by suggestion in some of Augustine's writings, it never came to be elaborated by the Church of Rome. Rome's disparagement of the natural, in contradistinction to the spiritual, accounts for that neglect. The anabaptists, instead of correcting that error, compounded it by positing an antithesis of the spiritual and the natural. To the present day a powerful strain of this persists in much of Protestantism. Hence, many Protestants —perhaps most of them—show little interest in the doctrine of common grace. The 16th-century Reformers, notably Calvin among them, may be said to have discovered that doctrine. Late in the 19th century and early in the 20th it was elaborated and strongly stressed by such Dutch Calvinists as Abraham Kuyper and Herman Bavinck. The former wrote three large volumes on this subject.

More recently, the present century witnessed considerable controversy on common grace among American Calvinists, particularly in the Christian Reformed Church. In 1920 Ralph Janssen, Professor of OT at Calvin Seminary, was charged with leanings toward higher criticism. Although he was exonerated by the Synod of that year, charges against him persisted. He retorted that his critics were neglecting the doctrine of common grace, and he quoted Kuyper and Bavinck to that effect, under both of whom he had studied at the Free University of Amsterdam. When he refused to defend himself at the Synod of 1922 because, as he contended, certain members of that Synod had by their denial of common grace disqualified themselves for proper evaluation of his teaching, that body found him guilty as charged. However, the very next Synod, that of 1924, found two of his most vehement critics, Henry Danhof and Herman Hoeksema, guilty of denying the historic Reformed doctrine of common grace. These men insisted that an attitude of favor on the part of God to the non-elect is out of the question and that they are incapable of doing any good whatsoever. Under three heads, Synod emphatically reaffirmed the doctrine of common grace. It also recommended further study of the subject. Attempts in that direction were subsequently made by Herman Kuiper, Cornelius Van Til, James Daane, William Masselink, and Alexander De Jong, among others. Discussion has brought to the fore the importance of the time factor. It is obvious that, although God from eternity decreed unalterably the damnation of certain men, so long as the non-elect have not in actual historical fact finally rejected Christ by unbelief, God does not exclusively regard them nor deal with them *qua* reprobate, but in many ways manifests His goodness to them. Yet that leaves the paradox of Divine reprobation and common grace unsolved. It has become increasingly clear that this paradox must be permitted to stand without modification. It behooves Christians to beware of detracting from either of its elements.

A significant question demanding further consideration than so far received is whether Christ merited the blessings of common grace for the non-elect by the Atonement. That God ever beholds His elect in Christ is perfectly clear. For Christ's sake He blesses them with natural blessings as well as spiritual. Does God also for the sake of Christ bestow some good things on the non-elect? Calvin has not answered that question explicitly. William Cunningham has said: "Many blessings flow to mankind at large from the death of Christ, collaterally and incidentally, in consequence of the relation in which men, viewed collectively, stand to each other" (*Historical Theology*, II, 333). Robert S. Candlish observed that the entire history of the human race from the Apostasy to the Final Judgment is a dispensation of forbearance in respect to the reprobate, in which many blessings, physical and moral, affecting their characters and destinies forever, accrue even to the heathen, and many more to the educated and refined citizens of Christian communities. He has asserted: "These come to them through the mediation of Christ" (*The Atonement*, 358 f.). Also, L. Berkhof, while admitting that Reformed theologians generally have been hesitant to say that Christ's atoning blood merited the blessings of common grace for the reprobate, has concluded that undoubtedly significant benefits accrue from Christ's death to the entire race of men (*Systematic Theology*, Grand Rapids, 1938, 438).

See ANTITHESIS, DEPRAVITY, GENERAL REVELATION, GRACE, IMAGE OF GOD, MERCY.

BIBLIOGRAPHY:

H. Bavinck, *De Algemeene Genade* (Kampen, 1894).

L. Berkhof, *De Drie Punten in Alle Deelen Gereformeerd* (Grand Rapids, 1925).

J. Calvin, *Institutes of the Christian Religion* (Grand Rapids, 1949).

J. Daane, *A Theology of Grace* (Grand Rapids, 1954).

A. De Jong, *The Well-Meant Offer of the Gospel* (Franeker, 1954).
J. L. Girardeau, *Calvinism and Evangelical Arminianism Compared* (Columbia, 1890).
V. Hepp, *Het Misverstand in zake de Leer der Algemeene Genade* (Grand Rapids, 1923).
H. Hoeksema, *A Triple Breach in the Foundation of the Reformed Truth* (Grand Rapids, 1925).
R. Janssen, *De Crisis in de Christelijke Gereformeerde Kerk in Amerika* and *Voortzetting van den Strijd* (Grand Rapids, 1922).
H. Kuiper, *Calvin on Common Grace* (Goes, 1928).
A. Kuyper, *De Gemeene Gratie* (Amsterdam, 1902-04).
W. Masselink, *General Revelation and Common Grace* (Grand Rapids, 1953).
J. Murray and N. B. Stonehouse, *The Free Offer of the Gospel* (Philadelphia, 1948).
S. Ridderbos, *Rondom het Gemeene Gratie Probleem* (Kampen, 1949).
K. Schilder, *Is de Term "Algemeene Genade" Wetenschappelijk Verantwoord?* (Kampen, 1947).
C. Van Til, *Common Grace* (Philadelphia, 1947).

R. B. KUIPER

COMMON LIFE, BRETHREN OF (*Fratres de communi vita*), a form of life in religious communion with common ownership, established by Geert Groote at Deventer, Holland. This movement differed from monastic orders especially in the fact that the participants did not have to bind themselves to the community for the rest of their lives but were allowed to leave it if they so desired. The leadership was exercised by a rector to whom the other participants, generally fewer than 20 in number, owed obedience. The first community of this type was one for women, established when Geert Groote offered his parental home to poor women (1374). It is evident from the articles of July 16, 1379, that the organization of this house was similar to that of the Beguines (*q.v.*). But quite soon there arose a life of communion with common ownership, so that one could speak of Sisters of the Common Life. Many sisters entered this community, so that by 1419, at the death of Johannes Brinckerinck, who was then spiritual leader of the group, there were 150. The number of individual homes for sisters also increased rapidly. The one at 's-Hertogenbosch had no fewer than 500 sisters by 1450.

As a home for men called Brethren of the Common Life, Florens Radewijns, a clergyman of the Church of St. Lebuinus at Deventer and a friend of Geert Groote, made available his vicarage. A larger house became available in 1396 and was called the Home of Master Florens after the original benefactor. Still during the life of Geert Groote a similar community was established in nearby Zwolle. This group received a new home in 1396, the Home of St. Gregory, under the leadership of clergyman Gerard of Calcar (d. 1409). Under the rectorate of Dirk van Herxen (1410-1457) this became the most important home of the Brethren. The Brethren did not increase nearly as rapidly as the Sisters. At first the movement had to cope with considerable opposition, especially from the Dominicans. The most important opponent was Matheus Grabow, lector at the Dominican Convent at Groningen. The matter was discussed at the Council of Constance. The Brethren community created the impression of being a new order; and a new order could be established only with the permission of the pope. Men like d'Ailly and Gerson disagreed with Grabow. When the Council had decided in their favor and Grabow had been forced to recant, the Community of the Brethren could expand peacefully. The expansion extended to S Netherlands and also to Germany. Two groups arose, the Western and the Eastern: the colloquium of Zwolle and that of Münster.

The Brethren of the Common Life led a devoted life and attempted to relate all of their work to God. Their activities consisted in the copying and binding of books, the exercise of pastoral care, and the education of the youth. For the latter purpose they had the custom of creating *bursae* or scholarships for the assistance of students who studied in the city schools. After the establishment of the Home of Master Florens in Deventer, a school was set up in the old vicarage. It is of interest that Erasmus began his training there. After 1460, in the period of the greatest expansion, the printing of books and the giving of instruction received most of the attention. However, it is not correct to consider the Brethren responsible for the establishment and maintenance of schools. Only in exceptional cases did this happen. The best-known examples of these are the schools at Utrecht—where Hinne Rode was rector in 1520, and later Macropedius—and the one at Liége, where Johannes Sturm, the famous humanist of Strasbourg, received his training.

At the beginning of the 16th century there were 29 homes. In the course of that century almost every one ceased to exist. Many were confiscated during the Reformation.

See Constance, Council of; Devotio Moderna; Groote, Geert De.

Bibliography:

E. Barnikol, *Studien zur Geschichte der Brueder vom gemeinsamen Leben.* Die erste Periode der deatschen Bruederbewegung: Die Zeit Heinrichs von Ahaus (Tübingen, 1917).

J. M. E. Dols, *Bibliographie der Moderne Devotie* (Nijmegen, 1941).

E. Van Gulik, *De Moderne Devotie in Hoorn,* in: *Nederl. Arch. voor Kerkgesch.,* N.S. XXXV (1946), 91-119.

L. Halkin, *Les Frères de la Vie commune de la maison St. Jérome de Liége* (1495-1595), in: *Bull. de l' Inst. archeol. liégeois* LXV (1945), 5-70.

A. Hyma, *The Christian Renaissance.* A History of the "Devotio Moderna" ('s Gravenhage, 1924).

A. Hyma, *The Brethren of the Common Life* (Grand Rapids, 1950).

J. Lindeboom, *Het Bijbelsch Humanisme in Nederland* (Leiden, 1913).

R. R. Post, *De Modern Devotie.* Geert Grote en zine Stichtingen (Amsterdam, 1940), 35-111; 123-131.

J. Traiecti alias de Voecht, *Narratio de inchoatione domus Clericorum in Zwollis,* ed. by M. Schoentgen (Amsterdam, 1908).

C. van der Wansem, S.C.J., *Het Ontstaan en de geschiedenis der Broederschap van het Gemene Leven tot 1400* (Leuven, 1958).

D. Nauta

COMMON PRAYER, BOOK OF, the name given to the Prayer Book of the Anglican Church. The first edition appeared in 1549, at a time when the Reformation was beginning to get under way under King Edward VI. The book of 1549 was something radically new. It provided within the compass of one book all that the worshipper would need to enable him to follow all the services. The "hour" services of the breviary were reduced to two, Morning and Evening Prayer, which meant that they could become services for all the people, not simply for monks. The mass became the Holy Communion (though *mass* was retained as an alternative title). Occasional offices like penance were dropped, but provision was made for baptism, confirmation, marriage, visitation of the sick, and burial of the dead.

The framers of the Book of Common Prayer were guided by certain principles. (1) *Preservation* of whatever was of value in the ancient services. They disclaimed producing anything new just for newness' sake. (2) *Simplification.* They did away with the multiplicity of service books so that the worshipper would find in one book all the services that were held. They also made the services easy to follow. The complexities and overelaboration of the pre-Reformation services were replaced by a studied simplicity, with the needs of ordinary men very much in mind. (3) *Primacy of Scripture.* This meant that readings from the Bible replaced legends of the saints, but it meant considerably more. It meant basing the whole of the services on Scripture. Although the compilers felt free to include elements not expressly commanded in Scripture so long as they were edifying, they carefully refrained from anything that was out of harmony with the teaching of Scripture. The actual wording of the services is often Biblical even where there is no attempt at quotation. And the lectionary provided for systematic reading from the whole Bible, so that the Psalter was read through every month, the OT each year, and the NT three times a year. This occurred in addition to the Epistles and Gospels at the communion service. (4) *Purification* of the services from un-Scriptural practices. This meant the removal of a good deal that had crept in through the years, such as prayer to the saints and superstitious ceremonies of various sorts. (5) *English* replaced Latin as the language of worship, since a cardinal point of the Reformers was that the people must be able to understand all that is done during divine service. (6) *Congregational Worship.* The services became congregational. Certain parts were provided for the minister, and other parts were for the congregation. Confession of sin, for example, was to be made by the whole congregation. In all the services it was plainly intended that the congregation be active. (7) *Uniformity.* There had been much diversity before the Prayer Book appeared. Now all England was to have one rite.

This book was a long step toward reform, though, not surprisingly in a first attempt, not everything the compilers wished was accomplished. We can see that the book was something of a halfway house when we reflect that the mass vestments were retained, that the holy table was sometimes called the *altar,* and that the name *mass* was permitted.

Such things made the book acceptable to those who opposed reform. They did not like it, but they felt that it could be interpreted in a non-Reformed way. But in 1552 it was replaced by a new book which systematically went through the 1549 book and removed everything that could not be reconciled with the Reformed view. The vestments of the minister were reduced to the surplice; the consecration prayer, which had been mainly the Roman "canon of the mass" translated, was now broken up; all prayer for the dead was removed; and the reservation of the sacrament was prohibited. By common consent the 1552 book is the high-water mark of Protestantism in the Prayer Book.

Subsequent revisions have preserved the essential character of the 1552 book, though with some modifications in the direction of 1549. The book of 1662 was the last one to receive official authorization, and it remains the legal Prayer Book in England. An attempt was made to replace it in 1927 and again in 1928, but these attempts were defeated in the House of Commons, which must authorize prayer books in England.

The importance of the books of 1549 and 1552 is more than historical. They represent two points of view which retain large followings within Anglicanism. The high church party in general favors something like the book of 1549 and would like to see a revision making this kind of worship the standard within the church. The evangelical party, on the other hand, stands by the doctrinal position of 1552 and would be most unhappy with anything like the 1549 book.

The provinces of Anglicanism outside England have mostly produced their own prayer books (but not all; Australia still uses the book of 1662 as in England). As a general rule it may be said that these to a greater or lesser extent represent concessions to the 1549 viewpoint. This means that evangelicals are usually less at home in such places than they are where the Prayer Book of England is in use.

In recent times there is a good deal of interest in liturgical revision, which is exemplified in the setting up of a liturgical commission to advise in such matters by the archbishops of Canterbury and York. The attempt is now being made to combine the insights of both wings of the church into a new and more comprehensive mode of worship, rather than seeking either a compromise that will satisfy nobody, or a rite dominated by one wing to the exclusion of the other. It remains to be seen whether such a procedure is feasible.

BIBLIOGRAPHY:

C. Adams, *The Prayer Book Pattern* (London, 1957).

J. H. Blunt, *The Annotated Book of Common Prayer* (New York, 1889).

F. E. Brightman, *The English Rite* (London, 1915), 2 vols.

E. Cardwell, *The Two Books of Common Prayer Set Forth by Authority of Parliament in the Reign of King Edward the Sixth* (Oxford, 1838).

E. Daniel, *The Prayer Book* (London, many editions).

P. Dearmer, *Everyman's History of the Prayer Book* (London, 1912).

G. Dix, *The Shape of the Liturgy* (London, 1945).

J. Dowden, *The Workmanship of the Prayer Book* (London, 1899).

J. Dowden, *Further Studies in the Prayer Book* (London, 1908).

T. W. Drury, *How We Got Our Prayer Book* (London, 1904).

H. Gee, *The Elizabethan Prayer Book and Ornaments* (London, 1902).

D. Hague, *The Story of the English Prayer Book* (London, 1949).

G. Harford and M. Stevenson (eds.), *The Prayer Book Dictionary* (New York, 1912).

C. Neil and J. M. Willoughby, *The Tutorial Prayer Book* (London, 1913).

F. Proctor, *A New History of the Book of Common Prayer*, rev. W. H. Frere (London, 1901).

L. Pullan, *The History of the Book of Common Prayer* (London and New York, 1901).

J. T. Tomlinson, *The Prayer Book, Articles and Homilies* (London, 1897).

LEON MORRIS

COMMUNION, HOLY. Holy Communion is a designation for the ordinance also called the Lord's supper, breaking of bread, and eucharist. It was instituted by Christ, administered by the apostles, and has been practiced universally by Christians in all ages. The NT records the direct institution in Luke 22; Mt. 26; Mark 14; as well as Paul's instructions in I Cor. 11. The supper is instituted both as a gift and a command. In its institution the Lord's supper had two primary motifs—*expiation* (the paschal lamb is slain) and the *eschatological hope* (the messianic banquet to come).

Holy Communion as a Paschal Feast

Because of the variant chronologies of the last week of Jesus' life between the Synoptics and John's Gospel, there has been considerable debate as to whether or not Jesus consciously linked the Lord's supper with the OT passover feast. Lietzmann, Otto, and others have advanced theories suggesting that the Lord's supper was not a passover meal. Supporters of the passover meal hypothesis include Dalman, Strack-Billerbeck, Jeremias, and others. Clearly the NT writers identify the supper as a passover meal, and key details of the accounts lend weighty evidence to support such an identification. For example, the Last supper involved an extended *evening meal* (obligatory for the passover; abnormal for other meals); the disciples used *red* wine (symbolic of blood—passover wine was red); the disciples *reclined* (symbol of *liberation* in passover meals); the meal concluded with a hymn (as in the closing Hallel).

By placing the Lord's supper in the context of the passover, the expiation motif of the paschal lamb which is slain can be clearly seen. As the Exodus was a saving act which conditioned the whole of Israel's history, so is the death of Christ the saving act which conditions the whole of the history of New Israel. In the meal Jesus attached a new significance to the unleavened bread. It was now to signify His body, which was to be broken in sacrificial death. The wine is used to signify His blood, which is shed for the sins of His people. Hence Jesus designates Himself as the fulfillment of the passover victim. With dramatic imagery, Jesus portrays His coming death as the Lamb without blemish—the *Agnus Dei* who takes away the sin of the world. Only by a method of radical selectivity can it be maintained that the expiatory motif of the Lord's supper was a later embellishment of the Jerusalem tradition by the Apostle Paul.

The Lord's Supper as a Sign of the Future Messianic Banquet

The Lord's supper not only is linked to Israel's past history, but it also has a strong thrust toward the future. In this context the supper has strong eschatological overtones. In instituting the supper Jesus points to the breakthrough of the Kingdom of God, which will be fulfilled at the Messianic banquet table. He said to His disciples, "I tell you I shall not drink again of this fruit of the vine until that day when I drink it new with you in my Father's kingdom" (Mt. 26:29). Also Paul says, "For as often as you eat this bread and drink the cup, you proclaim the Lord's death until he comes" (I Cor. 11:26). In both texts there is a clear forward thrust pointing to the future expectancy. Here a joyful note is incorporated into the supper as the church looks forward to the return of Christ and the resuming of fellowship with Him in His incarnational presence.

The Lord's Supper as a Dynastic Celebration

The elements of covenant language and actions are clearly present in the Last supper narratives. It was customary in the OT to follow the making of a covenant with a meal that was part of the ratification ceremony. Such elements are present in Jesus' words—"This is my blood of the covenant, which is shed for the remission of sins" (Mt. 26:28). Also Luke records, "This cup is the new covenant in my blood, which is shed for you" (Luke 22:20). The references to "covenant" and "blood" are important. In the OT a covenant (*berith*) was "cut" and ratified in blood, and instructions for future memorial observances given. All three of these elements are present in the Last supper as Jesus inaugurates and ratifies the new covenant. Of added import here is the abundance of references to the coming of the Holy Spirit in John's Gospel. The longest discourse Jesus ever gives on the person and work of the Holy Spirit is placed in the context of the Last supper (see John 14–17). Here there is a striking parallel between the events surrounding the death of Moses, the mediator of the old covenant, and those of the death of Jesus, the mediator of the new covenant. It was customary in the ancient Near East for the aged or infirm king or ruler to appoint his successor before he died and to institute a covenant renewal ceremony, where the people renewed their vows to the covenant and were bound by oath of allegiance to the dynastic successor. (See the covenant renewal ceremony at Moab in Deut. 31). In John's discourse Jesus speaks of His coming departure and the sending of the Comforter. Jesus, of course, is not completing His reign as was Moses—but rather is leaving to assume His place at the right hand of God. However, the Holy Spirit is sent to "represent" Christ's presence while He is absent in the body. So to some degree the Spirit and His work of completing the ministry of Christ parallels Joshua's conquest of Canaan in the absence of Moses. The authority of teaching and convicting of sin, etc., is given to the Holy Spirit, whom the church is bound by new covenant oath to obey. Hence the new covenant treaty (the NT) derives its authority not simply from the apostles but from the Holy Spirit who taught them.

The Lord's Supper and the Love Feast

Besides the Last supper, there are frequent references in the NT to a common meal which was shared by the followers of Christ. The designation "love-feast" (*agape*) is given to these meals by Jude and Peter (Jude 12; II Pet. 2:13). Apparently, as deduced from the events recorded in Acts 2 and 4 and I Cor. 11, the Christians gathered for a common meal wherein the rich believers shared their food in a communal way with the poorer brethren. This feast was usually followed by the celebration of the Lord's supper.

The Presence of Christ in the Lord's Supper

No aspect of the Lord's supper has engendered more controversy than the question of the mode of the presence of Christ in the sacrament. The classical RC view is called transubstantiation. In this view Christ is thought to be truly physically present in the elements of bread and wine. Appealing to the words of institution, "this *is* my body . . . ," the verb "is" is taken as a copula which renders the interpretation of the statement in such a way that requires an equation between the element and the body of Christ. Although the verb "to be" is frequently used by Jesus in a figurative way ("I am the Door . . ."), such a figurative interpretation of the words of institution is disallowed by the RC Church. Appeals are made to the Bread of Life discourse (John 6) and to Paul's statement of "discerning the Lord's *body*" (I Cor. 11:29) to substantiate the demand for literal interpretation.

Transubstantiation (changing of substance) is an expression used to indicate the way Christ becomes present in the Lord's supper. Here Aristotelian categories of metaphysical thought are used to make the miracle of the mass more transparent also. In the mass, the substance (or real essence) of the bread and wine are said to be supernaturally changed into the real substance of the body and blood of Christ. However, the *accidents* (external perceivable qualities) of the bread and wine remain the same. Thus, after the priestly prayer of consecration, the substance of Christ is present though outwardly the *accidents* of bread and wine are all that is visible and tangible. Some modern RC scholars have sought to replace the old Thomistic view of transubstantiation with a broader view of "transignification." However, Pope Paul VI in 1965 issued an encyclical entitled *Mysterium Fidei* in which the classic doctrine and its formulation were reaffirmed.

The most notable attack on transubstantiation was that launched by Luther during the Reformation. In scathing terms Luther charged the RC Church with teaching a magical and superstitious view of the sacrament in his treatise, *The Babylonian Captivity of the Church.* To avoid the "unnecessary" miracle of having the *substance* of one thing present with the *accidents* of another manifested, Luther replaced transubstantiation with his view of consubstantiation. He viewed the presence of Christ as not supplanting the elements but co-existing with them. Christ's substance was seen to be "in, under, and through" the substance of the elements. That is, the substance of Christ permeated the substance of the elements so that both Christ and the elements were really and substantially present.

Luther and Calvin could never agree on the question of the mode of Christ's presence. Their difference on this question was one of the most serious debates that divided the Reformation household. The issue raged not so much on sacramental grounds as on Christological grounds. Calvin questioned the possibility of the presence of the human nature in more than one place at the same time. Luther argued that the human nature of Christ (including body and blood) had the attribute of *ubiquity* (omnipresence) as the Divine nature could communicate its attributes to the human nature. (See *communicatio idiomata.*) Thus because of the communicated attribute of ubiquity, the human nature of Jesus could be present in several different masses at the same time. Calvin saw the communication of Divine attributes to the human nature as a violation of the Chalcedonian formula of Christology, which stated that the two natures of Christ were united without *mixture, change, division,* or *separation,* each nature retaining its own attributes. Hence Calvin saw in consubstantiation a confusion of the two natures of Christ, which ended in a kind of docetic or monophysite heresy.

In articulating the standard Reformed view of the Lord's supper, Calvin fought a two-front polemic. On the one side he attacked Rome and the Lutherans for exaggerating the real presence of Christ to include His human nature, and on the other side he attacked Zwingli and the more radical spiritualists who minimized the reality of Christ's presence by reducing it to a presence in the *memory* of the believer. In dealing with the former, Calvin studiously avoided using the word *substantial* in describing the presence of Christ for fear he would be understood to mean "physical"—yet on speaking to the latter group, he insisted on the word *substantial* to describe the presence of Christ as being *real.*

Calvin argued that the key to the presence of Christ in the Holy Communion is the Holy Spirit. In the person of the Holy Spirit Christ is really and truly present in the service, and the Holy Spirit links or connects the believer to the risen and ascended Christ, and the believer is then nourished by the resurrected body of Christ. Thus in Calvin's explanation, Christ is said to be truly present touching His Divine nature but not locally present touching His human nature. Where Calvin saw in Luther a *confusion* of the two natures of Christ, Luther saw in Calvin a *separation* of the two natures and consequently a view that bordered on Nestorianism. Luther insisted, however, that he did not intend to suggest confusion, and Calvin likewise maintained that he had no intent to suggest a separation. The issue between the adherents of both views continues to this day.

Other theological questions remain as controversial issues in Christendom on the matter of Holy Communion. They include such questions as the mode of operation (*ex opere operato* vs. *ex opere operantis*), the extent of the benefits conveyed, the character of the elements to be used, the treatment of the consecrated elements, etc.

The Lord's supper has been looked upon as a sacrament in most Christian groups. Since the term sacrament came to be used for that which conveys saving grace (whether in itself, as in the RC Church, or only in conjunction with the Word when it is preached and received, as in Protestant churches), this has been opposed by those who look upon the ordinance as only a remembrance. As the term has broadened in usage this objection is not as strong as it once was.

The fact that so much theological controversy in the history of the church has centered on the Lord's supper points out dramatically how seriously Christians have taken it. Where controversy abounds there still remains one basic point of agreement, i.e., the Lord's supper is indeed "holy" and touches the very heart of the life of the church. Because of the sanctity of the matter and the sober warnings of Paul that to eat and drink unworthily exposes a person to damnation, most churches have restricted participation in the supper to professing Christians who have reached an age of discernment and who recognize their need of being nourished by Christ.

Bibliography:

J. Calvin, *Institutes of the Christian Religion,* IV, xvii, xviii.

T. Cranmer, *Defence of the True and Catholic Doctrine of the Sacrament* (1550), reprinted in *The Works of Thomas Cranmer,* ed., G. E. Duffield (Appleford, Berks, 1964), pp. 45-231.

C. Hebert, *The Lord's Supper: History of Uninspired Teaching* A.D. 74-A.D. 1875, 2 vols. (London, 1879).

E. A. Knox, *Sacrifice or Sacrament?* (London, 1914).

ROBERT C. SPROUL

COMMUNION OF SAINTS, a term from the Apostles' Creed, "sanctorum communio." It is difficult to determine precisely when it received its place in the Creed of the church. In the 5th century it is found as a part of the Apostles' Creed as used by Faustus, bishop of Reji. Also, it is almost certain that Nicetas of Remesiana (*c.* 400) knew it as a part of the Creed. There are even indications that it was already in use in and around Antioch about the middle of the 4th century.

In regard to its meaning, there is a great difficulty lying in the fact that the word "sanctorum" may be translated as either "holy persons" or "holy matters." In the latter case, the reference would be to communion with the holy things of the church, particularly the sacraments; whereas in the former case, the reference would be either to the "saints" in a specific, RC sense, or to the communion among all believers mutually. This last view is supported by the fact that the words "communion of saints" immediately follow the confession about the holy, catholic church. They would then be epexigetical, and this would be of particular significance because of the Donatist heresy of that day. Since the Donatists distinguished between the "catholic church" and the "saints" (that is, their own followers), both of these expressions would then be consciously joined together here, so as to indicate that such a separation was completely unwarranted and that, to the contrary, it was exactly in the holy, catholic church that the communion of the saints receives stature and is experienced. But there is even a difficulty here, for in a number of the older texts the connection between these two elements of the Creed is not so direct. It is also certain that already with Faustus of Reji there were certain tendencies which pointed in the direction of the later RC view of saints. The thought of the *sancta* ("the sacred things," the sacraments) also appears from the beginning. At the time when these words, *sanctorum communio*, were included in the Creed, apparently no contradiction was seen between the two possible interpretations—the one, in a personal, and the other, in a sacramental sense. Indeed, an expert on the history of the Apostles' Creed such as Ferdinand Kattenbusch has even expressed the opinion that the term was purposely chosen because of the possibility of this double interpretation.

Nor can it be denied that both possibilities are closely bound up with each other. Even the conflict between Rome and the Reformation, however sharp it may have been in reference to this very element of the Creed, may not be reduced to the problem whether *sanctorum* refers to persons or things (sacraments). Both the Reformation churches and Rome have room for both views. The Heidelberg Catechism, for example, emphatically states that the *sanctorum communio* concerns the calling of believers to employ their gifts to the advantage and salvation of the other members, thus, the communion with each other as believers (Lord's Day 21). But it prefaces this statement with a reference to communion with Christ and all His treasures and gifts, and the Catechism includes in these treasures and gifts that which Christ grants to His people in the sacraments. The same is true in Calvin's catechism. By the "communion of the saints" he understands the unity which exists among the members of the church. But he would also include under this term all the benefits which the Lord confers to His church and tend to the advantage and salvation of every believer (par. 98).

In the Reformation church the term "saints" refers to the believers "all and every one" (Heidelberg Catechism, Lord's Day 21), who, according to the Holy Scriptures, partake of the holiness of Christ and are indwelt by Him through His Spirit. In Rome, however, attention is directed to a certain category of people called saints, consisting chiefly of those who had sealed their faith with the martyr's death, and later broadening out to others who excelled through a special devotion to the cause of Christ and His church and who, through their pious life, had acquired special merits. In the background of this view is the thought of the meritoriousness of good works, which makes it possible to ascribe to these saints-in-the-narrow-sense certain merits which can benefit not only themselves, but, via the "treasury of the church," also the saints-in-the-broader-sense. This refers then particularly to the dead in purgatory, the suffering church, which thus, through the intercession of the militant church, profits from the merits of the triumphant church. Thus, it followed that when the Reformation broke with the idea of the meritoriousness of good works, this view of the communion of the saints also had to be rejected: a view, after all, which could not be considered anything else than an attack upon the Mediatorship of Christ, about whose unique intercession the Belgic Confession speaks in the richest terms (Article 26). What remained, then, was the communion of every believer, personally, with Christ as the Head of His church and with everything that He grants to His people, and also the resultant union of all believers with each other, which must be expressed in mutual love, as befits the members of one body.

Y. FEENSTRA

COMMUNISM: ITS PHILOSOPHY AND PRACTICE

Christianity's basic affirmations are denied and opposed by communism. In contradiction to faith in God, it affirms that matter is the eternal and the sole reality. Dialectical materialism undercuts moral law. Economic determinism denies the possibility of the transformation of man through the Gospel and affirms that the change of the economic system changes human nature. Its worldwide mission brings it into conflict with Christ's great commission. Communism's utopian vision of an earthly paradise is a substitute for eternal redemption.

Christians need to understand the world's largest organized movement of atheism. Communism has grown from a few hundred followers to more than 50,000,000 party members throughout the world. Communists control about 26 percent of the land mass and about 35 percent of the world's population. As is true of all faiths, within their ranks Communists range from one hundred percent believers to opportunists. Although there is some division within and between Communist parties, about 90 Communist parties throughout the world are united on their basic philosophy, strategy, tactics, and ultimate goals.

Dialectical Materialism

In order to escape a mechanistic materialism, communism wedded materialism to the dialectic. The existence and struggle of opposites has been observed from ancient time. Heraclitus thought that "everything happens through struggle." Hegel (1770-1831) maintained that the Absolute unfolded itself in the dialectical pattern of movement (thesis), countermovement (antithesis), and the higher movement (synthesis) which arose out of the clash of contradictory movements. Marx claimed that Hegel was wrong in making the Idea instead of Matter primary. He taught that the Idea was "nothing else than the material world reflected by the human mind, and translated into forms of thought" (*Capital*, New York, p. 25). When applied to history and society, this philosophy is called historical materialism.

Laws of the Dialectic

The laws of the dialectic are: *First, potential or actual contradiction is universal,* existing in everything at every stage. *Second, the particularity of contradiction* means that a contradiction is definite and concrete. Flexibility of tactics is essential in order to exploit the contradiction so as to help communism. *Third, the unity of opposites* teaches that a contradiction does not exist in isolation. There is no antithesis without a thesis. Furthermore, the opposites can be transformed into one another in that the ruled (the proletariat) can become the ruler over the bourgeoisie. *Fourth, progress comes through the struggle of opposites* and the victory of the antithesis, which represents the future, over the thesis. Periods of relative rest may be followed by conspicuous changes. Coexistence is the period when the antithesis is bringing about the changes essential to the overthrow of the thesis. *Fifth, the transformation of quantity into quality* means that when enough changes have taken place the revolution occurs and society leaps to a new order; for example, the dictatorship of the proletariat occurs which builds socialism and finally communism. *Sixth, the negation of the negation* teaches that the antithesis (the proletariat guided by the Party) which brought an end to the thesis (the bourgeoisie) is negated by the progressive development into the synthesis (communism) (O. V. Kuusinen, ed., *Fundamentals of Marxism-Leninism*, 2nd revised edition, Moscow, 1963, pp. 77-81; Mao Tse-tung, *On Contradiction*, New York, 1953, pp. 44-51).

Dialectical Outline of Human History

Regarding history in the light of the dialectic, Communists come up with the following view of the past and vision of the future. *First*, primitive communism occurred, wherein lands, cattle, men, women, and children were in common. But the antithesis (private property) arose. *Second*, out of this developed the slavery of antiquity, which was the synthesis of the contradiction between primitive communism and private property. *Third*, as slave labor grew more and more unprofitable, and as freedmen arose, feudalism developed. This was a higher system than ancient slavery. *Fourth*, as manufactories, wage earners, and the urban bourgeoisie developed, they negated feudalism and created the synthesis called capitalism. *Fifth*, capitalism creates the proletariat (the working man in industrial society), which is capitalism's grave digger. The Party represents this class. As the general staff of the revolution, the Communist Party manipulates the proletariat so that the capitalist state is overthrown and the dictatorship of the proletariat is established. This is a transition stage to the final synthesis (communism). The dictatorship changes the economic system to socialism. Since Communists believe that the nature of man is shaped by the economic system, the change of the economic system results in the change of the nature of man. Since socialism is supposedly a cooperative system, man becomes cooperative. Under socialism the state (the dictatorship) exists, and men supposedly work according to their ability and receive according to their work. Finally the state withers away, for a classless society has no need, they say, of organized coercion. With the withering away of the state, there is the advent of communism, wherein men work according to their ability and receive according to their need.

The Philosophy of Revolution

Dialectical materialism is not just a theoretical contemplation of reality but is the guide to action, the ideological weapon of the working class, in the revolutionary transformation of the world. This philosophy of ceaseless conflict results in revolutionary action. "Marxist-Leninist theory provides a scientific basis for revolutionary policy." "In the proletariat the Marxist world outlook has found its material weapon, just as the proletariat has found in Marxism its spiritual weapon" (*Fundamentals of Marxism-Leninism*, pp. 18-19).

The revolution is threefold. *First*, the seizure of the state and the establishment of the dictatorship. *Second*, the state control, then, as far as possible, of the total life of the people. *Third*, the change of human nature through revolutionary struggle and the change of the economic system. All this is expressed in the closing words of the *Manifesto of the Communist Party*, which is viewed as a scientific document. "The Communists . . . openly declare that their ends can be attained only by the forcible overthrow of all existing social conditions. . . . The Proletarians have nothing to lose but their chains. They have a world to win. *Working men of all countries, unite!*"

The dictatorship is not a democracy, but it wages the fiercest and most merciless war against the bourgeoisie. The dictatorship is "untrammeled by law and based on violence . . ." (Joseph Stalin, *Leninism*, Moscow, 1934, Vol. I, pp. 43, 46).

How Communists Wage War

Communism wages war on us on various levels, including hot war, for example, in SE Asia. Their basic approach to the overthrow of all existing social conditions is based on dialectical materialism, which teaches that contradictions exist in everything at every stage. Progress results from the clash of contradictions wherein that which represents the future overcomes that which represents the past. Therefore, Communists seek to utilize every potential or actual contradiction in the forces arrayed against them. It has made a science out of the exploitation of real and imaginary grievances as it fans into revolutionary flames all possible points of tension within a society and between societies. As the International Conference of 75 Parties put it in 1969: "The Communist and Workers' Parties, the working class and the anti-imperialist forces, take into account all the contradictions in the enemy camp and strive to deepen and utilize them in the interest of peace and progress" (*World Marxist Review*, Toronto, July, 1969, p. 10). These sources of antagonism, and of conflicts of interest, are exploited in order to create the conditions for revolutionary conquest of power in one country after another until the world is subdued. The Communist countries, therefore, work with Communists in other countries, and with anyone else whom they can directly or indirectly motivate to agitate and exploit grievances.

Three Revolutionary Forces

A scientist does not create the forces which he manipulates, although he may bring them to bear in situations where, left to themselves, they would not operate. Communists view themselves as social scientists who understand the laws of society and are able to manipulate existing forces for revolutionary purposes.

The International Conference of 75 Parties (June 5-17, 1969) declared that three revolutionary forces are arrayed against imperialism, with the United States being the leader and mainstay of imperialism. "Three mighty forces of our time—the world socialist system, the international working-class and the national liberation movement—are coming together in the struggle against imperialism. The present phase is characterized by growing possibilities for a further advance of the revolutionary and progressive forces" (*World Marxist Review,* July, 1969, p. 5).

The world socialist, or Communist, countries constitute the main revolutionary force, and the leader is the Soviet Union. Although there are points of conflict between Communist countries, most of them believe it is their duty to strengthen the Soviet Union. To function as bases for world revolution, Communist countries must strengthen themselves in every way possible. Therefore, they tell us they "are building up their political, economic and military might" (*Information Bulletin*, Toronto, Nos. 5, 6, 7, May 14, 1967, p. 77). Economic strength is of vital importance, for their competition with us "is now an important front in the class struggle in the international arena" (B. N. Ponomaryov, ed., *World Revolutionary Movement of the Working Class*, Moscow, 1967, pp. 39-40). Of course, they welcome any sort of aid, even from their enemies, which strengthens them in economic warfare. The Communist parties in non-Communist countries are a part of international communism and constitute, as it were, foreign troops in civilian clothes.

The national liberation movement constitutes the second revolutionary force. A national liberation war is any war designed to overthrow a colonial power or a government which is not friendly to communism. Although they may unite with non-Communists to overthrow an unpopular regime, the aim of the Communists is to establish a Communist government. This is done either immediately or through forming a coalition government which they then subvert (*World Marxist Review*, June, 1969, pp. 40-41). Although this tactic is as old as Lenin, it has been refined in our own day (State Department, *Russia*, Washington, 1918, Vol. I, p. 359; Joseph Stalin, *Marxism and the National and Colonial Question,* New York, 1934, pp. 115, 234, 235, 246; *Problems of Leninism*, Moscow, 1954, pp. 27-73). In January, 1966, the Tricontinental Conference took place in Havana. Red China, the Soviet Union, and other Communist countries set up organizations designed to stimulate and direct revolutions in Asia, Africa, and Latin America. The ultimate design is to encircle and defeat the United States. As Lin Piao put it, they intend to split up and defeat "this colossus of U.S. imperialism." "That is why the greatest fear of U.S. imperialism is that people's wars will be launched in different parts of the world, particularly in Asia, Africa and Latin America, and why it regards people's wars as a mortal danger" (*Long Live the Victory of People's War!* (Peking, 1966, pp. 48-57). Vietnam is one of the important testing grounds of the national liberation wars (*ibid.*, pp. 57-58, 66; *World Marxist Review*, July, 1969, pp. 27-28; August, 1970, pp. 78-79).

The third revolutionary force is the working class movement, as Communists label it, which engages in mass struggle in non-Communist countries. The Party in each of these countries is regarded as the vanguard of the revolution. As a matter of fact, the working class is not communistic, so the Communists utilize disgruntled intellectuals, or anyone else whom they can convert or manipulate, to alienate and manipulate any segments of society in order to create chaos and subvert the society. They utilize the motivations of others to accomplish Communist purposes, regardless of the intentions of those whom they use. In every society and every individual there are tensions and grievances. Communists endeavor to exploit these so as to bring people into such confrontations with the established authorities that these people will be further alienated. Communists must "educate the working class in a revolutionary spirit, to develop their revolutionary class consciousness . . ." (*Communist and Workers' Parties' Manifesto*, Washington, 1961, p. 72). However, their efforts are not limited to the working class. Efforts are made to build united fronts on a wide variety of issues. As Gus Hall, General Secretary of the Party in the United States, put it: "Independent political action by the masses is a necessary and inevitable path of struggle. Hence our policy is to struggle for, to urge, to agitate for, to initiate every possible form of organization—the very maximum that each stage of development and each specific political level permit" (*Information Bulletin*, No. 95, May 9, 1967, pp. 11-12). Henry Winston thought that with sufficient wisdom and work the "merger of the three major currents of struggle—for peace, civil rights and economic welfare—can develop into a mighty anti-monopoly coalition" (*World Marxist Review*, October, 1968, p. 19). Communists constantly escalate centers of conflict within societies.

While Communists work within non-Communist countries to divide and destroy, on the international level they also endeavor to exploit the conflicts which exist between non-Communist nations. Through dividing their enemies both within nations and between nations, through the national liberation wars, and through the efforts of Communist countries, the Communists are confident that as these three revolutionary streams merge they will overflow the world and cover it with the dictatorship of the proletariat.

Communism and Christianity

Communism's antagonism to Christ is not a surface antagonism as a result of a reaction against corruptions in Christendom. There are basic elements in its philosophy, such as the following, which make it unalterably opposed to Christianity. *First,* militant atheism. *Second,* a world view in which all religion is considered to be superstition. *Third,* the doctrine that religion is a tool of the ruling class to keep the masses submissive. *Fourth,* the doctrine that religion is the opiate of the masses which deadens them to the pain caused by the misery and mystery of life under non-Communist systems. "Every religious idea, every idea of God, even every flirtation with the idea of God, is unutterable vileness . . . vileness of the most dangerous kind, 'contagion' of the most abominable kind" (V. I. Lenin, *Selected Works*, New York, 1943, Vol. XI, pp. 675-676). *Fifth,* the doctrine that religion is a sign of man's alienation from himself. Man, in affirming God, is denying that he, man, is the supreme being. *Sixth,* denial of Christianity's affirmation of the moral law. Communism maintains that morality is but a means of protecting class interests. The Communist moral system is the reverse of ours, for their interests are in opposition to ours (Howard Selsam, *Philosophy in Revolution,* New York, 1957, pp. 136-137). *Seventh,* since communism demands the total loyalty of the individual, there is no room for God (Liu Shao-chi, *How To Be A Good Communist*, Peking, 1965).

These things enable us to realize why communism considers Christianity to be one of its main enemies. Since Christians are for God, Christ, and the Bible, they must stand against communism, while seeking to convert Communists to Christ.

How does communism express its antagonism to religion? Lenin emphasized that "a Marxist must be a materialist, i.e., an enemy of religion; but he must be a dialectical materialist, i.e., one who puts the fight against religion not abstractly, not on the basis of abstract, purely theoretical, unvarying propaganda, but concretely, on the basis of the class struggle which is going on *in practice* and educating the masses more and better than anything else" (*Selected Works*, Vol. XI, pp. 668-669). In other words, the law of the particularity of contradictions teaches that one must be flexible, study the concrete situation, and see what one must do in a specific situation in order to advance communism and ultimately eliminate religion. This may necessitate in one time and place the exact opposite of what one does at another time and place. According to the circumstances, they do this in the following ways. *First*, they disseminate anti-religious propaganda both before and after they capture a country. In some countries, they may soften their propaganda when they are trying to manipulate religious people into doing something which the Communists believe will be helpful to them. *Second*, when possible, Communists form united fronts with religious people in order to work for some supposedly common objective. However, the ultimate objective of the Communist is not a reform within a system, but the revolutionary overthrow of the system. Today the dialogue with religious people is a Communist means of trying to get them to work with Communists. *Third*, the Communist front differs from the united front in that in the united front people consciously work with the Communists. The Communist front is a deceptive organization which dupes join without recognizing that it is being manipulated from behind the scenes by the Communists. They are especially happy to get clergymen to join fronts. These fronts perform such functions as raising money, spreading positions which the Communists want spread —but which would not be as acceptable to the public if they knew this—as a means of destroying or neutralizing opposition to communism. *Fourth*, when possible, Communists infiltrate religion, both in Communist countries and in non-Communist countries, in order to use this fortress of the enemy as effectively as possible. *Fifth*, when Communists conquer a country, they usually refrain from persecuting religion until they have consolidated their power. Then they persecute religious people in a wide variety of ways, including murder. Through the elimination of leaders who will not obey them, through infiltration, and through intimidation, the Communists bring organized religion under their control so as to use it for their own purposes. When they have changed the economic system, they claim, they will eliminate the need for religion by abolishing the mystery of life and the misery of life, and then religion will die, for its roots have been destroyed.

What can the Christian do? *First,* Christians should pray for the church, for their enemies, for those whom their enemies persecute and exploit, and for the spread of the Gospel. *Second*, Christians should be informed not only concerning the Bible, but also concerning such movements as communism. *Third,* Christians should be articulate in the spread and defense of the Gospel, as well as in exposing and opposing error. *Fourth*, Christians should increase righteousness, not just because it exalts a nation, but because it glorifies God to do so. *Fifth*, as citizens, Christians should do those things which help perpetuate and enlarge the borders of true freedom. *Sixth*, Christians should keep in mind that their negatives grow out of their positives. They are against communism and other forms of evil because they are for God, Christ, the Bible, and humanity.

BIBLIOGRAPHY:

D. M. Abshire, R. V. Allen, *National Security* (New York, 1963).

J. D. Bales, *Communism: Its Faith and Fallacies* (Grand Rapids, 1962).

J. M. Bochenski, *Handbook on Communism* (New York, 1962).

W. Chambers, *Witness Whittaker Chambers* (New York, 1952).

J. E. Hoover, *Masters of Deceit* (New York, 1958).

House Committee on Un-American Activities, *Soviet Total War* (Washington, 1956).

E. Lyons, *Workers' Paradise Lost* (New York, 1967).

W. C. Skousen, *The Naked Communist* (Salt Lake City, 1962).

JAMES D. BALES

COMPARATIVE RELIGION

Definition of Religion

Before religions can be studied the nature of religion must be defined. Many works on comparative religion uncritically assume that the various world religions have a common essence which enables them to be placed upon the same coordinate level. It is careless to assume that all religions are essentially the same simply because certain accidental features may be shared.

The concept of religion is not adequately defined by simply pointing to its extension, i.e., to such historical phenomena as Buddhism, Shintoism, Taoism, Hinduism, Judaism, and Islam. To give an example of what is included within the extension of the concept of religion does not yet state what characteristics, if any, are held in common. A denotative definition does not explicate the intensional or connotative definition of a concept of religion. To state what something is, is to state its essence or the basic qualities necessary and sufficient to constitute a thing as of a certain type. In this article we shall divide religions into Christian and non-Christian religions.

To the Christian there is only one correct relationship that man has to God. All non-Biblical or non-Christian religions are simply human distortions of God's self-disclosure, of true religion. The religions of the world are to be judged in terms of their relation to the one true religion. Such a procedure will appear arbitrary to anyone employing a different basis of division.

Basically there are two types of definitions of religion that purport to be real definitions. The first assumes that there is some basis for religious beliefs and practices outside of man. The second simply denies that there is any non-human fact or factor to which man is related. A person's concept of religion will vary, depending on which side he chooses. The Christian believes not only that God exists but that He has disclosed Himself, revealed Himself to man through the person of His Son, Jesus Christ. He therefore holds that there is an objective basis for the Christian religion.

Within the Biblical tradition, "religion" denotes man's relation to God. Special honor is due to God, since He is the first principle of all things. Religion is, therefore, a virtue, since it is a part of being good to render to God what we owe Him. It is, of course, impossible for man to pay God as much as he owes Him, yet his whole life ought to be devoted to God's honor. Thus man's relation to God gives rise to certain acts, e.g., to devotion, where men subject themselves wholly to God; and to prayer, where a man confesses his need of God and surrenders his mind to Him. Religion is here more than worship; it is the service of God with one's whole being throughout the entire course of one's life. It is in this sense that the religious man's whole life is a prayer and an offering to God.

The Ancient Near East

The view that religion is a subjective projection of the human fantasy is supported by the religions of the ancient Near East and the religions of India. The ancient Near East included Mesopotamia, Palestine, and Egypt, and there is evidence that Greece was also closely related to it. (See Cyrus Gordon, *The World of the Old Testament*, 2nd ed., New York, 1958, pp. 15 ff., especially pp. 20-21.) The first literature in Asia was the Sumerian, written from about 3000 B.C. in Mesopotamia. It was replaced as a spoken language by Acadian, sometimes known as Babylonian or Assyrian. Hittite is included in Acadian. The most recent language to be deciphered is Ugaritic, a branch of Canaanite. Some of the other languages to be found in this area of the world were old Persian, Phoenician, Aramaic, Egyptian, and, of course, Hebrew. For our studies of the religions of the ancient Near East we are fortunate in having a number of written sources available as well as numerous archeological remains. (See *Ancient Near Eastern Texts Relating to the Old Testament*, edited by James D. Prichard, Princeton, 1955.) The religions of the ancient Near East are typical of non-Biblical religions. The various aspects of nature are deified and personified. The gods were not all-powerful beings, nor were they creators of the universe. In fact, the gods came into being. An inscription carved inside the pyramids of Mer-ne-Re and Nefer-ka-Re of the 6th Dynasty, 24th century B.C., is typical. The text was a part of the dedication ritual of a royal pyramid. It begins by evoking Atum-khepren, the god of Heliopolis, who is compounded of two phases of the sun. It recalls the first "re-creation," when the god Atum stood on a primeval hillock, arising out of the waters of chaos, and then brought the first gods into existence: Shu, god of air; Tefnut, goddess of moisture; Geb, god of earth; Nut, goddess of the sky; the gods Osiris and Seth, and the goddesses Isis and Nephephys. Atum is not eternal; he states simply that "I am the great god who came into being by myself." When Atum Re named the parts of his body, the other gods then came into being. Variations on this theme are numerous. Much light has been shed upon the OT from recent studies of the ancient Near East. It is difficult, however, to see how anyone can accuse the Israelites of borrowing the idea of creation *ex nihilo* from any of the surrounding nations.

The religions of the ancient Near East do, in fact, display certain formal similarities to that of the OT. All are concerned with the origin of man and with the origin of the present world. All are concerned with man's relation to what is to be worshipped. The similarity ends with such formal agreement. With respect to content there are only striking contrasts. Similar language is used, but the concepts expressed are essentially different. To see the differences, the text of the first chapter of Genesis need only be compared with the religious texts of the surrounding ancient Near Eastern nations. When the Israelites read their Scriptures, they were made conscious of the difference between their faith and that of the nations. The Genesis account is the denial of the essential notions of the non-Biblical religions of the ancient world. The gods of the non-Biblical religions have a beginning. They usually arise out of the waters of a primeval, primordial chaos; they are totally lacking in moral qualities. They kill and are killed; they eat, drink, and engage in sexual intercourse. They literally display like passions with men. They are angry and afraid. They may, in fact, eat each other, as the god Mot eats puissant Baal (*ibid.*, p. 140). They are deceitful and treacherous, engaging in plots and conspiracy. They are finite deities whose power and knowledge is limited. In fact, such "supernatural" beings are more or less controllable by magic and ritual. The gods are neither eternal nor immortal, and they are subordinate to the chaos out of which they arose. The gods had a beginning, but apparently the waters of chaos, out of which they arose, did not.

The creative acts of Genesis refer to the acts of an omnipotent God. The phenomenal universe (heaven and earth) is brought into being (created) by Him. The chaos mentioned does not precede God, but God creates the chaos. All order, all law, all structures, the heavens and the earth, the sun, the moon, the stars, the world of plants and animals, the seas, in fact everything else is not a god, but a part of the created world which God alone has made. In Genesis man occupies a special place. He is made in the image and likeness of God, in holiness and righteousness, but he is not a part of God. He is neither the tears nor the blood of a slain deity. The world is not the body of a dead goddess; the cycles of drought and famine do not depend upon the death and reliving of Baal. Man need not fear the violence of the goddess Hathor, who seeks to destroy him, for God is good. The world is not the abode of half-men and half-bulls; there are no gods who eat each other and rule the regions of the universe. There is no need to fear the dragon of the world below who each day threatens the sun with destruction. For all of nature is the creation of God, and man has been given dominion over nature. The animals are not incarnations of God to be worshipped, but they are to be controlled by man.

Man's present misery is not a result of the whims of arbitrary deities. It is the result of his own willful transgression of God's holy law. There are no cruel deities that desire human sacrifice and arbitrarily threaten man's destruction. For this is the world that God has made. It is very unlikely that a person who lives within Western civilization will today believe in such gods as Marduk, Ea, Re, Osiris, or Baal. What we are apt to forget, however, is that one of the main reasons why we do not take such gods seriously is that our ancestors, whether Jews or Gentiles, came to believe in Biblical religion. In many regions of the modern world there are still great masses of people who live in a world like the religious world of antiquity. The religions of the ancient world today find much affinity with certain religions of India.

India

India does not have a single religion, but there are combinations of related religions based upon different phases of the Vedic tradition. The oldest Vedic texts are composed of four collections known as the *Vedas*. Other literature based upon one of the collections is also referred to as Vedic when the term is used broadly. The four *Vedas*, the *Sruti*, or "revelation," are the *Rig-Veda*, the *Sama Veda*, the *Yajur Veda*, of which there are two recensions, and the *Artharva-veda*. In addition, certain prose treatises, the *Brahmanas* that interpret Brahman, the *Aranynkas* or forest teachings, and the *Upanishads* belong to the Vedas.

Other Vedic documents are the *Smrti*, which include the *Sutras*, collections of aphorisms; the *Dharmasastra*, law manual; the *Itihasas*, or epic poems. The *Bhagavagita* is also considered to be sacred; and the *Puranas*, ancient traditional history sometimes grouped with similar works called *Tantaras*. From the number of hymns addressed to him, Indra appears to be the most popular god of the *Vedas*. It is to be noted that, like the other gods of antiquity, Indra himself came into being. In addition to Indra there are minor deities who represent the wind, Vata or Vayu, and the terrible storm gods, the Maruts and

Rudra, who later becomes Siva. There are also many goddesses. Other gods of importance in the hymns of the *Rig-Veda* are Agni, the god of fires, and Prajapati, the unknown god. Varuna, the god of the sky, is the supreme god whom others obey. In this he is like Marduk of the Babylonians. Varuna watches the world; the sun is his eye, the sky his garment. The universe follows his law.

The law he determines is the Rta, the order of the world. It is difficult to see how Varuna is often thought to represent the beginnings of a monotheism that is any way comparable with the omnipotent Creator of the heavens and earth in Genesis 1. Sin and forgiveness in the Biblical world refer to the violation of the divine law and the pardon of a single, unique, holy, all-wise God. The notion of a high god, who rules the gods, is entirely foreign to the Biblical tradition, and strikes at the very heart of Israel's faith; "Hear, O Israel, the Lord, your God is one." The Rta or moral order of the world which the gods uphold is external to their nature. The notion that the Vedic conception of sin is analogous to the Biblical sense of sin overlooks the very essence of sin in the Biblical sense. For within the Biblical tradition there is no moral standard apart from God. God's very nature is moral. His moral attributes are the expression of His Being. To sin in the Biblical sense is not to violate some moral order, but it is to sin against God. What is of significance in understanding the Vedic is that the numerous high gods and minor deities came into being like the gods of the ancient Near East, the gods of Egypt, Babylon, and Greece. "What was the germ primeval which the waters receive where all the gods were seen together? The waters, they receive that germ primeval wherein the gods were gathered all together . . ." (*A Source Book in Indian Philosophy*, Princeton, 1957, X.82 [p. 18]).

The hymn to the unknown god (Prajapti) is sometimes said to be as purely monotheistic as a Psalm of David. (See the remarks of Fetiphanus Wilson, in his *Introduction to Sacred Books of the East*, New York, 1945, p. 4.) Such remarks, which are frequently made, fail to distinguish the essential from the superficial. The following quotations from the hymn indicate that the god referred to came into being: "as the golden germ he arose in the beginning; when born he was the one lord of the existent . . . whose command all the gods wait upon . . . when the great waters came, bearing all as the germ . . . then arose the one life spirit of the gods . . . who through whose greatness beheld the waters, that bore power and generated the sacrifice, who is the one god of the gods" (*Source Book*, p. 24). The highest principle of the Rig-Veda is an impersonal, unknown "creative force." The gods to whom the hymns are addressed are secondary. Even the gods cannot know from whence came this world. In any case, no claim is here made that the highest principle is a personal, omnipotent Being who is infinite, eternal, and unchangeable, whose very nature is wholly just and good, and who has revealed what men are to believe concerning himself and what duties he requires of them. The world of the Rig-Veda, like most non-Christian religions, is the world of timeless myth; it is the world of subjective phantasy. The world of strange incantations, spells, charms, witchcraft, hymns to inanimate things, devils, and demons.

The concluding portions of the *Vedas* are the *Upanishads*, the basis of Vedanta philosophy. It is difficult to find a logical and coherent system of metaphysics in the *Upanishads*. They provide an example of speculative metaphysics which serves a religious function. They do not in any way claim to be a revelation of a personal God in the Biblical sense. Indeed, the highest principle that they reach is an impersonal absolute. A man may become aware of Brahman, but Brahman is not aware of man. Brahman is not aware of anything, for there are no "things." Brahman is in highest wisdom everything and nothing. Brahman cannot be apprehended by the mind. It is the one self-subsistent reality beyond logical categories or linguistic symbols. Within every being there is a portion of Brahman, the Atman. Brahman is like a primeval ocean, all arising out of it and fading away again. The manifold world does not exist apart from Brahman, although, as long as knowledge of Brahman being the self of all has not arisen, the world of phenomena is considered true, like the phantoms of a dream before the dreamer awakes. The ultimate aim of Hinduism is to overcome the illusion that the self is distinct from Brahman. Release (*moksa*) from error and from the wheel of rebirth is attained by knowledge. The many gods of the Vedas are subordinated to or made a part of Brahman. At death the soul that knows Brahman escapes further incarnations. Nothing is uncertain in human destiny, for it is governed by the causal law of *karma.* Every act or thought produces its result, whether it is good or bad. One cannot escape from the karma, or from retribution for one's actions. We become what we think or do; our present life is determined by what we did in our past life, and our future life depends upon what we do now. Our karma can be escaped only if we extinguish in the self all thirst for existence, so that we escape a new karma, which must in turn be fulfilled. Selfish action binds us to the chain of birth and rebirth. But we can break free by following a prescribed path. We can merge into Brahman and gain relief.

The concept of release or salvation in Brahmanism is to be contrasted sharply with the concept of salvation within the Biblical tradition. Frequently the word "*moksa*" is translated as salvation. But here this similarity ends. Moksa and salvation have a comparable function. Such functional correspondence lends itself to superficial comparisons. Hindus pray and Christians pray; Hindus offer sacrifice and the Israelites offered sacrifice; Hindus seek moksa and Christians seek salvation; therefore, so the argument frequently runs, there is no difference between the major religions of the world.

Such a contention merely overlooks what is important, namely, the content and significance attached to prayer, sin, salvation, and sacrifice. When a Hindu prays, he may pray to any number of deities, or if he is sophisticated he may regard "god" as a manifestation of one impersonal essence. When the Christian prays, he prays to one God who is infinite, eternal, and unchangeable. The Biblical concept of salvation is concerned with the restoration of proper relationship between a sinful man and a holy and just God. It is possible for a Hindu to violate "Dharma," a law of religious merit. That is to say, a Hindu may fail to fulfill the role assigned to him by karma. He may fail to obey the laws of universal harmony and follow the dictates of his own egoism. If he fails to fulfill his Dharma, the soul will not work off its residue of karma, and thus will not escape the endless round of rebirth. There is not one Dharma for everybody. Every person has his own individual Dharma, determined by race, caste, family, and private aspirations. This Dharma the Hindu may violate, but he cannot disobey or fail to conform to the law of the supreme, holy, personal god, for such a being has no existence within the Hindu tradition. Karma is an impersonal law of moral order. There is here no personal god to show mercy to the sinner, or to forgive his transgressions and to punish his iniquities. The consequence of violating the impersonal moral law of a particular soul (Dharma) is punishment by an impersonal law of retribution (karma). The soul is born and dies many times. Its life is a series of deaths and rebirths. Reincarnation is a necessity because the soul that has not secured release from the wheel of birth must return to work off its karma. The Hindu may violate Dharma, but he does not believe that he can sin, not in the Biblical sense.

Within the Biblical perspective salvation consists of the attainment of forgiveness of sin and the enjoyment of everlasting life. The redeemed in heaven will continue to be the same individual persons that they were on earth. They will never cease to be. In fact, they will not simply be disembodied souls, but they will be persons—body-souls; the body of the believer is to be resurrected. Those who have attained salvation will live forever with God, but they will never be God. Their personal identity is never at an end. Within Hinduism "salvation," Moksa, release, is the cessation of personal identity; it is not everlasting life, but everlasting death. The individual ceases to be. In a sense he never really was, but in any case, now he is no more. He is Brahman.

What is the essence of sin within the Biblical tradition? To try to be god is the essence of salvation in Hinduism, that is, to be Brahman. Within the Biblical tradition salvation depends upon the Divine favor of God; it is God who takes the initiative in making a covenant with Abraham; it is God who delivers His people out of Egypt; it is God, in the person of the Son, who enters into human history and redeems His people by His death and resurrection. God here takes the initiative in the history of redemption. Within Hinduism a man may accomplish his own "release" by following one of the paths, for which practical methods are prescribed. The discipline of Yoga may lead to release, to identification with the absolute, to freedom from the determinism of transmigration; within Hinduism there is no conception of the unique person, distinct from every other person, with a single earthly life to live. The Hindu does not appeal to the evidence of unique historical events to support his "faith," for in a sense there are no unique events. What could an endless series of existences prove? There is nothing unique. A linear concept of history, with a beginning and an end, is replaced by visions of cosmic cycles divided into world ages. The duration of our world is limited; it ends and begins again. Hinduism appeals solely to personal experience; it makes no appeal to historical evidence of an objective sort. It cannot make an appeal to history, for in the highest wisdom there is no history, nothing is unique, there is only one single reality. There are no objective historical states of affairs that are relevant to the truth or falsity of Hinduism. Hinduism is not verifiable even in principle by an appeal to any objective non-personal experience. If the Christian faith is true, then everyone will know it, including the non-believer. The non-believer will know this after death, when he meets Christ as his judge. If, however, Hinduism is true, no one will know it, since ultimately there will be no one. Upon reabsorption into Brahman the individual will no longer be conscious of himself.

Much of what we have said concerning Hinduism applies also to Buddhism, an offshoot from classical Hinduism. Buddhism has spread beyond the borders of India throughout Asia. It has given rise to many traditions, conflicting schools and sects. In many forms it is a religion without god, it is a way of life, designed to give ethical guidance. In other forms, for all practical purposes, at least on the popular level, it simply makes Gautama Buddha, the enlightened one, into a god—the highest of the gods, to be sure, but one who differs little from the gods of the Hindu Pantheon. Gautama was neither the first nor the last to become a Buddha. There have been others before him and there will be others after him. Buddhas will appear to lead men to *Nirvana* as long as they need to be liberated from the wheel of rebirth. Buddhism rejects the authority of the Vedas, but it retains the notion of the wheel of birth. The purpose of the Buddha is to teach men to fulfill their duty (Dharma) so that they can enter into Nirvana, a state which is difficult to define but which in any case means an end to the chain of temporal existence. Nirvana is the goal of all Buddhists.

Buddhism is a religion in which man attains his own release from the bondage of ignorance. It has a vast literature in Sanscrit and Pali. Certain Buddhists do not worship images or pray to Buddha expecting any answer. Sin is the consequence of man's ignorance of certain laws. One characteristic of Buddhism is its indifference to the gods of other religions. Many Hindu gods and goddesses have been incorporated into Buddhist ceremonies; many Buddhists observe festivals associated with nature's spirits. In China many Buddhist shrines are semi-Taoist; in Japan the common people do not distinguish between Buddhist gods and Shinto gods. What is common to all schools of Buddhism is a state of Nirvana, no matter how conceived. The notion of Dharma, the path of enlightenment, is conceived of in various ways. Theravada Buddhism holds to four stages of enlightenment; Mahayana Buddhism assumes many stages varying in number with the different sects. Zen Buddhism teaches that enlightenment can come by means of a direct intuition of one's own nature. There is no uniformity of teaching.

The most widely accepted doctrine is that of universal suffering, to be overcome by the cessation of desire, usually by our own efforts, but in some instances with external help. The non-ego principle (anatta) that life is a series of becomings and extinctions, rather than man being an entity with a substantial soul, is also held throughout Buddhism. The belief in rebirth, with some liberal exceptions, was taken over by the Buddhists from Hinduism. The principle of karma, that the individual is a result of a multitude of causes carried over from the past and extending into the future, is believed in some form by all Buddhists.

Disagreement among Buddhists is most prevalent in their attitude toward their sacred writings, which differs essentially from the Biblical concept of an authoritative word of a personal, supreme, omnipotent creator God. Within Buddhism there is no one scripture accepted by everyone. The Zen sect emphasizes great insight and pays little attention to the writings; Theravada Buddhism accepts Pali writings as authoritative but rejects Mahayana writings. Another point of difference between Mahayana and Theravada Buddhism concerns the Buddha. The Pali writings speak of seven Buddhas including Gautama, and some of the books mention 24 Buddhas, although Gautama is the most popular. Pure Realm Buddhism prefers Amitadaha Buddha to Gautama. The main difference between Theravada and Mahayana Buddhism is that the former holds to the historical Buddha, whereas the latter introduces the notion of the eternal Buddha and regards the earthly form of Gautama as quite temporary. There are innumerable Buddhas in Mahayana Buddhism; there were many in the past, there are now many, and there will be many in the future. Every Buddha shows a passion for the suffering that helps him along the path to Nirvana, usually by bringing the disciple to a heaven where he can hear the preaching of the doctrine that leads to enlightenment.

Buddhism is not a guide for attaining eternal life; it is rather a guide to no life at all. It is a guide to Nirvana. On its own principles Buddhism can exist only as long as it is unsuccessful, for if everyone were to follow the path, then there would be only Nirvana. If ignorance ceased at once, the cause of the world would cease; rebirth would end, and we would be left with nothing, enjoying nothing. The illusion of the self would end.

Certain superficial comparisons may be drawn between Buddha and Christ and between Buddhism and Christianity. To pass over essential differences as though they did not exist does not do justice to any religion. In what sense is Christianity like Buddhism? Only in the superficial sense that both are to be regarded as religion. The former believes in the creator God, the latter does not. Christianity believes in the non-illusory created world order and the everlasting existence of persons, Buddhism does not. When the Christian uses the word "sin," he means disobedience to the supreme Being who has revealed Himself in the OT and NT. For Buddhists, existence itself is evil; thus to desire to be is "sinful."

A comparison between the many Buddhas of Buddhism and the Christian conception of the unique person of Jesus, the Second Person of the Trinity, the Messiah, again, as in the case of Hinduism, results in superficial functional similarities and in essential contrasts. The many Buddhas are of importance to Buddhism, but Jesus is essential to Christianity. The Buddhas are the subject of Buddhism, but Jesus is also the object of Christian faith. Jesus is called the Savior, and the Buddhas are compassionate. Jesus had followers, and the Buddhas had followers. Jesus taught and the Buddhas taught. The difference, however, is that for Buddhists anyone or many can become Buddha, whereas no Christian can become Christ. Buddha wants to make other Buddhas. Jesus did set a moral example by keeping the moral law perfectly, and the Christian is to be like Him in this respect, but he is never to become the Second Person of the Trinity.

As the Savior, Jesus sacrifices Himself, a substitutionary offering for sin, to satisfy divine justice. The repentant believing Christian is pardoned his disobedience and accepted as righteous in God's sight solely because of the righteousness of Christ, which is received by faith alone. The Christian is saved from sin and its consequences. At death he is not reborn nor does he enter into a state of Nirvana, but he is made perfect in holiness. At the resurrection he does not cease to exist but is made perfectly blessed. He does not become God, nor does he lose his personal identity in a cosmic soup. He lives forever as a person in the full enjoyment of God. Jesus' love for man is a sacrificial love for real men, not simply a compassion for non-real men who suffer because they are deluded by their ignorance and pass through endless cycles of non-real existence. Jesus is not a god among gods; He is God and man, in two distinct natures and one Person. He is unique. There can be no other Christ; there can be many Buddhas.

What we have said of Hinduism, Buddhism, and the religions of the ancient Near East could readily be expanded. To this list we could add Shinto and a host of primitive religions with their many gods and goddesses. Such religions may satisfy the psychological need for security. They may relieve anxiety and despair, but they are hardly credible to anyone who demands logical consistency and some historical evidence for what is believed.

Christianity lends itself more readily to a comparative study with Judaism and Islam. For both Judaism and Islam are based upon the claim that God has disclosed Himself to man. Few of the religions of the world claim to be religions of revelation. By revelation in the religious sense is meant the disclosure of a message to men by a personal, true, and loving God. Many religions lay claim to believe in the existence of an absolute and ascribe to it attributes which transcend men. But such religions lay no claim to having received from God a written document that discloses His Being and mind. They rely upon man's own powers to discover what the ultimate is and what is required of men; so that man's own reson and insight furnish all that is necessary for an understanding ing of himself, of God, and of the world. Islam, Judaism, and Christianity share the claim to have a written, transmitted Word in the form of a book upon which man can rely for his knowledge of God.

Islam

The Koran, the "revelation" of the Moslem, is regarded by the orthodox Moslem as the supernatural dictation of God. The OT and NT are also regarded as revelation, but their teaching has allegedly been distorted by Jews and Christians. The definitive form of revelation is to be found in the Koran. To the non-Moslem the sources upon which the Koran draws are recognized to be pre-Islamic Arabian religion, Talmudic Judaism, and oriental Christianity. The cornerstone of Mohammedan belief is the insistence on the unity of god. God is so different from his creatures that very little can be postulated of him. Nothing is right or wrong by nature but becomes such by the fiat of Allah. What Allah forbids is sin, even if it appears right and good to us. If Allah allows it, it cannot be sin at the time he allows it, though it may have been sinful before and may be sinful after. Reformation of character is insignificant compared to the repetition of the creed. Just to repeat the Kalimet, "There is no god but Allah and Mohammed is the prophet of Allah," constitutes one a true believer and opens the door into the religion of Mohammed. The will of Allah is an irresistible force. It is equated with fate. There can be no prayer for god's will to be done. Allah reveals his will and accomplishes it, and all that man can do is submit. He must bow to the inevitable necessity. God is so merciful that what appears to be sinful in his favored ones is not really sinful. The moral law is not the expression of god's moral nature but of his arbitrary will.

General beliefs of Moslems are belief in angels, in prophets and apostles, in the resurrection of all the dead to judgment either to eternal bliss or to eternal fire, and in predestination by Allah of both good and evil.

Religious observances and social practices of Islam may be briefly noted. The Creed, the Kalimah, is to be recited; ritual prayer five times a day is required, as well as congregational prayer at noon on Fridays. During the ninth month of the Moslem year, Ramadan, Moslems, with the exception of the incapacitated, are required to fast from dawn to sunset. Legal alms are also to be given. When possible, at least once in a lifetime, a pilgrimage to Mecca is made by the faithful. The true believer is also enjoined to fight the cause of Allah. Fighting is obligatory. If you do not fight, Allah will punish you. Mohammed is Allah's apostle. Those who follow him are ruthless to unbelievers but merciful to one another. Every Moslem is enjoined to answer any legally valid summons to war against infidels. The duty of Jihad, or holy war, is not limited to the inception of Islam, for Islam is to be spread by the sword. The world where Islam does not reign supreme is *dar al harb*, the abode of war.

As to the ethical practices, Moslems are enjoined to marry no more than four legal wives at one time; any male shall cohabit with as many slave concubines as he may possess. Married women are forbidden to the Moslem unless they are slaves. A Moslem may divorce his wife at any time for any reason, but women can never divorce their husbands. Islam sanctions slavery and the slave trade. Of course, many of these practices, while sanctioned in the Koran, are disappearing in modern Islam. And yet the thief may still have his right hand cut off, and the adulterer may be stoned. Islam, at least to the non-Moslem, is simply to be regarded as a perversion of Judaism and Christianity.

Judaism

For many Jews today, the Scripture, that is, the Scriptures of the OT, is still what the OT claims to be, the true and authoritative word of God. In OT times the Jews were surrounded by "cultural forces." On all sides there were peoples with religion and a way of life all their own. We have pointed out that similarities in concepts and practices between the ancient Jews and those of their neighbors are only superficial, since at crucial points there are vast and significant differences. The OT exhibits a struggle to maintain its distinctive faith and life, for to many Jews the ways of the nations were attractive.

When the OT was completed, about the middle of the fifth century B.C., a body of writings started to emerge that have taken a prominent place in the development of Judaism. These writings embody traditions which purport to be very ancient and in the course of time assumed a place of pre-eminence in the religious life of the Jews. As early as 200 B.C. these traditions existed and were promoted by the Pharisees, a prominent sect, and they, although professing adherence to the law and the prophets, rigidly followed the traditions of the fathers, which were codified regulations for all aspects of life. Conformity to these laws took a prominent place, so that in time, for many, these became the essence of their religion.

About A.D. 200, these traditions were gathered and committed to writing by Judah Harcase (The Prince) as the *Mishnah*, which signifies the "second exposition of the Law." The Mishnah is divided into five parts, containing what is purported to be the oral Law of Moses and deductions from the written law. Also embodied are the decrees of the learned rulers of the Sanhedrin and customs for which Divine sanction is claimed.

The text of the Mishnah was amplified by many additions. These took literary form in the *Talmud*, which means "teaching or learning." The Talmud (both Palestinian and Babylonian about A.D. 500) marks the culmination of Jewish tradition. For many modern Jews it has come to have the place of supreme authority in religion. The religion and worship of Judaism under Talmudic influence consists in learning and practicing 613 commandments of the Talmud. The commonest functions of life are regulated. There are also many directions for the observance of the Sabbath, the festival seasons, and ceremonies in the synagogue and the home. The Talmud has assumed a position of importance, in spite of reaction from time to time, the most notable being that of the Karaites in the eighth to the eleventh centuries, a body of Eastern Jews who rejected the Talmud and adhered to Scripture alone.

A description of Judaism would be incomplete if we left out the part that the expectation of a Messiah has had in it. The "Targums," which are ancient paraphrases and interpretations of the Biblical text, interpret Messianically such passages as Genesis 3:15; Num. 24:17; Deut. 18:15-19; Isa. 2:4; 4:2; 9:6; 33:1; Jer. 23:5; Hos. 3:5; Micah 5:2; Zech. 3:8. Jewish believers in Jesus Christ as the Messiah of the Jews appealed to the Jewish Scriptures to justify their belief. In this faith they looked upon themselves as continuing the OT tradition. And they regarded the NT itself as the fulfillment of the Jewish Scriptures.

The great majority of Jewish people

have rejected the Messiahship of Jesus of Nazareth. They have found it difficult to reconcile Christ as a man and sufferer with the OT predictions of a Messiah possessing the attributes of Deity. However, those Jews who did reconcile the seemingly contradictory views of the Messiah pointed to the prediction of these two elements within the OT itself. (Compare Gen. 3:15; 22:18; Ps. 22:6; Isa. 9:6; 7:14; 53:9; Dan. 9:9; Zech. 9:9; 13:7 with Ps. 2:6-8; 45:6, 7; Jer. 23:6; Dan. 7:13, 14.)

There are essentially two types of Judaism—Orthodox and Reform. Orthodox Judaism is the same as it has been for about two millenniums. The OT tradition, the OT Scriptures, are held to be Divine revelation, but tradition as embodied in the Mishna and Talmud also possesses Divine authority for faith and practice. Salvation is attained by repentance and by observance of the laws, both Biblical and Talmudical. Much importance is attached to diet and dress, the festive seasons, and the tokens of the covenant, which are circumcision, the sabbath, and the Passover.

Reform Judaism resembles so-called liberal Christianity and marks a departure from the old pattern. The Torah or the Bible is tested by human judgment. The enlightened modern mind determines what is factual and what is meaningful. Miracles are excluded and ought to be interpreted allegorically or teleologically. There is some claim that the Jewish Scriptures are inspired, but only to the extent that they present truth and goodness. And in the doing of good, man works out his own salvation. Reform Judaism still clings to ancestral pieties, sentiments, and group loyalties. Tradition is respected because it contains the findings of men in quest for the true and good. Nationalism and idealism are the unifying principles.

What is known as conservative Judaism is not so well defined. It seeks to maintain a mediating position between the Orthodox and the Reform. On the other hand, Zionism is essentially political, aimed at the repatriation of Jews to Israel and development of communal societies for them. Even atheists can be Zionists.

Liberalism

In conclusion it must be noted that genuine Christianity is not always believed within churches which historically were Christian. For many, Jesus is the example of faith rather than the object of faith, or He is the first existentialist. In any case, He is not the Christ of the Bible. The miracles recorded in the NT, including Christ's virgin birth and His bodily resurrection, are denied. Jesus is no longer regarded as the Son of God who redeems man by virtue of what He did, by bearing the guilt of his sins upon the cross. The resurrection, final judgment, and heaven and hell are all denied.

Whatever be the differences in other respects—whatever be the distinction in outward form or administration, in ordinances, in government, in worship — these things are subordinate to the one criterion of the profession of the true faith, which marks, by its presence, a true church, and declares, by its absence, an apostate one. In contrast to all non-Christian religions, "the only true and infallible mark of the church of Christ is the profession of the faith of Christ."

DAVID H. FREEMAN

COMPLUTENSIAN POLYGLOT BIBLE, a magnificently printed, six-volume, early Renaissance Bible, taking its name from Alcalá (Latin *Complutum*), Spain, the place of its origin. The work was promoted by the enlightened Cardinal Ximenes de Cisneros, probably in 1502. The volumes were printed between 1514 and 1517, but not authorized by the Pope till 1520, and probably not published till 1522.

The four OT volumes contain the Vulgate in the center, flanked by the Septuagint with interlinear Latin translation and the Hebrew. Numerous introductions are included in volume one, and notes on Hebrew roots are given in the margins. The Targum of Onkelos is reproduced with Latin translation. Volume five contains the NT, actually printed before Erasmus' famous *Greek New Testament*, but published after it. Volume six provides a Hebrew grammar, dictionary, and section on the interpretation of Hebrew and Aramaic names. Ximenes spent much time and money collecting and borrowing manuscripts, especially from Venice and the Vatican. He employed famous Jewish scholars like Nebrija and Alfonso de Zamora, but Ximenes himself died in 1517. Alcalá was a center of Renaissance studies in the tradition of Biblical humanism, and the Complutensian or Alcalá Polyglot is one of the earliest Renaissance landmarks, both in Biblical texts based on the original languages and in the splendor of its printing. The prefaces and introductions together with the apparatus in the final volume show scholars anxious to lead the reader to serious study of the Bible text based on sound scholarship and study of the original language rather than the endless glosses of the medieval commentators.

G. E. DUFFIELD

COMRIE, Alexander (1706-1774), Dutch Reformed theologian. Born in Perth, Scotland, he went to Rotterdam in 1727, studied theology in Groningen and Leiden, took his doctor's degree (in philosophy) in 1734, and entered the ministry in Woubrugge (South-Holland) in 1735, where he remained for 40 years.

Comrie was an able, doctrinal, and practical preacher, who was almost always to be found in his study and who very seldom visited the meetings of the classis. He was most important in Holland as one of the last defenders of the genuine Reformed theology, which was succumbing in those days to the penetrating influences of Rationalism and Toleration. The main subjects expounded by Comrie were (1) the character of faith, (2) justification by faith, and (3) the dangers of religious toleration.

(1) *Character of faith.*—In those days the Arminian idea that the will of man precedes the will of God in accepting Christ was being presented in the Reformed churches. Comrie distinguished between the faculty and the act of faith (*habitus et actus fidei*). Answer 20 of the Heidelberg Catechism speaks of the faculty of faith (being ingrafted into Christ), and Answer 21 speaks of the act of faith (having sure knowledge and firm confidence). Implicitly, the knowledge and confidence of faith are included in the faculty of faith.

(2) *Justification by faith.*—Some were putting forth the Arminian idea that man first has to believe and to repent, and that God rewards that act of man by sitting in judgment and acquitting the believer. Comrie considered this way of reasoning as a new kind of nomism (living by the law and not by grace), and he defended the thesis that there is a justification from eternity, because Scripture speaks of "names written in the book of life of the Lamb slain from the foundation of the world" (Rev. 13:8, AV). This idea of a justification from eternity had been opposed in the Dutch Reformed Churches because it seemed to detract from the necessity of the act of personal faith. The Synod of Utrecht (1905) "earnestly warned against every position which detracts from either Christ's placing Himself as Surety for His people from eternity, or from the demand of true faith for the sake of being justified at the bar of conscience before God's righteousness."

(3) *Religious toleration.*—Comrie, together with his friend N. Holtius, wrote

a series of tracts under the title *Examination of the Concept of Toleration.* In these tracts he warned against a departure from the Forms of Unity of the Dutch Reformed Churches. The government stopped this publication in 1761, and gradually liberalism became dominant in these churches.

BIBLIOGRAPHY:
A. G. Honig, *Alexander Comrie* (Utrecht, 1892).
A. Kuyper, "Alexander Comrie," *The Catholic Presbyterian* (Jan., March, and April, 1882).

LOUIS PRAAMSMA

CONANIAH (spelled *Cononiah* in some versions), "Jehovah established," the name of two Levites:

(1) A ruler appointed by Hezekiah over the tithes and gifts brought to the Lord's house after Hezekiah's reformation work in Judah (I Chron. 31:12, 13). Shemei, Conaniah's brother, assisted him, as did ten other subordinate overseers. This indicates the great volume of offerings spontaneously presented by the Lord's people.

(2) One of the chiefs of the Levites during Josiah's reign, who supplied the Levites the necessary offerings for the Passover feast. These offerings were received as freewill offerings from the princes and distributed in turn to the Levites (II Chron. 35:8-10).

CONCEPTION, IMMACULATE

The Dogma and Its Importance

On December 8, 1854, in a meeting of fifty-four cardinals and 140 bishops in St. Peter's Church in Rome, Pope Pius IX pronounced the following dogma: "In honor of the holy and undivided Trinity, for the glory of the Virgin Mother of God, for the exaltation of the Catholic faith and the Christian religion, by the authority of our Lord Jesus Christ, of the blessed apostles Peter and Paul, and of our own office, we declare, pronounce, and define the doctrine which holds that the most blessed Virgin Mary was, in the first instance of her conception, by the singular grace and privilege of Almighty God, with regard to the merits of Christ Jesus the Savior of the human race, preserved free from every stain of original sin, has been revealed by God, and therefore is to be firmly and constantly believed by all the faithful" (Bull *Ineffabilis Deus*). Mary, therefore, is (besides Christ Himself) the only exception to the universal law of original sin. Grace made her holy and immaculate from the moment of her conception in the womb of her mother.

This dogma is not a subordinate point in the development of the RC system of doctrine. It is of the utmost importance in at least three respects: (1) It opened a new era in Mariology and strongly promoted the further development of this doctrine, leading to the dogma of the Assumption of Mary (1950) and, as is to be expected in the not too distant future, the dogma of co-redemption. (2) It promoted and authenticated a new view of the evolution of dogma. (3) It was a kind of "test case," exhibiting the authority of the pope in interpreting divine revelation and so naturally led to the definition of papal infallibility in 1870. Together with the latter dogma the immaculate conception is the most characteristic feature of modern Romanism and has not only widened the gap between Rome and the Reformation, but also between Rome and Scripture.

Historical Development

The decision of 1854 was both the end of a long, protracted controversy within the RC Church itself (especially since the 11th century) and the capstone of a Mariological development which started as early as the fourth century. The Church Fathers of the first three centuries knew nothing of a sinless Mary. Some of them (Irenaeus, Tertullian, Origen, and Chrysostom) openly stated that Jesus' words in John 2:4 contained a rebuke for Mary. Augustine was the first to express the notion that Mary was free from all actual sin, and even he spoke only tentatively. After the decision of the Council of Ephesus (431), which, in a Christological context, called Mary the Mother of God (*Theotokos*), the church began increasingly to concentrate on the person of Mary. From the 7th century onward the E theologians taught that Mary was free from all actual and original sin. In the W, Augustine's emphasis on the universality of sin retarded this development for centuries. But the holiness of Mary became more and more the object of reflection and veneration, and in the beginning of the 11th century the feast of the conception of Mary on December 8, taken over from the E Church, was already celebrated in some English monasteries. The Normans suppressed it again and as late as 1211 the Synod of Oxford declared the feast unnecessary. In Lyons, France, it was introduced *c.* 1140, but Bernard of Clairvaux opposed it.

Most of the great schoolmen (Anselm, Albert, Bonaventura, and Thomas) were against the doctrine. They did recognize Mary's sanctification before birth, but declared that she, being conceived in the natural way, was not exempt from the law of original sin. The great defender of the immaculate conception was Duns Scotus, mainly on the grounds that it would enhance God's glory and was most fitting for the mother of Christ. In his wake the Franciscans became the great protagonists of the doctrine, whereas the Dominicans (following Thomas) became its opponents. Although the Synod of Paris (1837) and the schismatic Council of Basel (1439) affirmed the Scotist position, the controversy continued. It even became so disturbing that Sixtus IV (who in 1476 had approved the feast) in 1483 threatened anyone with excommunication who called either opinion heretical. Although later on the Jesuits joined the forces of the Franciscans, the Council of Trent (1546) left the matter undecided by declaring that it did not intend to include in its decree the immaculate conception of the Virgin Mary. Consequently, in 1617 Paul V forbade public disputes, and later on Gregory XV prohibited even private discussions. Yet all these papal interventions became more and more markedly in favor of the doctrine. Alexander VII (1661) called it an ancient and pious view. Other popes emphasized and expanded the feast. In 1806 the Franciscans were permitted to insert the word *immaculata* in the mass for December 8. The natural result was the decision of 1854 by Pius IX, who during all his life had a highly romantic devotion to Mary. The decision was preceded by the report of a special commission, declaring that for such a dogma no direct evidence from Scripture was needed, but the testimony of tradition alone sufficed, and that not an unbroken line of tradition from the time of the apostles was strictly necessary.

Theological Basis

At first, RC theologians usually attempted to adduce Scripture proofs. They often appealed to texts as Gen. 3:15; Ps. 45:12 ff.; Song of S. 1:6-16; 2:2; 3:6; 4:1 f.; 6:9; Eccles. 1:4; Luke 1: 28, 41, 48; Rev. 12 and to types such as the ark of Noah, the dove with the olive branch, the burning bush, etc. Besides this they used the argument of "fittingness": it was becoming to Mary, God could give it to her, therefore He did in fact do so (*decuit, potuit, fecit*).

In more recent times the argument has been different. RC theologians now frankly admit that the doctrine lacks any clear Scriptural evidence and also any explicit patristic tradition; it even seems to be contrary to clear statements of Paul (Rom. 5) and Christ Himself (Luke 5:32). Besides, several of the greatest theologians declared it heretical; while popes, when pressed to decide the question, replied that "the Holy Spirit has not yet opened to His Church the secrets of this mystery" (Gregory XV, 1622). Yet the doctrine is vigorously defended, on the ground of the modern theory of the evolution of dogma. According to this theory, the teaching office of the church, through the infallible assistance of the Holy Spirit, is able to recall what was contained implicitly (i.e., in a preconceptual and unformulated manner) in the primitive deposit of Scripture and oral tradition, and is able to make it explicit (i.e., to bring it forth in a conceptual and formulated manner). In this light, Scripture is interpreted as implicitly teaching the exceptional place of Mary in the church, derived from her virginal motherhood, and the recapitulation of all the glories of the church in Mary. Passages referred to, among others, are Luke 1:26-38, 46-55; Rev. 12, and John 2. They all are supposed to speak of Mary's unique place and glory, implying her unique holiness.

Evaluation

The RC doctrine is nothing else than a heresy. Scripture does not provide any support to it, but rather contradicts it. The early church knew nothing of it. In addition, it leads to unsolvable dogmatical difficulties. How can one explain the *Magnificat*, where Mary herself calls God her Savior (Luke 1:47)? The heart of the whole Mariological dogma, however, is nothing else than Rome's synergism and semi-Pelagianism. In the RC system of doctrine Mary is the "symbolization of the relation between God's work and human cooperation" (Berkouwer). The dogma of Mary, including that of her immaculate conception, is therefore not only the denial of *sola Scriptura*, but also of the *sola fide* (cf. Heidelberg Catech. A. 80).

See MARY; INFALLIBILITY OF POPE.

BIBLIOGRAPHY:

B. Bartmann, *Maria im Lichte des Glaubens und der Froemmigkeit* (Paderborn, 1925).

K. Barth, *Church Dogmatics*, I, 2 (Edinburgh, 1956), 139-146.

G. C. Berkouwer, *The Conflict with Rome* (Philadelphia, 1958).

D. Bertetto, *Maria Immacolata* (Roma, 1953).

J. Carol (ed.), *Proceedings of the Fifth National Convention of the Mariological Society of Amerika, held in Washington, D.C.* (New York, 1954).

R. Garrigou-Lagrange, *Mariologie* (Montreal, 1948), esp. 30-82.

M. Jugie, A.A., *La Immaculée Conception dans l'Ecriture Sainte et dans la Tradition Orientale* (Roma, 1952).

B. A. McKenna, *The Dogma of the Immaculate Conception* (Washington, 1929).

E. D. O'Connor, *The Dogma of the Immaculate Conception* (Notre Dame, 1958), containing 86 pp. of bibliography in all major languages.

Pareri dell'Episcapato Cattoloico . . . sulla definizione dogmatica dell'Immacolato Concepimento, etc. (Roma, 1851-54), 10 vols.

M. Schmaus, *Katholische Dogmatik* (Munich, 1955), vol. V.

Summa Aurea de laudibus Beatissimae Virginis Maria, Dei Genitricis sine labe conceptae, ed., J. J. Bourassé (Paris, 1862-66), 13 vols.

"Virgo Immaculata," *Acta Congressus Internationalis Mariologici et Mariani, Romae anno MCMLIV celebrati* (Rome, 1955-58), 18 vols.

O. Zoeckler, "Maria," in *PRE* XII (1903), 309-336.

KLAAS RUNIA

CONCEPTUALISM, the philosophic doctrine that universals do not exist in themselves, whether before things or in the essences of things, but that they have their origin in the activity of the human spirit. Conceptualism also refers to the doctrine that general ideas are proper to thought and are not simply words or signs which denote a group of individuals.

Traditionally Abelard (*c.* 1079-1142) is thought to be the founder of conceptualism, in opposition to the extreme realism of his teacher, William of Champeaux. Conceptualism definitely appears in the Middle Ages, the term being used by Duns Scotus. It is considered to be a preparation for the moderate realism of the high Middle Ages.

Conceptualism is correct in holding

that what is called a universal does not exist in itself apart from the mind of man. It is also correct in maintaining that the general concept is proper to thought and is not simply a lingual sign for a group of individuals. Nevertheless, conceptualism errs at a critical point, in locating the source of universals in the human spirit in contrast to "things."

In our concrete, everyday experience we ascribe general characteristics (qualities), e.g., "red," "good," to things without setting them at a distance or making them into a problem. These qualities belong to individual things objectively, and should not be said to have their origin in something which is set over against these things.

Conceptualists have attempted to account for the relation of the general concept to the thing by saying that, although the general concept does not exist apart from the activity of spirit, things manifest identical or similar (logical) characteristics, which the mind abstracts in forming the general concept. The logical, however, cannot itself act as the general denominator of meaning. It is only one aspect of human activity, even including the act of thinking itself. That the logical is one aspect among others is also at the foundation of its possibility. The theoretical-logical concept is possible only on the foundation of a created order of reality. It abstracts from the fulness of concrete experience, but both this abstraction itself and the unity in diversity, which is the hallmark of the theoretical concept, are possible only because this theoretical-logical activity is not original but is rooted in a structure that is itself not logically qualified.

The notion that there are certain identical or similar traits, that things have of a logical character, does not provide an adequate basis for the construction of unambiguous theoretical-logical concepts. General concepts are vague and scientifically useless unless they are formed with an understanding of the created order of reality. Thus the concept "power" is ill-defined unless one designates what power is in its original signification and unless he is aware whether he speaks, e.g., of social, economic, historical power, or even of the power of faith.

ROBERT D. KNUDSEN

CONCORDANCES. A concordance is a reference work that lists passages of a book in which a given word occurs. Usually part of the passage is quoted, showing the word in its context. The most valuable are those that list all of the passages in which a given word appears. Since a concordance is such a valuable tool for close study of the text of the Bible, it is no wonder that concordances of the Bible have been in use for centuries. The only matter for surprise is that they were not invented earlier.

The first concordance appears to have been one on the Latin Vulgate, compiled by Antony of Padua, who died in 1231. But nothing of this survives, and the first concordance of which there is real knowledge is that of Hugo of St. Caro (d. 1263). The Vulgate was, of course, the standard text in the Middle Ages, and a Vulgate concordance was more useful than any other would have been.

Concordances to the Hebrew text of the OT appear to have begun with one compiled by R. Isaac (or Mordecai) b. Kalonymus during the years 1437-45, and published in Venice in 1523. This was revised by others, notably John Buxtorf, whose work was published in 1632. This led to the concordance by Julius Fürst (1840), then to those of B. Davidson in England (1876) and S. Mandelkern in Germany (1896).

A number of concordances to the Septuagint have been produced, but the standard is that by E. Hatch and H. A. Redpath (three vols., 1892-1900).

Concordances to the Greek NT began

with that of S. Birck, published in Basle in 1546. Other editions followed, of which particular mention should be made of that of C. H. Bruder (Leipzig, 1842). The standard work has come to be the concordance of W. F. Moulton and A. S. Geden (Edinburgh, 1897).

There have been many concordances to the English Bible. The first (on the NT only) seems to have been that of Thomas Gybson, published before 1540. But three concordances stand out, all based on the AV. The first is that of Alexander Cruden. This was published in 1737 and represents a tremendous labor in the face of mental illness and other difficulties. Many editions of this famous work followed, and it is still printed and valuable for the English Bible. Warning should be made to get the unabridged edition. Robert Young brought out his *Analytical Concordance to the Bible* in 1873, the distinctive feature being the arrangement of words under their Hebrew or Greek original. A Hebrew and Greek index is included which shows all the various ways a word in the original language has been translated. The third is James Strong's *Exhaustive Concordance to the Bible.* This includes references to the variants in the RV of 1881, and the Hebrew or Greek word in the original is also indicated by code numbers to a brief lexicon at the back, which includes the English translations of the AV.

LEON MORRIS

CONCORDAT, an agreement between a secular state and an ecclesiastical authority on ecclesiastical matters. Probably the principle of sovereign rights is assumed on both sides.

Many matters in dispute between church and state fall within both jurisdictions. In earlier centuries the spiritual sword claimed authority over the temporal and caused much conflict. The rise of national sovereign states compelled the RC Church to seek to protect its material and spiritual interests by constitutional agreements involving concessions, guarantees, etc., on both sides. Thus it was hoped that many grounds of conflict might be avoided.

The *pactum concordatum* or *solemnis conventio* grants state recognition to the official status of the church, its clergy, and its tribunals. Privileges are conferred, and sometimes payments are made to compensate for church properties acquired by the state. A recent instance of this is the Lateran Treaty. The church grants recognition to the existing regime in the state and agrees to cooperate. Insistence on traditional claims and rights are replaced by agreements which accept the actualities of a situation. In short, concordats are contracts.

From 1801 to 1830 more than 30 concordats were made with different states. Two famous concordats of modern times are—(1) Pope Pius VII's concordat with the French government in 1801. He sought to reconstruct the church after the Revolution: the religion of France was recognized to be RC; its public observance was assured; the canonical institution of bishops was reserved to the pope; church buildings were restored and emoluments were given to the clergy. The pope on his side conceded to the police some surveillance over worship; accepted the new diocesan divisions; allowed the nomination of bishops to be made by the First Consul (Bonaparte); and consented that purchasers of church lands would not be disturbed.—(2) The Lateran Treaty of 1929 between Pius XI and Mussolini ended the hostility of church and state in Italy by restoring the pope's temporal power, though only in the sovereign state of Vatican City. This concordat is part of the treaty between Italy and the pope. Article I of the treaty declared Roman Catholicism to be the sole religion of the state. On this is founded the opposition of Rome to evangelical propaganda in Italy.

D. N. EMERSON

CONDÉ, LOUIS I DE BOURBON, PRINCE DE (1530-1569), French Huguenot political and military leader. Fifth son of Charles de Bourbon and younger brother of Antoine, king of Navarre, Louis, after his father's death, was educated in the principles of the Reformed faith. He distinguished himself in the various wars of the time, but suspicion and jealousy at the French court caused his services to be ignored. On the accession of Francis II in 1559, Condé and his brother joined the French Protestant party, the Huguenots, and in the following year he took part in the unsuccessful Conspiracy of Amboise, the aim of which was to achieve recognition for the Reformed religion in France. For this, he was condemned to execution, and was saved only by the death of Francis.

The new king, Charles IX, was a minor, and the country was ruled by Catherine de' Medici, a bitter enemy of the Guises, who had hitherto been the ruling force in the land. She began by making concessions to the Huguenots. Condé was appointed governor of Picardy, and in January 1562 an edict assured religious liberty to the Protestants. Two months later the country was plunged into civil war when the Guises massacred at Vassy a group of Huguenots who had assembled in a barn for worship. The duke of Guise took Paris and removed the court to Fontainebleau, in defiance of the queen-regent.

Condé, with other Huguenot leaders, signed a manifesto in April 1562 at Orléans, declaring their loyalty to the crown, but stating that as good and loyal subjects they were compelled to resort to arms for liberty of conscience—the precise position taken in the following century by the Covenanters in Scotland. The Huguenot army was defeated, and Condé found himself again for a time in captivity. From this time on his story is part of the larger narrative concerned with the wars of religion in France (see HUGUENOTS).

In what became known as the Second Huguenot War (1567-69), Condé had coins made with this inscription referring to himself, "Louis XIII, first Christian king of France." But he did not long survive. His superb generalship having temporarily deserted him, he tried, at the battle of Jarnac with only 400 men, to charge the whole RC army which confronted them. Taken prisoner, he was treacherously shot through the head by an enemy officer.

BIBLIOGRAPHY:

H. Noguères, *The Massacre of Saint Bartholomew* (London, 1962).

JAMES DIXON DOUGLAS

CONFESSION. The role of confession in connection with the development of the sacrament of penance can be traced back to early practices in the life of the church. One was the use of public confession and penitential practices in dealing with the lapsed (those who renounced the faith during the persecutions in the early church). Another was the claim of the clergy to the power of the keys. The *Didache* (early second century) is quite clear that at that time confession was an act *publicly* performed in the church. The first allusion to any power in the clergy to forgive sin is found in Tertullian (*c.* 160-*c.* 220), and we do not find any traces of the practice of confessing to a priest until about 250. The Apostolic Fathers knew nothing of the power of the keys in the forgiving of sin. In fact, Cyprian (*c.* 254) disclaimed all power to absolve from sin. An often-quoted passage from him makes it quite clear that he required public confession of sin on the part of the lapsed as a necessary prerequisite for re-admission into the fellowship of the church.

Traces of the practice of private confession to a priest are found, however, in Cyprian's discussion of pardon. Yet as late as the first quarter of the 5th century, Augustine insisted that the power given to Peter in the famous discourse in Matthew 16 was transmitted to the church as a whole rather than to the clergy through Peter. In his controversy with the Donatists Augustine declared as heretical their claim that the priest had the power to forgive sin. Private confession to a priest was permitted in some cases by Ambrose (d. 397), but it was not required. Later, in the 5th century, Pope Leo I (440-461) ascribed to the clergy a mediating role between the faithful and God.

The rise of sacerdotalism brought with it the practice of private confession. The action of the Council of Toledo of 398 shows that in Spain confession was already becoming a recognized function of the priesthood, and there is evidence that it was growing in favor in the E as well. In 452 Leo I insisted that confession was necessary for reconciliation with God, but he did not specify what kind of confession was required. However, in 462 in a letter to the bishops he abolished public confession in the W but retained public penance. "I mean that in the matter of the penance which is demanded of the faithful there should be no public recitation of the nature of particular sins. . . . For it sufficeth that the accusation of conscience be indicated to the priest alone in secret confession." By 600 Pope Gregory I looked on confession as necessary for the remission of sins and to be made before a priest.

The practice of confession came to be regulated in great detail with the appearance of the Penitential Books. One of the first to be written in the W was that of Columbanus, the missionary (*c.* 550-615). Another influential one was written by the Venerable Bede (*c.* 673-735). Although the Frankish reformers of the Carolingian era sought to restore the ancient practice of public confession, the auricular mode was too firmly established by this time to be set aside.

Nevertheless, for the next two centuries much uncertainty continued concerning the mode and the sacramental status of auricular confession. Both in his writings and in his sermons, Bernard of Clairvaux (1090-1153) emphasized its necessity, but he was far from clear as to how it should be carried out. He emphasized, however, that confession must be to God.

Richard of St. Victor was one of the first Schoolmen to set forth a definition of confession as the detestation of sin with a vow of amendment of life, further confession to a priest, and satisfaction. In this form it required the priestly function. The indecision of the church on its importance before 1175 is clearly seen in the interesting fact that the monastic orders, even the very strict Cistercians and Carthusians, placed very little emphasis on its necessity for their own members. But with Richard of St. Victor, Peter Lombard, and Alexander of Hales, its necessity for pardon from sin was clearly asserted. In 1215 the Fourth Lateran Council declared that it was the duty of all Christians to confess to a priest at least once a year. In 1227 Gregory IX granted to the Dominican Order the right to preach, to hear confessions, and to grant absolution. Soon afterwards the same privileges were given to the Franciscan Order. The Council of Trent (1545-1563) elevated this decision into an article of faith and made failure to go to a confession at least once a year a mortal sin.

According to RC theology, confession is a divinely ordained institution defined as the "avowal of one's own sins made to a duly authorized priest for the purpose of obtaining forgiveness through the power of the keys." Its supposed Biblical sanction is John 20:23. It is a practice which is totally at variance with the Biblical doctrines of justification by faith alone and the priesthood of all believers. At an early date Lutheranism dropped the practice, although it was not entirely forbidden. The Anglican Prayer Book does not prescribe it but does advise its use in certain cases involving "exceedingly troubled consciences." The Oxford Movement of the 19th century sought without success to revive its use in the Church of England. The Reformed Churches have not allowed auricular confession, but have relied upon public confession, either in the liturgy or in the pastoral prayer.

Bibliography:

T. T. Carter, *The Doctrine of Confession* (London, 1885).

T. W. Drury, *Confession and Absolution* (London, 1904).

L. Duchesne, *Early History of the Christian Church From Its Foundations to the End of the Fifth Century* (New York, 1899), 3 vols.

H. C. Lea, *The History of Auricular Confession and Indulgences in the Latin Church* (Philadelphia, 1896), 3 vols.

A. G. Mortimer, *Confession and Absolution* (London, 1906).

O. D. Watkins, *A History of Penance* (London, 1920), 2 vols.

C. Gregg Singer

CONFESSIONALISM, the attitude of those who theoretically regard and accept a confession of faith as standing under the supreme authority of the Holy Scripture but actually and practically treat it as perfect and unalterable expression of Scriptural truth. They act as if the confession itself is infallible and consider even the smallest deviation from the terminology of the confession as heretical. The confession is dealt with as the final court of appeal. Every appeal from the confession to Scripture is met with suspicion and regarded as virtually unnecessary, even as lack of faithfulness.

In this extreme form, confessionalism will rarely be found. Usually it reveals itself in a sterile conservatism and traditionalism that neglects or ignores the spiritual nature and authority of a confession and treats it first of all as a legal document to safeguard the deposit of faith and uphold cherished traditional views. In most cases the truth of Scripture and dogma are understood in a one-sidedly intellectual way.

The danger of confessionalism is particularly great in the periods that follow days of ecclesiastical reformation. The epigoni, inferior successors that they are, want to retain the gains of reformation by all means and try to do this by rigidly maintaining a confession. Confessionalism is absolutely contrary to the Reformation conception of a confession. According to the Reformers the confession of faith has, first of all, a spiritual authority, grounded in its nature of being the exposition of God's Word. As such it is, of course, binding on the church. Yet this binding authority is never absolute. Holy Scripture is and remains the supreme and final authority, to which the confession is subordinate (cf. West. Conf., I, x). Every attempt at equating the confession with Holy Scripture must be opposed. For this very reason Calvin opposed Caroli, when the latter demanded subscription to the exact terminology of the creeds, although the content itself was not in dispute.

It is unfortunate that the term confessionalism is often misused. Liberal and Neo-orthodox theologians use it to describe the attitude of the truly confessional churches, those which take their confessions seriously. This charge can only be rejected as a caricature. On the other hand, a confessional church must realize that it is permanently in danger of falling into confessionalism. This can be escaped only by constantly remembering that the truly confessional church is at the same time the truly confessing church, the church that hears, trusts, and obeys only the revelation of Jesus Christ.

See Dogma, Dogmatism, Caroli.

Klaas Runia

CONFESSIONS AND CREEDS

I. INTRODUCTION
  A. Origin and Character
  B. Necessity
  C. Authority and Preservation
  D. Revision

II. ECUMENICAL CREEDS
  A. Apostles' Creed
  B. Nicene Creed
  C. Athanasian Creed

III. THE DECISIONS OF THE ECUMENICAL COUNCILS

IV. THE CREEDS OF THE EVANGELICAL REFORMED CHURCHES
  A. In the Netherlands
    1. Belgic Confession
    2. Heidelberg Catechism (Catechismus Palatinus)
    3. Canons of Dort
  B. In Switzerland
    1. Sixty-Seven Articles
    2. Ten Theses of Berne
    3. Confessions to Charles V
    4. Exposition of the Christian Faith
    5. Tetrapolitan Confession
    6. First Confession of Basel
    7. First Helvetic Confession
    8. Second Helvetic Confession
    9. First Catechism of Calvin
    10. Catechism of Geneva
    11. Consensus of Zurich (Consensus Tigurinus)
    12. Consensus of Geneva
    13. Helvetic Consensus Formula
  C. In France
    Gallican Confession
  D. In Germany
    1. Brandenburg Confessions (Confessiones Marchicae)
      a) Confession of Sigismund
      b) Colloquy at Leipzig
      c) Colloquy of Thorn
    2. Confession of Frederick III
    3. Confession of Anhalt (Repititio Anhaltina)
    4. Confession of Nassau
    5. Bremen Confession
    6. Hessian Confession
  E. In Bohemia, Poland, and Hungary
    1. Bohemian Confession of 1535
    2. Bohemian Confession of 1575
    3. Consensus of Sendomir
    4. Hungarian Confession (Confessio Czengerina)
  F. In England, Ireland, and Scotland
    1. Thirty-Nine Articles
    2. Anglican Catechism
    3. Lambeth Articles
    4. Irish Articles
    5. Scottish Articles
    6. National Covenant or Second Scottish Confession
    7. Scottish Catechisms
    8. Westminster Confession
    9. Westminster Catechism

V. OTHER PROTESTANT CREEDS
  A. The Presbyterians
    1. In England
    2. In America
  B. The Congregationalists
    1. Savoy Declaration
    2. Declaration of 1833
    3. Cambridge Platform
    4. Declaration of Faith of the National Council of Boston
  C. The Baptists
    1. Confession of the Seven Churches of London
    2. Confession of 1677
    3. Declaration of Faith
    4. Confession of the Free Will Baptists
  D. The Methodists
    1. Twenty-Five Articles of Religion
    2. Book of Discipline and Catechisms
    3. Welsh Calvinistic Methodists
    4. Doctrine of Wesleyan Methodism
  E. The Quakers
    1. Apology of Robert Barclay
    2. Catechism of 1673
  F. The Waldensians
  G. The Socinians
    1. Greater Catechism of Racow
    2. Shortest Institute of the Christian Religion
    3. Shorter Racow Catechism
    4. Confession of the Christian Faith
    5. Socinian Doctrine

VI. THE CREEDS OF THE EVANGELICAL LUTHERAN CHURCH
  A. Augsburg Confession (Confessio Augustana)
  B. Apology of the Augsburg Confession

I. INTRODUCTION

A. Origin and Character

From its inception the church has been a confessing church. The genuineness of our faith becomes evident in our confession; it shows that the truth has taken possession of our hearts and that we are related to Christ. Whenever the Holy Spirit gives new life to a man, there also comes the urge to confess. Thus believers know each other by a true confession (Rom. 10:9,10; I John 4:2; Heb. 4:14).

This does not mean that the church is founded upon the creed; for then it would rest upon a human basis, however excellent that might be. But the Apostle Paul calls the church the house of the living God, "built upon the foundation of the apostles and prophets, Jesus Christ himself being the chief corner stone" (Eph. 2:20). The firm foundation of the church is Christ, His person, His work, and His Word.

The creed or confession bears the mark of the time and the historical circumstances in which it arose. It must confess the truth to its contemporaries. Thus the church is, as it were, naturally obligated to distinguish between truth and falsehood in its confession.

Until the time of the Reformation in the 16th century, the church found no occasion to formulate new symbols. At the councils the church made pronouncements about many matters which concerned natural and ecclesiastical life, and attempted to order all of life, but it did not express itself in new confessional statements. But when the church in the 16th century returned to the Word of God to oppose error and corruption in its ranks, it was compelled to give utterance to its faith. Thus new confessions or creeds came into being which were linked to the symbols of the ancient church and interpreted the truth openly.

Only after its adoption by the church does the confession become an ecclesiastical symbol. Such an ecclesiastical symbol must never be a confession for theologians only, but for the entire body of believers. It must indeed be the fruit of study and reflection, but the form and manner of expression should be such that it is never a scholarly exposition of doctrine, but the confession of the faith of the church even as the church has found it objectively in the Word of God and has experienced it subjectively. Thus the Belgic Confession begins: "We all believe with the heart and confess with the mouth . . ." (Art. 1).

B. Necessity

Reformed believers consider confessional statements to be necessary for the following reasons:

"1. The first reason lies in the existence of the church itself. As a gathering of true believers, led by God's Spirit and Word, the church naturally confesses its faith. This faith in the heart can never remain hidden. Out of the treasures of God's Word come forth old things and new. The church attempts to realize the kingdom and to define it in lucid terms. The richer the reflection of the church, the fuller and deeper the tone of its confessions becomes. This confession is the fruit of the work of the Spirit which controls all of its life.

"2. The second reason lies in the necessity of self-defense. Wherever the church witnesses and struggles, it demands a decision from each individual. Its witness allows for no neutral position, but occasions hostility, slander, and persecution. Thus the confession of the church becomes one of its principal weapons.

"3. The third reason lies in the public affirmation of unity in doctrine. In the days of the Reformation it was a generally held conviction that a common confession is one of the most excellent means of affirming and establishing the existing unity of doctrine. In the case of Guido de Brès the apologetic motive may have been very strong; nevertheless, the church immediately recognized and adopted his confession as a form of unity. Dr. Schokking (*De Leertucht in de Geref. Kerk*, p. 183) rightly remarks: 'The confession was recognized as a form of unity, because it was the expression of a common faith.'

"4. The fourth reason lies in the preservation of purity of doctrine. Heretics have compelled the church to probe ever deeper into the Holy Scriptures. Without Arius, Athanasius would not have completed his great life's work. Augustine would never have drawn from the Word of God his profound views on grace, free will, predestination, and the church, without a Donatus and a Pelagius. Thus, heresy has compelled the church to engage in careful exegesis and serious reflection. Tolerance at this point would have indicated lack of character. Thus the confessions developed, not only as forms of unity, but also of purity" (P. S. G. de Klerk, *Gereformeerde Simboliek,* Pretoria, 1954, pp. 22-23).

It is never the intention to place the creed or confession beside the Scripture as another *principium cognoscendi,* but to formulate and express what the Scripture teaches about certain matters, and to do that under the special circumstances, according to the demands of a specific period of time.

C. Authority and Preservation

The church has never placed the creed beside or above Scripture, but always beneath it; and it has confessed that the creed was always subject to the test of Scripture, which is the only rule for life and faith. The confession is not *norma normans,* but *norma normata,* not a rule with an intrinsic norm, but a rule derived from faith. It is a human product, wholly subordinate to the Word of God (Belg. Conf., Arts. 5 and 7; Gallic Conf., Art. 4; Helv. Conf., II, 2). Not the church, but the Scripture is *autopistos.* As the Word of God, it has intrinsic authority. No human word may be placed on a par with that of Scripture. Yet the Reformation attributed authority to the confession because it was convinced and affirmed that whatever it professed in the confession was based wholly upon the Word of God.

Thus the Formula of Concord (2nd part) states that the ecumenical confessions are based on God's Word. In the Augsburg Confession we read that "this was taken from the Word of God and is founded fast and firmly therein." And the Dort subscription form says, that "all the articles and heads of doctrine included in the confession and catechism, together with the declaration on certain points of doctrine made by the Synod of Dort, conform in every respect to the Word of God."

Within the church the confession has authority as the concurrence of the community of believers because it is the expression of what the church believes to be the truth in regard to certain matters. Still, the church believes and upholds the confession only on the basis of God's Word. The confession can be tested by the Word of God at any time. The Reformed churches have viewed the Scriptures as the only source of knowledge and rule for faith and life. Consequently, they have considered it necessary for all members of the church to express agreement with the confession, and to submit to its discipline, whereas they especially require of ministers and elders subscription to the confession as the assurance of the right exercise of their offices. To that end the Reformed churches in the Netherlands and in South Africa also have demanded subscription to the confession by professors of theology. Accordingly, the church has the right to judge the convictions of a member or minister of the church and to test them by the Word of God.

When the church ordains a minister it has the authority to ask of him that he agree in doctrine and life with the confession of the church. The church must guard the honor of God, the salvation of souls, and the purity of the congregation. A church which does not bow before the Word of God is not faithful to its King. A church which does not uphold its confession does not give proper nourishment and direction to the sheep, permits them to wander in wrong paths, and runs the risk of dying out. Arbitrariness in doctrine is divisive; stability in doctrine produces unity and builds the church.

Freedom of conviction is upheld by the Reformed churches. Thus the Reformed churches are opposed to false confessionalism which aims to crystallize the confession and obstructs doctrinal development. In accordance with the words of à Lasco they "do not desire to cut off the development of future ages by the greater light which God might choose to kindle." The statement of Ursinus "that whatever needed improvement had to be improved" has constantly been the watchword of the Reformed churches.

D. Revision

Revision of the confession is always possible, but such revision is profitable only if the church itself is on a high spiritual plane and is capable of sharply ascertaining out of the Scriptures the expression of its faith. The confession of the church is certainly not in constant movement with time and history. The great truths of the confession stand fast, however the times may change and whatever drastic changes history may still disclose. Therefore, the Reformed church in the 17th century strongly resisted the revisionism of the Remonstrants. Trigland said: "The confession is certainly subject to review, but not to revision. Lawfully submitted gravamina against certain pronouncements of the confession, the church is willing to consider and to test by Scripture. But revision opens the door to all kinds of new confessions which today satisfy the one, tomorrow the other, while the church will be in a constant state of unrest" (Dr. A. Kuyper, *Revisie der Revisielegende,* p. 164). We affirm: The link with the past may never be broken, the leading of God's Spirit may never be denied. All the talk about contemporary relevance of the confession ignores the fact that essentially the questions always remain the same and that God's answers to them in His Word do not change. Therefore we do not need reform or renewal in order to make the old confessions relevant. In our spiritually impoverished times this is a hazardous undertaking and a dangerous experiment. Groen van Prinsterer said: "The forms are a series of memorials of the militant church, unimpeachable witnesses of the faith, which once was delivered to the saints, links in the same chain, mileposts along the one road, marking the way which has been traversed, not in order to remain stationary, but to go forward in the direction in which the church is being led with an unmistakable tendency" (*Adres aan de Algemeene Synode der Nedl. Herv. Kerk,* Leiden, 1842, p. 50).

II. ECUMENICAL CREEDS

A. Apostles' Creed

(*Symbolicum Apostolicum*)

This name is given to the well-known "twelve articles of our undoubted, catholic Christian faith." It is pure legend to say that these twelve articles were personally composed by the apostles, a view that was first found in Rufinus at the end of the fourth century.

In recent times the Apostles' Creed has been the object of study in a long and vehement controversy. Zahn and Harnack especially opposed each other. The controversy concerned the question: Where and when did the Apostles' Creed originate? One thought that it developed from the Jerusalem baptism creed, the other that it developed from that of Rome. Time of origin of this latter is in all likelihood the end of the first century or probably about the year 120. Harnack posits the date of origin to be about 150.

Although the apostolic confession of faith may not be from the hand of the apostles, still it has preserved in broad outline the essence and content of the apostolic preaching and tradition. In this sense there is no historical or material inaccuracy in speaking of the apostolic confession of faith. As far as the *origin* of these articles is concerned, we note at once that the confession of the Trinity controls the entire composition. We ask ourselves the question: At what occasion could such a personal confession of the Trinity have been more appropriate than at adult baptism, administered with the Trinitarian formula, after a confession of faith had been made? Thus various baptism forms developed. The baptism creed of the church at Rome is well known, but it was not used before about 120. This *Symbolum Romanum* became the foundation on which the apostolic articles were built. Bit by bit the Apostles' Creed was formed around this scriptural baptism formula, or rather, it developed as a creation of the Holy Spirit. This was a confessional miracle which can never cease to amaze and gladden us.

After various stages of development, which began as early as the second century, it was completed about the year 500, and in the eighth century it became an official confession with ecclesiastical authority. It first existed in a more abbreviated form. Later, particularly in the struggle with Gnosticism, new elements were added such as creation, descent into hell, the conception and death of Christ, and everlasting life. The present form as a *textus receptus* dates from the sixth century and was framed in S Gaul. The Reformers emphatically clung to the Apostles' Creed and incorporated it into the worship service. The Apostles' Creed is of great significance as a matrix creed. Through the ages it has enjoyed great respect. Augustine called it: *regula fidei brevis et grandis.* It is still the bond of all Christendom. Since the middle of the last century Biblical criticism has been pointed especially at the Apostles' Creed. The criticism concerned in particular the virgin birth of Jesus. In the forefront were Harnack, Kohnstamm, Emil Brunner, and Althaus. (Cf. G. C.

Berkouwer, *Het Probleem der Schriftkritiek,* ch. 3.)

B. Nicene Creed

(*Symbolum Nicaeno-Constantinopolitanum*)

Nicea began the series of ecumenical councils in the E. This was of great significance because the decisions reached there held for centuries. The creed formulated there differs from that of Eusebius of Caesarea only in a few omissions and alterations. However, the changes are of such great importance because it is clear from them that the party of Athanasius refused to compromise. In Art. 9 of the Belgic Confession we read that we also accept the creed of Nicea. It is printed after the rhymed Psalms of the three Afrikaans churches of South Africa, also after those in the Psalter Hymnal of the Christian Reformed Church of the U.S.A. In the Anglican Book of Common Prayer it is incorporated in the service of Holy Communion.

At the beginning of the fourth century the conflict with Arius broke out, the struggle in which the church father Athanasius played such an important role. Had not Arius taught that the Son had a beginning? that Christ, as the Word of God, came into being from the non-existing, so that there was a time when He was not? (Athanasius, *Against the Arians,* I, 5). This conflict culminated in the ecumenical council of Nicea in 325. There the confession was formulated that Jesus is the Logos of God, the only-begotten Son, begotten of the Father before all worlds. At the insistence of the Homoousians the expression was incorporated: "very God of God, begotten, not made, being of one substance with the Father." This confession of Nicea bears an Athanasian stamp from beginning to end. The conflict, however, did not terminate with the decision of Nicea. It flared up anew until the Council of Constantinople assembled in 381. At this council the true, complete humanity of Christ was maintained over against Apollinaris of Laodicea. The council is responsible for the familiar Nicene Creed, which further developed and confirmed the symbol of 325 (A. D. R. Polman, "De Strijd om het Dogma," in *Christus de Heiland,* p. 115). Müller, Hepp, and Biesterveld deny that this creed of Constantinople is a development of that of Nicea. The latter has greater resemblance to the baptismal creed of Jerusalem. Nor was it edited in 381. Not until the middle of the fifth century was it connected with the council of 381. Thus there is no certainty about the origin. The creed of Cyril of Jerusalem closely resembles the Nicene Creed, but it is shorter. That of Cyril dates from about 350. In the E Church it is still *the* creed. In the W Church, however, it did not so soon become accepted. The oldest traces of its use have been found in Spain. The Synod of Toledo decided to permit the singing of this creed at the mass even as was done in the E. The Church of Rome did not immediately follow this example. In the W, meanwhile, the word *Filioque* was incorporated into the creed, that the Holy Ghost proceeds from the Father *and the Son.* Not until 1014 was it included in this form in the singing of the mass in Rome. For the text see Schaff, II, pp. 57-58.

C. Athanasian Creed

(*Symbolum Athanasium*)

This creed of Athanasius is also called the *Quicunque Vult* after the opening words. Since the ninth century, this creed has been attributed to Athanasius, bishop of Alexandria. Athanasius in particular was the defender of the deity of Christ and the orthodox doctrine of the Trinity. Since the middle of the17th century the Athanasian authorship has been given up by both Roman Catholics and Protestants. This much is certain: Athanasius is not the author of this creed. No reference to it is found in the writings of Athanasius, nor do any of the councils state that he wrote it. The persistent legend of Athanasian authorship was conclusively disproved by G. Vossius in the 17th century. The principal reasons against Athanasian origin are these:

The *Filioque* is included in it, a problem which was still unknown to Athanasius. It includes expressions first found in Augustine. It includes expressions which have their origin in the Council of Chalcedon and which presuppose the heresies of Nestorius and Eutyches. It was originally composed in Latin and not translated into Greek until 1200.

Quite likely, its origins are in the church of Gaul or in N Africa, from the school of Augustine; it does not appear in completed form until the eighth century. In all likelihood it was drawn up at that time from two already existing expositions. Two parts can be clearly distinguished, a Trinitarian and a Christological part. In this creed, which was of the greatest importance for the entire W, the doctrine of the Trinity is completed and concluded.

The first part sets forth the orthodox doctrine of the Holy Trinity in its Augustinian form (3-28). The second part contains the doctrine concerning the person of Christ as it was established by the councils of Ephesus and Chalcedon (29-43). According to Harnack, the two parts first existed separately. Kattenbusch is of the opinion that the first part must have been known to Augustine, and may have received its present form shortly before his death. The big problem is to ascertain when the two parts were united.

This creed was also included in church song and is called *Psalmus Quicumque.* It is less ecumenical than the other two creeds. The Greek church never adopted it on account of the *Filioque.* It was accepted by the Reformation. Luther approved it and Calvin did so later. It is mentioned approvingly in the Augsburg Confession, in the Belgic Confession (Art. 9), the Formula of Concord, the Thirty-nine Articles, the Second Helvetic Confession, and the Bohemian Confessions. It is also acknowledged in the Gallican Confession and is included in the Book of Common Prayer. It is most dogmatic and apologetic in character. For the text see the back section of various Psalters and Schaff, II, pp. 66-70.

III. DECISIONS OF THE ECUMENICAL COUNCILS

We must distinguish carefully here. The church has never officially approved the decisions of the ecumenical councils. Theologians have done so, but the judgment of theologians is not that of the church. The pronouncements of the various councils may never be equated with a creed. Still, it is well that in symbolics we take cognizance of the pronouncements of the ecumenical councils. Reformed theology has, in general, been willing to adopt the decisions of the first six ecumenical councils.

1. Nicea, 325
2. Constantinople, 381
3. Ephesus, 431
4. Chalcedon, 451
5. Constantinople, 553
6. Constantinople, 680

The Roman and Eastern Orthodox Churches declare many more statements to be binding, but they differ in their estimate of which councils were lawful ones. The Lutherans generally do not go as far as the Reformed in their appreciation of what the councils have done. They prefer to restrict themselves to the three ecumenical symbols.

IV. CREEDS OF THE EVANGELICAL REFORMED CHURCHES

The Reformed confessions are much more numerous than those of the Roman, Greek, and Lutheran churches. This is largely because they embrace several nationalities: Swiss, German, French, Dutch, English, Scottish, Polish, Bohemian, and Hungarian. Each of these nationalities formulated its own creed because of its geographical and political isolation. The Reformed churches allowed greater freedom in the development of several dogmas, but always remained within the framework of the Word of God, to which they strictly adhered.

Schaff mentions 30 Reformed creeds of which some had no more than local authority. Müller in his *Bekenntnisschriften der Reformirten Kirche* refers to no fewer than 58. The *Harmonia Confessionum* appeared in Geneva in 1581. At Geneva too the *Corpus et Syntagma* appeared in 1612. In the edition of 1654 the Canons of Dort and the Confession of Cyril Lucaris are also included. In addition to Schaff and Müller, Reformed creeds are also given in Böckle.

A. In the Netherlands

1. *The Belgic Confession (Confessio Belgica), 1561*

This is the Netherlands confession of which Guido de Brès is the principal author. Guido de Brès was born in Mons in 1522. He died a martyr's death in 1567. De Brès drew up the Belgic Confession in imitation of the Gallican Confession (*Confessio Gallicana*), which in turn largely followed Calvin's design. The Belgic Confession was composed in French and as a creed it had appeared already in 1561. The first Dutch translation appeared in 1562. Assistance was rendered De Brès by Saravia and Herman Moded. Various ecclesiastical assemblies dealt with the confession. Thus it was reviewed at the Synod of Antwerp in 1566. Later it was translated into German and Latin. The first Latin translation was made according to the revised French text of 1566, apparently by Beza. The French text is also included in the *Harmonia Confessionum* of 1581. An official translation of this text into Dutch was prepared in 1581 by Cornelissen at the request of the Synod of Middleburg 1581. The Synod of Veere in 1610 decided to publish an authentic edition, which appeared in Middleburg in 1611 with the Dutch and French versions side by side. Since the 1611 edition is the only one in which the confession is printed in both languages in parallel columns, it follows that this edition was used at the Synod of Dort (H. H. Kuyper, *De Post-Acta,* Amsterdam, p. 353).

The Remonstrants wanted a completely free revision of this creed. The Synod of Dort then demanded that the Remonstrants present their objections to the Synod. The objections raised were of such minor significance that they were not deemed worthy of special consideration (*ibid.,* pp. 319ff.). Nevertheless, the question of revision came up, being raised by the States-General. It was their wish that the theologians from at home and abroad be asked whether there was anything in the creed which was in conflict with the Word of God or with the unity of the Reformed churches.

After having received this advice, the creed was adopted unanimously. The chairman then promised that an authentic text would be prepared in special sessions. The commission for revision included Thysius, Hommius, Faukelius, and Udemannus. The commission prepared the Dutch and French editions which were also approved by the Synod. Hommius was charged with the preparation of a Latin text which was included in the Latin Acts in 1621, whereas the Dutch edition was printed in 1619 by Canin. In 1654 the Latin revision was incorporated into the second edition of the *Corpus et Syntagma* with the title *Ecclesiarum Belgicarum Christiana atque Orthodoxa Confessio.*

The most useful and reliable text of the *Three Forms of Unity of the Reformed Churches of the Netherlands* was prepared by F. L. Rutgers with the cooperation of A. Kuyper and H. Bavinck. It is called the Flakkee edition because it was published by the Flakkee Printers of Middelharnis in 1898. Schaff considers the Belgic Confession "the best symbolic statement of the Calvinistic system of doctrine, with the exception of the Westminster Confession" (I, p. 506).

Content

First we have a long letter to Philip II which points out that the Reformed believers have different principles from the Anabaptists and that they are prepared to die for their principles. Then we have the 37 articles in *theological order,* proceeding from God, and after describing God's work, returning to God. It is more systematic than the Heidelberg Catechism and more Calvinistic in its method. The divisions are as follows:

a. God and the means whereby He is known (Arts. 1-11).
b. Creation, providence, the Fall and its consequences (Arts. 12-15).
c. Election and the restoration of fallen man (Arts. 16, 17).
d. Christ (Arts. 18-21).
e. The blessings of salvation (Arts. 22-26).
f. The church and the means of grace (Arts. 27-35).
g. Government and eschatology (Arts. 36, 37).

The French and English texts are in Schaff, *Creeds*, III, pp. 384-436; Bakhuizen presents in 4 columns the Confessio Gallicana, the French text, the Latin text, and the Dutch text. The Belgic Confession is used in the Nederlands Hervormde Kerk and in the Gereformeerde Kerken in the Netherlands and in Belgium, also in the Reformed and Christian Reformed Churches in America, and in the three Afrikaans churches in South Africa.

Literature about the creed can be found in Schaff, I, p. 502. A standard work is that of A. D. R. Polman, *Onze Nederlandsche Geloofsbelijdenis,* 4 vols., Franeker. There is also a popular commentary by Polman: *Woord en Belijdenis,* 2 vols., Franeker. Further: Arnoldus Rotterdam, *Zions Roem en Sterkte*, a commentary on the creed, 2 vols., Kampen, with an introduction by A. Kuyper.

2. *The Heidelberg Catechism (Catechismus Palatinus), 1563*

We treat the Heidelberg Catechism with the symbols of the Netherlands because it is one of the three "forms of unity" of the Gereformeerde and the Hervormde churches in the Netherlands.

Origin

Frederick III, elector of the Palatinate, soon after his coronation in 1559, carried out the Reformation in the Palatinate in a decidedly Reformed spirit. In order to have a textbook that could be used in churches and schools, he appointed a commission composed of professors and other scholars. The chief framers of the Heidelberg Catechism, Zacharias Ursinus and Caspar Olevianus, were also members of this commission. Ursinus was born on June 18, 1534, in Breslau. His father was Andreas Bär. When he was only 16, he went to Wittenberg to study. In 1557 he traveled with Melanchthon to Worms. He attended several universities and made the acquaintance of Calvin, Bucer, and Bullinger. Later he became professor at Heidelberg. Olevianus was born on August 10, 1536, in Trier. His father was Gerhard van de Olewig. When only 13 he went to Paris to study jurisprudence. There he joined up with Reformed men. In Geneva he became acquainted with Calvin and Beza. From there he went to Basel, where he made the acquaintance of Martyr and Bullinger. In 1559 he was back at Trier, where he taught the dialectic of Melanchthon. Later he became professor at Heidelberg and then a preacher. He was the principal adviser of the elector in ecclesiastical matters. In 1576 he was banished from there on account of his faith.

The preparation of the Heidelberg Catechism was assigned to these two men. It is also called the *Catechismus Palatinus* after the region, the Palatinate, for which it was intended. Even earlier, Frederick III had commissioned Ursinus to prepare a Latin catechism, out of which later developed a shorter one with 108 questions. This became the basis for the Heidelberg Catechism. The framers in all likelihood consulted existing Reformed catechisms such as those of Leo Judae, Calvin, and à Lasco.

Authorship of the material content is usually attributed to Ursinus, composition and redaction to Olevianus. Frederick speaks of counsel and cooperation of the entire theological faculty and the principal ministers of the church. Frederick himself wrote the introduction. The catechism is divided into 52 Sundays with 129 questions. In the margin reference is made to at least 700 Scripture proof texts. The division into Sundays did not appear until the 4th edition. In 1562 the Synod of Heidelberg approved the catechism.

Editions, Authority, and Importance

Early in 1563 the first edition appeared with the title: "Catechismus oder Christlicher Unterricht, wie der in Kirchen und Schulen der Churfürstlicher Pfaltz getrieben wirdt," printed in Heidelberg in 1563 by Joh. Mayer. Upon instruction of the elector the words "accursed idolatry" were inserted in respect to the mass in Q. 80. Apparently this was caused by the reprehensible action of the Council of Trent, which completed its sessions in 1563. The catechism was divided into nine reading sections, one of which was to be read every Sunday before the sermon. It was also laid down in the Church Order that the catechism should be preached every Sunday afternoon. The complete text of this copy in the church order is to be found in Müller, pp. 682-719. A Latin translation appeared on orders of the elector in 1563. In the same year a Saxon (Low German) translation appeared, as a result of which the catechism could be read in the greater part of Germany.

In the Netherlands the first translation, following the text of the second Lutheran edition, appeared in 1563, but the translation was not popular. The translation of Petrus Dathenus of the same year had a better reception. In 1566 the translation was printed in the back of the rhymed Psalter of Datheen. On order of the Zeeland Synod of Veere in 1610, the Heidelberg Catechism, like the Belgic Confession, was also republished by Herman Faukelius in 1611. The Synod of Dort in 1619 devoted two sessions to the catechism and made subscription mandatory. A Greek translation came out in 1597. Several English translations had wide circulation in Scotland, England, and America. The "New American Version" appeared in 1863. It is the symbol of the Reformed and Christian Reformed Churches.

The Heidelberg Catechism also appeared in all of the European languages and in many oriental ones as well. Schaff states: "It has been more widely circulated than perhaps any other book except the Bible, *The Imitation of Christ* by Thomas à Kempis and Bunyan's *Pilgrim's Progress.*" It is used even in Hungary and Poland. In South Africa it has been used in the churches since 1652.

Content, Text, etc.

In Sunday 1 there is an introduction which deals with our only consolation; Sundays 2-4 deal with our misery; Sundays 5-31 with our gratitude. Schaff and Klatsche observe that this division is in accordance with that of the Epistle to the Romans. Romans presents an organic doctrinal system in three parts: (a) misery (1:28 - 3:20); (b) deliverance (3:21 - 11:36); and (c) gratitude (12 - 16). Thus in the catechism we first have the content of faith and then the practice of faith. There is an organic system in the Heidelberg Catechism. In the doctrine of salvation the Apostles' Creed forms the basis. The introduction occurs in Sunday 7, which deals with faith proper. Sunday 23, which deals with justification, and Sunday 24, about good works, may be regarded as additions. Sundays 25-30 deal with the sacraments, and Sunday 31 with the keys of the kingdom of heaven. The doctrine of gratitude does not begin until conversion (Sunday 33), and then follow the commandments (Sundays 34-44) and prayer (Sundays 45-52). For further divisions see Biesterveld, *Schets van de Symboliek,* pp. 34-39.

Literature

For literature cf. P. Biesterveld, pp. 41-42, and Schaff, I, pp. 529-531.

The first commentary was by Ursinus himself, and was published by Festus Hommius as *Schatboek* in 1617. Then there were commentaries by Alting, Leydekker, Schotanus, and Van Alphen. Among the later commentaries we note the standard work of A. Kuyper, *E Voto Dordraceno,* 4 vols.; J. Bavinck, *De Heidelbergsche Catechismus,* 2 vols.; H. A. Van Andel, *De Eenige Troost,* 2 vols.; J. J. Knap, *De Heidelbergsche Catechismus.* Besides, there are the volumes of sermons on the catechism by Gezelle Meerburg, Van Oosterzee, and Hoekstra. The most practical commentary is that of B. Wielenga, *Onze Catechismus,* 2 vols. An important work is that of Tazelaar, *De Heidelbergsche Catechismus als het Leerboek onzer Vaderen.*

The definitive Dutch text was prepared by Rutgers in the Flakkee edition. Important is the *Tercentenary Monument* and the *Gedenkbuch der dreihundert jährigen Jubelfeier des Heidelberger Catechismus.* Both publications appeared in Philadelphia in 1863.

3. *The Canons of Dort, 1619*

These are the Canons of the Synod of Dordrecht, 1618–1619.

Occasion of the Meeting of the Synod of Dordrecht, 1618–1619

The reader is referred to J. Reitsma, *Geschiedenis van de Hervorming en de Hervormde Kerk der Nederlanden,* and H. Kaajan, *De groote Synode van Dordrecht in 1618–1619.* The conflict flared up between Arminius (Jakob Hermandszoon) and Gomarus, both professors at Leiden. Gomarus accused Arminius of being unreformed in the doctrine of justification. Arminius died in 1609 but the struggle was by no means over. Vorstius took his place at Leiden. He was under strong suspicion of holding Socinian heresies. A cry of indignation now arose in the ecclesiastical world. James I of England finally intervened in the conflict. At his insistence Vorstius was dismissed by the States-General of Holland. After the departure of Gomarus from Leiden, the curators appointed Johannes Polyander and Simon Episcopius, who was a disciple of Arminius.

In 1610 the Arminians, under the leadership of Johannes Uytenbogaert, held a secret meeting at which a remonstrance was formulated. The remonstrance dealt with these five points of doctrine:

a. the conditional decree of election.
b. the universal merits of Christ.
c. the free will of man.
d. the resistibility of divine grace.
e. the possibility of falling away from grace.

The text of this remonstrance in Dutch, Latin, and English can be found in Schaff, III, pp. 545-549. In 1611 the Contra-Remonstrance of the Gomarists appeared. The government intervened, and a schism in the church resulted. But a sudden change came about when Prince Maurice openly chose the party of the Gomarists.

The Synod

There were representatives on behalf of the particular synods, the Walloon churches, delegates representing the States-General, and Dutch professors in attendance. Foreign delegates came from England, the Palatinate, Hesse, Switzerland, Geneva, Emden, and Nassau. The French and Brandenburg delegates never appeared. Johannes Bogerman was chairman, and Hommius and Damman acted as secretaries. Acting as assistant examiners were Rolandus and Faukelius. This synod was extraordinary in character. In respect to doctrine, decisions were reached which concern the Reformed churches of all countries. For that reason foreign delegates were given not merely an advisory vote but full voting rights on matters doctrinal. The synod was national; that is why no new synodical board was elected after the foreign delegates departed. Nevertheless, this synod was in principle a Reformed ecumenical council, and in any case a *synodus extraordinarium.*

Drafting of the Canons

The five articles of the Remonstrants were unanimously rejected. After the several *judicia* had been reported, Bogerman began to formulate the canons. At the 126th session he was able to read the first draft of Article 1, but a storm of indignation arose. It was then decided to appoint a redaction committee consisting of the chairman and the assistant examiners, Bishop Carleton, Scultetus, Deodatus, Polyander, Walaeus, and Trigland. This commission worked with haste. In the formulation of the first article Bogerman proceeded from the thought: the canons aim at the establishment of the Netherlands churches; the order and style must be suited to these churches; matters must be presented in a simple manner. First the orthodox convictions must be formulated and then the rejection of errors must follow.

The canons proceed from the historical fact of man's fall and then explain why only a few among fallen humanity have faith. At the session of April 23, 1619, each article was signed by every one of the members of synod. The text of the canons, together with the *Acta Synodalia,* was presented to the States-General on May 30, 1619, by the delegates Bogerman, Faukelius, Hommius, Polyander, and Rolandus.

The canons were drawn up in three languages. Hommius received the authentic Latin text from Damman and prepared the Latin edition. Bogerman improved a few words in the Dutch text, while Colonius and Polyander prepared the French translation. These articles were adopted by the Netherlands churches. The Reformed churches in France and the Presbyterians in England were in agreement with them. Only the Episcopal church did not agree. The

Swiss churches and the Palatinate expressed their approval. It also became a recognized confession of the Reformed and Christian Reformed churches in America and of the three Afrikaans churches. The complete Latin and Dutch texts are presented in *De Netherlandsche Belijdenisschriften* by Bakhuizen van den Brink. The Latin text is also in Müller, pp. 843-861. T. Bos has written a popular commentary and given the complete text in *De Dordtsche Leerregelen,* 1915.

Content

The canons consist of a positive constructive part and a negative critical part. The subject matter is derived from the Remonstrance of 1610. The division is the same, the only difference being that articles 3 and 4 have been combined into a single heading as is consonant with the nature of the subject matter.

The *first article* deals with divine election and reprobation. Election is the unchangeable purpose of God. God has left some in the misery into which they have plunged themselves.

The *second article* deals with the death of Christ and the deliverance of man by His death. The righteousness of God requires eternal punishment for sin. This punishment cannot be escaped unless the righteousness of God is satisfied. Many do not repent, but this is their own fault; those who believe owe this to the grace of God.

The *third* and *fourth articles* deal with the corruption of man and conversion to God. Man became so corrupt through the Fall that only a few small glimmerings of natural light remain in him. Our Confession speaks of *vestigia* and *scintillae.* We can be saved only by the ministry of reconciliation. God pours new qualities into our will and makes the will, which was dead, alive. This happens in regeneration. All those in whose hearts God works efficaciously are effectually reborn and they actually believe. The will is renewed and man begins to believe and to repent.

The *fifth article* deals with the perseverance of believers. Perseverance is a result of the grace and work of God. This doctrine gives believers the certain assurance that they shall finally obtain the victory.

Finally, all ministers are exhorted to conduct themselves piously and religiously in dealing with the doctrine of election in school and church.

B. In Switzerland

1. *The Sixty-Seven Articles, 1523*

These are the articles which Zwingli formulated for the council of Zurich. He defended them against Joh. Faber in a public disputation on January 18, 1523. Faber tried to cover himself by appealing to the authority of the church and the Church Fathers. Zwingli fought with the Holy Scriptures as his only weapon. The council was deeply persuaded that Zwingli had gained the victory. It then announced that "Zwingli and the other preachers should continue to preach the Gospel until anyone should convince them of error." By this decision the Reformation in Zurich became an accomplished fact. Two other disputations followed. The result was that the entire canton of Zurich went over to the side of the Reformation. These articles are short theses which greatly resemble those of Luther, but they do indicate substantial progress in the development of Protestant belief. They are filled with Christ, the Redeemer, and clearly acknowledge the Word of God as the only rule of faith. The primacy of the pope is denied, the mass and the intercession of the saints are rejected. The merit of good works is repudiated, as are pilgrimages, celibacy, and purgatory.

The Sixty-Seven Articles are given in German and Latin in Schaff, *Creeds,*

III, pp. 192-207; title of the Latin text is: *Articuli sive Conclusiones LXVII, H. Zwingli, A.D. 1523*, German text, Müller, pp. 1-6; Niemeyer, pp. 1-13.

2. *The Ten Theses of Berne (Theses Bernenses), 1528*

After the conference of May, 1526, the Reformation triumphed in Berne. Berthold Haller and Frans Kolb prepared ten theses for a convocation held in Berne, January 6-26, 1528. They were drawn from Zwingli's articles and were revised by him. Many cities and cantons were represented; Zwingli, Oecolampadius, Bucer, Megander, and others were present. The result was that the canton of Berne joined the Reformation. The ten Bernese articles were adopted as a corporate basis by the Swiss Reformed cantons. One can find them in Niemeyer, pp. 14-15; Schaff, III, in German and Latin, pp. 208-210; Müller, pp. 30, 31.

3. *The Confession to Charles V, 1530*

The Latin title is *Ad Carolum Romanum imperatorem Germaniae Comitia Augustae celebrantem Fidei Huldrychi Zwinglii Ratio, 1530.* The occasion for which Zwingli wrote the *Ratio Fidei* was the Imperial Diet of Augsburg in 1530. It was never read at the diet. This is a personal confession of Zwingli which he directed to the emperor. Eck combated it and wrote the *Repulsio Articulorum Zwinglii.* The Lutherans were also opposed to the Confession, especially because Zwingli took a position against the bodily presence of Christ in the Lord's supper. In this Confession one finds Zwingli's deviations in respect to election, original sin, the church, and the sacraments.

On election Zwingli taught that all children, even those of pagans, are saved. The Canons of Dort and the Westminster Confession, however, taught that only the children of believers are saved if they die at an early age.

Regarding original sin, Zwingli also held a divergent point of view. He argues in the *Ratio* that sin really is transgression of the law alone. Thus original sin is not really sin, for it is not a violation of the law. It is a sickness, a condition. Indeed, it may be called sin, but never in the sense of guilt. Zwingli also transfers all the power of the church to the civil authorities. Therefore the church is nothing more than the religious side of the state.

Zwingli deviates also in the doctrine of the sacraments. To him the sacraments are merely visible signs of invisible grace. He condemns the Roman and Lutheran views. Whereas they erred *in excessu,* Zwingli erred *in defectu.* The sacraments are only signs, not seals, to him. The Lord's supper is merely a remembrance.

The Confession of Zwingli was never confirmed as an ecclesiastical symbol. The text is given in Latin by Müller, pp. 79-94; by Niemeyer, pp. 16-35.

4. *Exposition of the Christian Faith (Fidei Expositio) by Zwingli, 1531*

Zwingli wrote the Exposition in July, 1531. It is his swan song, written three months prior to his death. He wrote it at the request of Maigret, French ambassador to Switzerland, and sent it to Francis I of France. For political reasons Francis I supported the Protestants in Germany and Switzerland, while he persecuted them in his own country.

In 1536 Calvin also dedicated his *Institutes* to Francis I. But Francis I did not heed the warning voices. Had he done so, how different the history of France would have been! In 1536 the Exposition was published without any changes by Bullinger, while Leo Judae produced a free German translation. It is more like a personal testimony than an ecclesiastical creed. The text can be found in Niemeyer, pp. 36-37.

5. *Tetrapolitan Confession (Confessio Tetrapolitana), 1530*

Though this confession was not written by Zwingli, we may detect his spirit in it. It was composed by Bucer with the assistance of Capito and Hedio and was handed to Charles V at the Imperial Diet of Augsburg on August 28. It is called the Tetrapolitan Confession because it was submitted in the name of the four cities Strasbourg, Constance, Lindau, and Meiningen. These four cities could not agree with the eucharistic teaching of Luther.

The confession consists of 23 articles. In general, it agrees with the Augsburg Confession, but in Art. 18 it presents the views of Zwingli respecting the Lord's supper. In 1531 these four cities adopted the Augsburg Confession and joined the Smalcaldic league. Thus the Tetrapolitan Confession formally ceased to be an ecclesiastical creed. Today it has little more than historical significance. The text in German is in Müller, pp. 55-78.

6. *The First Confession of Basel (Confessio Fidei Basiliensis Prior), 1534*

Like the "Second Confession of Basel," it belongs to the Zwinglian group of creeds. The chief reformer of Basel is Johannes Oecolampadius, whose relationship to Zwingli was as that of Melanchthon to Luther.

In 1522 he became preacher and professor in Basel. The Reformation was formally introduced in that city on February 9, 1529. The First Confession of Basel was framed by Oecolampadius and was revised further by his successor Oswald Myconius in 1532. It contains only 12 articles. It was published in 1534 by the government of Basel with an introduction by the mayor of the city. In 1537 it was adopted by the city of Mühlhausen and consequently it is also known as *Confessio Mühlhusana.* In 1826 it was made binding upon preachers. It is composed in the Zwinglian spirit, although it has a more profound conception of the Lord's supper. Article 12 combats the Roman doctrine of transubstantiation and professes that our souls are fed and nourished by the flesh and blood of Christ through true faith in the crucified Christ.

This confession really constitutes the transition from Zwingli to Bullinger. Its standpoint is no longer purely Zwinglian in Articles 1, 5, and 6. The Latin text is in Niemeyer, pp. 78-104; the German text in Müller, pp. 95-100.

7. *The First Helvetic Confession, 1536*

It is also known as *Confessio Helvetica prior sive Basiliensis posterior.* It is called the Second Confession of Basel because it was drawn up in that city. The name First Helvetic Confession is preferable, however, because this is the first confession which was intended for all of Switzerland. It owes its origin both to the renewed efforts of Bucer and Capito to bring about a union between the Lutherans and the Swiss and to the fact that the pope had promised to call a general council. Preparations had to be made for such a council. Therefore the magistrates of Zurich, Berne, Basel, Schaffhausen, St. Gall, Mühlhausen, and Biel instructed a number of theologians to assemble in the Augustinian monastery at Basel on January 30, 1536. Bullinger, Myconius, Grynaeus, Judae, and Megander were appointed to draft a confession which could serve all the Swiss churches at the promised council. Capito and Bucer had an advisory role. It was signed by all the delegates. The official text is in Latin. A German translation was made by Leo Judae.

A copy was sent to Luther by Bucer. Luther was then under the influence of the Wittenberg Concord and consequently he expressed his satisfaction with this Helvetic Confession and promised to do whatever he could to promote unity with the Swiss.

This is the first Reformed confession with national authority in Switzerland. A peculiarity of the confession is the weakening of the Zwinglian point of view regarding the Lord's supper. This was done not so much to make a compromise with Luther, as it was to dispose Luther somewhat more favorably. Latin and German text in Schaff, III, pp. 211-231; Niemeyer, pp. 104-122; Müller, pp. 101-109 (German).

8. *The Second Helvetic Confession (Confessio Helvetica Posterior), 1566*

It was drawn up by Heinrich Bullinger, who was the principal author of the First Helvetic Confession. Next to Calvin, he had the greatest influence in the Swiss churches. He could not agree with the views of Luther but felt more attracted to those of Calvin.

The elector of the Palatinate, Frederick III, was threatened with expulsion by the Lutherans because he had become Reformed and had published the Heidelberg Catechism. In order to defend himself, he asked Bullinger to prepare a clear exposition of the Reformed faith. Bullinger had composed a Latin confession in 1562 as a testimony of his faith. When the plague broke out furiously in Zurich in 1564, Bullinger lost his wife and three children. He then worked out his confession in greater detail and appended it to his will. He recovered, however, and then handed his confession to Frederick III, who was so pleased with it that he had it published in Latin and in German. In March, 1566, Frederick III defended himself so brilliantly at the Diet of Augsburg that even his Lutheran opponents marveled at his piety.

Meanwhile, the need for a confession which could draw the bond of unity closer in Switzerland developed. The First Helvetic Confession was too brief. There were two other confessions available: the Consensus of Zurich and the Consensus of Geneva. But they only dealt with the Lord's supper and predestination. Accordingly, several conferences were held. Beza came to Zurich for this purpose. Bullinger permitted several changes to be made in his confession. The consent of Geneva, Berne, Schaffhausen, Biel, St. Gall, and Mühlhausen was received. Subsequently Basel also agreed. The result was that a new confession appeared in Zurich in 1566 in German and in Latin. Soon a French translation by Beza was published. It was adopted in the Palatinate, France, Scotland, Hungary, and Poland. It was held in high regard in the Netherlands and in England.

Next to the Heidelberg Catechism this is the most widespread confession of the Reformed churches. Schaff calls it "the most authoritative of all the Continental Reformed symbols, with the exception of the Heidelberg Catechism" (I, p. 394). All characteristic dogmas such as predestination are professed in a positively Reformed manner, which is "adverse to all Lutheranism and Melanchthonism." Through this confession Calvinism triumphed over Zwinglianism. This confession is living proof of the unity of the Swiss Reformation. It is a confession in which the doctrine of the Lord's supper and the doctrine of predestination are emphatically confessed in the spirit of Calvin.

The several heads of doctrine are treated in 30 chapters. The text is in Niemeyer, pp. 412-536; Schaff, III, pp. 233-306; Müller, pp. 170-221. Schaff in vol. I gives a brief summary in English, pp. 396-420.

Literature

Cf. Schaff, I, p. 390. For Bullinger,

cf. *Christelijke Encyclopaedie* I, p. 401 (1st edition).

9. *First Catechism (Catechismus Prior) of Calvin, 1536*

This brings us to *the symbolical writings of Calvin.* Calvin himself drew up most of them. They did not remain in use as confessions of the first order. Except for the Gallican Confession, the real symbolical writings of Calvin are local in character and were used only temporarily. Even his two catechisms are no longer used. Still, Calvin's theological and ecclesiastical views had tremendous influence in other countries. One need think only of France, the Netherlands, Scotland, the Lambeth Articles, the Irish Articles, and the Westminster Confession and Catechism.

The First Catechism was drawn up in Latin for local use in 1536. In 1537 it appeared in French. Schaff holds that it appeared in French in 1536. It is a concise summary of the Christian religion, a popular abridgement of the *Institutes.* It was intended for adult members of the congregation rather than for the instruction of children. It is not composed in question and answer form, but thetically in propositions. From this catechism Calvin formulated a short confession of faith, *La Confession de la Foy,* which consists of 21 articles. Church members were required to express their agreement with it by oath.

10. *The Catechism of Geneva, 1541*

It also goes by the name *Catechismus Genevensis* or *Posterior.* After his return to Geneva, Calvin revised his catechism, changing its form to questions and answers. It was supposed to serve for catechetical instruction, but was intended more as a manual for catechumens. This is Calvin's famous catechism which is used in various countries and which had great influence on the composition of other catechisms. It appeared in French in 1542 and in Latin in 1545. It was translated into Italian, English, Spanish, German, Dutch, Hungarian, Greek, and Hebrew. It is divided into five parts: concerning faith, the law, prayer, the Word of God, and the sacraments. The Apostles' Creed, the Law, and the Lord's Prayer are its basis. This catechism was long used in the Reformed churches and schools in France and Scotland. Appended to the catechism are a few prayers.

The text is in Niemeyer, pp. 123-190; in Müller, pp. 117-153 in Latin; in French under the title "Le Catéchisme de L'Église de Genève" in Niesel's *Bekenntnischriften,* pp. 1-41.

11. *The Consensus of Zurich (Consensus Tigurinus), 1549*

The sacramental controversy flared up anew in Switzerland as a result of Luther's vehement attack on the Zwinglians in 1545 and their sharp retort. Calvin realized that it was necessary to achieve uniformity.

The occasion for this Consensus of Calvin was primarily the fact that the Reformed believers in Berne had increasingly come under Lutheran influence. Some chose the Zwinglian view of the sacraments. It became more and more clear to Bullinger that there was no essential difference between him and Calvin. In 1545 he wrote his treatise on the sacraments and sent it to Calvin and à Lasco. There followed a correspondence between Calvin and Bullinger from 1547 to 1549 which led to the Consensus of Zurich. Haller meanwhile arranged for a synod to be held at Berne. Calvin sent 20 propositions concerning his doctrine of the sacraments, which were not dealt with at the synod, however. Bullinger then invited him to come to Zurich. Calvin accepted the invitation and left for Zurich with Farel. After a conference there in 1549, Bullinger, Farel, and Calvin reached agreement on the 20 propositions which Calvin had submitted to the synod of Berne. These 20 articles were increased by six. Thus the famous *Consensus Tigurinus* or Consensus of Zurich came into being, which makes it very clear that there was no difference between Zurich and Geneva on the doctrine of the sacraments.

This Consensus was adopted by the churches of Zurich, Geneva, Neuchatel, Schaffhausen, St. Gall, and Basel. It was published in Geneva and Zurich in 1551. It also appeared in Latin. The same year French and German translations appeared, the German one being by Bullinger himself. Berne refused to sign it.

In these 26 propositions position is taken not only against the *nuda signa* but also against the Lutheran, Roman, and Baptist views. Calvin here took a compromising position. He does not relinquish his convictions, but neither does he express them pointedly. For that reason one must be careful with the consensus. Nevertheless, it exercised great influence. For the text see Niemeyer, pp. 191-217; Müller, pp. 159-163. Proposition 20 teaches that the efficaciousness of the sacrament is not limited to the moment that it is being enjoyed.

The Latin text is in *Registres de la Compagnie des Pasteurs de Genève au temps de Calvin*, ed. J.-F. Bergier, Vol. I, Geneva, 1964, pp. 64-70. English translation, P. E. Hughes, *Register of the Company of Pastors of Geneva in the Time of Calvin*, Grand Rapids, 1966, pp. 115-123.

For literature consult Schaff, I, p. 471.

12. *The Consensus of Geneva (Consensus Genevensis), 1552*

It deals only with the doctrine of predestination. Calvin was vehemently attacked on his doctrine of predestination by Albert Pighius in 1542. Pighius was a proponent of free will and conditional predestination. In answer, Calvin wrote a *Defensio* in 1543. In 1551 he was violently attacked by Jerome Bolsec, who had returned to the Roman church. He accused Calvin of being blasphemous and un-Scriptural in his teaching. His attacks were the impetus for the formulation of the Consensus of Geneva. Calvin published it in the name of the preachers at Geneva. It is more like a theological treatise. In the introduction Calvin speaks contemptuously of Bolsec, without mentioning his name, because Bolsec had borrowed all his arguments from Pighius and Georgius.

The consensus is, accordingly, really the second part of the refutation of Pighius. It had appeared in Latin in 1552. The approach is supralapsarian. Outside of Geneva the consensus had no symbolical significance. It consists of two parts: the first deals with predestination and the second with providence.

It is largely because of this consensus that subsequent Reformed confessions dealt at length with the doctrine of absolute predestination as the *cor ecclesiae.*

The text can be found in Niemeyer. Schaff does not give the text of the Consensus of Zurich or of the Consensus of Geneva because the sacraments and predestination are considered broadly and sufficiently in the Second Helvetic Confession, the Gallican, the Belgic, the Scottish, and other Reformed confessions.

13. *The Helvetic Consensus Formula, 1675*

The short name is *Formula Consensus.* It is the last Swiss confession and in general concludes the confessional period of the Reformed churches. It was drawn up by J. H. Heidegger of Zurich with the assistance of Lukas Gernler of Basel and F. Turrettinus of Geneva. This Helvetic Consensus Formula is aimed especially against the errors of the theological academy of Saumur. This academy was established by the famous statesman Du Plessis Mornay in 1604. But error crept in under the professors De la Place, Cappel, and Amyraldus (Amyraut). They deviated especially at three points: the doctrines of inspiration, predestination, and original sin.

The Errors of Saumur

Louis Cappel (Cappellus) advocated a somewhat critical treatment of the text of Holy Scripture. De la Place denied the immediate imputation of Adam's sin. The stain or taint of sin is primary and becomes the ground for guilt. Amyraldus attacked the Reformed confession by his un-Scriptural view of predestination. According to him, God makes a double decree. God first decreed that all, without distinction, who believe in Christ are saved. This decree precedes election and is in reality the same thing as the *voluntas antecedens* of Rome. But this must be followed by a second decree, that of election. Because God has foreseen by His *praescientia* that no one can come to faith of himself, He added to the general and conditional decree a second absolute and special decree to give a few people the grace of faith. This error is known as hypothetical universalism. God wants to save; but, since He knows beforehand that man is incapable of faith, He decides to grant it only to a few people. Thus grace is universal as far as the will of God is concerned, but in respect to the condition it is particular. By means of this twofold decree Amyraldus attempts to maintain the sovereignty of God and our responsibility, but his effort failed. For in the first place the first universal decree has no power at all, and in the second place this view posits a dualism in God which is in direct contradiction to His simplicity and immutability.

Confessional Action

The school of Saumur thus became a focal point of heresy, particularly of Arminianism. Various theologians, including Molinaeus, Rivetus, and Heidegger, attacked the academy of Saumur. Long after the synods, such as that of Charenton, 1645, rejected these heresies, their influence lingered at Saumur. Therefore, it was considered necessary to combat these errors in a separate symbol. The idea was not to make a new confession, but to provide an explanation with respect to these several points which could serve as an appendix to the earlier confessions. It appeared in Latin under the title *Formula Consensus ecclesiarum helveticarum Reformatorum.* It was first printed in Zurich in 1714 as an appendix to the Second Helvetic Confession. The Latin text is in Niemeyer, pp. 729-739, and the German text is in Böckle, pp. 348-360.

This Helvetic Consensus Formula consists of 26 articles. In Arts. 4-6 it is stated that Amyraldianism is in conflict with the Scriptures. As regards inspiration, even the inspiration of vowels and accents is taught. Over against these errors the Reformed doctrine is set forth. Predestination is dealt with in an infralapsarian spirit. The cantons of Zurich, Basel, and Geneva adopted the Helvetic Consensus Formula and made it a binding rule in the instruction of professors and preachers.

Outside of Switzerland it never had symbolical authority. Even in Switzerland it gradually began to lose its symbolical significance at the beginning of the 18th century. For literature see Schaff, I, pp. 477-478.

C. In France

The Gallican Confession
(Confessio Fidei Gallicana), 1559

The founder of French Protestantism in its unorganized form is Jacques Lefèvre d'Etaples, professor at the Sorbonne. He translated the Bible from the Latin of the Vulgate. But there were other Reformers who were driven out of French Switzerland to France and there continued the work of the Reformation, namely Calvin, Farel, Viret, Froment, and Beza. Calvin and his successor Beza are regarded as the founders of the Reformed Church of France.

On May 26, 1559, all the Reformed churches existing in France assembled at a synod in Paris. The occasion was the visit of Antoine Chandieu of Paris, who had spoken in Poitiers with other preachers about the necessity of agreement on doctrine. He persuaded the church of Paris to call a synod. Calvin was consulted, and he and three delegates sent to Paris the draft of a confession. This confession was then altered somewhat and expanded and adopted by the Synod of Paris, 1559. Two editions of the confession exist: a shorter one, consisting of 35 articles, and a longer one, with 40 articles. The latter, published together with the church order under the title *Confession de Foy et Discipline Ecclésiastique des Èglises Réformées de France,* is the official edition. It includes a preface addressed to the king. The confession and its preface were presented to King Francis II at Amboise, 1560. At the religious conference at Poissy in 1561 they were presented to Charles IX by Beza. It is known as the *Confessio Gallicana.* Because it was revised and ratified by the seventh national synod in La Rochelle, at which Beza presided, it is also called the *Confession of La Rochelle.* This is the principal confession of the French Reformed churches. In it Calvin gives fullest expression to his convictions. Generally speaking, it was the basis for the Belgic Confession.

The text is given by Schaff, III, pp. 356-382 (French and English). Wilhelm Niesel in his *Bekenntnisschriften* gives the text of the *Confession de Foy* and also the *Discipline Ecclésiastique*, pp. 65-79. See also Müller, pp. 221-232 (French) and Niemeyer, pp. 313-326. For literature, cf. Schaff, I, pp. 490, 491.

D. In Germany

1. *The Brandenburg Confessions (Confessiones Marchicae)*

Brandenburg first became Lutheran, but in the early 17th century the elector, and many others with him, became Calvinists. Brandenburg has three confessions:

(a) The Confession of Sigismund, 1614
(b) The Colloquy at Leipzig, 1631
(c) The Colloquy of Thorn, 1645

a. *The Confession of Sigismund (Confessio Sigismundi), 1614*

Johann Sigismund, elector of Brandenburg, was taught in the strict Lutheran teachings of the Formula of Concord. Through his connections with Holland, Cleve, and the Palatinate, he came under Reformed influence, so that he adopted the Reformed faith in 1613. On Christmas, 1613, he publicly professed the Reformed faith by receiving the Lord's supper in the cathedral church of Berlin according to the Reformed ritual. This created a great sensation and aroused a storm of protest among Lutheran princes and preachers. In May, 1614, Sigismund published his personal confession, composed with the assistance of Pelargus, superintendent-general in Frankfurt-am-Oder. It is a further explanation of those points on which there were differences. In a genuinely Reformed manner, he affirms that he accepts the Holy Scriptures as the true, infallible Word of God and the only rule for faith and life. Then he accepts as being in agreement with the Word of God the ecumenical creeds and the Augsburg Confession. He rejects the Lutheran teaching of the *ubiquitas* of the body of Christ, exorcism at baptism, and the use of the wafer at the Lord's supper. He professes the Reformed doctrine on the points of predestination and the sacraments. In the conclusion the elector expresses the wish that God may illumine his faithful subjects by His truth, but that he would refrain from binding their consciences. For those days this was a very liberal position which was never adopted by the Lutheran princes. It was published in 1614. The text can be found in Niemeyer, pp. 642-652; in Böckle, p. 425ff.; in Müller, pp. 835-843.

b. *The Colloquy at Leipzig (Colloquium Lipsiense), 1631*

On account of the horrors of the Thirty Years' War, the thought of a union of Protestants against Rome came to many minds. In 1629 Ferdinand II, a supporter of the Jesuits, promulgated an edict which aimed at the eradication of Protestants. He would have succeeded in this if Gustavus Adolphus had not soon thereafter appeared on German soil. Something had to be done from the Protestant side. For that reason, Christian William, elector of Brandenburg, took the initiative in calling a conference at Leipzig on March 3, 1631. Representing the Reformed position were the elector and Landgrave William of Hesse and the theologians Bergius, Crocius, and Neuberger. The Lutherans were represented by the elector of Saxony and the theologians Höenegg, Leyser, and Höpfner.

The Altered Augsburg Confession was the basis for the negotiations. On most points agreement was reached, except on the *ubiquitas* of Christ and the *manducatio* of His body in the eucharist by unbelievers. In respect to the doctrine of predestination they were able to agree on the proposition that only a part of humanity is saved.

The sessions lasted until March 23, 1631. In conclusion, the theologians declared that the only purpose of the conference was to determine to what extent the two parties agreed on the Augsburg articles. The conference was strictly private in character.

The conference excited considerable sympathy among the Reformed, but not among the Lutherans, so that all these efforts remained fruitless. The Lutherans were intolerant in their attitude towards the Calvinists. Leyser even wrote a book in order to show that fellowship with Roman Catholics was preferable to that with Calvinists. The confession which was drawn up at Leipzig had symbolic authority in Brandenburg until the Union of 1817.

c. *The Colloquy of Thorn (Colloquium Thoruniense), 1645*

In Poland the Lutherans, Calvinists, and Moravians formed a conservative union in the Consensus of Sendomir in 1570. A peace treaty, the so-called *Pax Dissidentium,* afforded equal rights to Protestants and Catholics. But this peace was declared to be null and void by the pope, who labelled it a covenant between Christ and Belial. The king of Poland, Wladislaus IV, who himself was a Catholic, then desired to make another effort to bring about religious unity among all his subjects. To that end he invited Catholics and Protestants to a *fraterna collatio* in Thorn in West-Prussia. Three parties met on April 18, 1645. It was an assembly of 28 Catholics, 24 Reformed, and 15 (later 28) Lutherans. Of the Reformed the most important men were Bergius and Reichel of Brandenburg and the Moravian bishop Amos Comenius; on the Lutheran side, Calovius, Hülsemann, and Calixtus. The chairman was Ossolinski, chancellor of the king. Each party had to formulate a theological system. On September 16, 1645, the declarations of the Roman Catholics and of the Reformed were read. That of the Lutherans was never read. The Lutherans and Reformed were divided among themselves, so that the conference ended on November 20 without having attained its goal. The declaration of the Reformed was included in the Brandenburg Confessions. It is divided into a *Generalis Confessio* and a *Specialis Declaratio.* In the first part the canonical books of the Scriptures in the original text are professed to be the most perfect rule for faith. Agreement with the earlier creeds is professed at length. The second part deals with the several heads of doctrine in six chapters. It is signed by the preachers from Poland, Lithuania, and Brandenburg. The text is in Niemeyer, pp. 669-689; Böckle, p. 865ff.

The three confessions of Brandenburg did have an influence within their own circles but not outside them. They had symbolic authority in Brandenburg until 1817, when the Lutheran and Reformed churches of Prussia were united under Frederick William.

2. *The Confession of Frederick III of the Palatinate, 1577*

The confession, published after the death of Frederick III of the Palatinate by his son Johan Casimir, was the pious elector's last will and testament. It can be considered a supplement, a kind of explanatory appendix, to the Heidelberg Catechism. It was included in the *Corpus et Syntagma* of Geneva in 1612. A strong and clear testimony to the unshakable convictions of this hero of faith, it contains serious admonitions against the intolerance of the princes and theologians of his day. The text is given by Heppe, pp. 1-18. A Latin translation is included in the *Corpus et Syntagma* of 1612.

3. *The Confession of Anhalt (Repetitio Anhaltina), 1579*

This is a "repetition" of the Augsburg Confession and is principally the work of Wolfgang Amling, superintendent of Anhalt. It was presented to a conference of Hessian theologians in 1579 and published in 1582. This confession is really not Reformed. Not until 1596 did the duchy adopt the Reformed faith. Although it is directed against the Formula of Concord, it accepts the Smalcald articles and Luther's Catechism. In the doctrine of the Lord's supper it professes the *manducatio oralis* and the *manducatio indignorum.* Nor is it sound in respect to the doctrine of predestination. We do better to include this confession among the Lutheran ones which are Melanchthonian in spirit. The text can be found in Niemeyer, pp. 612-641, and in Heppe, pp. 19-67.

4. *The Confession of Nassau, 1578*

At the request of Count Joh. von Nassau Dillenburg, the Confession of Nassau was drawn up by Christopher Pezel, who had been banished from Saxony on account of his Crypto-Calvinism. It was presented to a synod in Dillenburg in July, 1578, where it was approved. It did not appear in print until 1593. It is written in the Melanchthonian spirit following the Altered Augsburg Confession. It rejects the doctrine of *ubiquitas.* The text is in Heppe, pp. 68-146; Müller, pp. 720-739.

5. *The Bremen Confession (Consensus Bremensis), 1598*

This confession was also drafted by Pezel, who had meanwhile moved to Bremen. He drew up this consensus as an expression of doctrinal agreement among the preachers of Bremen. He is more positive in this document than in the Confession of Nassau. The doctrine of predestination is taught lucidly and clearly in the Reformed sense while several times he appeals to the *Harmonia Confessionum* of Beza. The text is in Heppe, pp. 147-243; Müller, pp. 739-799.

6. *The Hessian Confession, 1607*

The Confession of Hesse was established at the Synod of Cassel in 1607 and was published in 1608. It treats only five articles: the law, the abolition of Roman image veneration, the person of Christ, eternal election, and the Lord's supper. In its doctrine of the sacraments it is positively Reformed. The text may be found in Heppe, pp. 244-249.

E. In Bohemia, Poland, and Hungary

1. *The Bohemian Confession of 1535*

In Bohemia the Catechism of the Waldensians, formulated in 1489, was used before the Reformation. The Bohemian Catechism was not drawn up until 1521. Between 1467 and 1671 no fewer than 34 confessions were written in Bohemian, Latin, and German. There are only two which had some influence. The Bohemian Confession of 1535 was drawn up in the spirit of the Augsburg Confession, in all likelihood by Johan Augusta. It was written in Latin and then translated. The nobility of the *Unitas Fratrum,* or Bohemian Brethren, signed it as proof of their orthodoxy and on November 14, 1535, presented it to King Ferdinand in Vienna. It consists of a long apologetic preface and 20 articles. After a number of corrections were made, Luther approved it, and upon request had it published in 1538. This is not, therefore, a Reformed creed as such. The text is in Niemeyer, pp. 771-818, and in Böckle, pp. 780-830.

2. *The Bohemian Confession (Confessio Bohemica), 1575*

Emperor Maximilian was favorably disposed toward his Protestant subjects and was somewhat sympathetically inclined toward their doctrine. He permitted all non-Catholic Bohemians to submit a confession at the Diet in Prague. The Reformed, the Lutherans, and the Moravian Brethren together submitted a confession which was drawn up by Paul Pressius and Markus Crispin. With a few alterations, it was adopted by the Diet and on May 17, 1575, it was presented to Maximilian II. This is the Bohemian Confession. Later it was again presented to Maximilian's son and successor, Rudolph II, who granted the Protestants equal rights with the Roman Catholics. This confession includes a preface to Maximilian II and 25 articles, which agree with the Augsburg Confession and the Bohemian Confession of 1535. Only the article on the Lord's supper agrees with the later views of Melanchthon.

A German translation was approved on November 3, 1575. The Latin translation appeared in 1619. The text can be found in Niemeyer, pp. 818-851, and in Böckle, pp. 780-850. For literature cf. Schaff I, pp. 577-580.

3. *The Consensus of Sendomir (Consensus Sendomiriensis), 1570* (Poland)

After the death of à Lasco and Prince Radziwill the Protestants in Poland no longer had a leader. For reasons of security the Lutherans, Calvinists, and Bohemian Brethren joined in a union. This confederative union was realized at the Synod of Sendomir on April 14, 1570. There the Consensus of Sendomir came into being. Both a Polish and a Latin edition were authorized in 1586. The preface is signed by Paulus Gilovius for the Reformed, by Erasmus Gliczner for the Lutherans, and by Johannes Laurentius for the Bohemian Brethren. The Consensus sets forth that the three groups agree on the doctrines of God, the Trinity, the incarnation and person of Christ, justification by faith, and other fundamental articles as they are taught in the Augsburg Confession and in the Bohemian and Helvetic Confessions. In respect to the sacramental controversy, they adopt that explanation of the words of institution which distinguishes between the earthly form and the heavenly substance in the Lord's supper, and regard the visible elements not as *nuda signa* (mere signs) but as conveying to true believers that which they represent.

The Consensus therefore adopted the later Melanchthonian or Calvinistic view. The doctrine of predestination is not dealt with.

Some weeks later, on May 20, 1570, another synodical assembly was held in Posen, where 20 supplementary articles were adopted with the purpose of confirming the Consensus. One of these articles prohibits polemics in the pulpit. The Consensus was subsequently reaffirmed by the synods of Cracow, 1573, of Petricow, 1578, of Wladilaw, 1583, and Thorn, 1595. The Synod of Thorn was the greatest synod ever held in Poland. The Lutherans, who clung to the Formula of Concord, withdrew. The text is found in Niemeyer, pp. 551-591. For literature cf. Schaff, I, p. 581.

4. *The Hungarian Confession (Confessio Czengerina), 1557*

During the Reformation the Calvinists were at least twice as numerous as the Lutherans and were mostly Hungarians (Magyars). In 1545, 29 Lutheran preachers assembled in Erdöd and drew up a confession of 12 articles in accordance with the Augsburg Confession. Another Lutheran synod convened in Medswisch in 1548 and formulated the *Confessio Pentapolitana.* It represented five cities in upper Hungary. The Magyar version was Reformed. The Hungarian Confession was framed at the synod of the Reformed in Czenger in 1557. Accordingly the name is *Confessio Czengerina.* It was published at Debreczin in 1570. In short articles it deals with the Trinity, the Son of God, the Holy Spirit, the Holy Scriptures, the sacraments, Christian freedom, election, the origin of sin, and the Mediator. This confession is very strong in its opposition to the Roman and Lutheran teaching on the Lord's supper. It teaches unconditional election, but is silent on reprobation. Later synods were more explicit on the doctrines of predestination and the perseverance of the saints. However, this confession was soon replaced by the Heidelberg Catechism and the Second Helvetic Confession, which were adopted at Debreczin in 1567. The text is given in Latin by Niemeyer, pp. 539-550; in German by Böckle, pp. 851-863. For literature cf. Schaff, I, p. 589.

F. In England, Ireland, and Scotland

1. *The Thirty-Nine Articles of the Church of England, 1563*

The confessional development of England can be sketched according to the several periods through which the Reformation as a whole passed there. Under Henry VIII the issue was exclusively a political one, a change in the highest ruling of the church. This is reflected in the writings of the time. Under his regime several confessions came into existence which are of minor symbolical significance. The English Reformation was nobly led by scholarly churchmen such as Cranmer, Latimer, Ridley, Hooper, and Rogers. Under Edward VI and Elizabeth the Episcopal system was dominant, whereas thereafter the Puritan movement gained ground. It achieved its noblest development in the Westminster Standards.

The history of the principal confession of the Church of England, namely *The Thirty-Nine Articles*, begins with the *42 Articles* of Edward VI. With the coronation of Edward VI in 1547 the influence of Cranmer and the Reform Party prevailed. The *Six Articles* of Henry VIII were then abolished. Cranmer intended to draw up an evangelical catholic confession which could serve as a bond of unity among the Protestant churches, a project that was never achieved. Cranmer's *42 Articles* were published, together with a short catechism, in 1553 with royal consent and with the approval of the Synod of London. These are also known as the Edwardian Articles. Cranmer sent extracts for evaluation to English and foreign theologians who were then residing in England. John Knox was also consulted.

The 42 Articles were replaced in their entirety by the *Thirty-Nine Articles,* which are merely a revision of the former. The 39 Articles were formulated by Archbishop Parker with the assistance of Cox and Guest. Parker presented this version of the Latin Articles of 1553 to a convocation which was called by Elizabeth in January 1553. After examination by both Houses of Parliament, it was signed by the 49 bishops and the members of the House of Commons and was published by the Royal Press in 1563.

The Latin text of the 42 Articles and that of the 39 Articles are printed side by side in Müller, pp. 505-522. The authorized English text was adopted by a convocation in 1571 and published under the supervision of Bishop Jewel. It contains not a few variations from the Latin edition of 1563. Charles I wanted to put an end to theological disunity. For that reason he had the 39 Articles published in 1628 with a foreword entitled, "His Majesty's Declaration." An American revision was prepared in 1801 by the Protestant Episcopal Church in the United States of America. Schaff presents the Latin edition of 1563, the English edition of 1571, and the American revision in parallel columns, III, pp. 487-516.

Content and Nature

First the ecumenical dogmas are presented, and then the rule of faith and the soteriological dogmas are dealt with. Thereafter predestination and Christ are discussed, followed by the church and the sacraments. The last three articles (37-39) deal with the state.

In the doctrines of predestination and the Lord's supper the 39 Articles are Reformed. From the article on baptism, Schaff concludes that baptismal regeneration is taught. But in Art. 27 baptism is called the *sign* of regeneration. And concerning the effect of baptism it teaches that by this sacrament "faith is confirmed and grace increased." This, however, is not Lutheran, but solidly Reformed. The text is also given in Niemeyer, pp. 601-611, and is included in all editions of the Book of Common Prayer.

Literature

E. Tyrrel, *The Thirty-nine Articles and the Age of the Reformation.* It also provides an extensive summary of literature. Cf. also Schaff, I, pp. 592-593.

2. *The Anglican Catechism*

Cranmer's Catechism made its appearance in 1548. It was in the main a translation of the catechism of Justus Jones. When, under Edward VI, the Book of Public Worship was ready, the Shorter Catechism was included in it.

In the Prayerbooks of 1549, 1552, and 1559 this catechism bears the title "Confirmation wherein is contained a Catechism for Children." This catechism underwent several changes. It is certainly an improvement over earlier English catechisms, but it is very meager in comparison to the catechisms of Luther and Calvin and the later Heidelberg Catechism.

The need for a longer catechism for more advanced age-levels was felt in England. Such a larger catechism was composed by Ponet, bishop of Winchester, together with the 42 Articles of 1553. It is formulated in Latin and in English with the evident approval of Cranmer and the Convocation. The authority of the catechism was disputed later. Following this model of the catechism, Nowell in 1562 prepared still another catechism, which was published in

1570. The text of the shorter Anglican Catechism, as it was published in the Prayer Book of 1562, is available in Schaff, III, pp. 517-522, and in Müller, pp. 522-525.

3. *The Lambeth Articles, 1595*

Controversy flared up in Cambridge University about predestination. Art. 17 of the Thirty-Nine Articles did not shed sufficient light on this doctrine. Men like Thomas Cartwright, William Perkins, and William Whitaker were teaching at Cambridge, but opposition to the Calvinistic doctrine of predestination arose there. Through Lord Burghley's influence, Baron, a Frenchman, was appointed professor. It soon became evident that he was an ardent opponent of Calvinism.

Dr. Goade, vice-chancellor of the university, then summoned Baron to call him to task. However, through the intervention of Burghley he never appeared. In 1596 he left for London, where he died after a few years. But this was not the end of opposition to the doctrine of predestination. The battle was joined even more vigorously by William Barrett, a fellow of Caius College. In a *Concio ad Clerum* on April 29, 1595, he vehemently opposed election, reprobation, and perseverance of the saints (*perseverantia sanctorum*) and attacked Calvin, Beza, Peter Martyr, and Zanchius. This academic controversy was first dealt with by the vice-chancellor and the senate, and then by Archbishop Whitgift of Canterbury. Whitgift was at first inclined to side with Barrett. However, he did not approve of Barrett's answers and proposed a second meeting at Lambeth Palace. Barrett was there interrogated in the presence of a deputation from Cambridge led by Whitaker. He was compelled to admit his lack of knowledge and to acknowledge his error. He then left the Church of England and joined the RC Church. In order to put an end to this controversy the heads of the university sent Whitaker and Tindal to London for an interview with the archbishop and other religious scholars.

The result was the adoption of the Nine Articles. On November 20, 1555, these Articles were sent for approval to Whitaker, who gave his complete approbation to them. They were also signed by Hutton, archbishop of York, and by Young, bishop of Rochester.

Whitgift sent the Articles to the University of Cambridge, not as a new confession, but as an explanation of certain points which had been established earlier. The Articles follow the formulation of Whitaker in the main, however with a few minor changes. These modifications led Hardwich and Schaff to conclude that they were intended to conciliate the anti-Calvinists. Nevertheless, we must recognize that the Lambeth Articles are definitely Calvinistic in dealing with predestination. The queen refused to sign these Articles because the Conference at Lambeth was called without her permission. She even demanded that Whitaker recall the Articles and prevent their distribution. Accordingly, in the real sense of the word, they did not have symbolical authority for the Church of England. Still, they continue to be of great significance. In Ireland they did have symbolical authority. Schaff points out that it is important to compare these articles with the *Articuli de Praedestinatione* of Calvin, which were discovered by the Strasbourg editors. In vol. III, pp. 524, 525, he includes a copy of Calvin's Articles. The Latin and English texts are given in Schaff, III, pp. 523, 524; and in Müller, pp. 525-526.

Literature

Strype, *Life and Acts of John Whitgift,* 2 vols. Cf. also Schaff, I, p. 658.

4. *The Irish Articles, 1615*

The Irish Articles belong to the Episcopal creeds and therefore we consider them before the Scottish Confessions. In Ireland the Book of Common Prayer was not adopted until 1560. Whether or not its adoption included the 39 Articles is a matter of uncertainty. It is evident, however, that these Articles never wholly satisfied the Irish. Ireland had to have its own Reformed confession. To that end a convocation of Irish Protestant preachers convened at Dublin in 1615. James Ussher, archbishop of Armagh, had already drawn up the Articles of Religion. These Articles were confirmed at the convocation in Dublin by the archbishops, the bishops, and preachers of Ireland. Appended was a decision of the synod that the Articles were to be a rule of public doctrine. The Irish Articles consist of 104 articles, divided into 19 chapters. In them the Calvinistic spirit is expressed much more strongly than in the Anglican Catechism. These Articles constitute one of the most systematic of our Reformed creeds; their tenor is strictly Reformed except on the relationship of church and state, on which they take a strictly Episcopal position. Because these Articles are so important and are the basis for the Westminster Confession, we present the headings of each chapter: chap. 1 deals with the Holy Scriptures and the first three ecumenical creeds; chap. 2 deals with the Trinity; chap. 3, with predestination; chap. 4, with creation and providence; chap. 5 deals with the Fall and original sin; chap. 6, with Christ; chap. 7, with the mediation of the grace of Christ; chap. 8, with justification and faith; chap. 9, with sanctification and good works; chap. 10 deals with *cultus Dei;* chap. 11, with civil government; chap. 12, with our duty toward our neighbor; chap. 13, with the church and the ministry of the Word; chap. 14, with the authority of the church; chap. 15 distinguishes the dispensation of the OT from the NT; chap. 16 deals with the sacraments; chaps. 17, 18, with baptism and the Lord's supper; chap. 19, with eschatology. The text is given in Schaff, III, pp. 526-544, and in Müller, pp. 526-539.

Literature, cf. Schaff, I, p. 662

5. *The Scottish Confession (Confessio Scoticana Prior), 1560*

John Knox was the father of the confessional movement in Scotland. He believed in the sovereignty of God and in the rights of the people. The Reformed Church of Scotland was not recognized by law and was not made a state church until 1567, seven years after the adoption of the first Scottish Confession. Yet it existed as a voluntary body from December 3, 1557, when a number of Protestant noblemen and private individuals signed a covenant in Edinburgh to defend the church of Christ even unto death. In principle, therefore, the Reformed Church already existed. The need was then felt for a sound Calvinistic confession.

On August 1, 1560, the Scottish Parliament assembled in Edinburgh before the arrival of Queen Mary. This was the most important assembly in the history of Scotland. In answer to the petition requesting the abolition of popery, Parliament instructed six preachers to draw up a confession: John Winram, John Spottiswoode, John Willock, John Douglas, John Rowe, and John Knox. They completed it within four days. John Knox was the principal author. The document was read twice, and on August 17, 1560, Parliament approved it "as a doctrine grounded upon the infallible Word of God." The adoption of this confession had as its consequence the abolition, on August 24, 1560, of the Catholic mass, the authority of the pope, and the abrogation of all former laws which served the interest of the RC Church. A messenger was sent to Queen Mary in Paris with the confession, but it was not well received. Mary's plan was to restore her own religion at a suitable time. In December, 1560, the first General Assembly met and approved the Book of Discipline, which was drawn up by the framers of the confession. In 1567 Parliament formally declared the Reformed Church to be the state church.

The Scottish Confession was the only legally recognized confession of both the Presbyterian and Episcopal churches in Scotland. In addition to this confession, the General Assembly also gave its approval to the Second Helvetic Confession, the Catechism of John Calvin, and the Heidelberg Catechism. Subsequently the confession was overshadowed by that of Westminster, which was also adopted in Scotland. It consists of 25 articles with a preface. Müller in his *Symbolik* (p. 418) declares: "The peculiarity of this confession consists in its weakening of Calvinistic doctrine." In all probability Müller has in mind that the confession did not express itself with sufficient clarity on election in Art. 8. But that was not the point of conflict at the time. Schaff is more appreciative: "It exhibits a clear and forcible summary of the orthodox Reformed faith" (I, p. 683). The Confession is soundly Reformed, but is characterized by vigorous expressions, such as "the pope is the antichrist." The Latin edition is by Patrick Adamson and was published in 1572. Together with the English text it is given by Schaff, III, pp. 437-479. The Latin text is given by Müller, pp. 249-263. It has a peculiar place among Reformed confessions. The idea is prominent that besides individual election one can speak of the election of a race and nation. God, for instance, concluded a covenant with Scotland. Moreover, Knox was zealous for the separation of church and state. Nevertheless, he demanded that the state should support a particular church. For literature, cf. Schaff, I, pp. 669, 680.

6. *The National Covenant, or the Second Scottish Confession (Confessio Scoticana Posterior), 1580*

"National Covenants" for the preservation and defense of Protestant principles are a mark of the history of the Church of Scotland. They are solemn declarations to defend the doctrine and organization of the Reformed church against all hostile attacks. The most important National Covenant was that of 1580, also called the Second Confession or "The King's Confession." It was drawn up in English and Latin by John Craig and is a solemn confirmation of the Confession of 1560. It is phrased in strongly anti-popish language: "against the usurped tyranny of the Roman antichrist upon the Scriptures of God, upon the Kirk," etc. It is also a protest against "his five bastard sacraments" and "his devilish mass."

This Confession was signed at Edinburgh on January 28, 1580, by James VI and his court and a number of noblemen and preachers. It was repeatedly renewed: in March, 1581, then in 1590, 1638, and 1639. It was put into effect by a decision of Parliament in 1640 and by the signature of Charles II, first in exile in 1650, then at his coronation in 1651. The text can be found in Schaff, III, pp. 480-485 in English and Latin; also in Niemeyer, p. 357ff. For literature cf. Schaff, I, p. 685.

7. *The Scottish Catechisms*

Quite a number of catechisms were written in Scotland. We mention only the catechism of John Craig, who was also the author of the Second Scottish Confession. The *Larger Catechism* of Craig was first printed at Edinburgh in 1581 and at London in 1589. The General Assembly adopted it in 1590, but it also instructed the author to prepare an abridgement. This *Shorter Catechism* was in general use until the Westminster Catechism took its place. It begins with several historical questions and then explains the Apostles' Creed, the Law, and prayer. It concludes with the means of grace and the way of salvation. The questions and answers are brief. For literature cf. Schaff, I, p. 696.

8. *The Westminster Confession, 1647*

The *Westminster Standards* includes the Westminster Confession, the two Westminster Catechisms, the Directory of Public Worship, and the Form of Presbyterian Church Government and Ordination of Ministers.

Occasion for the Westminster Confession

It is impossible to sketch in brief the conflict between Puritanism and the Episcopal Church. This ecclesiastical struggle was involved in the political struggle between the king and parliament. James I caused the aversion of the Puritans to the Anglican Church to increase. There were especially three matters which grieved them. First, the king attempted to reintroduce the episcopal system in Scotland. Second, he militated against the strict observance of the day of rest by publishing a list of permissible Sunday activities, the so-called Book of Sports. Third, the successor to the throne had married a RC wife.

Under Charles I the situation did not improve (1625). Spurred on by his RC wife, Charles I suppressed the Puritans still more and reintroduced into the Anglican Church many Roman practices. He was supported by his counselor William Laud, archbishop of Canterbury.

In 1638 the Scots made a covenant to oppose the covert introduction of Roman Catholicism. Now civil war erupted. Parliament was reconvened by the king, for the first time in eleven years. Because this Short Parliament was not well disposed toward the king, it was quickly disbanded. But the advancing Scots compelled the king to convene another parliament. This is known as the Long Parliament, which opened in 1640. The political revolt now became a religious one. In 1642 both episcopacy and its liturgy were repudiated. Charles I was compelled to sign this decree. By this action episcopacy as an integral part of the state was done away with. The House of Commons, which was composed especially of Presbyterians, now decided that it would regulate ecclesiastical matters since the revolt had already broken out. In 1643 the *Solemn League and Covenant* was formed, a solemn covenant between England and Scotland.

Now that the position of the House of Commons was strengthened, it decided to convene the Westminster Synod (1643–1648). The purpose was "an entire purification of the Church from the very foundation": it was a difficult time for a synod to be meeting. The leaders of despotism, Strafford, Archbishop Laud, and Charles I were condemned to death between 1641 and 1649. With the approval of parliament, the Westminster Synod opened on July 1, 1643, in Westminster Abbey.

The aim was to achieve a more complete reformation of the churches of England, especially in liturgy, discipline, and government, in order thus to bring the churches of England into a closer relationship with the churches of Scotland and those on the Continent. Schaff makes the following observation about the synod: "It forms the most important chapter in the ecclesiastical history of England during the seventeenth century" (I, p. 728). It was composed of 151 members—121 theologians and 30 lay assessors. Parliament appointed all the members. The Scottish delegates were designated by the Synod of the Scottish churches, but they did not go to London merely as delegates of the Scottish churches, "but as the accredited representatives of the Scottish people" (Warfield, VI, p. 31). Altogether there were 1,163 sessions, lasting until February 22, 1649. Even after that it still met irregularly. Finally the synod came to an end at the same time as the Long Parliament. The last minutes are dated March 25, 1652.

The Synod

The Westminster Synod began by revising the 39 Articles, but this task was interrupted on order of parliament October 12, 1643. The Synod was first to deal with church order and liturgy. Now differences of opinion began to appear. For indeed all parties were represented: Episcopalians, Presbyterians, Independents, and Erastians. Soon the Episcopalians refused to attend further sessions. The Independents and Erastians were by far the minority and departed before the Book of Discipline was completed. The first part of the Synod's work was the *Directory of Ordination,* which was presented to parliament on April 20, 1644. It was followed by *Propositions Concerning Church Government.* Meanwhile the doctrinal work proceeded. As early as October 12, 1643, an order came from parliament "to frame a Confession of Faith for the three Kingdoms according to the Solemn League and Covenant."

On August 20, 1644, a commission was appointed to write up a new confession. This commission was composed of the Scottish delegates, led by Henderson, and nine other delegates. On September 4, 1644, the commission was expanded to 23 members. The work of this commission had been interrupted meanwhile. The theologians under the leadership of Henderson then drew up the *Practical Directory for Church Government,* which on July 7, 1645, was presented to parliament.

In the space of two years and three months the task of writing the Confession, of which Henderson was the principal author, was completed. Repeatedly there had been interruptions in the work because of discussions concerning the catechism and church order. On December 4, 1646, the Confession was presented to parliament, where it was approved by the House of Commons on March 22, 1648, and by the House of Lords on June 4, 1648. The Synod of Scotland had already adopted it on August 27, 1647. This is called *The Humble Advice of the Assembly of Divines.* Not until March 5, 1660, was it declared to be the "Public Confession of the Church of England" by the "Rump Parliament." This confession is strictly Calvinistic in doctrine and anti-episcopal in church government. It embraces the complete authority of Holy Scripture, the sovereignty of God, freedom of conscience, and the complete jurisdiction of the church within its own domain. Of all existing confessions, it is most clear on all points. This results from the fact that it was formulated after the struggle with the Arminians. It bears the stamp of Dutch theology, for many members of the Synod had sojourned in the Netherlands. On all points it is a definitely Reformed revision of the 39 Articles in the spirit of the Lambeth and Irish Articles. In respect to church order, it is positively presbyterian as a result of Scottish influence. In Scotland it took the place of the First Scottish Confession. Later on the Book of Common Prayer and the Thirty-Nine Articles were restored.

Content, Text, Translations

The Westminster Confession consists of 33 chapters. Chap. I includes 10 articles which in a very clear manner affirm the authority of Holy Scriptures and divine inspiration. For content the reader is referred to the content of the Irish Articles, which forms the basis of the Confession and Catechism. A Latin translation of the Confession and Catechism appeared at Cambridge in 1656. More than 200 editions appeared in Britain and about 100 in America. As early as 1648 it was translated into German. Altogether it was translated into 17 languages. As a confession it is professed by more Protestants than any other.

For the history and origin consult Warfield, VI, and A. F. Mitchel, *The Westminster Assembly, Its History and Standards,* 1883. The text is given in Schaff, III, pp. 600-673 (English and Latin); Müller, pp. 542-612 (English and Latin); Latin text in Niemeyer. This confession also served as a basis for the Reformed Ecumenical Synod of Grand Rapids. For literature cf. Schaff, I, pp. 701, 702, 727, 728, 753, 754.

9. *The Westminster Catechism*

The Westminster Assembly also decided to write a new catechism. In the course of its labors the assembly became convinced that two catechisms were needed. A larger catechism was required for explanation in the pulpit and a shorter one for instruction of children. The *Larger Catechism* was completed on October 15, 1647, and was presented to parliament on October 22. It was the work especially of Anthony Tuckney. Tuckney also summoned the commission which drew up the *Shorter Catechism.* On November 22, 1647, it was ready and was immediately presented to parliament. This shorter catechism was approved by parliament on December 22-25 and was published under the title: "The Grounds and Principles of Religion, contained in a Shorter Catechism." The Larger Catechism never received authorization from the House of Lords. Both catechisms were approved by the Synod of Edinburgh in 1648. They depart from the usual catechetical tradition of taking the Apostles' Creed as the basis for discussion of doctrine. The Apostles' Creed is included in the Shorter Catechism as an appendix. Schaff calls the Shorter Catechism "one of the three typical Catechisms of Protestantism, which are likely to last to the end of time." The other two are Luther's Catechism and the Heidelberg Catechism.

Schaff gives the text of only the Shorter Catechism in English and in Latin, III, pp. 676-704. Müller gives the text of the Larger Catechism in Latin, pp. 612-643, and the text of the Shorter Catechism in English, pp. 643-652. For literature cf. Schaff, I, pp. 783 f.

V. OTHER PROTESTANT CREEDS

A. The Presbyterians

1. *In England*

There was a strong presbyterian element among the English Puritans. This became evident especially at the famous Westminster Synod of 1643.

By legislation of parliament in 1648 they were denied all civil and religious rights. In 1876 the English congregations of the United Presbyterian Church of Scotland united with the English Presbyterians. This became the Presbyterian Church of England. It adopted *Twenty-four Articles of Faith,* which are in complete agreement with the Westminster Confession.

2. *In America*

(a) In the United States of America there are several Presbyterian church organizations. The first presbytery was organized in Philadelphia in 1706 by Makemie and six other ministers. After only eleven years the first synod could be constituted. In 1729 the confessional standards of Westminster were formally adopted. In 1788, after the Revolutionary War, the united synods decided to organize a General Assembly with four synods. It adopted a revised form of the Westminster Standards. Thus the Presbyterian Church of the U. S. A.

came into existence. At the close of the 18th century there was a revival in the congregations of the presbytery of Transylvania, Kentucky. It produced much division, out of which the Cumberland Presbyterian Church arose in 1810. It repudiated the "fatalistic" character of the Westminster doctrines.

(b) In 1813 the Confession of the Cumberland Presbyterian Church was formulated, a semi-Pelagian revision of the Westminster Confession. The 33 chapters of the Westminster Confession were retained, with American revisions of chapters 23 and 31. It differs from the Westminster Catechism in rejecting unconditional election and reprobation. Strangely, the chapter on the perseverance of the saints was kept. The change in chapter 10 is also peculiar: "All infants dying in infancy are regenerated and saved by Christ through the Spirit," whereas the Westminster Confession reads "Elect infants." This confession was revised in 1829. Comparative textual readings are given by Schaff, III, pp. 771-776. Cf. Müller, pp. 912-927.

The United Presbyterian Church of North America was organized in Pittsburgh in 1858. It adopted the Westminster Standards, somewhat modified in respect to civil government. Moreover, a "Judicial Testimony" of 18 articles was incorporated, in which several points that are not clear in the Confession are explained.

(c) *The Auburn Declaration, 1837*

The Declaration owes its origin to the conflict which in 1837 produced a break in the Presbyterian Church when it was divided into the "Old School" and the "New School." The Declaration was drawn up by Dr. Baxter Dickenson in 1837. The complaint against the "New School" was that it deviated on sixteen points from the true Calvinism of the Westminster Standards.

The accusation is refuted in 16 articles. This refutation was adopted at an important convention in Auburn in 1837. Hence the title, the Auburn Declaration. This Declaration is not a creed, but only an authoritative declaration of the interpretation which the "New School" gave to the Westminster Symbols. It was endorsed by the General Assembly in 1868 "as containing the fundamentals of the Calvinistic Creed." The text is available in Schaff, III, pp. 777-780.

B. The Congregationalists

The Congregationalists proceed from the principle of the autonomy of the congregations or the local gatherings of believers. These congregations are completely free and independent of any church organization and civil authority. The congregations can, to be sure, assemble in conferences, but these are merely advisory. There is only one authority and that is Christ and the Holy Scripture. The church council does not rule, but executes the will of the congregation. The validity of the decisions of the church council is dependent upon the approval of the congregation. In accordance with their principles, the Congregationalists can have no creeds of general authority. Actually, there should be as many confessions as there are congregations. The "Congregational Union" does not have legislative power, but has only an advisory voice. Each confession is therefore only a declaration of the common faith at a given time. It is not a binding formula to which one must subscribe. Thus there is a host of confessions among American Congregationalists which have only local authority. Still, there are a few such documents which have more than ordinary authority.

1. *The Savoy Declaration, 1658*

This is the oldest and most fundamental Congregationalist confession. It is called the Savoy Declaration for the Savoy Palace in London, where an important meeting was held which lasted from September 29 to October 12, 1658. Shortly before his death Cromwell gave permission for the formulation of a creed for the entire kingdom. Twenty-six days after his death 200 delegates from 120 congregations were assembled. The Savoy Declaration is the work of a commission including Goodwin, Owen, Nye, Bridge, Caryl, and Greenhill. All, with the exception of John Owen, were members of the Westminster Assembly. Their decision about the confession and church order was unanimous. The confession is really nothing more than a copy of the Westminster Confession with a few slight changes. A long preface of 14 pages precedes and there is appended a "Platform of Church Polity." In the preface the Congregational view of the confession is set forth. The Declaration itself establishes that the Congregationalists wholly agree with the Westminster Confession. The changes concern in particular the Presbyterian system of church government and the authority of the magistrate in ecclesiastical affairs. The Westminster Confession granted the government a measure of authority over the church.

The Savoy Declaration teaches that the civil authority must indeed protect those who confess the gospel, but denies the government the right to restrict freedom when there are doctrinal differences. The Savoy Declaration was adopted also by the American Congregationalists at their synods in Boston in 1680 and in Saybrook in 1708. In the section dealing with church order, Art. 6 reads as follows: "Besides these particular churches there is not instituted by Christ any church more extensive or catholic intrusted with power for the administration of his Ordinances or the execution of any authority in his Name." The text is given in Schaff, III, pp. 707-729. Müller gives only the text of the *Institution of Churches,* pp. 652-656.

2. *The Declaration of 1833*

This Declaration is a popular compendium of older confessions, but "presents a milder form of Calvinism" (Schaff). It was drawn up by Dr. Redford of Worcester and other members of a commission of the "Congregational Union of England and Wales," which was organized in 1831. In 20 short articles the "Principles of Religion" are set forth. Art. 1 professes the divine inspiration of Scripture, but it must be studied "by the aids of sound criticism." Art. 6 deals with original sin and declares that it is "a fatal inclination to moral evil." In Arts. 7 and 14 election is reflected only weakly. In general the doctrinal conceptions are vague. To these articles there is appended "Principles of Church Order and Discipline," in 13 articles. The text can be found in Schaff, III, pp. 730-734; also in Müller, pp. 889-903.

3. *The Cambridge Platform, 1648*

The Congregationalists in America settled for the most part in Massachusetts. In America the Synod of Cambridge in 1648 drew up a church order based on the doctrinal teaching of Henry Barrowe. The Cambridge Platform also adopted the Westminster Confession, except "those things which have respect to church government and discipline." The Synod of Boston in 1680 adopted the Savoy Declaration together with the Cambridge Platform.

4. *Declaration of Faith of the National Council of Boston, 1865*

This Declaration was drafted by the National Council of Congregational Churches which was held in Boston in 1865. The draft was made by a commission of three theologians including Thompson, Lawrence, and Fisher. This commission did not wish to draft a new confession, but wanted only to refer to the Westminster Confession and the Savoy Declaration for those doctrines on which Congregationalists agree. The second draft by Fisher sought to emphasize the doctrines of the Trinity, incarnation, and atonement over against modernism. The third draft by Quint was adopted. The same assembly also adopted a new "Platform of Discipline." The Declaration first gives a historical introduction and then a short explanation in very general terms. The text is given in Schaff, III, pp. 734-736.

The confessional position of Congregationalism, also known as New England Theology, is in America no longer that of the Puritans. In the first half of the 18th century the Congregationalists underwent the influence of Arminian theology with Arian and Socinian leanings. Jonathan Edwards resisted this tendency and advocated a moderate Calvinism. His influence did not permeate very far. The doctrinal positions of the new theology were tolerated, although never adopted by the Congregationalists. "The old Calvinistic positions have one by one been abandoned, but something of the old Calvinistic spirit is left" (Selbie, *Congregationalism,* p. 177). For literature cf. Schaff, I, pp. 820, 821.

C. The Baptists

The Baptists came into existence in England under Charles I. In 1643 there were seven congregations in London. They suffered very much from persecution. A division between the Particular Baptists, who were Calvinistic, and the General Baptists, who were Arminian, developed in 1691. Not until 1891 was this division formally removed. The Baptists had the same judgment about the authority of creeds as did the Congregationalists, namely, they are mere declarations of faith, having no binding authority. Their view of church government is also the same as that of the Congregationalists. The Calvinistic Baptists differ from the Reformed position in infant baptism, and the Arminian Baptists also in the doctrine of election.

1. *The Confession of the Seven Churches of London, 1644*

This is an important confession of the Calvinistic Baptists. Daniel Featley, a prominent Episcopalian of the Puritan Party, in 1644 had a disputation with the Baptists, which he published. This was the occasion for a Confession of Faith which appeared in the name of the seven Baptist congregations of London. It appeared in 1644, three years before the Westminster Confession. In 1646 it was republished with several additions and changes. It consists of 52 articles and agrees with Reformed dogma everywhere except in respect to the sacraments and church government.

2. *The Confession of 1677*

This is the principal and most authoritative confession of the Calvinistic Baptists. It first appeared in London with the title: "A Confession of Faith put forth by the Elders and Brethren of many congregations of Christians baptized upon profession of their faith." Reprints appeared in 1688 and 1689; it was approved and recommended by preachers and "messengers" of more than a hundred congregations which met in London, July 3-11, 1689.

According to Dr. Angus it is still adhered to by all Baptists who hold to the doctrine of election and the perseverance of the saints. In America it was adopted by the Baptist Association which met in Philadelphia on September 25, 1742. Hence it is known in America as the *Philadelphia Confession.* It consists of 32 chapters, which begin with the doctrine of Holy Scripture and end with the Last Judgment. It is simply a Baptist recension of the Westminster Confession, just as the Savoy Declaration is the Congregationalist recension.

The principal differences are in the doctrines of the church and of the sacraments. At the end there is an appendix, which deals with baptism. The main differences from the Westminster Confession can be found in Schaff, III, pp. 738-741.

3. *Declaration of Faith, 1611*

The Arminian Baptists differ from the Calvinistic Baptists in the following points: they reject unconditional election and the perseverance of the saints, and they teach freedom of the will and the possibility of falling from grace. The Declaration of Faith was drawn up by Smyth and Helwisse for English refugees in Holland. It consists of 27 articles.

4. *Confession of the Free Will Baptists, 1834*

The Free Will Baptists were organized in 1780 by Randall as a separate Baptist Church. They also incline toward Arminianism. Their Confession of Faith was adopted by a general conference of Free Will Baptists of America in 1834. It was revised in 1848, 1865, and 1868. It consists of 21 articles of which the text is given in Schaff, III, pp. 749-756. For literature, cf. Schaff, I, pp. 845-858.

D. The Methodists

The founder of Methodism is Wesley. The Arminian principles of Wesley soon became dominant in the movement. In America we find the Methodist Episcopal Church, which is definitely Arminian in doctrine and episcopal in church government. The Methodist Protestant Church of America, established in 1830, differs radically in respect to church government. Since 1850 there has also been a Free Methodist Church of North America.

1. *The Twenty-Five Articles of Religion, 1784*

These 25 Articles were drawn up by Wesley for the American Methodists and were adopted at a conference in 1784. They are really an abridgement of the Thirty-Nine Articles. Wesley omitted article 23 on government. He also left out articles 13 and 17, which deal with justification and predestination. In 1804 an article about the state was incorporated. The text is in Schaff, III, pp. 807-813.

2. *The Welsh Calvinistic Methodists*

Some of the Calvinistic Methodists later joined the Congregationalists. In Wales they became a separate congregation. The revivals of the second half of the 18th century prepared the way for church organization. In 1823 they published their own confession. The English edition was published in 1827. This confession consists of 44 chapters and in its spirit and manner of composition it resembles the Westminster Confession but is inferior to it. In Arts. 5, 12, and 34 it differs from the *25 Articles* of Wesley. These three articles deal with God, election by free grace, and the perseverance of the saints. The text of these three articles can be found in Schaff, I, pp. 903, 904.

3. *The Doctrine of Wesleyan Methodism*

Wesley was never greatly concerned about doctrine. He reduced the gospel to a minimum and thus the clear-cut delineation of the church was increasingly obscured. He was more interested in the application of Christian principles. Wesley posited as a condition of faith an abrupt break with the past and a public declaration that one had been saved. He taught the universality of divine grace. In Adam, our first covenant head, we all fell; in Christ, the second covenant head, we are all restored.

Regarding Wesley's doctrine of original sin Schaff remarks: "By virtue of the universal atonement, man, though born in sin, is held guiltless until he arrives at the point of personal responsibility" (I, p. 898). His view of conversion is unscriptural. One must be able to point to a given moment, one must have experienced something specific at that time, and one must be able to make a public declaration about it. Living faith is never wrought directly by divine power in the heart, but by man himself. One can lose his faith again if he falls into sin. Sanctification really belongs together with regeneration and is the work of a moment. Penitence and repentance precede faith and regeneration not only in order of time but also of sequence. Thus regeneration also becomes the work of man. Justification has too much of an ethical-subjective significance and too little juridical-objective significance. Wesley takes an anthropological point of view, for in everything he is concerned first of all with man.

Literature

Dr. J. D. du Toit, *Het Methodisme,* Amsterdam, 1903.

J. G. Bürkhardt, *Volständige Geschichte der Methodisten*, 2 Bande, 1795.

I. Taylor, *Wesley and Methodism.*

For further literature, cf. Schaff, I, pp. 882, 903.

E. The Quakers

We are dealing here with the *Religious Society of Friends,* of which George Fox was the founder. In 1650 Fox had to appear before Judge Bennett on the charge of blasphemy. Fox called upon the judge to quake before God. Bennett then mockingly called Fox a quaker. Thereafter the Religious Society of Friends was generally known by this name.

One of the supporters was William Penn, who moved to America and founded the Quaker state of Pennsylvania. The city of Philadelphia became a haven of refugs for persecuted Quakers.

The Quakers are more radical than the Congregationalists and the Baptists. They broke with historic Christendom and repudiated all external authority in religion. They are an ultra-subjective movement. Their dominant principle is the universal inner illumination. They reject the doctrine of predestination. Atonement through Christ has receded into the background, giving way to illumination. The atoning death of Christ has been set aside for the birth of Christ in the heart. Justification has been replaced by sanctification, which leads to perfection on this earth. Baptism has been wholly abolished, because one needs only the baptism of the Spirit.

The Lord's supper is a commemoration which those who have been born by the Spirit no longer need. Only those who have been illumined and called by the Holy Spirit can be ministers, whether they be men or women, learned or unlearned. Quakers have no confession which has binding authority. Creedal statements were drawn up for apologetic purposes.

1. *The Apology of Robert Barclay*

This is the most authoritative exposition of the teachings of the Quakers. It was drawn up by Robert Barclay in 1675 and addressed to King Charles II. This apology embraces 15 theological theses. It first appeared in Latin in 1675 and then in English and other languages. It was widely distributed by the Society as a standard doctrinal treatise. The text is found in Schaff, III, pp. 789-798.

2. *The Catechism of 1673*

Robert Barclay also wrote a Catechism in 1673. It deals with the teachings of the Christian faith in 14 chapters. The answers consist of quotations from the Holy Scriptures. The purpose is to show the complete agreement of the Quakers with Scripture. A short confession which is appended to the catechism consists of 23 articles.

F. The Waldensians

The Waldensian movement arose as a practical protest against the secularization of the church. Its founder is supposed to be Pierre Valdez (Valdo).

In N Italy we find the Lombardy Waldensians, who must be distinguished from the French Waldensians. After the Reformation they organized their church life according to the example of the French Swiss Reformation. The confession of faith which they sent to King Francis I was completely Reformed. In 1535 a violent persecution against them broke out in Provence. In vain did they appeal to the German princes for assistance.

In 1545 the persecution began anew. The persecution of the Waldensians in Dauphine and Piedmont began in 1570. They were persecuted everywhere. They became impoverished, their property was confiscated, and their villages were destroyed by fire. The news of this barbarous cruelty aroused the indignation of the entire Christian world. Oliver Cromwell proclaimed a day of humiliation and fasting. Financial assistance was rendered.

After these bloody persecutions a confession was drawn up by the Waldensians in 1655, in all likelihood by Jean Leger, who was the moderator of the congregations in Piedmont. Thus the text is given in Leger's *Histoire des Èglises Vaudoises,* 1669, I, pp. 112-116. The French and English translations appeared later. The confession, based on the Gallican Confession, is entitled *Briève Confession de Foy des Èglises Reformées de Piémont* and consists of 33 articles. The doctrines of predestination, justification, original sin, good works, etc., are on the whole genuinely Calvinistic. The Waldensian church has a presbyterian form of church government.

Literature

Preger, *Beiträge zur Geschichte der Waldenser.* Comba, *De Waldenzen, Hun Oorsprong en Geschiedenis.* Kampen, 1927.

G. The Socinians

Unitarianism, which was already widespread in Italy, Zevenbergen, and Poland, received its first comprehensive and scientific form from Laelius Socinus. His system was taken over by his nephew, Faustus Socinus. This system of dogma gradually became the theological property of all Unitarians in various countries. They are most numerous in Zevenbergen, England, and North America. Socinianism is more important for the rationalistic influence that it exercised on the science of theology than for its formation of separate sects. In Racow the *Gymnasium Bonarum Artium* was established. Famous Socinians came from this school. After 1625 Socinianism lost ground because of the very powerful activity of the Jesuits. In 1658 they were even threatened with death. Many then took refuge in Sicily. In Holland the Socinians later joined the Remonstrants or the liberal Mennonites.

The Socinians officially repudiated all conferences. Their deviations from the universal Christian faith we find in the following:

1. *Greater Catechism of Racow*

It appeared in Polish in 1605, after the death of Faustus Socinus. It consists of 10 sections, the latter part of which was written by him. After his death, it was completed by prominent men like Valentine Schmalz and Hieronymus Moskorovius. In 1608 it was published in German.

2. *Shortest Institute of the Christian Religion (Religionis Christianae Brevissima Institutio)*

This work was written by Faustus Socinus himself and was published in Racow in 1618. This and other works of Socinus can be found in *Biblio Fratrum Polorum*, vols. I and II.

3. *The Shorter Racow Catechism*

This shorter catechism was prepared by Schmalz "for the exercise of children." It first appeared in Polish and German in 1605, later in Latin, entitled *Brevis Institutio Religionis Christianae*.

4. *Confession of the Christian Faith (Confessio Fidei Christianae)*

This confession was formulated in 1642 by Jonas Schlichting in the form of a commentary on the Apostles' Creed, with a host of quotations from Scripture. Its only purpose is a defense of the Socinian beliefs before the secular authorities. In 1646 Polish and French translations appeared, in 1651 an improved Latin translation, in 1652 a Dutch, and in 1653 a German translation.

5. *Socinian Doctrine*

The Catechism of Racow nowhere speaks expressly of inspiration of Holy Scripture, but only refers to the credibility of the Scriptures. The NT alone is considered as the real source of revelation concerning the Christian religion. In their attitude toward the Scriptures the Socinians stand for free, rational, scientific enquiry. According to them the doctrine of the Trinity is contrary to Scripture and to reason. The Holy Ghost is not a personal, Divine Being. God is not omnipresent, nor is He omniscient. Predestination is rejected, for this would mean the negation of human freedom. Creation out of nothing is denied. God created the world from "pre-existing matter." Christ is the Son of God by adoption. The deity of Christ must be rejected, although on earth He was more than we are. Jesus is true man, but not an ordinary man. Before He assumed His ministry He ascended into heaven and was instructed there concerning all things He was to reveal to men about God. Substitutionary atonement for man is out of the question. The manner in which Christ accomplishes salvation presupposes the cooperation of man and faith as a condition of salvation. Since the moral strength of man has only been weakened by the Fall, it does require divine support, but it must and can cooperate to attain salvation. Man was created mortal. The image of God in man constitutes his dominion over all creatures on earth. Mankind as it presently exists is distinguished from the first human beings only in the fact that it is no longer sinless. Because of the continuation of sin, such a *habitus peccandi* has become so rooted in mankind that every natural man is polluted with the inclination to sin. However, this must not be construed as *peccatum originale*. Baptism and the Lord's supper are not means of grace, but useful ceremonies, although they are not necessary. Baptism really was ordained only as a solemnity for the Jewish and pagan converts; it was never intended for those who are born within Christendom. The Lord's supper was indeed instituted for all time, but only as a solemnity which gratefully reminds us of the death of Christ. There is no resurrection of the body; we shall have a spiritual body. The godless and Satan and his devils shall one day be destroyed. There are, therefore, no eternal punishments. The true church is "the company of those who hold and profess sound doctrine." From all this it is apparent that the Socinians are the predecessors of the Rationalists.

VI. CREEDS OF THE EVANGELICAL LUTHERAN CHURCH

With the Lutheran creeds we return to the Reformation. In its essence the issue in the Reformation was a decision pertaining to authority. The source of authority does not reside in the church but in the Word of God. That is the formal principle of the Reformation. And from it follows the material principle, namely, justification of the sinner by faith only. The formal and material principles of the Reformation are the basis of all Lutheran and Reformed creeds. The Reformation was not only a restoration, but also a regeneration. It was the greatest emancipation from the slavery of the medieval hierarchy, and the establishment of that freedom with which Christ has made us free.

The Lutheran churches are found especially in Germany, Denmark, Sweden, Norway, and the United States. The Evangelical Lutheran Church has manifested two tendencies. There was a more rigorous party represented by Flacius, Amsdorf, and Wigand. Initially, they were called "Flacians." Then there was a mediating party with Melanchthon as its leader. They have been called the Philippists. The difference between these two movements has concerned especially the relationship of the Lutherans toward Roman Catholics on the one hand and toward Calvinists on the other. Melanchthon sought union with both sides, but the rigorous Lutherans would have no part in this.

The creeds of the Lutheran Church have been published several times in a collection entitled *Concordiënbuch (Concordia).* The first edition appeared in Dresden in 1580. It was published in German and in Latin. It appeared in Dutch in 1715 as *Concordia* or *Lutherse Geloofsbelijdenis.* In 1922 it appeared in America as *Concordia* or *Book of Concord,* in which are included in English all the Lutheran creeds. Also included is a substantial historical introduction of 254 pages. In addition to the three ecumenical creeds, the *Concordia* also contains the Augsburg Confession, the Apology of the Augsburg Confession, the Smalcaldic Articles, the Smaller and Larger Catechisms of Luther, and the Formula of Concord.

A. Augsburg Confession

(Confessio Augustana), 1530

It was the wish of Charles V that religious questions should be settled once for all. He wanted to negotiate with the Protestants, and therefore he summoned a diet which was to assemble at Augsburg on April 8, 1530. The elector of Saxony then instructed Luther, Melanchthon, Buchenhagen, and Jonas to summarize Protestant doctrines with Scripture references. This was done in Torgau. Thus the Torgau Articles came into existence. When the arrival of the emperor was delayed, Melanchthon made use of the opportunity to revise the Torgau Articles as the second part of the Augsburg Confession. But Melanchthon had still another document, the 15 Articles which Luther had drawn up at Marburg on October 5, 1529, and which he a little later revised as the 17 Swabian Articles. This document constituted the first part of the Augsburg Confession. All this was done with the consent of Luther.

Charles V arrived in Augsburg on June 15, 1530. On June 20, 1530, the Diet was opened. The confession of the Protestants, the Augsburg Confession, was read on June 24. There was a copy in German and one in Latin. The emperor demanded that it be read in Latin, but at the insistence of the elector it was read in German. It made a favorable impression on many, for it was framed in a moderate tone. German and Latin copies were presented to the emperor. But even during the sessions of the Diet copies appeared which displayed greater or lesser variations. For this reason the Protestants decided to publish an authentic text. For the standard text of this confession we must rely wholly on Melanchthon's *editio princeps,* which he published in German and Latin in 1531. Melanchthon also prepared several other editions, and in his German text he revised several articles. These revisions concern form rather than content. But in the edition of 1540 he also made changes in the text. These changes have to do with human nature and justification, on which he inclined toward Roman Catholicism, and also with the tenth article about the Lord's supper, in which he sought to gain the good graces of the Reformed. This edition of 1540 is called the *Variata* (Altered), whereas the unrevised edition of 1531 is known as the *Invariata* (Unaltered). The elector of Saxony was dissatisfied with the *Variata,* and it was never officially recognized in Lutheran circles. Accordingly, the Augsburg Confession was included in the *Concordia* in 1580 in the Unaltered edition. It is the principal Lutheran creed. Schaff remarks: "The Augsburg Confession is the fundamental and generally received symbol of the Lutheran Church which also bears the name of the Church of the Augsburg Confession." It consists of two parts: the first part has 21 articles which are positive and dogmatic, based on the Swabian Articles. The second part is based on the Torgau Articles. It comprises 7 articles which deal with religious and ecclesiastical malpractices. The treatment is not systematic. The text is given in all editions of the *Concordia.* Schaff has the text in Latin and English. In the *Book of Concord* the text is in English, pp. 11-26. For literature on Lutheran symbols in general cf. Schaff, I, pp. 220, 221; on the Augsburg Confession, p. 225.

B. Apology of the Augsburg Confession

(Apologia Confessionis Augustanae), 1530, 1531

After the Augsburg Confession had been submitted, the emperor and the Diet of Augsburg of 1530 decided to have a refutation of the confession of the Lutherans drawn up. A commission of 20 members was appointed including, among others, Faber, Eck, Wimpina, and Cochlaeus. This refutation was framed in such a way that it repeatedly had to be revised. Finally it was revised in a form acceptable to the emperor. On August 30, 1530, it was read to the Diet as the confession of the emperor under the title *Responsio Augustanae Confessionis.* The Protestants later called it *Confutatio Pontifica* (Confutation). The Protestants were permitted to have a copy of the Confutation only on the express condition that they would make no public use of it, nor write anything against it. When the Protestants were asked to declare their agreement with it, they refused. Several articles of the Augsburg Confession were revised as a result of the Confutation, especially Art. 7 on the church, Art. 20 on faith, and Art. 21 on the veneration of saints. The second part of the Augsburg Confession was completely revised except for minor ecclesiastical practices. The Protestants urged Melanchthon to refute the Confutation. Melanchthon then formulated an "Apology of the Confession." The first draft was presented to the emperor on September 22, 1530, but he refused to accept it. Meanwhile Melanchthon had gotten hold of a copy of the entire Confutation. He left Augsburg with it and went to Wittenberg to revise the entire Apology. In 1531 he published it in Latin under the title *Apologia Confessionis Augustanae.* A German translation was prepared in the same year by Justus Jonas. In 1532 the Apology was officially adopted at a convent in Schweinfurt, and in 1537 it was officially subscribed by the Evangelical or Lutheran theologians at Smalcald. In this way it was formally declared to be a confession of the Lutheran Church and was included in the *Concordia.*

The Apology is a triumphant defense of the Augsburg Confession. It is seven times as long as the Confession and is the most learned of the Lutheran confessions. It is strongly polemic in character. All hope of reconciliation with the church of Rome was now frustrated. Consequently, we do not find in it a conciliatory tone toward Rome. The complete text is given in Müller, *Die Symbolische Bücher der Ev. Luth. Kirche Deutsch und Lateinisch,* 1890, pp. 71-271; and in *Book of Concord* in English, pp. 37-135.

For literature cf. Schaff, I, p. 243.

C. Articles of Smalcald *(Articuli Smalcaldi), 1537*

After the Diet of Augsburg in 1530, the Protestants cherished the expectation that a general council would soon be called. It appeared that this expectation would be realized when Pope Paul III summoned a general council which was to assemble at Mantua about May 23, 1537. Although the Protestants had formed no illusions about this council, nevertheless they did feel they should be prepared to make a witness. For this reason the elector of Saxony received the task of drawing up articles of faith which could become the basis for negotiations at the Council of Mantua. Before the end of 1536 Luther had completed his articles and presented them for review to Jonas, Buchenhagen, Amsdorf, Spalatin, and Melanchthon. These theologians signed the articles and on January 3, 1537, presented them to the elector. On February 15, 1537, they were presented to an assembly of Lutheran princes and theologians at Smalcald. There, without any public discussion, the articles were subscribed by the theologians. However, these articles were never used at the Council of Mantua. The Smalcaldic League decided not to send a representative. Moreover, the council was postponed until 1545, when it was held at Trent.

These articles of Luther were never officially adopted by the Smalcaldic League, but privately they were subscribed by all Lutheran theologians and preachers in Smalcald. This took place at a private meeting on February 26, 1537. Melanchthon alone added a declaration about the authority of the pope, which was challenged by Luther. He believed that the pope must be allowed supremacy over the bishops of Christendom, a supremacy which he possesses *originis jure humano.* This was for the sake of peace and common concord. Upon instruction of the princes Melanchthon wrote a treatise, *De potestate et primatu papae.* This treatise must be regarded as a supplement to the Augsburg Confession and the Apology. It was subscribed separately from the Smalcaldic Articles by the theologians. The first part of the treatise refutes the contention of the pope that he has supreme authority in church and state by Divine right. In the second part there is an exposition of what the authority and jurisdiction of bishops are.

From the outset the Smalcaldic Articles have had great authority and have been equated with a confession. Accordingly, they were subsequently included in the *Concordia* with Melanchthon's treatise as an appendix. The articles are obviously polemic in nature and differ from the Augsburg Confession as much as Luther differs from Melanchthon. They are aggressive and written in a tone which makes any reconciliation with Rome impossible. They are divided into three parts. The first part deals with the Trinity and the person of Christ. The second concerns those articles which pertain to the office and work of Christ. The third includes 15 articles dealing with other heads of doctrine. The first edition of 1538 is in Luther's own language, but with many changes. The other edition is a copy by Spalatin. This manuscript was placed in the archives at Weimar.

When the Weimar theologians later defended the strict teaching of Luther against the Wittenberg theologians, they published these articles in 1553 according to this manuscript. This edition is also included in the *Concordia*. The text is available in Müller, pp. 295-344. In the *Book of Concord* it is given in English together with the treatise of Melanchthon, pp. 136-156.

For literature cf. Schaff, I, p. 253.

D. Smaller and Larger Catechisms of Luther

During his Saxon visitation in 1527-1529 Luther was impressed by the ignorance of religious matters and the immorality prevalent among preachers and people. This induced him to compose his Larger Catechism in 1529. It is based on his catechism sermons of 1528. It became quite lengthy and is a continuous exposition without questions and answers. Thus it was not suited for young people, nor even for adults. He decided to prepare a shorter text which would be more on the level of the common folk. This Smaller Catechism he published as *Enchiridion* before the Larger Catechism. The Larger Catechism followed in April, 1529, and was intended more as a guide for fathers and pastors in their instruction of the children of the congregation. The Smaller Catechism soon became more famous than the Larger Catechism. It was used in schools, churches, and homes. The first Latin translation was made by Sauermann in September, 1529. Thereafter it was used in various Protestant countries. This catechism is excellent for the following reasons:

(a) it is free from all polemics;
(b) it contains the simple Christian faith and does not attempt to provide a complete doctrinal system;
(c) it avoids all scholastic language and tends to render Biblical truths in simple language for common people.

Although not originally intended as a confessional statement, nevertheless, it did acquire that status. Thus the Smaller and Larger Catechisms were included in the *Corpora Doctrina,* were sanctioned as symbols by the Formula of Concord, and were incorporated into the *Concordia.* The Catechisms consist of five parts: the Decalogue, the Apostles' Creed, the Lord's Prayer, Baptism, and the Lord's supper. In the later editions of the Smaller Catechism there has been added, since 1654, a sixth part, which deals with confession of sin and absolution. Usually this part is inserted between the sections dealing with baptism and the Lord's supper. The text is given in Müller, pp. 295-344; the Book of Concord, pp. 159-215; Schaff has only the text of the Smaller Catechism in German and English, III, pp. 74-92.

For literature cf. Schaff, I, p. 245.

E. Formula of Concord
(Formula Concordiae), 1577

Origin

This confession owes its origin to the doctrinal controversies in the Lutheran Church, particularly after the death of Luther. There were three main parties in the Lutheran Church:

1. The strict Lutheran party, also called Gnesio-Lutherane, with Magdeburg and the University of Jena as centers. The principal proponents were Amsdorf and Flacius.

2. The supporters of Melanchthon, the Philippists, also known as the synergistic and Crypto-Calvinists, with headquarters at the universities of Wittenberg and Leipzig. The chief supporters were Buchenhagen, Major, Strigel, and Pfeffinger.

3. Between these two extremes there was a central party, which played an important role in the great task of unification. Its supporters included Brenz, Andreä, and Chemnitz.

Religious Controversies in the Lutheran Church

To understand the content of the Formula of Concord we must briefly note the religious conflicts. They are described at length by Schaff, I, pp. 268-307. We mention only the various controversies.

1. The controversy with Flacius regarding original sin.
2. The synergistic controversy, especially in respect to free will. Melanchthon was synergistic.
3. The controversy with Osiander about justification by faith. Osiander taught that Christ is our justification only according to His Divine nature, whereas Stancarus said only according to His human nature.
4. The controversy regarding good works. Major affirmed that good works were necessary to salvation. Amsdorf said, "Bona opera perniciosa ad salem."
5. The controversy about law and gospel. Agricola was antinomian.
6. The eucharistic controversy between Luther and Zwingli and later with Melanchthon regarding the Lord's supper. Westphal was the strict Lutheran who called all who denied the bodily presence of Christ in the Lord's supper heretics.
7. The Christological controversy, which dealt with the *communicato idiomatum.* On this point there was disagreement between the followers of Melanchthon and those of Luther.
8. The Hades controversy, dealing with the descent of Christ into hell. The difference between Aepinus and Flacius was about time and manner.
9. The adiaphoristic controversy, relating to several ecclesiastical practices. Luther at times retained certain forms of RC worship.
10. The predestination controversy between Zanchius and Marbach.

Origin

In order to make an end to all these controversies, it was imperative that a general *corpus doctrinae* for the entire Lutheran Church be determined. Several theological conferences were held for this purpose. Especially Andreä and Augustus of Saxony were zealous in trying to restore the peace, but their efforts were of no avail. Nevertheless, Andreä persisted and published a document with 11 positive and 11 negative articles. This document met the approval of Chemnitz and Chytraeus and was amended by them. It is known as the *Swabian and Saxon Formula.* Meanwhile, at the urging of Prince George Ernst a form of unity was drawn up at Henneberg by the two Wittenberg theologians, Osiander and Bidenbach.

This formulary was approved by several theologians at the Maulbronn monastery. It is called the *Maulbronn Formula.* These two forms of unity became the basis for the Formula of Concord. The Swabian and Saxon Formula was considered too long and the Maulbronn Formula too short. Consequently Andreä advised that these two be combined into a single formula. The elector followed this advice and recommended a new meeting of Lutheran theologians. The result was that 18 theologians met at Torgau. The two formularies were utilized for preparing the so-called *Torgau Book* (Torgischen Buche). It is especially the work of Andreä and Chemnitz and was reviewed by the 18 theologians. On June 7, 1576, it was presented to the elector. Despite hostile objections, many expressions of approval were also received. This moved the elector to instruct Andreä, Chemnitz, and Selhecker to revise it again, but to make only the most necessary changes. They met at the Bergen monastery in Magdeburg. After numerous conferences, including some with Musculus, Chytraeus, and Körner, their work was completed. The result was the *Bergen Book,* which was sent to the electors of Brandenburg and Saxony. This *Bergen Book* is the *So-*

lida Declaratio. However, a brief summary was also prepared, the *Epitome*, which was included at the beginning. The whole constitutes the Formula of Concord. But now sanction and signature were still needed. The subscribing took place before 1577 in the greater part of the Lutheran lands.

Content and Text

Upon instructions of Augustus, it was not published until June 25, 1580, in commemoration of the 50th anniversary of the Augsburg Confession. Together with the other Lutheran creeds it was bound in a single volume under the name *Concordiënbuch* (or *Concordia*).

The Formula of Concord was drawn up in German. The final revision of the Latin text took place in 1584. The texts of the *Epitome* and the *Solida Declaratio* in English are given in the *Book of Concord*, pp. 216-296. Schaff presents only the text of the *Epitome* in Latin and in English, III, pp. 93-180.

The *content* concerns the several points of controversy previously mentioned. Only controversy 5 on antinomianism is dealt with in two articles:

5. the law and the gospel and
6. the third use of the law, its significance for the regenerate.

This leaves 11 articles. A 12th article was added which combats the Anabaptists, Schwenkfeldians, Arians, and Antitrinitarians. The Formula of Concord is the most controversial of Lutheran creeds. It never achieved general authority and was rejected by a number of Lutheran princes. Hesse, Anhalt, Tweebruggen, a part of Mecklenburg, and various cities did not adopt it. It was rejected also by Denmark. Many of the princes who repudiated it later became Reformed. It encountered vehement opposition from the Reformed camp.

F. Symbols of the Lutheran States' Churches

1. *Saxon Confession (Confessio Saxonica), 1551*

In the electorate of Saxony Melanchthon had the greatest influence. In 1551 the *Repetitio Confessionis Augustanae Saxonica* appeared, drawn up by Melanchthon. During the sessions of the Council of Trent, the German emperor invited the Protestant states to send delegates. Melanchthon did not expect anything to come from it, but he heeded the emperor's invitation none the less. He was requested to prepare a statement and exposition of the Augsburg Confession. In order to do this he and his friend Comarius went to the Prince of Anhalt in Dessau. Thus the Saxon Confession was formulated for the Council of Trent in May, 1551. It is not merely a repetition of the Augsburg Confession, but a revision which Melanchthon adapted to the changed circumstances. However, the confession does not reveal any tendency to deviate from the doctrinal positions adopted at Augsburg. This confession was not signed by princes, as was the Augsburg Confession, but only by the theologians: Buchenhagen, Pfeffinger, Camerarius, Major, Eber, Melanchthon, and the superintendents of the electorate of Saxony.

2. *The Würtemberg Confession (Confessio Würtembergica), 1551*

The Würtemberg Confession was drawn up for the same purpose, at the same time and in the same spirit by Brenz in the name of his prince, Duke Christopher, who had also decided to send delegates to the Council of Trent. Würtemberg also was on the side of Melanchthon. The first Reformers who labored there were Blaurer, a definite Zwinglian, and Schnepf, a Lutheran, and this naturally led to a controversy about the sacraments. In 1535 Brenz went to Würtemberg. He appended to the Würtemberg Church Order in 1536 a catechism which is definitely in the spirit of Melanchthon. In addition to the *Augustana* and the Apology, the *Loci* of Melanchthon were introduced as doctrinal norms in 1546.

In 1551 Brenz formulated the Würtemberg Confession, which was adopted in the same year by the Synod of Stuttgart and was also approved by Melanchthon. It is not as precise and clear as the Saxon Confession, but the point of view is the same. In respect to the Lord's Supper the *cum* is taught but not the *sub,* nor the *manducatio oralis.* In the same year Brenz also published a larger catechism in the same spirit. In March, 1559, Brenz subscribed a "Bekenntnis und Beicht" at the the Synod in Tübingen, in which the doctrine of ubiquity is fully professed.

For literature cf. Schaff, I, pp. 340, 341, 343.

VII. CREEDS OF THE ROMAN CHURCH

It is extremely difficult to make a listing of the creeds of the RC Church. This fact is related to the infallibility of the pope, which is a retroactive authority. Later Roman symbolists have collected all papal *ex cathedra* pronouncements and from them have drawn up the doctrines of the Roman Church. In part the ecumenical councils adopted the papal proclamations. And one must bear in mind that the word *creed* has a different meaning for Catholics from what it has for the Lutherans and the Reformed.

In the Roman Church creeds are more directly intended for the clergy, for they must believe and preach them. Only indirectly are they intended for the laity. If the laity only agrees to trust the church, that is sufficient.

The Roman Church accepts not only the Apostles' Creed, but also the decisions of the ecumenical councils. Rome has a large number of ecumenical councils, of which Trent is the 18th.

A. The Council of Trent

For the history of this important council cf. Schaff, I, pp. 90-96. This council was called in opposition to the Reformation and to introduce reform in the Roman Church. The necessity for reform was generally recognized. But political and ecclesiastical difficulties prevented such a council from meeting. Not until December 3, 1545, could the council assemble in Trent. It was opened by Pope Paul III. The sessions, with long intervals, lasted until December 4, 1563. Usually the sessions are divided into three periods: the first period under Paul III from 1545 to 1547; the second under Julius III from 1551 to 1552; and the third period under Pius IV from 1562 to 1563.

The decisions are divided into decretals and canons. Thus the subjects were dogma and church discipline. The decretals are divided into those which deal with faith, with reform, and with discipline. They are the positive statements about Roman dogma. Besides the decretals there are the canons, which condemn the doctrinal positions of dissenters with an *anathema sit.* Actually, the Jesuits dominated. Charles V and France demanded reform, but the council decided first to discuss doctrine and then the necessary reforms. Quite understandably, the doctrines of the Protestants were presented in a very one-sided manner, sometimes so much so that Protestants would scarcely have recognized them. The views of the Protestants were also partially mixed with heresy, heresies which the Protestants condemned with all their might. The official name of this Roman confession is *Canones et Decreta Dogmatica Concilii Tridentii, 1564.* The Council was concluded with a twofold damnation of all heretics, a double anathema.

The Council was recognized by Italy,

Portugal, Spain, France, Holland, Poland, and the Roman part of the German Empire. No attempt was made to introduce it in England. The Confession of Trent was also sent to Scotland, but without any result.

The Council of Trent was not an ecumenical council as Rome alleges. It was simply a Roman Synod at which the Greek Orthodox and Protestant churches were not represented. The Greek Orthodox were never invited, and the Protestants were condemned without a hearing. In the history of the Roman Church this is the most important ecclesiastical assembly. Not only was church reform brought about, but various ecclesiastical abuses were abolished; disciplinary reforms were introduced in respect to indulgences and the morals of the clergy. Thus the Council had good results for the Roman Church because many evils were banished. The original acts, drawn up by Bishop Angelo Massarelli, were deposited in the Vatican and remained there three centuries before they were published. The complete Latin text of the confession and an English translation are given in Schaff, II, pp. 77-206. The first extensive criticism of the decisions of Trent was written by Chemnitz in his *Examen Concilii Tridentii, 1565–1573.*

Content

Three matters were on the agenda:

a. settlement of religious differences;
b. reform of ecclesiastical abuses;
c. a crusade against unbelievers.

The influence of the Reformation is clearly evident at some points, although the council basically did not deviate from medieval Roman Catholicism. Under the influence of the Reformation, the Holy Scriptures are highly regarded, but the same authority is attributed to the apocryphal books as to the canonical. In addition to the Holy Scriptures, tradition was designated as a source of special revelation, and the Vulgate was declared to be the only authentic translation. In the fifth session original sin was discussed. Original sin is considered to be completely removed by baptism. The remaining lust (*concupiscentia*) is indeed fuel for sin but, viewed in itself, is not sin. This is the notable decision regarding *concupiscentia*: "This concupiscentia, which the Apostle sometimes calls sin, the holy Synod declares that the Catholic Church has never understood it to be called sin, as being truly and properly sin in those *born again,* but because it is of sin and inclines to sin" (Session V, c. 5). At this point Trent elevates the authority of the Roman Synod above the Holy Scriptures. Justification is the changing of the sinner into a righteous person. It is not the forgiveness of sin, but the inner renewal of man. This does not happen at once, but continues until death. The Council of Trent also taught that by every mortal sin the grace of justification is lost.

Session 15 dealt with the possibility of falling away from grace. This does not mean, however, that faith is lost. The fact that Rome rejects the perseverance of the saints does not prevent her from regarding a final perseverance as possible.

By baptism one partakes of justification. According to Trent this is *causa instrumentalis justificationis* (Session VI, c. 7).

In the sacrament grace is communicated *ex opere operato,* never only by faith in God's Word (Session VII, c. 4). At the Council of Trent the doctrine of transubstantiation was established (Session XIII, c. 4). The sacrifice of the mass effects penance and is satisfaction for all sins (Session XXII, c. 1). Confession is dealt with at length in Session XIV, c. 5. Rome also has the authority to absolve one from the punishment of sin. This is the basis for the theory of indulgences. Trent deals with indulgences in Session XXI. The pope "is possessed of that infallibility with which the divine Redeemer willed that His Church should be endowed for defining doctrine, regarding faith or morals" (Session IV, c. 4).

As a result of the Council of Trent morals in Rome improved visibly, and a sigh for reform passed through all lands. The Roman Church was mindful of its self-preservation.

Literature

Paolo Sarpi, *Istoria del concilio Tridentino, 1619.* Also in Schaff, I, pp. 90, 91.

B. Profession of the Tridentine Faith (Creed of Pius IV)
(Professio Fidei Tridentinae), 1564

At its last two sessions the Council of Trent expressed the necessity of a binding formula of faith (*formula professionis et juramenti*). This creed must be binding for all clergy and teachers. It was prepared by order of Pius IV in 1564 by a college of cardinals. It consists of twelve articles. The first article includes the Nicene Creed, and the remaining 11 articles in short propositions summarize all that was settled at Trent. Later, two articles were added, one on the immaculate conception of the Virgin Mary, and the other on the infallibility of the pope.

This formula of faith also has become the creed for Protestant converts who join the Church of Rome. From this Profession it is evident that the pope is placed above the councils. This appears in Art. 10, where the oath to the pope is made: "I promise and swear (*spondeo ac juro*) true obedience to the Bishop of Rome, as the successor of St. Peter, prince of the Apostles, and as the vicar of Jesus Christ."

Art. 12 clearly states that no one can be saved outside the Catholic faith (*extra quam nemo salvus esse potest*).

Art. 2 first deals with "the apostolic and ecclesiastical traditions." Characteristically, the Scriptures come after tradition in this confession. The doctrines of original sin, the mass, the sacraments, the eucharist, the adoration or veneration of the saints, the efficacy of indulgences, etc., all agree with the decisions of Trent. Schaff provides an English translation of the Profession in I, pp. 98, 99. The original text is in Schaff, II, pp. 207-210. For literature cf. Schaff, I, pp. 96, 97.

C. Roman Catechism
(Catechismus Romanus), 1566

The Council of Trent also proposed that a new catechism should be prepared for religious instruction in harmony with the decrees of the Council. The Roman Catechism was published under Pius V for the benefit of the clergy. It is a popular manual of theology. The first draft was by a commission appointed by the pope which included Leonardo Marini, Egidio Foscarari, Muzio Calini, and Francesco Fueiro. Several catechisms appeared before and during the sessions of the Council of Trent. Thus, two catechisms of the Jesuits appeared, prepared by Peter Canisius; a larger catechism for teachers (1554) and a shorter one for students (1566). But not a single catechism was satisfactory to the Council of Trent. The Council then requested Pope Pius IV to supervise the preparation of a catechism which would summarize in brief the doctrines of Trent. Of the four theologians to whom this task was assigned three were Dominicans. This explains the subsequent hostility of the Jesuits. Cardinal Borromeo directed the writing of the catechism.

Pius IV did not live to see the publication of the catechism. His successor, Pius V, submitted the text once again to another committee for revision. Finally it appeared in 1566 in Latin and Italian.

The catechism was intended primarily

as a manual for the clergy. It is divided into four parts: de Symbolo Apostolico, de Sacramentis, de Decalogo, and de Oratione Dominica. In brief outline it sets forth the entire Roman theology and for that reason this catechism remains an important source for our knowledge of Roman doctrine.

Because it was drawn up under Thomistic influence, there was opposition to it from the Jesuits. Accordingly, the official sanction of the RC Church was never received; but since Trent had committed its preparation to the pope, it was published with his authority. Therefore it must be considered as one of the witnesses to genuine Roman Catholicism. In addition to this catechism, several other catechisms are in use in the Roman Church. Almost every diocese has its own catechism.

D. Roman Bulls and Decrees

A. Kuyper observed: "In addition to concrete dogmatic pronouncements, we must also point to liturgies and church ordinances as having even stronger secondary symbolic authority" (*Encyclopaedie der heilige Godgeleerdheid,* III, p. 370). Of tertiary importance are the decisions of organic groups within the church as a denomination. As far as the Roman Church is concerned, the Roman bull definitely has symbolical authority because it really is on a par with the decision of a council. A bull is a papal ordinance which is issued on matters of great importance. Important bulls are prepared in the consistory of cardinals and are signed by the pope and the cardinals. They are called *bullae consistoriales.* A bull does not become legally binding upon signature, but upon proclamation. Well known is the bull "Unigenitus," which was issued by Pope Clemens XI against the Jansenist Paschasius Quesnel in 1713.

Thus Pope Pius IX on December 8, 1854, in St. Peter's Church at Rome proclaimed the immaculate conception of Mary in the bull "Ineffabilis Dei."

The bull "Syllabus" or encyclical was proclaimed by Pope Pius IX on December 8, 1864. This extraordinary document is a mixture of truth and error (Schaff). It is a protest against atheism, materialism, and other forms of error. It condemns religious and political freedom and indirectly confirms the infallibility of the pope.

Among the Roman *Liturgical Formularies* the *Missale Romanum* should be mentioned first. This is the official book of the Roman Church which contains the liturgy of the mass. The liturgy was issued by Pope Pius V in 1570 in compliance with a decree by the Council of Trent. It has received public, ecclesiastical approval in all countries and provinces. The *Brevarium Romanum* differs in that it gives the liturgy for the service of the mass. It consists of four parts and includes the public prayer and also the legends of the saints and martyrs. For literature cf. Schaff, I, p. 189.

E. The Vatican Council

More than 300 years after the Council of Trent Pope Pius IX decided to call a new ecumenical council. What the Council of Trent did in opposing the Reformation of the 16th century, the Vatican Council did against the radical and dangerous enemies—modernism, liberalism, and rationalism. Pope Pius IX even dreamed that he might be able to bring about a reconciliation with the schismatic Greek Orthodox Church and the heretical Protestant churches. However, that failed and so the Vatican Council was nothing more than a general Roman council. This council was opened in the Vatican on December 8, 1869, the festive anniversary of the immaculate conception of Mary. The council reached its climax when the decree of the infallibility of the pope was proclaimed on July 18, 1870. There was strong opposition to the proclamation of papal infallibility. According to the episcopal system in France, so-called Gallicanism, the bishops together with the pope represent the church at general councils. The judgment of the pope does not become valid until it is confirmed by the approval of the church. The Ultramontanists, a strong element in the RC Church, opposed this view. They strove for the complete independence of the pope from the bishops. The declaration of papal infallibility was thus a triumph for the Ultramontanist point of view.

Pope Pius IX himself read the decree relating to his infallibility in the *Constitutio Vaticana* or the bull *Pastor aeternus*. This decree consists of four parts: the institution of the primacy, the continuation of the primacy of Peter in the pope, the power and character of the primacy of the pope, and the infallibility of the pope.

At the third session on April 24, 1870, the dogmatic constitution of the Roman Church was established, the *constitutio dogmatica de fide catholica,* which consists of four chapters dealing with (1) God as creator, (2) revelation, (3) faith, (4) faith and reason. Then follow 18 canons in which the errors of pantheism, naturalism, and rationalism are condemned.

At the fourth session of July 18, 1870, the decree concerning papal infallibility was adopted: *The First Dogmatic Constitution of the Church of Christ* (*Constitutio Dogmatica Prima de Ecclesia Christi*). It consists of the four parts mentioned above. The sinlessness of Mary and the personal infallibility of the pope are the characteristic dogmas of modern Romanism. The doctrine of the immaculate conception of Mary "perverts Christianism into Marianism." The dogma of papal infallibility "resolves the church into the Pope." "The worship of a woman is virtually substituted for the worship of Christ, and the man-god in Rome for the God-man in heaven" (Schaff, I, p. 164).

Before the vote on this decretal, 115 delegates of the Council had already departed, for though they were opposed they did not dare vote against it. The result was that 533 voted for it. Thus the Jesuits triumphed. Those opponents who were theologians continued their opposition. Söllinger and Friedrich of Munich, Reinkens and Weber of Breslau, and Reusch and Langen of Bonn never did consent, but gave the impetus toward the formation of the Old Catholic Church in Germany.

Literature:

J. Friedrich, *Geschichte des vatikanischen Concils,* Bonn, 1877–1883.

E. de Pressensé, *Le Concil du Vatican, son histoire et ses conséquences,* Paris, 1872.

S. H. ten Cate, *Het Vaticaansche Concilie,* Zwolle, 1872.

K. Marten, *Die Arbeiten des Vatikanischen Concils,* Paderborn, 1873.

C. Manning, *The True History of the Vatican Council,* London, 1877.

For further literature cf. Schaff, I, pp. 134, 135. For the decretals and text cf. Schaff, II, pp. 234-271.

F. The Old Catholics

The Old Catholic movement began at the time of the Vatican Council. But it was not organized as a church until 1873, at Constance. The Old Catholic Church in Germany and Switzerland arose especially as a protest against Roman absolutism and the infallibility of the Vatican Council. Leaders included Döllinger, Reinkins, and Huber. Döllinger could not abide by the Vatican decrees, and publicly so declared. On April 17, 1871, he was excommunicated because he was guilty of "the crime of open and formal heresy." Later on, other differences with Rome also developed, such as the *perspicuitas Scripturae.* In 1874, 14 theses were formulated at a conference in Bonn. This conference was attended by Greek and Episcopal theologians. A second conference at Bonn in 1875 dealt with the *Filioque* in the Greek spirit. The decrees of the two conferences are given in Schaff, II, pp. 545-554.

For literature cf. Schaff, I, p. 191.

VIII. CREEDS OF THE EASTERN ORTHODOX CHURCH

The official name of the Eastern Orthodox Church (often called the Greek Orthodox Church) is the Holy Orthodox Catholic Apostolic Eastern Church. This church includes the Greek Church in Turkey, the national Church of Greece, and the national Russian Church. They call themselves orthodox because they reject all confessional development after the ecumenical councils as heterodox. In 867 a council was held in Constantinople. Even at that early time the W Church was accused of falsifying doctrine by the inclusion of the word *filioque* in the confession. The tension between E and W mounted until a schism arose on July 16, 1054. The one apostolic church was rent and the Eastern Orthodox Church came into being. The great difference with the W Church is the confession that the Holy Spirit proceeds only from the Father, and thus not from the Son. Besides, there are the following points of difference: The E Church recognizes no visible vicar of Christ on earth and rejects the dogma of an infallible head of the church. It teaches one visible, infallible church. In the sacraments a distinction is made between sacraments of a higher order (baptism, Lord's supper, confession) and those of a lower order (the other four). Only bishops are forbidden to marry.

No one within the Eastern Orthodox Church has prepared a collection of its later confessions. A Protestant, E. J. Kimmel, in 1843 published such a collection: *Libri Symbolici ecclesiae orientalis; nunc primum corpus collegit* (Jena).

The E Church adopts the doctrinal decrees of the first seven ecumenical councils. Reformed theologians in general have also been willing to adopt the decisions of the first six ecumenical councils. The E Church annually commemorates these seven "sacred" councils. Since the seventh ecumenical council this church has undergone no essential dogmatic changes.

We must distinguish the Greek-Catholic Church from the Eastern Orthodox Church. The Greek-Catholic Church is that of the united Greeks in Poland, Gallicia, Hungary, etc. Subject to certain conditions, it united with the Roman Catholic Church. We are now dealing with the Eastern Orthodox Church.

A. John of Damascus

The last intellectual product of the Eastern Orthodox Church was the 8th-century work of John of Damascus entitled *Exposition of the Orthodox Faith.* In this work he attempts to organize the doctrine of the orthodox fathers into a system. This work almost possessed symbolical authority.

B. Orthodox Confession of Mogilas

This is the *Confessio Orthodoxa* which was prepared in the form of a catechism for use in the Russian Church.

Occasion

Since 1595 the Jesuits in Poland have succeeded in causing a large number of the clergy in Lithuania and in the W provinces of Russia to become apostate. Various synods even promised submission to the pope. Moreover, a Calvinistic movement developed under Cyril Lucaris. This became the occasion for Petrus Mokilas, Metropolitan of Kiev, to prepare a document which would make an end of this confusion. The actual text was prepared by Kosslowski in

1640. It is called "The Orthodox Confession of the Catholic and Apostolic Oriental Church." It combats both Protestantism and Roman Catholicism. At the Synod of Moldau in 1642 it received official sanction and was signed by the patriarchs of Constantinople, Alexandria, Antioch, and Jerusalem. In 1672 it was once again expressly adopted at the Synod of Jerusalem.

In 1723 Peter the Great had it included in the Russian Church Order. It consists of three parts: faith, hope, and charity. The first part is an exposition of the Nicene Creed; the second part consists of the Lord's Prayer and the Beatitudes; and the third part deals with the Decalogue. It was printed in Greek and Latin in 1662. The complete text is given in Schaff, II, pp. 275-400. Although it is a collection of pronouncements without any connection, this document has the character of a creed. Apologetically, it is conservative.

Content

The confession professes that baptism washes away sins and confers regeneration conformable to the dead and risen Christ. Concerning the Lord's supper, it teaches that the holy eucharist is the body and blood of Christ under the form of bread and wine, Christ being truly and actually or *kata ta pragma* present.

Whereas baptism remains absolutely essential, this cannot be said of the eucharist. Baptism again stands higher than the eucharist in the sense that its content communicates greater things. Baptism is the first step, the eucharist is the objective as far as life in the church is concerned. Those who die after baptism can be saved without the eucharist. But those who remain living cannot do without the eucharist, for through it they receive while on earth full possession of all that Christendom and the church give. For in the eucharist one learns to know and to enjoy Christ. In the eucharist Christ is on earth; otherwise He is in heaven.

The eucharist has these effects: "remembrance of Christ's suffering, reconciliation with God, propitiation for the sins of the living and the dead, and deliverance from the temptation of the Devil" (Q. 107).

Priests have the authority to forgive sins and to teach (Q. 109). The Greek priesthood is more mystagogical than hierarchical.

In respect to good works the Orthodox Confession professes: "For eternal salvation the essential conditions are *recta fides et bona opera* [right faith and good works]" (Q. 1). Faith is based on the written word of Christ and the apostles in the Holy Scriptures and on *oral tradition* (Orth. Conf., p. 169).

The Holy Spirit proceeds only from the Father, not from the Son (Orth. Conf. p. 69). Human nature is not totally depraved, but weakened to a high degree (Orth. Conf. p. 87). Purgatory does not exist (p. 132).

C. Confession of Cyril Lucaris

Cyril Lucaris was a man who traveled extensively. In Switzerland he became acquainted with the doctrines of the Reformation. He then conceived the plan to ingraft the Protestant doctrines into the ecumenical creeds of the E Church. He ever sought the reformation of his church. He constantly kept in correspondence with foreign theologians, including the Archbishop Abbot of Canterbury. In succession he was the Patriarch of Alexandria and Constantinople. He opposed the papacy and jesuitry. His desire was to combat superstition and to raise the academic level of Greek theology and of the church. For this reason he prepared a creed, first in Latin in 1629 and then in Greek in 1631. It was published in both languages at Geneva in 1631. His creed was never adopted by any party in the E Church, but was repeatedly condemned as being heretical. In his creed there appears the highly significant expression concerning the Holy Spirit: He proceeds from the Father through the Son. The author was definitely Reformed in his sympathies. His doctrine of salvation in particular is distinctly Reformed in character. The confession aroused a great deal of opposition, notably among the Jesuits.

And thus Lucaris did not achieve his goal. He was strangled to death in 1638 and his body cast into the Bosphorus. His creed is considered so important that it was included in the 1654 edition of the *Corpus et Syntagma* of the Reformed.

For literature cf. Schaff, I, p. 54.

D. Confession of Dositheus

The creed of Cyril Lucaris was condemned as heretical and godless at the Synod of Constantinople in 1638 and of Jassy in 1642. Later the synod met at Jerusalem in 1672 for the consecration of the restored Church of the Holy Nativity at Bethlehem. E Orthodoxy was represented by prominent leaders in the church. The chairman was Patriarch Dositheus. Schaff calls this synod the most important one in the modern history of the E Church and comparable to the Council of Trent. This synod, like that of Trent, condemned the doctrines of Protestantism.

The Synod of Jerusalem followed the order of the Confession of Cyril Lucaris exactly, but in an anti-Calvinistic spirit. The Confession of Dositheus, also called *Aspis Orthodoxias* (shield of orthodoxy), was formulated. Under this title it was published at Paris in 1676. Schaff says of this confession: "It is the most authoritative and complete doctrinal deliverance of the Modern Greek Church on the controverted articles" (I, p. 62). It consists of 18 articles which present "a positive statement of orthodox faith." The first six chapters are directed against the Confession of Cyril Lucaris; then follows an exposition of the orthodox faith as prepared by Dositheus. This therefore is the *shield* which must guard against Protestant attacks. Biesterveld calls it "a good representation of the Greek Orthodox tradition."

Content

Art. 1 deals with the doctrine of the Trinity and states that the Holy Spirit proceeds only from the Father. Art. 2 points out that the Scriptures must be interpreted only according to the tradition of the Catholic Church. Art. 3 teaches that God elects those "who would, in his foreknowledge, make good use of their free will in accepting salvation." Arts. 4 and 5 deal with creation and providence. Art. 6 relates to the Fall. Christ and the Virgin Mary are sinless. Arts. 7 and 8 are concerned with the incarnation and the work of Christ and also the intercession of Mary and the saints. Art. 9 points out that no one can be saved without faith. Art. 10 deals with the Holy Catholic and Apostolic Church which, with Christ as its only head, is ruled by bishops in an unbroken succession. Arts. 11 and 12 also deal with the church. Art. 13 states that man is not justified by faith alone, but also by works. Art. 14 states that man is debilitated by sin, but has not lost his intellectual and moral nature. He still has a free will to do the good. Art. 15 deals with the seven sacraments; Art. 16 with the necessity of baptism for "baptismal regeneration." Art. 17 deals with the eucharist. The Lutheran doctrine is rejected and the Roman doctrine of transubstantiation is most emphatically taught. Art. 18 states that there is no purgatory. Those who die in the state of penitence go to Hades, but they may be delivered by the prayers of the priest and especially by the unbloody sacrifice of the mass.

The complete text is given in Greek and Latin in Schaff, II, pp. 401-445.

To these articles there are appended four questions and answers. The first prohibits the general and indiscriminate reading of the Holy Scriptures. The second denies the perspicuity of the Holy Scriptures. The third establishes the number of books in the canon. The fourth teaches the veneration of the saints, but especially of the mother of God, who is the object of *hyperdulia.*

E. Confession of Metrophanes Cristopulus

This confession appeared a little earlier than that of Lucaris: Cristopulus attended several European universities and later became a patriarch. At the synod of 1638 he chose sides against Lucaris. He formulated a confession during his stay at Helmstadt in 1625. It was published later, in 1661. In 23 loosely related chapters, it presents Greek doctrine and ritual. It polemizes strongly against Rome, but not against the Protestants.

Although it is a private exposition of the Greek faith and cannot be considered an authoritative source for Greek doctrine, nevertheless it is of special importance for symbolics. It never received ecclesiastical sanction. Though it is generally orthodox, it does present a more liberal and progressive aspect of Eastern theology.

It excludes the apocryphal books from the canon. A distinction is made between the sacraments of a higher order (baptism, communion, penance) and those of secondary significance (the remaining four).

For literature cf. Schaff, I, p. 52.

F. Confession of Gennadius

The *Confession of Gennadius* is of subordinate importance. After the capture of Constantinople in 1453, Sultan Mohammed II authorized the election of a new patriarch. Georgius, named Gennadius, was then elected.

After a conversation with the Sultan, Gennadius prepared and presented a creed in defense of Christian doctrine. It provides a survey of the faith of the church in those matters in which the conflict with Mohammedanism stands out. These do not touch the differences between the Greek and Roman churches. The confession provides no particulars about the Greek faith, but gives expression only to the general truths of the Christian religion. The original text is in Greek. Although it is not a normative, ecclesiastical symbol, it is highly esteemed. In 20 short sections it deals with the fundamental doctrines of God, the Trinity, the two natures of Christ and His work, the immortality of the soul, and the resurrection of the body.

For literature cf. Schaff, I, p. 46.

G. Doctrinal Standards of the Russian Orthodox Church

This church is the Russian branch of the Eastern Orthodox Church.

1. *The Catechism of Platon, 1764*

This catechism can be designated as a subsidiary symbol. Platon was the Metropolitan of Moscow. He drew up the catechism more particularly for his student, the Grand Duke Paul Petrowitsch. It was published in Russian.

2. *The Catechism of Philaret*

Philaret was Metropolitan of Moscow. In 1839 his catechism, which had been approved by the Synod of Petersburg, appeared. It was translated into several languages and was used in schools and churches. It follows the plan and division of the Confession of Mogilas, but it is clearer and more practical. It was sent to all the E patriarchs and was unanimously approved by them. At present it is the most authoritative norm of the Russian Orthodox Church.

Schaff provides only the English translation (II, pp. 445-542). Like the Orthodox Confession of Mogilas, it consists of three parts. The first part is an exposition of the Nicene Creed. In the doctrine of the church the [Protestant] distinction between the visible and invisible church was adopted in slightly modified form. Christ is the only head of the church. The heading of Part I is faith.

The second part deals with hope. It is an exposition of the Lord's Prayer and the nine Beatitudes of the Sermon on the Mount. The third part concerns love or charity. It is an exposition of the Decalogue, which concludes with Luke 17:10: "When ye shall have done all those things which are commanded you, say, we are unprofitable servants; we have done that which it was our duty to do."

The following are Philaret's answers in respect to the sacraments. The definition of a sacrament is given in Q. 284: "A mystery or sacrament is a holy act, through which grace, or in other words, the saving power of God, works mysteriously upon man." Baptism washes away sin and grants regeneration conformable to the dead and risen Christ. Baptism is a sacrament by which man "dies to the carnal life of sin, and is born again of the Holy Ghost to a life spiritual and holy" (Q. 288). Why are children baptized? "For the faith of their parents and sponsors, who are also bound to teach them so soon as they are of sufficient age to learn" (Q. 292).

Concerning communion he states: The priest may administer the eucharist only on an altar with an altar cloth. The water and the wine must be mixed (Q. 332). In answer to the question what is required of the penitent, it is said: "Contrition for his sins, with a full purpose of amendment of life, faith in Jesus Christ and hope in His mercy" (Q. 353).

Penitence is exercised by *epitimia.* To the question what *epitimia* is, the answer is: "The word means punishment. Under this name are prescribed to the penitent, according as may be requisite, diverse particular exercises of piety, and diverse abstinences or privations, serving to efface the unrighteousness of sin and to subdue sinful habit, as, for instance, fasting beyond what is prescribed for all, or for grievous sins suspension from the holy communion for a given time" (Q. 356).

For literature cf. Schaff, I, p. 68.

P. J. S. de Klerk

CONFIRMATION. In its beginnings, confirmation (from the Latin *confirmare,* "to establish or make firm") consisted in the laying on of hands and the anointing of the forehead of the baptized confessor with oil in the form of a cross. This was to symbolize that he was endued with the Holy Spirit and consecrated to the spiritual priesthood of believers. As time went on the authority to confirm was restricted to bishops, supposedly in accordance with Acts 8:17, as those who were successors of the apostles. This meant that the rite was frequently delayed after Baptism until the bishop could be present. The W church extended this delay until the age of puberty, when the children who were baptized as infants were to say the Lord's Prayer and the Ten Commandments as taught by the priest and were to confess their faith in the words of the creed. The E church extends to priests and deacons the authority to confirm. They give the rite even to infants, so that Baptism and confirmation have remained together in the Greek usage. Cyprian, in the earlier part of the 3rd century, was the first of the Fathers to speak loosely of two sacraments. But especially in the W, where Baptism and confirmation were ordinarily separated in time, the latter evolved into a full sacrament with all the proper accoutrements. The name "confirmation" is a W usage, dating from about the 5th century. It is officially defined in the RC Church as "the sacrament through which the Holy Ghost comes on us in a special way to enable us to profess our faith as strong and perfect Christians and as soldiers of Jesus Christ." It is ordinarily to be administered by a bishop who shall pray for the Holy Ghost, laying hands on each person's head, signing them with the cross in the name of the Holy Trinity, and using holy chrism on the forehead. Holy chrism is defined as "a mixture of olive oil and balm, blessed by the bishop on Holy Thursday. This act, which is limited to those in a state of grace, increases this grace and imprints a lasting character on the soul" (cf. *A Catechism of Christian Doctrine*, rev. ed. of *The Baltimore Catechism*, Paterson, 1941, ques. 330-342).

The Reformers minced no words concerning this pseudo-sacrament. Luther, in his *The Babylonian Captivity of the Church* in the section on confirmation, called it "foolery and lying prattle devised to adorn the office of the bishops that they might at least have something to do in the church." Going beyond Luther's evocative satire, Calvin scorched the page with his pen as he wrote of that preposterous mimicry by which men seek salvation in oil: "They have so far lost all shame as to deny that Baptism can be rightly performed without confirmation" (*Institutes*, IV, xix, 8); "Sacrilegious mouth, dost thou dare to place an unction which is only defiled by thy fetid breath and enchanted by the muttering of a few words, on a level with the sacrament of Christ, and to compare it with water sanctified by the Word of God?" (*ibid.*, IV, xix, 10). In spite of this, confirmation in some form or other has been maintained by several Protestant churches. In 1539, Bucer reintroduced among the Lutherans of Hesse an ordinance of confirmation as an antidote to anabaptist protests that infant Baptism led nowhere because no one taught the children the need of repentance and faith. From this beginning confirmation spread to all parts of the Lutheran communion. In 1548 Melanchthon acquiesced when the Augsburg *Interim* went so far as to style it "a sacrament necessary to salvation." Flacius vigorously protested, and others sought to eradicate the superstition and emphasize the thought of instruction as the chief matter (cf. W. Diehl, *Zur Geschichte der Konfirmation*, as cited in Johannes Warns, *Die Taufe*, Cassel, 2nd ed., p. 166 f.). Thus confirmation has become a permanent feature of Lutheranism down to the present day, occurring at the time that a child renews his baptismal vows and is received into full membership in the church.

Of all the churches stemming from the Protestant Reformation, the Anglican Church has given the most attention to confirmation. The "Order of Confirmation" was retained in the Book of Common Prayer for the first and is obviously written from the standpoint of infant Baptism. The child confirms what his sponsors did for him in Baptism.

There have been those who feel that this deprives confirmation of its true status and makes it simply an appendix to Baptism. One Anglican work which explores this question is A. J. Mason's *The Relation of Confirmation to Baptism.* In this treatise Mason argues that the Reformed tradition in its repudiation of Roman confirmation went too far and thus enriched Baptism at the expense of the doctrine of the laying on of hands. He then proceeds to argue from the receiving of the Spirit by the laying on of apostolic hands, as in the case of the Samaritans in Acts 8, that we have here the true NT basis for confirmation. The laying on of hands is not, indeed, a third sacrament, but it is a constituent element of holy Baptism in the broader sense of Christian initiation. Baptism should be a double sacrament, even as in the Eucharist we ought to communicate in both bread and wine.

More recently, in a document entitled "Confirmation Today, Being the Schedule Attached to the Interim Reports of the Joint Committees on Confirmation as Presented in the Convocations of Canterbury and York in October, 1944," the position is taken that confirmation is a kind of lay ordination which may be postponed even beyond the time of first communion. The position Mason had espoused is rejected: "It is difficult to believe that any of the gifts needful to fulfill the blessings conferred by Baptism are withheld until the later rite of confirmation is received. We cannot but believe they are included in the original grace and are operative from Baptism onwards" (*ibid.*, p. 11.) L. S. Thornton calls this an "astonishing pronouncement" and complains that it removes all theological significance from confirmation (*Confirmation Today*, p. 6 f.). Dom Gregory Dix concurs. In his Oxford Lectures, *The Theology of Confirmation in Relation to Baptism*, he regards the dissociation of confirmation from Baptism as a medieval error which degrades the Baptism of the Spirit to a mere augmentation of the grace of Baptism. For all these protests, it seems that in the Church of England, as in other communions practicing the rite, confirmation will be regarded for a long time to come as the way in which infant Baptism is most properly brought to completion.

It does not appear, however, that it will ever be reinstated as a full sacrament in any Protestant church. Indeed, we might say that any communion which gives confirmation such status would no longer be truly Protestant, since the Scripture is the final norm of faith and practice and since it is not possible to find a definitive, clear basis for it in the NT.

CONGREGATION, a term used to translate several words denoting the idea of a "gathering."

A word found over 200 times in the OT, מוֹעֵד *mō'ēdh*, meant "an appointed time," "appointed place" or "meeting," and occurred in this sense in the Hebrew phrase translated "tent of meeting" (AV "tabernacle of the congregation"). A related form עֵדָה (*'ēdhâ*) described a company of people assembled together by appointment (cf. Ex. 16:1-2), occurring nearly 150 times in the OT. It designated the responsible citizens of the nation with Moses as their head.

The word קָהָל (*qāhāl*), derived from a root meaning "assemble together," was used in the sense of Israel as a theocratic community being gathered together by God (cf. Deut. 5:22). In Ezekiel it was applied to foreign military and naval forces (Ezek. 17:17; 24:36; etc.). In post-exilic Biblical literature the use of the term was virtually identical with that of עֵדָה (*'ēdhâ*).

A rare term, עֲצֶרֶת (*'asereth*), from a root "to restrain," "to confine," was rendered "solemn assembly" in the context of the important Israelite feasts (Lev. 23:36; Deut. 16:8) and underlies the "general assembly" of Hebrews 12:23.

In the LXX (Septuagint translation), ἐκκλησία (*ekklēsia*) was used to render both קָהָל (*gāhāl*) and עֵדָה (*'ēdhâ*), though συναγωγή (*synagōgē*) was also employed for the latter. Where ἐκκλησία (*ekklēsia*) occurs in the NT it is normally translated "church," but it is found in the classical sense of a "convened political gathering" in Acts 19:39.

The AV of Acts 13:43 rendered συναγωγή (*synagōgē*) by "congregation" (RV, RSV, "synagogue"). To mark their distinctiveness the early Christians described themselves as ἐκκλησία (*ek-*

klēsia), since συναγωγή (*synagōgē*) had come to be used of both the congregation and the church.

See SANHEDRIN, SYNAGOGUE.

CONGREGATIONAL CHURCH, THE, a further development in Colonial America of Congregationalism (*q.v.*) which had risen in England. It had its colonial origins in the founding of the Plymouth Colony by the Pilgrims under John Robinson, their pastor. Robinson had already moved from the first nonseparatist stage of Puritan dissent into the second stage of dissent known as independency or semi-separatism, or the Middle Way. This Middle Way was a mediating position between Presbyterianism on the one side and Brownism or strict democracy on the other.

The nonseparatist congregationalists, who came to Massachusetts Bay under John Winthrop in 1630, were Puritans who regarded themselves as part of the Church of England and under the jurisdiction of the Bishop of London. However, since they were separated by such a great distance from London, in practice they were operating under principles little different from the separatists in Plymouth. In addition, the basic Calvinism of the Pilgrims tended to dissipate suspicion.

An advanced party had established a church on the congregational model at Salem in 1629 on the basis of a simple covenant: "We covenant with the Lord and with one another, and do bind ourselves in the presence of God, to walk together in all his ways, according as he is pleased to reveal himself unto us in his blessed word of truth." In 1630 two additional churches were formed on this model at Boston and Watertown.

However, when the colony grew, the action of the Massachusetts General Court in 1631, requiring that the franchise should be limited to those who were members of the Congregational Church, had the effect of making the churches into a state church, a result quite contrary to the cherished convictions of the English separatists. It is to be noted here that there was a contradiction between the classical statement of congregationalism and the actual practices of the churches at that time. Instead of an association of independent congregational churches, a single Congregational Church came about. This connection between the franchise and membership in the Congregational Church became characteristic of the congregationalism of the Massachusetts Bay and New Haven colonies. There was a growing tension between the original position of the dissenters in England in their demand for religious toleration and local autonomy for the church and their intense conviction that theirs was the one true faith, with the resulting intention to found a Bible Commonwealth in which that true faith could be zealously guarded in the New World.

This determination on the part of the Puritan leadership is a major factor in any attempt to understand the rigidity of Massachusetts Bay policy during the seventeenth century toward Roger Williams and other forms of dissent from the Puritan position. Williams not only posed a threat to the church, but to the state as well. When he arrived in Boston in 1631, he refused to have fellowship with the churches because of their refusal to repent publicly for having communion with the Church of England before they came to New England. He also opposed the Puritan contention that the magistrates were responsible for enforcing the first table of the Decalogue. He did, however, become pastor of the church at Salem. In 1635 the controversy between Williams and the General Council came to a head because of a certain letter he had written. The General Council ordered Williams to be deported in 1635. This dispute became a factor in the early movement of the churches of Massachusetts Bay away from separatism. The impulse was further strengthened by the antinomian controversy involving Anne Hutchinson, Henry Vane, and John Wheelwright, all of whom had arrived in Boston in the years from 1634 to 1636. The controversy involved not only the relationship of the Christian to the law of God but also the claim of extra-Biblical revelation. It was decided to hold a general synod at Cambridge. Ministers and elders from the various churches gave forceful expression to the sense of community which was slowly developing. In accordance with the findings of this synod, the General Court passed sentence on Anne Hutchinson, and she was banished to Rhode Island.

The doctrinal unrest and the meeting of the Westminster Assembly in England had a profound effect on the development of New England congregationalism. The Massachusetts General Court summoned another synod to meet at Boston in 1646 for the purpose of considering problems of church government and discipline. Because of disagreements and the outbreak of a plague in Boston it was not able to get down to business until 1648. By this time the Westminster Confession of Faith had been completed and was approved by the General Assembly of the Church of Scotland and by the English Parliament. The synod, meeting at Cambridge, adopted the Cambridge Platform, which had been drawn up by John Cotton as a statement of congregational polity in contrast to the presbyterianism of the Westminster Confession. Nevertheless, the Westminster Confession was accepted as an adequate expression for congregational theology. The Cambridge Platform remained as the model for polity in Massachusetts throughout the colonial period but was replaced in Connecticut in 1708. A synod in Boston in 1680 adopted the Savoy Confession (a recension of the Westminster Confession) as a more suitable doctrinal standard for Massachusetts congregationalism. Also the Synod of Saybrook in Connecticut adopted the Savoy Declaration along with the Westminster Confession for its standards.

The year 1648 marks the end of the formative era in the history of American congregationalism and the beginning of a new period in which the doctrine and the polity agreed upon at Cambridge would be subjected to a severe testing. The immediate cause of the first great crisis is to be found in the demand that church membership should be a prerequisite for the franchise in Massachusetts Bay. To broaden the franchise it was necessary to modify the requirements for church membership. Baptized children of church members were also recognized as members of this covenant community, as well as professing saints. This extension of membership to children was not the result of Baptism itself but birth into a covenant family. It had been agreed early that this covenant blessing extended only to the immediate offspring of professing Christians. The increasing number of immigrants who claimed membership in the Church of England created a serious problem. The vital principle of requiring visible evidence for church membership would be destroyed. The children of such people constituted an additional dilemma. Synod, in 1662, worked out a compromise known as the "Half-way Covenant." It allowed the children of church members who themselves had been baptized to present their children for Baptism. The nonregenerate were thought sufficiently within the covenant relationship by virtue of their own Baptism to warrant some degree of church membership, but they were not recognized as possessing a full membership. This compromise was a serious modification of the congregational requirement of visible evidence of regeneration for church membership. However, most authorities take the position that religious causes rather than political pressure lay behind this crucial decision.

The Half-way Covenant was symptomatic of problems to arise in the future. Solomon Stoddard, pastor at Northampton from 1669 to 1729, advanced the theory, at the Reforming Synod of 1679, that the Lord's supper was designed for all adult members of the church who were not living scandalous personal lives and that it had been instituted as a means of regeneration. In spite of the vigorous opposition of Cotton Mather this position became very influential in W Massachusetts and to a degree in Connecticut.

Congregationalism in the Eighteenth Century

The eighteenth century witnessed the unfolding of the implications of the Half-way Covenant in the appearance of two movements which, although diametrically opposed in character, can be directly traced to it. The first was the development of consociations of churches. The Connecticut churches, in order to preserve their historic congregational orthodoxy, founded Yale College in 1701, to offset the growing liberalism of Harvard. Their determination also led to the calling of the Saybrook Synod in 1708, at which the fifteen articles of the Saybrook Platform were adopted. These articles provided that the churches of Connecticut should be grouped into "consociations" or standing councils that were given the right to decide cases of discipline brought to them from local churches. In much the same way ministers in the colony were to be grouped into associations for the purpose of ordaining candidates for the ministry. And finally, they provided for a general association for the churches of the colony. The platform was adopted and put into effect in 1709. But this drift toward presbyterian polity on the part of Connecticut congregationalism did not go unchallenged in Massachusetts, where considerable opposition arose. Many rightly recognized it as an attempt to create an ecclesiastical organization as a safeguard for traditional Calvinism.

John Wise in his very provocative *The Churches Quarrel Espoused* (1710) and *Vindication of the Government of the New England Churches* (1717) rose to defend traditional polity, but in so doing he introduced a new element which ultimately changed the whole direction of congregational theological development. In his defense he appealed to the Natural Rights philosophy of Baron Pufendorf and John Locke, calling for democracy in the government of the church as well as in the state. In so doing he attacked traditional congregational insistence on the sufficiency and supremacy of the Scriptures and prepared the way for the entrance of deism and unitarianism. This was also a harbinger of the use of Locke in colonial political theory during the American Revolution. During the eighteenth century congregationalism in America was shaken to its foundations by the Great Awakening on the one hand, and the rise of deism on the other.

The Great Awakening began in 1734 at Northampton, where Jonathan Edwards was the pastor. In December Edwards began a series of sermons on justification by faith alone to meet the growing trend toward Arminianism and the decline of a warm religious zeal in his congregation There followed a revival which spread over most of New England and had a great impact on the middle and southern colonies as well. Edwards was aided by the arrival of George Whitefield from England in 1740, and later by Gilbert Tennant. In 1741 Edwards preached his famous sermon, "Sinners in the Hands of an Angry God," which produced a tremendous emotional response on the part of many who heard it. Although the estimates for the number of those converted during the Great Awakening run as high as 300,000, such a claim is quite unrealistic, and a figure of 25,000 or possibly 30,000 would seem to be much more reasonable. The impact of the movement, however, did not depend on the number of conversions alone, for it renewed the zeal of many others so that it is well called the Great Awakening.

But the revival brought almost at once a reaction resulting first in a major theological division into the New Lights and the Old Lights. (This division was paralleled by a similar split in presbyterianism.) In New England the New Lights defended the emotional revivalism of Edwards and Whitefield, whereas the Old Lights opposed it. The leaders of the opposition were Charles Chauncy (1705-1787), pastor of the First Church, Boston, and Jonathan Mathew (1720-1766). In 1743 Chauncy published his *Seasonable Thoughts on the State of Religion in New England*, which set the tone for the ensuing criticism of the Great Awakening. In spite of the fact that Edwards felt that he was defending traditional Puritan Calvinism, it is also apparent that the evangelical emphasis following him underwent important changes under thinkers such as Joseph Bellamy (1719-1790), Samuel Hopkins (1721-1803), and Jonathan Edwards, the younger (1745-1801). They insisted on the necessity of conversion and regeneration but also denied that men may be certain of their eternal redemption. They also tended to accept the governmental theory of the Atonement—the death of Christ satisfied the requirements of good government rather than the strict demands of God's judgment against man's sin. But on the other hand, out of the opposition came both universalism and unitarianism. The trend toward universalism is evident in the changes taking place in Chauncy forty years after writing against Edwards, who published an anonymous tract, *Salvation for All Men Illustrated and Vindicated as Scripture Doctrine.* In 1784 he reinforced his position with his *The Mystery Hid From the Ages.* The followers of Edwards answered Chauncy but had difficulty in doing so because they had surrendered historic Calvinism by adopting views that the death of Christ was of general application.

The Nineteenth Century and Beyond

Nineteenth-Century congregationalism was characterized by several developments: (1) a movement westward, (2) a new era of missionary activity at home and abroad, and (3) a further deterioration of the Calvinistic theology. The stirring of missionary zeal was quite strong in Connecticut by 1800, and in 1801 it resulted in the formation of the Plan of Union with the Presbyterian Church for the more effective evangelization of the W. In 1810 the American Board of Commissioners for Foreign Missions was organized with Noah Porter as its first president. An agreement for cooperation remained in full force until 1837, when it was repudiated by the Old School Presbyterians, and then it was maintained by the New School Presbyterians until the Congregational Convention at Albany brought it to an end in 1852.

Paralleling this renewal of missionary activity was the continuous deterioration of congregational theology. After 1750 there was a growing cleavage between conservatives and liberals, but there was no open rupture until after 1800. The first of the series of events that brought this uneasy truce to an end was the election of Henry Ware, an avowed unitarian, to the Hollis Chair of Divinity at Harvard. Within four years the unitarians were able to gain control over four other chairs, and as a result, Harvard soon became the stronghold of unitarianism. By 1815 the unitarians were sufficiently strong to gain control of most of the older and larger churches of Boston. In Massachusetts 96 churches became unitarian. In protesting against the unitarian capture of Harvard, the evangelicals founded Andover Seminary as a bastion of Calvinism in 1808. The final step in the division came in 1815, when Jedediah Morse published his *American Unitarianism or a Brief History of the Progress and Present State of the Unitarians in America.* This pamphlet made it impossible for the unitarians to conceal their identity any longer, and the actual division, almost entirely confined to Massachusetts, took place between 1817 and 1840. By 1819 William Ellery Channing had emerged as the leader of the movement. He actually held to the ancient Arian or Socinian view of Christ. When the Unitarian Association was formed in 1825, it could claim only a few churches, and most of these were in Massachusetts.

But within the ranks of Trinitarian congregationalism a deteriorating influence was at work and became evident in the theology of Nathaniel Taylor and Horace Bushnell. At the national council meeting in Boston in 1865 the congregationalists adopted a confession which made a sharp break with Calvinism, disowning the name. Since then, in 1931, the General Councils of the Congregational and Christian Churches united to form the Congregational Christian Church, and in 1957 this denomination merged with the Evangelical and Reformed Church to create the United Church of Christ.

Bibliography:

L. W. Bacon, *The Congregationalists* (New York, 1904).

R. Browne, *A Platform of Church Discipline gathered out of the Word of God and agreed upon by the Elders and Messengers of the Churches Assembled in the Synod of Cambridge in New England* (Cambridge, 1939).

J. Cotton, *The Keys of the Kingdom of Heaven* (Boston, 1832).

A. E. Dunning, *Congregationalists in America* (New York, 1894).

E. S. Gaustad, *The Great Awakening in New England* (New York, 1957).

P. Miller, *Jonathan Edwards* (New York, 1949).

P. Miller, *The New England Mind: The Seventeenth Century* (New York, 1939).

H. M. Morais, *Deism in Eighteenth Century America.*

E. Morgan, *The Puritan Dilemma* (Boston, 1958).

W. W. Sweet, *Religion in Colonial America* (New York, 1949).

W. W. Sweet, *The Congregationalists* (New York, 1939).

W. Walker, *Creeds and Platforms of Congregationalism* (New York, 1893).

C. Wright, *The Beginnings of Unitarianism in America* (Boston, 1955).

C. Gregg Singer

CONGREGATIONALISM, one of the distinct forms of church polity (see Church, Nature and Government—Autonomous) within Protestantism having its origins in the English Reformation. Some authorities would place its beginnings in the reform movement of John Wycliffe and the Lollards, and other dissenting groups of the Middle Ages. However, it did not become a significant force in England until the rise of the Puritans during the reign of Elizabeth, when the more radical dissenters refused to accept the Elizabethan Settlement. Although all Puritan groups wished to purify the Church of England, they were in sharp disagreement on the extent to which the church should be changed in its doctrine, government, and liturgy; and they could not agree on the means by which reforms should be accomplished. Congregationalism had its roots among those Puritans who placed a greater emphasis upon the freedom of the individual congregation. On the other hand, they are to be distinguished from the Separatists and the most radical opponents of the Elizabethan Settlement. Some authorities hold that the separatist Robert Browne was the real founder of the English free church movement, but more recent scholarship has tended to question this assumption. It is true that a congregational or free church was organized at Norwich as early as 1581 and that Robert Browne was associated with it. But in 1583 he returned as a clergyman to the Church of England, and the leadership of the movement passed to other hands. More consistent in his support of the principles of congregationalism was another separatist, Henry Barrow, who became the leader of the movement and who in 1589 set forth the principles of the free church movement in his *A True Description of the Visible Congregation of the Saints.* He took the position that each church should be an independent religious community composed of only "the gathered ones," those consciously and conscientiously Christian in their convictions. Those who are united in such a covenant with Christ thus form a self-governing body, electing their own pastor and elders according to the pattern that Barrow professed to find for the church in the NT. In essence, such churches were designed to be pure democracies in both theory and practice. Neither the state nor higher church organization should have the power to demand conformity of any kind from these congregations. Each congregation should be independent and of equal status with all others. Within each congregation all members were to be equal in status, and pastors and officers should have no position of prestige but only the spiritual authority to preach and admonish. Henry Barrow and his fellow-separatist, John Greenwood, were both imprisoned for their activities and executed by hanging in 1593. Francis Johnson, like Barrow and Greenwood, a Cambridge graduate, assumed the leadership of the movement after this. He led his group to Holland in 1597, finally settling in Amsterdam.

Many congregationalists were not separatists like Barrow, Greenwood, or Johnson. Henry Jacob (1563-1624) was a leader who advocated a state church in which each congregation would be free to determine its own policies and choose its own pastor without interference. Those like Jacob became quite numerous within the nonseparatist dissenters or Puritans of the English church.

Congregationalism, as with Puritanism in general, suffered from the persistent opposition of James I, Charles I, and Archbishop Laud. But after the opening of the Long Parliament in 1640, a group of exiles returned from Holland to England, apparently in the expectation that all dissenters would find a favorable atmosphere for their forms of worship. But the Parliament, under the control of presbyterian Puritans, called the Westminster Assembly for the purpose of creating a Presbyterian Church for both Scotland and England. Not until after 1650 were other dissenting groups able to gain a hearing. In 1658 a meeting was held at the Savoy Palace which produced for English congregationalists the Savoy Declaration, comprising a Confession of Faith and a Platform of Discipline. This was the work of a committee called by Cromwell and composed of such leaders as Goodwin, Nye, Owen, and Greenhill. It was essentially the Westminster Confession of Faith of 1643-47 with modifications in the interests of the congregational principles. There is a more liberal view of the role of creeds in the life of the church, and it specifically changes the polity of the Westminster Confession in Articles XXX, XXXI, XXXIII, and XXXIV. The return of the Stuarts to the English throne in 1660 brought about a drastic change in the status of congregationalism in England, and the

Act of Uniformity of 1662 ushered in another period of great hardship. More than two thousand ministers who could not accept its requirements were driven from their parishes and congregationalists, like other dissenters, were forced to worship in secret. The Glorious Revolution of 1688-89 and the resulting Act of Toleration brought the religious liberty which they had been seeking and by which they were able to assume their proper place in the religious life of England.

See CHURCH, NATURE AND GOVERNMENT—Autonomous.

BIBLIOGRAPHY:

C. Burrage, *Early English Dissenters*, Vol. 1 (Cambridge, 1912).

H. W. Clark, *History of English Nonconformity*, Vol. 1 (London, 1911).

H. M. Dexter, *The Congregationalism of the Last 300 Years as Seen Through Its Literature* (New York, 1880).

W. H. Frere, *The English Church in the Reign of Queen Elizabeth and James I* (London, 1904).

W. Payne, *The Free Church Tradition in the Life of England* (London, 1944).

G. Westin, *The Free Church Through the Ages* (Nashville, 1958).

C. GREGG SINGER

CONSCIENCE

I. THE WORD 'CONSCIENCE'

The word *conscience*, transmitted through the French from the Latin *conscientia*, had at one time the sense of consciousness, especially of one's own thoughts or actions. Its current usage is for the moral sense of consciousness of right or wrong together with the judgment one passes on one's own acts.

II. BIBLICAL TEACHING

A. *Old Testament Teaching.*—In Biblical language the words *heart, spirit*, and *mind* are used as synonyms for *conscience* (I John 3:20; I Cor. 2:11; Rom. 14:5). The Hebrew OT has no word for *conscience*. But the reality of conscience is evident in the OT from the first chapters of Genesis. Conscience is evidently intended by *heart* (לְבָבִי) in Job 27:6, as well as in I Sam. 24:5 and II Sam. 24:10 (cf. I Sam. 25:31). I Kings 2:44 may be taken as an appeal to Shimei's conscience, the knowledge of his heart.

B. *New Testament Teaching.*—Although *συνείδησις* "conscience" occurs in classical Greek, its specific ethical and religious meaning is made explicit only in the NT, and particularly in the classic passage, Rom. 2:14, 15, in which the basis of conscience in natural law is set forth. Heathen, though ignorant of the Mosaic law, do by nature things prescribed by that law. The elements of the moral law are not unknown to them, but are innate, "the work of the law written in their hearts." This law of nature provides the foundation for the activity of conscience as an inward witness and judge. Conscience witnesses together with the law and judges, accusing or excusing, the actions performed.

Infallibility of judgment is not ascribed to conscience. Scripture teaches that there may be a weak and erroneous conscience (I Cor. 8:7, 10, 12; cf. 10: 25, 28, 29; and Rom. 14), a defiled conscience (Titus 1:15), or a seared conscience (I Tim. 4:2). The servant of Christ has a pure conscience (I Tim. 3:9; II Tim. 1:3), and a good conscience associated with a pure heart and sincere faith (I Tim. 1:5, 19; cf. Acts 23:1; Heb. 13:18) is the fruit of the Gospel promise and the effect of the sprinkling of the blood of Christ (Heb. 9:9, 14; 10:22). The testimony of conscience has reference to the mind and will of God (I Pet. 2:19).

Though obedience to God takes precedence over that due to human rulers, the magistrate is to be obeyed for conscience' sake (Rom. 13:5). The word *conscience* is characteristically Pauline (cf. also Acts 24:16), but the word *heart* is used by John for the testimony of conscience (I John 3:19-21). It is also associated with conscience in Rom. 2:15 and Heb. 10:22.

III. Teaching of the Church Historically

A. *Pre-Reformation Teaching.*—The Church Fathers laid the foundations of later systems of Christian ethics, as well as dogmatics. The legal emphasis of Tertullian contrasts with the allegorical and mystical in Clement of Alexandria. Stoic insistence on natural law blends with the Platonic vision of eternal ideas to provide the framework for the classical formulation of the doctrine of conscience. Augustine speaks of *conscientia* in relation to the transcript of the eternal law written in the heart (*Enarr. in Ps. 57,1*). Jerome, commenting on Ezekiel 1, found the three Platonic powers of the soul symbolized by three of the animals; and the eagle represented *synteresis*, a supernatural knowledge identified with the Divine Spirit in man. From this text the term "synteresis" (sometimes "synderesis" in the Scholastics) was taken by Alexander of Hales to represent a *potentia habitualis*, a native power of the soul liable to be obscured, which he identified with higher conscience. It is a *lumen innatum* in the intellect and a nondeliberative natural volition (*Summa Theol.*, Pt. II, QQ. 71-77). Bonaventura follows the same lines (*Comment. on II Sent.*, dist. 39) but locates conscience in the practical intellect and synteresis in the will. Conscience for Bonaventura is an innate habit, cognitive of moral principles, concerned also with particular applications of the general principles.

Whereas the Franciscans tended to give prominence to the emotional and volitional elements, the Dominicans, represented by Thomas Aquinas, laid stress on the intellectual aspects of conscience. Aquinas regards conscience as the mind passing moral judgments. Its two elements are *synderesis*, the intuitive grasp of first principles rooted in the natural law; and *conscientia*, the application of this law to particular acts (*Summa Theol.* I q 79 a.13, *De Veritate*, XVIII, 1).

B. *Reformation Teaching.*—The Reformation stressed the freedom of the individual conscience, bound only by the will of God revealed in Scripture. Luther's heroic behavior at the Diet of Worms exemplifies the powerful reality of the Reformation conscience. Calvin, treating conscience in relation to Christian liberty, defines it in concrete religious terms. He derives the definition from the etymology of the word. As *scientia* is an apprehension of the knowledge of things in the mind, so conscience is "a sense of Divine justice, as an additional witness, which permits them not to conceal their sins, or to elude accusation at the tribunal of the supreme Judge" (*Inst.*, III, xix, 15; cf. IV, x, 3). Conscience is a medium between God and man, a sentiment (*sensus*) placing man before the Divine tribunal, an essential ingredient in the sense of Deity implanted in the human heart (*Inst.*, I, iii). My conscience, he says, has respect to God alone, even if no other man existed in the world. With respect to human laws, conscience is not bound by every particular law but by the general command of God, which establishes the authority of magistrates (*Inst.*, IV, x, 5). Conscience, however, is not in the least bound by human traditions in the worship of God, for "the whole tendency of the doctrine of the apostles was that men's consciences should not be burdened with new observances, or the worship of God contaminated with human inventions" (*Inst.*, IV, x, 18). Reformation principle and practice as to freedom of conscience has received classical formulation in the Westminster Confession of Faith: "God alone is Lord of the conscience, and hath left it free from the doctrine and commandments of men which are in anything contrary to his Word; or beside it, in matters of faith or worship. So that to believe such doctrines, or to obey such commandments out of conscience, is to betray true liberty of conscience; and the requiring of an implicit faith, and an absolute and blind obedience, is to destroy liberty of conscience, and reason also" (Chap. XX, Sect. II).

C. *Puritan Teaching.*—The classic expression of the Puritan doctrine of conscience is found in Book I of the *De Conscientia* of William Ames. Ames's teacher, William Perkins, had written a *Discourse on Conscience*, as well as a work on cases of conscience. Whereas Perkins had defined conscience as a faculty, Ames identifies it with an act of the understanding, a practical judgment of oneself according to God's judgment. This judgment may be represented in the form of a practical syllogism. The major premise treats "of the law, the minor of the fact and state and the conclusion of the relation that ariseth from our fact or state, by reason of that Law; which is either guilt or spiritual Joy" (Divine Positions concerning Conscience, 7). The major is given by the synteresis, "an intellectual habit, whereby we give our consent to the principles of moral actions" (Position 10), containing the law of nature, its consequences, and Divinely revealed precepts. Then the minor is a witness that reviews our actions or state, and the conclusion is a judgment as to them in the light of the law. God alone is Lord of the conscience, but the judgment of conscience is binding, for one always sins in acting contrary to conscience (Rom. 14:23). Conscience, however, may be in error; and if conscience errs by pronouncing a sin to be a duty, acting according to conscience may be more sinful than the contrary course. (Cf. Pictet's *Christian Ethics*, II,X,7 f. Pictet also contends that a good action performed against conscience is not always a greater sin than an evil action in obedience to it [*op. cit.*, II,X,11], but Jeremy Taylor argues the contrary in *Ductor Dubitantium*, I, III, rule 4.)

In discussing the problem of the doubting conscience, Ames adopts the position of probabiliorism or tutiorism, that in things not necessary to salvation, it is lawful to follow a certain or even the most probable opinion. "In doubtful cases, the surest part is to be chosen; now that is the surest part, in doing which, it's sure there is no sin" (Divine Positions, 26). For what he calls scrupulous conscience, Ames has little patience. By a scruple he means "a fear of the mind concerning its practice, which vexeth the conscience" arising from slight or no arguments. Scruples ought to be removed by reason, or even by violence if one refuses to consider them. Such behavior is not against, but according to conscience, since a scruple is an ungrounded fear, the overcoming of which strengthens conscience.

The Thomistic intellectualism of Ames's approach to conscience and its problems is qualified by his reply to the difficult question of the possibility of a man's acting against the antecedent and concomitant judgment of his conscience (*De Conscientia*, I, VII). The undeniable fact of action contrary to conscience is hardly reconcilable with the doctrine that the will is determined by the judgment of the practical reason. Ames resolves the problem by introducing a voluntaristic doctrine of the will, while holding to the intellectualistic conception of conscience. Although the object of the will is the good which the intellect has conceived, the will may choose its object without a preceding judgment of the understanding to determine it. Error in the understanding may itself be due to the act of the will directing the attention.

Although Ames has defined conscience as belonging to the intellectual and not to the emotional side of human nature, he devotes Chapter XI to a consideration of the emotions or affections arising from the judgment of conscience. Joy and confidence proceed from a good conscience, whereas an evil conscience gives rise to feelings of shame, sorrow, fear, despair, and finally, the never-dying spiritual worm of overwhelming misery.

IV. Modern Views on Conscience

A. *Philosophical Doctrines.*—Modern ethical thought, so far as it has retained a concern about conscience, has tended to neglect the objective aspect of the natural law and its source in God and to stress emotional factors, identifying conscience with the "moral sense" (Shaftesbury, Hutcheson).

A transition between the Christian and the modern philosophical outlooks on ethics may be found in the ethical sermons of Bishop Butler (1692-1752), who ascribes primacy to conscience as a principle of reflection in man: "But there is a superior principle of reflection or conscience in every man, which distinguishes between the internal principles of his heart, as well as his external actions: which passes judgment upon himself and them; pronounces determinately some actions to be in themselves just, right, good; others to be in themselves evil, wrong, unjust: which, without being consulted, without being advised with, magisterially exerts itself, and approves or condemns him the doer of them accordingly: and which, if not forcibly stopped, naturally and always of course goes on to anticipate a higher and more effectual sentence, which shall hereafter second and affirm its own" (*Works*, ed. by Gladstone, II, 59). Butler speaks of the authority of conscience in such a way as to suggest its infallibility: "Had it strength, as it has right; had it power as it has manifest authority; it would absolutely govern the world" (*ibid.*, 64). The blindness of the enlightenment to original sin affects Butler's view of conscience, in spite of his scriptural acknowledgment of natural law and the ultimate authority of God.

Kant stresses the rational element in conscience onesidedly; he renders it independent of any natural law imposed by God, and thus makes it radically subjective, though universally valid.

The subjectivity and irrationality of conscience is consistently asserted by contemporary existentialists, e.g., Sartre on the "mauvaise foi," with the nihilization (*néantisation*) of conscience accompanying his rejection of all moral law (*L'être et le néant,* pp. 85-111).

B. *Attacks of Philosophy and Psychology on Conscience.*—Influential currents of modern thought have minimized or undermined the authority of conscience. Utilitarianism, proceeding from the empiricist denial of innate knowledge, subordinates conscience completely to the exigencies of society. Thus Alexander Bain argued that conscience is a complex fact of the mind, an extensive code of regulations, to be identified with our education, subjection to government, or authority (*Moral Science*, pp. 34-45).

Modern psychology has contributed much to the undermining of the authority of conscience. The mechanistic denial of consciousness on the part of behaviorism has proved less influential than Freud's naturalistic account of the genesis of conscience, from which psychoanalysts and laymen alike reason fallaciously to the invalidity of judgments of conscience. Freud regards conscience as the judicial activity of the "super-ego," an entity emerging in the child through the "introjection" of parental authority: "The establishment of the super-ego can be described as a successful instance of identification with the parental function. The fact which is decisively in favor of this point of view is that this new creation of a superior function within the ego is extremely closely bound up with the fate of the Oedipus complex, so that the super-ego appears as the heir of the emotion tie, which is of such importance for childhood" (Freud, *New Introductory Lectures on Psychoanalysis*, pp. 90 ff). Freud's alleged "fact" when subjected to critical analysis will, however, be found full of assumptions expressing an anti-rational as well as an anti-Theistic prejudice.

See ADIAPHORA, AMES, ANTHROPOLOGY, CASUISTRY, ETHICS (MORAL LAW), PERKINS, RUTHERFORD.

BIBLIOGRAPHY:

W. Ames, *Of Conscience with the Power and Cases Thereof* (London, 1639).

A. Augustine, *Ennarationes in Psalmos* (Turnholti, 1956), 3 vols.

A. Bain, *Moral Science: A Compendium of Ethics* (New York, 1869).

J. Butler, "Three Sermons on Human Nature," in *Works*, ed. Gladstone (Oxford, 1896), vol. II.

J. Calvin, *Institutes of the Christian Religion*, III, xix; and IV, x.

F. Delitzsch, *A System of Biblical Psychology*, trans. by R. E. Wallis (Edinburgh, 1899).

S. Freud, *New Introductory Lectures on Psychoanalysis*, quoted and discussed in E. Vivas, *The Moral Life and the Ethical Life* (Chicago, 1950).

T. H. Green, *Prolegomena to Ethics* (Oxford, 1883), II, v; and IV, i.

T. Kant, *Critique of Practical Reason*, translated by Thomas K. Abbott, 6th ed. (London, 1909).

B. Pictet, *De Christelyke Zedekunst*, transl. by Francois Halma (Leeuwarden, 1720), II, 10, 11.

W. Perkins, *A Discourse on Conscience* (1597), in *Works* (Cambridge, 1603).

S. Rutherford, *A Free Disputation against Pretended Liberty of Conscience* (London, 1649).

R. Sanderson, *De Obligatione Conscientiae Praelectiones Decem.* (London, 1660), trans., *Lectures on Conscience and Human Law* (Lincoln, 1877).

J. Sharp, "Two Discourses of Conscience," in *Sermons*, Vol. II (London, 1729).

T. Aquinas, *Summa Theologica* (Chicago, 1952-4), 3 vols.

WILLIAM YOUNG

CONSECRATION, the dedication of persons or things for the service of God.

The translators of the AV have used the noun "consecration" and verb "consecrate" to represent the following, each representing some aspect of devotion to God:

(1) *Fill the hand.* This is the commonest equivalent, and usually refers to priests. The verb is used of Aaron and the priests in Ex. 29:9, 29, 33, etc., and Ezek. 43:26, and the noun in Ex. 29: 22, 26, 27, etc., of the ram used at their consecration, and in Lev. 8:28-33 of other items used on this occasion. The verb is used of illegal priests (Judges 17:5, 12; I Kings 13:33; II Chron. 29: 31). The origin of the phrase must lie in some part of a ceremony when a person took up a portion of the sacrifice, or some sign of office, in his hands and symbolically gave it back to God. The term remained even when the act did not form part of the ceremony. Other versions use the terms "ordination" (RSV), "investiture" (Jer..), "installation" (NEB). The term is also used of people who dedicate themselves and their gifts to God (I Chron. 29:5; II Chron. 29:31). NEB here has "give with open hand."

(2) *Separate, separation,* connected with the root found in Nazarite (Nazirite), of whom it is used in Num. 6:7, 9, 12. Elsewhere in this chapter the AV translates the word as "separate" or "separation" instead of "consecrate," "consecration."

(3) *Set apart,* from the root commonly translated "holy," used of Aaron and the priests (Ex. 28:3; 30:30; II Chron. 26:18), of vessels set apart for religious use (Josh. 6:19), of animals for sacrifice (II Chron. 29:33), of tithes (II Chron. 31:6), and of festival days (Ezra 3:5).

(4) *Devote,* used only in Micah 4:13 of enemy spoils. But the verb and noun have other translations in the AV, including "accursed things" (Josh. 7:1 ff.), "devote" (Lev. 27:21; Num. 18:14), "dedicate" (II Sam. 8:11), and "utterly

destroy" (Num. 21:2, and about 40 other times). The thought is that things are handed to the Lord so that He can use the good and destroy the evil.

(5) *Make new,* used only in Heb. 10:20 of the new way opened for us by Christ. The same word in the original is translated "dedicated" in Heb. 9:18, but "inaugurated" would fit both passages.

(6) *Make perfect,* used of Christ in Heb. 7:28. The AV is misleading, since elsewhere it nearly always translates the Greek word as "perfect" or "make perfect." Here Christ is perfect where the OT types fell short.

CONSTANCE, Council of (1414-18). This council, counted as ecumenical by the RC Church, met for a threefold purpose: to heal the schism of the church, to reform ecclesiastical government and life, and to eradicate the Wycliffite "heresy" which had made great gains in Bohemia.

The most pressing problem, that of schism of the church, resulted from the Babylonian Captivity, during which the papacy had established itself at Avignon under French tutelage. When Pope Urban IV attempted in 1378 to re-establish the papal see in Rome, division disrupted the college of cardinals, part of whom elected a pro-French pope. In 1409 at the Council of Pisa some of the cardinals attempted to heal the division by having both popes resign and electing another. This only succeeded in establishing a third pope. However, the scandal became so great that eventually the Emperor Sigismund forced John XXIII, a Pisan pope, to call a council at Constance. The Council was composed of clergy: 29 cardinals, 3 patriarchs, 33 archbishops, 150 bishops, 100 abbots, 50 provosts, and 300 deans, along with some 18,000 other clergy and numerous visitors including princes, kings, and the emperor, the estimated total amounting to between 80,000 and 100,000. In a sense the council initiated the beginning of the modern period. It marked the end of the old medieval papacy and empire, the recognition of humanism, and the appearance of a reform movement within the church which manifested both the nationalistic and evangelical motifs so important in the Protestantism of the sixteenth century.

To bring about the reunion of the church by the elimination of the three popes and the acceptance of one, John XXIII, about whose legitimacy the Roman Church has never made up its mind, and Benedict XIII suffered deposition, whereas Gregory XII resigned to become Cardinal Bishop of Porto. The College of Cardinals, along with thirty deputies of the council, then chose as pope Odo Colonna, who assumed the name of Martin V. It was only at this point, according to many canon lawyers, that the council became truly an ecumenical gathering of the church.

The second objective was the reform of the church's government and life. A large group in the council, headed by French thinkers such as Gerson, d'Ailly, and others, insisted that the council and not the pope held the supreme position in the ecclesiastical body politic. With this Martin V did not agree, and he succeeded in blocking the "conciliarists" in their attempts to make the church a democracy. Various commissions also attempted to bring about the abolition of simony, nepotism, pluralism as well as immorality within the ranks of the clergy, but in vain. Consequently no reforms were initiated, conditions in the church generally becoming worse until the Reformation.

As a third objective the council aimed at the rooting out of the teachings of the English theologian, John Wycliffe, which had become popular in Bohemia under the preaching of Jan Hus and Jerome of Prague. In the eighth session the council condemned 45 of Wycliffe's propositions, later adding another 260, ordering all his writings to be burned and his body to be removed from consecrated ground. The final act was the burning of Hus, who had come to defend his views under the protection of an imperial safe-conduct. Claiming that the protection applied only to illegal treatment, the church tried him for heresy and on July 6, 1415, burned him at the stake, his principal supporter, Jerome, receiving the same treatment on May 30, 1416.

The only real achievement registered by the council was the re-establishment of papal unity. No true reforms resulted, and the Roman Church now officially declared itself opposed to the evangelical doctrines of Wycliffe and Hus. From this point on it became evident that only a violent disruption of the church could bring about a return to truly Biblical teaching.

BIBLIOGRAPHY:

E. Bonnechose, *Les réformateurs avant la réforme* (Paris, 1946), 2 vols.

H. Finke, ed., *Acta Concilii Constanciensis* (Munster, 1896-1928), 4 vols.

G. Picotti, "Il Concilia da Constanza," *Enciclopedia Italiana*, 1931-39, XI, 632-633.

T. J. Shahan, "Council of Constance," *CE*, 1908, III, 288-294.

N. Valois, *La Crise religieuse du XVe siècle, le pape et le concile* (Paris, 1909), 2 vols.

J. H. Wylie, *The Council of Constance to the Death of John Hus* (London, 1900).

W. S. REID

CONSTANTINE THE GREAT (274-337), the illegitimate son of Constantius, emperor of the Roman empire. When, in 306, Emperor Constantius died at York, Constantine was proclaimed emperor by the army, but he had to fight Maxentius and others to hold the throne. The story has been told that before his victory at Milvian Bridge near Rome, on October 27, 312, he saw in the sky a flaming cross with the inscription "In this sign conquer." Many explanations have been given, but it is clear that he had a remarkable experience of some kind which led him to favor Christianity. The fact that he later murdered those who might have a claim to the throne (including his own son), that he retained his position as chief priest of the pagan state religion, and that he delayed baptism until shortly before death indicates that his support of Christianity was a matter of political expediency by which he hoped to consolidate the empire. By the Edict of Milan in March, 313, Constantine and the joint emperor Licinius, who ruled in the E, proclaimed full toleration to all religions, including the Christian faith, and compensated Christian churches for losses suffered in the persecutions. At Adrianople in 323 Licinius fought against Constantine, was vanquished, and put to death; then Constantine became sole emperor. Though Christianity did not become the state religion under Constantine, as many have thought, it did receive direct support through subsidies to the clergy, exemption of the clergy from public service, and exemption of church lands from taxation. Other edicts of Constantine suppressed soothsayers, established Sunday as a day of rest, and established laws to protect marriage and give greater protection to slaves and animals.

The effect of Constantine's policies was to gain state control over church affairs, a result that he did not discourage. Large numbers of nominal professors of Christianity came into the church and exerted great influence in the selection of clergy who held to heretical teachings. But more important, Constantine stepped in to take a direct hand in ecclesiastical and theological affairs of the church. To settle and reconcile the opposing parties concerning the views of Arius (see ARIANISM), he called a church council, the First Council of Nicea, in 325. In this council he presided as a "bishop of bishops" and even suggested the wording that finally went into the creed which was agreed upon.

BIBLIOGRAPHY:
N. H. Bayne, *Constantine the Great and the Christian Church* (London, 1930).
C. B. Coleman, *Constantine and Christianity* (New York, 1914).
Eusebius, *Life of Constantine*, trans. by E. C. Richardson in *Nicene and Post Nicene Fathers* (New York, 1890), Vol. I.

CONSTANTINOPLE, First Council of (381). This, the Second Ecumenical Council, was called by Emperor Theodosius I to provide for the succession to the patriarchate of Constantinople, to confirm the Nicene Creed of 325, and to deal with the heresies that continued to trouble the church. It was attended by 150 orthodox and 36 heterodox bishops. Theodosius, who had become emperor in the E in 379, was determined to govern the church as Constantine had, and to be the champion of a strict orthodoxy. He called the council without seeking either the advice or the consent of the bishop of Rome. Although no W bishops attended, it has been regarded even by the W as the Second Ecumenical Council.

The decisions of the Council of Nicea had not brought peace to the church, and for much of the intervening period it had seemed as if the semi-Arian position would triumph over the Nicene theology. This half-century of theological and political tension formed the immediate background of this council. Theodosius appointed Meletius, bishop and leader of the orthodox party at Antioch, to preside over its deliberations, and this was a cause of serious offense to the W. Meletius died, however, soon after the council's commencement. Its acts and proceedings have been lost, and its work is largely known through the writings of such ecclesiastical historians as Socrates and Sozomen. Seven canons are attributed to it, but many scholars question the validity of the last three. Its first official act was to confirm Nectarius as patriarch of Constantinople instead of Gregory of Nazianzus. Further, it prescribed "that the bishop of Constantinople should have the next prerogative of honor after the bishop of Rome" (Socrates, *EH*, vii, 8).

The main concern of the council was the settlement of the Arian controversy. It is generally agreed that the creed usually ascribed to it and known as the Niceno-Constantinopolitan Creed of 381 was not the work of this council, but was probably composed by Cyril of Jerusalem about 362 as the baptismal symbol of the church at Jerusalem.

There is no doubt that at certain points this creedal statement is much more complete than that of 325, both in its Christological definition and particularly in its expanded affirmation regarding the Holy Spirit. Together with the creed of 325, it was formally adopted by the Council of Chalcedon, which in its dogmatic utterances was recognized by Gregory the Great as one of the four general councils. The *filioque* clause, concerning the procession of the Holy Spirit from both the Father and the Son, was added by the Council of Toledo in 589, but this clause was never accepted by the E Church.

The council anathematized not only Arians and Apollinarians, but also Macedonians or Pneumatomachi (who denied the deity of the Holy Spirit) and Sabellians.

BIBLIOGRAPHY:
J. C. Ayer, *A Source Book for Ancient Church History from the Apostolic Age to the Close of the Conciliar Period* (New York, 1903).
L. Duchens, *Early History of the Christian Church from Its Foundations to the End of the Fifth Century* (New York, 1904-24), 3 vols.
A. Harnack, *History of Dogma*, trans. from the third German ed. by E. B. Speirs, J. Miller, *et. al.* (London, 1874-79), 7 vols.
C. J. Hefele, *A History of the Christian Councils*, trans. from the German by W. B. Clark (Edinburgh, 1872-75), vols. 1-4.
E. H. Landray, *A Manual of the Councils of the Holy Catholic Church* (Edinburgh, 1909), rev. ed., 2 vols.
P. Schaff, *History of the Christian Church* (Grand Rapids, 1952), 8 vols.

CONSTANTINOPLE, Second Council of (553). This, the Fifth Ecumenical Council, was called by Emperor Justinian and was attended by 165 bishops, all but five of whom were from the E. Justinian called it to deal with Nestorianism, for he was convinced that this heresy was still being nurtured by the writings of Theodore of Mopsuestia, Theodoret of Cyros, and Ibas of Edess. It is generally assumed that it was the purpose of the emperor to set forth a more moderate monophysite interpretation of the Chalcedonian formula of 451 in order to bring about a reconciliation between the churches of the E and of the W. For this reason the writings of these three theologians (the so-called Three Chapters) were condemned; but this council also saved the authority of Chalcedon at the same time by decreeing an anathema against any who should declare that its formula gave countenance to error condemned by the council of 553. This was, to say the least, an ambiguous position, and the council failed in its purpose of restoring harmony between E and W, partly because its decisions were carried out in a violent manner. Pope Vigilius was banished, and the council's decrees were not recognized as authoritative by many of the W bishops. In its affirmations it departed from the high Biblical position adopted at Nicea in 325, Constantinople in 381, and Chalcedon.

Bibliography:
See Constantinople, First Council of.

CONSTANTINOPLE, Third Council of (681). This, the Sixth Ecumenical Council, was called to deal with the monophysite heresy, which had vexed the church for several centuries. During the seventh century this controversy took a new turn with the rise of monothelitism in the E. The council was called by Emperor Constantine Pogonatus and was attended by 174 bishops of the patriarchates of Constantinople and Antioch. It was presided over by three papal legates, who brought with them a letter from Pope Agatho which identified Rome with the cause of true orthodoxy in this dispute. The statement of faith which this council drafted was intended to reassert the Chalcedonian formula, and it accordingly appealed to the Creeds of 325 and 381. The letter from Agatho was used to support the orthodox doctrine that there were in Christ two natural wills or "willings" which were not contrary to one another. The human will of Christ was declared to follow the Divine will and neither resisted it nor followed it reluctantly. This council condemned Macarius, Patriarch of Antioch, and Pope Honorius I, who in 634 had written a letter in which he had set forth a monothelite position. This conciliar condemnation of Honorius I has been the cause of embarrassment to RC apologists, since it reflects adversely on the doctrine of papal infallibility. But it is also true that, in the issue at hand, Rome secured a theological triumph over the E in the acceptance of its formula. This acceptance must be regarded as the logical completion of the doctrinal position set forth by the Council of Chalcedon in 451.

Bibliography:
See Constantinople, First Council of.

CONSUBSTANTIATION. The term "consubstantiation" is a word used to describe the Lutheran view of the mode of the presence of Christ in the Lord's supper. Though the term is usually applied to the Lutheran view by non-Lutherans, it has become a classical method of distinguishing the Lutheran view from that of the RC Church. The term has reference to the co-existence of the substance of the body and blood of Christ with the substance of the elements of bread and wine. The substance of Christ is said to be really present *in,* *with,* and *under* the bread and wine. In this view the real, substantial presence of Christ in the sacrament is confessed without any metaphysical change of the substance of the bread and wine as is the case in transubstantiation. In the Lutheran view both the "substance" and the "accidents" of bread and wine remain intact. In consubstantiation there is co-existence but no *mixing* of the two substances into a third heavenly-earthly new substance of deified bread and wine. The substance of the elements remains present and metaphysically distinct from the substance of Christ. The Lutheran view is articulated clearly in Article Ten of the Augsburg Confession and in the Formula of Concord. The doctrine was based on Luther's concept of the ubiquity of the glorified human nature of Christ which was made possible by the communication of the attributes of the Divine nature of Christ to the human nature. This point was the focal point of the controversy that separated the Lutherans and the Calvinists during the Reformation.

See TRANSUBSTANTIATION, HOLY COMMUNION.

R. C. SPROUL

CONTARINI, Gasparo (1483-1542), RC diplomat and reformer.

After studying at Pavia, Contarini served Venice, his native town, as a diplomat. From 1521 to 1525 he was ambassador to the court of Charles V, and in 1521 he attended the Diet of Worms. From 1528 to 1530 he remained in Rome at the Vatican.

On May 20, 1535, Pope Paul III elevated him to cardinal although he was only a layman. In 1536 he became bishop of Belluno. With Caraffa he became a member of the committee of cardinals whose main concern was the reform of the church. As papal legate he witnessed the religious discussion at Regensburg in 1541. From May, 1542, until his death in August, he was papal legate at Bologna. Contarini was the leader of that group in the RC Church which pressed for a definite improvement and which strove for a compromise with the Lutherans. The reforms of the church had to begin with the pope, as was stipulated in the *Consilium de emendanda ecclesia* (1537), published in 1538. This work was later placed on the Index. Contarini agreed with the conception of the doctrine of justification as it was explained by Gropper (1538). In this sense he collaborated at Regensburg for the acceptance of Article 5 of the Book of Regensburg, which dealt with this topic. He defended his views in his *Epistola de justificatione* (1541). However, Contarini maintained the RC view of the eucharist, so that a real agreement with the Lutherans was impossible for him.

In his doctrine of justification, Contarini followed Augustine and Thomas. As early as 1511 he had personally found comfort in trusting Christ to conquer inner doubt.

BIBLIOGRAPHY:

G. Contarini, *Opera* (Paris, 1572; Venice, 1578, 1589), critical edition by F. G. Huenermann, in: *Corpus Catholicorum* VII (Münster, 1923).

F. Dittrich, *Contarini* (Braunsberg, 1885).

H. Hackert, *Die Staatschrift Contarinis und die politischen Verhaeltnisse Venidigs im sechzehnten Jahrhundert* (Heidelberg, 1940).

F. Huenermann, "Die Rechtfertigungslehre des Contarini," in *ThQ* CII (1921), 1 f.

H. Jedin, *Geschichte des Konzils von Trent* I & II (Freiburg, 1949, 1957).

H. Jedin, *Kardinal Contarini als Kontroverstheologe* (Münster, 1950).

H. Jedin, "Ein 'Turmerlebnis' des jungen Contarini," in: *HJb* LXX (1951), 115 f.

F. Lauchtert, *Die italienischen litterarischen Gegner Luthers* (Freiburg, 1912), 371 f.

H. Ruckert, *Die theologische Entwicklung Contarini* (Berlin, 1926).

D. NAUTA

CONTRA-REMONSTRANTS, the name given to the Dutch Calvinists of the 17th century in their struggle with the Arminians.

THE REMONSTRANCE. After the death of Arminius (1609) the leadership of his followers fell to Johannes Wttenbogaert, who convoked the most important Arminian ministers to a secret meeting at Gouda (Jan. 14, 1610). At this meeting they adopted a Remonstrance, written by Wttenbogaert himself. In the introduction they defended themselves against some of the charges against them, adding a rather distorted account of the Calvinist views. The Remonstrance itself contained five points: (1) conditional predestination; (2) unlimited atonement; (3) saving faith as due to the Holy Spirit; (4) resistible grace; (5) the uncertainty of perseverance.

THE CONTRA-REMONSTRANCE. On Aug. 3, 1610, the synodical deputies of N and S Holland met and prepared a Contra-Remonstrance, which was not made public until the Conference at The Hague (1611), convoked by the States-General of Holland. In the presence of the magistrates, the leading points were discussed by six representatives of each party. On behalf of the Calvinists Festus Hommius read the Contra-Remonstrance.

In the introduction they renewed their charge that the Arminians aimed at a change of religion, as clearly appeared from their request for a permanent revision of the confession and their refusal to submit their views to the proper ecclesiastical assemblies. They further stressed that they as well as the Arminians saw the confession as subordinate to Scripture; yet they held that a confession has binding authority and is necessary for the true unity of the church. Consequently, every minister is bound by his subscription; if any objections arise in his mind, he should lodge them with the general assembly. To ask for revision of the confession and release from subscription before evidence of errors in the confession has been submitted would only arouse unrest in the church. They summarized the teaching of the Reformed Church in the following points: (1) Man is universally and totally depraved. (2) There is a double predestination, consisting of election and reprobation (the latter seen as preterition). (3) Covenant children are to be regarded as elect; and, if they die in their infancy, believing parents should not doubt their salvation. (4) Election does not rest on foreseen faith, but faith is the fruit of election. (5) The Atonement, while sufficient for all, is efficient for the elect only. (6) Faith and conversion are results of regeneration by the Holy Spirit. (7) The saints will persevere in their faith. (8) These doctrines do not result in carelessness on the part of believers. In the conclusion they reject some Arminian distortions of the Calvinist view and make again a strong plea for a national synod. After this meeting these Calvinists were called Contra-Remonstrants.

FURTHER DEVELOPMENTS. On the whole the States-General of Holland, under the leadership of Oldebarnevelt, favored the Arminian party, mainly because of its Erastian views. Yet the Contra-Remonstrants continued the battle. Their most important leaders were Gomarus, Plancius, Hommius, and Bogerman. The great change came in 1618, when Prince Maurits of Orange chose the side of the Calvinists. A national assembly was called in Dort. At this synod, which was attended by delegates from Reformed churches in many countries (e.g., England, Switzerland, and Germany), the Arminians and their teachings were condemned and the Calvinism of the Contra-Remonstrants was upheld.

See ARMINIUS; DORT, SYNOD OF; REMONSTRANTS.

BIBLIOGRAPHY:

W. Cunningham, *Historical Theology* (Edinburgh, 1863; London, 1960), II, 371-513.
K. Dijk, *De Strijd over Infra-en Supralapsar-*

isme in de Gereformeerde Kerken van Nederland (Kampen, 1912), 57-115.
H. Kajaan, *De Groote Synode van Dordrecht in 1618-1619* (Amsterdam, n.d.).
P. Schaff, *The Creeds of Christendom* (New York, 6th ed.) I, 508-523.
T. Scott, *The Articles of the Synod of Dort; with a History of Events Which Made Way for That Synod* (London, 1818).
L. H. Wagenaar, *Van Strijd en Overwinning. De Groote Synode van 1618 op '19, en wat aan haar voorafging* (Utrecht, 1909), 85-239.
KLAAS RUNIA

CONVENT, Latin *conventus*, "assembly," an ascetic community, either male or female, or the buildings in which they live. The original pattern of the ascetic life was solitary existence, especially in Egypt and Syria. Carthusians and Camaldolese are the main W orders which continue the hermitage system. This was succeeded by the coenobitic life (life in community). Since the 9th century Benedict of Aniane, a follower of Benedict of Nursia, was especially influential in the convent form of community life.

Nowadays the term *convent* is used mainly for *nunnery*, though it may be used for communities of men, e.g., Franciscans. Canon Law (which has extensive legislation on convents) uses the term *enclosure* as applicable to women's orders. Cloister life prohibits or carefully limits further association with the outside world. Applicants usually spend a period as *postulants*, i.e., inquirers. They must then be at least 15 years old to join the novitiate. A year is spent as a novice, but perpetual vows are not taken under the age of 21. Each of the steps is supposed to be voluntary.

The law of enclosure does not apply to many orders today because of the kind of work they do. Members of these may be bound by simple vows as distinct from solemn ones. Such convents are technically *conservatoria.*

Some orders following the law of enclosure are strictly contemplative. Others engage also in educational, hospital, or social work. Devotions, services, work, and recreation occupy the time. Making vestments and church embroidery are normal occupations. The choir offices are frequent, and some orders have their own special offices, such as Poor Clares (Franciscan nuns) and Cistercians. Sisters may be divided into choir sisters and lay sisters. The latter are under separate regulations and do the domestic work.

Dowry is the money or property brought into the convent by a new member as a contribution to the community fund. Rules of dowry vary.

In England and Wales in 1960 there were about two hundred separate RC women's orders with one or more branches. In the U.S.A. the number of separate orders is a little greater.

D. N. EMERSON

CONVENTICLE ACT, an act passed in 1664 by the Cavalier Parliament in an attempt to make English nonconformists accept the Act of Uniformity, which included the use of the Book of Common Prayer and submission to episcopal authority. It forbade all meetings in private houses, or elsewhere, of more than five persons in addition to the household for any worship not according to the Book of Common Prayer. It imposed heavy fines for disobedience, the ultimate penalty being death. Only one informer was needed to give evidence, and magistrates received the widest authority for its enforcement. Since the act as originally passed had force for only three years, Parliament renewed it in 1670 with slightly modified penalties but with greatly extended powers granted to the enforcement officers.

Along with other laws such as the Five Mile Act, this statute formed part of the attempt of the high church party to force all Englishmen into the Church of England. Although many nonconformists submitted, many refused, choosing rather to suffer imprisonment and even death. The tragic part was that it finally alienated the nonconformists completely from the Church of England. At the time of the Restoration (1660) some hope had existed that Robert Baxter and others of the Presbyterians might succeed in obtaining some form of accommodation with the episcopal authorities. The Conventicle Act and similar laws, however, destroyed any such hope and politically sealed the fate of the Stuart monarchy. The law was repealed in the Act of Toleration of 1689.

CONVERSE, James Booth (1844-1914), Presbyterian home missionary and journalist. Converse was born in Philadelphia, and, after graduating from the College of New Jersey in 1865, he attended Union Theological Seminary in Virginia (1866-69), and was ordained by E Hanover Presbytery on April 8, 1870. He served the Makemie Church in Virginia for a brief time. From 1872 to 1879 he edited the *Christian Observer,* which his father had founded. He was a home mission evangelist in Tennessee, 1879-81; pastor at Blountville, Kentucky, 1881-87; evangelist and stated supply in Holston Presbytery (Tennessee), 1888-94; and a home missionary at Morristown, Tennessee, 1895-1914, where he died, October 31, 1914. Influenced by Henry George, he advocated the single-tax; but he turned to the Bible to study the relationship between Christianity and economics. He held that obedience to the Mosaic law was sufficient to solve economic problems and to banish poverty. Among his published works were *A Summer Vacation: Sketches and Thoughts Abroad* (Louisville, Ky., 1878), *The Bible and Land* (Morristown, Tenn., 1889), *Uncle Sam's Bible; or, Bible Teachings about Politics* (Chicago, 1899), and *There Shall Be No Poor* (1914). From 1890 to 1895 he published the periodical *Christian Patriot* to advocate the authority of Christ and the Bible as supreme in civil affairs. His social views precluded him from more important pulpits, but his labors were well received by the mountain people in East Tennessee among whom the latter part of his ministry was performed.

ALBERT H. FREUNDT, JR.

CONVERSION. The term "conversion" is commonly used to denote the change in an individual or group to a new mode of life, religion, beliefs, morals, or politics. It is frequently associated with a conscious, climactic crisis. Both religious and other forms of conversion are often marked by a unification of character and personal goals.

In Christian thought the term commonly refers to the once-and-for-all act of becoming a Christian, which involves repentance, faith, regeneration, and a conscious awareness of the grace and love of God in Christ. In the NT, "conversion" appears only once. It is used to describe "the conversion (ἐπιστροφή) of the Gentiles" (Acts 15:3) through the preaching of Paul and Barnabas. The root meaning of the noun here, like that of the more commonly used verb ἐπιστρέφω, denotes a *turning, turning around*, or *turning back.* Ἐπιστρέφω and its cognates are regularly used in the LXX to render the OT Hebrew שׁוּב, which means to *turn back* or *return* both literally and metaphorically.

The Old Testament

The OT writers speak of *turning* rather than "conversion." The expression is used of the turning from evil to God of the pagan community, Nineveh (Jon. 3:8, 10); of individuals like the penitent Psalmist (Ps. 51:13) and King Josiah (II Kings 23:25); and also of the prophecy of the turning of the nations to God (Ps. 22:27). The story of Naaman the leper (II Kings 5) stands out as a case of conversion of a non-Jew;

and that of Manasseh (II Chron. 33: 12 f.) as that of a notoriously wicked individual.

For the people of Israel in the OT *turning* meant turning to Jehovah, their covenant God. In virtue of the solemn pact made with Abraham and renewed from time to time in their history, they were the people of God (Gen. 17; Ex. 24; Deut. 7:6-11). God bound Himself to be their God, and they were pledged to live as His children in fellowship and obedience. For the Israelite, sin was essentially backsliding, breaking the covenant relationship by turning aside from Jehovah's statutes and love. Therefore, both the law and the prophets called upon Israel to return to the Lord their God and to His statutes (Deut. 4:30; 30:2, 10; Ezek. 18:21), so that the relationship and the blessings might be restored.

Such acts of returning occurred on a national scale, when a leader such as Joshua and later certain kings made or renewed covenants on behalf of the people. These involved both sacrifice and solemn repentance and profession of loyalty (Josh. 24:25; II Kings 11:17; II Chron. 19:10; 34:31; Ezra 10). When men humbled themselves, turning from their sin, and sought God with their whole heart, they found a deeper knowledge of God and fuller experience of His blessings (Deut. 4:29 f.; 30:1-10; II Chron. 33:13; Jer. 24:7).

The New Testament

The thought of *turning* to God as a condition of spiritual healing and seeing the kingdom of God is taken up in the teaching of Jesus and the early church (Mt. 13:15; 18:3; Mark 4:12; Luke 8: 10; John 12:40; Acts 3:19; 26:18; cf. Isa. 6:10).

In Acts repentance and faith are both described as turning. Repentance is turning from wickedness, idols, darkness, and the power of Satan, whereas faith is turning to God (Acts 3:19, 26; 9:35; 11:21; 14:15; 15:19; 26:18, 20; cf. I Thess. 1:9; I Pet. 2:25). Elsewhere, though it is not directly identified, the same turning is described in terms of becoming a disciple (Luke 14:27, 33), becoming as a little child (Mt. 18:3), taking upon oneself the yoke of Christ (Mt. 11: 29-30), and receiving Christ as Lord (Col. 2:6).

The NT records several conversion experiences (though without using the word *conversion*). Some of them were highly dramatic, like Paul's; others were less so. They include those of Paul (Acts 9:5-19; 22:6-16; 26:12-23), Cornelius (Acts 10:1-48; 11:4-18; cf. 15:7 ff.), the Ethiopian eunuch (Acts 8:26:38), Lydia (Acts 16:14 f.), and the Philippian jailer (Acts 16:25-34). The conversions of Paul and Cornelius are referred to three times each in view of their importance for the history of the church. In the latter's case the gift of the Holy Spirit was the signal for the inclusion of Gentiles in the church.

This radical change in the individual is sometimes linked with Baptism (Rom. 6:2 f.; I Pet. 3:21; and possibly Titus 3:5), as the sacrament of Christian initiation. But the above instances of adult conversions show that in each case conversion preceded Baptism, which symbolizes the washing, burial, and regeneration in Christ of the believer.

Although the conversions recorded in the NT were sometimes accompanied by profound emotional experiences, in no case were the experiences sought or induced for their own sake. The fundamental characteristic of conversion, without which a man cannot become a Christian, is a changed relationship with God, which is effected through receiving Christ in the power of the Holy Spirit. Through conversion believers have access to the Father, through the Son, in the Holy Spirit (Eph. 2:18).

From one point of view turning to

God is a deliberate act of the individual. But both OT and NT make it clear that it is also the work of God in him. Paul urged the Philippians to work out their salvation with fear and trembling, for it was God who was at work in them to will and to do His good pleasure (Phil. 2:12 f.; cf. Jer. 31:18 f.; Lam. 5:21). When men turn to God, it involves an act of God comparable with raising the dead (Eph. 2:1 ff.), a new birth (John 1:13; 3:3 ff.), a creative act bringing light into darkness (II Cor. 4:4-6), the drawing of the Father (John 6:44; 17: 6 ff.; cf. Rom. 8:29 f.), and the convicting power of the Holy Spirit (John 16:8; I Cor. 2:4 f.; I Thess. 1:5). In short: "By grace you have been saved through faith; and this is not your own doing, it is the gift of God—not because of works, lest any man should boast. For we are his workmanship, created in Christ Jesus for good works, which God prepared beforehand, that we should walk in them" (Eph. 2:8-10).

Conversion in the NT is not an end in itself, but a turning point. It means reckoning reconciliation and union with God to be a fact and living accordingly (Rom. 6:1-14; Col. 2:10-12, 20 ff.; 3:1 ff.).

'Επιστρέφω is used of the return of Peter after his denial (Luke 11:32), but elsewhere the lapsed are exhorted not to conversion but to repentance (Rev. 2: 5, 16, 21 f.; 3:3, 19).

In some English versions the word *convert* is used as a convenient, generally understood term, whereas the original Greek has something different. Rom. 16:5; I Cor. 16:15; and some mss of II Thess. 2:13 have ἀπαρχή, "first-fruits" (RSV "first convert") an allusion to consecrating the first-fruits of a crop or first-born of an animal. Acts 13:43 speaks of the many Jews and Jewish προσηλύτοι, proselytes, who followed Paul and Barnabas. This word was a customary designation for a Gentile convert to Judaism who became a Jew by undergoing circumcision. In I Tim. 3:6 νεόφυτος means literally "newly planted," i.e., in the Christian faith (cf. RSV, "recent convert").

Conversion in Church History and Modern Psychology

The NT lays stress on the reality of the relationship implied by conversion, rather than on the term. Its writers were not interested in conversion experiences for their own sake. In subsequent church history men have oscillated between the extremes of denying any need for conversion and intense introspective analysis.

The conversion of Augustine (described in his *Confessions*, VIII) exerted considerable influence on his own and later ages. In general, the Reformers focussed attention on the realities of grace and justification by faith, but the term conversion figured little in their writings and in the classical Reformed confessions of faith. It gained increasing currency through pietism and the evangelical revival. It figured also in discussions of Puritan divines. The conversion of John Wesley on May 24, 1738, who was already an Anglican clergyman with missionary experience, contributed to the eventual formation of Methodism, with its distinctive emphases on evangelism, conversion, personal holiness, and church organization. But interest in conversion was not confined to the Arminian wing of the evangelical revival. One of the classical studies of the subject is Jonathan Edwards' *Faithful Narrative of the Surprising Work of God in the Conversion of Many Hundred Souls, in Northampton* (1738).

In certain forms of 19th-century evangelicalism, stress upon conversion became paramount. In the 1820's C. G. Finney introduced the intensive evangelistic campaign and the custom of appealing for decisions in response to the message.

With the rise of modern psychology, the psychological aspects of conversion have come under intensive study. Early works included E. D. Starbuck, *Psychology of Religion* (1889), and William James, *The Varieties of Religious Experience* (1902). The former contended that conversion occurs in females mostly between the ages of 13 and 16, and among males around 17. But his conclusions have been questioned on account of the fact that his evidence was largely confined to U.S. evangelical circles. It should not cause a surprise that many conversions do take place at an age when so many other basic decisions are made which affect the course of life. On the other hand, history and pastoral experience confirm that conversion is by no means limited to adolescence. Starbuck and James agreed that, so far as their evidence went, those who had passed through conversion, having taken a religious stand, tended to feel identified with it, however much their religious enthusiasm might decline.

More recently William Sargant in *Battle for the Mind* (1957) has compared conversion with brain-washing techniques. He has sought to explain how beliefs—whether good or bad, true or false—can be implanted in the human brain (indoctrination), and how people can be switched to arbitrary beliefs opposed to those beliefs previously held (brain washing). Sargant's explanations draw upon the hypotheses of the Russian physiologist, I. P. Pavlov, who made a study of the reactions of dogs under varied conditions of stress.

In the ensuing debate Ian Ramage's *Battle for the Free Mind* (1967) admits that certain forms of evangelism differ little from indoctrination and brain washing, and therefore urges caution and self-criticism in modern evangelism. However, he rejects on historical and psychological grounds the charge that John Wesley's evangelism was a form of brain washing. Although there is a close relationship between mind and brain, Sargant's work suffers from failing to distinguish adequately between the two. Ramage contends that there are two radically different kinds of personality change that man can undergo—one essentially crippling and restrictive, the other creative and liberating. In genuine Christian experience there is a strengthening of personal integrity and a liberation from repressive and inhibiting factors, and these stem from submitting to the Lordship of Christ. "If the Son therefore shall make you free, you shall be free indeed" (John 8:36).

Bibliography:

G. Bertram, στρέφω, etc., *TWNT*, VII, 714-729.

E. M. B. Green, *Evangelism in the Early Church* (1970), 144-165.

M. Luther, *On the Bondage of the Will*, Eng. tr. by J. I. Packer and O. R. Johnston (1957).

A. D. Nock, *Conversion* (1933).

I. Ramage, *Battle for the Free Mind* (1967).

Colin Brown

CONVOCATION, from the Latin *convocatio*, a calling together, a provincial synod of the Church of England. Some universities also have bodies of registered graduates called Convocations, but the word is mainly used of assemblies of clergy of a more or less representative character. The Convocations of the Church of England are constitutional as well as ecclesiastical. There are two of these provincial synods, the Convocation of Canterbury and the Convocation of York, which are summoned to meet by royal writs issued to the archbishops at the time writs are issued for the assembling of Parliament. When assembled, they continue till prorogued or dissolved. These have always been separate synods. Each consists of two Houses, the Upper, composed of the bishops of the province, and the Lower, representing cathedrals, universities, and the diocesan clergy. A 20th-century innovation has been occasional joint meetings. When joint meetings are held, a representative body of laity (under the Enabling Act of 1919) may be summoned to confer with the combined Upper and Lower Houses, thus forming the National Assembly of the Church of England.

Convocations are ancient, being traced back to regulations made in the 7th century by Theodore, archbishop of Canterbury; the separate provincial authority of York dates from the 8th century. Convocations had the right to settle what taxes the clergy should pay to the Crown. The taxing powers of Convocations lingered till 1664.

Medieval Convocations passed legislation by means of canons, with due regard for the royal prerogative. Under Henry VIII "the submission of the clergy" limited the powers of Convocation.

After the revolution of 1688 Convocations were beset by political controversies, Whig and Tory, Hanoverian and Jacobite. As a result, for more than a hundred years the Crown, although still summoning Convocation, did not allow it to undertake any business. At length in 1852 the Convocation of Canterbury again began to deliberate, and York followed in 1861. A wide variety of religious concerns is discussed.

D. N. EMERSON

CONYBEARE, Frederick Cornwallis (1856-1924), a distinguished scholar whose researches in ancient Armenian literature resulted in several important discoveries. On the other hand, his writings as a member of the Rationalist Press Association were strongly characterized by skepticism. Educated at Oxford University, he obtained a First Class in Classical Moderations in 1876 and became a Fellow in 1880. Later distinctions were F.B.A. (1903) and LL.D. (St. Andrews, 1913). Among his more important discoveries were a ms ascribing the last twelve verses of Mark to Aristion (first century), a translation of a *Commentary on the Book of Acts* by Ephraem Syrus, and *The Key of Truth,* the sole surviving monument of the Paulician Church of Armenia. He catalogued the Armenian mss in the British Museum and the Bodleian Library. His published works include *The Key of Truth* (1898), *Old Armenian Texts of Revelation* (1906), *Myth, Magic and Morals* (Rationalist Press Association, 1909), *The History of Christ* (Rationalist Press Association, 1910), and *A History of New Testament Criticism* (1910).

BIBLIOGRAPHY:
D. S. Margoliouth, *DNB* (1922-1930), 210 f.
M. Mariès, "Frederick Cornwallis Conybeare," *Revue des Études Arméniennes* 6 (1926), 185-332.

WILLIAM J. CAMERON

COOK, Frederic Charles (1804-1889), an Anglican Bible scholar. Having studied at Cambridge and Bonn, he held a number of high positions, including chaplain to the Queen. He had a reputation as a linguist and was editor of the *Speaker's Commentary* (also called the *Bible Commentary* or *New Bible Commentary*). This commentary was designed to counteract the effect of modern criticism. Besides serving as editor, Cook wrote the introductions to several of the books and parts of the commentary on others. He wrote the entire commentary on Job, Habakkuk, Mark, Luke, and I Peter. In criticism of the revision of the NT he wrote *The Revised Version of the First Three Gospels Considered in Its Bearings upon the Record of Our Lord's Words and of Incidents in His Life* (1882), and *Deliver Us from Evil* (1883). Other works of his were *The Origins of Religion and Language* (1884) and, on the same subject, *Letters Addressed to the Rev. H. Mace and the Rev. J. Earle* (1885).

HARRY BUIS

COOKE, Henry (1788-1866), Irish church leader. Born near Maghera, Ulster, Cooke entered the University of Glasgow at the age of 14, to prepare for the ministry of the Irish Presbyterian Church. Licensed by the Presbytery of Ballymena in 1808, he ministered at Duneane (2 years), Donegore (5 years), and Killyleagh (14 years), before entering on his main ministry in May Street Church, Belfast, built in 1829. An impressive orator and powerful debater, he championed the cause of orthodox Presbyterianism against the powerful Arian party in his denomination and witnessed the complete triumph of his principles. He was three times called to the moderator's chair in the General Assembly of the Presbyterian Church in Ireland. In 1847 he was elected President, and Professor of Sacred Rhetoric and Catechetics, of Assembly's College, Belfast. Jefferson College awarded him its D.D. in 1829; and Trinity College, Dublin, its LL.D. in 1837. A diligent student, he prepared an *Analytical Concordance of the Bible*, but the ms was destroyed by fire before publication could be arranged. Influenced during his early ministry by Caesar Malan of Geneva, he was ever warmly evangelical. He said to one who came to see him in his last illness: "You see an old man going home; you see a great sinner saved by Divine grace; you see a frail mortal about to put on immortality."

BIBLIOGRAPHY:

J. L. Porter, *Life and Times of Henry Cooke, D.D., LL.D.* (Belfast, 1888).

R. STRANG MILLER

COORNHERT, Dirck V. (1522-1590), Dutch humanistic theologian and man of letters. Born in Amsterdam, he made a journey to Spain and Portugal in his youth. Only when he was 30 years old did he make a study of the classics, patristic literature, and the humanistic works of his own time. He then translated much of Cicero, Seneca, Homer, and Boccaccio. His most renowned Dutch work is *Zedekunst dat is Wellenvenskunste* (*The Art of Morality*), which appeared in 1586. He supported William the Silent, was Secretary of Haarlem, and then for some time Secretary of the States of Holland. It has been rightly stated that if his ideas had prevailed, Roman Catholicism would have had an easy triumph and in the next generation the Reformed faith would have disappeared completely. Influenced by the so-called Biblical humanism of Erasmus, the spiritualism of the "Theologia Deutsch," and the liberal ideas of Castellio, he continually attacked the Reformed doctrines of original sin, predestination, justification by faith, and the supreme authority of the Bible. He acknowledged Reason as his only authority, believing that it bridles man's passions and that a constant, honest use of it leads to perfection. In his work *Verschooninghe van de Roomsche afgoderye* (*Apology for Roman Catholic Idolatry*), he took the position that it was quite acceptable to persist in Roman practices, to attend Roman worship, to assume the outward form of a Roman Catholic if only the inward spirit remained free. In the next year (1562) Calvin wrote against him his *Résponse à un certain Hollandais, lequel sous ombre de faire les Chrétiens tout spirituels, leur permet de polluer leur corps en toutes idolatries.* Coornhert is called "a prophet of tolerance," but his vehement mode of argumentation proved him to be very intolerant. In some respects he influenced the later Arminians.

BIBLIOGRAPHY:

G. Kuiper, *ChrE*, s.v.

F. L. Rutgers, *Calvin's invloed op de Reformatie in de Nederlanden* (Leiden, 1889).

LOUIS PRAAMSMA

COOS (in the RV and RSV, this appears as Cos), a large mountainous island bearing a city of the same name, located off the SW coast of Asia Minor near Halicarnassus. Famous for wines and silk, it was the location of the medical school of Hippocrates, of the 5th century B.C. Paul visited Cos after leaving Miletus at the close of his third missionary journey (Acts 21:1).

COPERNICUS, Nicolaus (1473-1543), founder of modern astronomy. Born Mikolaj Kopernik at Torun, a town on the Vistula which had a few years earlier come under Polish sovereignty, Copernicus entered Cracow University in 1491 as a student of mathematics and science. It was there that he first became interested in the geocentric system of Ptolemy. In 1496 he went to Italy to study canon law and astronomy at Bologna, where he became acquainted with and assisted the astronomer Domenico Novarra of Ferrara. Four years later he left Bologna, lectured on astronomy in Rome, paid a short visit home, and in 1501 went to study medicine at the University of Padua. Shortly afterwards, he took leave to take up canon law at Ferrara, receiving his doctor's degree there in 1503. Authorities differ at this point: some say he then returned to Poland, others that he resumed medical studies at Padua. What is clear is that when he did go back to his native country he possessed all the contemporary knowledge of mathematics, medicine, astronomy, and theology.

By 1506 we find him secretary and medical adviser to his uncle, Lucas Watzelrode, the influential bishop of Ermland, a post held till the bishop died in 1512. Copernicus then went to Frauenburg Cathedral, of which he had been made a canon in 1501, took up ecclesiastical duties, and used his medical skill chiefly in the service of the poor. He remained in Frauenburg for the rest of his life, becoming in 1523 administrator-general of the diocese where he had become known also as a stout opponent of the marauding activities of the Teutonic Knights.

His Heliocentric System

During his stay in Bologna, Copernicus had studied the original texts of ancient writings on astronomy, and it may have been then that he began seriously to doubt the traditional (second century) Ptolemaic theory of the universe, which held that the earth was a central stationary body about which the sun, planets, and stars all revolved daily. Copernicus suggested that their apparent motions were more easily explicable by assuming that the earth rotated and moved around the sun. Instruments were then imperfect, and he could not prove his theory, but he was persuaded of its validity because it offered a much more logical explanation than did the Ptolemaic theory.

His fame spread, but when ecclesiastical authorities consulted him on the long-considered question of calendar reform he declined to commit himself, holding that the positions of sun and moon were not accurately enough known to allow a proper reassessment. He became increasingly dissatisfied with the Ptolemaic system (a conclusion shared by some other scholars of the day), and about 1530 he completed his great work *De Revolutionibus Orbium Coelestium* (*On the Revolutions of Celestial Bodies*). Publication was postponed because the church was committed to the Ptolemaic theory, but in the following year he did publish his *Commentariolus*, in which he illustrated his heliocentric system without calculations—to the evident approval of Pope Clement VII.

De Revolutionibus found its way to Nuremberg through the agency of Rheticus, a disciple and admirer of Copernicus, where it was published in 1543, just before Copernicus died. Unhappily, an anonymous preface by Andreas Osiander, a local pastor opposed to Copernicus' views, implied that the work was completely hypothetical. Partly because of this, the book's findings were not generally accepted for some time. Leaders of the Reformation, moreover, notably Luther and Melanchthon, opposed it because they thought it was at variance with the Bible.

Lasting Influence

The Copernican system as originally propounded was not entirely accurate, chiefly because it assumed that the planets revolved in circles, rather than ellipses, around the sun. Copernicus was, however, the first to locate the sun correctly among its planets. Some writers of antiquity had taught that the earth rotated but had been scoffed at; Copernicus provided what his predecessors could not: a logical basis for this view. He is a profoundly significant figure in history, not only because of his astronomical achievements, but because he effected a shattering and salutary change in human thought and outlook. He gave great stimulation to man's inquiring mind, which is a prerequisite for the advance of knowledge.

Copernicus produced also an exposition of currency reform, which was not published till 1816 at Warsaw. He held that bad money always drives out good —a principle now incorporated in Gresham's Law.

BIBLIOGRAPHY:

A. Armitage, *Copernicus, Founder of Modern Astronomy* (London, 1939).

S. P. Mizwa, *Nicholas Copernicus* (Kosciuszko Foundation, 1943).

J. Rudnicki, *Nicholas Copernicus* (Copernicus Quatercentenary Celebration Committee, London, 1943).

JAMES DIXON DOUGLAS

COPTIC CHURCH

I. The Term "Coptic"
II. Beginnings and History of the Church
III. Characteristics of the Church and Modern Trends

I. The Term "Coptic"

The Coptic Church is the Monophysite Church of Egypt. The term is sometimes used popularly, but inaccurately, of the Ethiopian Orthodox Church, which is likewise monophysite and related historically to the Egyptian form (see ETHIOPIC CHURCH). The words *Copt* and *Coptic*, derived from the Arabic through Greek, denote both the people indigenous to Egypt and the language which they spoke in the centuries before the invasion of the Muslim Arabs imposed upon the land the Islamic culture that has existed there since the 7th century. Arabic is now the vernacular of the Copts as well as of all other Egyptians, and while opinions vary on the question of whether the Copts have distinctive physical characteristics, a strong case seems to have been made for the view that since intermarriage has almost always resulted in the Coptic person's turning to Islam, their stock has not been diluted much over the centuries.

II. Beginnings and History of the Church

The origins and early development of the church comprised of Coptic-speaking believers remain a problem to the historian. The important figures and the general course of events in and around Alexandria are accessible, but source materials are wanting regarding the considerable Christian community in Upper (southern) Egypt during the first three centuries of our era, and even the details of church life among the Copts of the N are not as full as could be wished. The Arian controversy of the 4th century, which raged in Alexandria among the Greeks, had but little effect on the Copts, who vigorously supported Athanasius and the high Christology of Nicea. In the next century, however, Byzantine politics and an unfortunate looseness in Christological terminology by the brilliant and influential Cyril of Alexandria (whose views were developed by Eutyches and supported in their Eutychian form by Dioscurus, Cyril's successor to the Alexandrian patriarchate) combined to drive the Coptic-speaking Christians to repudiate the formulations of Chalcedon in 451 (at which council Dioscurus was deposed, excommunicated, and banished). The Egyptian Church thus became officially monophysite, and communion was severed between it and orthodox Christendom.

These developments had serious civil as well as ecclesiastical results. The orthodox party (the "Melchites") appointed its own patriarch and began a vigorous persecution of the monophysite heretics. Most of the latter, unable to defend themselves against the power of the Byzantine court, left Lower (northern) Egypt in large numbers and settled in the S. There ensued almost two centuries of more or less constant strife between the two groups, now relieved, now heightened by the monothelite debate (see MONOPHYSITISM, MONOTHELITISM). At the end, the Christian cause in Egypt became so weakened that when in 640 the Arab Muslims invaded, the Copts, welcoming them as liberators, supported them against the orthodox. Within two years the whole country had passed into Islamic hands, where it remains until this day.

The history of the Coptic Church from the Arab conquest to the modern period consists of a series of persecutions interspersed with some years of comparative quiet. (The persecutions, notably those under the Caliph al Hakim at the beginning of the 11th century, resulted in considerable numerical losses for the Copts.) As the 19th century dawned, the lot of the Copts became less difficult, and the church has for some years enjoyed official toleration. This, it may be remarked, although it allows freedom of worship, is not the equivalent of religious liberty and assuredly does not include the unrestricted right to proselytize. Modern Egyptian governments are frankly Islamic; all types of Christianity are restricted, and the lot of the Muslim convert is hard. At present there are about 1,900,000 Christians of all kinds out of a total Egyptian population of some 24 million. Copts constitute the large majority of this group, which also includes Greek Orthodox, a Uniat Coptic Church (in communion with Rome), and several Protestant churches. The main strength of Coptic Christianity is in Upper Egypt, notably around Assiut.

III. Characteristics and Modern Trends

The Coptic Church shares many features with other ancient E churches and with Rome. It is highly liturgical; the altar-centered services are conducted in the ancient Coptic language (Sahidic dialect), which is understood by practically none of the Arabic-speaking populace and by few of the clergymen themselves, among whom educational standards are not high. In modern times, however, the practice of Scripture reading and preaching in the vernacular at the services has grown. Monasticism has played an important part in the church's life from the beginning, and remains strong; the patriarch of Alexandria is always chosen from among the monks. Priests and inferior clergy may marry. The church enjoins a rigorous system of fasting (the longest period is the 55-day Lenten fast, but Copts observe more than one third of the days of the year in abstinences of one kind or another). The church practices infant baptism; it as well as the Baptism of adult converts is performed by the total immersion of the candidate, unclothed. Communion, on which a view of transubstantiation approximating that of Rome is held, is given in both kinds, but the members of the laity do not commonly receive it after reaching the age of puberty. Circumcision of male infants is practiced, but evidently for customary rather than religious reasons. The church buildings contain paintings of various religious subjects but not much statuary. Veneration of images or icons is not practiced, although prayers to the saints are offered and much emphasis is given to the intercession of the Virgin Mary. The training of the clergy consists almost exclusively in liturgical studies; knowledge of the Scriptures is not common among the priests and even less so among the people.

Understandably from the foregoing, the impact of the Coptic Church upon Muslim Egypt has been negligible; indeed, the flow is in the other direction, for defections to Islam take place at the rate of more than six hundred persons per year. In the 19th century, when Protestant missionary enterprise in Egypt was begun, it was the hope of some evangelical societies that a reformed and awakened indigenous church would become the means of bringing light to that country's millions of unevangelized Muslims. However, several decades of effort in that direction proved fruitless. Since Coptic Christianity was moribund and content to be so, there was no choice but to bring new churches into existence. In recent years there have been some hopeful signs: a group of priests and laymen with evangelical tendencies and dedicated to the promotion of the knowledge of Holy Scripture has become active within the Coptic Church. It remains to be seen, however, how great will be the influence of those of such persuasion in restoring the Egyptian church as a whole to the understanding and service of the truth of the Gospel.

Bibliography:

D. Attwater, *Christian Churches of the East* (Milwaukee, 1947-48).

E. L. Butcher, *The Story of the Churches of Egypt* (London, 1897), 2 vols.

A. J. Butler, *The Ancient Coptic Churches of Egypt* (Oxford, 1884), 2 vols.

"Coptic Church," *ODCC*, s.v.

W. E. Crum, "Coptic Church," *New Schaff-Herzog Encyclopedia of Religious Knowledge*, III, 267 ff.

Herbert Bird

CORBAN, a Hebrew word meaning an "offering" given to God. Mark 7:11 duplicates in the Greek (*κορβᾶν*) the sounds of this Hebrew word (קָרְבָּן), which has been subsequently also transliterated into the English word "corban" found in the AV.

The Hebrew word is used in Lev. 2: 1, 4, 12, 13, where it refers to an "offering." In each of these verses the root verb קָרַב ("to come near") is also used, occurring in the Hiphil stem in which it means "to offer." Hence a "corban" in OT usage was a gift offered to the Lord.

From Mark 7:9-13 it is seen that in NT times a practice had become acceptable in the casuistry of the scribes and Pharisees in which a man could take the funds which he had set aside to take care of his parents in their old age and donate them to an approved religious project. Through pronouncing them "corban" it was then to be understood that he had given the funds to a higher cause and was to be considered as released from his obligation to his now-infirm parents. Christ denounced both this and the reasoning behind it as an open disobedience to God's law. He cited this custom as an example of the pharisaic and rabbinic legalism that set aside God's laws through the traditions and reasonings of men (Mark 7:9-13; I Cor. 3:19-20; Mt. 5:20 ff.).

CORINTH, the chief commercial city at the W end of the isthmus between central Greece and the Peloponnese. Artifacts from the site show that it was settled in the Neolithic period, and was subsequently reoccupied by the Dorians about 1000 B.C. In the 7th century B.C. Corinth attained great prosperity under Cypselus and his son Periander, becoming renowned for its bronze and pottery work as well as its commercial activity. From the fourth to the second centuries B.C. Corinth was controlled mainly by the Macedonians but joined the Achaean League in 196 B.C. The city was destroyed fifty years later for its opposition to Rome, but a century later was rebuilt by Caesar as a commercial center. Under Augustus it became the capital of the province of Achaea, having its own proconsul.

The Apostle Paul's 18-month stay in Corinth (Acts 18:1-18) has been dated by reference to an inscription from Delphi indicating that Gallio came as proconsul to Corinth in A.D. 51 or 52 (Acts 18:12-17). His "judgment-seat" (Acts 18:12) has been identified, as has also the "meat-market" (AV, "shambles," I Cor. 10:25). An inscription near the theater mentions an aedile (Roman official), Erastus (cf. Rom. 16:23), and another fragmentary one found on the lintel of a Jewish synagogue may indicate the successor to the one of Acts 18:4.

CORINTHIANS, FIRST EPISTLE TO THE

I. City and Church

The geographical position of the city of Corinth was on the isthmus, the narrow neck of land connecting the Peloponnesus with central Greece. On either side of it was a harbor city, Lechaeum and Cenchreae. This famous location made ancient Corinth the major merchant city of commerce between E and W, and consequently a prosperous city. In 146 B.C. the Romans destroyed ancient Corinth. The city had become a member of the Achaian confederation that tried to recapture the freedom of Greece. In 46 B.C. Corinth was rebuilt by Julius Caesar, who populated it mainly with people who had been given their freedom. Now the city was a Roman colony and it was also made the seat of the proconsul of the province of Achaia. Soon it flourished again. Many came from Egypt, Syria, and Asia, also among whom were Jews who settled there. The mixed character of the population is evident from the several strange religions that became part of Corinthian life. New Corinth was no longer a Greek city. It was now genuinely Hellenistic. It was a meeting place of E and W, culturally, religiously, and commercially. This increasing prosperity was, however, accompanied by a growing moral corruption. Corinthian immorality became proverbial. Great wealth as well as much poverty and an impoverished proletariat were also found there side by side.

Paul arrived in this city on his second missionary journey, probably in the year 51 (Acts 18:1-17). Travelling from Athens, he found lodging with Aquila and Priscilla, Jews who had come from Rome. At first Paul preached to the Jews only. When, however, they rejected the Gospel, he left the synagogue. Using the house of the proselyte Titus Justus as his new base, he now directed his efforts to the Gentiles. He did not sever all relations with the Jews, as the conversion of Crispus, chief ruler of the synagogue, shows. His results among the Gentiles caused resistance among the Jews. They brought him before the new proconsul, Gallio, accusing him of going against their law. Gallio, realizing that this was a Jewish religious question, refused to act.

With much difficulty, in about a year and a half Paul gathered together a large Christian congregation, which developed a rich spiritual life. After Paul's departure Apollos, a learned Jewish Christian, educated in Alexandria, carried on his work (Acts 18:24-28). Aquila and Priscilla had heard his preaching in the synagogue in Ephesus and taught him a more accurate understanding of the Gospel. He received Christian Baptism and then went to Corinth, where, after Paul's departure, he continued his work.

On his third missionary journey Paul remained three years in Ephesus (54-57), a city opposite Corinth, separated from it only by the heavily sailed Aegean Sea. Messengers and letters busily went back and forth. Some are mentioned by name, but there were no doubt many others.

II. Occasion and Purpose

In those years Paul wrote at least four letters to Corinth, of which only two are in the NT (unless these letters include parts of those other two). It appears from I Cor. 5:9 and 11, where Paul speaks of an earlier letter, that before writing I Corinthians he had written an earlier letter which apparently was misunderstood by the congregation. At least it seemed necessary to correct it and send another one in its stead. This unknown first letter is lost.

Reports from Corinth were the occasion for Paul's writing I Corinthians. Messengers mentioned in it are those who "are of the house of Chloe." She must have been a well-to-do Christian woman from Corinth who is otherwise unknown to us. They told Paul about the unpleasant divisions in the church. Also, Apollos had sailed from Corinth to Ephesus (I Cor. 16:12). Three other Christians, Stephanas, Fortunatus, and Achaicus, also came to Paul (I Cor. 16:17). They, and probably others, had brought with them a letter for Paul (I Cor. 7:1) in which there were many questions. Paul considered the advisability of travelling to Corinth to solve the difficulties. Not willing to interrupt his successful work in Ephesus (I Cor. 16: 8, 9), he decided against it and instead wrote a letter. This epistle was probably carried to Corinth by the three messengers just mentioned.

No doubt exists about the authenticity of this epistle. Clement of Rome was acquainted with it as coming from Paul (47:1-3), and it is regularly cited by the fathers of the 2nd century. The question, however, has been raised whether this letter was written originally in the form it has now. There are those who think that parts from other letters written by Paul to the church in Corinth have been added to it.

III. Authenticity

The epistle itself supplies the information that it was written in Ephesus (I Cor. 16:8). From that city and via Macedonia Paul intended to go to Corinth. This plan he carried out on his third missionary journey (Acts 20:1- 2).

IV. Time and Place of Origin

There is little difference of opinion about the time of composition. Most are agreed that this was during the final months of Paul's long stay in Ephesus (third missionary journey) and before the Jewish Pentecost of the year 54 (according to some, 55).

V. Contents

In the introduction to the letter (1: 1-9) Paul greets the church and thanks God for her well-being. Then he points out the existing internal divisions and quarrels (1:10–6:20) which had been reported to him. Pointing to his own behavior as an apostle, he shows that the Gospel is not human wisdom but God's wisdom, so that the congregation has no reason to be proud. Paul has laid the foundation, which is Christ, and the congregation, being the temple of God, must build on it.

Against the background of another report (5:1), Paul discusses a number of questions dealing with sexual matters and emphasizes to the congregation that the body belongs to the Lord.

Further, the apostle discusses questions which had been put to him in a letter from Corinth (7:1–11:1), concerning marriage, the eating of meat sacrificed to idols—the latter in connection with the freedom of the Christian—and some other matters. In the next section

(11:2-34), Paul takes up a number of disorders in the church—women who pray and prophesy with uncovered head and the abuses at the communal meals.

The place of spiritual gifts in the meetings of the congregation is the subject of the next section (12–14) with its climactic hymn in praise of love. Paul makes it clear that persons with charismatic gifts, and particularly those who are able to speak in tongues, were demanding too large a place for themselves. He also has something to say to those who were denying the resurrection from the dead (15:1-58). He proclaims the Resurrection of Christ as a genuine event in history. The risen Christ is also the firstfruits of a great many who will be raised, and His Resurrection gives meaning to the life of the church. Having discussed some possible objections against this, Paul describes what will happen at the Parousia.

Concluding his letter (16:1-24), Paul mentions a collection for the poverty-stricken Christians in Jerusalem and his plan to visit Corinth. He commends Timothy and gives some information concerning Apollos. He ends his letter with a number of admonitions and a commendation of Stephanas and his family.

CORINTHIANS, SECOND EPISTLE TO THE

II Corinthians is the third longest of the thirteen letters in the NT which bear the name of Paul, only Romans and I Corinthians being longer.

1. Authorship

The Pauline authorship of II Corinthians is uncontested, excepting such eccentric schools of thought as that represented by the Dutch scholar W. C. van Manen (cf. his contribution to the article "Paul" in *Encyclopaedia Biblica*, columns 3620 ff., especially 3626 f.) and certain modern reservations about the six verses 6:14–7:1 (see below, 5. Structure). With Romans, I Corinthians, and Galatians, it belongs to the four "capital" epistles which provide us with the foundation of Pauline theology.

2. Destination

The addressees are specified with all desirable clarity: they are "the church of God which is at Corinth"—a church planted by Paul himself (Acts 18:1-18—together with "all the saints who are in the whole of Achaia" (1:1). Achaia (S Greece) was the Roman province of which Corinth was the capital; the Gospel evidently had spread from Corinth into every part of this province (cf. 9:2; 11:10), including, for example, Cenchreae, the E seaport of Corinth (Rom. 16:1).

3. Background

At least two letters, and probably three, had been sent by Paul to the Corinthian church before II Corinthians. One was the "previous letter" of I Cor. 5:9, warning the Christians in Corinth against association with fornicators; next came the letter which we call I Corinthians, written from Ephesus. When Paul sent I Corinthians, it was his intention to follow it up with a personal visit, some time after Pentecost in A.D. 55. He sent Timothy ahead of him as his representative; he himself planned to pass through Macedonia (the province N of Achaia) during the summer and fall of that year and so come to Corinth, where he would perhaps spend the winter (I Cor. 16:5-9).

Shortly afterwards he changed this plan somewhat and decided to visit Corinth twice—once before going on to Macedonia and then on his way back from Macedonia before he set sail for Judaea with the collection for the Jerusalem church (II Cor. 1:15 f.; 8:1 ff.; cf. I Cor. 16:1-4; Rom. 15:25 ff.). He seems to have kept the Corinthians in touch with his plans as they took shape.

But several factors combined to prevent him from carrying out these plans as he had hoped. In addition to dangers which beset him in Ephesus and elsewhere in the province of Asia, news from Corinth became increasingly disquieting. It appears that I Corinthians was not immediately effective in checking those trends in the church which caused Paul such concern, and Timothy, when he arrived, was not strong enough to enforce Paul's directives. It may have been Timothy's report that moved Paul to pay Corinth a flying visit for a personal confrontation with those members of the church who resisted his authority. The visit was a painful one for all concerned (II Cor. 2:1; 13:2). The opposition to Paul came to a head, and he felt humiliated among his own converts from whom he ought to have derived joy (12:21). He left Corinth and returned to Asia through Macedonia. At some point he sent the church a letter, written "out of much affliction and anguish of heart and with many tears" (2:3 f.). Another of his lieutenants, Titus, was entrusted with this letter, and no sooner had Titus set off with it than Paul began to regret that he had sent it (7:8). In it he assured the Corinthians of his love for them, and demanded that they should give proof of the love they claimed to have for him by submitting to his authority as the apostle of Christ and disciplining those who had led the opposition to him, among whom one man in particular appears to have played a prominent part. He told Titus that he had no doubt of the Corinthians' basic loyalty and that they would show their loyalty by rendering him the obedience he demanded. He now had to wait and see if this expression of confidence would prove to be well founded or not. Back in the province of Asia he was prey to external threats and inward distress. He tried to settle down at Troas, hoping that Titus would land there if he came back from Corinth across the Aegean. Although Troas presented him with splendid opportunities for preaching the Gospel, his spirit was too restless for him to take advantage of them. When at last it became clear that Titus would not come by sea, because navigation across the Aegean had closed down for the winter, he crossed over into Macedonia, expecting Titus now to travel N by road (2:12 f.). Troubles without and within still assailed him, until at last Titus arrived (perhaps at Philippi) and brought such good news that Paul's clouds melted away (7:5 ff.). Paul's sorrowful letter had proved completely effective: his boasting to Titus about his Corinthian converts had been vindicated. They were stung with such a sense of shame and indignation that now, in their zeal to show their love and loyalty to Paul, they were in danger of pressing to unwarranted extremes their disciplinary action against the opposition party and, in particular, its leader (2:5-11; 7:12). There were still a few murmurs about Paul's disconcerting changes of plan: why did he go back to Asia from Macedonia and not pay a further visit to Corinth, as he had promised? But the general mood was one of repentance and reconciliation: Titus was delighted with it and communicated his delight to Paul. In the joy and relief which flooded his soul when he received Titus' news, Paul sent this further letter (II Corinthians) to Corinth, in which he pours out his heart in unreserved affection.

4. Date

The date from which this middle period of Paul's apostolic career can be fixed is Gallio's arrival in Corinth as proconsul of Achaia (cf. Acts 18:12). On the strength of a Delphi inscription bearing a proclamation of the emperor Claudius (H. Dessau, *Inscriptiones Latinae Selectae* ii^3, 801), this was probably on July 1, 51 (or possibly just twelve months later). This enables us to date Paul's eighteen months in Corinth (Acts 18:11) from spring of A.D. 50 to fall of A.D. 52 and his ensuing residence in Ephesus—two and a quarter to three years (Acts 19:8-10; 20:31)—from fall of 52 to early summer of 55. "Pentecost" in I Cor. 16:8 would be that of A.D. 55; the events between the sending of I and II Corinthians would occupy the remainder of A.D. 55 and II Corinthians was probably sent early in A.D. 56. The references in II Cor. 8:10; 9:2 to the original Corinthian interest in the collection for Jerusalem (cf. I Cor. 16:1-4) as being manifested "a year ago" or "last year" may suggest an interval between the two letters of 9 to 15 months.

5. Structure

The foregoing discussion of the date of II Corinthians presupposes the substantial unity of the letter. If, however, it is a composite document in which portions of two or more letters from Paul to the Corinthian church have been preserved, then different dates would have to be assigned to the different parts.

The main structural problem is posed by the sudden change of attitude when we move from chapter 9 to chapter 10. The spirit of warmth and reconciliation which characterizes most of chapters 1 to 9 gives place suddenly to sharp polemic and self-defense. Paul denounces certain opponents who have made their way to Corinth and endeavored to alienate his converts' loyalty; he uses language of unsparing severity with regard to those members of the Corinthian church who refuse to submit to his authority. There is little sign here of the near-unanimous revulsion of feeling in Paul's favor which figures prominently in chapter 7, and even less of the apostle's consequent sense of relief. It looks indeed as if, between the dictating of chapters 9 and 10, disturbing and unpleasant news about the Corinthians reached Paul which convinced him that the recent improvement in their attitude had been but short-lived.

But another explanation of the change of mood in II Corinthians 10–13 has won widespread acceptance for the last 100 years—namely, that these chapters originally formed part of the "tearful letter" which was sent to Corinth soon after Paul's "painful visit" (II Cor. 2:1-4; 7:8-12), and therefore antedated II Cor. 1–9. In support of this view it is argued that several back-references to the "tearful letter" and its occasion in II Cor. 1–7 have actual counterparts in chapters 10–13 (cf., e.g., II Cor. 1:23 and 2:3 with 13:10; 2:4 with 11:11 and 12:15; 2:9 with 10:6; 3:1 with 10:8 ff.). There is the further, though uncritical, consideration that if II Cor. 1–9 follows II Cor. 10–13, Paul's Corinthian correspondence has a happy ending.

There are, however, some factors which tell against the identification of II Cor. 10–13 with the "tearful letter," or part of it. These four chapters may possibly have been written "with many tears," but they read as if they had been composed more in anger than in sorrow. Whereas in the tearful letter Paul called for the disciplining of those members of the Corinthian church who defied his apostolic authority, in II Cor. 10–13 he attacks those interlopers who came to Corinth masquerading as apostles of Christ (11:13), and his main complaint about the Corinthian Christians is that they are too ready to accept these impostors at their own valuation. The tearful letter called in particular for the disciplining of one individual (II Cor. 2:5-11; 7:12), but there is nothing of this in II Cor. 10–13. Above all, there is a reference in 12:18 to a recent financial mission of Titus to the Corinthian church which cannot be other than the mission to organize its contribution to the fund for Jerusalem, on which he sets out in 8:6, 16 ff., not long after his return from his happy mission of reconciliation. It is clear not only that 12:18 was written after chapter 8, but also that a sufficient interval has elapsed for Paul to be able to appeal to the Corinthians' knowledge of Titus' conduct during that visit. During this interval, it appears, Paul received news of the influence which interlopers (probably from Judaea) were exercising among his converts at Corinth: it was this news that occasioned II Cor. 10–13. This sequence of events would mean that Paul's Corinthian correspondence has no happy ending—but life, including church life, is often like that.

Another problem in the structure of II Corinthians relates to the short paragraph 6:14–7:1, which has been felt by some scholars to be intrusive in its present position, interrupting Paul's plea in 6:1-13 and 7:2-4. The theory that this is a misplaced fragment of the "previous letter" of I Cor. 5:9, first propounded, it appears, by A. Hilgenfeld in 1876, has to surmount the general obstacle of bibliographical improbability (shared with all interpolation theories of the paragraph) and the particular obstacle that, whereas the "previous letter" conveyed a warning against fornication, this paragraph conveys a warning against idolatry. On the other hand, this paragraph contains eight words not otherwise found in the letters of Paul or anywhere else in the NT, but also presents close affinities with leading themes and locutions in Qumran literature. However, Paul is quite capable of digression, and the resumption in 7:2 of the appeal of 6:13 ("open your hearts wide to us") suggests that in fact he had digressed at this point. Furthermore, he was no stranger to Hebrew thought and could easily incorporate in his letter material expressive of the truth he wished to bring out.

Arguments that the excursus on the apostolic ministry (2:14–6:10) breaks the flow of Paul's personal narrative, or that the exhortations about the collection for Jerusalem (8:1–9:15) represent one or two separate notes, not originally part of the same letter as chapters 1–7, do not weigh seriously against the unity of chapters 1–9. It is not easy to see how scribal or editorial activity could have been responsible for so many insertions of Pauline fragments from other compositions; and the circumstances of dictation, coupled with Paul's tendency to digress for longer or shorter periods, will account for most of the breaks in continuity.

6. Contents

OUTLINE:

- I. Removal of Misunderstanding (1:1–2:13)
  - A. Salutation (1:1-2)
  - B. Thanksgiving for Divine comfort (1:3-7)
  - C. Paul's deliverance from deadly peril (1:8-11)
  - D. Explanation of recent conduct (1:12–2:4)
    - 1. A plea for understanding (1:12-14)
    - 2. Answer to charge of vacillation (1:15-24)
    - 3. A painful visit and a tearful letter (2:1-4)
  - E. Call to forgive an offender (2:5-11)
  - F. Paul's unrest after sending the tearful letter (2:12-13)
- II. The Apostolic Ministry (2:14–7:1)
  - A. The triumphal progress of the Gospel (2:14-17)
  - B. The ministry of the new covenant (3:1-18)
    - 1. Paul's credentials (3:1-3)
    - 2. Letter and spirit (3:4-6)
    - 3. The fading glory of the old covenant and the excelling glory of the new (3:7-18)
  - C. Hardship and splendor of apostolic service (4:1–5:10)
    - 1. Paul's source of encouragement (4:1)
    - 2. Divine treasure in earthen vessels (4:2-15)
    - 3. Momentary affliction and eternal glory (4:16-18)
    - 4. The Christian's sure hope (5:1-10)

- D. The message of reconciliation (5:11–6:13)
  1. The preachers' motive (5:11-15)
  2. Ambassadors for Christ (5:16-21)
  3. Apostolic entreaty (6:1-13)
- E. Call to separation from idolatry (6:14–7:1)

III. Restoration of Mutual Confidence (7:2-16)
- A. Paul's affection for the Corinthians (7:2-4)
- B. Joyful sequel to the tearful letter (7:5-16)

IV. The Collection for Jerusalem (8:1–9:15)
- A. A new mission for Titus (8:1-24)
- B. Generous sowing, generous reaping (9:1-15)

V. Vindication of Paul's Apostolic Authority (10:1–13:14)
- A. Attack on citadels of rebellion (10:1-12)
- B. Spheres of service (10:13-18)
- C. False apostles (11:1-15)
- D. Paul boasts "as a fool" (11:16-29)
- E. A humiliating memory (11:30-33)
- F. An ecstatic experience and its sequel (12:1-10)
- G. Signs of an apostle (12:11-13)
- H. A third visit (12:14-21)
- I. Concluding admonition (13:1-10)
- J. Final exhortation, greetings, and benediction (13:11-14)

I. Removal of Misunderstanding (1:1–2:13)

Paul, conjoining Timothy's name with his own in greeting the Corinthian church, breaks out into an ascription of blessing to God for His consoling mercy. He himself had recently experienced Divine comfort in an outstanding degree and so was able to practice the ministry of comfort. As the sufferings he endured in the cause of the Gospel were accepted by him as a sharing in Christ's sufferings on His people's behalf (cf. Col. 1:24), so, when he enjoys the comfort of Christ, he communicates that comfort to them (1:1-7).

One signal form of comfort which Paul had recently experienced was his deliverance from a deadly peril somewhere in the province of Asia. Whether it was a near-mortal illness or some external attack that menaced him (and the language suggests the latter rather than the former), he had never been nearer death. In fact, death seemed quite certain—so much so that, when deliverance came unexpectedly, he greeted it as a miracle of resurrection, wrought by the power of God. The experience, whatever it was, permanently affected Paul's outlook on his personal future; for the present, he reflected that the God who had delivered him so signally would deliver him from further danger (1:8-11).

Now that the strained relations between Paul and his Corinthian converts had become more friendly, he explains why he had changed his mind about visiting them more than once on his recent tour. He had planned to visit them twice, once on his way to Macedonia and again on his way from Macedonia to Judaea, but he did not carry out his plan. This was not through worldly vacillation: they ought to know him better than that. He had learned consistency and trustworthiness in speech from the God whose Gospel he proclaimed—the God whose promises were sure and found their answering "Yes" in Christ. (That, he adds, is why Christians in worship add their own "Amen," or "Yes," when the promises of God are rehearsed in their hearing.) Paul is conscious of his responsibility to the God who commissioned him to be an apostle, anointing and sealing him with the Holy Spirit, even as the Corinthian Christians themselves had received the same Spirit as a guarantee of their future heritage of glory (1:12-24).

If he changed his mind about paying them a third visit, it was because the second one was so painful. Instead of paying a third visit, he wrote a further letter—wrote it weeping, as he urged them to prove the reality of their love to him. The unnamed offender of 2:5-11 has traditionally been identified with the incestuous man of I Cor. 5:1 ff., with the corollary that the tearful letter is our I Corinthians. But I Corinthians does not give the impression of a particularly sorrowful letter, and the offender of 2:5-11 is much more likely to have been an offender against Paul personally, to be forgiven at Paul's direction, than one whose behavior had damaged the church's reputation among its pagan neighbors. Paul might well be accused of "vacillating" if, after demanding the solemn sentence of I Cor. 5:3-5, he now urged the church to let bygones be bygones. Paul had apparently demanded sanctions against the offender of 2:5-11 in order to test the church's obedience; now that proof of its obedience was forthcoming, the sanctions could be dropped, the more so as the man was thoroughly penitent (1:23–2:11).

After the dispatch of the tearful letter Paul was so agitated that he could not settle down—even to exploit the opportunities for evangelism which lay before him at Troas. He waited anxiously for Titus to return and tell him how the Corinthians had reacted to his letter. When, after he crossed into Macedonia, Titus met him there with his good news, the relief was indescribable (2:12, 13).

II. The Apostolic Ministry (2:14–7:1)

Paul's thanksgiving to God for Titus' good news is caught up into thanksgiving for the glory of the gospel ministry with which he has been entrusted—a ministry in which Christ leads His servants in His triumphal procession. No human commendation is required for these servants: the effects of their ministry in the lives of men and women like the Corinthian Christians is commendation and seal enough. The glory of this life-bringing ministry of the new covenant surpasses the glory that attended the promulgation of the old covenant of Sinai, based on a law that pronounced death on the sinner. Great as that ancient glory was, it was a fading glory, of which the disappearing radiance on Moses' face after his confrontation with God (Ex. 34:29-35) was a parable. By contrast with the veiled and fading glory on Moses' face, believers under the new covenant see the unveiled and unfading "glory of God in the face of Christ" (4:6). Paul's methods were as open and above board as the Gospel he proclaimed; if that Gospel was obscure, it was so through no fault of his own but because of the veil which covered the eyes of unbelievers and prevented them from seeing the light of the new creation shining in Christ, the very image of God (2:14–4:6).

Yet, glorious as the apostolic ministry was, it was committed to frail human beings, who could never be suspected of responsibility for the glory and efficacy of the message they preached. They were exposed to mortal danger every day; but this they endured for Jesus' sake, so that not only His suffering and death, but His resurrection life, might be displayed in their mortal bodies. Their affliction was light and temporary, and was actually the means used by God to secure the excelling weight of eternal glory which would be their portion in Christ. "So we do not lose heart," says Paul (4:7-18).

One day the present mortal "tent" or "garment" will be discarded and replaced by the enduring "dwelling" which is even now being prepared. Paul looks forward, not to a disembodied existence, but to the "putting on" of this heavenly garment (the "spiritual body" of I Cor. 15:44). If the mortal body were even now transformed and "swallowed up by life," that would be best of all. But if death must intervene, then to be "absent from the [mortal] body" would mean being "at home with the Lord." In either case the judgment seat of Christ must be faced; therefore, to please Christ is Paul's present and constant concern (5:1-10).

Therefore it was from no motives of self-advertisement that Paul discharged his ministry; he was impelled by the joint constraint of "the fear of the Lord" (5:11) and "the love of Christ" (5:14). The Christ whom he proclaimed was no longer assessed by the worldly standards of the period before his conversion: it was in the light of the new creation brought into being by Christ's Resurrection that he now assessed all men and, as an ambassador of Christ, announced the message which called on men to be reconciled to God—the God who accepted men as righteous in His sight for the sake of the sinless one who was "made sin (a sin-offering) on their behalf (5:11-21).

Let Paul's readers, who have accepted the Divine amnesty, see to it that their acceptance of it is not futile. Paul and his companions have shown them all sincerity, putting up with discomfort, danger, and disrepute; it was but fair that they should be shown sincerity and grateful affection in return. Let them make room for Paul in their hearts, just as they have a warm place in his (6:1-13).

Paul is conscious of some reserve on their part, and he puts it down to their failure to heed his earlier pleas to have done away with all idolatrous associations (cf. I Cor. 10:14 ff.). He begs them anew to cut loose from all such defilements and go on to perfect holiness (6:14–7:1).

III. Restoration of Mutual Confidence (7:2-16)

Returning to the narrative begun in 2:12 f., he tells of the gratitude and relief which his meeting with Titus had brought him. His joy and comfort know no bonds. He was sorry when he sent the tearful letter but he cannot be sorry now, as he thinks of its reconciling effect. He had told Titus how loyal and loving the Corinthian Christians were at heart, and their response to the letter has proved him right. Paul has great cause for renewed gladness and confidence in them (7:2-16).

IV. The Collection for Jerusalem (8:1–9:15)

The new atmosphere of reconciliation makes it possible for him to resume the topic of the collection being organized in the Gentile churches for the relief of the Jerusalem Christians (briefly touched upon in I Cor. 16:1-4). He tells them of the generous and spontaneous response being made right now by the Macedonian churches out of their poverty, and recommends their example to the Corinthians: above all, he reminds them of Christ's perfect example of utter self-giving (8:9). Paul is sending Titus to Corinth to complete "this grace also" (8:7), as he has already completed another delicate task. With him he is sending two Christian men (8:18, 22) whose probity in the administration of money has already commended them to the esteem of the churches. Paul was always anxious to discharge financial responsibilities in a way that would stand up to the keenest scrutiny, lest he should be accused of lining his own pockets (8:1-24).

He has been encouraging the Macedonian Christians by telling them of the prompt generosity of the Corinthians and other Achaians; he knows they will not let him down. Their contribution should be given cheerfully and willingly. It is a gift to God, and they will not be impoverished by it. As a gesture of fellowship it will strengthen the bonds uniting the Gentile churches and the Jerusalem Christians: both sides will pray for one another the more eagerly in consequence. All Christian giving is a reflection of the grace of God, who has given the greatest gift of all (9:1-15).

V. Vindication of Paul's Apostolic Authority (10:1–13:14)

The sudden change of tone in 10:1 ff. is explained by a revival of disaffection against Paul in the church of Corinth, fostered by visitors who claimed to act by the authority of the Jerusalem apostles, whose status they represented as much higher than Paul's. The Jerusalem leaders were "superlative apostles" (11:5; 12:11). Paul echoes this designation ironically but is careful not to criticize them; although, if the visiting interlopers were indeed their emissaries, he could complain that the agreement of Gal. 2:6-10 was being breached. Corinth was included within the "limits" which God had appointed as his apostolic "field" (10:13-16). He did not appreciate the activity of intruders in his field, just as he made it his own policy not to "build on another man's foundation" (cf. Rom. 15:20).

The interlopers themselves are denounced unsparingly. They are "false apostles . . . disguising themselves as apostles of Christ"; servants of Satan, who "disguise themselves as servants of righteousness" (11:13-15). They proclaim "another Jesus, . . . a different spirit, . . . a different gospel" (11:4). They are boastful, self-assertive, dictatorial; yet some Corinthian Christians, so resentful of the fatherly discipline of their own apostle, submit meekly to these men's authority. At the instigation of these men, they even make disparaging remarks about Paul. He can write strong letters from a distance, they say, but cannot impose his authority at close quarters: "his bodily presence is weak, and his speech is of no account" (10:10). Even Paul's virtues are turned into vices: his refusal to live at the expense of the Corinthian church shows lack of self-confidence; he is not all that sure of the validity of his apostolic vocation. At the same time his organization of the Jerusalem fund is misrepresented to his disadvantage.

What can Paul do to win his converts' allegiance back? Must he boast of his attainments, as the interlopers do? If he did, he could draw up a list which would far outdo not only their attainments but those of the "superlative apostles" whose authority they claimed. But such boasting would be a foolish and fruitless business—even boasting of the hardships and dangers he underwent in the cause of Christ, for these too could minister subtly to an un-apostolic pride (11:1-29). No, he will boast rather in experiences which were completely humiliating, like the occasion when he was let down in a basket through a window in the Damascus city wall (11:30-33). Or—since visions and revelations of the Lord have been appealed to—he will recall an ecstatic experience in which, caught up to the third heaven, he heard indescribably wonderful revelations. He does not boast in this experience, but in its sequel. It left him with a recurring physical affliction of a peculiarly humiliating kind. After he had three times prayed for its removal, he was given additional grace to endure it. Now he can boast in this humiliating infirmity, because it is when he himself is weakest that the power of Christ most manifestly rests upon him (12:1-10). And the Corinthians themselves saw this power at work, when "the signs of an apostle" were performed among them during Paul's ministry in their city. He has no need of any argument but an appeal to their own personal recollection (12:11-13).

Now he is about to pay them a third visit. Let them see to it that they are in the right spirit to receive him, in the name of the Lord whose apostle he is; otherwise he will be as bold face to face with them as he is in writing, and the power of Christ will be displayed in the exercise of apostolic discipline (12:14–13:10). With a final exhortation, salutation, and benediction, he bids them farewell (13:11-14).

Whether the Corinthian Christians themselves benefited by this correspondence is uncertain. "But Paul, who learnt at Corinth what it is to be weak in Christ, shows there perhaps more clearly than elsewhere his full stature of Christian intelligence, firmness, and magnanimity" (C. K. Barret, "Christianity at Corinth," *Bulletin of the John Rylands Library* 46, 1963-4, p. 297).

BIBLIOGRAPHY:

E. B. Allo, *La deuxième Epitre aux Corinthiens*, Etudes Bibliques (Paris, 1937).

P. Bachmann, *Der 2. Korintherbrief*, Zahn-Kommentar (Leipzig, 4th ed., 1922).

C. K. Barrett, "Christianity at Corinth," *BJRL* 46 (1963-64), 269-297.

J. H. Bernard, *The Second Epistle to the Corinthians*, Expositor's Greek New Testament (London, 1910).

G. Bornkamm, "The History of the Origin of the So-called Second Letter to the Corinthians," in K. Aland and others, *The Authorship and Integrity of the New Testament* (London, 1965), 73-81.

F. F. Bruce, *First and Second Corinthians*, Century Bible (London, 1970).

R. Bultmann, *Exegetische Probleme des zweiten Korintherbriefes* (Darmstadt, 1963).

J. Calvin, *The Second Epistle of Paul the Apostle to the Corinthians* (1547), translated by T. A. Smail (Edinburgh, 1964).

J. Denney, *The Second Epistle to the Corinthians*, Expositor's Bible (London, 1894).

F. V. Filson, *The Second Letter of Paul to the Corinthians*, Interpreter's Bible (New York, 1953).

G. Friedrich, "Die Gegner des Paulus im 2. Korintherbrief," in O. Betz, etc. (eds.), *Abraham Unser Vater: Festschrift für O. Michel* (Leiden, 1963), 181-215.

D. Georgi, *Die Gegner des Paulus im 2 Korintherbrief* (Neukirchen-Vluyn, 1964).

H. L. Goudge, *The Second Epistle to the Corinthians*, Westminster Commentaries (London, 1927).

R. P. C. Hanson, *II Corinthians*, Torch Bible Commentaries (London, 1954).

J. Héring, *The Second Epistle of Saint Paul to the Corinthians* (1950), translated by A. W. Heathcote and P. J. Allcock (London, 1967).

C. Hodge, *An Exposition of the Second Epistle to the Corinthians* (Edinburgh, 1860; reprinted, Grand Rapids, 1950).

P. E. Hughes, *Paul's Second Epistle to the Corinthians*, New International Commentary on the New Testament (Grand Rapids, 2nd ed., 1962).

W. H. Isaacs, *The Second Epistle of Paul the Apostle to the Corinthians* (London, 1902).

E. Käsemann, "Die Legitimität des Apostels," *ZNW* 41 (1942), 33-71.

W. Kelly, *Notes on the Second Epistle of Paul the Apostle to the Corinthians* (London, 1882).

J. H. Kennedy, *The Second and Third Epistles of St. Paul to the Corinthians* (London, 1900).

H. Lietzmann, *An die Korinther I-II*, Handbuch zum Neuen Testament (Tübingen, 4th ed., revised by W. G. Kümmel, 1949).

T. W. Manson, "The Corinthian Correspondence," *Studies in the Gospels and Epistles* (Manchester, 1962), 190-224.

A. Menzies, *The Second Epistle of the Apostle Paul to the Corinthians* (London, 1912).

A. Plummer, *A Critical and Exegetical Commentary on the Second Epistle of St. Paul to the Corinthians*, International Critical Commentary (Edinburgh, 1915).

K. Prümm, *Diakonia Pneumatos*, 3 vols. (Rome, 1960-67).

W. Schmithals, *Die Gnosis in Korinth* (Göttingen, 2nd ed., 1965).

A. M. G. Stephenson, "A Defence of the Integrity of 2 Corinthians," in K. Aland and others, *The Authorship and Integrity of the New Testament* (London, 1965), 82-97.

R. H. Strachan, *The Second Epistle to the Corinthians*, Moffat New Testament Commentary (London, 1935).

R. V. G. Tasker, *The Second Epistle of Paul to the Corinthians*, Tyndale New Testament Commentaries (London, 1958).

M. E. Thrall, *The First and Second Letters of Paul to the Corinthians*, Cambridge Bible Commentary (Cambridge, 1965).

H. Windisch, *Der zweite Korintherbrief übersetzt und erklärt*, Meyer-Kommentar (Göttingen, 9th ed., 1924).

F. F. BRUCE

CORNELISZ, Arent (or Cornelii, Arnoldus), also Kroese, Croesius, or Crusius (1547-1605), a Dutch Reformed theologian. Some incorrectly give him the name Van der Linden. His father was Cornelis Huygensz of 's Gravesande; Cornelisz is sometimes also named after this place. His birthplace, Delft, was an early center of Reformation activity. In 1565 Cornelisz went to study in Heidelberg. After June 10, 1568, he was a student of Beza in Geneva. In the summer of 1570 he left for Wezel, to which his father had fled. Shortly after his ecclesiastical examination at Heidelberg (November 8, 1570), he became pastor of the refugee church at Frankenthal, succeeding Petrus Dathenus. He visited Delft in 1573 and received a call from the church there, his native town. Cornelisz played a leading role in the life of the church; he was a regular delegate to both particular and national synods, serving as president of the Synod of 1581 at Middleburg and assessor of the one at The Hague in 1586. Although he declined an appointment to a professorship at Leiden in 1578, he was later asked to reconsider more than once. He was not an original theologian but closely followed Calvin (one of whose commentaries he translated) and especially Ursinus. Cornelisz rejected supra-lapsarianism on the basis of Ursinus' views. His activity was generally characterized by thoughtfulness and balance. He had friendly contacts with such men as Regius, Lydius, Menso Alting, and Helmichius, with whom he had become acquainted while a student. A respected personage in the palace of Prince William of Orange, he baptized Prince Frederik Hendrik and conducted the funeral service of Prince William on August 3, 1584. Cornelisz also participated in the preparations for a new Bible translation.

CORNELIUS (Lat., "of a horn"), a centurion of the auxiliary cohort stationed at Caesarea and known as the Italian cohort (Acts 10:1). Being a centurion, Cornelius would have been a Roman citizen. His name suggests that his citizenship resulted from the liberation of 10,000 slaves by Publius Cornelius Sulla in 82 B.C., since these manumitted (freed) persons subsequently adopted the name of their liberator's gens or clan. His freedom could not have been purchased in the same way as that of Claudius Lysias (Acts 22:28), for in that case he would have borne an imperial name. The fact that his relatives and close acquaintances were at Caesarea (Acts 10:24) seems to indicate a considerable period of residence there. Notwithstanding the strongly Hellenistic character of the city, he appears in a favorable light, reminding us of the centurion at Capernaum (Luke 7:1 ff.). Though a Gentile, he became deeply interested in Judaism, shared in synagogue worship and almsgiving, and formed a habit of private prayer to God. Clearly, however, he remained a proselyte of the gate (Acts 11:3), not fully becoming a Jew nor circumcised. Luke's object in narrating his conversion is not simply to tell a good story. By the space Luke devotes to the story in Acts 10 and to its rehearsal in Acts 11, it is plain that he recognized it as marking an important step in the progress of the church. Moreover, he later mentions that Peter recalled the incident in his speech at the Council at Jerusalem (Acts 15:7).

The story itself narrates how Cornelius and Peter were brought together in consequence of two visions. Cornelius, when at prayer in his house at the time of the evening sacrifice, was surprised by the appearing of an angel who assured him that his service was acceptable to God and that he would receive further instruction by sending for Peter. Three things are noticeable about the angelic message. It is related to the immediate circumstances of Cornelius by sacrificial terminology (cf. Lev. 2:2, LXX; Ps. 141:2); the task of instruction is left to the church (cf. Acts 9:6); and if, as is possible, Philip the evangelist had already settled in Caesarea (Acts 8:40), the choice of Peter rather than one in a lower office indicates the importance of the occasion. On the following day Peter was prepared for the request of Cornelius by a vision of a very different kind. Having gone to pray about noon beneath the awning on the roof of the house where he lodged, and being hungry at the time, he saw a sheet let down from heaven containing clean and unclean animals. Thereupon, a voice invited him to kill and eat. Shocked at the mixture of animals, he replied that nothing unclean had ever passed his lips. The interchange occurred three times before the vision terminated, leaving Peter with a disturbing problem vividly before his mind. But it was quickly solved by the arrival of the messengers and the express command of the Holy Spirit. The difficulty involved for Peter in accompanying the servants of Cornelius was twofold. First, there was the question of proclaiming the Gospel to the uncircumcised, contrary to an earlier command of the Lord (Mt. 10:5-6), and second, there was the awkward matter of table fellowship with them (Acts 11:3). From the special instruction given him in such an impressive manner, it may be inferred that he had not so far fully comprehended the implications of the post-resurrection commission of Jesus (Mt. 28:19; cf. Acts 1:8). Being aware, however, that the views of the church in general coincided with what his own had been up until now, he took the precaution of taking along with him six brethren to whose knowledge of the facts he afterwards appealed when his conduct was challenged (Acts 11:12).

The earnest sincerity of Cornelius is evinced by the company which he assembled to await Peter's arrival and by the reception which he gave him. The speech of Peter affords an example of the early *kerygma* (preaching) addressed to a Gentile audience. Even the summary form in which it appears suggests greater fulness of detail than is found in Peter's earlier speeches, but at the same time it assumes considerable knowledge of the career of Jesus. All that was required was some amplification accompanied by an authoritative interpretation. Possibly Cornelius and his friends had already pondered the facts but were at a loss as to how they should be evaluated. Martin Dibelius regards the speech as an interpolation in the narrative, but the roughness of its composition and the fact that, when translated into Aramaic, it reads well, indicate that Luke obtained it from an authentic source. The most remarkable event of the meeting was the descent of the Holy Spirit upon the audience, with evident Pentecostal effect, before the conclusion of Peter's address. This development astonished Peter's companions, but it amply proved that Gentile faith had received the seal of Divine approval apart from circumcision. Baptism, however, followed as the outward seal of admission to the church.

BIBLIOGRAPHY:
F. F. Bruce, *The Speeches in the Acts of the Apostles* (London, 1948), 9.

WILLIAM J. CAMERON

CORNERSTONE, a Messianic metaphor of Scripture (Ps. 144:12; Job 38:6; Eph. 2:20; I Pet. 2:6). Moulton and Milligan (*Vocabulary of the Greek New Testament*, p. 19b) quote W. W. Lloyd's comment on Eph. 2:20-22: "The cornerstone (ἀκρογωνιαῖος) here is the primary foundation stone at the angle of the structure by which the architect fixes a standard for the bearings of the walls and cross walls throughout." The appropriateness of this idea is further seen in the relation of the foundation to the temple and the city. These great unifying figures run through Scripture, portraying Christ and His redeemed people, and culminate in the sublime pictures of Rev. 21 and 22.

G. A. Barton, in his article, "Corners," in *HERE*, has collected references from the literature of the ancient Near E showing the religious significance of the cornerstone in ancient architecture. The association of the cornerstone and foundation with sacrifice is particularly significant. (T. C. Cheyne has a selection of possible parallels from other cultures in the article "Hiel" in *EB*, cols. 2062-3.) The laying of the temple of Solomon is described in I Kings 6:37, and the foundation stones are mentioned as especially large and costly (I Kings 7:9,10; 5:17). The laying of the foundation of the post-exilic temple under Zerubbabel is an event of great significance (Ezra 3:8-13), possibly the laying of a cornerstone. When this account is compared with the references in Hag. 2:18 and Zech. 3:9; 4:9, 10; and 8:9, the allusions to the foundation and a stone having seven eyes bring to mind the reference to Christ in Rev. 5:6.

These hints from antiquity are harmonious with the more explicit statements of Isa. 28:16 and Ps. 118:22, and the use of these statements in the NT. Isa. 28:16 is quoted by Paul in Rom. 9:33 and 10:11, and by Peter in I Pet. 2:6. Rom. 9:33 combines these words and ideas with words from Isa. 8:14, giving the idea of Jehovah as a stone of refuge for those who trust Him, but a stone of stumbling for many.

The word ἀκρογωνιαῖος is used in the LXX of Isa. 28:16 and is used by Paul in Eph. 2:20 and by Peter in I Pet. 2:6. The connection in the context of Isaiah is with the idea of a foundation, and therefore it makes good sense in Eph. 2:20 and I Pet. 1:6 to think of Christ in the apostolic metaphor as the *corner foundation stone*, holding together both walls and foundations. Both Peter and Paul conceive of believers as "stones" built on the foundation. Believers constitute a "spiritual house" or "habitation of God by the Spirit," and, formed into a temple on the foundation stone, also constitute a priesthood to offer up sacrifices acceptable to God through Jesus Christ (I Pet. 2:5; Heb. 13:15, 16).

In Ps. 118:22, the idea of a stone is again used as a Messianic metaphor, though the word ἀκρογωνιαῖος is not used, but rather λίθος. This is cited by the Lord Himself in Mt. 21:42 (cf. Luke 20:17; Mark 12:10, 11). It is referred to by Peter in Acts 4:11 and I Pet. 2:7. In all these cases the Scripture clearly speaks of Christ Himself in His rejection by the leaders of the people. The idea of rejection is paralleled by the opposition, offense, and stumbling of the Isaiah passages already mentioned; and the idea of His being the *corner foundation stone* is paralleled by the expression "head of the corner." In both Isa. 28:16 and Ps. 118:22 the word *pinnah* ("corner") is used and probably the same idea is meant: Christ is the corner foundation stone of the spiritual temple constructed of His redeemed.

The ideas of *foundation* and *temple* lead to the ideas of priestly service and sacrifice. Christ's sacrifice is the infinitely precious thing which is at the foundation of all the hopes of His people, and He, risen from the dead, is the guarantor of the fruition of their hopes. In Rev. 21:22 the Lamb is said to be the temple of the new Jerusalem. The Lamb indicates sacrifice in connection with temple service. On the other hand in Rev. 21, the idea of foundations or foundation stones is connected with the apostles, as in Eph. 2:20. Here the foundation of prophets and apostles is the foundation of the city.

WILBER B. WALLIS

COSAM, a name in the genealogy of Jesus Christ (Luke 3:28), otherwise unknown.

COSIN, John (1595-1672), English High Church divine. Born November 30, 1595, into a wealthy Norwich family, he was educated at Caius College, Cambridge. Cosin helped Richard Montague with his *Appello Ceasarem,* 1625, to set out the Arminian position that Rome was a church, though in error. Two years later he published his *Collection of Private Devotions* at the instigation of Charles I. In 1635 he became Master of Peterhouse, Cambridge, a college in the High Church tradition, whose chapel he decorated with ritual and ceremony, though details are obscure. He became vice-chancellor of the university, and in 1640 was appointed Dean of Peterborough. The Long Parliament deprived him of his offices for his popish sympathies, and after spending some time in hiding to avoid arrest, he fled to the Continent, where he became chaplain to the Laudian exiles. Though a High churchman, he was friendly to the Huguenots and denounced Rome for transubstantiation (*Historia Transubstantionis Papalis*) and for including the Apocrypha in its Canon of Scripture (*A Scholastical History of the Canon of Holy Scripture*). He even disowned his own son when he became a Catholic. At the restoration he became bishop of Durham. He attended the Savoy Conference and was a leader in the revision of the Prayer Book. Cosin stood in the Laudian theological tradition, though some think he later modified this, anxious to persuade dissenters, Roman or Puritan, into conformity. His main literary work was either liturgical or polemical, but his High Church Arminian stance should not be confused, as is sometimes the case, with Tractarian theology. This is implied by the misleading title of the *Library of Anglo-Catholic Theology*, in which his complete works are included.

His *Correspondence* is published in the Surtees Society, and a new edition of *A Collection of Private Devotions* was edited by P. G. Stanwood, Oxford, 1967. A biography appears in the *Dictionary of National Biography*, volume 12, by J. H. Overton, and a life was written by P. H. Osmond, London, 1913. *The Durham Book*, edited by G. J. Cuming, Oxford, 1961, is also relevant.

G. E. DUFFIELD

COSMOLOGICAL ARGUMENT. See PROOFS FOR EXISTENCE OF GOD.

COSTA, Isaac da. See DA COSTA, ISAAC.

COTTON, John (1584-1652), leading New England Puritan clergyman, theologian, and writer. Born at Derby, Derbyshire, England, son of a Puritan lawyer, Roland Cotton, he received his A.B. in 1603 and his A.M. in 1606 from Trinity College. He became head lecturer and Dean of Emmanuel College, Cambridge, which granted him a B.D. in 1613. In 1612 he was appointed vicar of the large parish of St. Botolph's in Boston of Lincolnshire. Facing a summons before the High Commission for omitting forms and ceremonies offensive to his increasingly Puritan convictions, he fled to London in 1632, resigning in 1633. His friendship with John Davenport, John Winthrop, and other Puritan leaders in New England drew him to the Massachusetts Bay Colony in 1633. Five weeks after his arrival, on October 10, he became teacher of the First Church of Boston. Such was his influence that many believed "God would not suffer Mr. Cotton to err." Winthrop stated that what was pronounced in the pulpit "soon became either the law of the land or the practice of the church." Winthrop noted the "special testimony" of the Lord's presence in the church with the addition of 117 new members in the first year under his ministry, so that "more were converted and added to that church than all the other churches in the Bay."

Cotton and the Commonwealth were shaken by two major controversies. He believed that the OT set forth the ideal pattern for the state, in which all political rights should be subordinated to religious conformity, enforced by godly magistrates subject to God's law as interpreted by learned ministers. Roger Williams objected, maintaining that a magistrate's power extended "only to the bodies, and goods, and outward state of men." He also charged that the New England church erred in not breaking with the "false" Church of England. Cotton was instrumental in having Williams banished from the Commonwealth in 1635, for threatening the foundations of the state.

Cotton's position of leadership was more seriously challenged by the "Antinomian Controversy." He sought to minimize the role of moral effort in the regenerative process, and propounded that the strongest evidence for regeneration and union with Christ was not outward works or acts of faith but the "witness" of the Holy Spirit. Anne Hutchinson, center of the controversy, claimed that her brother-in-law, John Wheelwright, and John Cotton, her minister, were the only two in the colony preaching a "covenant of grace" as opposed to a "covenant of works." But she went to the extreme so that two dangerous errors were introduced: that a believer could receive a revelation from God superior to the Bible (which she subsequently claimed for herself), and that mere inner assurance, not good works, could authenticate one's spiritual estate before God. All the ministers of the colony were summoned to the Newtowne Synod of 1637. As a result Wheelwright was banished; another supporter, Governor Henry Vane, was defeated; and other followers were disenfranchised. Mrs. Hutchinson was excommunicated and banished in 1638. Cotton, her most formidable supporter, was won over to the majority opinion and delivered her sentence.

In 1646 Cotton was one of three chosen to assist in framing a model of church government. In connection with this he wrote *Keyes of the Kingdom of Heaven, and Power Thereof* (2 eds., 1644); *The Way of the Churches of Christ in New England* (1645), a justification of the New England churches against the Presbyterians; and the *Way of Congregational Churches Cleared* (1648), a further defense of these same views.

His son-in-law, Increase Mather, and a grandson, Cotton Mather, were noted New England theologians.

CALVIN MALEFYT

COUNCILS, GENERAL. The ecumenical or general councils of the church are those bodies or assemblies which supposedly represent the whole of the Christian church. For Rome, the official general councils include 21 in all from Nicea through Vatican II; the Eastern Church (Greek Orthodox) reckons seven as official, most Protestants six, some Anglicans seven or eight, and the Church of Armenia three. These are councils beyond those of the apostolic age and the book of Acts (chapters 1, 6, 15, 21).

The purpose of the six councils accepted by Protestants was essentially theological, to define and defend the faith against heresies. Subsequent church councils rather gradually came to have an ecclesiastical concern, to deal with problems of church order, rites, discipline, and corruption. The gatherings of the World Council of Churches have had unity and union as their purpose rather than any precise formulation of faith. They are not ranked among the ecumenical or general councils of the church.

The first of the general councils, the Council of Nicea, 325, was called to combat the heresies of Arius. Arianism sought to introduce the humanistic philosophy of an unknowable, unconscious god, and to deny the deity of Jesus Christ. The first formulation of the Nicene Creed resulted, which stated the orthodox faith with respect to God the

Father and God the Son, who was declared to be of the same or of one substance with the Father.

The second council, the First Council of Constantinople, 381, continued the same battle and expanded the creed. monarchianism, Sabellianism, the newer forms of Arianism such as Eunomianism, Semi-Arianism, Macedonianism, and Apollinarianism were all condemned. These heresies were anti-Trinitarian.

The third council, the Council of Ephesus, 431, fought the attempt to introduce man-worship into the church by the condemnation of Nestorianism. Nestorius, although allegedly denying the Incarnation of God the Word, insisted on the worship of Jesus, whom he regarded as merely man. The elements of the Eucharist were worshipped by the Nestorians, the bread and wine being regarded as the real flesh and blood of Jesus. The Council of Ephesus affirmed the Incarnation and declared that only the Deity of Christ can be worshipped, never His humanity. A much misunderstood term from this council is the declaration of Mary as "Theotokos," usually mistranslated as "Mother of God" but meaning literally the "Bringer Forth of God"; it was thus an affirmation of the reality of the Incarnation. Nestorius replaced the Incarnation with a conjunction or connection of God and man. The man Jesus progressed spiritually to the point where He united Himself with God.

The fourth council, the Council of Chalcedon, 451, was marked by the absence of the Church of Armenia. The council defined the nature of Christ carefully as two natures, one fully human, one fully Divine, in true union but "without confusion, without change, without division, without separation." The door was thus barred against Eutychianism, which held that the natures of Christ became fused into one Divine nature.

The fifth council, the Second Council of Constantinople, 553, applied the implications of Chalcedon to a variety of new and old heresies, condemning certain opinions of long-dead churchmen like Theodore of Mopsuestia (semi-Pelagian), Ibas, and others, behind which the monophysites were taking refuge.

The sixth council, the Third Council of Constantinople, 680-681, dealt with monothelitism, which sought to reduce Christ to one will, the human being absorbed in the Divine. The Definition of Faith was a precise declaration of the doctrine of Incarnation as against the various forms of the doctrine of deification.

The first six councils, with their definitions of the orthodox theology, have been regarded legitimately as faithful to the Biblical doctrines. Although their canons with respect to church government have not been accepted by all churches, their theological definitions have been largely recognized as standards of orthodoxy.

Bibliography:

F. J. Badcock, *The History of the Creeds* (London, 1938).

J. Chrystal, *Nicea, A.D. 325* (Jersey City, 1891).

J. Chrystal, *The Third World Council, Ephesus, A.D. 431*, 3 vols. (Jersey City, 1908).

C. J. Hefele, *A History of the Christian Councils* (Edinburgh, 1872-1895), vols. 1-4.

P. Hughes, *The Church in Crisis*, A History of the Twenty Great Councils (London, 1960).

H. Jedin, *Ecumenical Councils of the Catholic Church* (Edinburgh-London, 1960).

G. B. Ladner, "Origin and Significance of the Byzantine Iconoclastic Controversy" in *Mediaeval Studies* (New York, 1940), vol. II.

E. H. Landon, *A Manual of Councils of the Holy Catholic Church* (Edinburgh, 1909), 2 vols.

J. H. Leith, *Creeds of the Church* (Chicago, 1963).

H. R. Percival, *The Seven Ecumenical Councils, Their Canons and Decrees, in Nicene and Post-Nicene Fathers*, Second Series, vol. XIV.

R. J. Rushdoony, *The Foundations of Social Order, Studies in the Creeds and Councils of the Early Church* (Nutley, N.J., 1968).

P. Schaff, *The Creeds of Christendom* (New York, 1887), vol. I.
H. M. Scott, *Origin and Development of the Nicene Theology* (Chicago, 1896).

ROUSAS JOHN RUSHDOONY

COUNSELING, PASTORAL. The modern pastoral-counseling movement in America is of recent origin, and may be said to have begun with the publication of an article entitled "Challenge to Our Seminaries," by Anton Boisen (*Christian Work*, 1926), which stressed the need for counseling. In that article Boisen set forth the thesis that "in mental disorders we are dealing with a problem which is essentially spiritual" (p. 8). Ten years later in his book, *The Exploration of the Inner World*, Boisen argued (against Freud, *q.v.*) that mental disorders arise from a bad conscience occasioned by real guilt rather than an inner conflict over false guilt (guilt feelings). Boisen rejected the Freudian notion that guilt feelings stem from the conflict of the *Id* (natural impulses: sex and aggression) and an overly severe *Superego* (conscience).

Had the pastoral counseling movement developed along the lines suggested by Boisen, its subsequent history might have been considerably different. Although Boisen was liberal in theology (e.g., he held the moral influence theory of the Atonement), he at least considered mental disorders subject to theological discussion. But the movement soon was re-directed into Freudian channels and early succumbed to the idea that the pastor's major task is to defer and refer to the psychiatrist. Ministers of all theological descriptions bowed to the unending stream of propaganda published and widely disseminated under the aegis of the Mental Health campaign, which insisted upon the medical model advocated by Freud. According to this model, counselees must be considered as mentally ill persons, their problems the result of sickness rather than sin. This medical model removed responsibility from the counselee (he was now considered a victim rather than a violator of his conscience) and necessitated referral by the pastor, who was thought to be incompetent to counsel persons suffering from difficulties more severe than a psychic scratch.

Those with mere scratches could indeed be helped by the Christian minister if he was careful not to intrude his theological categories into counseling. Carl Rogers' nondirective method was pressed into service and widely propagated as most adaptable to the ends of such counseling. According to Rogers, man has all of the resources he needs to solve his problems within himself. Thus the counselor merely reflects the counselee's own thoughts back toward him in order to help him clarify his problem and come to his own solution to it. Directions and advice are taboo. The counselor is taught, and may quickly learn (a fact that largely accounts for the phenomenal acceptance of the method), to rephrase the counselee's statements as his own response. Mixed with existential philosophy, nondirective counseling all but became the authorized version of pastoral counseling during the 1940's and 1950's. The chief advocates of this approach have been Seward Hiltner, Rollo May, and Wayne Oates. Rogerianism has come to be accepted not only by liberals and the neo-orthodox, but by conservative Christians of various sorts, who have hesitantly, but assuredly, followed its main outlines. Only during the 1960's has a belated challenge to this direction in pastoral counseling been issued. At Westminster Theological Seminary, in Philadelphia, under the impetus of Cornelius Van Til's insistence that every movement be examined presuppositionally, basic questions have been asked concerning the foundation principles of Freudian and Rogerian thought. Both the fundamental principle of Freud that man is not responsible for what he does and the basic presupposition of Rogers that man has all of the resources in himself have been rejected as un-Scriptural. Both presuppositions undercut the Biblical doctrines of human depravity and Christ's Atonement.

A new movement, sometimes known as nouthetic counseling, calls for the return to a system built upon Biblical presuppositions. Apart from organically caused difficulties (brain damage, chemical malfunctions, toxic problems, etc.), nouthetic counselors hold that the basic problem of the so-called mentally ill is not sickness but sin. Rejecting the medical model, proponents challenge the right of the Freudian to attack value systems in the name of medicine and declare that the theology of Rogerians who claim that man is essentially good and self-sufficient is heretical. This attack upon the roots of the pastoral-counseling movement has stimulated a growing interest among some conservative Christians to return to a more Biblical approach to pastoral counseling.

Briefly stated, nouthetic counseling sees the work of pastoral counseling as part of the work of sanctification, i.e., putting off the old sinful life patterns and putting on new Biblical response patterns (cf. Eph. 4:22-24). The counseling of unbelievers (which is not strictly pastoral work) must primarily focus upon evangelism. Nouthetic confrontation is one way in which God has ordained that believers may grow by His grace. In Colossians 3:16 (lit. "teaching and confronting one another nouthetically") and Rom. 15:14 ("you yourselves are able to confront one another nouthetically") nouthetic confrontation is clearly depicted as the proper activity of all believers to some extent. In passages like Col. 1:28 ("we proclaim Him, nouthetically confronting each man and teaching each man") and Acts 20:31 ("day and night for a period of three years I did not cease to confront each one of you nouthetically with tears") nouthetic confrontation is described particularly as the work of the pastor.

The word *noutheteo* ("to confront nouthetically") has no one adequate English equivalent. The term contains three elements: (1) the person confronted is involved in attitudes or behavior that must be changed; (2) the change is to be effected by appropriate verbal means; (3) the change is sought for the benefit of the one confronted.

Biblical counseling demands counselor involvement, taking counselees seriously about their sin and using the Scriptures, prayer, and the discipline, fellowship, and worship of the church, all in the context of the activity of the Holy Spirit, who was called by Christ "another Counselor" (paraclete) like Himself (John 14:15). We find that the desirable personality changes listed in Gal. 5:22, 23 are described as the "fruit" (result of the work) of the Spirit and cannot be attained apart from Him. In Gal. 6:1 the counseling of erring Christians is restricted to "those who are spiritual" (i.e., those who possess the Spirit). This restriction clearly prohibits the seeking of such counsel from non-Christians. Plainly all counseling that claims to be Biblical, therefore, must take account of the work of the Holy Spirit in counseling. The Spirit ordinarily uses His Word (the Bible) in achieving His purposes. Indeed He has described the purposes of the Scriptures to be (1) "to make wise to salvation" and (2) "to teach, to reprove, to correct, and to train one to do what is right" (II Tim. 3:15, 16). These purposes are essentially nouthetic in nature. Consequently, counseling that by-passes the Scriptures runs the risk of by-passing the Holy Spirit. (See bibliography, Adams, *Competent to Counsel.*)

Modern acceptance of group counseling techniques has frequently failed to take into consideration Christ's injunction in Matthew 18:15 that if a brother has wronged another the latter is to go to him "alone" and discuss the matter. Then Jesus indicates that the broadening of the confrontation is to include persons not involved only in the event that the offending party refuses to be reconciled. And two or three others are to be called in to act first as arbiters (vs. 16). If the offender fails to hear them these two or three become witnesses as the offended brother carries the matter officially before the representatives of the church (vs. 17). Group counseling that ignores Matthew 18 does so at the peril of slandering Christian brethren and thus driving greater wedges between them. Any group sessions that involve the disclosure of personal offenses between brethren are un-Scriptural in principle and practice and must be avoided. Other group "therapy" methods that involve disrobing, fondling, or other forms of bodily contact plainly have no place in Biblical counseling. Equally non-Christian are methods that in the name of openness or honesty degenerate into verbal dissecting contests. Confession groups which encourage the disclosure of the sordid details of deviant and sinful behavior are likewise to be shunned as un-Scriptural.

There is a proper use of "groups" in Biblical counseling. Groups must be comprised of those directly involved in the offenses and problems that are to be discussed (Mt. 18:15; 5:23-25). Thus husbands ought to be counseled together with their wives, children together with their parents, etc., so that the counselor himself does not become a party to slander by encouraging one person to talk about another behind his back. Counselees themselves are already so widely separated from one another that it is only adding insult to injury to further widen the gap by driving the wedges of suspicion that so often arise from slander in one-to-one counseling sessions. Thus the uncritical adoption of group counseling techniques by Christian pastors is but additional evidence of what can only be described as an incredible gullibility and strong propensity to grasp hold of the current fads in non-Christian counseling, whatever they may be, rather than to re-examine the entire question afresh from the Biblical perspective.

Bibliography:

J. E. Adams, *Competent to Counsel* (Nutley, N.J., 1970).

A. T. Boisen, *The Exploration of the Inner World* (New York, 1936).

W. Glasser, *Reality Therapy* (New York, 1956).

O. H. Mowrer, ed., *Morality and Mental Health* (Chicago, 1967).

O. H. Mowrer, *The Crisis in Psychiatry and Religion* (Princeton, 1961).

E. L. Phillips, and D. N. Wiener, *Short-term Psychotherapy and Structured Behavior Change* (New York, 1966).

T. S. Szasz, *The Myth of Mental Illness* (New York, 1967).

Jay E. Adams

COUNTER-REFORMATION, a movement extending roughly from 1560 to 1648 (the end of the Thirty Years' War) in which the RC Church endeavored to bring about reforms within itself. RC writers generally hold that the movement did not arise because of the Reformation, because they claim it had already begun before Luther nailed his 95 Theses to the door of the Castle Church in Wittenberg (Oct. 31, 1517). They often hold that Luther himself was in the reform tradition but went astray because he rejected the church's authority. Protestants, while recognizing some truth in this position, hold that the Counter-Reformation represented primarily a reaction to the Reformation, and in making its reply the Roman Church found itself obliged to formulate its doctrine more thoroughly, to make its organization more efficient, and to strengthen its system of discipline.

In 1560 RC fortunes seemed to have reached their lowest point. Papist forces were in retreat everywhere. England, Scotland, the N Netherlands, N Germany, much of Switzerland, and Hungary had accepted the Reformation, and in France and Poland strong bodies of bourgeois and lesser nobles had also become Protestant. RC education had everywhere suffered from the humanism of the Renaissance, but Protestant academies and the universities of Strasbourg, Wittenberg, Geneva, and others were pouring out Protestant ministers and missionaries. Moreover, governments looking at the large amounts of land held by the Roman Church saw in the Protestant movement an opportunity to secularize much of this valuable property. Yet despite all these portents of ultimate disaster, a spirit of reform or rather counter-reform was stirring within the Roman Church.

One of the first and most important means for countering Protestant expansion was the Society of Jesus, founded by Ignatius Loyola. Wounded at the siege of Pampeluna, Spain, in 1521, Loyola during his recovery resolved to organize a small body of men to go to the Near E as missionaries. But when this proved impossible because of war, he went to Rome, where he placed his group directly under the pope's orders. Out of this beginning came the Jesuits, a closely knit, thoroughly trained, and absolutely selfless body of men. Turning their attention to the education of the young, missions, and the direction of the spiritual lives of political rulers, they became one of the most effective organs of opposition to the Protestant movement.

To the Jesuits goes most of the credit for the calling and continuance of the Council of Trent. This gathering took place at three different periods: 1545-49, 1551-52, and 1562-63; and despite Protestant refusal to attend as well as much lukewarmness on the part of many Roman Catholics, it greatly strengthened the stand of the church. On the foundation already laid by Thomas Aquinas in the 13th century, the Council of Trent erected an impressive system of sacramental doctrine that it declared necessary for salvation. It also drew up a catechism for popular instruction, instituted the preparation of the Indices of Prohibited Books and of Expurgated Books, and revivified the Holy Office of the Inquisition, which did so much to prevent the rise of Protestantism in Spain, Portugal, and Italy. The council also reimposed discipline and set up an adequate organization for its enforcement. Making no concessions to Protestantism, it formulated unmistakably its own position.

The council reached its climax during the time of the first of three very able reforming popes. Pius V (1566-1572) heartily endorsed the work of the Council of Trent and of the Jesuits, so that they were able to go forward with their plans. He also took the step of excommunicating Elizabeth of England (1570) and of absolving her subjects from the oath of allegiance. He was followed by Gregory XIII (1572-1585), who concentrated upon gaining the support of civil governments for the Roman Church by working closely with such men as Philip II of Spain, Catherine de Medici in France, and Mary Queen of Scots. Finally, Sixtus V (1585-1590), a businesslike and aggressive individual, did much to encourage the use of the most violent methods for the suppression of Protestantism.

One of the primary interests of the Roman reformers was missions. The Jesuits, Capuchins, and others travelled far and wide teaching the doctrines of

Rome. Some reached China and Japan in the E, while others travelled to the New World of America, where they endeavored to establish truly RC states. The names of François Xavier, Vincent de Paul, Brebeuf, Lallement, and a host of others, many of whom died for their faith, come from this period. Even more important for the cause of the Counter-Reformation, however, were those who went as missionaries to newly Protestant areas. Trained either as Jesuits or at seminaries such as the English colleges at Douai and Reims, the Scots college at Paris, or the Irish at Madrid and Salamanca, with almost certain death facing them, they attempted to regain these countries and others for Rome. At this time religion and politics were not distinguished; so when they were discovered and arrested they suffered the fate of subversives or traitors. By means of their schools in Austria, S Germany, Poland, and elsewhere they succeeded in winning back many of the children of Protestants. Thus Protestantism, weakened by internal troubles, was gradually contained.

Comparatively peaceful missionary endeavor, however, could not usually bring back a country to the Roman fold. More was needed. Since the 4th century the Roman Church believed in the use of physical force, as demonstrated by the medieval crusades. In the Counter-Reformation, Spain and the Holy Roman Empire formed the twin prongs of a political fork against Protestantism. Philip II of Spain aided the Roman Catholics in their fight against Protestantism in France, and they were triumphant. He also supported Mary Queen of Scots against Elizabeth of England, but failed when his Armada met defeat and destruction in 1588. He also failed to crush the Dutch under William of Orange in the N seven provinces of the Netherlands. In Germany, with the accession of Emperor Rudolph (1576-1612), the conflict began in earnest, leading eventually into that destructive holocaust known as the Thirty Years' War (1618-1648). By 1631 RC power had reached its peak in Germany, and after that time it gradually declined, partially due to French intervention on the Protestant side.

By 1650 the driving force of the Counter-Reformation was largely spent. The movement had produced some able theologians, such as Bellarmine, Suarez, and Vasquez; an effective organizer and leader, Ignatius Loyola; and some important mystics, such as François de Sales and Teresa. But its whole effort was in the direction of conserving, defining, and exalting the church's teachings rather than of real reform. Even the art forms which partially grew out of the movement, the Rococo and Baroque, stressed the importance, glory, and power of the RC Church. One may see this in the poetry of Tasso and Calderón, in the music of Palestrina and Lassus, and in the painting and sculpture of Michelangelo and Bernini. The movement laid its great emphasis upon the place of the Roman Church as the mediator between God and man, while Christ's unique position as mediator fell into second place. Such has been the position of the Church of Rome ever since.

Bibliography:

J. Hashagen, *Das Zeitalter der Gegenreformation und der Religionskriege, 1555-1660* (Constance, 1950).

P. Hughes, *Rome and the Counter-Reformation in England* (London, 1944).

P. Janelle, *The Catholic Reformation* (Milwaukee, 1949).

H. Jedin, *Katholische Reformation oder Gegenreformation?* (Lucerne, 1946).

B. J. Kidd, *The Counter-Reformation, 1550–1600* (London, 1942).

T. M. Lindsay, *A History of the Reformation* (New York, 1906-07), II.

M. Philippson, *La Contre-revolution réligieuse au 16e siecle* (Brussels, 1884).

J. H. Pollen, *CE*, IV, 437-445, s.v.

A. W. Ward, *The Counter-Reformation* (New York, n.d.).

W. S. Reid

COURT, Antoine (1696-1760), French Protestant minister. Born in the province of Vivarais, he observed much persecution during his youth because of the revocation of the Edict of Nantes (1685). The pastors had been driven out, and lay preachers held secret assemblies. These earnest men and women upheld the Reformed churches in those times but occasionally led them away from their traditional clear thinking and discipline. After being a companion to such preachers, Court was himself at the age of 19 put in charge of the congregation at Nîmes.

Court planned to bring the churches back to their former discipline. In 1715, a few days before Louis XIV's death, he brought together and presided at a provincial synod, where it was decided that women would no longer be allowed to preach and that Scripture should be the standard of faith.

For a few years Court was able to carry on his work in France. But a bounty of 10,000 pounds had been put on his head, and in 1729 he felt compelled to take refuge at Lausanne, where, with the aid of the government of Berne and the archbishop of Canterbury, he founded a seminary especially intended to prepare young French students for the ministry in the persecuted churches, the churches "of the Desert." This seminary existed until 1812. Four hundred and fifty ministerial students studied there, many of them crowning their testimony with martyrdom. From 1729 on, Court lived chiefly at Lausanne and died there in 1760; but he paid some visits to the French churches in spite of mortal danger. His only son, Antoine Court de Gébelin, who was ordained in 1754, left the ministry and devoted himself to science and literature, never missing an opportunity, however, to work for his fellow believers' liberty, often successfully.

Bibliography:

A. Court, *Histoire des troubles des Cévennes ou de la guerre des Camisards sous le règne de Louis le Grand* (Geneva, 1760), 3 vols.

A. Court, *Mémoires d'Antoine Court* (Toulouse, 1885).

H. M. Baird, *The Huguenots and the Revocation of the Edict of Nantes* (New York, 1895).

E. and E. Haag, *La France Protestante* (Paris, 2nd ed., 1884), IV, 809-817.

E. Hugues, *Antoine Court, Histoire de la restauration du Protestantisme en France au XVIII siècle* (Paris, 1872), 2 vols.

E. Hughes, *Les Synodes dut Désert* (Paris, 1881), 3 vols.

N. Peyrat, *Histoire des pasteurs du désert* (Paris, 1842), 2 vols.

P. Rabaut, *Lettres à divers* (Paris, 1891), 1884), 2 vols.

P. Rabaut, Lettres á divers (Paris, 1891), 2 vols.

J. Viénot, *Antoine Court* (Rotterdam, 1929).

J. Nicole

COVENANT, HALF-WAY. The Half-way Covenant was the expedient adopted by New England Congregationalism at the Synod of 1662, by which parents who were themselves baptized but who admittedly did not possess evidences of God's saving grace were allowed to present their children for baptism. This compromise was adopted after some 30 years of heated discussion and virtually approved the radical changes which the churches had undergone since the time of their being founded.

The significance of these changes can best be understood in the light of Congregationalism's original principles. Although an ecclesiastical matter, the half-way covenant had profound implications for New England's social and political life. The early churches were largely Calvinistic in doctrine, embracing the "federal" or covenantal theology. In church polity they approximated the Anabaptist "pure church" ideal, which allowed membership only to "visible experiential believers." This was intimately related to the civil or political covenants, acknowledged by the inhabitants as the instrument for attaining the ideal of a "holy commonwealth." The former ideal demanded rigid selection for church membership, but the latter was supposed to be entered into by all the colonists to insure God's favor upon the colony. Complications arose when the Massachusetts General Court in 1631 decided to limit the franchise to church members.

Most first-generation colonists could in good conscience enter both church and civil covenants, since they were assured of their place in God's covenant of grace. The coming of enthusiastic dissenters and the decline of fervent piety within the first decade filled the church leaders with alarm. A double problem arose. Many baptized adults no longer entered the church covenant voluntarily, being unable to meet the high standard of experiential religion stressed by the clergy. Regarding themselves as devoid of grace, they claimed inability to enter the civil covenants sincerely. This was resolved by the admission that such civil contracts with God involved external duties alone, to which "graceless" persons could pledge themselves. Thus the commonwealth was never so holy as originally intended.

Far greater was the problem concerning church covenants. Originally, only "visible experiential believers" who had voluntarily entered church covenant could present their children for baptism. Within a few years it became apparent that many children remained unbaptized, since their parents could not meet the standards. Fearing that the church would die out, the leaders felt constrained to devise some method by which such children could be baptized and thus assured of a place in church and community. The Ministerial Convention (1637) approved the presentation of such children by covenanting grandparents, thus safeguarding experiential religion as the standard for church membership and access to the sacraments.

When this failed to meet the need, John Cotton first argued that all parents who did not openly renounce God's covenant or lead ungodly lives might safely present their offspring for baptism, since they were "yet in a more hopefull way of attayning regenerating grace." To salvage the pure church ideal, he prohibited such parents from coming to the Lord's Supper. Thus the two sacraments were radically divorced. His position won growing support, although several older ministers and many church members bitterly opposed it.

Cotton's position then became official church doctrine by the decisions of the Synod of 1662. Seven propositions were endorsed. In the fourth, the churches admitted to two kinds of members: those having saving grace and others admittedly "graceless." In the fifth, it was argued that parents "but in the lowest degree" of church membership could and should pass this on to their children by means of baptism. Charles Chauncy, John Davenport, and Increase Mather argued that this expedient would serve only to harden the unregenerate in their sinful state. Cotton was vigorously supported by Richard Mather, Jonathan Mitchell, John Higginson, and especially John Allin.

For 20 years controversy raged in the churches, although measurably reduced when Increase Mather capitulated in 1671. By reducing the position of baptized children in the church to a purely formal one, a meaningless half-way house was erected between the church as God's people and the world. Bitter dissensions compelled the organization of second churches in many towns. Preaching often degenerated into arid, scholastic speculation on the distinctions between external and internal covenant, and natural and spiritual ability. Respectability rather than religious conviction became the standard for church membership. Moral laxity and lack of interest in the church compelled preachers to urge repeatedly a public renewal of the church covenants, an expedient adopted by the Reforming Synod of 1680. The failure of the Half-way Covenant to strengthen the churches led Solomon Stoddard to make the Lord's Supper available to noncovenanting adults as a "converting ordinance." Against his views, which many regarded as a low Arminianism, the Mathers fought in vain. Here Congregationalism's original ideals received their death-blow. Jonathan Edwards sought to revive the ideals in his discussions of the nature, propriety, and efficacy of revivals, but largely in vain. The last case of baptism administered on the basis of Half-way Covenant was recorded at Charlestown, Mass., in 1828.

BIBLIOGRAPHY:

P. Y. De Jong, *The Covenant Idea in New England Theology* (Grand Rapids, 1945).
S. Fleming, *Children and Puritanism* (New Haven, 1933).
J. Haroutunian, *Piety versus Moralism* (New York, 1932).
P. Miller, "The Half-Way Covenant," *New England Quarterly*, vol. IV, no. 4.
The New England Mind: The Seventeenth Century (New York, 1939).
The New England Mind: From Colony to Province (Cambridge, Mass., 1953).
W. Walker, *Creeds and Platforms of Congregationalism* (New York, 1893).

PETER Y. DE JONG

COVENANT OF GRACE. See COVENANT THEOLOGY.

COVENANT OF SALT, an expression used in Num. 18:19 and II Chron. 13:5 to designate an indestructible divine agreement. The preservative properties of salt made it a symbol of permanence. Orientals "ate salt" together to seal friendships and ratify treaties (see Ezra 4:14, RV). Arabs used the same word for salt as for treaty. As an emblem of incorruption it was a prescribed part of OT offerings (Lev. 2:13; Ezek. 43:24). Hence its appropriateness to describe God's covenants.

COVENANT, SOLEMN LEAGUE AND

I. Historical Background and Origin

The Solemn League and Covenant had its origin in the conflict between the king and the parliament of England in the fourth decade of the 17th century. The Long Parliament began in 1640, and by 1642 it was involved in civil war with the king. Feeling the need of support in this conflict, the parliament in August 1643 proposed to the Estates of Scotland, and also to the General Assembly of the Church of Scotland, that a military treaty for mutual defense be formed between the nation of Scotland and the parliament of England. Though the Scottish Presbyterians had much sympathy for the English Puritans in their struggle against the tyranny of the Stuarts, still the general sentiment in Scotland favored a religious bond rather than a civil or military pact. The result of this was the formulation of the Solemn League and Covenant.

Originally drafted by Alexander Henderson, the document was approved by the General Assembly of the Church of Scotland. It was then sent to England, where, after some minor changes had been made, it was publicly sworn and subscribed in a joint meeting of the House of Commons and the Westminster Assembly of Divines. Following this the document was returned to Scotland, where it was sworn and subscribed by the Commission of the General Assembly of the Church of Scotland and the Committee of the Convention of Estates of the Scottish Parliament. Following this it was signed by large numbers of people throughout Scotland, though it was opposed by the minority that favored prelacy in the church and absolutism in the state.

II. Aims and Provisions

The Solemn League and Covenant provided for the preservation of the Reformed religion in Scotland, and the reformation of religion in England and Ireland according to the Word of God and the example of the best reformed churches. It also bound the covenanting parties to undertake the extirpation of popery and prelacy. The precise nature of the reformation aimed at was not stated, nor was it specified which were "the best reformed churches." It was generally understood at the time, however, that the Church of Scotland and the Continental bodies holding the Calvinistic theology and the Presbyterian system of government were intended.

III. Analysis of Contents

A. *Introductory Paragraph.* The Solemn League and Covenant contains an introductory paragraph, six articles, and a concluding paragraph. The introduction sets forth the reasons for the establishment of the bond:

We Noblemen, Barons, Knights, Gentlemen, Citizens, Burgesses, Ministers of the Gospel, and Commons of all sorts, in the kingdoms of Scotland, England, and Ireland, by the providence of GOD, living under one King, and being of one reformed religion, having before our eyes the glory of GOD, and the advancement of the kingdom of our Lord and Saviour JESUS CHRIST, the honour and happiness of the King's Majesty, and his posterity, and the true public liberty, safety, and peace of the kingdoms, wherein every one's private condition is included: And calling to mind the treacherous and bloody plots, conspiracies, attempts, and practices of the enemies of GOD, against the true religion and professors thereof in all places, especially in these three kingdoms, ever since the reformation of religion; and how much their rage, power, and presumption are of late, and at this time, increased and exercised, whereof the deplorable state of the church and kingdom of Ireland, the distressed state of the church and kingdom of England, and the dangerous estate of the church and kingdom of Scotland, are present and public testimonies; we have now at last (after other means of supplication and remonstrance, protestation, and sufferings) for the preservation of ourselves and our religion from utter ruin and destruction, according to the commendable practice of these kingdoms in former times, and the example of GOD'S people in other nations, after mature deliberation, resolved and determined to enter into a mutual and solemn League and Covenant, wherein we all subscribe, and each one of us for himself, with our hands lifted up to the Most High GOD, do swear.

B. *Body in Six Sections.* Article I binds the covenanting parties to endeavor the preservation of the Reformed religion in Scotland, and the reformation of religion in England and Ireland, in doctrine, worship, discipline, and government "according to the Word of God and the example of the best reformed churches," and to seek to bring the churches of the three kingdoms to the greatest possible degree of uniformity in "religion, confession of faith, form of church government, directory for worship and catechising."

In Article II the parties engage to endeavor the "extirpation" of popery, prelacy, superstition, heresy, schism, profaneness "and whatsoever shall be found to be contrary to sound doctrine and the power of godliness."

In Article III the swearers promise to endeavor, with their property and their lives, to preserve the rights and privileges of the parliaments, and the liberties of the three kingdoms, "and to preserve and defend the King's Majesty's person and authority, in the preservation and defence of the true religion, and liberties of the kingdoms; that the world may bear witness with our consciences of our loyalty, and that we have no thoughts or intentions to diminish his Majesty's just power and greatness."

Article IV binds the parties to seek the discovery and public prosecution of enemies of the reformation of religion and active opponents of the ends of the Solemn League and Covenant.

Article V binds the parties to seek "a firm peace and union to all posterity" of the three kingdoms, and requires "that justice may be done upon the wilful opposers thereof."

In Article VI, the parties bind themselves to mutual assistance and pledge that they will not permit themselves "directly or indirectly, by whatsoever combination, persuasion, or terror, to be divided and withdrawn from this blessed union and conjunction, whether to make defection to the contrary part, or to give ourselves to a detestable indifferency and neutrality, in this cause which so much concerneth the glory of GOD, the good of the kingdom, and honour of the King. . . ."

C. *Concluding Paragraph.* The final paragraph contains a confession of sins and promise of amendment, and ends with a solemn protestation of sincerity in the sight of God, "with a true intention to perform the same, as we shall answer at that great day, when the secrets of all hearts shall be disclosed; most humbly beseeching the Lord to strengthen us by his HOLY SPIRIT for this end, and to bless our desires and proceedings with such success, as may be deliverance and safety to his people, and encouragement to other Christian churches, groaning under, or in danger of, the yoke of anti-christian tyranny, to join in the same or like association and covenant, to the glory of GOD, the enlargement of the kingdom of JESUS CHRIST, and the peace and tranquillity of Christian kingdoms and commonwealths."

IV. The Parties Bound by the Covenant

In the first instance, the Solemn League and Covenant purports to be binding on the individual swearers and subscribers: "We all subscribe, and each one of us for himself. . . ." Inasmuch as it was adopted by the parliaments of England and Scotland, as well as by the Westminster Assembly of Divines and the Church of Scotland, it became binding upon the nations of England and Scotland as such. In addition, it was subscribed by Charles II upon his coronation as king. Thus the bond became in the most explicit manner a part of the basic national structure of England and Scotland. (The inclusion of Ireland was formal rather than actual. The importance of the bond chiefly concerned England and Scotland.)

V. Kind of Reformation Intended for England and Ireland

From the standpoint of the Reformed faith, the cause of reformation in Scotland was in advance of the progress made in England and Ireland. From the beginning the Reformation in Scotland had been a movement of the people—the Reformation was not imposed from above but earnestly promoted by the people themselves. Moreover Scotland had advanced far beyond England and Ireland in setting up a truly Scriptural structure of worship, discipline, church government, and indoctrination as envisaged by the Reformed or Calvinistic interpretation of Christianity. Thus the professed aim was to bring England and Ireland up to the level of reformation already attained, in large measure, by Scotland. This appears from the statement of aim to *preserve* the Reformed religion in Scotland, while *undertaking* the reformation of religion in England and Ireland. Scotland, of course, had followed the Calvinistic churches and reformers on the Continent. Thus the expression "according to the Word of God, and the example of the best reformed churches" was generally understood, at the time, to mean "according to the Word of God as implemented by the Church of Scotland and similar bodies on the Continent."

VI. The Presuppositions of the Bond

It is obvious that beyond what is explicitly stated, certain things are presupposed in the Solemn League and Covenant. It is assumed as axiomatic that there can be but one church in each of the three kingdoms, that that church must be established by the state as the official church of the nation, and that no rival church or churches can be permitted to exist alongside the established church. The idea of separation of church and state was foreign to the thinking of the Christian world of that time, as was the idea that distinct denominations, each claiming to be a manifestation of the true church, could exist side by side in a single country.

Article II of the bond actually binds the parties to the "extirpation," not only of Roman Catholicism and the episcopal form of church government, but also of heresy and schism, i.e., of all open dissent from the officially established church. Those minority bodies in Scotland and elsewhere which still adhere to the validity and binding character of the Solemn League and Covenant, interpret the word "extirpation" as something not involving the use of force or violence. This must be regarded as straining the language of the document, however. At the time it was all but universally believed that it was the duty of the civil government to suppress schism and heresy. And the Solemn League and Covenant was formally entered into, not only by private citizens and church assemblies, but by the national parliaments of England and Scotland. Thus "extirpation" can hardly mean anything less than legal suppression enforced by the power of the state. No one, presumably, would advocate this today, but it was set forth as a proper and valid aim by the Solemn League and Covenant.

VII. Outcomes in the Church and Nation of Scotland

A. *Imposed by Civil and Church Authority.* It was in Scotland that the Solemn League and Covenant was originally formulated, and it was in Scotland that it had the greatest historical effect. While originally it was voluntarily subscribed by multitudes of all classes in Scotland (excepting those who favored prelacy and absolutism), it was soon being required of people by civil and ecclesiastical authority. In 1644 the General Assembly of the Church of Scotland decreed that ministers should report to the presbyteries the names of any newcomers in their parishes who might be opposed to the National Covenant of Scotland or the Solemn League and Covenant. Large numbers of people, of various classes, were required to sign the bond. For example, no one could enter a university in Scotland as a student without accepting it. Even King Charles II on his coronation was required to sign the Covenant. The infliction of both religious and civil censures on any who might refuse to sign it was justified by many of the ministers and people of Scotland.

B. *Accepted Hypocritically by Many.* It was typical of the psychology of those times that those who were most zealous for the Solemn League and Covenant were, apparently, quite unaware of the inevitable outcome of requiring acceptance of the bond by civil and church authority—namely, that multitudes would conform to the requirement hypocritically, with a feigned or merely formal acceptance, in order to gain status or to avoid disabilities. The Rev. James Guthrie in 1651 alleged that one of the causes of the Lord's wrath against Scotland was the hypocritical acceptance of the National Covenant and the Solemn League and Covenant by many, yet he held that the imposition of the Covenant by civil and religious censures was proper and legitimate.

C. *Eliminated by the Stuart Restoration.* The restoration of Charles II as king, following the Commonwealth period, meant the abolition of the Solemn League and Covenant so far as the state was concerned. Charles had accepted the National Covenant of Scotland and the Solemn League and Covenant when he was crowned King of Scotland in 1651. At his restoration in 1660 these religious qualifications were not mentioned. The Scottish parliament in 1662 declared the Solemn League and Covenant to be an unlawful oath, and contrary to the fundamental laws of the kingdom. The same act of parliament required all persons holding responsible public office in Scotland to take an oath renouncing the two Covenants. It was further declared unlawful to subscribe to either Covenant in the future. In addition to this act of parliament, King Charles II had the Solemn League and Covenant publicly burned by the hangman. This was done in England in 1661 and in Scotland in 1662. Thus the Solemn League and Covenant was abolished so far as it was in the power of the king and government of Scotland to do so.

A considerable body of people in Scotland—the Covenanters—continued to hold to the validity and binding character of the Solemn League and Covenant. After 28 years of increasingly violent persecution, freedom dawned with the Revolution of 1688. In the reconstitution of the church and nation of Scotland, the Solemn League and Covenant was ignored. Its binding obligation has continued to be held down to the present day by the Reformed Presbyterian Church and some other Presbyterians in Scotland.

Bibliography:

S. Cheetham, *A History of the Christian Church Since the Reformation* (1907), pp. 34 ff.

J. Cunningham, *The Church History of Scotland from the Commencement of the Christian Era to the Present Time* (1882), 2 vols.

W. M. Hetherington, *History of the Church of Scotland* (1852).

J. K. Hewison, *The Covenanters: A History of the Church of Scotland from the Reformation to the Revolution* (1908), 2 vols.

J. C. Johnston, ed., *Treasury of the Scottish Covenant* (1887), pp. 97-105, 116.

T. M'Crie, *Sketches of Scottish Church History* (1841 and 1849), 2 vols.

Solemn League and Covenant, The (1643), included in many editions of the Westminster Standards.

Testimony Bearing Exemplified (Paisley, 1741; New York, 1834), pp. 122-124, 175.

B. B. Warfield, *The Westminster Assembly and Its Work* (New York, 1931), pp. 3-35.

Johannes G. Vos

COVENANT THEOLOGY

I. Definition
II. The Covenant of Works
III. The Covenant of Grace
IV. The Covenant of Redemption
V. The External Dispensation of the Covenant of Grace
VI. The Sacraments of the Covenant of Grace

Covenant theology denotes a development of theological thought and construction within the Reformed or Calvinistic tradition. This does not mean that the idea of God's covenantal relations with men has been ignored in other theological traditions. The term *covenant* is a Biblical term, and any theology which regards the Scripture as the rule of faith is compelled to recognize the frequency with which the relationship that God established with men is set forth in covenantal terms. Hence, within Protestant churches both Lutheran and Arminian theologians have taken account of the covenant form in which God has revealed Himself to men (cf. J. A. Quenstedt, *Theologia Didactico-Polemica,* Leipzig, 1715, II, 1298 ff.; D. Hollazius, *Examen Theologicum Acromanticum*, Leipzig, 1763, 1045 ff.; M. Chemnitz, *Examen Concilii Tridentini,* Frankfort, 1609, 242b; P. Limborch, *Theologia Christiana*, The Hague, 1736, 195 ff., 203 f., 603 f.; S. Episcopius, *Opera Theologica*, London, 1678, 31 f., 45 f., 155 f.; S. Curcellaeus, *Opera Theologica*, Amsterdam, 1675, 188-196, 347 ff.; R. Watson, *Theological Institutes*, London, 1846, II, 337 f., 611; III, 472-493; W. B. Pope, *A Compendium of Christian Theology*, London, 1880, II, 13, 60, 93-96; III, 100 ff.).

Covenant theology is, however, a distinguishing feature of the Reformed tradition because the idea of covenant came to be an organizing principle in terms of which the relations of God to men were construed.

From the beginning and throughout the development of covenant theology, covenant has been defined as a contract, or compact, or agreement between parties. From the earliest Reformed treatise on the subject, that of Henry Bullinger (*De Testamento seu Foedere Dei Unico et Aeterno Brevis Expositio*, 1534), through the classic period of formulation, and continuing to recent times this concept has exercised a great influence upon the exposition of God's covenant relations with men. Hence, in the words of Zachary Ursinus, God's covenant is "a mutual promise and agreement, between God and men, in which God gives assurance to men that he will be merciful to them. . . . And, on the other side, men bind themselves to God in this covenant that they will exercise repentance and faith . . . and render such obedience as will be acceptable to him" (Eng. tr., G. W. Williard, *The Commentary on the Heidelberg Catechism,* Grand Rapids, 1954, 97). And Charles Hodge, three centuries later, insisted that since covenant "when used of transactions between man and man means a mutual compact" we must give it the same sense "when used of transactions between God and man" (*Systematic Theology*, II, 354). The formulation of a covenant, therefore, took the form of a fourfold division—contracting parties, conditions, promises, threatenings. It was also defined in terms of *stipulation*, denoting the demand of God placed upon man, of *promise* on the part of God to man, of *astipulation*, referring to the acceptance on man's part of the conditions prescribed by God, and, finally, of *restipulation,* whereby man could claim the promise on his fulfilment of the prescribed demands.

I. Definition

This formulation became the occasion of ardent dispute when it was applied to the Covenant of Grace. This dispute concerned particularly the matter of condition, the question being: Is the Covenant of Grace to be construed as conditional or unconditional? The controversy continues up to the present time, and it is not apparent that a solution can be obtained without a reorientation in terms of a revised definition of the Biblical concept of covenant (see Covenants, Biblical).

II. The Covenant of Works

Towards the end of the 16th century the administration dispensed to Adam in Eden, focused in the prohibition to eat of the tree of the knowledge of good, had come to be interpreted as a covenant, frequently called the Covenant of Works, sometimes a covenant of life or the Legal Covenant. It is, however, significant that the early covenant theologians did not construe this Adamic administration as a covenant, far less as a covenant of works. Reformed creeds of the 16th century such as the French Confession (1559), the Scottish Confession (1560), the Belgic Confession (1561), the Thirty-Nine Articles (1562), the Heidelberg Catechism (1563), and the Second Helvetic (1566) do not exhibit any such construction of the Edenic institution. After the pattern of the theological thought prevailing at the time of their preparation, the term "covenant," insofar as it pertained to God's relations with men, was interpreted as designating the relation constituted by redemptive provisions and as belonging, therefore, to the sphere of saving grace.

It might appear from certain expressions that John Calvin enunciated the doctrine of what came later to be known as the Covenant of Works. He uses such terms as "the covenant of the law" and "the legal covenant" (*foedus legis, pactum legis, foedus legale*; cf. *Inst.*, II, xi, 4; *Comm. ad* Jer. 32:4). In these references, however, it is clear that it is the Mosaic covenant, in distinction from the new covenant of the Gospel age, that he calls the covenant of the law and the legal covenant. There is no allusion to the Adamic administration, nor can there be any suggestion to the effect that the Mosaic covenant was legal or one of works in contrast with grace; Calvin is insistent that the covenant of all the fathers is identical with the new in substance and differs only in the mode of administration (*Inst.*, II, x, 2 and 8; II, xi, 1). This use of the terms to designate the Mosaic covenant or, more inclusively, the OT should guard us against the assumption that they have any affinity with or give any support to what, later on, had come to be called the Covenant of Works.

There is, however, another sense in which Calvin uses the expression "covenant of the law." The law of God as commandment does prescribe the rule of a devout and perfect life, and promises the reward of life to perfect fulfilment of its demands (*Comm. ad* Gen. 15:6; *Inst.*, II, ix, 4). It must be noted, however, that this kind of righteousness or the merit accruing therefrom is for Calvin purely hypothetical. For in this connection he says that such observance of the law is never found in any man. Nevertheless, in view of Calvin's use of the expression "covenant of the law" with this import, and since he believed that Adam had been created in righteousness and holiness, there would appear to be good ground for applying the term "covenant" to that administration which had been constituted with Adam in the state of innocence. It is noteworthy that he does not make this application and evinces great restraint in this regard. The interpretation of Hosea 6:7 in which allusion might be found to an Adamic covenant he vigorously rejects, and he is insistent that there was no *covenant* answering to the requirements of justification and acceptance with God prior to the covenant with Abraham (*Comm. ad* Gal. 3:17).

This restraint on Calvin's part does not mean that the doctrine of Adam's representative headship, which later on came to be formulated in terms of the Covenant of Works, is absent from his teaching. He maintains that all men were created in the first man, that what God designed for all He conferred on Adam, that the condition of mankind was settled in Adam's person, and that Adam by his fall ruined himself and drew all mankind into the same ruin (*Comm. ad* I Cor. 15:45; Rom. 5: 12 ff.). But he did not construe this Adamic constitution as a *covenant* of works or of law.

It is difficult to discover the genealogy of the doctrine of the Covenant of Works which appeared in fully developed form in the last decade of the 16th century. It may be that the earliest suggestion is found in Gaspar Olevianus. After the pattern of what we find in Calvin, Olevianus speaks of the legal covenant as the eternal rule of righteousness to which man is obligated and to which is annexed the promise of life on the fulfillment of perfect obedience and the threat of death in the event of transgression. This is a principle always recognized in covenant theology. But in Olevianus we find what goes beyond this application of the term "covenant." He applies the term to the administration under which Adam fell by the temptation of Satan: "For we see that Satan, in order to destroy that first covenant or relationship which existed between God and man created in the image of God, set before man the hope of equality with God" (*De Substantia Foederis Gratuiti inter Deum et*

Electis, Geneva, 1585, 9 f.). He then speaks of the "impious covenant" by which man sold himself to the devil. It is more likely that he construed the "first covenant" as a special administration to Adam rather than as merely the legal covenant insofar as it applied to Adam (cf. also F. Junius in *Theses Theologicae*, XXV, 3, *Opuscula Theologica Selecta*, Amsterdam, 1882, 184).

But by whatever processes in the course of covenant thinking the doctrine of the Covenant of Works came to occupy a place in the formulation of covenant theology, we find it clearly enunciated in all its essential features in Robert Rollock, first in his treatise *Quaestiones et Responsiones Aliquot de Foedere Dei* (Edinburgh, 1596) and then in his *Tractatus De Vocatione Efficaci* (1597; Eng. tr. by Henry Holland, London, 1603). It is significant that the premise of Rollock's thought is that all of God's Word pertains to some covenant; God speaks nothing to man without covenant.

The Covenant of Works, also called the Covenant of Nature, Rollock defines as the covenant in which God promises to man eternal life on the condition of good works performed in the strength of nature, a condition which man in turn accepts. The *foundation* of this covenant was the holy and perfect nature with which man was endowed at creation and is thus to be sharply distinguished from the foundation of the Covenant of Grace, which is in Christ and the grace of God in Christ. The *condition* was good works performed in virtue of the holy nature with which man was created and not faith in Christ or the works of grace. The heads of this condition are the commands of the Decalogue written first of all upon man's heart. The *promise* is eternal life accruing to man not on the basis of his original righteousness or integrity but on the basis of the good works performed in the strength of this integrity. As regards *repetition*, the covenant is repeated again and again from the creation and fall of man to the coming of Christ but particularly in the promulgation from Mount Sinai by the hand of Moses (Ex. 19:5-8). The end of this repetition, however, was not that men might be justified and live by this covenant but that, being convicted of sin and of the impossibility of good works in the strength of nature, they might take refuge in the Covenant of Grace. The *threat* of the covenant was the curse epitomized in the twofold death which followed upon the breach, death corporal and spiritual (see W. M. Gunn, ed., *The Select Works of Robert Rollock*, Edinburgh, 1849, I, 33-38).

The concept of legal covenant, found in Calvin but not applied by him to the Adamic administration, is here in Rollock clearly utilized in the interpretation and construction of the Adamic institution. From this time on the rubric of the Covenant of Works is part of the staple of covenant theology. M. Maternus Heyder, in theses presented to Grynaeus, Stuckius, and Pareus, dated November 25, 1602, and titled *De Foedere Dei et Conjunctis Aliquot Capitibus,* says that there is a twofold covenant, of works and of grace. The Covenant of Works he defines as that in which God promises to man immortality and eternal life on the performance of the most absolute and perfect obedience to the law of works, a covenant entered into between God and men immediately upon the first creation. Heyder also propounds the notion of repetition and the purposes fulfilled thereby in a way similar to that of Rollock. Amandus Polanus in his *Syntagma Theologiae Christianae* (Hanover, 1609) follows the same pattern in respect of definition, repetition, and the purposes promoted by repetition. But he also becomes more explicit respecting the time and persons involved when he says that God made this covenant from the beginning with our first parents, Adam and Eve, in the state of primitive integrity (*Lib.* VI, *Cap.* XXXIII, 2904 ff.).

It is not certain that William Perkins, though he plainly speaks of the Covenant of Works as God's covenant made on the condition of perfect obedience and expressed in the moral law (*A Golden Chaine*, London, 1612, 32), conceived of the special administration to Adam in these terms. There is no mention of a covenant with Adam at an earlier point in his treatise where he deals with Adam and the consequences of his sin (*ibid.*, 19 ff.). The Covenant of Works may have been for Perkins another way of describing what in Calvin, for example, was a hypothetical legal covenant. In John Preston, however, Perkins' younger contemporary, the Covenant of Works is expressly stated to have been made with Adam and expressed by Moses in the moral law but which now by reason of sin is no more than the ministration of naked commandment, of servile fear, and of death (*The New Covenant or the Saints Portion*, London, 1639, 314 ff.).

This interpretation of the Adamic administration in terms of covenant found expression in creedal formulation for the first time in The Irish Articles of Religion (1615). Article 21 reads: "Man being at the beginning created according to the image of God . . . had the covenant of the law ingrafted in his heart, whereby God did promise unto him everlasting life upon condition that he performed entire and perfect obedience unto his Commandments, according to that measure of strength wherewith he was endued in his creation, and threatened death unto him if he did not perform the same." In more explicit form it is set forth in the Westminster Confession of Faith and Catechisms. In Chapter VII, Sections I and II, the Confession says:

> The distance between God and the creature is so great, that although reasonable creatures do owe obedience unto Him as their Creator, yet they could never have any fruition of Him as their blessedness and reward, but by some voluntary condescension on God's part, which He hath been pleased to express by way of covenant.
>
> II. The first covenant made with man was a covenant of works, wherein life was promised to Adam; and in him to his posterity, upon condition of perfect and personal obedience.

In Chapter XIX, Section I, we read:

> God gave to Adam a law, as a covenant of works, by which He bound him and all his posterity to personal, entire, exact, and perpetual obedience, promised life upon the fulfilling, and threatened death upon the breach of it, and endued him with power and ability to keep it (cf. The Larger Catechism, 20-22; The Shorter Catechism, 12).

The doctrine of the Covenant of Works was more extensively unfolded in the classic Reformed theologians of the 17th century. New aspects or at least emphases appear. Francis Turretine may be mentioned as representative of the more detailed expositions (*Institutio Theologiae Elencticae, Loc.* VIII). A few features are worthy of special attention.

Adam, as a *contracting party*, is to be regarded in the bond of union that existed between him and the whole human race descending naturally from him. This bond of union is twofold, *natural* because he is the common father of all and *forensic* because he was a public person and constituted the representative prince and head of the human race. The *obligation* of the covenant was partly general and partly special, general in respect of the moral law and special in respect of abstinence from the forbidden tree. The *promise* was that of the greatest felicity in heaven. The obligation which God assumed in this promise was wholly gratuitous; God had no debt, strictly speaking, from which a right could belong to man. The only debt was that of His own faithfulness to the promise. And as for man, he could not, strictly and properly, obtain merit from his obedience and could not seek the reward as a right. The worthiness of works could bear no proportion to the reward of life eternal.

In these features we can see that the conception entertained moved away from that of a *legal covenant*, and the gracious character of what was still called the Covenant of Works came to be recognized and accented. This is the emphasis which appears in the Westminster documents when covenant is construed as "voluntary condescension" and "special act of providence." And the designation "covenant of life" in both Catechisms is much more in accord with the grace which conditions the administration than is the term "covenant of works."

III. The Covenant of Grace

It is with the Covenant of Grace that the covenant theologians of the 16th century were concerned almost exclusively. And even in later developments of covenant theology it was not the Covenant of Works that claimed the chief interest; the latter was but the preface to the unfolding of the Covenant of Grace, which is constitutive of the history of redemption.

The Covenant of Grace from the earliest period of the Reformation was conceived of in terms of the administration of grace to men and belonging, therefore, to the sphere of historical revelation. It was regarded as having begun to be dispensed to men in the first promise given to Adam after the fall, but as taking concrete form in the promise to Abraham and progressively disclosed until it reached its fullest realization in the New Covenant.

Henry Bullinger in his tractate of 1534 mapped out the lines along which the thinking of covenant theologians proceeded. He found the essence and characterizing features of what he calls "the one and everlasting testament" or "covenant in the covenant made with Abraham" (Gen. 17).

> Here God, of His ineffable mercy and grace and moved by nothing else than mere goodness, entered into covenant with the seed of Abraham, promising to be a God to them and requiring of them that they walk perfectly before Him, a covenant that is perpetual in its reference and confirmed by a bloody ceremony. Here he says is the mystery that surpasses human comprehension, that the eternal God, the Creator and Preserver of all, should join Himself in covenant with miserable mortals corrupted by sin, to the end that He should not deal with them after their sins nor execute His wrath upon them. It was this covenant that Christ confirmed. It is confirmed by the fact that He is God-with-us, that we are complete in Him in whom dwells all the fulness of the Godhead, and that out of His fulness we all receive grace for grace. The condition, likewise, is confirmed by Christ; there is no retraction of the demand that we walk before Him and be perfect. He that says he abides in Christ ought to walk even as He walked. Hence the covenant of God with men is one and it is perpetual, as was indicated to Abraham when God said "and between thy seed after thee in their generations for an everlasting covenant" (*op. cit.*, 155-161).

It was noted above that Calvin regarded the covenant made with Abraham as the first *covenantal* administration answering to justification and acceptance with God. Calvin, like Bullinger, finds in the Abrahamic covenant substantial features of all that is involved in God's covenant relationship with men. It is the promise of the covenant with Abraham that Christ fulfils, and fulfilment constitutes the New Covenant. But of particular interest in connection with unity and continuity is Calvin's insistence that the Mosaic covenant was not of a different character or governed by a different principle but was a confirmation of the Abrahamic. "It then follows," he says, "that the first covenant was inviolable; besides, he had already made his covenant with Abraham, and the Law was a confirmation of that covenant. As then the Law depended on that covenant which God made with his Servant Abraham, it follows that God could never have made a new, that is, a contrary or a different covenant. From whence do we derive our hope of salvation, except from that blessed seed promised to Abraham? . . . These things no doubt sufficiently show that God has never made any other covenant than that which he made formerly with Abraham, and at length confirmed by the hand of Moses" (*Comm. ad* Jer. 31:31, 32, Eng. tr. by John Owen, Grand Rapids, 1950; cf. *ad* Gal. 3:17, 18, 19, 23; Heb. 8:6, 10; Ex. 24:5). Even the New Covenant is not so called because it is contrary to the first covenant but because there is a clearer and fuller manifestation of the gratuitous adoption which the Abrahamic covenant revealed and the Mosaic confirmed (*idem*).

It is necessary to observe the extent to which Calvin recognized the principle of historical progression in the disclosure of covenant grace. The recognition of progressive revelation long antedates Cocceius. Nothing surpasses the following excerpt from Calvin's greatest work:

> For this is the order and economy which God observed in dispensing the covenant of his mercy, that as the course of time accelerated the time of its full exhibition, he illustrated it from day to day with additional revelations. Therefore, in the beginning, when the first promise was given to Adam, it was like the kindling of some feeble sparks. Subsequent accessions caused a considerable enlargement of the light, which continued to increase more and more, and diffused its splendour through a wide extent, till at length, every cloud being dissipated, Christ, the Sun of righteousness, completely illuminated the whole world (*Inst.*, II, x, 20, Eng. tr. by John Allen).

Calvin devotes two chapters to the subject of the similarities and differences between the two Testaments (*Inst.* II, x and xi), and subsequent discussions follow the pattern delineated in these chapters. The formula adopted to express the three features of unity, continuity, and consummation in Christ was oneness in substance but difference in mode of administration (*Inst.*, II, xi, 1).

This tradition received its most succinct formulation in the Westminster Confession of Faith in Chapter VII, Sections V and VI:

> V. This covenant was differently administered in the time of the law, and in the time of the gospel: under the law, it was administered by promises, prophecies, sacrifices, circumcision, the paschal lamb, and other types and ordinances delivered to the people of the Jews, all fore-signifying Christ to come; which were, for that time, sufficient and efficacious, through the operation of the Spirit, to instruct and build up the elect in faith in the promised Messiah, by whom they had full remission of sins, and eternal salvation; and is called the Old Testament.
>
> VI. Under the gospel, when Christ, the substance, was exhibited, the ordinances in which this covenant is dispensed are the preaching of the Word, and the administration of the sacraments of Baptism and the Lord's Supper: which, though fewer in number, and administered with more simplicity, and less outward glory, yet, in them, it is held forth in more fulness, evidence, and spiritual efficacy, to all nations, both Jews and Gentiles; and is called the New Testament. There are not therefore two covenants of grace, differing in substance, but one and the same, under various dispensations.

The covenant theologians who followed Calvin such as Jerome Zanchius, Zachary Ursinus, and Gaspar Olevianus adhere to a rather uniform pattern in expounding the doctrine of the Covenant of Grace. First of all, it is noteworthy that they do not orient their exposition to a comparison and contrast with the Covenant of Works, as later theologians were wont to do. The following summary, in terms largely of Olevianus' exposition, will serve to illustrate the pattern pursued.

The covenant is that by which God reconciles us to Himself in Christ and bestows upon us the twofold benefit of gratuitous righteousness in the remission of sins and renovation after God's image. The emphasis falls to a large extent upon the gratuitous character.

It is gratuitous in three respects: in respect of the Mediator, in respect of us, and in respect of the ends contemplated. (1) It is gratuitous in respect of the Mediator because He was given freely for us, the Father accepts from Him the price of reconciliation, the merit of the Mediator is freely imputed to us, and the promise of grace in Christ is gratuitous. (2) It is gratuitous in respect of us because the faith by which we embrace the gift of reconciliation is given to us freely by the Holy Spirit. (3) It is gratuitous in respect of the ends contemplated—God willed reconciliation that all the glory might redound to Himself, and the peace of conscience we enjoy can be gained only by God's free favor and provision.

The foregoing emphasis upon the gratuitous character is correlative with unconditional character. Since the covenant as to substance consists in the remission of sin and the renovation of our hearts (Jer. 31:31 ff.), this twofold promise belongs to the elect and to them alone. And the faith itself by which we are ingrafted into the seed of Abraham is the gift of God freely bestowed by the Holy Spirit. Even in the administration of the covenant, as distinct from its substance, the Holy Spirit prepares the hearts of the elect in due time, by His internal efficacy, imparts the gift of faith and repentance. The whole covenant, therefore, is merely of grace.

Christ is the Mediator. Since He was constituted such by the Father, He came with the *mandate* of the Father, ordained as high priest to make sacrifice and intercession, received the *promise* from the Father that the sacrifice and intercession would be accepted and the Holy Spirit given, and became, in turn, *sponsor* to make satisfaction for the sins of all whom the Father gave Him and to insure for them peace of conscience and renewal in the image of God.

The gratuitous and unconditional character of the covenant is not construed in any way as prejudicing the demand for faith. Zanchius, for example, is equally insistent that as the covenant pertains to God's promise it is altogether gratuitous, absolute, and without any condition, that God fulfils the promise out of mere mercy and goodness. But he also recognizes that from the side of man there are the stipulations imposed by God. These are twofold: (1) faith by which man believes that God for Christ's sake is a Father to him and that his sins have been pardoned, and (2) obedience in conformity of life to the good pleasure of God (*Opera Theologica*, Geneva, 1613, Tom. V, 43b).

In this early period there had not emerged the tension which developed in the 17th century on the question whether the covenant was to be conceived of as conditional or unconditional. It is apparent, however, that the question which was the occasion for so much debate later on had already been posed in the insistence of these 16th century theologians upon the unconditional nature of the covenant and at the same time upon the stipulations arising for the beneficiaries of covenant grace.

In Robert Rollock, who, as noted above, formulated the doctrine of the Covenant of Works, we find that the formulation of the Covenant of Grace is from the outset oriented to the contrast between the two covenants. To give but one example, the ground of the Covenant of Grace is, first, the Mediator Jesus Christ and, second, the grace and mercy of God in contrast with the strength of nature, which was the ground of the Covenant of Works. It is of particular interest to observe how Rollock answers the question of *condition* as it pertains to the Covenant of Grace. "The very name of the Covenant of Grace," he says, "might seem to require no condition, for it is called a free covenant, because God freely, and, as it might seem, without all condition, doth promise herein both righteousness and life. . . . But we are to understand that grace here, or the particle freely, doth not exclude all condition, but that only which is in the Covenant of Works, which is the condition of the strength of nature, and of works naturally just and good . . . which can in no wise stand with God's free grace in Christ Jesus" (*Select Works*, Edinburgh, 1849, I, 39). This condition is none other than faith as that which comports with Christ and with God's free grace. And faith itself is also of grace and is the free gift of God. So we are to remember "that whereas God offereth righteousness and life under condition of faith, yet doth he not so respect faith in us, which is also his own gift, as he doth the object of faith, which is Christ, and his own free mercy in Christ, which must be apprehended by faith. . . . Wherefore the condition of the Covenant of Grace is not faith only, nor the object of faith only, which is Christ, but faith with Christ, that is, the faith that shall apprehend Christ, or Christ with faith, that is, Christ which is to be apprehended by faith" (*ibid.*, 40). The viewpoint here set forth is essentially the same as that of Rollock's predecessors mentioned above, but faith as the condition is brought into clearer focus and its relation to the covenant carefully defined so as in no way to prejudice free mercy and grace.

In the confessions of the 16th century, as was noted, the Edenic institution is not construed in terms of covenant. But there is also a marked paucity of the use of the term "covenant" in reference to the provisions of redemptive grace. When the term is used, it occurs most frequently in connection with the sacraments, particularly with reference to the baptism of infants (cf. Heidelberg Catechism, 74; Belgic Confession XXXIV; Second Helvetic Confession, XX, 2 and 6). On occasion the term "testament" is used with covenantal signification. It is surprising, however, that the term "covenant" should be used with such infrequency, especially when we remember that the confessions were framed in terms of the truths which covenant grace represents and that both the concept and the term occupied so important a place in the thinking of those whose influence was paramount in the preparation of them. The Westminster Confession of Faith and Catechisms evince a marked change in this respect. The scheme of salvation is in these documents expressly set forth as the provision of the Covenant of Grace (Confession, VII, iii-vi; XIV, ii; XXVIII, i; L. C., 30-36, 166; S. C., 20, 94).

In the theology so far delineated the Covenant of Grace had been conceived of and formulated as the covenantal relation established on God's part with *men* and the grace dispensed to them. This continued to be the definition throughout the classic period of covenant theology, and the doctrine was unfolded in these precise terms. It is stated expressly thus in the Westminster Confession: "Man, by his fall, having made himself uncapable of life by that covenant, the Lord was pleased to make a second, commonly called the covenant of grace" (VII, iii). That the words "make a second" are to be understood in the sense of "make a second with man" is plain from the title of the chapter, "Of God's Covenant with Man," and also from the terms of the preceding section, where we read, "The first covenant made with man," which implies that the second was also made with man. In theologians such as Amandus Polanus, John Ball, Johannes Cocceius, Francis Turretine, Edward Leigh, Samuel Rutherford, and John Owen this designation is maintained and, with qualifications to be noted later, this may be said to have been the prevailing view. Turretine's formulation, herewith summarised, is representative.

"The Covenant of Grace is a gratuitous pact between God the offended one and man the offender, entered into in Christ, in which God freely on account of Christ promises to man the remission of sins and salvation and man in dependence upon the same grace promises faith and obedience" (*op. cit., Loc.* XI, *Q,* II, v). With respect to the nature of this covenant there are four things to be observed: (1) The *author* is God, of His goodness and free good pleasure, so that it is always called God's covenant and never man's. It is common to the whole Trinity but with the distinction that each Person, in a way suited to this economy, has His own peculiar way of working. God the Father instituted the covenant and sends the Son and Holy Spirit. God the Son is the cause and foundation. The Holy Spirit is the witness and earnest of the heavenly inheritance. The instruments of God's administration are the Word and sacraments and the ministers of both. (2) The *contracting parties* are God as the offended one, man as the offender, and Christ as the Mediator—God, not as Creator, Lord, and Lawgiver but as merciful Father and Redeemer; man, not as creature but as sinner; and Christ, as reconciling man the offender to God the offended one. (3) The *things covenanted* are, on the part of God, the promised benefits and, on the part of men, the duties prescribed. The promised benefits are principally: reconciliation and communion with God, the communication of all good gifts of grace and glory of this life and of the life to come, conformity to God's likeness so that as far as can apply to finite creatures we are made partakers of the Divine nature, and, finally, the eternal possession and fruition of the blessings bestowed. (4) The duties prescribed are faith and repentance, worship and obedience, separation from the world and consecration to God, all of which may be summed up in the obligation to be God's people and live as His redeemed.

The question which aroused the most ardent dispute in the 17th century, especially in the British Isles, was whether the covenant is to be conceived of as conditional or unconditional. Lest the nature of the dispute be misunderstood, there are certain considerations that must be kept in mind. (1) No theologian within the Reformed camp took the position that, in the saving provisions of which the Covenant of Grace is the administration, the thought of condition is to be completely eliminated. Those who were most jealous for the unconditional character of the covenant as an administration of grace to men were insistent that for Christ as the Mediator of the covenant there were conditions which had to be fulfilled. It was customary for those holding this position to appeal to Christ's fulfilment of the conditions as a reason, if not the main reason, why the covenant, as it respects men, is without condition. (2) Those who maintained the conditional nature of the covenant were jealous at the same time to maintain that the fulfilment of the conditions on the part of men was wholly of God's grace. There was no thought of the covenant as contingent upon human autonomy or as deriving any of its ingredients from a contribution which man in the exercise of his own free will supplied. In the words of John Ball, "the covenant of grace doth not exclude all conditions, but such as will not stand with grace" (*A Treatise of the Covenant of Grace*, London,

1645, 17). (3) The dispute was to a large extent focused upon the relation which faith, repentance, obedience, and perseverance sustained to the covenant. None held that the covenant relation obtained or that its grace could be enjoyed apart from those responses on the part of the person in covenant fellowship with God. However, in this connection, there was no disposition to exclude infants and others uncapable of being outwardly called by the ministry of the Word from the embrace of the covenant blessing.

One of the most outspoken exponents of the covenant as unconditional was John Saltmarsh. He expresses the viewpoint thus:

> God makes no Covenant properly under the Gospel as he did at first. . . . Man is not restored in such a way of Covenant and Condition as he was lost, but more freely; and more by Grace and Mercy; and yet God Covenants too; but it is not with Man only, but with him that was God and Man, even Jesus Christ; he is both the Covenant, and the Messenger or Mediator of the Covenant. God agreed to save Man, but this Agreement was with Christ, and all the Conditions were on his part; he stood for us, and performed the Conditions for Life and Glory. . . . God takes us into Covenant, not upon any Condition in us before; he brings with him Christ, and in him all the Conditions, and makes us as he would have us; not for the Covenant, but in it, or under it. . . . A Soul is then properly, actually, or expressly in Covenant with God, when God hath come to it in the Promise; and then when it feels itself under the Power of the Promise, it begins only to know it is in Covenant . . . so as they that believe, do rather feel themselves in that Covenant which God hath made with them, without any thing in themselves, either Faith or Repentance (*Free Grace: or, The Flowings of Christ's Blood Freely to Sinners*, London, 1700, 101-103).

Saltmarsh had deviated in several respects from Reformed patterns of thought. But the viewpoint reflected in these quotations was one espoused by others who could not be classified with Saltmarsh in other respects. Tobias Crisp is equally emphatic in maintaining the unconditional character of the Covenant of Grace and, in this respect, the total difference between this covenant and all other covenants in which there is "mutual agreement between parties upon certain articles, or propositions, propounded on both sides; so that each party is bound and tied to fulfil his own conditions" (*Christ Alone Exalted, Complete Works*, London, 1832, I, 83). "But in this covenant of grace, to wit, the new covenant, it is far otherwise; there is not any condition in this covenant . . . the new covenant is without any conditions whatsoever on man's part" (*ibid.*, 86). Crisp will not allow that faith, though indispensable to a state of salvation, can be regarded as the condition of the covenant. Christ alone justifies, he insists, and therefore a man is justified before he believes (*ibid.*, 90 ff.). In answer to the objection that this doctrine encourages license Crisp replies: "You must make a difference between doing anything in reference to the covenant, as the condition thereof, and doing something in reference to service and duty, to that God who enters into covenant with you" (*ibid.*, 89).

Thomas Blake was one of Crisp's chief opponents on this issue. He devotes much space and argument to the thesis that the Covenant of Grace is conditional. He does not question the covenant between God and Christ in respect of which there are no conditions fulfilled by men. But the Covenant of Grace is between God and man, and astipulation on the part of man is integral to such a covenant relationship. The conditions he specifies are chiefly faith and repentance (*Vindiciae Foederis, or, A Treatise of the Covenant of God Entered with Mankind*, London, 1653, 74, 93 ff., 105 ff.). Blake stresses the place occupied by the command of God's law in the Covenant of Grace and the corresponding sincerity in the way and work of God which the covenant requires and accepts (*ibid.*, 112). He inveighs against the severance of promise and duty "so that Christ is heard only in a promise, not at all in a precept, when they hear that Christ will save; but are never told that they must repent. These are but delusions; promise-Preachers, and no duty-Preachers; grace-Preachers and not repentance-Preachers" (*ibid.*, 144).

One of the most polemic opponents of the position adopted by Crisp was Daniel Williams. In his *Gospel-Truth Stated and Vindicated* (1692) a chapter is devoted to the conditionality of the Covenant of Grace in which he maintains that faith and repentance are acts of ours which, though performed by the grace of Christ freely given to sinners, are nevertheless required of us in order to the blessings of the covenant consequent thereupon and are required in accordance with the covenant constitution. In a later work, *A Defence of Gospel-Truth* (1693), Williams is largely concerned with a reply to Isaac Chauncy and develops his thesis with still greater vigour and fulness. He distinguishes between the Covenant of Redemption, which allows for no conditions to be fulfilled by men, and the Covenant of Grace, which requires our believing consent as a condition of pardon and glory. In terms of the former, God absolutely promised and covenanted with Christ that the elect will believe and persevere in faith and holiness to eternal life. But in terms of the latter, it is God's will that duty and benefit are so connected that the enjoyment of the benefit is conditioned upon the fulfilment of the duty, not because any merit attaches to the duty nor because the benefit is less of grace but because the duties required comport with grace and avail for the bestowment of grace by the promise of God. He is also careful to distinguish between "the promise of grace, which is absolute, and the promises to grace, which are conditional" (*ibid.*, 313).

Herman Witsius, the noted continental theologian, agrees with those who take the position that the Covenant of Grace has no conditions, properly so called. Witsius is aware that none come to salvation except in the way of faith and holiness, that it is impossible to please God without faith, and that many have for these reasons called faith and a new life the conditions of the covenant. But, he continues, "they are not so much conditions *of the covenant*, as *of the assurance* that we shall continue in God's covenant, and that he shall be our God" and thus, "to speak accurately, and according to the nature of this covenant, they are, on the part of God, the execution of previous promises, and the earnest of future happiness, and, on the part of man, the performance of those duties, which cannot but precede the consummate perfection of a soul delighting in God" (*The Economy of the Covenants between God and Man*, Eng. tr., Edinburgh, 1771, I, 389 f.). He appeals to the testamentary nature of the covenant as consisting in God's immutable purpose, founded on the unchangeable counsel of God, and ratified by the death of the testator. Thus it is not possible for it to be made void by the unbelief of the elect or made stable by their faith. "The Covenant of Grace is *testamentary*, and to be distinguished from a covenant founded on a compact, agreement, or law" (*ibid.*, 386 f.). This unilateral character of the covenant does not, however, remove the obligations descending upon him who accepts the promises of the covenant. He binds himself to the duties, and only thus can he assure himself of the fulfilment of the promises. In this respect the covenant is mutual (*ibid.*, 391 f.). And Witsius does not regard the unilateral character as interfering with the free overtures of grace in the Gospel nor as toning down the threatenings pronounced upon unbelief (*ibid.*, 393 ff.).

In the more recent development of covenant theology, Herman Bavinck represents this same position that the Covenant of Grace is unconditional. He does not tone down the responsibilities devolving upon those embraced in the covenant; it comes to us with the demand for faith and repentance. But "taken by itself the covenant of grace is pure grace, and nothing else, and excludes all works. It gives what it demands, and fulfills what it prescribes. The Gospel is sheer good tidings, not demand but promise, not duty but gift" (*Magnalia Dei*, Kampen, 1931, 261; Eng. tr., *Our Reasonable Faith*, Grand Rapids, 1956, 278). "We have to note particularly therefore that this promise is not conditional. . . . God does not say that He will be our God if we do this or that thing. . . . People can become unfaithful, but God does not forget His promise. He cannot and may not break His covenant; He has committed Himself to maintaining it with a freely given and precious oath: His name, His honor, His reputation depends on it" (*ibid.*, Eng. tr., 274 f.; cf. *Gereformeerde Dogmatiek*, Kampen, 1918, III, 210 f.).

Francis Turretine resolves the question by his characteristic method of distinguishing the different respects in which the term *condition* may be understood. If condition is understood in the sense of meritorious cause, then the Covenant of Grace is not conditioned: it is wholly gratuitous and depends solely upon God's good pleasure. But if understood as instrumental cause, receptive of the promises of the covenant, then it cannot be denied that the Covenant of Grace is conditioned. The covenant is set forth with an express condition (John 3:16, 36; Rom. 10:7): there would otherwise be no place in the Gospel for threatenings, and it would follow that God would be bound to man but not man to God, which is absurd and contrary to the nature of all covenants. Furthermore, there is the distinction between the promises respecting the *end* and those respecting the *means*, namely, salvation in the former case and faith and repentance in the latter. The promises respecting salvation are on the condition of faith and repentance, and no one can deny that these promises are conditional. But when the promises respect the means (faith, regeneration, repentance), then they are not conditional but simple and absolute: otherwise the process would be infinite, which again would be absurd.

When it is said that faith is the condition of the covenant this is not to be understood *absolutely* but *relatively and instrumentally* as embracing Christ and through His righteousness obtaining the title to everlasting life. Only thus would it comport with the grace of God, with the condition of the sinner, with the righteousness of the Mediator, with life eternal as the gift of God, and with the promises which set life before man not as something to be acquired but as something already acquired (*op. cit., Loc.* XII, *Q.* III).

The construction exemplified in Turretine, whereby the covenant is conceived of as conditioned upon faith and repentance, is in accord with the classic formulation in terms of *stipulation, promise, astipulation,* and *restipulation* (cf. Francis Burmann: *Synopsis Theologiae*, 1687, I, 476; J. H. Heidegger: *Medulla Theologiae Christianae*, 1696, I, 238 ff.). This same viewpoint is reflected in the *Synopsis Purioris Theologiae* of 1624 (see *Disp.* XXIII, xxix). It is clearly stated in the Westminster Larger Catechism (Q. 32) and is implied in the Confession of Faith (VII, iii). It should be understood that the insistence upon this conditional feature of the Covenant of Grace, within the frame of thought espoused by these theologians, impinged in no way upon the sovereignty of God's grace nor upon the covenant as a disposition of grace, and they were unanimous in maintaining that the fulfilment of the conditions proceeded from operations of grace which were not themselves conditional.

IV. The Covenant of Redemption

The covenant theologians of the 16th century and early 17th conceived of covenant, as it applied to the provisions of God's saving grace, in terms of administration to men. By the middle of the 17th century, however, the relations of the Persons of the Godhead to one another in the economy of redemption came to be formulated under the rubric of covenant. The eternal counsel of God as well as the relations of the Persons to one another in the temporal execution of that counsel were construed in covenantal terms. This signalized a distinct development in the formulation of covenant theology. At the end of the 16th century the Adamic administration came to be construed in covenant terms, and so there was an extension of the covenant idea in that direction. Now we find expansion in a different direction; the covenant concept was applied to the Trinitarian counsel and economy of salvation.

The term "Covenant of Redemption" was not, however, a uniform designation. It cannot be said to be sufficiently descriptive to serve the purpose of distinguishing the aspects of God's counsel denoted by it. For this reason the use of other terms by some of the most representative covenant theologians is easily understood. Furthermore, in some cases, the avoidance of the term "covenant" to identify the intertrinitarian arrangements no doubt reflects hesitation as to the legitimacy of this use of the term.

Johannes Cocceius, though he on occasion uses the word "covenant" in reference to this convention between the Persons of the Godhead, more characteristically speaks of it as a pact. He takes over the language of Zech. 6:13 and calls it "the counsel of peace." It is construed as "the ineffable economy" in terms of which the Father requires obedience unto death on the part of the Son and promises to Him in return a kingdom and spiritual seed. The Son gives Himself to do the will of the Father and in turn demands from the Father the salvation of the people given to Him from the foundation of the world. In this mystery of our salvation the Father sustains the character of both Legislator and Governor—Legislator in demanding the demonstration of justice and punishing sin in His own Son, and Governor in giving His Son as Sponsor for the exercise of mercy towards His creatures. The Son represents the mercy of God by assuming flesh and condemning sin in it. He is the Testator by whose death we receive the inheritance. The Holy Spirit exercises the power of God in the regenerate, and through Him the Father and Son dwell in those whom He seals for the heavenly inheritance.

In this pact of salvation the will of the Father and Son is the same. But since the Father and Son are distinct, this one will must be viewed distinctly, on the one hand as giving and sending, and on the other as given and sent. Thus in this mystery, God is the one who judges and is judged, who satisfies justice and accepts that satisfaction—God Himself satisfies Himself by His own blood. The Son, being one with the Father, satisfies the justice of the Father and at the same time satisfies His own justice (*Summa Doctrinae de Foedere et Testamento Dei, Cap.* V, *Summa Theologiae*, Amsterdam, 1701, Tom. VII, 60 ff.).

Francis Turretine calls this aspect of

the counsel of redemption the pact between the Father and the Son. He thinks that it is superfluous to dispute whether the covenant was made with Christ and in Him with all His seed or whether it was made in Christ with all the seed. These alternatives amount to the same thing. But that there is a twofold pact, the one between the Father and the Son to execute the work of redemption, the other with the elect in Christ on the condition of faith and repentance, is not to be disputed.

For Turretine, the pact between the Father and the Son consists in the will of the Father in giving the Son as Redeemer of His mystical body and the will of the Son in giving Himself as Sponsor for the redemption of the members of His body. In this "economy of salvation" the Father is represented in Scripture as demanding obedience unto death and promising the reward, the Son as presenting Himself to do the Father's will, as promising faithful execution, and at length demanding in return the kingdom and glory promised. This formulation follows the pattern found already in Cocceius.

Of peculiar interest is what Turretine calls the three periods of this covenant. The first concerns *destination* when, from eternity in the counsel of the holy Trinity, Christ was given to the church (Prov. 8:23; I Pet. 1:20; Ps. 2:8); the second has respect to the *promise* when, immediately after the Fall, Christ offered Himself for the actual performance of what He had promised from eternity and, in His actual appointment as Mediator, began to do many things pertaining to this office; and the third respects *execution* when, in the incarnate state, Christ accomplished the work of salvation. Thus, Christ perfectly fulfilled all that was necessary to the consummation of the Covenant of Grace (*op. cit. Loc.* XII, *Q.* II, xi-xvi).

Peter van Mastricht uses the terms "eternal" and "temporal" to express the distinction. The former was made in eternity between the Father and the Son, the latter is made in time between God and the elect sinner, the former being the prototype, the latter the ectype. He construes the eternal covenant after the usual pattern as a transaction between the Father and the Son, comprehending the mutual demands and promises as they pertain to the eternal salvation of the elect, and insists upon the distinctness of the capacity in which each Person of the Trinity acts in this economy (*Theoretico-Practica Theologia*, 1698, *Lib.* V, *Cap.* I, vii-xi; cf. J. H. Heidegger, *op. cit.*, 234 ff.).

Herman Witsius develops this phase of covenant theology in great detail and with characteristic clarity. He calls it the compact (*pactum*) between the Father and the Son, and distinguishes it from the testamentary disposition by which God bestows upon the elect eternal salvation and all things relative thereto. This compact he regards as the foundation of our salvation, and it consists in the will of the Father in giving the Son to be the Head and Redeemer of the elect and the will of the Son in presenting Himself as Sponsor for them (*op. cit.*, 222-381).

In Samuel Rutherford the designation "Covenant of Redemption" is the characteristic one. It is to be considered in two ways, he says: as transacted in time by the actual discharge on Christ's part of His offices as King, Priest, and Prophet, and as an eternal transaction in the compact between Father and Son. In respect of the latter there are three eternal acts—designation, ordination, and delectation. Rutherford is jealous to maintain the distinction that the Covenant of Redemption is eternal as one of *designation* but temporal as one of *actual* redemption. And he likewise develops the differences between the covenant of suretyship and redemption made with Christ and the Covenant of Grace and Reconciliation made with sinners. The latter is no more eternal than is the creation itself; it was made in paradise. Though decreed from everlasting, it had no existence as a covenant until revealed to Adam after the Fall (*The Covenant of Life Opened: or, A Treatise of the Covenant of Grace*, Edinburgh, 1655, 282 ff.).

Edward Leigh is another representative. "The whole business of man's salvation was transacted between the Father and the Son long before it was revealed in Scripture, there was a covenant of redemption between God the Father and the Son for the salvation of the Elect" (*A Systeme or Body of Divinity*, London, 1662, 546; cf. also T. Goodwin, *Works*, Edinburgh, 1863, V, 3 ff.; T. Jacomb, *Sermons on the Eighth Chapter of the Epistle to the Romans*, Edinburgh, 1868, 187; A. Hamilton, *A Short Catechism Concerning the Three Special Divine Covenants*, Edinburgh, 1714, 8).

As noted, in the earliest formulations of covenant theology, the Covenant of Grace was conceived of historically as God's administration to men. Later on, when the inter-Trinitarian counsel of salvation came to be construed in terms of covenant, the term "Covenant of Grace" continued to be used to denote the covenant made with men and thus distinguished from the Covenant of Redemption. But there is a further development, exemplified in Thomas Boston, whereby the Covenant of Grace itself is conceived of in terms of the inter-Trinitarian counsel and economy. In Boston's words, "The Covenant of Redemption and the Covenant of Grace are not two distinct covenants, but one and the same covenant. . . . Only, in respect of Christ, it is called *the Covenant of Redemption*, forasmuch as in it he engaged to pay the price of our redemption; but in respect of us, *the Covenant of Grace*, forasmuch as the whole of it is of free grace to us" (*The Complete Works*, London, 1853, I, 333 f.). Since Boston constructs the Covenant of Grace in terms of purpose, appointment, commitment, and fulfilment on the part of the Persons of the Godhead, he is insistent that "the Covenant of Grace is absolute, and not conditional to us" (*ibid.*, 334). All the conditions were laid upon Christ, and He has fulfilled the same. Boston is careful to distinguish between conditions of connection or order in the covenant and conditions of the covenant (*idem*). Here again we meet the same kind of insistence found earlier in Crisp, Witsius, and others. In this case, however, the demand that the Covenant of Grace be regarded as unconditional *for us* is relieved of the objection which it readily encounters in the context of the earlier debates. Once the Covenant of Grace is interpreted in terms of the "eternal compact" between the Father and the Son (*ibid.*, 317), it is obvious that requirements devolving upon men cannot be construed as conditions of its execution.

Herman Bavinck uses "Counsel of Redemption" and "Covenant of Grace" as terms to designate the distinction. But he also maintains that "the Counsel of Redemption is itself a covenant—a covenant in which each of the three Persons, so to speak, receives His own work and achieves His own task. The Covenant of Grace which is raised up in time and is continued from generation to generation is nothing other than the working out and the impression or imprint of the covenant that is fixed in the Eternal Being. . . . The Counsel of Redemption and the Covenant of Grace cannot and may not be separated, but they differ from each other in this respect, that the second is the actualization of the first. The plan of redemption is not enough in itself. It needs to be carried out" (*Magnalia Dei*, 256; Eng. tr.,

273). The interrelationship between the eternal and the temporal is thus established, and it is readily seen how, as noted earlier, Bavinck can maintain the monopleuric and unconditional character of the Covenant of Grace. The Covenant of Grace must be viewed in its organic relation to the whole Counsel of Redemption.

V. The External Dispensation of the Covenant of Grace

Covenant theologians, though maintaining the particularity of the Covenant of Grace, nevertheless distinguished between the internal essence and the external dispensation, the former corresponding to the effectual call and the latter to the external in promulgation and presentation. In this external administration it is extended even to the reprobate who are within the visible church and includes the external benefits which accrue from the promulgation of the Gospel and obtain within the sphere of profession (cf. Turretine, *op. cit., Loc.* XII, *Q.* VI, v, vi). In the words of Witsius, "Moreover, as we restrict this covenant to the elect, it is evident, we are speaking of the *internal*, mystical, and spiritual *communion* of the covenant. For salvation itself, and every thing belonging to it, or inseparably connected with it, are promised in this covenant, all which none but the elect can attain to. If, in other respects, we consider the *external* oeconomy of the covenant, in the communion of the word and sacraments, in the profession of the true faith, in the participation of many gifts, which, though excellent and illustrious, are yet none of the effects of the sanctifying Spirit, nor any earnest of future happiness; it cannot be denied, that, in this respect, many are in the covenant, whose names, notwithstanding, are not in the testament of God" (*op. cit.*, Eng. tr., 384 f.; cf. M. Leydecker, *Synopsis Theologiae Christianae, Lib.* V, *Cap.* I, ix, x; P. Mastricht, *op. cit., Lib.* V, *Cap.* I, xxviii, xxix). Herman Bavinck, recognizing that not all were Israel who were of Israel and that there are evil branches in the vine, expresses this distinction by saying that there are persons "who are taken up into the Covenant of Grace as it manifests itself to our eyes and who nevertheless on account of their unbelieving and unrepentant heart are devoid of all the spiritual benefits of the covenant." Thus there are "two sides to the one covenant of grace," the one visible to us but the other visible perfectly to God alone. Bavinck, however, rejects the distinction between an internal and external covenant (*Magnalia Dei*, 261 f.; Eng. tr., 278 f.; cf. Louis Berkhof, *Systematic Theology*, Grand Rapids, 1941, 284 ff.).

VI. The Sacraments of the Covenant of Grace

In covenant theology the sacraments were always construed as holy signs and seals of the Covenant of Grace. Since the covenant was conceived of as one in substance under both dispensations, circumcision and the passover under the OT were regarded as having essentially the same significance as baptism and the Lord's supper under the NT. As signs and seals they possessed no virtue in themselves but derived all their efficacy from the spiritual realities signified by them. As seals of the covenant they were confirmations of God's faithfulness to the promises which the covenant enshrined.

The most distinctive feature of covenant theology in connection with the sacraments is the inference drawn from the nature of the covenant in support of paedobaptism. The argument, reduced to its simplest terms, is that the seals of the covenant pertain to those to whom the covenant itself pertains. But that the covenant pertains to infants is clear from Gen. 17:7 and Acts 2:39. From God's ordinance His grace extends from parents to children. Since the things signified in baptism, namely, remission of sins, regeneration, and the kingdom of heaven, belong to infants, there is no reason why the sign should not also be added (cf. F. Turretine, *op. cit., Loc.* XIX, *Q.* XX, v).

Of particular importance is the emphasis placed on the unity and continuity of the covenant. In covenant theology the argument for infant baptism falls into its place in the schematism which the organic unity and continuity of covenant revelation provided. In the words of Calvin: "For it is most evident that the covenant which the Lord once made with Abraham continues as much in force with Christians in the present day, as it did formerly with the Jews; and consequently that that word is no less applicable to Christians than it was to the Jews. . . . Now, as the Lord, immediately after having made the covenant with Abraham, commanded it to be sealed in infants by an external sacrament, what cause will Christians assign why they should not also at this day testify and seal the same in their children? . . . Since the abrogation of circumcision, there always remains the same reason for confirming it, which we have in common with the Jews. . . . The covenant is common, the reason for confirming it is common. Only the mode of confirming it is different; for to them it was confirmed by circumcision, which among us has been succeeded by baptism. Otherwise, if the testimony by which the Jews were assured of the salvation of their seed be taken away from us, the effect of the advent of Christ has been to render the grace of God more obscure and less attested to us than it was to the Jews" (*Inst.*, IV, xvi, 6; Eng. tr. by John Allen). "But if the covenant remains firm and unmoved, it belongs to the children of Christians now, as much as it did to the infants of the Jews under the OT. But if they are partakers of the thing signified, why shall they be excluded from the sign? If they obtain the truth, why shall they be debarred from the figure?" (*ibid.*, IV, xvi, 5).

John Murray

COVENANTERS, those who entered into one or more of the public covenants connected with the Scottish Reformation and those who subsequently adhered to those bonds and held the obligations involved in them to be perpetually binding.

I. The National Covenants of Scotland

It was characteristic of the Reformation movement in Scotland for the godly to band themselves together under the Lord by solemn oath for mutual assistance and support in the defense of the Gospel and the reformation of the church according to the Word of God. The earliest known "band" or "covenant" was made in 1556 under the leadership of John Knox. This was followed by several others through the years 1557-1572.

The first covenant of epoch-making significance in Scotland was the National Covenant written in 1580, occasioned by fear of Jesuit plots to destroy the Reformation. It was signed by King James VI and by many persons of all ranks in 1581 and again in 1590.

The National Covenant of 1580 contained about 1,000 words. It is a profession of faith in the Gospel, an acceptance of the Scots Confession of Faith of 1560, and a renunciation of the whole RC system, including a detailed list of rejected errors and abuses. Soon James VI adopted the doctrine of the divine right of kings, however, and believed he was set up by God to rule both church and state. As a result, in 1584 he established episcopacy in the Church of Scotland by the Black Acts of Parliament. Now the battle shifted from Romanism to prelacy. And after much struggle, the king in 1592 agreed to and ratified an act known as the "Charter of Presbyterianism," which nullified the Black Acts and approved the Presbyterian Book of Discipline. In spite of the law, bishops were appointed again, and in 1610 the Court of High Commission was set up that suppressed any minister who opposed episcopacy. When Charles ascended the throne and then came to Scotland accompanied by Archbishop Laud, he was surprised at the extent of open opposition. So in 1636 a book of ecclesiastical order was prepared, and all who opposed it were excommunicated. Ministers were forced to accept and use a new liturgy, and all meetings of church officers and presbyteries were held illegal.

A large convocation was held in Edinburgh in reaction to the oppression from the king and his bishops, and the National Covenant of 1638 was adopted and signed by great numbers of people. Against his will King Charles allowed a General Assembly to be held, in which the Church of Scotland ratified the covenant and abolished episcopacy. The king immediately sent his army but finally made treaties conceding Scottish demands.

This covenant consisted of three parts: first, the Covenant of 1580 *verbatim;* second, a legal section listing many acts of Parliament, to show that the adoption of the covenant was in keeping with the national law; third, an application to the special conditions existing in 1638.

When, as a result of civil conflict, the English Parliament appealed to the Scottish Parliament and Church for help against the king, Alexander Henderson, who had led the Scottish people in 1638, drew up the Solemn League and Covenant. This was approved in 1643 at the General Assembly of the Church of Scotland and at a joint session of the English House of Commons and the Westminster Assembly. It aimed at securing uniformity of religion on a Reformed and Presbyterian basis in the three lands of England, Ireland, and Scotland. It consisted of an introductory paragraph followed by six articles. The subscribers swear to endeavor to preserve the Reformed religion in Scotland, in doctrine, worship, discipline, and government, and aid the reformation of religion in England and Ireland, according to Scripture "and the example of the best reformed churches." They also bind themselves to endeavor the "extirpation" of all contrary systems and practices, including Romanism, Episcopacy, superstition, heresy, and schism. There are pledges of unity and mutual assistance against all opponents.

II. The Solemn League and Covenant

When the Church of Scotland became officially Episcopal under Charles II, true Presbyterianism could be practiced only in dissenting conventicles and unofficial society meetings until the Revolution of 1688. This begins the history of the Covenanters as a dissenting group distinct from the Church of Scotland. After 1688 Presbyterianism was restored by law in Scotland but on a somewhat different basis.

III. The Covenanters as a Dissenting Minority

In 1662 an act of the Privy Council (one of the Acts of Uniformity) required all ministers installed since 1649 to obtain approval of the Episcopal bishops or be removed from their pastoral charges. The result of this action was that nearly 400, or about one-third, of the ministers of Scotland were forced out of their churches. Later enactments of a similar character forced even more to leave their charges for conscience' sake.

Many of the ministers ejected in 1662 and subsequent years continued to preach, conducting services in private homes and also addressing large audiences in open fields. These activities incensed the bishops and the king, resulting in a series of increasingly severe laws against conventicles, or unauthorized religious meetings. Fines were imposed for failure to attend the parish churches. Later a Court of High Commission, authorized by no law but proceeding from the royal prerogative, was set up to deal in drastic fashion with offenders. Many were fined, imprisoned, banished, or sold as slaves. Finally persons attending the conventicles were declared to be outlaws. All protection of the laws was denied them. An act decreed the penalty of death, not merely for preaching at a conventicle, but even for attending one. In 1685 giving, taking, or writing in defense of the National Covenant or the Solemn League and Covenant was declared to be treason and was to be punished accordingly. The period from 1685 to 1688 became known as "the killing time." Many were put to death by soldiers, without process or form of law. The fact or presumption of having been at a conventicle was sufficient ground for instant execution without legal prosecution. Ensnaring and contradictory oaths and questions were proposed to persons apprehended, and in the event of unsatisfactory answers, or refusal to answer, immediate death by shooting was the outcome.

Concurrently with the use of armed force to intimidate and subdue the Covenanters, the government sought to divide them through "indulgences." These were royal offers to permit selected ones of the expelled ministers to resume their ministry in the parish churches under certain regulations and stipulations laid down by the government, upon acceptance by the ministers. The effect of the indulgences was to weaken the Covenanters' cause by driving a wedge of division into their ranks. From 1669 on, the presbyterian ministers of Scotland were divided into the indulged and the non-indulged. The indulged compromised with episcopacy and Erastianism, while the non-indulged avoided these compromises at the cost of suffering and sacrifice. The indulgences proceeded from the king's alleged supremacy over the church, and to accept the indulgence meant to accept the principle of Erastianism. As time passed, more and more of the ministers returned to their pulpits by accepting the indulgences. A dwindling minority of the ministers, however, and thousands of people scattered throughout Scotland realized that accepting the indulgence meant accepting the king as head of the church and prelacy as the lawful government of the church. In the face of the most savage and bitter persecution, these loyal Covenanters held out to the end against such sacrifices of principle.

Many of the ministers, as well as other Covenanters, were shot, hanged, or sent into banishment. Finally only a handful of ministers was left. Richard Cameron was killed in 1680 in a clash with the king's troops soon after the posting of the Sanquhar Declaration, which declared that the king had violated his coronation oath and was not qualified to occupy the throne. Donald Cargill, an elderly minister, was hanged in 1681. James Renwick, a youth of 24, was hanged in 1688 on the verge of the Revolution. This left the Covenanters almost without ministers. They had paid the price of their testimony in anguish and blood.

Doctrinally, the Covenanters adhered to the Westminster Standards. Their special claims, which resulted from the persecutions which they suffered, were set forth in published declarations, sermons, and the dying testimonies of their martyrs.

IV. The Principles of the Covenanters

They stood for—(1) the continuing obligation on the church and nation of the National Covenant and the Solemn League and Covenant; (2) the sole headship of Christ over the church, in opposition to the Erastian claim of the king to ecclesiastical headship; and (3) Christian civil government, in opposition to the tyranny of absolutism under which they had suffered.

Freedom came at last with the end of the Stuarts and the accession of William of Orange. The episcopal form of government of the state Church of Scotland was abolished and the presbyterian form restored. However, the obligations of the great covenants of the Scottish Reformation were not reaffirmed. The Covenanters who had witnessed and suffered through 28 years of persecution attempted to get a hearing but were haughtily brushed aside by those in positions of leadership and authority. Covenanters were especially grieved that the king still claimed, and was granted, a degree of headship in the reconstituted Church. As a result they elected to remain outside the Church of Scotland and to continue their worship in "society meetings." By 1743 they were able to attain ecclesiastical organization as the Reformed Presbytery, from which has come the Reformed Presbyterian Church as it exists today.

V. The Covenanters Since the Revolution of 1688

See CAMERONIANS AND CAMERON, RICHARD; CARGILL, DONALD; CONVENTICLE; COVENANT, SOLEMN LEAGUE AND; ERASTUS; LAUD, WILLIAM; REFORMED PRESBYTERIAN CHURCH, under PRESBYTERIANS; RELIGIOUS LIBERTY; RUTHERFORD, SAMUEL.

BIBLIOGRAPHY:

Act, Declaration, and Testimony, for the Whole of our Covenanted Reformation (Ploughlandhead, 1761; Philadelphia, 1876).
S. Cheetham, *A History of the Christian Church Since the Reformation* (1907).
J. Cunningham, *The Church History of Scotland from the Commencement of the Christian Era to the Present Time* (1882), 2 vols.
G. Grub, *An Ecclesiastical History of Scotland from the Introduction of Christianity to the Present Time* (1861), 4 vols.
T. Henderson (ed.), *Testimony Bearing Exemplified* (Paisley, 1791; New York, 1834).
W. M. Hetherington, *History of the Church of Scotland* (1852).
J. K. Hewison, *The Covenanters: A History of the Church of Scotland from the Reformation to the Revolution* (1908), 2 vols.
C. S. Horne, *A Popular History of the Free Churches* (1903).
J. Howie (ed.), *Sermons Delivered in Times of Persecution in Scotland, by Sufferers for the Royal Prerogatives of Jesus Christ* (1880).
J. Howie, *The Scots Worthies* (1781).
M. Hutchison, *The Reformed Presbyterian Church in Scotland. Its Origin and History, 1680-1876* (1893).
J. C. Johnstone (ed.), *Treasury of the Scottish Covenant* (1887).
D. Maclean, *Aspects of Scottish Church History* (1927).
T. M'Crie, *Sketches of Scottish Church History* (1841 and 1849), 2 vols.
A. Smellie, *Men of the Covenant* (1903).
J. Spottiswoode, *History of the Church of Scotland, 203–1625* (1851), 3 vols.
A. P. Stanley, *Lectures on the History of the Church of Scotland, Delivered in Edinburgh in 1872* (1872).
Summary of the Testimony of the Reformed Presbyterian Church of Scotland (1932).
Testimony of the Reformed Presbyterian Church of Ireland (1912), 2 vols.
J. H. Thomson (ed.), *A Cloud of Witnesses for the Royal Prerogatives of Jesus Christ* (1871).
J. G. Vos, *The Scottish Covenanters: Their Origins, History and Distinctive Doctrines* (1940).
P. Walker, *Six Saints of the Covenant* (1901), 2 vols.
R. Wodrow, *The History of the Sufferings of the Church of Scotland from the Restoration to the Revolution* (1829-1835), 4 vols.

JOHANNES G. VOS

COVENANTS, BIBLICAL

A covenant (Lat. from *con* and *venire* "coming together") in general means a solemn agreement between two parties. In the OT, the word "covenant" is a translation of the Hebrew word בְּרִית (*berith*), which is also rendered in the AV "league" (Josh. 9:6; Judges 2:2, etc.) and once as "confederacy" (Obad. 7). It is not only used with great frequency (about 280

I. Biblical Words for "Covenant"

times), but it is used again and again in every major section of the OT, thus testifying to its great importance.

The etymology of בְּרִית (*berith*) is very uncertain. Some scholars derive it from the Akkadian word *baru*, which means to bind, relating the idea that covenants bind parties involved in mutual obligations to each other. Others find the source in the verb ברה (*bara*), which means to eat, referring to the idea that the participants commonly ate a meal together as a symbol of the pact they were making. A few scholars connect it with ברה (*barâ*), meaning to perceive or determine. Still other scholars find the source of *berith* in the verb ברא (*bara'*), meaning "to cut," since often an animal was cut in pieces and the parties involved in making the covenant walked between the halves perhaps to indicate that if they broke their pledge they would suffer a fate similar to that of the slain animal. The term "covenanted" used twice in the AV translation of the OT (II Chron. 7:18; Hag. 2:5) is כָּרַת בְּרִית (*karath berith*), meaning literally "to cut a covenant." The same two words are translated "to make a covenant" in a number of OT passages such as Gen. 15:18 and Jer. 34:8, 18, indicating that the idea of cutting is involved.

The Septuagint translators rendered *berith* as διαθήκη (*diathēkē*) in every occurrence except Deut. 9:15, where they used μαρτύριον (*marturion*) "testimony," and I Kings 11:11, where they translated it as ἐντολή (*entolē*) "commandment." Διαθήκη (*diathēkē*) is derived from διατίθεσθαι (*diatithesthai*) meaning "to order or dispose for oneself." It is especially significant that the Septuagint translators used this word when the word συνθήκη (*sunthēkē*) was available as the ordinary word for covenant. This latter emphasizes the legal equality of the parties involved in the agreement, whereas *diathēkē* emphasizes the inequality of the parties and the authority of the one party to impose his conditions on the agreement.

Διαθήκη (*diathēkē*) thus also became the word used in the NT to describe the arrangement which God made in His relationship to His people. He retains the right to set all the conditions of the arrangement between Himself and men. The AV introduces confusion by translating διαθήκη (*diathēkē*) "covenant" in 21 instances but "testament" in the other 12 cases. Although "testament" expresses the fact that there is a unilateral initiation of the agreement, it is better to use the term covenant consistently, except in Heb. 9: 16-17, with the realization that the term does not indicate a mutual agreement between equals but rather a specific agreement by God that men have no right to alter. The word "testament" indicates the legal will of someone, which becomes valid at death; and it is only in the Hebrews passage above that διαθήκη (*diathēkē*) is used in that sense.

II. Biblical Usage in the OT

In the OT, the term בְּרִית (*berith*) "covenant" is used in some instances to describe an arrangement between men and in other instances an arrangement between God and man. In the former instances, the covenant is sometimes concluded between individuals and sometimes between groups of individuals. Even where the covenant was between just two men it had a deeply religious aspect, since the participants always called upon God as a witness of the agreement who would surely punish anyone who violated its stipulations. Such covenants were not limited to those involved in the Biblical narrative but were common throughout the Near East; our growing knowledge of the elements involved in these covenants through archeological discoveries has cast increasing light on the human covenants found in the Bible.

The Semitic concept involved the relationship of blood brotherhood. The entrance into such an agreement sometimes involved drinking blood from the other party, but in many instances a number of other rituals evolved as substitutes for this. Because of the strong sense of relationship among these people, such a covenant involved not only the individual himself but the adoption of such individuals into the other party's family and tribe. Those steeped in views of modern W individualism must struggle to appreciate this emphasis on the group if they are to understand Biblical covenants.

The OT gives several illustrations of covenants between individuals but also involving their families. Apparently Abimelech was uneasy concerning Abraham's intentions toward him, so he requested Abraham to "swear unto me here by God" (Gen. 21:23) that he would not deal falsely with him or with his descendants. The mutuality of the agreement was described in the words "both of them made a covenant" (vs. 27) and the term *covenant* was repeated in vs. 32. The ratification of the covenant included the transfer of the ownership of animals between the parties involved as a visible symbol of the transaction. Later Abimelech made a similar approach to Isaac (Gen. 26:28). The covenant involved mutual oaths and in this case the eating of a meal together.

After considerable tension between Laban and Jacob, the former suggested the making of a covenant (Gen. 31:44). in this case a heap of stones was used as the visible symbol and then significantly they ate a meal together on this pile of stones. The pile also formed a boundary marker, and if either party to the covenant crossed this boundary God was entreated to punish the offender. As a further ritual to confirm the covenant, animals were killed and were eaten.

Another illustration of a covenant between individuals was that between Jonathan and David (I Sam. 18:3). Jonathan gave David some of his clothing and military equipment as a visible symbol of their agreement. Later David urged Jonathan to treat him with kindness, and reminded him of the covenant between them as the basis for such treatment (I Sam. 20:8). At a later period in the narrative, the two reaffirmed their covenant (I Sam. 23:18).

Another form of covenant between individuals was the institution of marriage. This was specifically called a "covenant" *berith* in the later part of the OT (Prov. 2:17; Mal. 2:14).

Covenants between nations were also common. These were of two types, mutual covenants between nations treating each other as equals, and covenants between ruling states and their vassals. Within recent years archeologists have uncovered much evidence of the later type of treaty. Such treaties were made by the Egyptians, the Hittites, the Assyrians, and others with the nations they had conquered. The texts of the Hittite agreement reveal a pattern amazingly similar to that of the covenant which God made with Israel. This pattern began with an identification of the ruling state and an enumeration of the kindnesses it had shown in its dealings with the subject state. This was followed by a series of statements stipulating the future relations which were to exist between the two parties, a call on the gods to witness the treaty, and a series of curses and blessings resulting from breaking or keeping the agreement. Often the documents were deposited in a temple, they were read periodically, there was an oath by which the conquered king accepted the agreement, and there was a ratification of the covenant by means of animal sacrifices.

Covenantal arrangements between victor and conquered peoples are also mentioned in the OT. In Joshua 9, in the arrangement made between Joshua and the Gibeonites, the term "covenant" (*berith*; translated "league" in the AV) is used four times. In II Sam. 8, such an arrangement between David and the conquered Syrians and Edomites is mentioned, but the word "covenant" (*berith*) itself is not used. Omri treated Moab in similar fashion (II Kings 3:4 f.), although again the term itself is not used. Later in their history, Israel and Judah were subjected to such agreements by their more powerful neighbors.

The OT also contains illustrations of covenants between equals or near equals, such as that between Hiram and Solomon in I Kings 5:12. The word "covenant" (*berith*) is translated in the AV here by the word "league." A similar situation prevailed between Baasha and Benhadad as recorded in I Kings 15:19.

Covenants were also made between a king and his people. After the death of Ishbosheth, the elders of Israel met David at Hebron, "and David made a covenant with them there before the Lord" (I Chron. 11:3). The visible sign of this covenant was the ceremony in which David was anointed.

Another interesting illustration of a covenant between a king and his people is found in Jeremiah 34, where Zedekiah made a covenant with the people of Jerusalem which required them to free all Hebrew slaves held. Later, after promising such freedom, some of the slave holders reneged and as a result Jeremiah was sent by God to remind them that the original covenant that God had made with His people at Sinai had included the stipulation of freeing Hebrew slaves every seven years. The covenant made by the slave holders on this occasion had included the ancient ritual of cutting an animal in half and passing between the halves (Jer. 34:19, 20). As a result of this incident of covenant breaking, Jeremiah prophesied that these violators would suffer death at the hands of their enemies.

The Covenants between God and Man in the OT

The first specific mention of a covenant between God and man in the OT is found in Genesis 6, where God promised that He would save Noah, but the rest of the human race would be destroyed in a flood (Gen. 6:18). After the flood, the covenant was actually made with Noah and with his descendants (Gen. 9:9). Never again would such a flood destroy the human race. The rainbow was specifically called "the token of the covenant," a covenant called "an everlasting covenant." The fact that God was the initiator of this covenant and that it was a covenant not between equals is emphasized by the frequency with which God called it "my" covenant (Gen. 6:18; 9:9 11, etc.). This same emphasis should be noted in later instances of covenants between God and man. God says over and over, "*I will establish* my covenant" (Gen. 6:9; 9: 11; 17:7, etc.), or a similar formula (Gen. 17:2; Isa. 55:3, etc.).

The next covenant mentioned in the Bible is that which God made with Abraham (Gen. 15:18). Again in this instance, the establishment of the covenant included the ritual of dividing in half the bodies of animals. The narrative states that "a burning lamp," evidently symbolizing God Himself, passed between the pieces of the severed animals. The promise which was specifically mentioned was that Abraham's descendants would inherit the land. In the 17th chapter of Genesis the covenant between God and Abraham is discussed more fully. Again God called the covenant "my covenant" (Gen. 17:2, 4, 9, 10, 14, 19, 21). The emphasis of the promise in this passage is on the multiplicity of the descendants of Abraham, and his name was changed from Abram to Abraham as a sign of this promise. God called circumcision a "token of the covenant betwixt me and you" (vs. 11), which was to be administered to the male descendants of Abraham, and the purchased male slaves' male children born in his household. The ritual was to take place at the age of eight days, and if it was not performed the child was said to have broken the covenant so as to be cut off from his people (vs. 14). In this case also the promise was called "everlasting" and was made not only with Abraham but with his seed after him (vs. 7). The inclusion of the descendants is especially crucial as is shown by subsequent Biblical history. Included in the covenant relationship between God and Abraham was the requirement that Abraham was to be separated unto God, a requirement which was also placed upon the descendants who were the beneficiaries of the promises of the covenant. The covenant promises made to Abraham were reiterated in Gen. 22:15-18 after he had been willing to sacrifice Isaac, the one person through whom it seemed the covenant promises could be fulfilled.

Although the term *berith* is not used in the Biblical account, the Lord appeared to Isaac and identified himself as the God of Abraham and repeated to Isaac the same covenant promises He had made to Abraham (Gen. 26:24). In the dream at Bethel, God dealt similarly with Jacob (Gen. 28:13, 14). Later when Jacob returned to Bethel God repeated these same covenant promises (Gen. 35:11, 12), and as a visible symbol of this experience Jacob erected a stone pillar and poured a drink offering over it. Again these promises were repeated to Jacob at Beersheba when he began his journey to Egypt (Gen. 46:14).

After the years of slavery in Egypt on the part of the descendants of Jacob, descendants who had begun to multiply rapidly in accordance with the covenant promise in spite of the efforts of their enemies to prevent this, the narrative specifically states that God remembered "his covenant with Abraham, with Isaac, and with Jacob" (Ex. 2:24). In meeting with Moses at the burning bush, He distinctly identified Himself as the God of Abraham, Isaac, and Jacob, the patriarchs with whom He had made and reaffirmed His covenant (Ex. 3:6, 15, 16). And in discussing with Moses plans for the deliverance of Israel, He mentioned the covenant (Ex. 6:4, 5). As a result the characteristic covenant promise, "I will take you to me for a people, and I will be to you a God," was an essential part of Moses' message to the people.

Having delivered the people of Israel from Egypt and brought them to Sinai, just prior to giving them the Ten Commandments God gave this message to Moses for the people: "If ye will obey my voice indeed, and keep my covenant, then ye shall be a peculiar treasure unto me above all people" (Ex. 19:5). The conditional nature of the covenant is seen in this statement. The blessings would be theirs only *if* they obeyed God's covenant requirements. This significant "if" is also found concerning the promise of the land in Deut. 30:16-18 and Isa. 1:19, 20. There is a sense in which the covenant that God made with His people is unconditional, for Scripture emphasizes again and again that it is an "everlasting covenant." But nevertheless the blessings are to come upon the children of the covenant *if* they are faithful and obedient. Whether they will be these particular people depends on the condition of their obedience.

At Sinai the people of Israel accepted the covenant with the verbal response, "All that the Lord hath spoken we will do" (Ex. 19:8), and Moses reported this response to the Lord. After giving the Ten Commandments which evidently formed the basic statement of the way in which God expected this response to be expressed in daily life and after the giving of other commandments which described this response in greater detail, these covenantal agreements were put into writing and read to the people from "the book of the covenant" (Ex. 24:7). Animal sacrifices were made and the blood of these animals, called "the blood of the covenant" (vs. 8), was sprinkled partly on the altar and partly on the covenant people. This covenant formed the basis of the theocratic government of Israel.

Later the sabbath was called "a sign between me and you throughout your generations" (Ex. 31:13) and its observance was called "a perpetual covenant" (vs. 16). The Ten Commandments (literally "ten words") were called the "words of the covenant" (Ex. 34:28). The receptacle in which the Ten Commandments were placed for safe keeping by God's order was called "the ark of the covenant." The remainder of the Mosaic legislation made a great number of references to this covenant.

The "ark of the covenant" is mentioned again and again in the accounts of the activities of Joshua. In these accounts sin is described as a matter of having "transgressed my covenant" (Josh. 7:11) as it had already been described in Deut. 17:2. Near the end of his career, Joshua gathered the people together at Shechem for a renewal of the covenant (Josh. 24) and set up a stone as a witness to this covenant renewal.

The "covenant" (*berith*) with God and a "covenant" (*berith*) with a neighboring nation which served other gods had been declared mutually exclusive. It was prohibited in the covenantal arrangements made at Sinai (Ex. 34:12, 15). This idea was expressed even more clearly at the beginning of the period of the Judges. In Judges 2:1-2 God's punishment was threatened because of the failure of the Israelites to keep this requirement of the covenant, that they should not make a *berith* (in AV, "league") with their idol-worshipping neighbors.

The next significant stage in the history of the covenant is the covenant which God made with David. David had brought the ark of the covenant to a prominent place in the life of Israel. Having accomplished this, he wrote a Psalm which included these words: "Be ye mindful always of his covenant; the word which he commanded to a thousand generations; even of the covenant which he made with Abraham, and of his oath unto Isaac; and hath confirmed the same to Jacob for a law, and to Israel for an everlasting covenant, saying, Unto thee will I give the land of Canaan, the lot of your inheritance" (I Chron. 16:15-18). David was troubled, however, that the ark remained in a tent while he had built a permanent palace for himself. Therefore he planned to build a temple, and in the same message in which God's prophet told David that he was not to build a temple God promised David that his throne would be established forever. While the word "covenant" (*berith*) is not used here, the specific nature of the promises shows that God made a covenant with David. This is shown also in the last words of David: "He hath made with me an everlasting covenant" (II Sam. 23:5).

In the Psalms, the term "covenant" is used twenty times. Many of these references deal with the keeping (Ps. 25:10; 10:18) or breaking (Ps. 44:17; 55:20) of God's covenant, and with the certainty that God will keep His covenant (Ps. 89:28, 34). The parallelism of Hebrew poetry gives several insights into the significance of the term *berith* in the minds of the writers of the Psalms. For example, "covenant" is placed in a parallel relationship to "oath" and to "law" in Ps. 105:8-10, and in parallel with "multitude of his mercies" in Ps. 106:45. These show His faithfulness to His covenant and the special relationship that He had with the covenant people.

Like his father, Solomon was very covenant-conscious. After God made great promises to him in a dream, he "stood before the ark of the covenant of the Lord" to make sacrifices to God (I Kings 3:15). And his completion of the temple was a project to provide a place for the ark of the covenant (I Kings 6:19; 8:1, 21). Solomon began his prayer at the dedication of the temple with a description of God as one who "keepest covenant" (vs. 23). When Solomon was old and began to build temples to the gods of his pagan wives, God rebuked this activity as not keeping God's covenant (I Kings 11:11).

After the division of the kingdom, Abijah, king of Judah, criticized Jereboam, king of Israel, with a reminder that God's covenant was with David and with his descendants (II Chron. 13:5). The covenant with David is here called "a covenant of salt," a term which had been used in Numbers 18:19. This described the fact that the priests were to receive certain parts of the sacrificial animals, which, according to Mosaic legislation, were to be salted. But the "covenant of salt" may reflect that salt prevented decay, indicating that the covenant was to be permanent.

Israel's failure to live as the people of God can be described as a complete forsaking of the covenant as Elijah charged (I Kings 19:10, 14). Yet God continued to be gracious to the northern tribes for a time because of His covenant with Abraham, Isaac, and Jacob (II Kings 13:23). Their constant violation of the covenant, however, finally led to their destruction (II Kings 17:15; 18:12). The Samaritans who replaced them in the land likewise displeased God by their failure to keep the covenant (vss. 24-41). Throughout the history of Judah, revivals of true religion can be described as returnings to the keeping of the covenant. Although Jehoram was evil, God did not destroy his house "because of the covenant that he had made with David" (II Chron. 21:7). When young Joash was made king, Jehoida "made a covenant between him, and between all the people, and between the king, that they should be the Lord's people" (II Chron. 23:16). The result was the destruction of the temple of Baal and a renewal of the worship services held in the temple of the Lord. Recognizing that it was sin against God which had led to the punishment of his forefathers, Hezekiah determined to make a covenant with the Lord (II Chron. 29:10). Again, this covenant led to a reestablishment of temple worship. In the reign of Josiah, the renovation of the temple resulted in the discovery of "the book of the covenant" (II Kings 23:2; II Chron. 34:30). Upon reading its contents, Josiah "made a covenant before the Lord, to walk after the Lord, and to keep his commandments . . . to perform the words of the covenant which are written in this book" (II Chron. 34:31). The result was a campaign against idolatry and the renewal of the celebration of the passover (II Kings 23:21). The neglect of the covenant by Josiah's descendants, however, finally led to the exile of Judah.

The revival that accompanied the return of the Jews from exile in Babylon involved a renewed consciousness of the great significance of the covenant. When intermarriage with heathen wives led to another threat of idolatry, the suggestion was made "therefore let us make a covenant with our God to put away all the wives . . ." (Ezra 10:3). Nehemiah in his fervent prayer to God when he heard of the weakened condition of Jerusalem, addressed God as the one "that keepeth covenant and mercy for them that love him" (Neh. 1:5). On the occasion of another renewal of the spiritual life of the returned exiles, God was addressed in prayer as the God "who didst choose Abram, and broughtest him forth out of Ur of the Chaldees, and gavest him the name of Abraham; and foundest his heart faithful before thee, and madest a covenant with him to give him the land of the Canaanites . . ." (Neh. 9:8). And He was addressed as the God "who keepest covenant and mercy" (vs. 32).

The prophets made frequent references to the covenant. Isaiah stressed the fact that the covenant was everlasting (Isa. 24:5; 55:3; 61:8), which is stressed elsewhere as well (cf. Gen. 17:7; Lev. 24:8). God's faithfulness in keeping the covenant He made with Noah is used as a basis for assurance that He will keep His covenant promise to restore Israel after the exile (Isa. 54:9, 10). And the one who "keepeth the sabbath" was equated with the one who "taketh hold of my covenant" (Isa. 56:4, 6).

Jeremiah mentioned the term "covenant" (*berith*) more than any other prophet. He too was disturbed by its violation (Jer. 11:3; 11:10; 33:21; 34:18). Of greatest significance was the prediction of a new covenant (Jer. 31:31-34). A contrast is drawn between this new covenant and the old covenant which God had made with Israel. The same essential covenant promise, however, was to characterize this new covenant, "and will be their God and they shall be my people" (vs. 33). An important part of this new covenant, however, would be the inner change connected with it that would result in a personal experiential knowledge of God.

Although Ezekiel did not use the term "new covenant," he spoke of the future hope of God's people in terms of a renewal of the covenant (Ezek. 16:60, 62; 34:25; 37:26). Ezekiel compared the marriage covenant with God's covenant with Israel (Ezek. 16:8). He also used the term "covenant of peace" (Ezek. 34:25; 37:26; cf. Isa. 54:10). Daniel described the covenant as "holy" (Dan. 11:28, 30) and saw the action of the great enemy of God's kingdom as being "against" this holy covenant.

God spoke through Hosea saying that His people had "transgressed" the covenant, which he equates with breaking God's law (Hos. 6:7; 8:1). The entire book of Hosea is a comparison between the marriage covenant and God's covenant with Israel. God is pictured as initiating a marriage contract with Israel at the time of the exodus, a contract accepted by Israel at that time, but to which she was later unfaithful. Amos mentioned a covenant only once (Amos 1:9), referring to the covenant David and Solomon had made with Hiram of Tyre (II Sam. 5:11, 12; I Kings 5:12). Zechariah mentioned the term *covenant* twice (Zech. 9:11; 11:10). Malachi refers to the special covenant God had made with Levi (Mal. 2:4, 8), but also refers to the covenant in which the Messiah would be "the messenger of the covenant" (3:1).

In the intertestamental period the monastic community which produced the Dead Sea Scrolls considered themselves to be the only ones who were faithful to the covenant. In the Damascus Document they state that they are "the members of the New Covenant." This covenant, however, was in reality a turning back to the old covenant; the convert to this covenant took "a binding oath to return to the Torah of Moses." The members of the community renewed the covenant in a special annual ceremony. This may be related to that described in the apocalyptic Book of Jubilees (Jub. 6:17).

III. The New Covenant of the NT

In the NT the term "covenant" διαθήκη (*diathēkē*) is mentioned with much less frequency than the "covenant" *berith* in the OT. Furthermore, these occurrences are obscured in the AV by the ambiguous way in which the term is sometimes translated "covenant" and sometimes "testament."

It is mentioned only four times in the Gospels. Zacharias, the father of John the Baptist, was inspired to see the events which were soon to transpire as the fulfillment of the covenant that God had made with Abraham "to perform the mercy promised to our fathers, and to remember his covenant; the oath which he sware to our father Abraham" (Luke 1:72, 73). However, Mary certainly referred to God's covenant with Abraham even though she didn't use the word itself when she said, "He hath holpen his servant Israel, in remembrance of his mercy; as he spake to our fathers, to Abraham, and to his seed forever" (Luke 1:54, 55). The other three occurrences in the Gospels are in the parallel passages (Mt. 26:28; Mark 14:24; and Luke 22:20) which describe the institution of the Lord's Supper in which the contents of the cup are described as "my blood of the new testament." Here Jesus made deliberate reference to the supper and all it symbolized as the fulfillment of the promise in Jeremiah concerning the new covenant. He strongly implied that His blood which was to be shed would play a similar role in the new covenant to that which the blood of the animal sacrifices played in the old covenant.

The term "covenant" (*diathēkē*) is used twice in Acts. In his second sermon, Peter explained to his hearers that they were the children of the covenant, which God had made with Abraham and his descendants (Acts 3:25). He was implying that they should respond to his sermon by keeping that covenant and thus reaping its benefits. Although he had not mentioned the word "covenant" in his first sermon at Pentecost, it was implied when he said "the promise is unto you and to your children" (Acts 3:39). This was the promise made to Abraham when God entered into covenant with him. The other instance is found in the sermon of Stephen, where he described the history of God's people, including, "he gave him [Abraham] the covenant of circumcision" (Acts 7:8).

Paul used the term "covenant" several times in his letters. He listed "the covenants" as one of the benefits of being a Jew (Rom. 9:4). In Rom. 11:27, he quoted loosely from Isa. 59:21 to show that God still has a future for Israel, "for this is my covenant unto them, when I shall take away their sins." In his correspondence with the Corinthians, Paul gave a description of the institution of the Lord's supper using words which closely parallel the Gospels, "This cup is the new testament in my blood" (I Cor. 11:25). Paul also mentioned that God has "made us able ministers of the new testament" (II Cor. 3:6) in a passage in which he emphasized the superiority of the ministry of Christ to the ministry of Moses. And he explained the opposition of Jews to the Gospel as a result of the fact that they have a veil over their eyes "in the reading of the old testament; which veil is done away in Christ" (vs. 14). Writing to the Galatians, Paul stressed the immutability of a covenant as the basis for his teaching that the law could not annul the promises made to Abraham in the covenant God made with him long before the law was given (Gal. 3:15-17). The point here is that the covenant with Abraham is still in force and is the basis for the New Testament Gospel which makes Christians God's covenant people. Thus Christians become the true descendants of Abraham and heirs of the promises made in God's covenant with him (Gal. 3:29). In the next chapter, Paul made an allegorical comparison between the two covenants (Gal. 4:24). In his letter to the Ephesians, Paul magnified the grace of God in his dealings with Gentiles by pointing to the fact that they were once "strangers from the covenants of promise" (Eph. 2:12) but now through Christ they have been made the recipients of these covenant promises.

By far the greatest number of occurrences of the term "covenant" (*diathēkē*) in the NT are found in the letter to the Hebrews. When the author speaks of the promise and the oath God made to Abraham (Heb. 6:13-18), he is referring to the covenant. This reference to the covenant has the practical purpose of arousing God's people to energetic faith (vs. 12) and comforting hope (vss. 18, 19). The first use of the word διαθήκη (*diathēkē*) itself is in the seventh chapter: "By so much was Jesus made a surety of a better testament" (Heb. 7:22). A surety is a person who acts as the guarantor who is answerable for the fulfillment of the clauses of the contract. The new covenant, in which Christ is the high priest, is much better than the old covenant whose priesthood was administered by the sons of Aaron. It is better because the priesthood of Christ is after the order of Melchisedec, a priesthood confirmed by an oath made by God Himself (Ps. 110:4). A little later in the closely knit argument this new covenant is again called a better covenant in contrast to the old (Heb. 8:6). Christ is the mediator of this covenant, and it is better because it was "established upon better promises." In fact Christ is called the mediator of this covenant three times (Heb. 8:6; 9:15; 12:24). The very fact that there is a second covenant was seen by the author as evidence of the imperfection of the first (Heb. 8:7, 13).

Associated also with the first covenant there was a tabernacle (Heb. 9:1-10), but Christ's high priestly ministry is associated with "a greater and more perfect tabernacle, not made with hands" (vs. 11). Christ is the "mediator of the new testament" (vs. 15) so that by His death the called of God might receive the "promise of eternal inheritance." With this the author slides over into the usage of "covenant" (*diathēkē*) as the description of a will which is executed upon the event of death. Death then is a necessary event in order to bring the covenant into effect (vss. 16, 17) as a testament. Just as the blood resulting from the death of the sacrificial animals was a sign that the old covenant was in effect (vss. 18-20) so also the blood of Christ has this significance as evidence that the new covenant is now in effect (vss. 23-26). Later, reference is made again to Jeremiah's prophecy of the new covenant (Heb. 10:15-17). This time the remission of sins as included in the covenant promises is stressed, so it is made clear that the blood of Christ makes such remission possible. In yet another reference to the covenant, the author of Hebrews pointed out the seriousness of turning back into a life of sin after confessing Christ, because such an action is a matter of counting "the blood of the covenant, wherewith he was sanctified, an unholy thing" (Heb. 10:29). The final reference in this epistle is to "the blood of the everlasting covenant" (Heb. 13:20) found in the benediction near the conclusion of the book.

The only other use of the term "covenant" (*diathēkē*) in the NT is in Rev. 11:20, where a vision of the temple of God included "the ark of his testament." The description of the heavenly city in Rev. 21, however, includes the basic covenant promise, "They shall be his people, and God himself shall be with them, and be their God" (21:3).

This survey of the Biblical use of the concept of the covenant shows clearly that the concept is a central one in Scripture. It is so central that the books of the Bible have been divided according to their relationship to the old covenant made with the nation of Israel and the new covenant made with the church of Christ.

IV. Conclusion

The covenant idea stresses the legal element in the relationship between God and His people. The relationship is not ambiguous and vague. God makes definite promises to His people, and He in turn makes definite demands upon His people with whom He has entered into covenant. Involved in covenant making is reconciliation, the kind of relationship that God offers to us in the Gospel! The covenant concept is so significant that God can be described as above all a covenant-keeping God, "Know therefore that the Lord your God is God, the faithful God who keeps covenant . . ." (Deut. 7:9).

Although the covenant relationship places its stress on legal features which demand faithfulness as a duty, it is an agreement like the marriage relationship, which involves a loving relationship, a continuous fellowship between the parties involved. In fact, the warm affectionate word for love used in the OT, חֶסֶד (*chesed*), is a term which is so distinctively related to the covenant that some scholars specifically call it covenant-love. This word, which is commonly called "mercy" or "lovingkindness" in our English versions, carries with it the idea of faithfulness and loyalty, that is, a determination to maintain the covenantal relationship, even when the other party to the covenant does not act as he should. God not only has such love toward His people, but he persists in this love because of His determination to be faithful to the covenant. God is described frequently in Scripture as a God who keeps "covenant" (*berith*) and "covenant-love" (*chesed*) with those who respond in faithfulness.

The concept of covenant also reminds man of the necessity of ritual. The fact that God wisely associated visible signs with His covenants is a warning that no one should think he has become so "spiritual" that he does not need such visible evidences of the covenant relationship he has with God.

The covenant idea in Scripture also counteracts the excessive individualism often found in the church. Living the Christian life not only involves something within the individual person, but also involves the relationship between the individual Christian and God, and relationship with Christians who are members together of the same covenant with God. The Biblical covenant is never with the individual in isolation but always with the group of God's people, of which the individual is a part. H. Buis

COVERDALE, Miles (1488-1568), English Reformer, bishop, and Bible translator. He was born in Yorkshire, probably at York, ordained priest in 1514, and entered the house of the Augustinian friars at Cambridge, of which Robert Barnes became prior in 1520. As Barnes moved through Erasmian views towards the full Lutheran insight into faith in Christ to which Bilney brought him in 1525, Coverdale followed. In 1528, having preached against the mass, image-worship, and auricular confession, Coverdale was forced to leave the country for safety. He joined Tyndale at Hamburg and helped him to re-translate the Pentateuch, since Tyndale's original version perished through shipwreck in 1529. In 1535, while at Antwerp, Coverdale brought out the first complete English Bible, the fruit of a year's work, based upon a collation of Tyndale's Pentateuch and NT, the Vulgate and Pagninus' Latin OT, and the

German versions of Luther and the Zurich translators. Coverdale knew Latin and German well, but not Greek or Hebrew; hence he could only conflate his five versions and had to proceed by guesswork, or majority opinion, when they disagreed with each other. However, his smooth, clear, homely English gave distinction to his rendering.

In 1535 he returned to England. In 1537, on the instructions of Thomas Cromwell, his patron, he revised what was known as Matthew's Bible, and this revision became the "Great Bible" of 1539, ordered to be installed in all parish churches. In 1540, the year after the reactionary Six Articles Act was passed, Coverdale went abroad again. There, in 1543, he settled down as pastor at Bergzabern, a township 40 miles N of Strassbourg. When Henry VIII died, Coverdale came back to England, and after the suppression of the rebellion of Devon and Cornwall against Cranmer's English Prayer Book of 1549, he distinguished himself by preaching and teaching Reformation doctrine throughout these counties. His work was recognized by his appointment as bishop of Exeter in 1551.

In 1554, the year following Mary's accession, because of the intervention of the king of Denmark (to one of whose chaplains Coverdale was related by marriage), Coverdale was allowed to leave the country; otherwise he might well have been martyred. He travelled widely, again spending some time in his old pastorate at Bergzabern and then going on to Geneva, where he may have helped toward the making of the Geneva Bible. He returned to England in 1559 and took part in the consecration of Parker as archbishop of Canterbury, but declined the offer of his former position, perhaps because of his age or perhaps because of unhappiness with the Elizabethan settlement. It is known that he had scruples concerning surplice and the ceremonies to which the Elizabethan Puritans objected and that he never used them. In 1564 he became incumbent of St. Magnus, London Bridge, but resigned in 1566, the year of Parker's Advertisements, which enforced conformity.

In addition to his Bibles, Coverdale translated several works of continental theologians, including Calvin's *Treatise on the Lord's Supper*, Bullinger's *The Old Faith*, Luther's exposition of Psalm 23, and an abridgment of Erasmus' *Enchiridion*. He also issued a volume of letters of the Marian martyrs (1564).

Bibliography:

M. Coverdale, *Works* (Cambridge, 1844), 2 vols.

M. Coverdale, *Godly Letters of the Martyrs* (1564; reprinted with an introduction by E. H. Bickersteth, London, 1844).

H. Guppy, "Miles Coverdale and the English Bible," *Bulletin of John Rylands Library* 19 (1935), 300-336.

J. J. Lowndes, *Memorials of Myles Coverdale* (London, 1838).

J. F. Mozley, *Coverdale and his Bibles* (London, 1953).

H. R. Tedder, *DNB*, s.v.

B. F. Westcott, *A General View of the History of the English Bible* (New York, 1868; 3rd ed. revised by W. A. Wright, 1905).

James I. Packer

COVETOUSNESS. The proscription of covetousness reveals the extent of God's sovereign sway over man and the totality of the depravity of man. One might argue, At least my thoughts are my own affair. But Scripture clearly asserts that man must bring "into captivity every thought to the obedience of Christ" (II Cor. 10:5). Moreover, Scripture calls not only words and deeds sinful, but the radical character of sin is seen in the fact that "delighting in" something evil, even before it becomes a purposeful longing, is called iniquitous (see Concupiscence).

"Covet," "covetous," or "covetousness" appears 41 times in the AV. The English words translate a variety of Hebrew and Greek terms. These describe a subjective state of "taking pleasure in," "desiring," "being concerned about," or "greedy" (especially for money); or an objective act of "plunder," or "reaching out the hand." Although "desire" may be for something lawful and hence laudable (I Cor. 12:31; I Tim. 3:1), more often the connotation is of evil; that is, the desire for something itself forbidden (a neighbor's wife) or for the procuring of a lawful thing in an unlawful manner (a neighbor's house).

Julius Mueller finds selfishness near the root of sin, a selfishness which is covetousness (*The Christian Doctrine of Sin*, I, 147 f.), and this selfishness may be excited in different ways. Schultz notes this in his discussion of the two words used in the Commandments: חָמַד (*chamad*) is the Hebrew word for "covet" in Ex. 20:17; it "denotes the desire as founded on the perception of beauty, and therefore excited from without." On the other hand אָוָה (*awah*) is the Hebrew word for "desire" in Deut. 5:21, and denotes "desire originating from the very outset in the person himself and arising from his own want or inclination" (quoted by *KD*, on Ex. 20:17).

The heinousness of covetousness is seen from the following:

(1) Covetousness is characterized as an act of idolatry. This is so because "the commonest and most typical form is when one sacrifices another to the gratification of his own appetite. . . . Self takes the place of God" (Wescott on Eph. 4:19). Lightfoot, on Col. 3:5, says, "The covetous man sets up another object of worship besides God. There is a sort of religious purpose, a devotion to soul, to greed, which makes the sin of the miser so hateful."

It is in this connection that the spiritual or religious character of covetousness is most vividly seen. Apart from the holiness and omniscience of the Lord it cannot be judged a sin. It cannot be judged in a law court, civil or ecclesiastical; and it can lodge in the heart of those who seem to be most virtuous (Mark 10:27 f.; Rom. 7:7 f.). Covetousness is a form of practical atheism.

(2) God's judgments on covetousness are particularly severe, both in this life and hereafter. The seed which fell among thorns (Luke 8:7) was "*choked* with cares and riches and pleasures of this life" (vs. 14). (Cf. also James 5:1 f.) Moreover, covetousness is classed with particular sins which bar entry to heaven (I Cor. 6:9; Eph. 5:5, 6; Col. 3:5, 6).

(3) Covetousness breeds other sins, especially when money is involved. It made Jezebel a murderer and a liar (I Kings 21); Gehazi, a liar and a disobedient servant (II Kings 5); Balaam, a depraved and perverted character who typifies the ungodly in an extreme of heinousness (II Pet. 2:10 f.; Jude 11 f.). Lightfoot says, "Impurity and covetousness may be said to divide between them nearly the whole domain of human selfishness and vice" (on Col. 3:5). The poetical and prophetical books develop this theme in depth and breadth. When a soul in covetousness has turned from God, there is no effective curb against other sins.

(4) The OT commandments protecting the poor and workers are specific curbs on an ever-present covetousness in the heart. Thus, payment of wages is regulated; high interest rates are forbidden; total reaping of fields is banned (Ex. 21; 22; Lev. 18:11, 13). The great number of these statutes reveals God's concern for the covetousness of His people.

Though covetousness is prohibited as the 10th commandment of the Decalogue (Ex. 20:17), it would be a mistake to conceive of the commandment as teaching only a negative. Its positive aspect is to teach us to be content (Phil. 4:11; I Tim. 6:6; Heb. 13:5). The providence of God is based on His wisdom, power, and love. Since His providence governs every phase of our lives, to be covetous is to deny or call into question each of these attributes. This is why it is practical atheism. The commandment, however, teaches not merely a passive acquiescence but an active liberality toward God and man. Neither Achan (Judges 7) nor Saul (I Sam. 15) in their covetousness could allow God to have that which had been reserved to Him. The withholding of anything from God is an act of covetousness, whether it be money, children, abilities, or time. On the other hand, liberality toward God reaps manifold blessings (Mt. 19:27 f.).

To withhold from a neighbor what is due him or what he may need stems from covetousness (Prov. 3:27-29). This was the sin of the priest and Levite in the parable of the Good Samaritan (Luke 10:25 f.). The opposite of, and the cure for, covetousness is love. Notice how love is defined in the OT, by concrete examples which illustrate this point (Lev. 19:9, 10, 13, 14, 15, 18). "God therefore commands a strong and ardent affection, an affection not to be impeded by any portion, however minute, of concupiscence. He requires a mind so admirably arranged as not to be prompted in the slightest degree contrary to the law of love" (Calvin, *Institutes of the Christian Religion*, II, viii, 50).

Finally, the commandment involves a positive injunction to rejoice in as well as to promote the blessings of another. We are to "rejoice with them that do rejoice" (Rom. 12:15) because love "envieth not" (I Cor. 13:4).

Luther, whose full discussion of the 10th commandment in *The Large Catechism* is characteristically incisive and vigorous: "It is to be commanded, first, that we do not desire our neighbor's damage, nor even assist, nor give occasion for it, but gladly wish and leave him what he has, and, besides, advance and preserve for him what may be for his profit and service, as we should wish to be treated. Thus, these commandments are especially directed against envy and miserable avarice, God wishing to remove all causes and sources whence arises everything by which we do injury to our neighbor. . . . For He would especially have the heart pure, although we shall never attain to that as long as we live here; so that this commandment will remain, like all the rest, one that will constantly accuse us and show how godly we are in the sight of God!" Nevertheless, the very passages which speak of its heinousness speak of the power of the Gospel to bring forgiveness and victory (I Cor. 6:11; Col. 3:5 f.). When the covetous man is begotten anew, he finds the power to love God and man in the power of that new life.

JOHN W. SANDERSON, JR.

COWPER, William (1731-1800), Christian poet and hymn-writer, descended from John Cooper, alderman of London (d. 1609). His mother, Anne Donne, belonged to the family of the poet John Donne (*q.v.*). His father was chaplain to George II and rector of the parish of Great Berkhamstead, Hertfordshire, where William was born. Upon the death of his wife his father sent William, age six, to a boarding school. Later he was sent to Westminster School, where Warren Hastings was a schoolmate. Cowper was called to the bar in 1754. A crisis occurred when Cowper was nominated to a clerkship in the House of Lords. Anxiety over the preliminary examination drove him to attempt suicide. When friends learned of his attempts, he was committed to a private asylum, where he was gloriously converted to Christ through the visits of his brother John. Upon his release he went to reside with the Morley Unwin family, till Morley was thrown from his horse and killed. After this tragedy, he moved with Unwin's widow Mary to the village of Olney at the request of John Newton, where Mary faithfully cared for him. Here he spent many years assisting his friend Newton in parish work until 1773, when he again descended into despair and once more attempted to kill himself. After recovery he made his first appearance as an author with his Olney Hymns in 1779, written in conjunction with Newton and signed with a "C." At the suggestion of Lady Austen and Mrs. Unwin, he now began to write secular verse. His second volume, *The Task: A Poem in Six Books*, immediately caught fire, along with his frolicking *The Diverting History of John Gilpin*, his *On the Loss of the Royal George*, and his personal correspondence. He has been heralded as bringing a new spirit to English verse and pioneering the way for the poetry of Burns, Shelley, Wordsworth, and Byron. A third attack of melancholy and depression overtook the poet in 1787 and another in 1794. He died April 25, 1800, and was buried near Mrs. Unwin, who had passed away before him.

His greatest hymn, commonly known by the opening lines, "God moves in a mysterious way, his wonders to perform," was published in the *Olney Hymns*. It was the last hymn he ever composed, written after the breakdown of 1773. He also wrote the hymn, "There Is a Fountain Filled with Blood." Other fine hymns still sung are "O For a Closer Walk with God" and "Sometimes a Light Surprises."

BIBLIOGRAPHY:

R. Southey, *Life and Letters of William Cowper* (London, 1834-1837), 15 vols.

T. Wright, *The Complete Correspondence of Cowper* (London, 1904).

S. Brooke, *Theology in the English Poets* (London, 1874), 40-54.

COX, Richard (1499-1581), English Reformer and Elizabethan bishop. A native of Buckinghamshire, Cox was educated at King's College, Cambridge, and chosen by Wolsey as one of the junior canons for his new foundation at Oxford (1525). Next he became headmaster of Eton and chaplain to Henry VIII. His other preferments under Henry and Edward VI included an archdeaconry, two canonries, and two deaneries. When Henry refounded Wolsey's college as Christ Church (1547), Cox became the first dean and chancellor of the university. He assisted Cranmer in the liturgical work which resulted in the two English Prayer Books of Edward's reign (1549 and 1552). Imprisoned in the Marshalsea on Queen Mary's accession, Cox managed to get away to the Continent, where he became champion of the group of exiles at Frankfurt which demanded the use of the Prayer Book and "the true face of an English Church" instead of the Geneva-style order of service introduced by Knox and Whittingham. Elizabeth nominated Cox to the bishopric of Ely, and he was one of the first of a group of bishops to be consecrated after Parker (December 21, 1559). Called upon to celebrate the Lord's supper in the royal chapel at a time when its furnishings were causing some scandal, Cox wrote to Elizabeth: "I dare not minister in your grace's chapel, the lights and cross remaining." Although he was later prepared to side with Parker against Jewel and Grindal in a disputation over the use of a crucifix, this does not necessarily indicate a radical change of position. He remained a firm believer in all that Cranmer had stood for; but he was not in sympathy with the views Cartwright began propagating at Cambridge (in his own diocese) in 1570.

BIBLIOGRAPHY:

F. O. White, *Lives of the Elizabethan Bishops* (London, 1898), 78-95.

JOHN TILLER

COZ, of the posterity of Judah (I Chron. 4:8). Coz is not to be confused with Koz (Hakkoz) of the posterity of Levi. The ARV renders Coz as Hakkoz but there is no justification in the original text for this alteration. The clan to which Coz belonged is not revealed.

COZBI, "false," a daughter of Zur, a Midianitish chief. Zimri, the son of a prince in the tribe of Simeon, took her into the camp of Israel as a prostitute (Num. 25:6-18). Phinehas, loving the Lord and zealous for the sanctity of God's people, killed both offenders with the Lord's approval.

CRADOCK, Samuel (*c.* 1621-1706), English puritan Nonconformist. Educated at Emmanuel College, Cambridge, Cradock became a fellow there in 1645. His public performance on taking his B.D. degree in 1651 was highly applauded. He resigned his fellowship when appointed rector of North Cadbury, Somerset, in 1656. He was ejected in 1662 by Act of Uniformity (see UNIFORMITY, ACTS OF). He inherited the estate at Geesings in Suffolk and some years later took his family there. On the Declaration of Indulgence in 1672 he obtained a license as a "presbyterian teacher." He opened an academy, frequented by the sons of Presbyterian gentry. He moved in 1696 to Bishop's Stortford in Hertfordshire and soon became pastor in a congregational chapel in a nearby village, preaching twice a Sunday till his death on October 7, 1706. Among his works were *The History of the OT Methodized* (1683), *Knowledge and Practice* (1702), *Harmony of the Four Evangelists* (1688), *The Apostolical History* (1672), and *Exposition of Revelation.* Doddridge said *Knowledge and Practice* was one of the best manuals for young ministers, and that no other author helped him more in the NT field.

CRAIG, John (*c.* 1512-1600), Scottish Reformer. Born in Aberdeenshire, Scotland, he lost his father in the Battle of Flodden a year later. He graduated from the University of St. Andrews in Arts. After tutoring in England, he entered a Scottish Dominican monastery to train for the priesthood; but being suspected of Lutheran "heresy," he fled to England, and thence to the Continent. Reaching Rome in 1538, he came under the magnetic influence of Cardinal Pole, was confirmed in his inherited faith, and became rector of the leading Dominican school in Bologna. Having access to the Library of the Inquisition there, he came across a Latin copy of John Calvin's *Institutes of the Christian Religion* in 1557. To the careful reading of this work he owed his conversion to the Reformed faith. Boldly voicing his convictions, he was imprisoned and sentenced to death. But he escaped as the result of an amnesty on the death of Pope Paul IV in August 1559, and after many adventures reached his native land in 1561. There he threw in his lot with the newly reformed Church of Scotland.

At first he preached in Latin "to the learned sort, in the Magdalene Chapel at Edinburgh," but soon became a colleague of John Knox in the High Kirk of St. Giles. Here, in 1567, he courageously refused to read the banns of marriage between Queen Mary and the Earl of Bothwell. Having moved to Montrose in 1572, and Aberdeen in 1575, he returned to Edinburgh in 1580 as chaplain to King James VI, at whose request he prepared the Second Scots ("Negative") Confession (1581), rebutting the errors of Romanism. He composed metrical versions of a number of Psalms, including the 145th, "O Lord, Thou art my God and King"; compiled a classic Scots Catechism (1590); and abridged it at the request of the General Assembly, as *A form of examination before the Communion.* He died at Edinburgh at the age of 87, being survived by his son William, who became a professor of divinity in the French Reformed College of Saumur.

BIBLIOGRAPHY:
R. Chambers, *A Biographical Dictionary of Eminent Scotsmen* (Glasgow, 1855), I, 572 f.
H. Bonar, *Catechisms of the Scottish Reformation* (London, 1866), 175-285.
T. F. Torrance, *The School of Faith* (London, 1959), 97-165, 243-254.

R. STRANG MILLER

CRANACH, Lucas (1472-1553), German painter and engraver. Friend of the German reformers, Cranach was from 1504 court painter of Frederick the Wise, Elector of Saxony, and his two immediate successors. He became more widely known when in 1509 he painted the Emperor Maximilian and the boy who later became emperor as Charles V. Cranach produced also many woodcuts of religious themes in a style reminiscent of Albrecht Dürer. He is best known, however, for his portraits of Luther, Melanchthon, and other reformers and their princely adherents. Increasing demands on his time adversely affected his originality, and his portraits have been criticized for repetition, overcrowding, and an inordinate preoccupation with accessories such as dress. Twice burgomaster of Wittenberg, Cranach's reformed views are beyond dispute: one of his pictures, indeed, dated 1518 and now at Leipzig, features a dying man's soul rising to meet the Trinity, in illustration of the doctrine of justification by faith alone.

JAMES DIXON DOUGLAS

CRANMER, Thomas (1489-1556), English Reformer. After the normal course of scholastic studies at Cambridge University, he graduated B.A. in 1510 or 1511 and was elected a fellow of Jesus College. About 1517, under the influence of Erasmus' *Novum Instrumentum*, he commenced a careful study of the Scriptures. He was ordained and received his D.D. in 1523, and gained recognition as a foremost scholar in the Scriptures and the Early Fathers. Cranmer became involved in public affairs through a chance meeting with King Henry VIII's almoner and secretary. He suggested to them that the universities of Europe should be asked for their decisions on the validity of Henry's marriage to Catherine of Aragon, and that the English Church should pronounce sentence according to the majority view. He was therefore employed in negotiations on the continent, where he secretly married the niece of the Lutheran theologian Osiander. He was then recalled to become, though unwillingly, archbishop of Canterbury and was consecrated in 1533, taking the customary oath of obedience to the papacy, with openly expressed reservations. On April 23, 1533, Cranmer pronounced the marriage of Henry and Catherine contrary to Divine law and therefore null and void. A week later, he declared that Henry and Anne Boleyn were validly married. On subsequent occasions he was required to accede to the royal matrimonial wishes, but was careful to administer existing canon law. Cranmer welcomed the substitution of royal for papal headship of the Church in England but played little part in bringing it about other than participating in theological debates in support of that for which he had long prayed. The breach with Rome was essentially the work of the king in Parliament.

Free of Rome's control, Cranmer persuaded Convocation (*q.v.*) to petition the king for an authorized English Bible (1534) and encouraged Thomas Cromwell, Henry's vicar-general, to call for the provision of an English Bible in every church. This was accomplished through the injunctions of 1536 and especially 1538. First Coverdale's, then Matthew's, and finally the Great Bible were licensed. Cranmer contributed a preface to the numerous editions of the

Great Bible in 1540 and 1541. Cranmer's theological influence was limited by the slow, though steady, development of his own thought and even more by rival political considerations whose influence upon the king was even greater than his own. He attempted to secure the confiscated wealth of monasteries and chantries to worthy objects but with little success. The Ten Articles of 1536 show the influence of Lutheran theology upon him. The Six Articles of 1539, which were opposed by Cranmer in Parliament and Convocation, reveal the limitations of his influence. Under the terms of this latter act (which, among other things, upheld clerical celibacy), Cranmer found it necessary to remove his wife to Germany, and his own position was one of extreme difficulty. In July, 1541, he was able to secure the abrogation of certain saints' days, the abolition of some superstitious practices, and the prohibition of lights and candles except before the sacrament, but from this time until almost the end of Henry's reign he was in constant danger from his enemies. Only the king's favor saved him from three plots (1542-1545), enabling him to exert some influence on the composition of the *King's Book* (1543) and to avert the proposed revision of the Great Bible. In 1545 Cranmer was able to undertake the translation and revision of the litany in the comprehensive and impressive form in which it was authorized by royal injunction.

The death of Henry VIII in 1547 opened the way for more rapid and radical changes. The young king, Edward, and Protector Somerset were in full sympathy with Cranmer, whose views were still in process of development. By the repeal of the Six Articles and the heresy laws, a remarkable degree of freedom of action was provided, and for the purpose of providing instruction in Scriptural principles the Book of Homilies was issued in 1547. Its 12 sermons were edited by Cranmer; and those on salvation, faith and good works were undoubtedly written by him. The First Book of Common Prayer (1549) was drawn up by Cranmer in his incomparable English. The book drew its inspiration from the teaching and practice of continental reformers, and from Cranmer's knowledge of the Bible and the Fathers. It reestablished communion in both kinds. The controversies which were aroused led to Cranmer's *True and Catholic Doctrine of the Lord's Supper* and his *Answers* to Gardiner and Smith. He reiterated his conviction that "Christ's body and blood be given to us in deed, yet not corporally and carnally, but spiritually and effectively." In March, 1550, the Ordinal, drawn up largely by Cranmer, recognized only three orders of ministry, removed sacerdotal implications, and stressed the ministry of the Word and sacrament. Cranmer's Second Book of Common Prayer (1552) made explicit much that had remained implicit in the first book. In the key matter of the Eucharist, mass vestments were forbidden, the minister was to stand on the N side of the *table* in the body of the church, the canon was revised to avoid implying the substantial presence of Christ or prayers for the dead, ordinary bread was to be used, and reservation was forbidden. The Forty-Two Articles were largely the work of Cranmer and reveal the extent of the influence of Calvinistic doctrine upon him.

Two of Cranmer's projects were never implemented. First, his *Reformatio Legum Ecclesiasticarum* was an attempt to reconstruct canon law for the benefit of the English Church, but he was never able to present it to Convocation or Parliament. Second, Cranmer warmly welcomed contacts with foreign Reformed churches and the coming of men such as Peter Martyr, Martin Bucer, and Paul Fagius during the reign of Edward VI. He hoped to promote a conference of Reformation divines, but was unable to achieve this.

Cranmer experienced difficulties under the rule of Edward's adviser, Northumberland, whose policy of rapid change, dictated largely by uncontrolled greed, he found distasteful. The accession of Mary (1553) caused a temporary reverse in the progress of the Reformation and brought about Cranmer's martyrdom. He refused to flee, and offered to defend his liturgical and doctrinal work. He was tried and condemned on a charge of treason (reluctantly he had acknowledged Lady Jane Grey as Edward's successor), was ordered to take part in a farcical disputation on the Mass, and was formally pronounced a heretic. After the passage of heresy laws in January, 1555, he was tried and convicted, induced to sign a series of humiliating recantations, and finally brought out for execution. In his public "recantation" he made a triumphant renouncement of his former recantations and asserted his fidelity to Reformation teaching. He died courageously at the stake on March 21, 1556, in Oxford.

BIBLIOGRAPHY:

H. Belloc, *Cranmer* (London, 1931).
G. W. Bromiley, *Thomas Cranmer, Archbishop and Martyr* (London, 1956).
G. W. Bromiley, *Thomas Cranmer, Theologian* (London, 1956).
C. H. Collette, *The Life, Times and Writings of Thomas Cranmer* (London, 1887).
J. E. Cox (ed.), *Writings and Disputations of Thomas Cranmer relative to the Sacrament of the Lord's Supper* (Parker Society, 1844).
J. E. Cox (ed.), *Miscellaneous Writings and Letters of Thomas Cranmer* (Parker Society, 1846).
A. C. Deane, *The Life of Thomas Cranmer* (London, 1927).
C. W. Dugmore, *The Mass and the English Reformers* (London, 1958).
J. Gairdner, "Cranmer, Thomas," *DNB* XIII (1888), 19-31.
F. E. Hutchinson, *Cranmer and the Reformation in England* (London, 1951).
A. D. Innes, *Cranmer and the Reformation in England* (Edinburgh, 1900).
C. W. Le Bas, *The Life of Thomas Cranmer* (London, 1833), 2 vols.
M. L. Loane, *Masters of the English Reformation* (London, 1954), 179-242.
A. J. Mason, *Thomas Cranmer* (London, 1896).
J. G. Nichols (ed.), *Narratives of the Days of the Reformation* (Camden Society, First Series, LXXVII), 1859, 218-233.
A. F. Pollard, *Thomas Cranmer and the English Reformation* (New York and London, 1904).
C. C. Richardson, *Zwingli and Cranmer on the Eucharist* (Evanston, 1949).
C. H. Smyth, *Cranmer and the Reformation under Edward VI* (Cambridge, 1926).
J. Strype, *Memorials of Thomas Cranmer* (London, 1694; Oxford, 1848-54), 3 vols.
H. J. Todd, *Life of Cranmer* (London, 1831), 2 vols.

H. H. ROWDON

CRASHAW, Richard (1612?-1649), English mystical poet. Son of a Puritan divine, Crashaw came to Cambridge under high-church influence, and lost his fellowship at Peterhouse on refusing to sign the Solemn League and Covenant. Later he became a Roman Catholic, and having been found living in utter destitution in Paris by his friend Abraham Cowley, was introduced first to Queen Henrietta Maria, and by her to Cardinal Palotta, at whose residence in Rome Crashaw became an attendant. His sensitive, ascetic nature scandalized by the more licentious of the household, Crashaw was sent by the cardinal to a minor ecclesiastical post at Loreto. He died of a fever less than a month later. Crashaw's poetry was marked by fervent religious feeling, a markedly sensuous imagery, and the rhetorical devices favored by Italian poets. His style was otherwise idiosyncratic and uneven, and Samuel Johnson sneered at his "enormous and disgusting hyperboles." Yet Crashaw was capable of soaring to heights of devotion never surpassed, and he exercised significant influence on Milton, Coleridge, and Pope—though the latter considered him to have "writ like a Gentleman . . . [more] than to establish a reputation." His published works include a volume of sacred poems, *Steps to the Temple* (1648).

JAMES DIXON DOUGLAS

CRAWFORD, Thomas Jackson (1812-1875), Scottish theologian. Born at St. Andrews, Scotland, his father was professor of moral philosophy at the university there, being the immediate predecessor of Dr. Thomas Chalmers. He took his degree at St. Andrews in 1831 and in 1834 was licensed by the Presbytery of St. Andrews (Church of Scotland). He became successively minister of Cults in Fife (1834), Glamis in Perthshire (1838), and St. Andrew's in Edinburgh (1844). He received the D.D. degree from his *alma mater* in 1844. In 1859 on the death of Dr. John Lee he was appointed professor of divinity in the University of Edinburgh. His principal writings were on presbytery and prelacy, the Fatherhood of God, and the Atonement. His writings on prelacy in 1853 and 1867 led to a controversy with Bishop Wordsworth carried on in "The Scotsman." His work on "The Scripture Doctrine of Atonement" was first published in 1871 and passed through a number of editions. In it he gives an able exposition of Scripture passages relating to the Atonement and reviews the theories of Bushnell, Robertson of Brighton, etc. It is still one of the finest works on the subject. On the Fatherhood of God, he controverted certain views of Dr. Candlish (see CANDLISH, ROBERT S.). Candlish was the first to deliver a series of Cunningham Lectures (established after the death of Principal Wm. Cunningham in 1861). He chose the theme, "The Fatherhood of God and the Sonship of Believers." Dr. John Macleod is no doubt right when he says the conflict between the two was mainly a verbal one. He adds, "Crawford seems to us to do less than justice to the truth that the sinner is a child of wrath, is of his father the devil, and a child of disobedience. And his defense of the common teaching of Reformed divines, that in a certain diluted sense fallen man is still a son, though an apostate son, of God, might stress more than it does the exiguous character of this universal Divine sonship for which he pleads" (*Scottish Theology*, p. 274). Yet Dr. Macleod says that Crawford's work on the Fatherhood of God was "one of the most important contributions to the literature on a side of Christian truth that was widely discussed in the third quarter of the 19th century by different schools of theology—Broad and Orthodox alike." Crawford made his name "the best known (in that time) of the divines of his church as a sound and able theologian" (*Scottish Theology*, p. 268). In 1861 he became a chaplain to the queen and subsequently a dean of the chapel royal. In 1867 he was elected moderator of the General Assembly. He died at Genoa, October 11, 1875.

BIBLIOGRAPHY:
W. G. Blaikie, "Thomas Jackson Crawford," *SHERK* I (1891), 568.
T. Cooper, *DNB* XIII (1888), 55-56.
J. Macleod, *Scottish Theology* (Edinburgh, 1943), 268, 272-275.

WILLIAM JAMES GRIER

CREATION. The Biblical account of the creation of the world is found in the first chapter of Genesis and the first three verses of the second chapter.

According to the Bible God is the Creator of all things. Throughout the first chapter of Genesis this fact is prominent.

I. General Characteristics of Genesis Chapter One

In 31 verses the word God (אֱלֹהִים) is used, and in almost every instance as the subject of a verb. The first exception is the phrase "Spirit of God," in which the word is the object of a preposition, and yet even here the phrase itself is employed as a subject of "was hovering." Also, in verse 27 the phrase "in the image of God" occurs. Apart from these two occurrences, however, the word always occurs as a subject: "God created," "God said," "God saw," "God divided," "God called," "God set,"

"God blessed," etc. Thus the activity of God, His monergism in the work of creation, is emphasized.

In stressing His activity, the Bible does not preclude us from thinking about God's Being. We are not to conclude that we may say nothing about God metaphysically. Throughout the action which takes place it is God who acts. And since it is explicitly stated that He created heavens and earth, He is not a part of them but the Creator who exists in independence of His creation.

The account of the creation is given in terms of *fiat* and *fulfillment.* "Fiat" is expressed in the command, "let there be," and the "fulfillment" is expressed in the phrase, "and there was." Then there usually follows the statement, "And God saw that it was good," and seven times the expression, "And it was so" is added, and thus the assurance of the completion of God's fiat is given.

It is well to note the emphasis that is placed upon God's satisfaction with His handiwork. We read that "the Spirit of God was hovering over the waters" (Gen. 1:2), then, following the work of each of the days, the statement is made that "God saw that it was good," and at the conclusion of the entire chapter (vs. 31) the climactic declaration follows, "And God saw everything that He had made, and behold, it was very good." This vigorously excludes the doctrine that material things in themselves are evil. The creation is something in which God delights and which gives satisfaction to Him.

In order to understand the first chapter properly it is necessary at the outset to notice the relationship in which the first verse stands to what follows.

II. The Relation of Verse One to the Remainder of the Chapter

As a historical curiosity we may mention the view (propounded by Rashi, d. 1105), that the first verse is a temporal dependent clause, and that the second verse is the principal sentence. Upon this construction we might read, "When God began to create the heaven and the earth, then the earth was desolation and waste, etc." This rendering has not won many adherents. Far more widespread is a view which Ibn Ezra (d. 1167) set forth. It would also take the first verse as a temporal sentence, verse two being a parenthesis, with the third verse then constituting the main sentence. On such a construction the rendering would be, "When God began to create the heaven and the earth, . . . and the earth was desolation and waste, etc., . . . then God said, 'Let there be light.' " Thus the first act of creation and the command for light to spring into existence are made simultaneous. This translation would rule out a genuine *creatio ex nihilo*, for then, at the time when God began to create, matter was already in existence.

Basically, there are two reasons advanced for this translation. In the first place it is argued that in the cosmogonies of peoples of antiquity, and in particular of the Babylonians, the narrative begins with a temporal clause. Thus, the Babylonian account, popularly known from its first two words, *Enuma Elish* (i.e., When on high), is said to begin with a temporal or dependent clause. A literal rendering of the first two lines of this account would be:

"In the day on high (when) the heavens were not named,
And below the earth had not received a name"

For the proper understanding of them, an independent sentence is needed, and this sentence does actually occur some few lines farther on. The Sumerian account also begins in a similar way. Does it follow from this, however, that Genesis must also begin with a temporal clause? As a matter of fact, Genesis does not begin with a temporal word. Rather, its first word may be rendered "In the beginning," and there is nothing similar to this in any ancient cosmogony. This word and the following, translated "he created," form a remarkable alliteration in Hebrew. Both of these words begin with the three letters: ב, ר, and א.

In the second place, it is argued that the first word בְּרֵאשִׁית is actually in the construct state, and therefore must be rendered "in the beginning of," (i.e., "When God began. . . ."). It cannot be denied that the word is usually in the construct state, as for example, in phrases such as "the beginning of," "the first fruits of our dough" (Neh. 10: 37). Also the word may be in the absolute, as is clearly witnessed by Isa. 46:10 and Neh. 12:44. Thus, it need not necessarily be a construct. Some have suggested that as a matter of fact the second word of the verse should be emended to the form of the infinitive construct (בְּרֹא) in order to obtain the correct text. This is without warrant. It may be noted that the construct in Hebrew may be followed by a finite verb, so that such an emendation would not be necessary, even if the first word were to be taken as a construct. There is, however, a further consideration which is pertinent. In the Hebrew OT whenever a word is to be construed as construct, that fact is apparent either from the form of the word in construct, followed by a verb, or else from the context demanding such an interpretation. Neither of these conditions is present in the first verse of Genesis. The form of the word בְּרֵאשִׁית may be either absolute or construct; hence it certainly does not demand a construct. And surely the context does not demand it. Hence, in this verse neither of these conditions is met. In line with this thought it may also be pointed out that simplicity is a characteristic of Hebrew sentences. They may contain co-ordinate sentences or clauses, but they have comparatively few dependent clauses. Dependent clauses, which are so frequent, for example, in Latin and Greek, are not characteristic of Hebrew. And the ancient versions have not taken this verse as a dependent clause. All of them, without exception, have rendered it in the straightforward majestic manner which really befits it.

There are cogent reasons for believing that the first chapter of the Bible teaches absolute creation, *creatio ex nihilo;* and in line with these reasons we should hesitate to render the first verse in such a manner as to obscure that doctrine. If the first verse of the Bible is a temporal clause, it follows that the first chapter of the Bible does not teach such creation.

Another view of the verse is that it simply states the creation of the primeval matter from which the present well-ordered universe is formed, not the universe as we now know it but merely the creation of the original matter. In opposition to this view, however, is the fact that the phrase "the heavens and the earth" never refers to primeval material but always to the cosmos, the well-ordered world that we know today. It is right then to regard the verse as a simple declaration of the fact that God is the Creator of all things. When we look out upon the beauty of the created world that we now know and when we lift our eyes to the heavens and ask, "Who made these things?" Genesis is ready with an answer. In simple, straightforward terms it declares that the beginning of all things was through a creative act of God. The verse then answers the question that arises at one time or another in the mind of everyone, "Who is the Creator of all things?" or "What is the origin of all things?" It thus stands as a simple, grand, comprehensive statement of the fact of creation, the detailed account of which follows, and which does not exhaust it. This is indeed a common method of narration in

Hebrew; a comprehensive, general statement is followed by a detailed narration. The reader may compare I Kings 18:30b, the general comprehensive statement, and the following verses, the detailed statement of the repairing of the altar. (Note also Gen. 18:1 and following verses; and Psalm 139:1 and following verses.)

In Gen. 1:2 the detailed account of the creation begins. This verse consists of three descriptive or circumstantial clauses which may be rendered as follows: (1) "The earth was desolation and waste"; (2) "darkness was upon faces of abyss"; and (3) "the Spirit of God was hovering over the waters." Grammatically these three clauses are to be construed with the main verb of the third verse, "and he said." The thought is that at the time when God said, "Let there be light," this threefold condition was in existence. If we ask how long such had been the case, it must be replied that the Scripture does not answer the question expressly. In the light of the statement of the first verse, however, we may probably assume that this condition was in existence from the very beginning until the time when God commanded the light to spring into existence.

It must not be thought that the second verse represents an earth that is the result of Divine judgment. Those who hold such a view generally appeal to various passages of Scripture such as Jer. 4:23 ff.; Ezek. 28:12 ff.; Isa. 14:12 ff.; 24:1; and 45:18. These passages, however, are taken out of context, for none of them teaches that the earth which is described in Genesis 1:2 was an earth ruined by judgment. Furthermore, adherents of this view sometimes claim that the verse should be rendered, "And the earth became *etc.*" This rendering, however, is incorrect, for it is contrary to Hebrew grammar.

What the second verse teaches is simply that the earth was in such a condition that at that time man could not live upon it. It was "desolation and waste," there was an abyss covered by darkness, but "the Spirit of God was hovering over the waters." This is not a picture of chaos, if, by the word chaos, we mean that things were out of order. All was under the control of God's Spirit, and there is no reason to believe that God might not have described it as good, as He does with other unfinished stages of the earth.

The account of creation is presented as covering a period of six days, followed by a seventh of rest. This interpretation is supported by the Ten Commandments, in which it is explicitly stated, that ". . . in six days the Lord made heaven and earth," and "rested the seventh day." This is set as the pattern for man's week, namely, six days followed by a seventh. It is essential to grasp this fact, for it is the crucial point in any discussion of the nature of the days. A period of six days followed by a seventh is the picture given in the first chapter of Genesis and the first three verses of chapter two. Other questions concerning the nature of the days should fall within this framework.

III. The Days of Genesis

How long were these days? It is often argued that they were solar days such as we now know. But the first three days were not solar, inasmuch as the sun had not yet been brought into existence. A second view would assert that the days were much longer than 24 hours in length. Still a third view holds that the first three days may have been longer, but the last three were days as we now know them. Also, it has been held that each of the days represents an epoch of geology, and may be designated a geologic period.

Attention must be devoted to another view. Inasmuch as it presents the days as not sustaining a chronological relationship to one another, it may be designated a non-chronological view. This view regards the days as presenting different aspects of the creation, but not as necessarily following one another. Although designated the "framework hypothesis," such a label is not satisfactory, for other views also posit a framework in the first chapter of Genesis. Different arguments are employed to support this interpretation. Appeal is made to Genesis 2:5, in which it is stated that it had not yet rained. If this verse refers to the third day, and the days are 24 hours in length, then it is reasoned that the verse would not make sense. Hence, it is concluded, the verse teaches the existence of ordinary providence during the creation week, and so excludes the 24-hour day view. However, it may be noted that this position would not necessarily exclude the view that the days were longer than 24 hours. Furthermore, it is not correct to appeal to this verse as teaching ordinary providence during the creation week, inasmuch as in the following verses it is shown that the watering of the earth and the production of man were not ordinary providential works. But also to appeal to Genesis 2:5 in this way is to take the verse out of context, inasmuch as it belongs to a section of Genesis which deals not with the creation but rather with the preparation of the Garden of Eden. For the most part it appears that adherents of this view are motivated by a desire to avoid the difficulties posited by geology and astronomy. In particular, a question is raised about the existence of light before the sun. The answer may be stated somewhat as follows. It is not our prerogative to harmonize the Bible with what men at any given time may happen to teach. Our first and supreme task is to interpret the Bible correctly. If we do that, we may then notice what men say and what the relationship is, if any, which the Bible bears to their teaching. In this connection it must be stressed emphatically that men have no warrant, when they make observations concerning the nature of things as they are today, to lay down laws apodictically and to assert that conditions must always have been thus, and that God must be bound by these conditions. When we discuss the creation we are entering the realm of mystery. It is only God who can create and we are in no position, inasmuch as we are finite, to assert that the conditions which we see in existence today must always have prevailed.

Also in opposition to the non-chronological view is the express designation of the days, as day one, day two, etc., and the climactic "the sixth day." This surely emphasizes chronology. Again, one must consider the progression or development presented in the first chapter. The purpose of the six days is to remove the chaos of verse two and to lead up to the finished world which God may declare to be "very good." The non-chronological view of the days loses sight of this purpose completely. Step by step God brings into existence those things which are necessary for man's habitancy of the world. First we are given the account of the creation of inanimate things; then those that are animate but stationary; then follows, after the statement of the making of the heavenly bodies, the creation of those things that are animate and move about. With them the word בָּרָא, "create," is employed, and a blessing pronounced. Last of all God engages in deliberation concerning the creation of man. Again the word בָּרָא (*bara*) is employed, and a blessing is pronounced upon man. Also, man is commanded to subdue the entire earth. Thus, by means of the six days, the gap has been bridged between the condition of the second verse and that of the 31st verse. In the light of this remarkable progression, a non-chronological view of the days seems untenable. It is difficult to believe that the author intended his readers to accept such a view. Had that been his purpose, we might well have expected that he would have given some indication.

It is necessary, therefore, to hold that the days are chronological and follow one another in the sequence indicated in the first chapter of Genesis. But then there arises the question as to the length of these days. That is a question which is difficult to answer. Indications are not lacking that they may have been longer than the days we now know, but the Scripture itself does not speak as clearly as one might like.

IV. Exposition of Genesis One

Over the earth, enshrouded in darkness and apparently covered by water, the Spirit of God hovered. It was a time when man obviously could not live upon the earth, but when all was under God's control. Then God commanded the existence of light. Scripture, in speaking of God, naturally employs anthropomorphic language, for the finite mind cannot comprehend the Infinite and man can only speak of God from the standpoint of a finite being. Hence, he must describe God's actions with statements, such as, "God said, saw, divided, etc." When God commanded the light to shine out of darkness, we are not to understand that He uttered vocal, audible sounds or that He spoke in Hebrew or in some other human language. Rather, Scripture would have us understand that at this time God willed into existence light, and light immediately came into existence. God divides between the light and the darkness, and gives to each a name.

Can there be light apart from the sun? There was a time when this was advanced as an argument against the correctness of the creation account of the Bible. But it is now known that there can be light even apart from the sun. We do not know where this light in the Bible came from, whether it came from a lightbearer or whether it came from that body which was afterwards on the fourth day made to be the sun. It is, however, now widely acknowledged that light may come from sources other than the sun.

On the second day God created the "expanse" which divided between the waters that adhered to the earth and those that were above the expanse. Two interpretations may be mentioned. Some understand the waters above the expanse to refer to the clouds and atmosphere, whereas others think that the reference is to waters which are beyond our atmosphere. This latter theory would fit in with the idea of rain coming from outer space.

The third day presents two principal works. In the first place the oceans are formed and the dry land appears. Involved in this would have been great upheavals, in which the mountains were formed and many of the processes of erosion were set into motion.

On the fourth day the sun, moon, and stars are brought into existence. Scripture simply says that God made the sun, which it designates a lightbearer. How God formed the sun, we are not told, but it is possible that the sun had existed in some different form before and now is brought into the relationship to the earth which it has at present. It is possible that the fourth day indicates that the present constitution of the universe was then established.

In the fifth day we note the creation of those things which are both animate and move about. For them the word בָּרָא, "create," is employed, and a blessing is pronounced upon them.

Lastly, on the sixth day, animals are created upon which also a blessing is pronounced, and man is created, which involved Divine deliberation. God consults with Himself, "Let us make." This hortatory command is an indication that there is a plurality of persons in the speaker and thus foreshadows the doctrine of the Trinity to be revealed more fully in the NT. With respect to man the verb בָּרָא is also used, but also he is said to be created in God's image, thus distinguishing him from the lower creation. Upon him a blessing is pronounced, and he is set over the world to subdue it for the glory of God. Over the entire finished creation God pronounces the judgment "very good." On the seventh day (Gen. 2:1-3) God rests from His labors. Thus, the account of creation comes to a close. It is a section, complete in itself, designed to exalt God as the true Creator of heaven and earth and reject the notion that matter is inherently evil.

V. The Relation of Genesis One and Genesis Two

It has been widely held that the second chapter of Genesis is a second, duplicate account of creation, and that it differs essentially from the first chapter. Genesis, therefore, is said to contain two radically contradictory accounts of the creation. On the face of it, it would be strange that a compiler should put together two conflicting narratives of the creation. Would he not seek to smooth out the contradictions, so that his finished product would offer a consistent account? Such we might expect, but we are told that this was not the case. Modern critics of the negative school are insistent that the two accounts are contradictory on essential matters, such as the order of creation and the ideas concerning God expressed.

As a matter of fact, however, there are not two conflicting accounts. The heading to the second section of Genesis (Gen. 2:4–4:24) reads, "These are the generations of [i.e., the things produced by] the heavens and the earth." This phrase refers to those things which come from the heaven and earth, not to the creation of heaven and earth. It is an introductory phrase, a heading, which identifies the nature of the section which follows. It tells us that we are now going to deal not with the origin of all things, but with that which came from heaven and earth, namely, man. The heading itself therefore shows that the following is not an account of creation.

Furthermore, there is no essential conflict between this section and the first chapter. In this section the order of statement is topical or emphatic rather than chronological. In fulfillment of his purpose of showing the preparation of the Garden for man, the writer first states that there were no herbs or plants because it had not rained and there was no man to till the soil. These conditions were then met: a mist watered all the faces of the ground; and man, a responsible creature, one made in God's image, was formed. Then we are told that God planted a garden and placed man in it. Man's home was not to be on some barren spot but in a garden. Scripture then directs attention to the trees of the garden and in particular to two sacramental trees, followed by a description of the garden. Again it is stated that God placed man in the garden, but this time the purpose of doing so is announced; man is to dress and to keep the garden. The prohibition not to eat of the fruit of the tree of the knowledge of good and evil follows. Attention is called to man's need for a help. First a help in the animals is provided, but inasmuch as these are not sufficient for man's needs, a help that is suitable for him is created. Thus the chapter closes with the man and woman in the garden in perfect innocence. When the purpose of the chapter is considered, it will be seen that there is no conflict with the first chapter. The second chapter is dealing with a more restricted subject than the first.

As is well known, there was a cosmogony of the Babylonians, now known from its first two words as *Enuma Elish* ("When on high"). This account was discovered in the library of Asshurbanipal at Nineveh, which was excavated between the years 1848-1876. Claims have been made that Genesis is really influenced by this account. There are, of course, certain resemblances, notably, the philological equation between the Hebrew word תְּהוֹם *tehôm* (Gen. 1:2) and the name of the goddess Tiamat of the poem. At that point, however, the equation ceases. Far more significant are the differences. For one thing Genesis has greater unity than *Enuma Elish.* This is acknowledged even by those who claim that Genesis contains two accounts of creation. The two taken together, it is held, present greater unity than does *Enuma Elish.* Furthermore, in the Babylonian epic, there are no six days of creation followed by a seventh; creation is not told in terms of fiat and fulfillment; and the form of the account is not similar to that of Genesis.

VI. The Relation of Genesis One to the Babylonian Account of Creation

Of greater significance than these differences, however, are the respective ideas of God. The god of *Enuma Elish* has a long genealogy behind him; whereas the God of Genesis One is the true Creator of heaven and earth. The polytheism of *Enuma Elish* is of a gross and crude kind. The gods engage in rivalries and jealousies; they plot and counterplot and act generally like depraved human beings. In addition to all this, there is no true account of creation.

The relationship between Genesis and *Enuma Elish* cannot be explained as one in which Genesis is regarded as having borrowed from the Babylonian document. On the other hand, if the account given in the first book of the Bible is a Revelation from God, it is to be expected that God would have revealed its truth to Adam, and that Adam would have communicated it, so that it would be handed down until it received written form. Also, when Moses came to write, he was superintended by the Spirit of God. In so writing, he may have employed earlier written documents but was prevented by the Spirit of God from making errors in what he wrote.

This would also explain why so many peoples have a cosmogony and why it is that in these cosmogonies there are certain elements of truth preserved. The Babylonian and other cosmogonies represent a corrupted tradition, whereas Genesis One is a Divinely inspired Revelation of the truth. In this lies the profound difference between Genesis One and all other accounts of creation.

VII. Significance of the Creation Account

What is of particular significance about the narrative in Genesis is that it alone, of all cosmogonies, presents an account of creation. It asserts that God "created," which means that God brought into existence that which previously had no existence. This creation is a work of God alone. Furthermore, the creation is to be regarded as distinct from and dependent upon God. What is created is not a mere emanation of God, an extension of His Being. It is entirely distinct from Him. The creation can be properly understood and interpreted only when it is regarded as having been created by God. This doctrine is fundamental to the teaching of the entire Bible, for it explains why man is responsible before God and is a creature who owes his very life and existence to God.

EDWARD J. YOUNG

CREATIONISM

I. The term creationism (also creatianism) is used as the name of a theory about the origin of the human soul. In distinction from the other two theories (traducianism and pre-existentianism), creationism teaches that while the body of man is the result of the sexual union of the father and mother, the soul is created by God directly and *de novo,* either at the moment of conception or at the moment the foetus shows the first signs of independent life. Creationism was accepted by most of the church fathers (Jerome even called it "the doctrine of the Church," though important thinkers such as Tertullian taught traducianism), by the majority of the Greek, scholastic, and RC theologians (Thomas Aquinas regarded the opposite doctrine as heretical), and also by nearly all Reformed theologians. The Lutherans generally favored traducianism. Creationists usually appeal to the following passages of Scripture: Gen. 2:7 (the creation of Adam's soul); Eccl. 12:7; Zech. 12:1; and in particular Heb. 12:9 (cf. Num. 16:22; 17:16). Their main arguments are: (1) it is more consistent with the prevailing representations of Scripture; (2) it is more consistent with the nature of the human soul, which is immaterial and spiritual and therefore of an indivisible nature; (3) it does justice to the vertical-creative aspect in every man and thus respects the mystery of the human individual; (4) it avoids the pitfalls of traducianism in Christology and explains how Christ could be true man and yet without sin.

In recent Reformed theology creationism is no longer accepted as the best explanation of the origin of the human soul. This does not mean a shift to traducianism. On the contrary, both theories are rejected, because both proceed from a problem that as such is illegitimate in the light of Scripture. Behind both lies the Greek idea of a man as consisting of two separate "substances" (body and soul). In Scripture, however, man is seen as a unity and therefore the Bible does not even raise the question of the origin of his soul. E.g., Gen. 2:7 does not speak of this origin, but declares that when God breathes the breath of life (i.e., the principle of life) into man, this man *becomes* a "living *soul,*" i.e., a living being. Ps. 139, speaking of the origin of *man* as a totality, states that God is the Creator of the *entire* man *in* the horizontal relationship. Commenting on Heb. 12:9, Berkouwer rightly says: "The difference is not that God is the source of one 'part' of man, and earthly fathers the source of another 'part,' but rather that God is the Creator of life in His incomparable glory and majesty."

See also PRE-EXISTENCE OF THE SOUL; TRADUCIANISM; SOUL.

BIBLIOGRAPHY:

A. W. Argyle, "The Christian Doctrine of the Origin of the Soul," *SJT* VIII (1965), 3.

H. Bavinck, *Gereformeerde Dogmatiek* (Kampen, 1928), II, 541-550.

L. Berkhof, *Systematic Theology* (Grand Rapids, 1953), 196-201.

G. C. Berkouwer, *Man: The Image of God* (Grand Rapids, 1962), 279-309.

H. Heppe, *Reformed Dogmatics* (London, 1950).

C. Hodge, *Systematic Theology* (London, 1883), II, 65-77.

A. G. Honig, *Creatianisme of Traducianisme?* (Kampen, 1906).

J. Waterink, *De Oorsprong en het Wezen der Ziel* (Wageningen, 1930).

II. The term "creationism" is also used in reference to the whole doctrine of creation as opposed to evolutionism. Whereas evolutionism is an un-Scriptural philosophy which teaches that all things have come into existence in a purely natural way, according to autonomous principles and without any previous plan, creationism teaches that this universe and all that is in it owes its existence to the creative activity of God. Creationism has no place for absolute autonomy, and it utterly rejects the evolutionistic concept of pure chance. All that exists is made by God and is from the very beginning under His sovereign control.

Within the broad concept of creationism several theories can be distinguished. (1) According to some, the universe and all organisms in it were once and for all created *c.* 7000 years ago. (2) Others hold that over an exceedingly long period God performed successive acts of creation, each time producing new kinds of organisms *de novo.* (3) Others again believe that God added new elements to existing organisms; e.g., life was added to inorganic material so that living organisms came into existence; a soul was added to one of the primates so that man came into existence. (4) Others again believe that God created in one comprehensive act of creation ("in the beginning") the whole universe in one harmonious totality, and that under His providential guidance and control the created potentialities developed into the existing organisms. In this view there is no place for the addition of new elements, but all that exists has evolved from the original creation. Although this view leaves room for a great deal of development or evolution, it is opposed to evolutionism in that it rejects all autonomy and sees the process as constantly under the providential guidance of God as the Creator. For this reason it falls within the broad spectrum of creationism. The first two views are the more traditional conceptions, both accepting the idea of fiat-creation. A variation of the second view is Bernard Ramm's "progressive creationism." The great phyla and families came into being by the creative act of God, but within these, development took place. The third and fourth views gloss over the expressions of fiat in Gen. 1 and should not be accepted. The third view is commonly known as theistic evolution. It accepts a continuous line from the original cells on the pre-historic waters to man. The fourth view is defended by J. Lever and others. Though these views differ considerably among themselves, they all have in common the belief that the origin and differentiation of all that exists is a result of God's creative activity.

See also CREATION; EVOLUTION.

BIBLIOGRAPHY:

R. E. D. Clark, *Darwin: Before and After* (London, 1948).

J. Lever, *Creation and Evolution* (Grand Rapids, 1958).

A. Lunn, *The Flight from Reason* (London, 1932).

B. Ramm, *The Christian View of Science and Scripture* (Grand Rapids, 1953).

A. E. W. Smith, *Man's Origin, Man's Destiny* (Wheaton, 1968).

KLAAS RUNIA

CREEDS. See CONFESSIONS AND CREEDS.

CREMATION, the burning of human corpses.

Ancient Times. Although not the oldest form of disposal of the dead, cremation is found throughout the ancient world, with the important exceptions of Egypt, Israel, and China. The general background seems to have been fear of the dead and the corresponding desire to destroy completely their physical remains. The Greeks and Romans increasingly favored cremation in order to make the deliverance of the soul from the prison of the body more complete. The victory of the Christian church made the custom gradually disappear in the W world.

Modern Times. In the 19th century cremation was revived, mainly by humanitarians and liberal theologians. In 1876 the first crematory was built in the United States, and in 1884 Justice Stephen declared cremation to be a legal procedure in England, provided no nuisance was caused to others. Since then it has expanded enormously. Statistics of 1952 give the following numbers of crematoria: Great Britain, 62; United States and Canada, 193; Sweden, 29; Denmark, 21; Norway, 14; Australia, 13; New Zealand, 7; Holland, 1.

The arguments of the advocates are

usually that cremation is (1) more hygenic and sanitary; (2) more economical, as regards both the costs involved and the space occupied; (3) more aesthetic and in keeping with the dignity of the body. Moreover, it is nowhere forbidden in Scripture.

Scripture Teaching. Although the last point is correct, Scripture is by no means silent on this matter. It clearly points to burial as the proper custom. The OT records that the patriarchs and their wives, and later on the kings of Israel, were all buried. Deut. 34:6 tells that God Himself buried Moses. The great burnings at the burials of some kings (Jer. 34:5; II Chron. 16:14) are burnings of spices and furniture in the king's honor. The burning of the body of Saul and his sons (I Sam. 31:12, 13) is exceptional; it was probably done to prevent all risk of further insult. For the rest, burning is regarded as a curse (Lev. 20:14; 21:9; Josh. 7:25, 26; Amos 2:1; 6:10; II Kings 22:16).

The NT knows burial only. It records the burial of John the Baptist, Lazarus, and others. Above all, it records the burial of Christ Himself, who in this way sanctified the graves of all believers. Also in His own teaching Jesus referred several times to burial (Mt. 8:22; 23:29; John 5:28). Very important is Paul's metaphor in I Cor. 15:35 ff., where he compares the burial of the body to the sowing of the grain of wheat that is not quickened before it dies.

Conclusion. The Christian church has from the beginning to the present time followed these clear indications. Among the early Church Fathers, Tertullian called cremation a symbol of hell, and Cyprian regarded it as the equivalent of apostasy. The latter verdict still applies in many respects to our situation. Often (though not always) the modern advocates of cremation hold a philosophy which is hostile to orthodox, Scriptural Christianity. They either deny the resurrection of the body (sometimes even all life after death) or advocate a false dualism between body and soul. Over against this, the church, by insisting on burial as the proper custom, should witness to her belief in the resurrection of the body and life everlasting.

See Burial.

Bibliography:

L. Boettner, *Immortality* (Grand Rapids, 1956), 50-55.

P. Jasperse, *Zullen wij onze Doden begraven?* (Goes, n.d.).

P. H. Jones, "Cremation," *Enc. Brit.* (1959).

P. H. Jones and G. A. Noble, *Cremation in Great Britain* (London, 1931).

Klaas Runia

CRESCENS, a Christian who was with the Apostle Paul during his imprisonment in Rome and who left for Galatia (II Tim. 4:10).

CRESCENTS, the moon-shaped adornments, hung on the necks of camels (Judges 8:21) and also worn by people. They were worn, for instance, by kings (Judges 8:26) and by women (Isa. 3:18).

CRESPIN, Jean (d. 1572), French Protestant author and printer. Crespin's family was from Arras, at that time a city of the Netherlands under Emperor Charles V's rule. He came to Paris in 1540, and was deeply impressed by the courage of various Protestant martyrs such as Claude Le Peintre. On returning home, he was soon suspected of having Reformed sympathies and was banished. He fled to Strassburg in 1545, and later to Geneva (1548), where he received citizenship in 1555. He created there a printing office and died in 1572 of the plague. His main work is his *Book of Martyrs.* After learning of five students who were burned alive at Lyons in 1553, he decided to issue a narrative of various executions of Protestant martyrs, beginning with John Hus. The first edition came to light in 1554. Later he took advantage of John Foxe's *Acts and Monuments*, a Latin edition of which had appeared in 1554, to add some stories of English martyrs of the 15th century. And of course, as years and persecutions went on, he added new names. The last edition during his lifetime was published in 1570 and ran to seven books.

After his death his son-in-law, Jean Vignon, carried on the printing office, and a minister named Simon Goulard completed the *Book of Martyrs*. The issue of 1582 was divided into eight books, the first one devoted to the martyrs of the early church and the Middle Ages, and the last two to persons who suffered between 1569 and 1574. Later two more books were added, with stories of martyrs since 1574. The final edition was published in 1619. This book was an inspiration for countless Huguenots in the 16th and 17th centuries. After the Bible and the Psalter, it was the most widely read and the most influential support of faith and courage in the midst of danger and persecution.

BIBLIOGRAPHY:

A complete republication of the *Book of Martyrs* was made by Daniel Benoit (Toulouse, 1884), 3 vols. An abridged edition was issued by C. Bonifas and E. Petitpierre under the title *Galerie Chrétienne* (Grenoble, 1837), 2 vols., and another one by Theodore Monod, Jr., under the title *Le Livre des Martyrs* (Neuilly, 1930).

E. and E. Haag, *La France Protestante*, 2nd ed. (Paris, 1884), vol. IV, pp. 885-901.

J. NICOLE

CRETE, a mountainous Mediterranean island, 150 miles long, 3,120 square miles in area, and stretching across the S Aegean Sea. In spite of strategic position, fertile valleys, useful harbors, and the traditional glory of its remote antiquity, Crete never achieved political supremacy in the Mediterranean world.

Mount Ida, highest point in the central mountain chain, was the legendary home of Zeus. Early Cretans had a reputation for seamanship, and their semi-mythical ruler Minos was credited by Aristotle with suppressing piracy. Homer refers to Crete as "the island of a hundred cities." Its most important centers were Knossos, Gortyna, and Cydonia. In Greece's classical age, Cretans were mainly merchants and mercenaries.

There is evidence of an early connection with Palestine. Cretans were believed to have visited Canaan in Abraham's time (Petrie, *Palestine and Israel*, p. 62). Philistine "Cherethites" are generally identified as Cretans (I Sam. 30:14; Ezek. 25:16; Zeph. 2:5). Caphtor, an island from which the Philistines migrated, was probably Crete (Deut. 2:23; Jer. 47:4; Amos 9:7). Cherethites served in David's army (II Sam. 8:18; 15:18). In the intertestamental period many Jews settled in Crete (see I Macc. 10:67; 15:19-23). An appeal to Rome by Cretan Jews in 141 B.C. led to Roman intervention and ultimately (68-66 B.C.) to annexation.

NT connections with Crete include:

(1) A reference to Cretans present in Jerusalem at Pentecost (Acts 2:11).

(2) Report of a storm which forced a ship bearing Paul to Rome to take shelter in a Cretan harbor and later to skirt the S coast of the island (Acts 27). Nautical allusions in this record confirm its credibility (see J. Smith, *Voyage and Shipwreck of St. Paul*, for proofs of Luke's accuracy from a study of admiralty charts and Mediterranean tides).

(3) References to Crete in Titus spotlight the presence of Christian churches and the prevalence of Cretan vices. Paul's appraisal of Cretan character (Titus 1:10-13) agrees with ancient extra-Biblical estimates. Livy, Plutarch, Polybius, and Strabo refer to Cretan cupidity, fraudulence, and ferocity. Cretans were proverbially listed with Cilicians and Cappadocians as the world's worst, and were so notorious that the

Greeks coined an expression "to Crete-ize" to designate deception. The quotation in Titus 1:12 ("Cretans are always liars, evil beasts, idle gluttons") is from a Cretan poet Epimenides (600 B.C.), who crystallized common contempt for his fellow-islanders. Recognizing these natural defects, Paul emphasized his confidence in the Gospel by encouraging Titus to evangelize Crete.

From A.D. 823 on, the island was successively controlled by Saracens, the Byzantine Empire, Venice, Turkey, and Greece.

JOHN F. HOLLIDAY

CRISP, Tobias (1600-1643), rector of Brinkworth and author of *Christ Alone Exalted*, was educated at Eton, Cambridge, and Oxford (Balliol, 1626). After a period of legalistic Arminian preaching, he reacted so emphatically as to expose himself to the charge of antinomianism in doctrine, though not in practice. Samuel Rutherford preached against Crisp's doctrines of the laying of sin itself, not simply its guilt, on Christ and the consequent confusion of justification and sanctification, as well as the doctrine of the actual justification of the elect from eternity. Crisp's teaching, however, found favor in some High Calvinistic quarters, being approved by William Twisse, the Dutch professor Hoornbeek, and later by John Gill. With the good intention of encouraging Christians in trials, Crisp made such paradoxical statements as "There is not one sin you commit, after you receive Christ, that God can charge upon your person" (I, 73); "before a believer confesses his sin, he may be as certain of the pardon of it, as after confession" (I, 359); "they that have God for their God, there is no sin that ever they commit, can possibly do them any hurt" (II, 171). Yet Crisp may not be simply charged with antinomianism, for he admits the moral law as the Christian's rule of life (II, 124, 526 ff.). Nor may he be charged with hyper-Calvinism, for he ardently champions the free offer of the gospel (I, 112 ff., 213 f.) in terms disturbing to Rutherford as well as unacceptable to Gill. There is magnificence as well as a snare in the one-sidedness of Crisp's proclamation of the freeness of sovereign grace.

BIBLIOGRAPHY:

A. Burgess, *The True Doctrine of Justification* (London, 1648).

A. Burgess, *Vindiciae Legis* (London, 1646).

T. Crisp, *Christ Alone Exalted* with Gill's notes, 5th ed. (London, 1861), 2 vols.

S. Geree, *The Doctrine of Antinomians Confuted, in answer to the Sermons of Dr. Crisp* (London, 1644).

D. Neal, *History of the Puritans* (London, 1754).

S. Rutherford, *A Survey of the Spiritual Antichrist* (London, 1648).

S. Rutherford, *The Trial and Triumph of Faith* (Edinburgh, 1845), especially sermons 8, 14, 16, 18, 19, 24.

D. Williams, *Gospel-Truth Stated and Vindicated, wherein some of Dr. Crisp's opinions are considered and the opposite truths are plainly stated and confirmed* (London, 1692).

H. Witsius, *Irenical Animadversions*, trans. Thomas Bell (Glasgow, 1807).

WILLIAM YOUNG

CRISPUS (Lat., "curled"), a man mentioned in Acts 18:7, 8, and probably the person referred to in I Cor. 1:12. He was a ruler of the synagogue at Corinth, but on believing on Christ, he, along with his family, attached himself to the Christian congregation. He was one of the few Corinthians whom Paul baptized.

CROCE, Benedetto (1866-1952), idealist philosopher, literary critic, historian, statesman.

Croce is one of the most widely known Italian philosophers of art and of the spirit. He held to absolute historicism, i.e., that everything is involved in a historical process that has a controlling principle of immanence. Immanence he defined as the concrete inwardness of spirit to its own processes. His philosophy took shape in opposition to transcendence, including the idea of the transcendence of God. He regarded everything to be immanent to the spirit in its activity. In agreement with his historical orientation, Croce sought to develop a critique of historical reason. It is only to historical judgments, he said, that the predicates "true" and "false" can be applied. The only genuine knowledge is historical knowledge.

During the development of his views there was always an affinity between Croce's literary criticism and his theories of art and history. We understand the spirit only as we make present what has been realized by the spirit in the past, making spirit conscious of itself. What characterizes art is immediate, individual intuition. A greater universality is observed in the lyrical character of art, but its universality is truly apparent only in the context of the history of spirit. It is the place of literary criticism, therefore, to disclose the universal significance of the individual work of art in the history of spirit.

Croce's denial of transcendence and his exclusive attention to the process of spirit is reflected in his statement that history is God, and that God is the total real dialectic of the spirit in its concrete universality.

Of independent financial means, Croce was able to dedicate his entire life to philosophical studies and to literary criticism. Indeed, he thought of himself as being first of all a literary critic and wrote voluminously on modern and classical literature. In 1903 Croce founded the journal *La critica*, through which he exercised a wide influence throughout Italy and all of Europe for more than 40 years. He effectively criticized the tampering on the part of the Fascists with the Italian constitution. After World War II he was the dominant figure in the constitutional assembly from which the Italian republic finally emerged.

Bibliography:

H. W. Carr, *The Philosophy of Benedetto Croce: The Problem of Art and History* (London, 1917).

E. Ciono, *Bibliografia crociana* (Monza, 1956).

B. Croce, *Filosofia dello spirito* (1902-1917).

B. Croce, *History of Europe in the Nineteenth Century*, tr. Henry Furst (New York, 1933).

B. Croce, *History as the Story of Liberty* (London, 1941).

F. Nicolini, *Benedetto Croce* (Turin, 1962).

G. N. G. Orsini, *Benedetto Croce: Philosopher of Art and Literary Critic* (Carbondale, Illinois, 1961).

G. N. G. Orsini, "Theory and Practice in Croce's Aesthetics," *The Journal of Aesthetics and Art Criticism*, XIII (March, 1955), 300-313.

R. Piccolo, *Benedetto Croce* (London, 1922).

C. G. Seerveld, *Benedetto Croce's Earler Aesthetic Theories and Literary Criticism: A Critical Philosophical Look at the Development during his Rationalistic Years* (Kampen, 1958).

Robert D. Knudsen

CROMWELL, Oliver (1599-1658), Lord Protector. Born in Huntingdon into a Protestant family, Cromwell's formal education by Dr. Thomas Beard at Sidney Sussex College, Cambridge, was in a Puritan atmosphere. Leaving Cambridge prematurely on the death of his father in June, 1617, he assumed responsibility for the family estates, and in 1620 he married Elizabeth Bourchier, daughter of a prosperous city merchant, by whom he had eight children.

He was elected as member for Huntingdon to the Parliament of 1628-29, where he protested against the spread of ritualism in the Church of England. Charles I was angered by the attacks made on his ministers and policies in this parliament, and 11 years passed before he called another one. The king had to terminate this experiment in 1640 to seek support for his war to impose episcopacy on the Scots, but the opposition of the Puritan gentry in the Commons was more determined and better organized than before. Cromwell sat for Cambridge in the Short and Long Parliaments and seems to have been primarily, though not exclusively, concerned with church matters, such as advocating the destruction of the Anglican hierarchy "root and branch."

Cromwell's remarkable rise from nothing to be head of state was not deliberately sought by him. It was largely a result of the ability he showed in the Civil Wars as a cavalry officer and of his strength of purpose in prosecuting the war, as evidenced in the battles of Marston Moor (1644) and Naseby (1645). When they had defeated the Royalists, Parliament and its army fell out, and Cromwell, as political leader of the latter, was chiefly responsible for the execution of Charles I in January, 1649, and the dissolution of the Rump, as the remnant of Parliament was called, in April, 1653. In both cases he believed he was acting justly and in the interests of the nation, though contrary to tradition. Cromwell was now in a position to make himself dictator, had this been his ambition, since his popularity had been greatly enhanced by military successes in Ireland and Scotland. In fact, in December, 1653, he became Lord Protector on the initiative of Major-General Lambert and the army, after the nominated Parliament of "Saints" had re-signed its powers back to him.

Henceforth Cromwell regarded himself as called by God through a remarkable series of providences to govern. Thus, fundamentally, he would not permit his parliaments to change the constitution under which they had been summoned. Yet he was never, nor did he desire to be, a dictator. In 1657 he was offered the crown, but refused in deference to opinion in the army. But, although the Protectorate retained a military character to the end and as such was distasteful to the nation, Cromwell's rule was distinguished. Abroad he pursued religious and national ends rather than dynastic interests, as the Stuarts tended to. His two main objects were to crush the power of Spain, the political mainspring of the RC interest in Europe, and to organize a Protestant League. This latter dream was never realized, though Cromwell was able to exert his influence to protect the Protestant minority in Savoy. Though of a reforming disposition, Cromwell's achievements in domestic affairs were mainly negative: the destruction of arbitrariness in church and state, and the maintenance of peace and order. After his death in 1658, neither his son Richard, who succeeded him as Protector, nor anyone else was able to save the Commonwealth and prevent the restoration of the Stuarts, which took place in May, 1660.

Throughout his career, Cromwell was motivated, not by personal ambition, nor by political idealism, but by his religious convictions. His letters show a familiarity with the Scriptures, to which he was careful to submit his life and thought. Despite his upbringing, his conversion does not seem to have taken place until about 1627-28. As a husband and father, he showed himself chaste and loving. His spiritual home was the army, which he sought to fill with godly men. In it, a multitude of sects flourished, some of which abandoned the Biblical doctrine characteristic of true Puritanism for their own private fancies and utopian schemes. Though not personally in sympathy with their teachings, Cromwell was indulgent to such men because he admired their sincerity and emphasis on the internal character of true religion. Regarded as the "Great Independent," he did not oppose presbyterianism as such, but the policy of uniformity and religious persecution with which it had become associated. In seeking guidance at crucial times, such as before the trial of Charles I, Cromwell seems to have paid too much attention to his feelings while at prayer, and not enough to the objective Word of

God. A similar failing was his tendency to interpret success as necessarily a sign of Divine approval. Yet though Cromwell's judgment was faulty in these respects, it is just as true that subsequent generations of Christians have tended to lack that true sense of providence which sustained, energized, and humbled him.

Against Cromwell's mystical tendencies must be set his choice of such sober and orthodox chaplains as Caryl, Howe, Thomas Goodwin, and Owen. The Cromwellian religious settlement, of which Owen was the architect, provided for an established church including all orthodox Protestants, with each congregation free to choose its own order and government. Commissions tried ministers for their fitness and ejected them where necessary. On the testimony of Baxter, they did a considerable amount of good. Although the prevailing religious temper was against toleration, Cromwell did not wish to persecute the Roman Catholics, Anglicans, and heterodox sects, providing they were peaceful and law abiding. He realized that saving faith could not be compelled by the sword, and the cause of the Gospel would not be furthered by the savage repression of its opponents. His life's ambition was to promote the unrestricted preaching of the Gospel and the practice of godliness.

Oliver Cromwell's religious integrity and practical wisdom saved the Puritan Revolution from sterility and self-destruction. He struck lasting blows against tyranny and clericalism in England, and his rule made English Puritanism famed and respected in his own day and to succeeding generations.

BIBLIOGRAPHY:

W. C. Abbott, *A Bibliography of Oliver Cromwell* (Cambridge, 1929).

W. C. Abbott, *The Writings and Speeches of Oliver Cromwell* (Cambridge, 1937-47), 4 vols.

M. Ashley, *The Greatness of Oliver Cromwell* (London, 1957).

M. Ashley, *Oliver Cromwell and the Puritan Revolution* (London, 1958).

T. Carlyle, *The Letters and Speeches of Oliver Cromwell with elucidations* (London and New York, 1904), 2nd ed.

J. H. M. D'Aubigné, *Le Protecteur; ou la Republique d'Angleterre* (Paris and Geneva, 1846; Eng. trans., New York, 1846-7; London, 1847).

C. H. Firth, *Oliver Cromwell and the Rule of the Puritans* (London and New York, 1900).

S. R. Gardiner, *History of the Great Civil War 1642-49* (London, 1886-91), 3 vols.

S. R. Gardiner, *History of the Commonwealth and Protectorate 1649-60* (London, 1903), 4 vols.

R. S. Paul, *The Lord Protector* (London, 1955).

MICHAEL BOLAND

CROMWELL, Thomas (*c.* 1485-1540), Earl of Essex, and chief minister to Henry VIII.

The early life of Thomas Cromwell is obscure. Though associated with Cardinal Wolsey from 1524, Cromwell's career was not prejudiced by Wolsey's fall from favor in 1529. Shortly afterwards he entered the service of King Henry VIII, where his influence soon became supreme.

Cromwell did not hesitate to advocate more radical measures than Wolsey to obtain for the king a divorce from his Spanish wife, Catherine of Aragon. By parliamentary legislation in 1532-34, England severed its ties with the Pope, and Henry VIII was declared to be Supreme Head of the English Church. Cromwell presided over the dissolution of the monasteries, which tied the fortunes of the gentry to the Reformation and widened the breach with Rome. Thus far the Reformation was purely political. But Cromwell, to secure his work, supported moderate doctrinal change and worked for an alliance with the Lutheran princes of Germany. Though he had many enemies, Cromwell was safe while he retained the king's confidence, but he lost this in 1540 and was executed in July of that year.

A very able administrator, Cromwell initiated momentous ecclesiastical changes and gave official support to the circulation of the English Bible. Though his own outlook seems to have been secular and not evangelical, he instigated the irrevocable breach with Rome and so prepared the way for a reformation of the doctrine and practice of the English church.

BIBLIOGRAPHY:

A. G. Dickens, *Thomas Cromwell and the English Reformation* (London, 1959).

G. R. Elton, *England under the Tudors* (London, Reprint, 1957).

R. B. Merriman, *The Life and Letters of Thomas Cromwell* (Oxford, 1902), 2 vols.

MICHAEL BOLAND

CROSS, CRUCIFIXION. Death on the cross was one of the most horrible punishments to which a criminal could be condemned. Besides the Carthaginians, it was chiefly the Romans who applied this punishment to slaves who were guilty of insurrection or murder in the territories under their jurisdiction. Anyone who held Roman citizenship, although he was guilty of such an offense, might not be crucified. One condemned to death on a cross was scourged, stripped of almost all his clothing, and then at the place of execution, while the cross beam still lay on the ground, was nailed or bound to it. The cross beam with the dangling body upon it was then lifted up on the upright 10-foot beam that stood in the ground.

This was also probably the procedure at the crucifixion of the Lord Jesus Christ. We read in the Gospels that the Lord was scourged (Mt. 27:26), and that He bore the cross (John 19:17). On the hill of crucifixion, Jesus was deprived of His clothing (Mt. 27:35), and was nailed to the cross (John 20:25; Luke 24:39). In the event that the victim was not fastened to the cross with nails but with ropes, and that thus he did not directly receive any terrible open wounds in his hands and feet, his suffering could go on for several days. Now and then the victim was offered a stupefying potion. Such a potion, wine mingled with myrrh, was also offered to Jesus (Mark 15:23), but He refused it.

In some cases, the *crurifragium*, the breaking of the legs, was inflicted to shorten the death struggle. This was not necessary with Jesus (John 19:33) since He was already dead.

In all probability, the cross of the Lord was not a *crux commissa*, a cross with a cross beam on the end of the upright beam (St. Anthony's cross, in the form of a "T") but a *crux immissa,* a cross with a cross beam midway, or somewhat higher, on the upright beam. This is likely because a superscription was placed *above* Jesus' head: "This is Jesus, the King of the Jews" (Mt. 27: 37). On the basis of a few remarks by the ancient Christian writers Justin, Irenaeus, and Tertullian, we may safely assume that the cross of the Lord was fitted with a *sedile* or *cornu*, a crosspiece between the legs upon which the body could partially rest.

The crucifixion of Jesus was a proof that He bore the curse of sin (Gal. 3: 13). In the law of Moses it was already declared that the body of an evil-doer must be hung on a tree in order to make known that "he that is hanged is accursed of God" (Deut. 21:22, 23). Hanging on the tree, Jesus bore this curse with full consciousness. Thus He became obedient to the death of the cross (Phil. 2:8).

The gospel writers are unanimous as to the day on which the Lord was crucified. It was a Friday. Matthew (27:26) and Luke (23:54) say that it was the day of the preparation, the latter writer that "the sabbath drew on." Mark expressly mentions Friday, saying that it was "the day before the sabbath" (Mark 15:42). John likewise mentions the day of preparation and reports that the body might not remain on the cross on the sabbath (John 19:31).

There is, however, a problem in regard to the day. The first three evangelists say that Jesus celebrated the Passover with His disciples on the day before His death, which day according to Jewish chronology was 14 Nisan (Ex. 3:6), while it appears that John wishes to say that the Passover was still to be eaten after Jesus had been sentenced to death and consequently that the Lord was crucified on 14 Nisan. According to the synoptists, who place the Passover on 14 Nisan (Mt. 26:18, 19; Mark 14:12 ff.; Luke 22:7, 15), Jesus must have been put to death on 15 Nisan. John comments that the members of the Sanhedrin, after they had come to agreement that Jesus must be put to death, very early on the Friday morning of the crucifixion crowded before the hall of judgment where Pilate stayed during his residence in Jerusalem in order to deliver Jesus to this Roman procurator. They themselves did not enter the building so that they would not be defiled and so could eat the Passover (John 18:28). Moreover, just as Matthew and Luke, this evangelist speaks of the "preparation for the Passover" (John 19:14, cf. vs. 31). The principal difficulty in an attempt to bring the data of the Gospel according to John into agreement with that of the Synoptics occurs in John 18:28.

When this text is taken as a starting-point, then it must first of all be established that two groups of men played an important role in the arrest of Jesus Christ: in the first place, the company of soldiers with the servants of the Jews who took Jesus into custody in Gethsemane, and in the second place, the members of the Sanhedrin who passed the death sentence in their official session and thereupon proceeded to secure the execution of this sentence by the procurator as soon as possible (John 18:12, 13, 24). The procession that arrived at the praetorium was made up exclusively of these men, because it was early in the morning (Mt. 27:1), in the fourth watch. Pilate could expect the leaders of the people very early since they had conferred with him about Jesus' arrest and he had placed a detachment of soldiers from the citadel at their disposal (John 18:3, 12). Upon approaching the praetorium, the group divided: the soldiers, probably happy that the night action went off without very great difficulties, entered the inner court with their prisoner, but the members of the Jewish court remained standing outside so as not to be defiled.

Following the example of the members of the Sanhedrin, the men of the temple guard, who on the authority of the Sanhedrin took part in the arrest of Jesus, would also have remained outside (John 19:6). Thus, we read in John 18:28 nothing else than that the members of the Sanhedrin and the servants of the Jews still must eat the Passover. The celebration of the Passover, which according to the law already should have been eaten, they had postponed. The members of the Sanhedrin and their subordinates had deferred the celebration of the Passover so that they might take Jesus into custody without the interference of the multitude. There is but one reason that they went to such extremes: bitter animosity. Everything was permissible, if only Jesus could be put out of the way. All other considerations had to give way for this.

The Fourth Gospel also alludes to this. John, who so frequently spoke of the enmity of the Jews, draws attention in this case to the outrageous godlessness of the leaders of the people. He gives a striking illustration of the truth of the grave accusations that the Lord often brought against the leaders of the people. In order to arrest Jesus, the members of the Sanhedrin could indeed postpone the eating of the Passover for a day, from 14 to 15 Nisan, and that contrary to the law, but meanwhile they could not enter Pilate's judgment hall. Then they would have made themselves unclean! Here again the godlessness of the Jews is demonstrated. This procedure agrees with the characterization which the Lord Jesus Himself had given: "Even so ye also outwardly appear righteous unto men, but within ye are full of hypocrisy and iniquity" (Mt. 23:28). The Passover, of course, had to be celebrated strictly. The rules for exceptional situations were carefully defined in the law (Num. 9:9-12). It is clear that these rules could not be applied to the situation in which the members of the Sanhedrin suddenly came to stand through their postponement of the celebration of the Passover in connection with the arrest of Jesus. Anyone who did not eat the Passover was to be banished from the national community (Num. 9:13).

In this dilemma, the conflict between the leaders of the people and Jesus Christ reached a new peak. The members of the Jewish court desired the death of Jesus. At that point, the case was opened before Pilate. Concerning the course of events which the Synoptics report about the start of the trial, John speaks at the outset of the question of Pilate: "What accusation bring ye against this man?" (John 18:29), and the charge is: "If he were not a malefactor, we would not have delivered him up unto thee" (John 18:30). This accusation, that there was no longer a place for Jesus in society, is uttered by those who had carried their own godlessness so far that they had actually placed themselves outside the national community because they had not eaten the Passover at the appointed time. This is accentuated by John. He lays stress on some things the other Gospels omit, and in some respects gives a piquant supplement to the reports of the other evangelists.

Bibliography:

N. Geldenhuys, *Commentary on the Gospel of Luke* (Grand Rapids, 1951), 649-670.
E. G. Hirsch, *The Crucifixion* (New York, 1921).
U. Holzmeister, *Crux domini atque Crucificio* (Roma, 1934).
H. Mulder, "De datum der kruisiging," *GThT* (1951).

Harry Mulder

CROWN, something pre-eminent in the structure of things.

(1) As a significant part of architecture. In the structure of the human body, as fashioned by the Divine Architect (Gen. 1:27), the head becomes the "crown" (Gen. 49:27; Deut. 33:20; II Sam. 14:25; Job 2:7; Isa. 3:17; Jer. 2:16; 48:45). In a somewhat different sense, and yet still pregnant with implications of Divine majesty, the table of shewbread (Ex. 25:24 f.; 37:11 f.), the ark of the covenant (Ex. 25:11; 37:2), and the altar of incense (Ex. 30:3 f.; 37:26 f.) were fashioned with a "crown"—that is, gold moldings.

(2) As a significant part of adornment. Here the word is used figuratively of wisdom (Prov. 4:9), of a worthy woman (Prov. 12:4), of riches (Prov. 14:24), of the hoary head (Prov. 16:3), of grandchildren (Prov. 17:6), of blessings (Ps. 65:11; 103:4), and of personal (Job 19:9; 31:36) and national (Isa. 28:1, 3; Jer. 13:18; Lam. 5:16) honor and sovereignty.

(3) As a symbol of authority. It is thus used in a threefold way: (a) among heathen kings (I Chron. 20:2; Esther 1:11; 2:17; 6:8; 8:15); (b) among Hebrew kings (II Sam. 1:10; 12:30; II Kings 11:12); and (c) among the high priests of Israel (Ex. 28:36 f.; 29:6; 39:30 f.; Lev. 8:9; 21:12). The crown, worn on the head and set with jewels (Zech. 9:6), thus became a symbol of position and of authority (II Sam. 12:30).

(4) As a symbol of Christ's reign. The various aspects of His "crowning" may be noted thus: (a) His "crowning" was definitely predicted in the OT. This fact is latent in the description of rulership belonging to Israel's coming King (Gen. 49:10; Num. 24:17; Ps. 60:7; 108:8); it becomes patent in the references to the "crowning" of the coming Messiah (Ps. 21:3, 5; cf. 8:5; Song of S. 3:11). (b) His "crowning" was typified and pantomimed when Joshua, exercising the dual rights of leader and of high priest in the post-captivity period, was symbolically "crowned" as The BRANCH who "shall be a priest upon his throne" (Zech. 6:9-15). (c) His "crowning" was perniciously perverted by the Roman soldiers who derisively put "a crown of thorns" upon our Savior's head (Mt. 27:29; Mark 15:17; John 19:2, 5). They did this because they did not know "the Lord of glory" (I Cor. 2:8). (d) His "crowning" was gloriously perfected when He, after His resurrection, sat down "on the right hand of the throne of the Majesty in the heavens" (Heb. 8:1), "crowned with glory and honor" (Heb. 2:9). Then the words spoken to Mary by Gabriel (Luke 1:32 f.) were wonderfully fulfilled, as Peter faithfully shows (Acts 2:29-36; based upon II Sam. 7:12 f., 16). As the "crowned" King, our Lord now goes forth "conquering, and to conquer" (Rev. 6:2; cf. Mt. 24:14). In His blessed Second Coming He shall come forth, with "many crowns" on His head, as "KING OF KINGS, AND LORD OF LORDS" (Rev. 19:11-16). Then the church, like "the daughters of Zion" in the symbolic description, will be encouraged to "go forth" to their King Jesus "with the crown wherewith his mother crowned him in the day of his espousal" (Song of S. 3:11; cf. Ps. 24:7-10; Rev. 12:1). (e) His "crowning," however, will be ignominiously plagiarized by the powers of anti-Christianity (Rev. 9:7); both the "great red dragon" (Rev. 12:3) and the "beast" (Rev. 13:1) wear usurped "crowns" upon their heads. But as David, the spiritual prototype of our Lord, "took the crown of their king from off his head . . . and it was set upon David's head" (I Chron. 20:2), so our King Jesus, "having on his head a golden crown, and in his hand a sickle," will surely subdue the forces of the anti-Christ (Rev. 14:14-18; cf. Ps. 132:18).

(5) As a symbol of reward. Here a threefold distinction may be made: (a) The reward given as a "crown" to national Israel—"And I put a beautiful crown upon thine head" (Ezek. 16:12; cf. Rom. 9:4). (b) The reward to be given as a "crown" to spiritual Israel "in that day" (the Messianic age) when the Lord shall be "for a crown of glory, and for a diadem of beauty, unto the residue of his people" (Isa. 28:5; cf. 62:3; Zech. 9:16; Rom. 2:28 f.). (c) The reward to be given as a "crown" to members of the body of Christ. This "crown" is a "crown of rejoicing" (I Thess. 2:19; cf. Phil. 4:1), "of righteousness" (II Tim. 4:8), "of life" (James 1:12; Rev. 2:10), "of glory" (I Pet. 5:4), and "incorruptible" (I Cor. 9:25; cf. Prov. 27:24). In the beatific world, however, the saints of God will "cast their crowns before the throne" and worship the eternal God (Rev. 4:4, 10), though now and up until the time our King returns it is incumbent upon each of us to hold that fast which we have, that no man take our crown (Rev. 3:11).

Bibliography:

W. F. Boyd, *HDAC* I (1916), 269, s.v.
A. Israel and S. A. Cook, "Crown," *EB* I (1899), 961-963.
J. A. MacCulloch, *HERE* IV (1912), 336-342, s.v.
M. S. and J. L. Miller (eds.), *Harper's Bible Dictionary* (New York, 1952), 120, s.v.
G. T. Purves, *HDB* I (1898), 529-531, s.v.
W. E. Raffety, *ISBE* II (1930), 762-763, s.v.

M. F. Unger (ed.), *Unger's Bible Dictionary* (Chicago, 1959), 228-229, s.v.
E. Venables, *DCA* I (1875), 506-511, s.v.

WICK BROOMALL

CRUCIFIXION. See CROSS.

CRUCIGER, Caspar (1504-1548), Lutheran theologian. Cruciger studied first at Leipzig, where he witnessed the debate between Luther and Eck in 1519, and later at Wittenberg (where his parents had moved to escape the plague). In 1525 he became pastor and rector of the school at Maagdenburg, and in 1528 professor at the University of Wittenberg, where he also served as pastor. Cruciger was a co-worker of Luther, for example, in Luther's translation of the Bible. Theologically, however, he was closer to Melanchthon. Cruciger took part in the religious discussions at Hagenau, Worms, and Regensburg in 1540 and 1541, about which he sent reports to Justus Jonas. There he also met Calvin. Cruciger participated in the publication of the works of Luther.

D. NAUTA

CRUCIGER, Caspar (1525-1597) Lutheran theologian. Son of Caspar Cruciger (1504-1548), he also became professor at Wittenberg, at first in the philosophical but later in the theological faculty. He became the successor of Melanchthon and was viewed as the leader of the Philippists. He was accused of crypto-Calvinism (*q.v.*), so that he had to leave Wittenberg in 1576. Subsequently he was active as president of the Consistorium at Kassel.

D. NAUTA

CRUDEN, Alexander (1701-1770), compiler of the *Biblical Concordance*. Born in Aberdeen, Scotland, he graduated M.A. from Aberdeen University at the age of 19. He early showed the persistence in study which enabled him in later years to become a most accurate proofreader and to compile his famous *Concordance*.

The same characteristic in another direction proved his undoing. His unwelcome persistence in an unrequited love affair led to a mental breakdown, and for a short period he was confined as a lunatic. Soon afterwards (1737), while a bookseller in London, he published the first edition of his *Complete Concordance of the Old and New Testaments*, which is his lasting memorial, and an invaluable service to the cause of Bible study.

He suffered further confinements in asylums, but in later years his mental instability took the form of eccentricity. He was intensely concerned about the decline in morals throughout the country, and his work as a corrector of proofs gave him the idea that he might become an official corrector of public morals. He called himself Alexander the Corrector and vainly petitioned Parliament (1755) to have him officially appointed to this post.

In 1762 his persistent efforts to secure royal clemency for an unfortunate sailor who had been condemned to death for forging a seaman's will led to his visitation of Newgate Prison and to a sustained endeavor to improve the lot of prisoners. Throughout his life he was an assiduous tract-distributor. A servant in his house, whom he had rescued from a life of shame on the streets, found his body when he died in the attitude of prayer.

BIBLIOGRAPHY:
E. Olivier, *The Eccentric Life of Alexander Cruden* (London, 1934).
L. Stephen (ed.), "Cruden, Alexander," *DNB* London, 1888).

HUGH J. BLAIR

CRUELTY. In the AV the words *cruel*, *cruelly*, and *cruelty* appear only in the OT. They are used to translate several words in Hebrew having a similar meaning. There are a number of actions recorded in the OT which in their very nature merit the description of cruel. Some of these are prompted by revenge, as the slaughter of the men of Shechem by Simeon and Levi (Gen. 34:25); "Simeon and Levi are brethren; instruments of cruelty are in their habitations" (Gen. 49:5). Some are carried out by God's servants, such as the slaying of the prophets of Baal by Elijah (I Kings 18:40). Again, what may appear as cruel actions were commanded by God, as, for example, the destruction of the Canaanites (Deut. 7:2).

Because these cruel acts are recorded in the OT, certain critics have asserted that the spirit of Christ did not prevail in those times, that the moral standards were lower, and that the idea of "an eye for an eye and a tooth for a tooth" was abolished by Christ and replaced by the law of love. There is no need, however, to explain away these acts of cruelty or regard the OT Scriptures as inferior. They impress upon us at least three important facts: (1) the total depravity of the human heart and the terrible depths to which sin drags its victim; (2) the holiness of God manifested in His hatred of the abominations of the heathen and His judgment upon sin; and (3) The warning given to the Lord's people against the toleration of that which is false in their midst.

ALEXANDER BARKLEY

CRUSADES

I. Historical Background
II. The First Crusade
III. The Latin Kingdom of Jerusalem
IV. Later Crusades
V. The Failure of the Crusades
VI. The Results of the Crusades

The Crusades may be described, broadly, as the struggle in Palestine between Christianity and Islam, from 1096 to 1291. The name comes from the cross worked into the clothing of the Christian armies.

I. Historical Background

Since the end of the 10th century, W Christendom had been recovering ground lost to Islam, but E Christians had lost control of almost all of Asia Minor to the Seljuk Turks, who captured Jerusalem in 1071. Local Christians were subsequently persecuted, it became more difficult for pilgrims from the W to visit the Holy Land, and plans of W merchants for further trade with the Orient were frustrated.

The E emperor, Alexius Comnenus, appealed in 1095 to Pope Urban II for reinforcements to recover Asia Minor, but papal policy read this as an invitation to a holy war whose object was to recover Jerusalem. Urban was at the time having trouble with an upstart antipope; Philip I of France was excommunicate; the emperor, Henry IV, was at loggerheads with Rome; the English king, William Rufus, tended to ignore the papacy; and the kings of Spain were fully occupied in fighting the Moors. The church, in fact, seemed to be losing its grip on the policies of Europe.

Nothing unites people so much as a common antagonism, and Urban seized this as a solution to his problems. In a great speech he launched the First Crusade: Let the Truce of God be observed at home and Christian forces unite against the infidel, a deed which would count for complete penance. Urban, a great believer in channelling the fighting propensities of the laity, had visions of extending the Roman sway ultimately to the Holy Land itself.

The time was auspicious in other ways. In 1094 the plague was raging from Flanders to Bohemia; in 1095 there was famine in Lorraine. There was a restlessness abroad, seen both in a people seeking escape from inflexible feudalism and in aristocratic younger sons fired by adventure and realizing the necessity for making their own way in the world.

Many others saw the defense of the Holy Places as a quest after the eternal verities and a cause worth dying for.

II. The First Crusade

The First Crusade is the most important, and set the tone of much that was to follow. It represented all classes: as well as professional soldiers there were merchants, couriers, minstrels, medieval carpet-baggers, failures, malcontents, unfrocked monks, escaped serfs, beggars, and hoboes—a staggering proportion of the submerged tenth of humanity such as was involved in the gold rushes of modern times.

The enterprise posed many problems, with narrow roads jammed by Crusaders trekking across Europe. Food prices rocketed, a simple economic phenomenon for which Armenians and Greeks were conveniently blamed. Disorganization was further aggravated by the number of non-combatants—menials, peasants with their families, wives of Crusaders, adventuresses, pious pilgrims, clergy—who probably outnumbered the fighting men and greatly hindered the army.

Urban appointed his legate, Adhémar de Puy, as ecclesiastical head of the expedition, and the Crusaders elected Stephen of Blois as their first leader. Matters of policy were usually settled at a council of the leaders, lay and ecclesiastical. Even within each band matters were usually decided at a common council, but difficulties of discipline under the new conditions were enormous for those whose only basis of allegiance was the feudal oath. In addition, adventurous knights often went off on marauding expeditions without consulting their leaders.

Nevertheless, progress was made. The army learned much in the art of warfare, as is reflected in the stronger castles which appeared in Europe during the 12th century. The city of Nicea, capital of the Seljuk kingdom of Rūm, was the first to fall, and this was followed by victory at Dorylaeum. With many dropping by the wayside, the army crossed the arid highlands of Asia Minor and, after a long siege which reduced them to dire straits, took the strongly fortified Antioch in June, 1098. Although they were besieged and threatened with famine, their failing fortunes were revived by an alleged miracle which so boosted morale that they inflicted a crushing defeat on the Seljuks.

Petty jealousies among the Crusading leaders ensued there after the death of Adhémar, who had been a tremendous influence for good on the whole expedition. At last they restarted and, after abandoning a design to besiege Arkah, marched S along the coast via Beirut, Sidon, Tyre, Acre, Haifa, and Caesarea. Turning inland, they reached Ramleh on June 2 and Jerusalem on June 7, 1099. The comparative immunity from attack on their way to the Holy City (and the subsequent consolidation of Christian states) is partly explicable in terms of internal disruption among the Seljuks after the death in 1092 of the last of the three great sultans.

The first frenzied assault on Jerusalem failed, but another mystical incident occurred at an opportune moment. Peter the Hermit dreamed that Adhémar appeared to him and declared that if the besiegers, putting away all uncleanness and being reconciled to one another, would march around the walls, calling upon God and fasting, the city would be taken by the ninth day. The instructions carried out, a breach was made in the NE wall and another entry effected from the S. "There might no prayers nor crying for mercy avail," as 70,000 people, including women and children, died in the slaughter. Night came and, drenched in blood, the victors "came rejoicing, nay for exceeding joy weeping, to the tomb of our Saviour to adore and give thanks."

The First Crusade broke up the Seljuk kingdom of Rūm, restored to the Greeks the coastline and part of the interior of Asia Minor; gave the Crusaders several fortresses and vantage points; and led to the establishment of the Latin Kingdom of Jerusalem, with the dependent but not always subservient principalities of Antioch, Tripoli, and Edessa.

III. The Latin Kingdom of Jerusalem

We can do no more than sketch the salient features of a Kingdom that had 11 kings in a century. Perhaps its supreme defect was its lack of a sound financial basis. The church, the richest proprietor in the Holy Land, was virtually immune from taxation—thus helping to ruin the Kingdom which, above all others, it should have supported. The two greatest military orders—Templars and Hospitallers—took advantage of their half-lay and half-clerical position to evade the responsibilities of either. They amassed wealth, quarreled among themselves and with the clergy, interfered in political matters, and negotiated separately with the Mohammedans. Their force of arms made them indispensable (and they later rendered notable service in the prolonged rearguard action from 1187 to 1291).

Other factors contributed to the Kingdom's downfall. The climate sapped both the physical strength and the moral fiber of its rulers, and the work to be done was too much for them. Fresh blood from the W never came in any great quantity (the one thing which could have saved the day), and often those who did come were bad characters transported E as a penance.

In addition, the Crusading States were riddled with adventurers who robbed Saracen travelers and held them for ransom. Infidels the Mohammedan might tolerate, but not brigands. Moreover, over-taxation and intolerance estranged the indigenous churches, such as the Nestorian, and there is evidence to suggest that Jerusalem was betrayed to Saladin in 1187 by Christian Melchites. In contrast to the Christians, Saladin treated the people with great clemency.

IV. Later Crusades

The Second Crusade (1147-49) had been a complete failure, and subsequent years saw a gradual consolidation of Mohammedan power under Saladin, whose capture of Jerusalem sparked off the Third Crusade (1188-92). French-English rivalry proved its undoing, but Richard I of England in 1192 made a three-year peace with Saladin, and small groups of Crusaders were allowed to visit the Holy Sepulchre. The Fourth Crusade (1202-4) was diverted into attacking a usurping Greek emperor at Constantinople, and merely served to deteriorate further the relations between E and W Christians. The pathetic Children's Crusade in 1212 suffered tragically: the small number which did disembark from S France and Italy soon perished.

The Fifth Crusade (1217-21), during which St. Francis began a wide missionary activity, was largely an Egyptian campaign, but in the Sixth (1228-29) Emperor Frederick II secured by treaty possession of Nazareth, Bethlehem, and Jerusalem. In the latter city, control of which was retained for 15 years, he had himself crowned king in March, 1229. The Seventh Crusade (1248-54) was notable merely in that it was led by St. Louis of France and was carried out not only against the heathen but also against Frederick II, who was excommunicate. Louis and his brother undertook the Eighth and last Crusade (1270), but it became exhausted after Louis' death at Tunis, and soon the whole of the former

Kingdom of Jerusalem passed into Islamic hands.

V. The Failure of the Crusades

Various factors contributed to the failure of the Crusades. One glaring defect was the lack of sea-power, which would have obviated the long march overland through Hungary, the E Empire, and across the deserts and mountains of Asia Minor. Sea-power, which was in the hands of the Greeks or of the Italian cities, was largely denied them. The Greek Empire (for reasons mentioned below) soon became bitterly antagonistic to all Crusades; Venice had become the former's ally; and Genoa was intent on guarding its trade in the Crimea.

The division of Christendom was probably the chief cause of failure. From the start the Crusades were a French movement; thus the Germans did little. Even more serious were the strained relations with the E emperor. Right at the outset Alexius had insisted that whatever the Crusaders conquered was done in his name. Moreover, Westerners never forgot that the Greek emperors had earlier taken advantage of their protectorate of the Holy Places to impose taxes on pilgrims. The resultant wrangling helped to lose Edessa in 1144 and hastened the ruin of the Latin Kingdom. It should be added, however, that there was nothing in the first Crusaders' conduct to endear them to Alexius.

The Crusades ended not in the occupation of the E by the Christian W, but in the invasion of the W by the Mohammedan E. They began with the Seljuk Turk camped at Nicea; they ended with the Ottoman Turk entrenched by the Danube.

VI. The Results of the Crusades

Among the results was the colonization of the Kingdoms of Jerusalem and Cyprus, and the Latin Empire of Constantinople, and the emergence from military orders (once charitable societies) of commercial companies with banks, navies, and considerable lands. Trade was greatly stimulated by the incentive to find a route for the diffusion throughout Europe of the E commodities which began to pour into Venice and Genoa. The result was a long line of municipal development from Venice, over the Brenner Pass, and up the Rhine to Bruges. Along this route in Lombardy, Germany, and Flanders, the great towns of the Middle Ages were established.

Another sphere affected by the Crusades was geography in the discovery of the interior of Asia and also the composition of books written to guide the pilgrim in his travels from one sacred spot of Bible history to another. Impulse was given also to the writing of history, and this produced notably William of Tyre's *Historia Transmarina,* perhaps the greatest historical work of medieval times.

Looking at the three great powers most nearly affected by the Crusades, we find that France emerged at the end of the 13th century as the greatest power in Europe; the results of her colonization of the Levant can still be traced today. The E empire, having been virtually annihilated ironically by the movement it had instigated in 1095, survived tenuously into the 15th century as a pale shadow of its former self, with its hold on Asia Minor slight and with diminishing influence in Greece and the Archipelago, which the Latins occupied till driven out by the Ottoman Turks. The papacy, however, had grown as a result of the Crusades. Popes had preached them, financed them, sent legates to lead them, and through them had directed the foreign policy of Europe. But if the Crusades had magnified the papacy, they had also corrupted it, taught it the expediency of crying

Crusade when there was no Crusade, and of using this magic gimmick for its own purposes, which were all too often saturated with secular self-seeking.

In spite of all worldly motives, the Crusades stand as an astonishing symbol of Christianity's power and challenge. They caught men's imagination in a quite unparalled way. They were bound up with the age-old lie of popes that salvation could be bought at little price (a gross error that they shared with their Islamic adversaries). Yet no one can deny in them the element of jealousy for God's holy Name, a concern that sites associated with the Savior's earthly life should neither be desecrated nor barred to the faithful, and a desire to extend the kingdom of God upon earth.

BIBLIOGRAPHY:
E. Barker, *The Crusades* (Oxford, 1923).
R. D. Lobban, *The Crusades* (London, 1966).
S. Runciman, *A History of the Crusades,* 3 vols. (New York, 1951-54).
K. M. Setton, ed., *History of the Crusades* (University of Wisconsin, 1955).
H. B. Workman, "Crusades," in *HERE* (vol. 4, pp. 345-351).

JAMES DIXON DOUGLAS

CRYPTO-CALVINISM, a term used in the second half of the 16th century to designate the position of the followers of Melanchthon regarding the doctrine of the Lord's supper. In Germany, beginning with the violent attack by Joachim Westphal (1552), opposition to Calvin's doctrine of the Lord's supper broke loose with new strength and became the occasion for a whole series of local conflicts (for example, between Joh. Timann and Alb. Hardenberg in Bremen). Meanwhile, however, a totally different position was being developed by Melanchthon's followers at the University of Wittenberg. Melanchthon himself remained notably silent with respect to these renewed disputes. However, already during the latter years of his life and also after his death (1560), his followers supported Calvin's propositions in increasing measure. At first, they managed to persuade Elector August that they were only turning against certain extreme views of the Lutherans. But in 1574 the elector arrived at a different opinion, partly as a consequence of the appearance of an anonymously published writing of a physician, Joachim Curaens, in which he rejected the bodily enjoyment of Christ in the Lord's supper, the eating of His body by unbelievers, and the omnipresence of His human nature, and in which he set forth a program envisioning an agreement regarding the Lord's supper among all those who were committed to the Reformation. This opened the elector's eyes. At the diet of Torgau, strict rules for church visitation were enacted in order to check these notions. One of the influential figures in the background, Kaspar Peucer, Melanchthon's son-in-law and the elector's personal physician, ended up in prison. He was not released until 1586, upon the accession of the new elector, Christian I, during whose short rule the Melanchthonian school of thought at Wittenberg had a chance once more. However, with his death in 1591, the possibilities of crypto-Calvinism in Germany were over. Only in Denmark was it able to survive for a few more decades.

See LORD'S SUPPER, MELANCHTHON, PEUCER.

Y. FEENSTRA

CUDWORTH, Ralph (1617-1688), English divine. Son of an Anglican rector, he became Regius Professor of Hebrew at Cambridge in 1645 (a post he held till his death), to which was added in 1654 the mastership of Christ's College. Cudworth was in many ways the most distinguished exponent of the Cambridge Platonist school, which generally took up a middle position between Puritans and High Churchmen. Like his colleagues, he disliked religious dogmatism; but even less was he enamored of materialism, whether advocated by Hobbes or by Spinoza. The Platonists' philosophy was adequately summed up by one of them, John Smith: "To follow reason is to follow God." Cudworth, who is remembered as having formulated the theory of a "plastic nature," declared: "Things are what they are, not by Will but by Nature." He asserted the need for revealed religion, was a staunch advocate of the reality of moral freedom and responsibility, and was convinced that the "impossibility" of atheism was demonstrable. He was imperfectly understood, however, partly because of his habit of introducing much extraneous lore into his arguments, partly because of his scrupulously fair delineation of his adversaries' views—a procedure to which his controversial age was notably unaccustomed. A well-known if somewhat diffuse scholar, he was consulted in 1657 by a parliamentary committee exploring the need for a new translation of the Bible. Cudworth's chief works were *The True Intellectual System of the Universe* (1678); and a *Treatise concerning Eternal and Immutable Morality* (published posthumously in 1731), directed in part against Calvinism.

JAMES DIXON DOUGLAS

CULLMANN, Oscar (1902–), German NT scholar and theologian. Born in Strasbourg, Cullmann studied at the University of Strasbourg and at Paris. He then became lecturer in NT exegesis at Strasbourg and then professor of NT at the University of Basel (1938).

In early years, Cullmann tried to study the relationship of Jewish Christianity to gnosticism. He later became a leading exponent of the *Heilsgeschichte* (Salvation-history) movement (*q.v.*) in modern German critical theology. According to Cullmann certain points of time, *kairoi*, were chosen by God out of the time-line as a whole to have redemptive significance, and the central *kairos* is the life, death, and resurrection of Jesus Christ (see *Christ and Time*). To have authentic Christian faith one has to understand the redemptive *kairoi*, which can only be done through regeneration by faith in the Christ of the *kairoi*.

Cullmann, however, does not hold to the inerrancy and plenary inspiration of Scripture, in spite of the evangelical sounding position he puts forth. Whatever is found in the Bible that is not a part of the *Heilsgeschichte*, the *kairoi*, is not an item that can be depended upon. The story of Adam and the prophecies of the end-time are also not a part of *Heilsgeschichte*, but are *myths* (see MYTH). As a result, Cullmann is another who accepts destructive Bible criticism to a point where it tears the heart out of Christian theology. Desiring to hold on to Christ, he is unable to receive the sovereign plan of God and loses the fulness of the truth of Scripture.

G. R. JAFFRAY, JR.

CULTS. The terms *sect* and *cult* have been used synonymously in recent years (cf. Gerstner's *The Theology of the Major Sects* and Van Baalen's *Chaos of the Cults*) to designate any organized group originating on the fringes of the Christian church that consciously or unconsciously places tradition, human interpretation, or supposed revelations on a par with or above Scripture, and that claims, therefore, a monopoly upon essential truth (usually declaring itself to be the only true church). Such groups make such a basic error that they stray eventually, if not at the outset, into a denial of one or more fundamental doctrines of the Scriptures, perverting the Gospel, and showing that they are not a part of the Christian fold.

Originally the word *sect* (from Latin *sequi*, "to follow"; in Scripture *hairesis*, "an organized school of thought") always meant a division or school *within* a religion. An Acts 26:5, the Pharisees are called the strictest sect of the Jewish religion, and in I Cor. 11:19, Paul also speaks of "divisions *among you.*" The word *hairesis* etymologically refers to a "choice" that is "seized upon," a "selection of one party or idea from among others." The word *sect* is nearly equivalent to *denomination.* Only in the late second century did the term come to be used of other religions that should be excluded from the Christian church.

In contrast, the term *cult* (from Latin *cultus*) has never been used to describe parties or divisions *within* the Christian church, but has always designated organized heretical groups *outside* of the church and is the prefered term. *Cult* came to mean "a carefully cultivated system of religious worship or ritual." The term stresses *devoted* attachment or extravagant admiration for a person, principle, or cause. The word has especially come to designate a heretical religious group that claims to be Christian but is not.

The NT explicitly takes note of early cultic deviations and combats them. God commands, "Try [test] the spirits" (I John 4:1), and the "discerning of spirits" is said to be a gift from Him (I Cor. 12:10). Ministers are frequently enjoined to protect the flock from heretical wolves (cf. Acts 20:28-31; John 10; Titus 1:9-11; II John; Jude), and churches are commended for such alertness (Rev. 2:2; note in contrast Rev. 2:20).

Fundamentally, cults originate when the Scriptures are rejected as the only standard of faith and practice (cf. I John 4:1-6 with Deut. 13:1-4; the doctrine of the apostles recorded in the Scriptures is normative). The cults may therefore be divided into several categories:

A. *Those that add to the Scriptures*
   1. Revelation added
      a. Spoken (e.g., Spiritualism)
      b. Written (e.g., Mormonism)
   2. Infallible interpretation—or interpretation on a par with the Bible (e.g., Seventh-Day Adventists)

B. *Those that subtract from the Scriptures* (e.g., the Churches of Christ, who reject the OT).

The "Big Six" cults with a combined membership exceeding six million are:

1. Churches of Christ (Abilene group)
2. Seventh-Day Adventists
3. Jehovah's Witnesses
4. Christian Science
5. Mormonism
6. Unity

Probably today Herbert W. and Garner Ted Armstrong's "Radio Church of God" should be included as a seventh. Spiritism, in various forms, together with astrology, is also enjoying a world-wide resurgence.

The original Big Six may be classified in another manner—by the historical-doctrinal thrust of the movement with which each is associated. Three movements may be distinguished:

1. The Restoration Movement
2. The Healing Movement
3. The Adventist Movement

Restoration Cults

The Churches of Christ, founded by Thomas and Alexander Campbell, are doctrinally and historically related to Mormonism. Sidney Rigdon, one of the originators of Mormonism, delivered his congregation to Joseph Smith as the first Mormon assembly. The Mormon church was originally known as the Church of Christ, a specifically Campbellite designation, and early adopted the Campbellite definition of the Gospel (faith, repentance, and baptism) with but one addition: the laying on of hands for the reception of the Holy Spirit. Both groups claim to be the apostolic church *restored* (in contrast to *reformation* churches they claim *restoration* status). There are various groups—clustered rather than closely organized—that are known by the name Churches of Christ, and they are growing very rapidly also. The Mormons themselves are divided into a number of bodies, the most significant of which are The Church of Jesus Christ of Latter Day Saints (Salt Lake City) and The Church of Jesus Christ of Latter Day Saints, Reorganized (Independence, Mo.).

The healing groups are numerous, but Christian Science and Unity School of Christianity are two of the largest. Both schools stem from the healing practices of Phineas P. Quimby and, in the case of Christian Science, a manuscript by Franz Lieber on Hegel. The fundamental thesis of Christian Science is that "God is all." The entire system flows from this presupposition:

Healing Cults

If God is all . . .
- and God is sinless, then there is no sin;
- and God is impervious to sickness, then there is no sickness;
- and God is deathless, then there is no death;
- and God is spirit, then there is no matter.

Unity, until the Armstrongs began publication, was the largest mail-order religion in America, publishing over a dozen magazines and numerous books and pamphlets. The genius of this cult is found in the idea of the affirmation of truth sayings. Prayer, which plays a major part in this religion, is not prayer to a personal God, but instead the repetition of a positive affirmation or truth saying. Unity also stresses vegetarianism.

The third large movement is Adventism. Both Seventh-Day Adventism and Jehovah's Witnesses have a common origin in the Adventist movement begun by William Miller. After Miller repudiated his views following his failures to predict the date of Christ's second coming, Ellen G. White, in conjunction with several others, emerged as the prophetess of what came to be known as the Seventh-Day Adventist Church. Charles Taze Russell, the founder of the Jehovah's Witnesses (and the succeeding group called the Dawn Bible Study Movement) studied with Seventh-Day Adventists and even wrote a book, *The Three Worlds*, in conjunction with a Seventh-Day Adventist minister. Russell soon went his own way and took his turn also at predicting Christ's return (several times unsuccessfully). The Jehovah's Witnesses are once again predicting the end of all things in the middle or end of the 1970's.

Adventist Cults

Herbert W. Armstrong and his son, Garner Ted, the newest successful cultists, are not so much a part of any one of the above three movements as they are a result of the cultic picture in general. They offer a smorgasbord of beliefs similar to British Israelism, Seventh-Day Adventism, the Jehovah's Witnesses, etc., to which they have added an original element or two of their own. Armstrong's unique view that God is a family of which Christians become a part, is a particularly dangerous doctrine of which Christians should become aware. Precisely what he means is quite difficult to determine, because doctrine is treated sensationally rather than systematically in all his numerous free publications.

The cults may be studied with profit biographically, historically, critically (with special reference to changes in their unique documents; the cults have a history of altering their original publications), doctrinally, and practically (how they organize, evangelize, etc.). Such study reveals certain similarities among many of the cults. A list of these follows:

1. There was an explicit rejection of Calvinism on the part of many of the founders of the cults (e.g., Campbell, Eddy, Russell).

2. The cults offer "green stamps." Usually, the cults not only capitalize upon the failures of the Christian church (when prophetic study waned, Adventism prospered; when the church abandoned its ministry to the psychosomatically sick, the healing movement arose; when the church was torn by unloving factions, restorationism flourished) but usually go further in offering bonuses of various sorts.

3. The devotion and zeal of the adherents and their knowledge of its doctrinal system are apparent. However, if you speak to one Jehovah's Witness, you have spoken to them all. The training in the cults tends to be highly regimented. Adherents learn the party line in the interpretation of verses and in approach.

4. There has been a leading place given to women in the origin of many (not all) of the cults (e.g., Spiritism, Christian Science, Seventh-Day Adventism, Unity, Theosophy) that contradicts I Tim. 2:11-15, in which the two tasks of the eldership (ruling and teaching) are forbidden to them. It is informative to note in the passage that one of Paul's reasons for the prohibition was Eve's susceptibility to deception.

5. Fraud and deception occur in the beginning and history of the cult. Revelations supposedly from God have been tampered with, books have been altered without changing publication dates, and original materials have been suppressed by various cults.

A student of the cults is necessarily a student of doctrine and of church history. One fact he must face is that of the failures and weaknesses of the true church. The study is important in protecting the flock from error and in winning those ensnared in the heresies of the cults. For these reasons every pastor should instruct his people concerning the basic errors of the major cults.

Bibliography:

J. H. Gerstner, *The Theology of the Major Sects* (Grand Rapids, 1963).

A. A. Hoekema, *The Four Major Cults* (Grand Rapids, 1963).

W. R. Martin, *The Kingdom of the Cults* (Grand Rapids, 1965).

F. F. Mayer, *The Religious Bodies of America* (St. Louis, 1961).

J. K. Van Baalen, *The Chaos of the Cults* (Grand Rapids, 1956).

Jay E. Adams

CUMBERLAND, Richard (1631-1718), English moral philosopher and bishop. Educated at St. Paul's College, London (1653), and Magdalene College, Cambridge (1656), Cumberland took up the study of medicine, but never practiced it. Afterwards, he took up theological studies (B.D., 1663, and D.D., 1680). He became chaplain to the Lord Keeper of London, rector of Bampton, Northamptonshire, preacher to Cambridge University, rector of Allhallows, Stamford, and finally bishop of Peterborough.

Cumberland wrote *De legibus naturae disquisitio philosophica* (1670) (tr. by John Towers as *A Philosophical Enquiry into the Laws of Nature*, 1750). For him there was one fundamental law of nature to which all others could be reduced. That one law was the common good of all. By knowing the Existence of God as the cause of the laws of nature, Cumberland tried to derive on that basis this fundamental law from nature. In that way he tried to refute Hobbes's philosophy, which tried to determine what were natural laws by arguing only from a comparison of various cultures in different eras. He had great influence on Samuel Clarke and the Earl of Shaftesbury. He also influenced Butler,

Hutcheson, Hume, Adam Smith, Jeremy Bentham, and John Stuart Mill.

In rejecting Scripture as a foundation Cumberland only aided the development of anti-Christian humanistic thought.

CUN (in AV Chun), a city of Hadadezer, king of Zobah, whom David defeated. From this place and from Tibhath David took a great amount of bronze which was used by Solomon for the making of certain vessels of the temple (I Chron. 18:8). In the parallel passage, II Sam. 8:8, the names Betah and Berothai occur. It has been suggested that Cun might be the same as Berothai, which would be the same as the Berothah of Ezek. 47:16. On the other hand, Cun has been identified with the modern Râs Ba'albek, located between Hamath and Damascus.

CUNEIFORM WRITING. See WRITING, ANCIENT.

CUNNINGHAM, William (1805-1861), leader of the Free Church of Scotland. A native of Hamilton, Scotland, he had a distinguished career at Edinburgh University, and was greatly influenced in student days by the preaching of Dr. Robert Gordon, who became the means of winning his wholehearted support for the Evangelical cause. His first charge was at the Middle Church, Greenock, and his powers as a debater almost immediately brought him into prominence in the General Assembly. In 1834 he moved to Trinity College Church, Edinburgh. In the ecclesiastical controversies of those years he became a stout supporter of Dr. Chalmers in contending for the spiritual independence of the church. When the Church of Scotland split over this issue in 1843, Cunningham received appointment as a professor in the newly constituted Free Church College ("New College"), Edinburgh, and, on the death of Dr. Chalmers in 1847, he became principal. He was moderator of the Free Church General Assembly in 1859.

Cunningham has been bracketed with Thomas Halyburton as one of the two greatest theologians that Scotland has ever produced. He was undoubtedly the foremost exponent of the Reformed faith in his day. He took a leading part in the founding of the *British and Foreign Evangelical Review* and was its editor from 1855 to 1860. Many of the best articles which appeared in its pages and in those of the *North British Review* were from his pen. He edited an edition of Stillingfleet's *Doctrines and Practices of the Church of Rome* and added greatly to the value of the original work by the copious notes which he contributed. Shortly before his death he committed his manuscripts to his two colleagues in the New College, James Buchanan and James Bannerman, who prepared them for publication. They extend to four massive volumes: *The Reformers and the Theology of the Reformation, Historical Theology* (2 vols.), and *Discussions on Church Principles.* In the first of these, his essay on "Calvinism and the Doctrine of Philosophical Necessity" is competently regarded as representative of his best work. Another volume of Cunningham's writings was edited by Thomas Smith and appeared under the title *Theological Lectures.* A volume of his sermons, with a biographical sketch, was edited by his friend Dr. J. J. Bonar of Greenock.

See FREE CHURCH OF SCOTLAND.

G. N. M. COLLINS

CUPBEARER, an official of high dignity at ancient Oriental courts, appointed to serve the monarch his wine. After washing and filling the royal goblet, the cupbearer, supporting it with three fingers, handed it gracefully to his sovereign in such a manner that not a single drop would be spilled. Before serving the wine, he tasted it himself as evidence that to his knowledge it was not poisoned. When not engaged in this service, he guarded the royal chamber, with authority to admit or bar visitors at his discretion. The intrigues of Oriental courts necessitated that the cupbearer be of trustworthy character, although attractive appearance seems to have been a secondary qualification. The cupbearer often enjoyed the king's friendship, confidence, and favor (Neh. 2). Several of these officials come into prominence in the OT: (1) Pharaoh's chief butler, or cupbearer (Gen. 40, 41); (2) the cupbearers of Solomon (I Kings 10:5; II Chron. 9:4); (3) Sennacherib's Rabshakeh, Aramaic for "chief of the cupbearers" (II Kings 18:17; Isa. 36:2); and (4) Nehemiah, cupbearer to Artaxerxes Longimanus of Persia (Neh. 1:11).

CURSE. Several Hebrew and Greek words are translated into English as "curse." They have in common the meaning that, because a responsibility to God has been broken, a judgment is pronounced. A curse is thus the reverse of a blessing. Both curse and blessing presuppose man's absolute obligation to obey God and to serve Him with heart, mind, and being. Because God is man's Creator and Sovereign Lord, man is absolutely bound to obey God in His every word. And even as the disobedience of man in Eden brought about his Fall and the curse, so man's restoration depended on Christ's perfect obedience. Tempted in the wilderness, which man's Fall and the curse on it had made of the world, Jesus Christ answered the tempter, "It is written, Man shall not live by bread alone, but by every word that proceedeth out of the mouth of God" (Mt. 4:3).

A covenant with God all the more, therefore, carried its promises of blessings and curses (Deut. 27, 28). An oath within the covenant invoked the covenant sanctions, which meant also the covenant curse for violations. Christ as man's substitute suffered the curse for His elect (Gal. 3:13).

A curse thus assumed prior authority; for this reason, no child could curse his parents without suffering death (Ex. 21:17), because he thereby overturned the whole structure of authority. On the other hand, a parent could curse an incorrigible son (Deut. 21:18-21), being in authority over him.

Bibliography:
M. G. Kline, *By Oath Consigned* (Grand Rapids, 1968).

Rousas John Rushdoony

CURSIVE SCRIPT, a way of writing Greek in a "running" hand. It was used for rough notes and the like. It could be written quickly and had little beauty. For important writings a more careful script called uncial was used. At a later time an attractive form of running hand was devised, but this is better called minuscule.

CUSANUS, Nicolaus. See Nicholas of Cusa.

CUSH, CUSHITES. Cush is described as the eldest son of Ham (Gen. 10:6) and the father of Seba, Havilah, Sabtah, Raamah, and Sabtecah. The name of Cush came to be applied to the land of Cush, or Ethiopia (modern Nubia), the portion of the Nile Valley S of the First Cataract at Seyene (modern Aswan). The AV translates Cush by either Cush or Ethiopia (Isa. 11:11; 18:1; Ezek. 29:10).

Cush was conquered and annexed by Egypt during the Twelfth Dynasty and usually was subject to Egypt after that time. After the decline of the Twenty-second (Libyan) Dynasty, Cushites became powerful and gradually encroached on N Egypt. An Ethiopian (i.e., Cushite) Dynasty actually ruled Egypt as the Twenty-fifth Dynasty, according to Manetho's reckoning. Tirhakah of that dynasty attempted to defeat the Assyrian king, Sennacherib.

Although primarily referring to the district in Africa S of Egypt, Cush had important relations with Arabia, where several of the sons of Cush are said to have settled. Egypt and Cush are associated in a majority of the instances in which the word appears in Scripture (cf. Ps. 68:31; Isa. 11:11; 20:4; 43:3; 45:14). In other passages, however, Cush appears closely related to Elam and Persia (Isa. 11:11; Ezek. 38:5). In II Chron. 21:16, Arabs are described as dwelling "beside the Cushites," and both are mentioned in connection with the Philistines. These facts suggest that the term Cush was used of Cushites in Arabia as well as those across the Red Sea in Africa. Communication across the Red Sea was common in ancient times, and Cushites evidently settled in both areas.

In Gen. 2:13 and 10:8, mention is made of a Mesopotamian Cush. This is Biblically related to Nimrod, a son of Cush, who is said to have had a kingdom which included the cities of Babel, Erech, Accad, and Calneh "in the land of Shinar" or S Mesopotamia. These are among the oldest cities known to man and have histories going back to Sumerian and Akkadian times. Nimrod is said to have gone forth from Shinar to Asshur (i.e., Assyria), where he established Nineveh, Rehoboth, and Calah (Gen. 10:11; "He went forth to Asshur" is the better translation).

The Gihon, one of the rivers of Eden, is said to have compassed "the whole land of Ethiopia," i.e., Cush (Gen. 2:13). Since the Tigris and the Euphrates are two of the other rivers, it is presumed that the Gihon was related to the Asiatic rather than the African Cush. In the *Histories* of Herodotus (iii, 94; vii, 70) mention is made of the "Ethiopians of Asia" as distinct from the "Ethiopians above Egypt." He states that the two groups did not differ in appearance "but only in speech and hair." The E Ethiopians were straight-haired, but those of Africa "have of all men the wooliest hair." It is thought that the "Ethiopians of Asia" in Herodotus came from Baluchistan or its environs. Ancient peoples moved about a great deal, and it is not possible to define racial relationships exactly when peoples are in flux. The Scriptural picture of descendants of Cush in both Africa and Asia is in accord with the extra-Biblical notices.

BIBLIOGRAPHY:

J. B. Bury, S. A. Cook, and F. E. Adcock, eds., *The Cambridge Ancient History* (Cambridge, England, 1954), III.

T. G. Pinches, *ISBE*, II, 767-768, s.v.

J. A. Wilson, *The Burden of Egypt* (Chicago, 1951).

CHARLES PFEIFFER

CUSHI, "Ethiopian."

(1) The father of Zephaniah the prophet (Zeph. 1:1).

(2) The great-grandfather of Jehudi (meaning a man of Judah), who served as a messenger (to Ethiopia?) for the princes of Judah in Jeremiah's time.

(3) In the AV, Joab's first runner to bear news to David concerning Absalom's death (II Sam. 18:21-32). However, all but one of the references to the runner in the Massoretic text and the LXX have the definite article before the name: the Cushi(te). (See BV, ARV, RSV.) The Hebrew term *the Cushite* is translated *the Ethiopian* (AV, ARV, RSV) in Jer. 38:7. Thus Joab's runner could legitimately be regarded as an Ethiopian, and as such he did not know the shorter route native Ahimaaz took.

See CUSH, CUSHITES.

GERARD VAN GRONINGEN

CUTH, a city mentioned in II Kings 17:24 and 17:30. In the former passage the name is given as Cuthah and there it is mentioned as one of the places from which the Assyrian ruler had people brought to Samaria to repopulate the city after the deportation of the original inhabitants, Jews of the N ten tribes, into exile to Assyria. In Samaria the people who had formerly lived in Cuthah made Nergal, whom they had also served in Babylon, their god. The modern Tell-Ibrahim, NE of Babylon, has been identified as the site of the ancient Cuthah. In ancient days the city with its god Nergal must have been a city of considerable importance, ranking with Babylon and Borsippa.

CUTHAH. See CUTH.

CUTTINGS IN THE FLESH, as cited in the OT, concern either incisions, causing blood to flow (I Kings 18:28), or "marks," such as tattooing or branding (Lev. 19:28). Both are prohibited in the Mosaic codes as being contrary to conduct befitting "the children of Jehovah" (Deut. 14:1). Explanation for this prohibition has been sought in three directions: (1) Bodily defacement or injury debases "the temple of the Holy Spirit which is in you" (I Cor. 6:19; cf. the Pentateuchal precautions regarding leprosy, Lev. 13-14). Only figuratively may a believer "write on his hand, Unto Jehovah" (Isa. 44:5, ARVm; Ex. 13:9; Rev. 13:16). (2) Unrestrained emotion, particularly as cutting the flesh, demonstrates an abandonment to grief over the dead (Deut. 14:1), and reflects upon God's lordship over the lives of His own and upon His sustaining power (Ps. 23:4; 73:24; I Thess. 4:13). Levitical priests are especially warned against such infringement upon holiness or profanation of God's name (Lev. 21:5-6). (3) Association with pagan practice is forbidden (cf. the connection of cutting in the flesh with superstitious hair-trimming, Lev. 21:5).

Jezebel's priests who opposed Elijah cut themselves "after their manner" (I Kings 18:28) to procure the attention and favor of Baal; cuttings as a sign of mourning characterized the pagan Philistines and Moabites (Jer. 47:5; 48:37); and blood-letting to propitiate evil-intentioned spirits of the dead repeatedly accompany primitive funerary rites. Under such influence, pre-exilic Judeans not infrequently thus "cut themselves" (Jer. 16:6; 41:5), though even classic culture came in later years to forbid the practice (cf. the Laws of Solon and the Twelve Tables of Roman Law).

BIBLIOGRAPHY:

S. R. Driver, *A Critical and Exegetical Commentary on Deuteronomy* (*ICC*), 155-157.
G. B. Eager, *ISBE*, s.v.
A. R. S. Kennedy, "Cuttings in the Flesh," *HBD*, I, 537-539.
J. B. Payne, *Theology of the Older Testament* (Grand Rapids, 1961), chapter 26-D.
R. H. Pfeiffer, *Religion in the Old Testament* (New York, 1961), 718-719.

J. BARTON PAYNE

CYPRIAN (*c.* 200-258), bishop of Carthage. Comparatively little is known of the personal history of Cyprian. We know him chiefly through his public life. He is an outstanding example of a man who had an earnest desire to serve Christ and yet originated influences which have had an evil effect upon the history of the church.

He was born at Carthage of a noble and wealthy pagan family. Like Tertullian, whom he always called "the master," and who lived in the same city, Cyprian entered the legal profession. He quickly became renowned as an outstanding lawyer and administrator.

Under the guidance of an old friend, a presbyter, he took the decisive step of becoming a Christian and, as a token of the change in his life, sold many of his estates and gave the money to the poor. In 246 he was baptized, became ascetic in outlook, and began to study the Bible. Two years after he was baptized he was elected bishop of Carthage (248) by popular acclamation. By this time it had become the custom for the neighboring bishops to choose the man to fill a vacant see. In the case of Cyprian the call of the people was so unanimous and insistent that he could not refuse their demand, and the bishops felt they could not stand in the way. This procedure was similar to what was followed in the appointment of the great bishops Athanasius and Ambrose. During the first two years of his occupancy of the bishop's chair, he applied himself much to matters of discipline, and was firm and rigorous in his decisions.

In 250 the terrible persecution under the emperor Decius broke out. Cyprian thought it wise to retire from the scene from January 250 until March 251. He was accused of cowardice by enemies, but the charge was not true. The aim of Decius was to strike down the leaders of the church first, and then destroy the church itself when thus weakened. Cyprian was able from his hiding-place to guide and advise the church in a time of deadly peril. The persecution was the worst which had overtaken the church up till then. There had been peace from 212 to 249. Christianity had gained enormously in strength and popularity. There was now a vast number whose families had been Christians for generations. Many had little depth of conviction and easily denied the faith in the hour of peril, for they were only fair-weather Christians and easily fell away. They satisfied the Roman authorities by sacrificing to the heathen gods, or by offering a few drops of incense on a pagan altar. Sometimes they secured a certificate stating that they had sacrificed to the idols when they had not. This raised a grave problem when the persecution ended—how to deal with those who had denied the faith, the "lapsed" as they were called. As the manner of dealing with the situation had an enormous influence upon Cyprian and upon the whole church, the development of the situation must be carefully noticed. Two extreme attitudes manifested themselves. (a) In Carthage certain clergy, led by Novatus, were antagonistic to Cyprian because of his sudden elevation to the episcopate. They advocated a policy of laxity by which the lapsed could be received back into full communion on the easiest possible terms. They co-operated with the "confessors" in this movement—that is, the men who had suffered greatly in the persecution. Some, under sentence of death, had been liberated on the decease of Decius. Certain martyrs were supposed to have authorized friends to use their names in interceding for the lapsed. Thus, it became common for the confessors to issue "certificates of peace" without discrimination, and the merits of the confessors were regarded as conveyed to the account of those who had so recently denied Christ. It is obvious that such proceedings must have been embarrassing to Cyprian, the bishop. It was subversive of all rule and order in the church. (b) At Rome the difficulties arose from the opposite extreme—the rigorist party led by Novatian, a scholarly and brilliant presbyter who had much influence. Novatian was aggrieved because Cornelius had been elected bishop of Rome on March 5, 251. He was supported by many of the confessors and was put forward as a rival bishop, being consecrated to office by some country bishops. This party claimed to be the party of purity in the church. They maintained that "the admission into fellowship of those who by gross sin had violated their baptismal vows was to cease to be a true church." The attitude of Novatian and his supporters that the lapsed should never be received back into church membership was directly contrary to the teaching of Christ. The party became very troublesome at Carthage as well as Rome, and Cyprian described Novatian as "a foe to mercy, a destroyer of repentance, a teacher of arrogance, a corrupter of truth, and a murderer of love."

Cyprian, in dealing with the extremely delicate situation as between the opposing extremes, acted with much wisdom and courage. Before the persecution ended, he had laid down his plan for dealing with the problem. He proposed that every case concerning the lapsed, including those cases where the confessors had granted indulgences through "certificates of peace," should be reserved for consideration till after the persecution, when Councils of Bishops at Carthage and Rome should lay down terms for receiving back into communion the fallen church members; and that then the bishops with the help of presbyters and laymen should deal with each case on its merits and that when they were satisfied with the repentance and true penitence they should receive them back into the church. Although there was wide agreement with these proposals, the factious elements at both Carthage and Rome prevented their immediate acceptance; but Councils in both cities dealt with the situation in 251. They rejected the claims of the malcontents in Carthage, and recognized Cornelius as the legitimate bishop of Rome as against Novatian. As to the lapsed, their decision was that "certificates of peace" granted by the confessors should not be taken into account and that each case should be judged on its merits after penance was done, all the factors in each case being considered. Those who had not sacrificed to the pagan gods but had received certificates of having done so ("libellatici") were to be received one by one into communion, after penance. Those who had sacrificed to the gods ("sacrificati") were to do penance for life but were to be received back before death if penitent to the end. Those who only asked for penance at death, being previously impenitent, were not to be restored. These conditions seem very hard (although so much better than those of the Novatians), but at a second Council at Carthage in 252, in view of an outbreak of fresh persecution, all the lapsed of every kind who had continued penitent were received back into communion.

The triumph of Cyprian was an event in church history. He was victorious over the self-righteous and dictatorial confessors, over the party of laxity at Carthage, and over those who presumed to set up rival bishops, whether at Carthage or Rome. Above all, it was a triumph for the episcopate.

Three matters of vast importance in the history of Cyprian must be noticed:

(1) *His glorification of the Episcopate.* In his fight against schismatics, confessors, rebellious presbyters, and malcontents, he had to emphasize very strongly the unity of the church, as in his book, *De Unitate.* The decisions reached amounted to a declaration that finality rested with the bishops and that, further, the authority to retain or remit sin rested alone with the church organization of which the highest expression was the meeting of Bishops in Council. The center of the unity of the church lay in the bishop. For Cyprian he was the vicegerent of Christ in spiritual things. He raised the claims of the episcopate to a far higher level than ever before. His success in propagating this idea was a result of his personality and energy. Until Cyprian, then, the idea of the absolute supremacy of the bishop had been vague and only an assumption. The work of Cyprian thus had effects afterwards on the papacy of which he could not have dreamed. For Cyprian, the unity of the church was based upon Christ's words to Peter in Matthew 16: 18-19, but he held that all bishops had inherited Peter's prerogatives and held office by a direct decree of God.

(2) *His emphasis on the priesthood of the bishop.* He was the first to give

this idea definite shape. The church had been coming gradually to regard the eucharist as a *sacrifice*. Formerly the only sacrifice recognized in the Christian church was that of prayer, thanksgiving, and the offering up of the worshipper himself in connection with the Lord's supper. Cyprian turned the Communion into a sacerdotal performance, and roundly declared "the sacrifice we offer is the Passion of the Lord." The change thus introduced into the church was revolutionary and led on finally to the glaring errors of the sacrifice of the mass in the Roman Church. Cyprian's conception was based partly on pagan ideas of sacrifice and partly upon Jewish ideas. The clergyman now became a mediating priest, mediating between the people and God, and bringing them the grace of God. In Cyprian's system the grace of God came only through the episcopate.

This mightily increased the power and prestige of the bishop, but it was totally at variance with the Scriptural doctrine of the priesthood of all believers.

(3) *His insistence upon the autonomy of each bishop in his own church.* No man resisted more the arrogant claims of the bishop of Rome when he tried to lord it over other bishops. In particular he resisted sternly Stephen of Rome when he tried to browbeat other churches as to the rebaptism of heretics and schismatics. Unlike Cyprian, Stephen held that this was not necessary, and his view was upheld by the church in later ages. The interesting point, however, is that the bishops of Africa, Asia, Cappadocia, and other places were in complete accord with Cyprian in his argument that the bishop of Rome had no jurisdiction outside his own area. Cyprian strongly insisted that each separate church must be free from interference from the outside. In view of the claims of the papacy this should be noted.

When, in the Valerian persecution, he was beheaded at Carthage (September 14, 258) his dignity and Christian composure profoundly affected the multitude, Christians and pagans alike.

Bibliography:

Cyprian's Writings, *MPL* IV, English translation of selected works in *Ante-Nicene Christian Library*, vols. VIII and XIII (1873 and 1876).

P. Allard, *Histoire des Persécutions pendant la Premiere Moitié du Troisième Siècle* (Paris, 1894).

E. W. Benson, *Cyprian, His Life and Times* (London, 1897).

E. W. Benson, Art. on "Cyprian" in *DCB*.

W. H. C. Frend, *Martyrdom and Persecution in the Early Church* (Oxford, 1965).

H. M. Gwatkin, *Early Church History* (London, 1909), Vol. II, 254-303.

B. J. Kidd, *Hist. of the Church* (Oxford, 1922), Vol. I, 436-479.

J. B. Lightfoot, *Epistle to the Philippians* (London, 1868), Art. on "The Christian Ministry."

W. M. Sinclair, in *Lectures on Eccles. Hist.* delivered in Norwich Cathedral (London, 1896).

A. M. Renwick

CYPRUS, an island at the NE end of the Mediterranean, about 45 miles from the coast of Asia Minor and 60 miles from Syria. On clear days the mountains of the mainland can be seen from Cyprus. The island is 148 miles long, and its width varies from 5 to 50 miles. Its area comprises 3,600 square miles of largely mountainous terrain.

Since ancient times, Cyprus has been a source of timber and valuable mineral deposits. Its forests provided lumber for shipbuilding, and Cypriots boasted that they could build their vessels without aid from foreign countries. In addition to its valuable deposits of copper, the mountains of Cyprus yielded iron, lead, zinc, and silver. Pliny (*Natural History*, xxxiv, 2) states that brass was invented on Cyprus. Diamonds, emeralds, and other precious stones also were found there.

From prehistoric times Cyprus was exploited by its neighbors from the mainlands of Asia Minor and Syria. Shortly after 3000 B.C. the island's copper attracted settlers from Anatolia (Asia

Minor). Later it was subject to a succession of peoples including the Hyksos, the Egyptians, and the Hittites. Thutmose III of Egypt claims to have conquered it. Mycenaean traders and settlers came to the island, as Achaeans did later from Greece. The Greek settlements remained independent and emerged in historic times as separate kingdoms possessing Cypriot, Greek, and oriental elements.

After 1000 B.C., Cyprus suffered a period of eclipse, probably brought on by the use of iron, which replaced copper as the common metal. The Cypriots used their timber to construct ships and became a sea power until eclipsed by the Phoenicians. In the eighth century B.C. the Phoenicians established trading stations on Cyprus.

Subsequently, Cyprus was tributary to Assyria (under Sargon), Egypt (under Amasis II), and Persia (under Cyrus). The Cypriots supported Alexander the Great in his siege of Tyre and, after Alexander's death, Cyprus fell to Ptolemy and became part of the Egyptian kingdom. In 58 B.C. the Romans annexed Cyprus and made it a senatorial province under a proconsul. Salamis was its principal town and Paphos its administrative capital.

The Kittim (Gen. 10:4) listed among the sons of Javan (i.e., the Ionians) are primarily the people of Cyprus, designated as Chittim in Isaiah 23:1. Barnabas was a Cypriot (Acts 4:36), and the island was among the first places outside Palestine to hear the Gospel (Acts 11:19-20). It was visited by Paul and Barnabas during the First Missionary Journey (Acts 13:4-13). Later Barnabas and John Mark returned to Cyprus (Acts 15:39). Three bishops from Cyprus were present at the Council of Nicea (A.D. 325).

BIBLIOGRAPHY:

S. Casson, *Ancient Cyprus: Its Art and Archaeology* (London, 1937).
C. D. Cobham, *An Attempt at a Bibliography of Cyprus* (Nicosia, 1900).
G. P. Hill, *A History of Cyprus* (Cambridge, England, 1940).
L. and H. A. Mangolian, *The Island of Cyprus* (Nicosia, 1947).

CHARLES PFEIFFER

CYRENE, the chief city of Libya in N Africa (Acts 2:10), founded by the Greeks in 631 B.C. Alexander the Great gave the Jews equal rights of citizenship with the Greeks, and in the time of Josephus the Jews accounted for one quarter of the total population. The Cyrenians appear to have had a synagogue at Jerusalem along with the Libertines and Alexandrians (Acts 6:9). Simon the Cyrenian, who helped to carry the cross of Jesus, may have belonged to this synagogue. His two sons and probably his wife may have become Christians, if Rufus in Mark 15:21 is the person mentioned in Romans 16:13. Cyrenians were among the first to evangelize Gentiles at Antioch (Acts 11:19-21), and Lucius, a Cyrenian, became a prominent teacher in the church there (Acts 13:1).

WILLIAM J. CAMERON

CYRENIUS, mentioned in Luke 2:2 as the governor of Syria under whom the census of the population of Judea at the time of the birth of Jesus took place. The name is the Greek form of the Latin name *Quirinius*. It is known that Publius Sulpicius Quirinius was imperial legate of Syria-Cilicia from A.D. 6 to 9 and that during this period he carried out a census of Judea. This was not, however, the census of Luke 2:2, which must be dated some ten years earlier, but referred to the one mentioned in Acts 5:37 (see Josephus, *Ant.*, XVIII, i, 1). Some scholars, including Sir William Ramsay, basing their judgment mainly on the inscription of the *Lapis* Tiburtinus (*CIL*, XIV. 3613), have concluded that Cyrenius held the governorship on two occasions, the former of which would have coincided with the time of the birth of Jesus. The inscription, unfortunately, is damaged, and while it may be interpreted to mean that the officer whose deeds it records was governor of this territory on two occasions, the actual name of the officer in question is missing. The assertion of Tertullian (*Adv. Marcionem*, IV, xix) that the census in Judea at the time of the birth of Jesus was taken by Sentius Saturninus has given rise to the view, advocated by a number of scholars, that "Saturninus" rather than "Cyrenius" is the correct reading for Luke 2:2. Such a reading is unsupported in the mss. of the Third Gospel, however, and in view both of this consideration and also of the fact that Luke's use of names and titles is acknowledged to be accurate and reliable it is sensible to accept Cyrenius (Quirinius) as correct.

P. E. HUGHES

CYRIL OF ALEXANDRIA (d. 444), patriarch of Alexandria (412-444). Cyril was a member of the Alexandrian school of theology, which defended the Gospel in the spirit of the Nicene Fathers. Inevitably there arose between the school of Alexandria and the school of Antioch a conflict which came to a head in the personal and theological controversy between Cyril and Nestorius, who came from Antioch and became patriarch of Constantinople. Cyril was both learned and passionate in his defense of Biblical truth as he conceived it. He has frequently been accused of being both arrogant and violent in his attacks on Nestorius, and there is no doubt that personal motives did play a role in this controversy, but it would be misleading to reduce it to this level. However, a continuing ecclesiastical jealousy between Constantinople and Alexandria added fuel to the flames kindled by deap-seated theological differences.

Cyril sought to give particular emphasis to the mystery of the one Christ in a union of Deity and humanity, in the spirit of the Nicene tradition; and for this reason it was his purpose to warn the church in both the E and in the W about the dangers which he felt were inherent in the position assumed by Nestorius. Some scholars hold that Cyril is the last great Alexandrian theologian.

The immediate cause of the controversy between Cyril and Nestorius was Nestorius' insistence that Mary could be called *Christotokos*, "Christ-bearer," but not *Theotokos*, "God-bearer." In the ensuing correspondence between the two, Cyril accused Nestorius of heresy for dividing the Person of Christ. Cyril held that in Christ there were two complete, distinct natures, the Divine and the human, and that these found their unity in the Person of Christ, the Divine Logos. Some confusion arises in his writings because he applied the term φύσις, "nature," to the Divine Logos only, and not to the humanity of Christ, thus using it as a synonym for ὑπόστασις, "Person." It was this terminology that gave the monophysites a ready excuse to appeal to him for their doctrine that since Christ had only one Person He therefore had only one nature. The three points stressed by Cyril which are in harmony with the Bible and the great ecumenical creeds are these: (1) the indissoluble union of the two natures of Christ; (2) yet the unity of the Person of Christ (not a human as well as a Divine Person); and the necessary corollary, (3) the impersonality of the human nature of Christ. The only disagreement between him and the later Chalcedonian Creed (451) might possibly be found in the confusion of terminology as mentioned above.

It is also quite likely that Cyril saw in the heresy of Nestorius an opportunity to humiliate the rival patriarchate of Antioch as well as to strike a blow for orthodoxy. At first his letters to Nestorius were calm and dignified, fairly setting forth the issues between them, but when Nestorius supported those clergy in Alexandria who were opposing Cyril for other reasons, Cyril attacked the person of Nestorius as well as his doctrine. Thus, the controversy took a new turn toward a more violent character. In 429 Cyril wrote two treatises to influence Emperor Theodosius II, and his wife, against Nestorius; he also sent a letter to Bishop Celestine of Rome concerning the erroneous doctrines taught by the patriarch of Constantinople, phrased in such a way as to imply that Celestine had a degree of judicial supremacy and thus calculated to win his support in the conflict.

The quarrel now involved the prestige of Alexandria over Constantinople, and it became political as well as religious. Celestine ordered Nestorius to recant and to accept the Roman and Alexandrian doctrine or be excommunicated and deposed. Cyril decided to take the initiative and to carry out this sentence of excommunication decreed by Rome. In 430 he accordingly sent a letter to Nestorius in behalf of a synod which he held at Alexandria, ordering him to recant. For political reasons, Theodosius II was unwilling to have the issue settled at Rome, so he accordingly called the Council of Ephesus in 431 to deal with Nestorius.

Cyril and his followers arrived at this council and, with the aid of Bishop Memnon of Ephesus, organized the council. In one day, by high-handed measures, he was able to secure the desired condemnation and deposition of Nestorius. When the latter arrived at Ephesus, he, in turn, secured support at a separate council in deposing Cyril. But when the papal delegates arrived they supported Cyril, and Nestorius retired to a monastery. Under imperial pressure Antioch and Alexandria worked out a kind of compromise in 432 by which Antioch sacrificed Nestorius, and Cyril made one important concession in his own position when he signed a creed probably composed by Theodoret of Cyprus, one of the leaders of the Antiochene school, which declared Mary to be *Theotokos*, since "God the Word was made flesh and became man and from His conception united with Himself the temple received from her."

In signing this, Cyril did not retract any of his former position, and he was able to secure a general recognition of the Council of Ephesus. He was also restored to his patriarchate at Alexandria in 433.

Extremists in both parties, however, were dissatisfied with this compromise, and the followers of Cyril began to agitate for the doctrine of a single nature in Christ, the germ of which is found in the writings of Cyril himself. The new controversy came to a head when Eutyches succeeded Cyril as patriarch, and the monophysite heresy resulted.

BIBLIOGRAPHY:

Works of Cyril, *MPG*, LXVIII-LXXVII, P. E. Pusey, ed., 7 vols. (Oxford, 1868-77).

J. F. Bethune-Baker, *Nestorius and His Teaching* (Cambridge, 1908).

J. F. Bethune-Baker, *An Introduction to the Early History of Christian Doctrine* (London, 1903), Chapter XV.

J. N. D. Kelly, *Early Christian Doctrines* (Oxford, 1958), 310 ff.

R. L. Ottley, *The Doctrine of the Incarnation* (London, 1896), Vol. II, 68 ff.

C. GREGG SINGER

CYRIL OF JERUSALEM (*c.* 315-386), a defender of Nicene theology during the Arian controversy of the fourth century. He was ordained deacon in 335 and presbyter in 345 by Bishop Maximus. He attempted to be neutral in the early stages of the Arian controversy, but in 349, after the expulsion of Maximus by the Arian party, Cyril was consecrated bishop by Acacius, the Arian bishop of Caesarea. A controversy subsequently developed between these two men and when Acacius summoned Cyril to appear before him Cyril refused to obey. Cyril was deposed and banished by a council called by Acacius; but he was reinstated by the largely semi-Arian Council of Seleucia (359), which in turn deposed Acacius. In 360 a larger council of Arians meeting at Constantinople confirmed the deposition of Cyril; on the accession of Emperor Julian in 361, however, he was restored to his bishopric. Cyril was by this time fully committed to the defense of the Nicene orthodoxy. As a result, in 367 he was again deposed by the Arian Emperor Valens, along with other orthodox bishops. In 378 Theodosius allowed him to return once more to his bishopric. He attended the ecumenical Council of Constantinople of 381, which confirmed him in his office and lauded him for his staunch defense of orthodoxy. His most important work, the 24 *Catacheses*, written in 347 for the instruction of catechumens, offers a valuable insight into the sacramental and liturgical developments of the 4th century. In it he describes the vital union existing between Christ and the believer in a terminology which certainly foreshadows the later doctrine of transubstantiation.

BIBLIOGRAPHY:
"Works," *MPG*, XXXIII.
H. Leitzmann, *The Era of the Church Fathers*, 4 vols. (London, 1953).
P. Schaff, *History of the Christian Church*, Vol. 3 (Grand Rapids, 1953).

C. GREGG SINGER

CYRIL LUCARIS (1572-1638), Greek theologian and patriarch of Constantinople. This very remarkable man has become renowned by his attempt to introduce into the Greek Orthodox Church the main ideas of Calvinism. He was born at Candia in Crete and studied in Venice and Padua. From 1595 to 1602 he lectured at universities in Lithuania and Poland; in 1602 he succeeded the patriarch of Alexandria. In that city he showed himself sympathetic to Protestantism and sent one of his clergy, the monk Metrophanes Critopoulos, to study at Oxford in 1616. In 1621 he was appointed patriarch of Constantinople, a city in which both Protestantism and Roman Catholicism tried to gain influence among the clergy of the Greek Orthodox Church. The ambassadors of France and of the Austrian emperor worked in favor of a reunion with the Church of Rome; and the Dutch ambassador Cornelis Haga, assisted by the Dutch merchant David le Leu de Wilhelm, tried to stimulate Cyril's interest in Protestantism. They did so by giving him books from Dutch Arminians and by achieving a correspondence between Cyril and the famous Dutch Arminian theologian Vytenbogaert. But Cyril was not inclined to Arminianism; his heart was drawn to Calvinism. Through the English ambassador Thomas Roe he took up correspondence with the Archbishop of Canterbury, George Abbot, to whom he presented the newly discovered Codex Alexandrinus. In turn the archbishop called his newborn son Cyrille. After that, the minister of the Dutch embassy, Leger, brought Cyril into direct contact with Geneva. This contact resulted in negotiations for an official union between this mother-church of the Reformation and the Greek Orthodox Church. On both sides creeds were exchanged and attendance of worship in both kinds of churches was organized. Theologians in the Netherlands were greatly interested: the well-known Revius translated the Belgic Confession into Greek and the fervent Calvinist Hommius did the same with the Heidelberg Catechism. Cyril himself published in 1629 a personal confession of faith, a Calvinistic interpretation of the faith of the Greek Orthodox Church. He accepted the *filioque* clause, Divine election, justification by faith, and the doctrine of two sacraments; and he rejected the worship of images. It is small wonder that he had many enemies, including the members of his own clergy; but behind the scenes the Jesuits tried to undo him at the court of the Sultan. In 1638 he was accused of inciting the Cossacks against the Turkish government, was banished and strangled by the soldiers who accompanied him on board ship. After his death the tracks of his work were soon covered up. Synods of the Greek Church emphatically rejected Calvinism in 1638, 1642, and 1672.

BIBLIOGRAPHY:
C. Emereau, *DIC*, s.v.
G. A. Hadjiantonion, *Protestant Patriarch: The Life of Cyril Lucaris* (London, 1961).
G. Hofmann, *Patriarch Kyrillos Lukaris und die Römische Kirche* (Rome, 1929).
E. Kimmel, *Libri Symbolici Ecclesiae Orientalis* (1843).
P. Meyer, *PRE*, s.v.
P. Schaff, *The Creeds of Christendom* (New York, 1887), I, 54-57.
R. Schlier, *Der Patriarch Kyrill Lukaris von Konstantinopel* (Marburg, 1927).
V. Semnoz, "Les dernieres Annees du patriarche Cyrille Lucar," *EO*, VI (1903), 97-107.
A. A. Van Schelven, "Cyril Lukaris' poging tot Calvinisering van de Oostersche kerk," *De Stryd der Geesten* (Amsterdam, 1944), 137-160.

LOUIS PRAAMSMA

CYRUS (599-530 B.C.), king of Persia who conquered Babylon.

OUTLINE:
I. Background and Early Conquests
II. Conquest of Babylon
III. Cyrus and the Jews
IV. The Last Years of Cyrus

I. Background and Early Conquests

Cyrus is more accurately known as Cyrus II, the Great, to distinguish him from his grandfather Cyrus I (640-600 B.C.), the grandson of Achaemenes, founder of the Achaemenid dynasty of Persia). His father, Cambyses I (600-559 B.C.), was king of Anshan, a region in E Elam, and his mother was Mandane, a daughter of Astyages, king of Media (585-550 B.C.). When his father died in 559 B.C., Cyrus II inherited the throne of Anshan and, after unifying the Persian people, attacked the weak and corrupt Astyages. The Median general Harpagus, whom Astyages had previously wronged, deserted the king and brought his army to the side of young Cyrus. Astyages was soon captured and the Persians took the capital city of Ecbatana in 550 B.C. without a battle.

Cyrus succeeded in welding the Medes and Persians into a unified nation. Moving swiftly to the W, he absorbed all of the Median territories as far as the river Halys in Asia Minor. When Croesus, the fabulously wealthy king of Lydia, refused to recognize the sovereignty of Medo-Persia, Cyrus defeated him in battle and took over his empire (546 B.C.). Seven years later, he was ready to launch the great assault against Babylon itself.

II. Conquest of Babylon

The Neo-Babylonian empire was in no condition to resist a Medo-Persian invasian in the year 539 B.C. During the preceding fourteen years Nabonidus, the king, had not so much as visited Babylon, leaving the administration of that great city to his profligate son Belshazzar, to whom he also "entrusted the kingship" ("Verse Account of Nabonidus," *Anet*, p. 313). Nabonidus weakened the empire by incurring the wrath of the Babylonian priesthood through concentrating his favors upon the cult of the god Sin at Harran at the expense of Babylonian deities.

Realizing that danger was near, Nabonidus came to Babylon for the New Year's festival of April 4, 539 B.C., and began to bring the images of Babylonian divinities into the city from the surrounding areas. But it was to no avail. Toward the end of September, the armies of Cyrus under the command of Ugbaru, governor of Gutium, attacked Opis on the Tigris and defeated the Babylonians. Sippar was taken without a battle and

Nabonidus fled. Two days later on October 12, Ugbaru's troops were able to enter Babylon while Belshazzar, completely oblivious of the doom that awaited him, was engaged in a riotous banquet within the "impregnable" walls of the city (Dan. 5). In that same night Belshazzar was slain.

Cyrus himself entered Babylon on October 29, 539 B.C., and presented himself to the people as a gracious liberator and benefactor. He reversed the cruel policies of the Assyrian and Babylonian rulers by permitting transplanted populations to return to their homelands. The Jews who had been held as captives in Babylonia since the early part of Nebuchadnezzar's reign were not only permitted but were actually encouraged by Cyrus to return to Palestine and to rebuild their temple (II Chron. 36:22-23; Ezra 1:1-4). Furthermore, he gave them the vessels which Nebuchadnezzar had plundered from Solomon's temple (Ezra 1:7-11; 6:5), and contributed financially to the construction of their second temple (Ezra 6:4). About 50,000 Jews responded to this royal proclamation and returned to Palestine under the leadership of Zerubbabel and Joshua (Ezra 2:64-65).

III. Cyrus and the Jews

Nearly 200 years earlier, Isaiah had prophesied that Cyrus would be God's chosen instrument for liberating the Jewish exiles and for initiating the restoration of the temple (Isa. 44:28; 45:1-7, 13). Though he did this, it seems certain that Cyrus was not a true believer in Jehovah ("I have surnamed thee, though thou has not known me" [Isa. 45:4]). He probably recognized the God of Israel as one of the most important deities, especially if Daniel, who lived at least until the third year of Cyrus (Dan. 10:1), showed him these prophecies of Isaiah (Josephus, *Ant.*, XI, i, 1).

The famous Cyrus Cylinder, discovered by Hormuzd Rassam in the 19th century, harmonizes well with the Biblical account of Cyrus' benevolence toward captive peoples. In it, Cyrus tells how the Babylonian god Marduk had "scanned and looked through all the countries, searching for a righteous ruler willing to lead him (i.e., Marduk) in the annual procession. Then he pronounced the name of Cyrus, king of Anshan, declared him to become the ruler of all the world. . . . Without any battle, he made him enter his town Babylon, sparing Babylon any calamity. . . . I returned to sacred cities on the other side of the Tigris, the sanctuaries of which have been ruins for a long time, the images which used to live therein and established for them permanent sanctuaries. I also gathered all their former inhabitants and returned to them their habitations" ("Cyrus Cylinder," *ANET*, pp. 315-16).

The very day that Cyrus entered Babylon, Gubaru, (probably Darius the Mede in the book of Daniel), the newly appointed governor of Babylon and the Region Beyond the River, began to appoint sub-governors to rule with him over the vast territories and populations of the Fertile Crescent. Ugbaru, the general who conquered Babylon and had administered the city, was ailing and died on November 6. Turning the administration of the entire Fertile Crescent over to Gubaru, Cyrus left for Ecbatana toward the end of his accession year (A. T. Olmstead, *The History of the Persian Empire*, University of Chicago Press, 1948, pp. 57, 71).

IV. The Last Years of Cyrus

In the meantime, Cambyses, son of Cyrus, lived in Sippar and represented his father at the New Year's festival in Babylon as "the King's son." He was also given the task of preparing for an expedition against Egypt, which he conquered in 525 B.C. after his father's death. In 530 B.C., Cyrus finally appointed his son to be his co-regent and successor, just before setting out upon a campaign to the far NE in the Oxus and Jaxartes region. At the New Year's festival of March 26, 530 B.C., Cambyses assumed the title "King of Babylon" for the first time, while Cyrus retained the broader title, "King of the Lands" (cf. Waldo H. Dubberstein, "The Chronology of Cyrus and Cambyses," *American Journal of Semitic Languages and Literatures*, LV, 1938, p. 419). In the autumn of the same year news reached Babylon that Cyrus had died on the field of battle, leaving his vast empire to Cambyses. Cyrus was buried at Pasargadae, where his small tomb may still be seen near the meager ruins of his capital city.

See BABYLON; DARIUS; DISPERSION OF JEWS; EXILE; PERSIA.

BIBLIOGRAPHY:

G. C. Cameron, *Histoire de L'Iran Antique* (Paris, 1937).

A. T. Clay, "Gobryas, Governor of Babylonia," *JAOS* 41 (1921).

A. T. Clay, *Legal and Commercial Transactions Dated in the Assyrian, Neo-Babylonian, and Persian Periods* (Philadelphia, 1908).

G. Contenau, *Textes Cuneiformes. Tome 13: Contrats Néo-Babyloniens II, Achéménides et Séleucides* (Paris, 1929).

R. P. Dougherty, *Goucher College Cuneiform Inscriptions.* Vol. II, *Archives From Erech: Neo-Babylonian and Persian Periods* (New Haven, 1933).

R. P. Dougherty, *Nabonidus and Belshazzar* (New Haven, 1929).

W. H. Dubberstein, "The Chronology of Cyrus and Cambyses," *AJSLL* 55 (1938).

J. Finegan, *Light From the Ancient Past* (2nd ed.; Princeton, 1960).

R. Ghirshman, *Iran* (Baltimore, 1954).

F. R. B. Godolphin (ed.), *The Greek Historians* (New York, 1942), 2 vols.

B. G. Gray, "The Foundation and Extension of the Persian Empire," *The Cambridge Ancient History*, IV (Cambridge, 1940).

H. R. Hall, *The Ancient History of the Near East* (London, 1952).

A. T. Olmstead, *The History of the Persian Empire*, Chicago, 1948).

A. L. Oppenheim, "Babylonian and Assyrian Historical Texts," *Ancient Near Eastern Texts Relating to the Old Testament* (Princeton, 1950), 305-316.

T. E. Page and W. H. D. Rouse, *The Loeb Classical Library: Xenophon's Cyropaedia* (New York, 1914), 2 vols.

R. A. Parker and W. D. Dubberstein, *Babylonian Chronology 626 B.C.–A.D. 75* (Providence, 1956).

H. H. Rowley, *Darius the Mede and the Four World Empires of the Book of Daniel* (Cardiff, 1959).

W. Schwenzner, "Gobryas," *Klio* 18 (1923).

S. Smith, *Babylonian Historical Texts Relating to the Downfall of Babylon* (London, 1924).

J. N. Strassmaier, *Inschriften von Cambyses, König von Babylon.*

A. Tremayne, *Records From Erech, Time of Cyrus and Cambyses (538–521 B.C.).* Vol. VII, *Yale Oriental Series: Babylonian Texts* (New Haven, 1925).

J. C. Whitcomb, Jr., *Darius the Mede* (Grand Rapids, 1959).

D. J. Wiseman, "Nebuchadnezzar and the Last Days of Babylon," *Christianity Today*, II, 4 (Nov. 25, 1957), pp. 7-10.

E. J. Young, *The Prophecy of Daniel* (Grand Rapids, 1949).

JOHN C. WHITCOMB, JR.

CZECHOSLOVAKIA, THE CHURCH IN. The areas which in 1918 came to form the Czechoslovak republic have had a turbulent history, constantly contested by Slavs, Germans, and Magyars (Hungarians). Ecclesiastically much of the action took place in Bohemia, which can claim the first national Protestant church. This originated in the late 14th century, when both church and state were German-controlled. A national religious movement found its spokesman in Jan Hus, Prague University professor who became rector in 1402. A popular preacher in the vernacular, Hus had been deeply influenced by the Englishman John Wycliffe. Hus attacked the sale of indulgences, demanded church reforms, challenged papal primacy, and upheld the superior authority of Scripture. With Jerome of Prague he supported the nationalist movement in the university which culminated in the departure of the alien Germans. Excommunicated by the archbishop of Prague, Hus went to the Council of Constance in 1415, where, despite an imperial safe conduct, he was arrested, tried, and burned. His friend Jerome followed him to the stake in 1416. This clearly identified religious reform with Bohemian nationalism and split the country in the Hussite Wars (1420-33).

The reformers were themselves divided. The Calixtines or Utraquists, university-centered, favored separation of religious and political reform; and in the Four Articles of Prague (1420) sought full liberty of preaching, communion in both kinds (*calix* = cup), the punishment of immorality, and the secularization of ecclesiastical property. The Taborites, on the other hand, came largely from rural and artisan stock, and had learned from Waldensians, Cathari, and Wycliffites. They had no churches, rejected transubstantiation, and followed a program of apostolic communism with ruthless discipline.

Calixtines and Taborites

Papal opposition united the nation behind the Taborite John Ziska, a brilliant soldier who won a series of remarkable victories over the much larger imperial forces. Prokop the Bald continued the leadership and even carried the war into Germany. When civil war again divided Taborites and Calixtines, Prokop was killed, and a compromise made at the Council of Basel, when the Catholics accepted the Hussites as true sons of the church and conceded to them the cup in communion. In 1448 the moderate George Podebrad became head of the Hussites, and later king. He completely suppressed the Taborites and took stern action against those Hussites known as Bohemian Brethren (*Unitas Fratrum*).

In the 16th century Lutheranism came to Bohemia, but the Catholic influence was reasserted in 1547 when the Bohemian crown was vested in the House of Hapsburg. For a time the Protestants enjoyed religious liberty; then the fanatical Rudolf II (1576-1612) championed the Counter Reformation and set out to eradicate the opposition. The Thirty Years' War began (1618) with a revolt in Bohemia when one Utraquist church was closed and another destroyed. In 1620 the Hussites were defeated by imperial troops near Prague. Bohemia and Moravia lost their independence, and there followed three centuries of political, economic, and religious subjection. Many Protestants were forced into exile, among them J. A. Comenius, last bishop of the Bohemian Brethren. In 1624 all Protestant worship was forbidden and civil rights denied to all who would not conform to Roman Catholicism. Meanwhile in Slovakia, which since 1526 had been under the same alien domination as Bohemia, the Hungarian landlords stoutly resisted Hapsburg tyranny, efforts to extirpate Protestants failed, and religious traditions survived. Slovakia had also an E Church link, but many of its members had joined the Uniats in the 16th century.

Toward the end of the last century, Czech nationalism reasserted itself. One manifestation was an association of Catholic priests which sought the introduction of Czech into church services, the abolition of priestly celibacy, and more democracy in church administration. Their demands rejected by Rome, the group formed the Czechoslovak (National Catholic) Church on presbyterian lines, but with elected bishops. The post-World War I period saw also an Orthodox Church formed in Bohemia and Moravia, but as part of Nazi reprisals during World War II, its bishop and four clergy were executed and the church disbanded. Orthodoxy nevertheless survived in E Slovakia. During the Stalinist era the RC primate, Archbishop (later Cardinal) Berans, was expelled from his see and other bishops and priests imprisoned. Protestant churches are comparatively small and divided partly according to their national origins. Some Protestant churchmen have tried to come to terms with the Com-

Modern Times

munist state, notably those connected with the Prague-based Christian Peace Conference. However, this movement was shaken by the 1968 Russian invasion; and the CPC's founder, Josef Hromadka, died a disillusioned man in 1969.

Approximate church membership figures for Czechoslovakia: RC's, 10 million; Protestants, 1.3 million; Czechoslovak (National Catholic) Church, 1 million; E Orthodox, 500,000; and Jews (a pathetic remnant of their prewar representation), 18,000.

See HUS, JAN; CONSTANCE, COUNCIL OF; COMENIUS, J. A.

JAMES DIXON DOUGLAS

DABAREH. See DABERATH.

DABBASHETH or DABBESHETH, a town on the S boundary of Zebulun (Josh. 19:11). The boundary ran along the river Kishon. It is probably the modern Tell esh-Shammam.

DABERATH, a town marking the E border of Zebulun (Josh. 19:12), but reckoned as belonging to Issachar (I Chron. 6:72). It is probably the same as Dabareh (Josh. 21:28) and the modern Daburiyeh. The name means "pasture."

DABNEY, Robert Lewis (1820-1898), Southern Presbyterian theologian. Born in Louisa County, Virginia, Dabney studied at Hampden-Sydney College (1836-37), taught school (1838-39), received the M.A. degree from the University of Virginia (1842) and graduated from Union Theological Seminary, Virginia (1846). After brief service as a rural missionary, he was ordained as pastor of the Tinkling Spring Church, Virginia (1847-53), where he also conducted a classical academy. In 1853 Hampden-Sydney awarded him an honorary doctorate and he was called to Union Seminary as professor of church history and polity. In 1859 he was made adjunct professor of systematic theology, and from 1869 to 1883 full professor. He also served as co-pastor of the Hampden-Sydney College Church (1858-74). His numerous articles on religious and secular topics marked him as a man of extraordinary ability. In 1860 he declined calls from Princeton Seminary and from the Fifth Avenue Church in New York. For a while in 1861 he was a chaplain in the Confederate army; and, in 1862, a major and chief of staff to his friend General T. J. (Stonewall) Jackson. Before the Civil War he had opposed secession, but he became one of the strongest advocates of the righteousness of the S cause. In 1870 he was elected moderator of the Presbyterian, U.S., General Assembly. He was always active as a conservative in the church courts and strenuously opposed reunion with the N Presbyterians. For reasons of health he left Virginia in 1883 to become the professor of mental and moral philosophy at the University of Texas, where he remained until 1894. In this period he was also co-founder and professor of the Austin School of Theology (1884-95). From 1890 he was totally blind. He retired to Victoria, Texas, in 1896, and died there, January 3, 1898.

Dabney was a man of versatile gifts, of intense energy and conviction, and of wide and detailed learning. He combined keen perception and intellectual ability with clarity and terseness of expression. In philosophy he was influenced by the Scottish Common Sense school. Archibald Alexander called Dabney "the best teacher of theology in the United States, if not in the world." He was also recognized by Bavinck and Lecerf as one of the leading American theologians. He compares favorably with the thoroughgoing Calvinists of his century in the penetration and power of his thought and as a stimulator of thought. He approached the exposition of theology with a broader knowledge and a larger Biblical base than most of the old school Presbyterian theologians. There was also a practical bent to his theology; he therefore deplored as over-refinements and undue subtlety some of the abstract distinctions traditionally made, such as between supra- and infra-lapsarianism, and between mediate and immediate imputation.

Although he was personally modest and compassionate, he had a strong sense of duty and burned with moral indignation in the face of what he believed to be falsehood and wickedness, especially when he saw the S oppressed by political adventurers in Reconstruction days. Believing strongly in Calvinism and in the S and her institutions, he never doubted that they would at last be Divinely vindicated. Dabney has recently been seen as an accurate critic of modern industrialization, antedating the social gospel movement, perceiving agonizing social problems, and warning against the impersonality and immorality of business and the centralization of economic power in the late 19th century.

Among his numerous writings are *Memorial of the Christian Life and Character of Francis S. Sampson* (Richmond, 1855), *Life and Campaigns of Lieut-General Thomas J. Jackson* (New York, 1866), *A Defense of Virginia (and Through Her of the South) in Recent and Pending Contests Against the Sectional Party* (New York, 1867), *A Review of "Theodosia Ernest: or, The Heroine of Faith"* (3rd. ed., Richmond, 1869), *Sacred Rhetoric: or, A Course of Lectures on Preaching* (Richmond, 1870), *The Sensualistic Philosophy of the Nineteenth Century Considered* (New York, 1875), *The Christian Sabbath* (Philadelphia, 1882), *The Latest Infidelity: A Reply to Ingersoll's Positions* (Richmond, 1890), *Discussions* (vols. 1-3, Richmond, 1890-97; vol. 4, Mexico, Mo., 1897), *Five Points of Calvinism* (Richmond, 1895), *Christ Our Penal Substitute* (Richmond, 1897), *The Practical Philosophy, Being the Philosophy of the Feelings, of the Will, and of the Conscience, with the Ascertainment of Particular Rights and Duties* (Mexico, Mo., 1897), *Syllabus and Notes of the Course of Systematic and Polemic Theology Taught in Union Theological Seminary, Virginia* (6th ed., Richmond, 1927), and scores of periodical articles. Dabney has been recently rediscovered by Reformed circles, and two volumes of his *Discussions* have been re-issued by the Banner of Truth Trust (London, 1967). Collections of his papers and letters are held by the libraries of the University of Virginia, Charlottesville; Union Theological Seminary, Richmond; and the Historical Foundation, Montreat, North Carolina.

BIBLIOGRAPHY:

DAB, V, 20 f.
W. B. Hesseltine, *Confederate Leaders in the New South* (Baton Rouge, 1950), pp. 70-77.
T. C. Johnson, *The Life and Letters of Robert Lewis Dabney* (Richmond, 1903).
F. B. Lewis, "Robert Lewis Dabney, Southern Presbyterian Apologist" (dissertation, Duke University, Durham, N. C., 1946).
I. Murray, "Dabney of Virginia," *The Banner of Truth*, No. 47 (March-April, 1967), 1-4, 20.
D. H. Overy, "Robert Lewis Dabney: Apostle of the Old South" (dissertation, University of Wisconsin, 1967).
D. H. Overy, "When the Wicked Beareth Rule: A Southern Critique of Industrial America," *Journal of Presbyterian History*, 48, ii (Summer, 1970), 130-142.
Robert Lewis Dabney—In Memoriam (Knoxville, 1899).
M. H. Smith, *Studies in Southern Presbyterian Theology* (Amsterdam, 1962), 183-216.
C. T. Thomson, "Robert Lewis Dabney—The Conservative," *Union Seminary Review*, 35, ii (January, 1924), 154-170.
H. A. White, *Southern Presbyterian Leaders* (New York, 1911), 382-393.
H. M. Woods, *Robert Lewis Dabney: Prince Among Theologians and Men* (Richmond, 1936).

ALBERT H. FREUNDT, JR.

DA COSTA, Isaac (1798-1860), Dutch Jewish poet and Christian leader. Born in Amsterdam in a Portuguese-Hebrew family of notable merchants, he studied in Leiden and took two doctor's degrees: one in law (1818) and one in literature (1821). The private classes of Willem Bilderdijk, the greatest Dutch poet of that time and a romantic Calvinist, put their ineffaceable stamp on him. He and his young wife became Christians and were baptized in 1822. From then on he became an ardent and eloquent champion of orthodoxy, as was evidenced in his sensational brochure *Bezwaren tegen den geest der eeuw* (*Objections against the Spirit of the Age* [1823]). Although some of the ideas of this booklet are not well founded (he defended slavery because the Negroes were the children of Ham), it made an urgent appeal to all true believers to return to the God of their fathers and to ministers to bring the Gospel of the cross. The response of the Dutch intelligentsia was entirely negative. The courageous young man was avoided, stigmatized as an obscurantist, and for some time the police had to protect his home against the threats of the mob. Nevertheless, Da Costa followed his call to awaken the Christians of the Netherlands, and he gained friends who were influential in the movement of the Reveil (a continuous revival). His main contributions to this movement consisted in his poems and his Bible lectures, which resulted in an awakening in the state church. In 1834 a secession took place. Da Costa, however, was opposed to separation from the established church, and when, in later years, evangelical leaders of the state church pleaded for maintenance of the doctrinal standards in their essence and thrust, he did not join their ranks. He declared himself to be in harmony with the fundamentals of Christianity, but pronounced the Forms of Unity (the Belgic Confession, the Heidelberg Catechism, and the Canons of Dort) out of date in view of the progress made in knowledge of Scriptural revelation. He justified his position with an appeal to Zech. 4:16: "Not by might, nor by power, but by my Spirit, saith the Lord of hosts."

Bibliography:

W. G. C. Bijvanck, *De jeugd van Is. da Costa* (Leiden, 1894-96), 2 vols.

M. E. Kluit, *Het Reveil in Nederland* (Amsterdam, 1936).

D. H. Kromminga, *The Christian Reformed Tradition* (Grand Rapids, 1943), 80, 81, 114.

H. J. Koenen, *Levensbericht van Mr. Is. da Costa* (Leiden, 1860).

DAGON, the name of a pagan deity, which we encounter in the OT as an idol of the Philistines, e.g., Judges 16:23; I Sam. 5:2-7; I Chron. 10:10. Nevertheless, Dagon was not an exclusively Philistine deity. Even before the Philistines entrenched themselves in the Holy Land, Dagon was revered in all of Phoenicia. The Philistines adopted this veneration. Also, Dagon is mentioned in the texts of Ras Shamra as the father of the god Alyan (Baal). In addition, a god of this name was known from quite ancient times in Assyria and Babylonia. Traces of a Dagon-cult go all the way back to the time of the Sumerians.

Earlier it was thought that the meaning of his name was closely related to the Hebrew word *dag*, i.e., "fish." Therefore Dagon was viewed as a type of fish-god, and was depicted as a being that was half man and half fish. Some inferred from I Sam. 5:4 that the statue of Dagon ended in a fish-tail, but the text says nothing about it. In the Hebrew there is mention only of "Dagon": "only Dagon was still up above" (namely in his place); that yields no clear meaning, but probably traces of the Septuagint can be seen in the reading, "only the back (referring to the back support of the statue) was still up above." Others have entertained the idea that the name Dagon is closely related to the Hebrew word for "corn" (*dagan*) and that Dagon therefore should be considered as a corn-god. But again, there are no sufficient grounds for this. Some have seen Dagon as a god of the weather, which could account for the great proliferation of his cult. Even in the time of the Maccabees there was still a temple of Dagon in Ashdad, which was burned to the ground by Jonathan (I Macc. 10:83, 84; 11:4).

J. G. AALDERS

DAILLÉ, Jean (1594-1670), one of the most eminent pastors of the Reformed Churches of France in the 17th century. After he completed his studies at the famed Academy of Saumur in 1612, the governor of the city, Du Plessis-Mornay, noticed him and took him into his home as a tutor for his two grandsons. He spent seven years with this illustrious family and became good friends with Cameron and Amyraut, professors at Saumur. Ordained in 1623, he became Du Plessis-Mornay's chaplain and attended his death bed. In his "Dernières Heures de Mornay" he recounted the end of this great Christian, theologian, and statesman. Daillé then became pastor of Saumur and later, in 1626, pastor of the Consistory of Paris at Charenton, where he served as minister for 44 years, until his death.

Many of the eloquent sermons which he preached there have been collected into some twenty volumes: sermons on Calvin's Catechism, on the Lord's supper, on the Epistles to the Philippians, to the Colossians, to Timothy, and to Titus. The pure language in which they were written won for their author the close friendship of the Protestant Valentin Conrart, one of the founders of the French Academy. But the most important work of Daillé is his *Traité de l'emploi des Saints Pères pour le jugement des différends qui sont aujourd'hui en la religion* (Geneva, 1632). In this work, which Bayle calls a masterpiece, Daillé tries to show that the church Fathers cannot constitute a decisive authority in controversies, for it is difficult, if not impossible, to know their opinions on the matters in question. And, if one should know their opinions, they could not replace the only infallible authority, that of Holy Writ.

This work was followed by *La Foi Fondée sur les Saintes Ecritures* (1634), where he tried to show that all Christian doctrines are either explicit in the Bible or may be directly deduced from it. His other works are *De Pseudepigraphis Apostolicis* (1653); *Adversus Latinorum de Cultus Religiosi Objecto Traditionem* (1664); *De Scriptis Quae sub Dionysii Areopagitae et Ignatii Antiochenii Nominibus circumferuntur* (1666) (an attempt to disprove the authenticity of much Ignatian literature); and *De Cultibus Religiosis Latinorum* (1671).

JEAN CADIER

D'AILLY, Pierre (1350-1420), French theologian, philosopher, and conciliarist. Reared in Compiègne, D'Ailly entered the Nominalistic College of Navarre in the University of Paris in 1363. In 1380 he received his doctorate in theology, and four years later became director of the college. Strongly influenced by Occam and the Nominalists, he contended that the existence of God could not be strictly demonstrated, nor could the doctrine of the Trinity be deduced from Scripture. His expressed doubts on transubstantiation were later to influence the young Luther. Positive law alone he considered the basis of morality. Priest and bishop he regarded as holding authority from Christ, not the pope. The universal church, and not the occupant of the papal throne, was to be regarded as infallible. D'Ailly contended that the church, even without papal sanction, could summon a general council. The Council of Constance was convoked in 1414, and here D'Ailly played a leading role, being especially concerned with the reformation of the church "in both head and members" and the trial of John Hus. He examined the Bohemian Reformer and was present at his condemnation. D'Ailly's views on reform within the church are expressed in his *De reformatione ecclesiae* (1416). After the council elected a new pope, Martin V, D'Ailly, who himself had been a candidate, became papal legate to Avignon, where he died in 1420. His interests included many fields. In his *Imago mundi*, used by Columbus, he discussed the possibility of reaching the Indies by sailing W; and in his proposed revision of the calendar, he anticipated the work carried out by Gregory XIII.

Bibliography:

P. D'Ailly, *De reformatione ecclesiae Petri de Alliaco cardinalis Cameracensis* (Basel, 1551).
P. D'Ailly, *Imago mundi* (Paris, 1930-31).
P. D'Ailly, *Tractatus* (Paris, 1505).
L. Salembier, *Petrus de Alliaco* (Lille, 1886).
P. Tschackert, *Peter von Ailli* (Gotha, 1877).

Peter J. Klassen

DALAIAH. See Delaiah.

DALE, Robert William (1829-1895), English congregational preacher and theologian. He was pastor of Carr's Lane Chapel, Birmingham, from 1853 (assisting J. A. James until 1859) to his death in 1895. He was renowned for his forthright preaching, both doctrinal and topical. As a theologian, Dale may be described as a liberal evangelical. His lectures on *The Atonement* (1875) maintained the penal view of the atonement but veered unconsciously toward a Grotian interpretation. Despite a deep sense of sin, he held a modified doctrine of human depravity. He rejected limited atonement and, from 1874, maintained conditional immortality. Tireless in championing Nonconformist interests, he advocated the disestablishment of the Church of England. He was chairman of the Congregational Union (1869) and presided over the International Council of Congregational Churches (1891).

Dale also played an active part in national and municipal affairs, especially in education. He upheld the interests of Nonconformists in connection with the Education Act (1870); he served on the Birmingham School Board (1870-1880); as governor of the King Edward VI Foundation (1878-1895) he helped reorganize secondary education in Birmingham; and he played an active part in the transfer of Spring Hill College to Oxford and its reconstitution as Mansfield College (1889).

Bibliography:

A. W. W. Dale, *Life of R. W. Dale* (London, 1898).
R. W. Dale, *Works*. For full details see A. W. W. Dale, *Life of R. W. Dale* (London, 1898), 751-758.
A. Gordon, "Dale, Robert William," *DNB* Suppl. II (1901), 104-106.
C. S. Horne, "R. W. Dale," *Nine famous Birmingham Men*, ed. J. H. Muirhead (Birmingham, 1909), 253-292.

H. H. Rowdon

DALETH, "door," the fourth letter of the Hebrew alphabet. It has the numerical value of four, and with the dieresis, 4,000. In Biblical Hebrew it ordinarily represents the sound "d," but when preceded by a vowel it has the voiced sound "th."

DALMAN, Gustaf Hermann (1855-1941), German theologian and Orientalist. Dalman made a special study of the language, culture, history, and geography of Palestine in the time of Christ. He distinguished between Galilean and Judean Aramaic, conjecturing that Jesus spoke both. Born at Niesky, Silesia, he became a professor at the Delitzsch Institute, Leipzig, in 1895. From 1902 to 1917 he was director of the German Evangelical Institute for the Archaeology of the Holy Land, in Jerusalem. In 1917 he accepted a professorship of theology at Greifswald, but in 1925 he returned to Palestine as director of the Gustaf Dalman Institute for Palestinian Research. His works include *Christus im Thalmud* (1891); *Grammatik des jüdisch palästinischen Aramaeisch* (1894); *Aramaeisch-neuhebraeisches Wörterbuch* (1897-1901); *Christentum und Judentum* (1898; Eng. trans., 1901); *Die Worte Jesu* (1898; Eng. trans., 1902); *Petra u. seine Felscheiligtuemer* (1908); *Orte und Wege Jesu* (1919; Eng. trans., 1935); and *Jesus-Jeschua* (1912; Eng. trans., 1929).

BIBLIOGRAPHY:
A. Alt, "Palästinajahrbuch," *des deutschen evangelischen Instituts für Altertumswissenschaft des heiligen Landes zu Jerusalem* 37 (1941), 5-18.
O. Kaiser, *LThK* (1959), 3, 127.

WILLIAM J. CAMERON

DALMANUTHA, a place, probably a village, on the NW shore of Lake Galilee. Mark 8:10, the lone Biblical reference, shows it to be located on the shore of the lake. It was to this region that Christ and the disciples sailed after the miraculous feeding of the 4,000 (Mark 8:1-10; Mt. 15:32-39). When Mark 8:10 is compared with its parallel, Mt. 15:39, it is seen that Magdala is essentially the same as, if not identical with, Dalmanutha.

It may be that Mary Magdalene, who ministered to Christ and who came from Galilee, came from Magdala, that is, from Dalmanutha.

Today as one drives from Tiberias to Capernaum he passes a spot by the road not far from the water of the lake marked by a yellow sign *Magdala* (מגדלא in the Hebrew). The sign stands near an ancient stone tower about 11 feet high, and it explains that this was once *Migdal-Nunia*, "Tower of the Fisherman." It appears to have been a small haven for local fishermen, perhaps used when the lake suddenly became stormy.

DALMATIA, a Roman province located in the S portion of Illyricum. The Dalmatians bitterly opposed the Romans in 157 B.C., suffering the loss of their capital as a result. In 119 B.C. Dalmatia was again occupied by Rome, but in 50 and 48 B.C. the resurgent Dalmatians defeated Caesar and Gabinius. After several years' campaigning, Octavian subjugated Dalmatia in 33 B.C., and forty years later another revolt was crushed by Tiberius. Titus is asked to come to the Apostle Paul in Titus 3:12. Dalmatia is mentioned in II Tim. 4:10 as being the destination of Titus after being with him.

DALPHON, from an Akkadian root meaning "sleepless," this is the second of Haman's ten sons, who were slain by the Jews (Esther 9:7).

DAMARIS, a woman at Athens converted through Paul's preaching (Acts 17:34). Some think she was a foreigner or a woman of loose morals, since Athenian women would not be allowed to stand listening to speakers; but Luke does not say that the converts were drawn only from the audience on the Areopagus.

DAMASCUS, a city situated in a fertile plain, 30 miles by ten in extent at the E base of the Anti-Lebanon range of mountains. The Abana River (modern Barada), from its source on the W flank of the Anti-Lebanons, runs through the mountains and then turns E, where it brings fertility to the plain of Damascus. The plain abounds in gardens, orchards, and meadows. Damascus is on the W border of the Syrian desert and has served as a center for three important trade routes: one leading to the Mediterranean coast and, eventually, Egypt; a second leading to Arabia (now used by pilgrims en route to Mecca); and a third leading across the desert to Baghdad and the Tigris-Euphrates Valley.

Damascus is mentioned in the patriarchal records (Gen. 14:15). Abraham employed a steward who was a native of the city (Gen. 15:2). Later the Egyptian empire-builder, Pharaoh Thutmose III (1490-1436 B.C.), mentions *Timasqu* (Damascus) as subjected to Egyptian control. Still later the king of Qatna (1375-1370 B.C.) wrote a letter to Amenophis IV (Ikhnaton) in which mention is made of the loyalty of Damascus to the pharaohs. In the centuries that followed, Egyptians and Hittites vied for control over Damascus. When the Hittite Empire came to an end and Egypt was weakened as a result of attempts to repel invaders from the N, a series of Aramaean states arose in Syria.

During the reign of David we read that Aramaeans (AV, "Syrians") from Damascus sought to aid Hadadezer of Zobah, but David defeated the coalition and garrisoned the whole territory (II Sam. 8:6). Later we read that Rezon forsook his lord Hadadezer and established himself as king of Damascus (I Kings 11:23-25). During the latter part of Solomon's reign Rezon harassed Israel. With the division of the Israelite kingdom, the Aramaeans of Damascus exercised increasing power. Their king, Ben-hadad, joined Baasha of Israel against Asa of Judah (I Kings 15:19), and then reversed himself and joined Asa against Baasha (I Kings 15:20). Following the death of Ahab at Ramoth-gilead (I Kings 22:15-37), Aramaean bands ravaged Israel and besieged Samaria. A servant of Ben-hadad, Hazael, murdered his master (II Kings 8:15) but met opposition from Assyria. Hazael and his son successfully attacked both Israel and Judah, but Joash was able to recover Israelite cities from the Aramaeans (II Kings 13:3, 22-25). Under Jeroboam II, Damascus was temporarily occupied by Israel (II Kings 14:28). Later, Rezin, king of Damascus, joined Pekah of Israel in besieging Jerusalem (II Kings 16:5). Ahaz of Judah sought aid from the Assyrian king Tiglath-pileser (II Kings 16:7, 8), and the immediate threat to Judah was ended. The Assyrians marched against Damascus; Rezin was slain; the city of Damascus was destroyed; and the Aramaean kingdom was brought to an end (II Kings 16:9). The Assyrians could move against Israel and Judah with little difficulty after the fall of Damascus (732 B.C.).

We do not know when Damascus was rebuilt, but its excellent location could not be by-passed for long. For five centuries after its conquest by Tiglath-pileser it was simply a residence of Assyrian, Neo-Babylonian, and Persian governors. Strabo (xvi, 2, 19) says it was the most famous place in Syria during the Persian period. Darius III left his family and treasures in Damascus when he went out to defend his empire against Alexander the Great. Alexander's victories brought Damascus under his control and it became a provincial capital. Under the Seleucids, Antioch was established as the Syrian capital, and Damascus took a secondary place. In 64 B.C., the Romans under Pompey invaded and captured Syria, constituted it a province, and made Damascus the seat of government. Although the Roman procurators subsequently moved to Antioch, the importance of Damascus did not decline. About A.D. 37, Aretas of Arabia quarreled with Herod Antipas and seized Damascus. During the brief rule of Aretas, Paul visited the city (Gal. 1:16-17; II Cor. 11:32). Following his conversion, which took place on the road to Damascus (Acts 9:1-19), Paul's preaching stirred up opposition, with the result that he had to be let down from the wall of the city in a basket by night (Acts 9:25).

BIBLIOGRAPHY:

E. G. H. Kraeling, *Aram and Israel* (New York, 1918).

A. Malamat, *The Aramaeans in Aram Naharaim and the Rise of their States* (Jerusalem, 1952).
M. F. Unger, *Israel and the Aramaeans of Damascus* (London, 1957).

CHARLES PFEIFFER

DAMASUS, bishop of Rome, A.D. 366-384. His election caused riots by supporters of his rival, Ursinus, in which many were killed, but he was backed by the secular authorities. He became an expert in discovering and embellishing the tombs of martyrs and composed verse epitaphs for them, one of which states that Peter and Paul had once dwelt in Rome. He practically eliminated Arianism from Italy and Illyria, and at a small council, which he convened in Rome in 382, he issued 24 anathemas against doctrinal errors, including Apollinarianism and Macedonianism. Jerome became his private secretary, and Damasus encouraged him in his translation of the Vulgate. J. S. WRIGHT

DAMNATION. See FUTURE STATE.

DAN, "judge":

(1) Jacob's fifth son, borne by Rachel's servant Bilhah and named by Rachel because God had favorably judged her plea for sons (Gen. 30:1-6).

(2) The tribe of Dan, whose inheritance (Josh. 19:40-48) included the maritime plain of Joppa and southward, and the Sorek and Aijalon valleys inland to Benjamin. The Danites failed to overcome the Canaanitish population, especially the Amorites (Judges 1:34), and rapidly declined. Many were absorbed by their kinsmen or assimilated into the indigenous peoples such as the coastal seafarers, to which Judges 5:17 probably alludes, though some here understand N Danites in the service of Tyre.

A remnant held the upper Sorek about Eshtaol and Zorah (Judges 13, 16 and 18), but its precarious position constrained an early migration to Laish (Judges 18), during which the degeneracy of Israelite religion is so poignantly displayed in the incident of Micah and the Levite. Jacob's prophecy likening Dan to a serpent (Gen. 49:17) agrees with the stealth and suddenness which characterized the attack on Laish and also the stratagems of Samson in the later period of Philistine domination.

Although Dan contributed 28,600 troops to David's army at Hebron (I Chron. 12:35), its later history is clouded. The tenuous position Dan sometimes held as one of the twelve tribes may be traceable to an early disintegration and loss of tribal identity under Damascene subjugation throughout the 9th century, together with a religious apostasy engendered by the bull cultus established by Jeroboam. Thus, although included by Ezekiel (ch. 48), Dan is omitted by the genealogies of I Chron. 2–9 and by John in Rev. 7.

(3) A city located on the Nahr el-Leddan, a major source of the Jordan, identified with Tell el-Qadi, in which the Arabic "Qadi" also means "judge." Here Abraham overtook Chedorlaomer (Gen. 14). The later Phoenician settlement of Laish was unprotected and fell easily to the tribe of Dan, which rebuilt and renamed the city (Judges 18). Thereafter it was Israel's most northerly city and is thus frequently cited in the formula "from Dan to Beersheba."

Its choice as the site of one of Jeroboam's two royal chapels apparently was determined by its border location, an ideal place to invoke, and thus constrain and insure, divine protection of the kingdom's sovereignty and territorial integrity, as well as by the prior existence of a sanctuary and priesthood whose heritage was rooted in antiquity (Judges 18:30). Benhadad I seized the city from Baasha shortly after 890 B.C., but Israelite reoccupation before the reign of Jeroboam II is doubtful. In the last third of the eighth century Assyrian invasions and deportations brought fulfillment to the prophecy of Amos 8:14.

Bibliography:

A. Fernandez, "El Santuario de Dan," *Biblica* 15 (1934), 237-264.

Y. Kaufmann, *The Biblical Account of the Conquest of Palestine* (Jerusalem, 1953).

H. H. Rowley, "The Danite Migration to Laish," *ET* 51 (1940), 466-471.

H. H. Rowley, *From Joseph to Joshua* (London, 1950).

Joseph P. Duggan

DANCING. Dancing is associated with joyful celebration, such as the crossing of the Red Sea (Ex. 15:20); with the joyful homecoming of Jephthah (Judges 11:34) and the Prodigal Son (Luke 15:25); when the ark was brought into Jerusalem (II Sam. 6:14); at sacred festivals (Judges 21:21); and in some of the regular worship of praise in the temple (Ps. 149:3; 150:4). Dancing for sheer joy is implied in Ps. 30:11 and Jer. 31:4 and formed a part of children's games (Mt. 11:17). Later Jewish writings describe wholesale dancing at the Feast of Tabernacles, when even staid scholars showed their individual skill.

E practice, presumably followed by the Hebrews, was for the sexes to dance separately, or in lines, often moving spontaneously in time to percussion instruments like timbrels or tambourines (Ex. 15:20; Jer. 31:4). The exhibition dance by the daughter of Herodias (Mt. 14:6) was a degenerate introduction from Greece and Rome.

Early Christians in pagan society soon found it expedient to ban dancing altogether. J. S. Wright

DANIEL ("God is my Judge").

(1) Immediately we think of the famous prophet of this name, from whom we possess a book of the Bible bearing the same name. Various critical scholars attribute this book to some author who used a famous personality from the remote past as the hero of his story in order to lend stature to his material. This idea has been strengthened by texts found in Ras Shamra, because they contain a legend concerning a certain Danel who was generally renowned because of his help to widows and orphans. The Biblical writer could have identified the main character of the book of Daniel with this Danel. Others, who dismiss this theory, are nevertheless of the opinion that we encounter the legendary Danel in Ezekiel 14:14, 20; 28:3. Ezekiel must have had this person in mind and not the *prophet* Daniel, considering that he names him along with two other men of primeval time, namely Noah and Job. The prophet Daniel was a contemporary of Ezekiel and his fellow captive, and therefore, according to this opinion, could not yet have had such renown among these associates as the famous "righteous ones." Furthermore, it is pointed out that the striking name in the Hebrew text of Ezekiel is spelled differently than that of the prophet. This would be all the more reason to conclude that Ezekiel does not refer to his contemporary Daniel in the text but rather the above-mentioned hero of antiquity.

Against this opinion, however, is the great improbability that a prophet such as Ezekiel, who always turns sharply against all forms of idolatry, would put a heathen mantic (in the case of the legendary Danel) on the same plane with the "Righteous Ones," Noah (Gen. 6:9) and Job (Job 1:1). The mention of Daniel between Noah and Job does not in the least indicate that for Ezekiel he was a figure from the distant past; this indicates simply that the Daniel mentioned at the time of the Babylonian captivity at least enjoyed just as great a fame for his righteousness and wisdom as the ancient famous personalities Noah and Job. And with reference to the *prophet* Daniel this is indeed possible, if we consider that the prophecies of Ezekiel in question date at least from the sixth or ninth year of his captivity (see Ezek. 8:1; 24:1), that is, 592 and 589 B.C., and that the appointment of Daniel was as ruler over Babylon and chief over all the Babylonian wise men (see Dan. 2:48). By this his fame was everywhere established, which must, in all probability, be dated in the year 593 B.C.

In any case, there is no reason not to identify the main character of the book of Daniel with the historical prophet. What we know about this prophet otherwise, is known only from the book that bears his name. He was one of the Jewish men of noble origin who, during the reign of King Jehoikim, were carried away to Babylon (II Kings 24:1 ff.) to serve in the royal court. During the three years of his indoctrination he proved to be extraordinarily committed to the service of the Lord, for which he was rewarded by God with unique gifts of knowledge, understanding, and wisdom, and also with a deep insight into the meaning of all sorts of visions and dreams (Dan. 1). Thus he was given a particular insight by revelation and interpretation of a dream that Nebuchadnezzar had dreamed, the so-called monarchy dream (Dan. 2). A short time later he provided a similar service to Nebuchadnezzar on the occasion of another important dream. This dream involved a revelation concerning the king's future fate, namely, a temporary insanity which would result in his being removed from the kingship and the community (Dan. 4).

We know nothing about the experiences of the prophet during the reign of the three immediate successors of Nebuchadnezzar (Amel-Marduk, Nergal-Sharezer, and Labashi-Marduk, from 562 to 556). We hear of him again only under the rule of Belshazzar, the son of the last Chaldean king, Nabonidus (Nabu-Naid), who replaced his father for a short time during his absence (*c.* 550-545 B.C.; see Dan. 5). Daniel's interpretation of the writing on the wall caused him once again to occupy a very prominent position under the new authorities who had seized control over Babylon. Darius the Mede installed him as one of the three top functionaries who were to exercise supervision over the 120 princes of the whole kingdom. The jealousy of these princes is what brought Daniel to the lions' den (Dan. 6).

During the reign of the same Darius, another striking revelation came to the prophet concerning the "seventy weeks" or "seventy sevens" (Dan. 9). Darius the Mede was succeeded by Cyrus the Persian, under whose regime the edict was published which granted freedom to the Jewish exiles to return to their homeland. Daniel himself, however, made no use of this freedom, probably because of his advanced age or because his official position did not allow him to leave Babylon. In any case, Daniel continued to exercise his exalted office under the rule of Cyrus and was held in high esteem by the king (Dan. 6:28). In the third year of this monarch's reign the prophet received another new Divine revelation, which we find in the last chapters of the book of Daniel (Dan. 10-12).

(2) A son of David by Abigail, mentioned in I Chronicles 3:1. In II Samuel 3:3, however, he is called by the name of *Chileab*. Presumably this prince died at an early age.

(3) A contemporary of Ezra and Nehemiah (see Ezra 8:2; Neh. 10:6) about whom nothing further is mentioned.

J. G. Aalders

DANIEL, THE BOOK OF. The book of Daniel appears among the major prophets in the English and Greek Bibles. In the present Hebrew Bible it occurs near the end, among the "Hagiographa" or Writings. Written ostensibly by Daniel, the great statesman and prophet of the Exile, it would have been completed about 536 B.C. The tenth chapter records a vision of the third year of Cyrus, king of Persia, which was 536 B.C. The book has long been a favorite because of its intriguing story of God's blessing on this faithful man who came a captive lad to the court at Babylon and advanced to high position. It has also been an important book in discussions of prophetic teaching, for Daniel was given visions of far distant things. But the book has also been a battleground of critical attack, and it is confidently asserted by many to be late and spurious. The book, like Ezra but unlike any other OT writing, is partly written in Aramaic (Dan. 2:4b–7:28). The date and characteristics of this Aramaic have been much discussed. Some new material bearing on Daniel comes from the Dead Sea Scrolls.

The following is an outline of the book of Daniel:

- I. Daniel's captivity and youth, 1:1-21.
- II. Nebuchadnezzar's dream of the image, 2:1-49.
- III. Historical incidents at court, 3:1–6:28.
  - A. Nebuchadnezzar's idol and the fiery furnace, 3:1-30.
  - B. Nebuchadnezzar's madness, 4:1-37.
  - C. Belshazzar's feast, 5:1-31.
  - D. Daniel in the lions' den, 6:1-28.
- IV. Prophecies of future days, 7:1–12:13.
  - A. Four beasts and four kingdoms, 7:1-28.
  - B. Medo-Persia and Greece, 8:1-27.
  - C. The 70 years and 70 "weeks," 9:1-27.
  - D. Visions of the final days, 10:1–12:13.
    1. Daniel's prayer and vision, 10:1-21.
    2. Preview of the kings of the North and South, 11:1-35.
    3. The willful king of the end time, 11:36-45.
    4. The tribulation, resurrection, and finale, 12:1-13.

Date and Authorship

The traditional view held almost universally in Jewish and Christian circles until modern times is that the book was written by Daniel the prophet in the sixth century B.C. The skeptic Porphyry (*c.* A.D. 270), however, claimed that the book was written in the day of Antiochus Epiphanes, because it gives accurately the events of his reign. It will be noted that the arguments of Porphyry are quite similar to those of modern higher critics. Daniel does indeed speak of the events of Antiochus Epiphanes and the Maccabean revolt. The question is, does he do this as a contemporary, or does he as a prophet predict future events? The early date of Daniel cannot be held unless one holds to the possibility of supernatural revelation of events in the distant future. This watershed of opinion is most noticeable in connection with the book of Daniel and thus it has become a battleground of critical-orthodox study.

There is not sufficient external evidence for or against the early date of Daniel to decide the question. Daniel is referred to in I Maccabees 2:59-60, but the date of I Maccabees is not certain, perhaps about 100 B.C. The earliest positive evidence now comes from the Dead Sea Scrolls, among which are a dozen copies of the book. According to F. L. Cross (*The Ancient Library of Qumran,* 1961, p. 43), "one copy of Daniel is inscribed in the script of the late second century B.C. . . no more than about a half century younger than the autograph of Daniel." Cross here assumes the Maccabean date of Daniel (166 B.C.) and is surprised that it made its way so quickly into the library of Qumran. He does not even consider that it could have been older. It is alleged against the early date that "the book is not known by Sirach in the list of Israel's great persons (Ecclus. 44-49), which gives us a *terminus a quo* in about 180 B.C." (A.

Bentzen, *Introduction to the Old Testament*, 1958, Vol. II, p. 199). To be more accurate, an argument from silence can hardly give us a *terminus* before which there was no book of Daniel. The list of famous men in Ecclesiasticus is not considered to be complete. It includes others besides authors of Scripture (Noah, Abraham, Aaron), and omits authors of Scripture (Ezra, Job—fragments of Job from 200 B.C. are found at Qumran). There is no external evidence against the early date of Daniel.

Critical Arguments

The three lines of argument on which critics rely for their conclusions are the linguistic, the historical, and the canonical phenomena. These are very capably handled in introductions such as G. L. Archer, Jr. (*A Survey of Old Testament Introduction*, 1964) and may be summarized here.

The linguistic argument includes the nature of the dialect of the Aramaic portions, the presence of Persian loan words, and especially the presence of three Greek loan words which are said to force a date after Alexander the Great.

The dialect of the Aramaic is no longer considered so significant. It used to be said that the E Aramaic had a third masculine singular imperfect verb form beginning with "n" and that W Aramaic, including Ezra and Daniel, used a form beginning with "y." Therefore Daniel was written in Palestine, not Babylon. It is true that later Aramaic shows this division. But since the discovery of the Jewish Aramaic documents of the 5th century in Egypt and also the older royal inscriptions, this division into E and W cannot be maintained. Whole books have been written on the details of this linguistic argument. But the conclusion of critical scholars themselves is that "a generation ago the *Linguistic proofs* played a greater role than now. . . . the Persian government-language already from the time of *Darius I* (about 500 B.C.) has influenced the Aramaic dialects so that their differences have been blotted out" (Bentzen, *op. cit.*, Vol. II, p. 199 f.). Bentzen still relies on the loan words and claims that the use of the word *Chaldaean* indicates lateness. But the other old arguments are largely given up. After all, almost any student can see that the Aramaic of Daniel is quite close to that of Ezra and this in turn well paralleled by the fifth-century Aramaic from Egypt.

As to the presence of the loan words, it is true that Daniel contains about 15 Persian words and three Greek words. But the conclusion to be drawn from this fact is not clear. It seems to be assumed by critical scholars that no one in Mesopotamia knew any Greek until Alexander the Great nor any Persian until Cyrus. Such a view assumes that ancient cultures were primitive, isolated, and parochial, when it is as plain as can be that they were not. The Medians (related to the Persians) fought side by side with the Babylonians in the conquest of Nineveh in 612 B.C. Why should Persian words not have been well known at the Babylonian court? And moreover Daniel lived on at least three years into the Persian period. If he wrote his memoirs in his old age, he might well have used the terms which surely irrupted into Mesopotamia after the Persian conquest.

The arguments built on the three Greek words seem almost curious. These words (in 3:5, 10, and 15) are names of Greek musical instruments. If such instruments were not known and used in the Babylonian court, it would be strange indeed. After all, the Persian kings invaded Greece in 490 B.C. and took a whole city captive. Four hundred years later these captives near Susa still spoke their native Greek (A. T. Olmstead, *History of the Persian Empire*, 1948, p. 161). The Persian invasions of Greece had been preceded by years of contact and of friction between Greek colonists in Asia Minor and Mesopotamian governments from Nebuchadnezzar on down. If Daniel had been written in Maccabean times in Palestine, it might well have had no Persian words and many Greek words—or if it had been written by a patriot it might have had no foreign words at all. One should compare Ecclesiasticus, written in Palestine in 180 B.C., which has no Persian non-Biblical words and no Greek. Greek dialects were used in the Mediterranean area since 1400 B.C. One should not be surprised at a few Greek loan words in sixth-century Babylonian material.

The historical arguments against Daniel are still urged, although only two are of any force. The claim is made that the sixth-century history of Daniel is confused, but the later history of Palestine right up to the time of the Maccabees is impeccable. Actually all of its history can be defended. Bentzen (*op. cit.*, Vol. II, p. 195) claims that the dates of 1:1 do not agree with 2:1. But it is easy to answer that comparison of these verses with Jeremiah 25:1 shows that the discrepancy concerns only one year, and it is now known that a king's accession year was sometimes counted, sometimes not. Authors still claim that Belshazzar is not accurately pictured as the last king of Babylon. But this material has often been gone over, and since the research of R. P. Dougherty, it is clear that Belshazzar had royal prerogatives and was in fact at the helm while his father Nabonidus lived in retirement. That Nebuchadnezzar is called the father of Belshazzar means no more than that he was a predecessor. The details are given by Archer (*op. cit.*, p. 370 f.). Actually only Daniel of all ancient historians has the details of Belshazzar's reign correct. Herodotus and others do not mention him at all. It is not clear how a Maccabean author would have known that Belshazzar could only promise Daniel the *third* place in the kingdom (5:16).

The only significant historical errors that can be alleged are the matter of Darius the Mede and the madness of Nebuchadnezzar. Daniel says that Darius the Mede took the kingdom; Cyrus' own writings leave no room for Darius the Mede. It should be noted that Daniel is well aware of the existence of Cyrus, king of Persia (10:1 and 6:28). And the later Darius the Great is given as a Persian and successor to Cyrus in Ezra 4:5—a writing well known among the Jews. There is therefore small possibility that the author of Daniel, if he wrote at a later date, would be confused here. Rather it is probable that Darius the Mede is a representation of an earlier figure unknown to us, at least by that name. Two suggestions have been made, either of which is possible—first, that he was a subordinate king of Babylon under Cyrus the King of Kings. J. Whitcomb has argued this at length and shown that it is a definite possibility (*Darius the Mede*, 1959; also Archer, *op. cit.*, pp. 371-374). Another possibility, suggested by D. Wiseman, is that Darius is the throne name used by Cyrus in his Median domains, as Tiglath Pileser was called Pul in Babylon. Wiseman has discovered a tablet referring to the king of the Medes while Cyrus was on the Medo-Persian throne (see article "Darius" in *The New Bible Dictionary*, ed. J. D. Douglas, 1965).

The matter of Nebuchadnezzar's madness is reopened by the "prayer of Nabonidus" discovered among the Dead Sea Scrolls in which Nabonidus suffers from some disease for seven years in the oasis of Teima and is recovered by a Jewish magician (text in J. T. Milik, *Ten Years of Discovery in the Wilderness of Judea*, 1959, p. 36 f.). It is now often held that the Scroll is correct and Daniel wrong in attaching the story to Nebuchadnezzar. Of course the reverse could as easily be true, and it is not impossible that both were true. Kings suffer illnesses also. And many kings have been insane. There is another possibility which is not at all unlikely, although proof is wanting. It is not impossible that Nabonidus on occasion usurped the name of the great Nebuchadnezzar as he had usurped the throne. It is clear that one of Nabonidus' sons, Nidintu-Bel, took the name of Nebuchadnezzar in his bid for the throne in 522 B.C., as had another pretender in 521 B.C. (Olmstead, *op. cit.*, pp. 112, 115). It is not at all unlikely that Nabonidus bore two names, as many kings before and after him have done. Nabonidus' otherwise unexplained long retirement in Teima would thus be made more understandable.

The argument for a late date of Daniel because of its position in the third division of the Hebrew Bible is singularly weak. Few authors, conservative or critical, seem to realize that there is no evidence that Daniel was originally in the third division of the Hebrew Bible. Our present Hebrew Bible arrangement cannot be traced back of a passage in the Talmud of about A.D. 400. There is an earlier Christian listing by Melito (A.D. 170) which positions Daniel between the Minor Prophets and Ezekiel. A still earlier authority, Josephus (A.D. 90), clearly places Daniel in the second of three divisions, divisions that do not parallel the three divisions of the Talmud. Books clearly switched places in antiquity, and Daniel's position in later listings cannot be used as the basis of any argument for its early position or date of authorship. Prominent theories of canonical studies today founder on these few facts (cf. R. Laird Harris, *Inspiration and Canonicity of the Bible*, 1957, pp. 140-153).

The arguments for a late date being what they are, it seems very likely that the skeptical considerations of Porphyry are still determinative. If predictive supernatural prophecy is possible, the early date of Daniel may fairly be maintained. To a non-supernaturalist who cannot admit the possibility of a detailed preview of history, the Maccabean date is a necessity; for all agree that chapter 11 carries the history of the Jews right down to about 165 B.C.

The Histories of Daniel

The character of Daniel is beautifully illustrated in the opening scene, where Daniel, of the king's family in Jerusalem, is taken as a slave to the court of Babylon. Like many another godly youth, he maintained his faith in a foreign milieu, and God blessed him for his faithfulness. His rise to prominence, like Joseph's, resulted from his interpreting the king's dream (chapter 2). The king's wise men spoke to the king in Aramaic (2:4) and from there until 7:28 the language is in Aramaic, the *lingua franca* of the day. The change from Hebrew to Aramaic and back again at these junctures is attested by the Dead Sea fragments. R. D. Culver has the best explanation of this phenomenon in his excellent commentary: Aramaic is simply used for the "Gentile-slanted portion" ("Daniel" in *Wycliffe Bible Commentary*, 1962, p. 770). The king is given a preview of history which will be considered later. Daniel himself does not figure in the episode of Nebuchadnezzar's image. He may well have been away on state business. But his three friends stood true and their testimony was amply rewarded. The madness of Nebuchadnezzar has already been considered.

Belshazzar's feast has always been intriguing. The handwriting on the wall was not Hebrew (which would have given the second word as *shekel*). It was Aramaic and can have a variety of meanings. It may mean "counted," "weighed," "divided." It may also refer to weights as our "pound," "ounce," "half-pound." It could also mean items of money, like our "dollar," "quarter," "half-dollar." The last word includes a play on the word *Persian*. It is not necessary to think that Belshazzar could not read the words. It was the meaning of the frightening phenomenon that unnerved the king. Daniel gave the interpretation in its context of moral judgment. He was rewarded with hollow honors. Belshazzar's feast, life, and kingdom were come to an end.

Daniel in the lions' den is another instance of God's keeping His faithful servants in time of trial. Bentzen (*op. cit.*, Vol. II, p. 195) calls these histories "legends" because the same motif is found in chapters 3 and 6. He could have gone further. This motif is also to an extent found in chapter 1 and in many other parts of the Bible. God's deliverance is a recurring miracle. To some, all miracles are "legends." But the answer to such skepticism is given by Paul on the basis of a vibrant theism: "Why should it be thought a thing incredible with you, that *God* should raise the dead?" (Acts 26:8).

The Prophetic Sections

The prophecies of Daniel fall into five sections: Nebuchadnezzar's image (chap. 2), Daniel's four beasts (chap. 7), the ram and he-goat (chap. 8), the seventy weeks (chap. 9), and the future of Persia, Greece, and following times (chaps. 10-12). In general, these prophecies concern four great empires, followed by a fifth that comes from God. The interpretation of the visions can best be elucidated by comparing them in chart form (next page) so that their symbolism may be better appreciated.

Two questions particularly arise concerning the prophecies. What kingdoms do the four divisions represent, and does the Divine kingdom immediately succeed the earthly kingdoms, or does it concern eschatology? The critics' answer to the first question is that the four kingdoms represented are Babylon, Media, Persia, and Greece, with the Grecian empire coming to a head in Antiochus Epiphanes of Maccabean times. The conservative view is that the four empires are Babylon, Medo-Persia, Greece, and Rome. The chart follows the latter view. Note how the symbolism of the third beast in chapter 7 fits that of chapter 8, which is clearly labelled Greece. Also, the symbolism of the second beast of chapter 7 best fits that of Medo-Persia in chapter 8. Media as a kingdom is never given an independent status in Daniel, and indeed Media did not follow Babylon in history. Media was an ally of Babylon against Nineveh in 612 B.C. and fell to Cyrus in 550 B.C., before he conquered Babylon. The critical view, then, would thus distort both symbolism and history. Comments on the identification of the Divine kingdom and the interpretation of Daniel 9 follow the chart. The identifications given in the Biblical text are shown. The identifications inferred from symbolism and parallels are enclosed in parenthesis.

The interpretation of the 70 weeks has been an ancient problem. Many commentators take this to mean 490 days, with each day standing for a year. Others object to the year-day theory. Actually in Daniel the word *week*, when referring to seven days, is qualified *weeks of days* (10:2, 3, in the Hebrew). But the word *week* is used throughout the apocryphal book of *Jubilees* to refer to a period of seven years, a Hebrew sabbatical. How long before *Jubilees* this usage prevailed we do not know, but the sabbatical year was early. The claim therefore can be advanced that the prophet understood that a period of 70 sabbatical years was intended by the angel who came in answer to Daniel's prayer concerning the 70 years. The angel gives a word on 70 sabbaticals as a further revelation.

COMPARISON OF THE PROPHESIES OF DANIEL

Chapter 2	*Chapter 7*	*Chapter 8*	*Chapter 9*	*Chapters 11-12*
Head of gold Babylon	Lion with eagles' wings (Babylon)			
Chest of silver (Medo-Persia)	Bear rising on one side (Medo-Persia)	Ram with two horns, last higher Media & Persia	70 weeks 490 years starting 456 B.C.	3 kings remaining in Persia
Belly of brass (Greece)	Leopard with 4 wings and 4 heads (Greece)	He-goat 1 horn becoming 4 Greece	↓	Great king of Greece 4 divisions, not to sons
Legs of iron (Rome?)	Dreadful beast of 10 horns (Rome?)		↓	Fighting of King of South vs. King of North—till Antiochus Epiphanes, the vile person of 11:21
Toes of iron and clay			↓	
			A.D. 27 interval	
			70th week 7 years	Great Tribulation 12:1 Resurrection of Dead 12:2
			Abomination of Desolation. Cessation of sacrifice. 9:27	Abomination of Desolation. Cessation of sacrifice 12:11
Stone becoming a mountain	Judgment of the Ancient of Days & coming of Son of man			

The 70 sabbaticals, however, do not run to the Messiah. The last one, the 70th, is after His coming. From the command to build Jerusalem to the Messiah is to be 7 sabbaticals plus 62 sabbaticals—a total of 69 or 483 years.

Some students take these numbers as purely symbolic and claim that no calculation is possible. But Daniel did not himself so treat the prophecy of the 70 years of captivity. Neither did the Chronicler (II Chron. 36:21). A merely symbolic treatment of these figures cannot be proved. Others insert an unknown period between the 7 sabbaticals and the 62. This is not necessary. We do not know why the number 69 might be divided up, but there was a tendency to isolate the number 7. Ezekiel 45:12 strangely divides the *maneh* into 20, 25, and 15 shekels, and we do not know why. But the total is 60 shekels, as would be expected. A hiatus between the 7 and 62 is not indicated or necessary.

The start of the 483-year period has been variously understood. Some hold that it begins with the year when Jeremiah prophesied the return. That would be 605 (Jer. 25:12) and would yield a date of 122 B.C. Others hold more logically that the start was the time of Cyrus' permission to return. That would be about 539 and would yield a date of 56 B.C. Neither of these dates fits the reign of Antiochus Ephiphanes, but critical scholars merely reply that the author of Daniel was mixed up in his dates.

The other two obvious options are the returns under Nehemiah (444 B.C.) or Ezra (456 B.C.). Nehemiah did indeed build the wall of Jerusalem. But his date yields A.D. 39, which does not fit the time of Christ. Therefore some have adjusted the data by claiming that the 483 years were short prophetic years of 360 days (cf. Rev. 12:6, 14; 13:5). This figures out to an equivalent of 473 years and yields about A.D. 30, the year of Christ's crucifixion. This result is impressive, but it gives the impression that the figures have been juggled.

Actually the return of Ezra is satisfactory. Ezra 4:7-21 tells of an attempt to build the walls in the days of Artaxerxes, which was stopped. The work of Nehemiah in the 20th year of Artaxerxes succeeded. The unfortunate start could only have been made by Ezra, who returned in the seventh year of Artaxerxes, bringing 1,750 men with their families, and 7,500 pounds of gold and 50,000 pounds of silver, plus precious vessels. Ezra, with these resources, surely intended to do something. Ezra 4:12 says the wall was partly built in those times. It seems that the date of Ezra, 456 B.C., is a suitable starting point. It yields a date of about A.D. 27, just the time of the beginning of the ministry of the Messiah of Israel. Note that a literal, straightforward interpretation of Daniel's prophecy falls directly on the time of Christ's appearing to Israel. This says something, surely, for the possibility of supernatural prophecy and for the reality of Daniel's prophetic work.

The question remains as to the interpretation of the fifth monarchy, the Divine kingdom. Three main views have been held. First, the critical view claims that these visions were given by the unnamed author of 166 B.C., who thought, mistakenly, that he was living in the last time. He expected an immediate beginning of the heavenly kingdom of God and prophesied it in lurid detail to comfort and support his compatriots in the Maccabean wars.

The second view is that these prophecies refer to the Christian church, which was to follow the fourth empire, identified as Rome. The stone of chapter 2, the church, becomes a great mountain and fills the earth. This is the viewpoint especially of postmillennialism and amillennialism. The 70th week of Daniel follows immediately on the 69th week, which tells of His advent. The first half of the 70th sabbatical is the three-and-a-half-year ministry of Christ. Then the sacrifices ceased when Jesus died. Shortly the Abomination of Desolation was set up when Jerusalem was destroyed in A.D. 70. This view does not seem to deal adequately with the parallels from chapters 7 and 12.

The third view is held in premillennial circles. It holds that there is an interruption in the affairs predicted in Daniel's vision and that the stone of chapter 2 is the millennial kingdom at the end of this age. Likewise, the 70th week is held to be eschatological with the church period as an interval between. At first sight, this view seems to be unnatural, but the parallels above referred to are clearly eschatological with chapter 7 referring plainly to the eschatological judgment and 7:13 to the Second Coming of Christ (cf. NT references in Mt. 24:30; 26:64; Rev. 1:7; 14:14, 15, etc.). Furthermore, the events of chapter 12 are clearly eschatological, and the Abomination of Desolation links 12:11 with Daniel's 70th sabbatical in 9:27 and with Christ's eschatological warnings in Matthew 24:15.

There must be some interval between the historical and eschatological in chapter 7, for Greece is clearly spoken of followed by a fourth beast, which is logically Rome, followed in turn by the judgment. There must also be an interval in chapters 11-12, for the kings of Egypt and Antioch seem to end in Antiochus Epiphanes in 11:21-35. Whether the willful king of 11:36-45 is still Antiochus or the man of sin of II Thessalonians 2:3 of whom he is an illustration may not be certain. But, again, the next item is clearly eschatological. The precise beginning of this interval may be indicated by chapter 9, which carries history up to the coming of Christ and begins the 70th sabbatical with events connected with His Second Coming. There are many shades of opinion in all three of the views, for which the commentaries must be consulted.

The book of Daniel, as is obvious from the above discussion, is much used in the NT, and much of its symbolism is taken up in the book of Revelation. Similar divisions of opinion bear on the interpretation of that book. But, like the book of Revelation, there is much of a doctrinal nature of basic importance in Daniel apart from its prophetic message. Its teaching of the power and grace of God, the reality of angelic help, and the necessity of fidelity under trial are all themes that are vital to Christian thought and life.

BIBLIOGRAPHY:

O. T. Allis, *Prophecy and the Church* (Philadelphia, 1945).

G. L. Archer, Jr., *A Survey of Old Testament Introduction* (Chicago, 1964).

C. A. Auberlen, *The Prophecies of Daniel and the Revelation of St. John* (Andover, 1857).

C. Boutflower, *In and Around the Book of Daniel* (London, 1923).

R. D. Culver, *Daniel and the Latter Days* (Westwood, N. J., 1954).

R. P. Dougherty, *Nabonidus and Belshazzar* (New Haven, 1929).

R. L. Harris, *Inspiration and Canonicity of the Bible* (Grand Rapids, 1969, revised).

The Interpreter's Bible, Vol. VI, *Lamentations, Ezekiel, Daniel and the Twelve Prophets* (New York, 1956).

Jerome's Commentary on Daniel, translated by G. Archer (Grand Rapids, 1958).

C. F. Keil, *Biblical Commentary on the Book of Daniel* (Grand Rapids, 1949).

H. C. Leupold, *Exposition of Daniel* (Columbus, Ohio, 1949).

P. Mauro, *The Seventy Weeks and the Great Tribulation* (New York, 1919).

A. J. McClain, *Prophecy of the Seventy Weeks* (Grand Rapids, 1940).

J. A. Montgomery, *A Critical and Exegetical Commentary on the Book of Daniel,* International Critical Commentary (New York, 1927).

E. B. Pusey, *Daniel the Prophet* (New York, 1885).

J. C. Whitcomb, *Darius the Mede* (Grand Rapids, 1959).

R. D. Wilson, *Studies in the Book of Daniel* (New York, 1917).

R. D. Wilson, *Studies in the Book of Daniel,* Second Series (New York, 1938).

E. J. Young, *The Prophecy of Daniel* (Grand Rapids, 1948).

R. LAIRD HARRIS

DAN-JAAN, between Tahtim-hodshi in Gilead and Sidon (II Sam. 24:6), corresponds to the town mentioned in Abram's eastern pursuit of Chedorlaomer (Gen. 14:14; Dan-Laish, in the N, arose later, Judges 18:29) and seen by Moses from Pisgah (Deut. 34:1).

BIBLIOGRAPHY:

S. R. Driver, *Commentary on Deuteronomy (ICC)*, 421.

H. C. Leupold, *Exposition of Genesis* (Grand Rapids, 1958), I, 459.

H. P. Smith, *Commentary on the Books of Samuel (ICC)*, 389-390.

J. BARTON PAYNE

DANNAH, a city situated in the hill country of Judah (Josh. 15:49). Its location, in all probability, corresponds to that of the modern Idhna, about eight miles W of Hebron.

DANTE ALIGHIERI (1265-1321), Italian poet. From his youth Dante eagerly absorbed learning of all kinds. Becoming one of the chief magistrates of Florence, he opposed papal interference in the city's affairs. This led in 1302 to a false charge brought against him, banishment, loss of possessions, and threat of execution if he returned to Florence. He travelled widely. Henry of Luxembourg's election as emperor augured well for Dante, but before his hopes of a new régime in Florence had been realized Henry died. Dante passed the rest of his life in exile and died at Ravenna. His crowning achievement was the *Commedia* (*c.* 1300), to which the adjective *divina* was attached by Boccaccio. Portraying the author's journey through hell, purgatory, and heaven, *The Divine Comedy* is unique, its people and situations realistic (even identifiable), and its aim to warn men that policies and actions now would meet with a reward or penalty hereafter. More than 500 manuscripts of the *Comedy* have been preserved, and it has been translated into numerous languages. Dante's other works include *Vita Nouva* (1294), which relates his love for Beatrice; and *De Monarchia* (*c.* 1313), advocating a universal monarchy exercised by sacred and secular powers. Dante has long been regarded as the national poet of Italy.

DARA, the name of Judah's grandson born to Zerah (I Chron. 2:8). He is called Darda in I Kings 4:31, where Solomon as a wise man is compared with him.

DARBY, John Nelson (1800-1882), pioneer of the Plymouth Brethren. John Nelson Darby was the son of a well-to-do Irish landowner and merchant. The family home was at Leap Castle, Offaly. At fifteen he entered Trinity College, Dublin, where in 1819 he graduated as Classical Gold Medallist. Although he was called to the Irish Bar, he abandoned his career for the church, being ordained deacon in 1825 and priest in 1826. His only charge was as curate of Calary, County Wicklow (1825-27). After this he felt constrained to leave the Anglican church. Going to Dublin, he became associated with a devout group called the "Brethren," among whom were A. N. Groves and J. G. Bellett. The established church disillusioned Darby. A long and thoughtful convalescence enabled him to plot his own course. By 1830 in Plymouth, England, he had won many people to his views, including clergymen and the Biblical scholar Samuel Prideaux Tregelles. Starting as an extreme sacramentalist ecclesiastically, he moved outside the church to form a sect given to the supremacy of Scripture without tradition. In 1838 he went to live in French Switzerland, where many congregations were formed. Others also arose in France, Germany, and Italy. When he returned to England he found many divisions due to doctrinal deviations among the Brethren, beginning at Plymouth. To cope with this the "circle of fellowship" concept was developed, which resulted in the formation of the Exclusive Brethren or Darbyites. Later in 1881 this group split again on a point of discipline, and that pattern has not ceased. Throughout, Darby made many tours abroad to lecture and preach, including visits to North America and New Zealand. His works were numerous, including works on controversial, doctrinal, and devotional subjects, and hymns.

See BRETHREN, PLYMOUTH.

DARDA. See DARA.

DARGAN, Edwin Charles (1852-1930), Baptist pastor. Born in Springville, South Carolina, Dargan graduated from Furman University and the Southern Baptist Theological Seminary (1877). He held pastorates in Baptist churches in Virginia, California, and South Carolina, until he became professor of homiletics in the Southern Baptist Theological

Seminary, Louisville, Kentucky, in 1892, where he taught until 1907. From 1907 to 1917 he was pastor of the First Baptist Church of Macon, Georgia, and from 1917 to 1927 was the editor of Sunday School Lesson Helps for the Southern Baptist Convention.

Dargan is principally remembered for his two-volume work, *A History of Preaching*, Vol. I, 1905; Vol. II, 1912 (republished by Baker Book House, Grand Rapids, 1968, 1970). Largely by default, this history has become the standard work in the field.

JAY E. ADAMS

DARIUS:

(1) *Darius the Mede* (601-525 B.C.), ruler of "the realm of the Chaldeans" (Dan. 9:1) under Cyrus (Dan. 6:28) immediately following the death of Belshazzar (Dan. 5:30). He is best remembered for his decree which resulted in the prophet Daniel being cast into a den of lions (Dan. 6:7-18). He was of Median extraction, "of the seed of the Medes" (Dan. 9:1), and his father's name was Ahasuerus (the Hebrew equivalent of "Xerxes," the name of a later king of Persia; cf. Esther 1:1). He was born in 601/600 B.C., for at the fall of Babylon (October, 539 B.C.) he was 62 (Dan. 5:31).

One of the cardinal doctrines of negative criticism has been that the book of Daniel was written by an unknown author of the Maccabean age (*c.* 165 B.C.) who mistakenly thought that an independent Median kingdom ruled by Darius the Mede followed the fall of Babylon and preceded the rise of Persia under Cyrus. But Darius the Mede is not depicted in the book of Daniel as a universal monarch. In fact, his subordinate position is clearly implied in the statement that he "was made king over the realm of the Chaldeans" (Dan. 9:1). Also, the fact that Belshazzar's kingdom was "given to the Medes and *Persians*" (Dan. 5:28) and that Darius found himself helpless to alter the "law of the Medes and *Persians*" (Dan. 6:15) renders the critical view untenable.

The publication of additional cuneiform texts from this period has enabled us to gain a clearer understanding of the fall of Babylon in 539 B.C. It seems quite possible that Darius the Mede was none other than Gubaru, the governor under Cyrus, who appointed subgovernors in Babylon immediately after the fall of that city (cf. "Nabonidus Chronicle," *ANET*, p. 306). This same Gubaru (not to be confused with Ugbaru, governor of Gutium, the general under Cyrus who conquered Babylon and died three weeks later) is frequently mentioned in cuneiform documents during the following fourteen years as governor of Babylon and the Region Beyond the River. (It may be that the term "Darius" is a title that could be applied to any ruler and that it was applied to Gubaru as being from Media.) Gubaru thus ruled over the vast and populous territories of Babylonia, Syria, Phoenicia, and Palestine, and his name was a final warning to criminals throughout this area (cf. J. C. Whitcomb, *Darius the Mede*, Grand Rapids, 1959, pp. 10-24). The fact that he is called "king" in the sixth chapter of Daniel is not an inaccuracy, even though he was a subordinate of Cyrus. Similarly, Belshazzar was called "king," even though he was the second ruler of the kingdom under Nabonidus (cf. Dan. 5:29).

(2) *Darius I—Hystaspes* (521-486 B.C.), king of Persia, often referred to as Darius the Great because of his brilliant achievements as restorer of the Persian Empire of Cyrus II and his son Cambyses. Cambyses died, possibly by suicide, while returning from the conquest of Egypt, upon hearing that a pretender (who claimed to be Smerdis, another son of Cyrus whom Cambyses had secretly murdered for suspected disloy-

alty) had taken the throne in Babylon. The Achaemenid dynasty would have ended with Cambyses had not Darius, son of Hystaspes and great-grandson of Ariyaramnes (brother of Cyrus I), retained the loyalty of the Persian army. Within two months he succeeded in capturing and killing the Pseudo-Smerdis (522 B.C.), and during the next two years he defeated nine kings in nineteen battles. His own account of these victories is recorded in a large trilingual cuneiform inscription (in Old Persian, Babylonian, and Elamite) on the face of the Behistun Rock. The remaining years of his reign were occupied with the reorganization of the empire into satrapies; the conquest of NW India (*c.* 514 B.C.); the re-digging of the ancient Egyptian canal at Suez (*c.* 513 B.C.); the conquest of Lybia, Thrace, and Macedonia (*c.* 512 B.C.); the crushing of revolts among Ionian Greeks (500-493 B.C.); and the ill-fated expeditions against Greece (493 and 490 B.C.).

During the early part of his reign, when he was struggling to gain control of his vast empire, Darius Hystaspes found occasion to encourage the Jews in the rebuilding of their temple in Jerusalem. About 50,000 Jews had responded to the decree of Cyrus (Ezra 1) and had returned to Palestine. They succeeded in laying the foundation of the second temple by 535 B.C., but the constant opposition of Samaritans and other Palestinian tribes brought the work to a halt for fifteen years. In 520 B.C., God encouraged the Jews through the ministries of Haggai and Zechariah to begin their work again (Ezra 4:24–5:2). No sooner did they begin than Tatnai, Persian governor of W provinces, challenged them and sent a letter to Darius at Babylon asking whether Cyrus had indeed granted them the permission they spoke of (Ezra 5:3-17). Darius not only found the original decree of Cyrus at a branch library in Ecbatana, but also issued his own decree commanding Tatnai to assist the Jews in their work on the temple and to provide expenses from the tribute that came from the W provinces (Ezra 6:1-12). With this assistance, the Jews completed their temple in the sixth year of Darius (515 B.C.).

(3) *Darius the Persian*, a king mentioned in Nehemiah 12:22, during whose reign the names of some Jewish priests were recorded. Critics have attacked the authorship of Nehemiah by insisting that this king must have been Darius III Codomannus (335-331 B.C.), because the same verse mentions a high priest Jaddua, and Josephus states that a Jaddua was high priest in 332 B.C. (*Ant.*, XI, viii, 4). But if we assume that Josephus was accurate in this historical reference (an assumption that carries with it some embarrassing implications for the critics, since Josephus states in the following paragraph that this Jaddua presented a copy of the book of Daniel to Alexander the Great), he could have been referring to another high priest of the same name or to the same Jaddua at an advanced age. The Elephantine papyri mention Jaddua's father, Johanan, as being high priest in 408 B.C. Therefore, Jaddua could easily have been high priest by 404 B.C., especially since he was only five generations removed from the high priest Joshua (Neh. 12:10-11) and must, of necessity, have been over thirty years of age by this date. Consequently, there is no valid reason for denying that this king was Darius II Ochus (423-404 B.C.), and that Nehemiah could have written the book of Nehemiah at that time.

BIBLIOGRAPHY:

G. C. Cameron, *Histoire de L'Iran Antique* (Paris, 1937).

A. T. Clay, *Legal and Commercial Transactions Dated in the Assyrian, Neo-Babylonian, and Persian Periods* (Philadelphia, 1908).

G. Contenau, *Textes Cunéiformes. Tome*

13: Contrats Néo-Babyloniens II, Achéménides et Séleucides (Paris, 1929).
R. P. Dougherty, *Goucher College Cuneiform Inscriptions.* Vol II, *Archives From Erech: Neo-Babylonian and Persian Periods* (New Haven, 1933).
J. Finegan, *Light From the Ancient Past* (2nd ed.; Princeton, 1960).
R. Ghirshman, *Iran* (Baltimore, 1954).
F. R. B. Godolphin (ed.), *The Greek Historians* (New York, 1942), 2 vols.
B. G. Gray, "The Foundation and Extension of the Persian Empire," *The Cambridge Ancient History*, IV (Cambridge, 1940).
H. R. Hall, *The Ancient History of the Near East* (London, 1952).
A. T. Olmstead, *The History of the Persian Empire* (Chicago, 1948).
R. A. Parker and W. H. Dubberstein, *Babylonian Chronology 626 B.C.–A.D. 75* (Provdence, 1956).
H. H. Rowley, *Darius the Mede and the Four World Empires of the Book of Daniel* (Cardiff, 1959).
J. C. Whitcomb, Jr., *Darius the Mede: A Study in Historical Identification* (Grand Rapids, 1959).

JOHN C. WHITCOMB, JR.

DARKNESS in Scripture is most frequently representative of peril, bondage, ignorance, misery, death, and separation from God. The coming of Christ is light shining in darkness (Isa. 9:2; 60:2; John 1:5; 8:12; 12:46) and salvation is repeatedly described as deliverance from the darkness (Ezek. 34:12; Col. 1:13).

Darkness is the kingdom of evil (Luke 22:53; Eph. 6:12) and the way of evildoers (Prov. 2:13; 4:19; John 3:19) in which God's people are not to walk (II Cor. 6:14; I John 1:6; 2:8-11). It serves as a cloak for sin (Job 24:16) but only ineffectually (Isa. 29:15; Ezek. 8:12).

Darkness is the punishment which God lays on the wicked (Isa. 5:30; 8:22; 9:19; 47:5) both in this life (Ex. 10:21 f.) and in eternity (Mt. 8:12; 22:13; 25:30; II Pet. 2:4, 17).

See BLINDNESS; LIGHT.

DARKON, "bearer," or "scatterer," a servant of Solomon. He is recorded in Ezra 2:56, Neh. 7:58, and in the Apocrypha, I Esd. 5:3, as having covenant-conscious descendants who returned from exile to re-inhabit Jerusalem and other cities of Judah.

DARWIN, Charles Robert (1809-1882), popularizer of the theory of evolution. His early education at Shrewsbury, England, heavy in the classics, stimulated Darwin little. In 1825 he went to Edinburgh to study medicine but finally convinced his father that he was unfitted for this by nature. Consequently, in 1828 his father sent him to Cambridge to prepare for ordination. In 1831 he graduated, but by then his interest in outdoor sports and entomology and his friendship with older scientists led him to spend two terms of his still-required residence in studying geology under Adam Sedgwick.

On returning from a field trip to Wales in August, 1831, he applied for the position of naturalist on the survey ship *Beagle.* Accepted, he spent the five years until October, 1836, visiting islands of the S Atlantic, the coast of S America, Tahiti, the Australasian area, the Maldives, Mauritius, St. Helena, Ascension, Brazil, and the Azores. His observations on the trip resulted in a number of important geological publications. But above all, even as early as 1837, he began developing the epoch-making idea of the transmutation of species from his observations of S American fossils, Galapago speciation, and from his reading of Malthus.

From 1838 to 1841 he was secretary of the Geological Society and in close contact with Sir Charles Lyell, author of the important *Principles of Geology.* Married in 1839 to his cousin, it was not until late in 1842 that he could finish his report and leave London for Down, where he spent the rest of his life. Always in poor health, he spent his time until 1854 working chiefly on four monographs on paleontology. But then he continued his work on *The Origin of*

Species, already begun in notebooks in 1837, in a short sketch in 1842, and in an essay of over 200 pages in 1844, after he was urged by Lyell to turn these into a major treatise. In June, 1858, A. R. Wallace, also after reading Malthus, sent an essay to Darwin to review which turned out to be essentially an abstract of Darwin's unfinished treatise but developed independently. In July they therefore presented a joint paper on natural selection to the Linnean Society. Finally, in November, 1859, *The Origin of Species* appeared and stirred up considerable controversy. The general approval, however, of Lyell, T. H. Huxley, and Spencer in his later writings led to the theory's being widely influential beyond the technical area.

Darwin also wrote other major works on evolution, such as *The Variation of Animals and Plants Under Domestication* (1868) and *The Descent of Man* (1871), but he continued writing widely on other facets of geology and botany until 1880. Ill health caused most of his contact with the intellectuals of his time to be carried out in copious correspondence, which was stimulated by his notable writings and mutual friends. It is in these and in his *Autobiography* (written in 1876 and published only in 1887 with some of his stronger religious comments excised) that one sees Darwin best as a man. Here we find intense concentration, regularity of schedule, a patient wife, and financial independence leading to thought and writing far beyond what one might have expected from one so poor in health.

As to his religious attitudes, Darwin tells us that before his Cambridge days he persuaded himself that the creed of the Church of England was to be fully accepted and that the Bible was true literally in every word but, he adds nearly 50 years later, that "it never struck me how illogical it was to say that I believed in what I could not understand." Indeed, he never formally gave up the idea of becoming a country clergyman; the *Beagle* expedition simply diverted his interests. He says that on the *Beagle* he was laughed at "for quoting the Bible as an unanswerable authority on some point of morality," but he had gradually come to see the OT as no more inspired than the beliefs of any religion, and the NT as often incredible. Yet he tried to invent evidence that could convince him otherwise. This became more and more difficult until "disbelief crept over me at a very slow rate but was at last complete." He tells us in 1876 that he felt no distress and never doubted he had concluded correctly.

Nonetheless, he did feel compelled (at least about the time he wrote *The Origin of Species*) by the complexity of the universe to postulate an intelligent First Cause. This presupposition, however, gradually weakened as a belief in later years until he became, and remained, an agnostic in the latter half of his life.

BIBLIOGRAPHY:

N. Barlow (ed.), *Autobiography of Charles Darwin* (New York, 1958).
F. Darwin (ed.), *Life and Letters* (London, 1887), 3 vols.
F. Darwin and A. C. Seward (eds.), *More Letters* (London, 1903), 2 vols.
B. Glass *et al., Forerunners of Darwin, 1754–1859* (Baltimore, 1959).
G. Himmelfarb, *Darwin and the Darwinian Revolution* (New York, 1959).
W. Irvine, *Apes, Angels and Victorians* (New York, 1955).
A. Keith, *Darwin Revalued* (London, 1955).
B. J. Loewenberg (ed.), "Darwin Anniversary Issue," *Victorian Studies* (Sept., 1959).
M. Millhauser, *Just Before Darwin* (Middletown, Conn., 1959).
P. H. Rohmann (ed.), "The Origin of Species . . . One Hundred Years Later," *Antioch Review* (Spring, 1959).
B. Willey, *Darwin and Butler* (London, 1960).

THOMAS H. LEITH

DATHAN, a Reubenite, the son of Eliab. He was the brother of Abiram, and together they led a revolt against the leadership of Moses (Num. 16:1-35; Deut. 11:6). This was not so much a separate rebellion as part of a twofold attempt to challenge established authority. While Korah was protesting against the ecclesiastical role of Moses and Aaron (Num. 16:3), Dathan, Abiram, and On were rebelling against their civil authority. These rebels were entombed by the earth opening up under them.

DATHENUS, Petrus (1531-1588), Dutch Reformed minister and church leader in the days of the Reformation. Born in Mont-Cassel in Flanders, he became a Carmelite monk in his youth, but as early as 1550 he had sided with the Reformation. In 1553 he went into exile in England, but in a very short time he had to flee upon the accession of Mary Tudor to the throne. He went to Germany and ministered to a congregation of Dutch exiles in Frankfurt on Main (1551-61). There he met with Calvin to ask advice on questions raised by the intolerance of the Lutherans of Frankfurt. The Lutherans required the Dutch Calvinists to have their children baptized in the Lutheran Church. Calvin advised them to yield to this demand, but to confess at the same time in unambiguous terms the truth of the Reformed conviction on the Lord's supper. After that, the Reformed Church was closed by the local government, and Dathenus departed with 60 families to Frankenthal, where they resided in peace from 1562 to 1566. There he translated the Heidelberg Catechism into Dutch and published it together with his versification of the Psalms. Although the versification of the Psalms was far from perfect and hastily completed, it became the accepted Psalter of the Dutch Reformed Church until 1773. The congregations were attached to it because these Psalms were sung at open-air preaching services in the days of the most violent persecution.

From this time on Dathenus was constantly moving from one place to another, while holding the highest offices in the church. In 1566 he preached at open-air services in Flanders and presided at the Synod of Antwerp. Afterward he was banished. He returned to Frankenthal and then became a field-preacher in the army of the Huguenots. He presided at the Convent of Wesel (1568) and then became chaplain of Frederick III of Paltz, travelling in several capacities in the service of state or church. From 1578 to 1585 he lived in the Netherlands. He presided at the Synod of Dort in 1578 and was appointed by the synod, together with Marniz of St. Aldegonde, to produce an improved translation of the OT. Later he entered into a serious conflict with the Prince of Orange concerning religious toleration. The prince wanted to grant Roman Catholics freedom of worship, a policy which Dathenus strongly opposed. The conflict came to a head in Ghent, where he and his friend Hembyze brought about the expulsion of prominent RC laymen and monks, the imprisonment of priests, and the plundering of monasteries and churches. Two visits of William were necessary to quiet the city and, as Hembyze appeared to expose him, Dathenus had to flee to the Netherlands, where he was imprisoned for 50 days. He was not able to bear his shame, so he changed his name and went to Sleswick-Holstein in Germany, where he carried on a practice, without qualifications, as a physician for the last two years of his life.

Dathenus was a courageous and zealous Calvinist, extremely intolerant toward RC's, and an influential church leader, especially in liturgical matters.

LOUIS D. PRAAMSMA

D'AUBIGNÉ, Jean-Henri Merle (1794-1872), eminent historian of Protestantism. Born in Geneva of French stock, d'Aubgné studied theology and came under the influence of the Scotsman, Robert Haldane, who was one of the originators of the awakening of the 19th century through his influence on the young students in Geneva. When his studies were completed d'Aubigné was present at the third centenary of the Reformation at the Wartburg (1817) and resolved to devote his life to the history of Luther and Calvin. He continued his studies in Berlin under Neander and was pastor of the French Church in Hamburg from 1818 to 1822, and then pastor in Brussels from 1822 to 1831.

It was at this time that the Evangelical Society and its School of Theology were founded in Geneva on the principles of the Awakening. Merle d'Aubigné was dean of the school for nearly 40 years. His imposing figure, his voice, his learning, and his piety gave him great authority. The school experienced a serious crisis when its professor of dogmatics, Edmond Scherer, abandoned the position on the authority of the Bible held by his colleagues and resigned his post amid much publicity.

D'Aubigné's great work is his history of the Reformation in the 16th century. It comprises 13 volumes of which the first four are devoted to Luther and the fifth to the Reformation in England. These constitute the first part of the work. The second part is entitled *History of the Reformation in Europe in the Time of Calvin.* It continues the account of the effects of the Reformation in Geneva, in France, in Germany, in England, in Italy, and in Spain. The story is carried as far as the death of Luther in 1546. The work is incomplete, and in fact the two last volumes were published after the death of the author, based on notes which he left behind. It continues to be of great value. The style is lively, easy to read, and full of information. It is also characterized by the use of the imaginative faculty which Michelet had made fashionable. Over the intervening 100 years learned researchers have shown the need to modify certain of the opinions advanced by d'Aubigné, but in reality the work is very little dated. The English translation of these volumes has had a wide distribution in Great Britain and in the United States.

Merle d'Aubigné also wrote a book on Cromwell (entitled *Le Protecteur*) and a book on *Three Centuries of Struggle in Scotland.* Apart from his work as a historian, he was an outstanding worker for the Evangelical Alliance, which in 1846 brought together all the churches of Reformed persuasion and produced a profound unity in Christ.

BIBLIOGRAPHY:

J. Bonnet, "Notice sur la vie et les écrits de Merle d'Aubigné," *Bulletin d'hist. du prot. fr. t.*, XXIII, 158-184.

JEAN CADIER

DAVENANT, John (1576-1641), Bishop of Salisbury. By the age of 33 Davenant was D.D. and professor of divinity at Cambridge. In 1618, with Europe buzzing with the Calvinist controversy, King James I (himself not without scholarly pretensions) sent him and three other churchmen to represent the Church of England at the Synod of Dort. Despite his colleagues' uneasiness, Davenant on their behalf read to the synod a paper advocating the doctrine of universal redemption. His king evidently approved, for Davenant in 1621 was appointed Bishop of Salisbury. Even his very moderate Calvinism, however, proved unacceptable under a new king (Charles I) and the growing power of William Laud. In 1631 Davenant was summoned before the Council for preaching a sermon on predestination and election which provoked the royal displeasure. Thereafter Davenant in his W country diocese meekly carried out Archbishop Laud's high church commands in ecclesiastical matters. His works include a well-received commentary on Colossians.

JAMES DIXON DOUGLAS

DAVENPORT, John (1597-1670), New England Puritan divine. Born in Coventry and educated at Oxford, he was ordained in the Church of England and in 1624 became a vicar in London. Embracing Puritan views, he fled to Holland when William Laud became archbishop of Canterbury. Four years later, after a brief return to England, he sailed to Boston; and in April, 1638, with others founded the colony of New Haven, where he served as pastor in a somewhat theocratic society. In 1642 Davenport declined an invitation to the Westminster Assembly. In 1662 he opposed the Boston Synod's adoption of the "Half-way Covenant." His stand was to split the First Church of Boston, where he became minister in 1668. It was his last controversy, for he soon died of apoplexy. Davenport was the author of a number of works, including *A Catechism Containing the Chief Heads of the Christian Religion* (1659).

JAMES DIXON DOUGLAS

DAVID. The name David means "beloved," and the son of Jesse was the only Bible personality with that name. The source of our knowledge of David is the continuous narrative beginning at I Samuel 16, continuing through the entire book of II Samuel and concluding in I Kings 2, and the parallel passage in I Chronicles 11–29, which begins its narration of the life of David at the point when he became king of all Israel and which takes special interest in David's relation to arrangements for worship. A total of about 60 chapters provides more information about David than about any other OT personality. There are also many other references to David throughout the remainder of Scripture.

I. DAVID AS A YOUTH

A. *His Genealogy.* One of the main purposes of the book of Ruth was probably to explain the background of David. Having traced several generations of the ancestry of Ruth's husband Boaz, the concluding verses of the book of Ruth explain that Boaz was the father of Obed, who was the father of Jesse, the father of David (Ruth 4:17-22). Significantly, David's ancestry thus included the non-Israelite Moabitess, Ruth.

The genealogy of Jesus in Matthew begins by calling Jesus "the son of David" (Mt. 1:1). It traces the ancestry of David, beginning with Abraham. It then goes on to trace David's descendants down to Joseph, the husband of Mary. It specifies that there were fourteen generations from Abraham to David and fourteen more generations from David to the exile in Babylon (Mt. 1:17). Luke's genealogy traces backward through David back to Adam (Luke 3:23-38). David, whose family belonged to the tribe of Judah, was the youngest of eight brothers and grew up at Bethlehem. Almost every scholar gives slightly different dates for David's life, all in the years around 1000 B.C.

B. *A Shepherd Boy.* When Samuel came to anoint one of the sons of Jesse, David was not at first present because, as Jesse explained, "he keepeth the sheep" (I Sam. 16:11). Later, when Saul called for him to come to the palace, he described him as one who was "with the sheep" (I Sam. 16:19). After playing his musical instrument for Saul, David "returned from Saul to feed his father's sheep" (I Sam. 17:15). When he was told by his father to take food to his brothers who were in the army, he left his sheep with a keeper and was criticized by his brother Eliab for doing so (vs. 28). In the course of his work of keeping the sheep, David defended them against attacking animals (I Sam. 17:

34-36). After David rose to prominence God reminded him of his lowly beginnings as a shepherd (II Sam. 7:8; I Chron. 17:7). Scripture draws a comparison between David as a shepherd of sheep and as a shepherd of God's people (Ps. 78:70, 71).

C. *Anointed King.* While no spectacular miracles occur in the narrative of David's life, there is abundant evidence of the constant guidance of God. Such guidance was evident when Samuel was sent by God to anoint one of the sons of Jesse to be king in Saul's place. After God had indicated that none of the older brothers was God's chosen one, David was sent for. When he arrived he was described as one "ruddy, and withal of a beautiful countenance, and goodly to look to" (I Sam. 16:12). The term "ruddy" probably referred to reddish hair, which was unusual for an Israelite. When Samuel anointed David with oil, "the Spirit of the Lord came upon David from that day forward" (vs. 13). It was to be a long time after this anointing, however, before David was actually to begin his reign as king.

D. *The King's Musician.* Some time after this, Saul, being troubled by an evil spirit, was advised to call for a musician who would be able to calm him. One of his servants suggested David, who then became Saul's armor bearer (I Sam. 16:21) and played his harp whenever Saul became troubled, to soothe his spirit. Critics once rejected the possibility of David's role as a musician at this early date, but archaeology has given evidence of instruments like the harp even preceding this period.

II. David as a Soldier

A. *Victory over Goliath.* When the Philistines attacked Israel, while both sides were facing each other separated by a ravine located about 16 miles SW of Jerusalem, Goliath, a Philistine giant over nine feet tall, walked up and down between the lines ridiculing the Israelites and challenging them to a duel. David had returned home from his visit to the palace to play his harp for Saul and had resumed his role as a shepherd. But then his father sent him to take food to his three older brothers who were serving in the army and to bring back word concerning their well-being (I Sam. 17:17, 18). David was deeply troubled when he saw what was happening and especially that Goliath's challenge constituted a mockery of the power of God. When he offered to fight Goliath, he was brought to Saul (vs. 31). David tried on Saul's armor, but he preferred not to use this armor. Instead he went forward against Goliath with the weapons he was accustomed to use when protecting his sheep —his staff, his sling, and five smooth stones which he chose from a nearby brook.

When Goliath with an armored coat weighing almost 160 pounds saw this mere boy advancing, he didn't consider him a worthy adversary. David made it clear on what power he was depending when he said, "I come to thee in the name of the Lord of hosts" (vs. 45). With his first shot, David hit Goliath with a stone with such force that it sank into his forehead. After Goliath fell, David rushed forward, took Goliath's own sword and cut off his head.

B. *Saul's Jealousy.* Even before he was called to be the king's musician, David had a reputation for courage, for he was described as "a mighty valiant man, and a man of war" (I Sam. 16: 18). When David had killed Goliath, Saul inquired who he was (I Sam. 17: 56-58). The reason for such a question is difficult to understand. Perhaps some time had elapsed since David's previous encounter with Saul in which he had changed considerably in appearance as he was growing up. Or perhaps Saul was really asking for more background information concerning David. A problem is raised by the statement in II Sam. 21:19 that a man named Elhanan killed Goliath. One possibility is that there were two men named Goliath. Another possibility is that Elhanan was another name for David. But a more likely possibility is that Lahmi, the brother of Goliath, was killed by Elhanan, as stated in I Chron. 20:5 and that the words "Lahmi, the brother of" were lost in the process of copying II Sam. 21:19.

After the death of Goliath, Saul made David an officer in his army (I Sam. 18:5). When David returned from a victory over the Philistines, he was greeted by a group of singing women who credited David with having killed ten thousands of the enemy and Saul with only having killed thousands (vs. 7). This tactless song understandably made Saul very angry, and from that time onward he regarded David with increasing suspicion. The day after Saul's jealousy was stirred by this incident he was filled with an evil spirit and tried to pin David to the wall with his javelin, but missed twice (vs. 11). Saul then transferred David from his duty in the palace, appointing him an officer over a thousand men, but in this new responsibility David did so well that he only became more popular.

At this point Saul offered his daughter Merab to David as a wife if he would fight against the enemy, hoping that the enemy would kill David. However, Saul gave Merab to someone else. He then offered David another daughter, Michal, if David would give him evidence that he had killed a hundred Philistines, hoping David would be killed in the battle to meet this test. But David brought evidence of having killed two hundred Philistines and thus became Michal's husband (vs. 27). This only made Saul more fearful and more determined to kill David.

C. *His Friend Jonathan.* In the meantime David had become a very close friend of Saul's son Jonathan (I Sam. 18: 1-3), who was considerably older than David. The two made a solemn covenant of friendship with each other. Therefore, when Saul planned to kill David, Jonathan warned him of the plot (I Sam. 19). When Saul made another attempt on David's life, he was forced to flee. Michal helped him escape by placing an image in his bed, thus leading Saul's servants to think he was still present and giving him time to get farther away. While in hiding, David continued to keep contact with Jonathan (I Sam. 20).

D. *Pursued by Saul.* Having fled from Saul, David went to Samuel at Naioth in Ramah. When Saul attempted to capture him there, God thwarted his efforts (I Sam. 19:20-24). David then fled to Ahimelech, the priest at Nob. Having obtained the bread dedicated to the Lord for food and Goliath's sword as a weapon, David fled to Achish, the Philistine king of Gath. Becoming suspicious of Achish's intentions toward him, David escaped from him by pretending insanity. He then went to a cave called Adullam, believed to be Aid-el-Ma, 12 miles SW of Bethlehem. There he was joined by about 400 other men. As the years of his exile passed, he was joined by an increasing number of men, the names of some of which are given in I Chronicles 12. It is noteworthy that a number of them were Benjamites, from Saul's own tribe. David and his men travelled from Adullam to Mizpeh, where he left his parents for safe-keeping. Perhaps this was made possible because of Jesse's descent from Ruth the Moabitess.

On the advice of the prophet Gad, David left Mizpeh and went to the forest of Hareth (I Sam. 22). When Philistines attacked Keilah, David sought God's leading and defeated them. He had been joined by Abiathar, the priest who had fled when Saul executed the priests who had been at Nob for aiding David. Abiathar brought with him the priestly ephod which was used in some way by David to determine the will of God.

With his followers, who had now grown to 600 in number, David travelled to the wilderness near Ziph, about three miles S of Hebron. Betrayed by the men of Ziph, David retreated to the wilderness of Maon. However, Saul had to abandon his pursuit temporarily because of the attacks of Philistines.

In the meantime David moved to Engedi (I Sam. 24), now called Ain-Djedy, on the shore of the Dead Sea. There David had an opportunity to kill Saul, and when Saul learned that David did not take advantage of this opportunity, his attitude temporarily softened and he returned home. At this time Samuel died. David again moved, this time to the wilderness of Paran. After protecting Nabal's flocks from marauding bands but then being mistreated by Nabal, David planned to attack him but was persuaded not to do so by Nabal's wife Abigail. After Nabal died David married Abigail. He also took as his wife about this time Ahinoam of Jezreel. Also, his first wife Michal was given to another man.

Again Saul took up his pursuit of David in the wilderness of Ziph (I Sam. 26). When David again spared Saul's life and proved it to him by showing him his spear and water bottle which he had taken from him while he slept, Saul again temporarily discontinued his pursuit of David. David, however, not trusting Saul, joined with Achish king of Gath, who was probably a successor to the Achish he had previously evaded by pretending insanity. Achish gave David and his men the town of Ziklag to live in, a town probably located in the desert border S of Judah. There he stayed for a period of 16 months. From this headquarters David attacked the Geshurites, the Gezrites, and the Amalekites, tribes living on the S border of Judah. But he left no survivors who could tell Achish what he was doing. Meanwhile he lied to Achish by telling him that he was attacking Judah, convincing Achish that he had incurred the hatred of his own people.

Achish invited David to join the Philistines in attacking Israel at Mount Gilboa, but other Philistine chiefs would not permit this. Returning to Ziklag, David and his men discovered that the city had been burned and their families and possessions captured by the Amalekites. His men were so upset by this disaster that they considered stoning him, but significantly Scripture states: "David encouraged himself in the Lord his God." He attacked the Amalekites, recovering what belonged to his own people and much more besides. Some of this was graciously shared with those of his men who were too exhausted to continue pursuing the enemy, and some of it was sent to the elders of Judah as a present.

At the battle on Mount Gilboa, when Saul saw that his army was being defeated by the Philistines, he fell on his sword. An Amalekite who saw this incident, hoping for a reward, told David that he had killed Saul. When David heard of the death of Saul and Jonathan, he slew the Amalekite who claimed to have killed Saul. He also grieved publicly for Saul and Jonathan (II Sam. 1). But with Saul dead, David was able to return to Judah from his exile.

III. David as King

A. *His Rule from Hebron.* After his return to Judah, David settled at Hebron, which had a significant historical background. There the leaders of Judah anointed him as king (II Sam. 2) at the age of 30. He reigned there for 7½ years while Saul's son, Ishbosheth ("man of shame," also Ishbaal, "man of Baal"), was king of the N tribes with his headquarters in Transjordania. Abner, Saul's cousin, was Ishbosheth's general. David strengthened his hand by sending congratulations to the men of Jabesh–gilead for giving Saul an honorable burial and by marrying Maacah, daughter of the king of Geshur, thus making an alliance with a nation to the rear of Ishbosheth.

Abner's army was defeated in a skirmish with David's men, following an engagement at Gibeon in which each side was represented by 12 men and in which all 24 perished. This began a lengthy conflict between David's forces and Ishbosheth's. As a result of trouble between Abner and Ishbosheth over Abner's desire to marry one of Saul's widows, which probably represented an attempt to take Saul's place in the kingdom, Abner offered to join David and to bring Israel over to David's side. David agreed on the condition that Michal, Saul's daughter, be returned to him as his wife. However, Joab, David's military leader, who had a score to settle with Abner for killing his brother in the engagement at Gibeon, murdered Abner. Shortly thereafter Ishbosheth was murdered by two of his own captains. David was not guilty of having any part in either of these two murders and made his innocence public.

B. *His Rule at Jerusalem.* The elders of Israel, accompanied by a large army representing each of the tribes, had come to Hebron and anointed David king of the entire nation. David then captured Jerusalem (about 20 miles N of Hebron) through Joab's ingenuity. Jerusalem tended to unify the country by its central location, and greater unity was essential if David was to succeed as king. This choice of Jerusalem also had far-reaching consequences in the history of God's people.

The Philistines now saw David as a serious threat, but when they attacked him he defeated them in several decisive battles. This was the end of a long Philistine domination over Israel.

David was now very anxious that the ark of the covenant should be brought to Jerusalem from Kirjath-jearim, where it had been left neglected for years. He gathered together representatives from each of the tribes to move the ark, but his efforts were delayed when one of the men helping to transport the ark died because he steadied it with his hand. After some time David renewed his efforts. This time they were more careful to follow the instructions given by God to Moses in moving it to Jerusalem. There is no reason to believe that David had any other than the most sincere religious reasons for doing this, but this move also strengthened his position as king. David had been reunited with Michal, but his dance of joy at the return of the ark caused her to despise him, and she played no later significant role in his life. David defended himself against Michal's charges that he had made a spectacle of himself by explaining to her his devotion to the Lord, but she could not appreciate this.

David then decided to build a temple in which to house the ark of the covenant (II Sam. 7). Nathan the prophet approved the plan, but God then told Nathan that He did not want David to proceed with the building because he was a man who had been involved in much bloody warfare. Instead, David was promised by God that his son would carry out this project. Moreover, God promised that David's descendants would reign on the throne forever, which evoked a wonderful prayer of thanksgiving from his lips. This promise is fulfilled in the kingship of Jesus Christ.

C. *His Victories and Organization.* A series of military victories under David's leadership brought Israel to its Golden Age, a period which following generations used to describe the future glory they hoped for so eagerly. David had brought the Philistines and the Moabites into subjection. He had defeated Hadadezer, king of Zobah, and when the Syrians came to try to rescue him he defeated them also. This led to treaties with other nations to the N accompanied by rich gifts. Following a slaughter of Edomite leadership, David established garrisons in Edom. When the Ammonites insulted his ambassadors, David defeated them together with another band of Syrians whom they had called to their aid. The result of these conquests was real control of Israel over the promised land for the first time in history.

After relative peace was attained, David remembered his pledge to Jonathan to look favorably on his friend's children. Discovering that lame Mephibosheth, Jonathan's son, was still alive, David restored Saul's lands to him and invited him to share his table as one of his own sons.

All of the expansion which had taken place added further strain to the tenuous unity of the nation, so that it was imperative for David to organize both the civil government and the army. He did so by choosing capable men who were appointed to various tasks (II Sam. 8: 16-18; 20:23-26). This organizing effort is described in considerable detail in I Chronicles 11 and 12. That it was not completely successful apparently lay behind Absalom's ability to gather a following of dissatisfied people later. A number of David's military leaders were men of exceptional bravery. His tremendous ability to arouse the loyalty of his subordinates is illustrated in an incident when David was still in exile and three of his men broke through the Philistine lines to get him a drink from the well at Bethlehem because he had expressed a longing to taste that water. On the other hand, Joab, David's step-nephew and his general for most of his career, was a strong-willed vengeful man who often caused David trouble, although he was of exceptional help to him on several important occasions.

D. *His Adultery and Murder.* The most tragic event in David's life was his affair with Bathsheba (II Sam. 11), an incident which teaches that it is possible for a godly man to fall into great sin if he grows spiritually careless. The chronicler does not include this event in his narrative of the life of David, but the writer of II Samuel gives a frank account of this terrible sin of David. While the army, under Joab, laid siege to Rabbah, David remained in Jerusalem. Upon arising in the evening and looking out from his roof to a house below, he saw a beautiful neighbor woman, Bathsheba, bathing herself. David had her brought to his palace and committed adultery with her. When it became evident that she was expecting a child, David ordered her husband, Uriah, who was classified as one of David's "mighty men," home from the battle so that no one would suspect that the child was not Uriah's. However, Uriah refused to live with his wife while his comrades were facing danger in battle. Therefore David ordered him back to the battle and arranged with Joab to have him placed in the heat of the conflict and exposed to attack so that he would be killed. Having Uriah killed in this way, David took Bathsheba to be his wife after her period of mourning was over, and she bore him a son. David had apparently remained unrepentant over this terrible sin. Finally, God sent the prophet Nathan to him with a parable concerning a rich man who took his neighbor's one pet lamb and through this parable revealed the dimensions of his sin to David so that he became genuinely repentant (II Sam. 12; Ps. 53). David's acceptance of this rebuke from the prophet reveals a relationship very different from that which prevailed in the courts of the despots of the other nations of the Near East at that time.

The child born to David and Bathsheba became ill and died as part of David's punishment. God also said that David would be punished by the death of some of the members of his own household in battle and by others committing adultery with David's own wives. This threat of poetic justice was fulfilled in David's trouble with his son Absalom. Scripture points out that another serious consequence of David's sin was that by this deed he had "given great occasion to the enemies of the Lord to blaspheme" (II Sam. 13:14). Later Bathsheba bore David another son, Solomon.

E. *The Rebellion of Absalom.* David's son Amnon had a half sister, Tamar, with whom he fell in love. Amnon forced Tamar into intercourse and then despised her. Absalom, Tamar's brother, hated Amnon and waited two years for a chance of revenge. Finally, Absalom had his opportunity and killed Amnon. Absalom then fled to Geshur, his mother's country, for three years.

Joab saw that David longed to have Absalom return, so he arranged for a reconciliation through the services of a woman from Tekoa (II Sam. 14). However Absalom, upon his return, began to wean the loyalty of the people away from David. Finally, when he felt strong enough, he gathered an army, had himself anointed king at the traditional spot, Hebron, and forced David to flee from Jerusalem to a position E of the Jordan River accompanied by his foreign mercenaries. Several people who had scores to settle with David, as well as some of his former friends such as Ahithophel, joined the rebellion. At this low point in his career David continued to show a wonderful spirit of submission to the Lord (II Sam. 15:25, 26).

By means of the advice of David's friend Hushai, which he deliberately gave to Absalom to help David, Absalom postponed his attack on David, giving him time to prepare. The result was the defeat and death of Absalom. Joab killed Absalom contrary to David's specific orders, thus increasing the tension between the two. David became unpopular by mourning so long for Absalom while neglecting those who had been loyal to him, and this strengthened the position of those who wished to divide the nation. A period of turmoil followed. David, angry with Joab, chose Amasa in his place; but Joab killed Amasa. Sheba, a Benjamite from the same tribe as Saul, rose up and led the N tribes in rebellion against David but was killed by the people (II Sam. 20). Shortly afterward, a three-year famine was seen as Divine judgment for Saul's extermination of the Gibeonites, and David ordered seven of Saul's sons slain as a reparation (II Sam. 21).

F. *David's Numbering of Israel.* Another tragic incident in the life of David was his decision to take a census of the people, an action which was probably motivated by pride and may have been the first step in the development of a tyrannical plan for heavy taxation and military draft. Joab resisted the idea but was overruled. According to II Samuel, the result of the census showed that there were 800,000 men of Israel and 500,000 men of Judah capable of bearing arms. The figures are different in Chronicles. There are many possible explanations for the discrepancy besides the possibility of miscopying of manuscripts of the Bible. The Bible explains that David was stirred by Satan (I Chron. 21) to commit this sin because God (II Sam. 24) was angry with Israel.

When David realized that this had been a serious sin, he made confession to God. God sent the prophet Gad to David to give him a choice of three alternatives as his punishment: (1) seven years (or three years according to Chronicles) of famine, (2) three months of military defeats, or (3) three days of pestilence. Since David was convinced that he could expect more mercy at the hand of God than at the hands of men, he chose the third alternative. After 70,000 people had perished in the pestilence, as the threat was approaching Jerusalem itself, David saw the angel of the Lord with drawn sword and pleaded for mercy. In response, God stayed His hand and through Gad instructed David to build an altar on ground which he purchased for this purpose from Ornan (Araunah) the Jebusite. The record in Chronicles seems to imply that this spot became the site of Solomon's temple.

G. *His Last Days.* In his old age David became ill. His son Adonijah, whose mother was Haggith, decided to take over the throne with the help of Joab (I Kings 1). Having promised Bathsheba at an earlier date that her son Solomon would be the next king, David responded to the news concerning Adonijah's attempted coup with an energy which indicates that the crisis aroused him from the lethargy into which he had fallen due to his illness. He quickly summoned Zadok the priest and Nathan the prophet and made plans for the public anointing of Solomon.

Before he died, David gave careful instructions to Solomon to obey God's commandments (I Kings 2:3) and to build the temple using materials that David himself had been gathering for that purpose. Setting the example himself, he also encouraged large donations on the part of the leaders of the nations, and, when the response was gratifying, he offered a beautiful prayer of thanksgiving (I Chron. 29:10-19). David also gave Solomon strict orders to take vengeance upon people like Joab and Shemei, the man who had cursed him when he fled from Absalom. One of the last acts of David was a final organization of the work of the Levites in their temple service, ordering that the age at which they were to begin their service should be lowered from 30 to 20. After having reigned in Jerusalem for 33 years, David died at the age of 70 and was buried there.

IV. David as a Poet

A. *Poems in the Narratives.* Several of David's poems are included in the narratives of his life. The first, entitled "The Bow," is found in II Sam. 1:19-27 and was composed on the occasion of the death of Saul and Jonathan. The author of II Samuel especially states that his source for this poem is the book of Jasher, which also contained the story of Joshua's long day. This poem is generally acclaimed as one of the outstanding poems of ancient literature, with its solemn refrain "How are the mighty fallen" (vss. 19, 25, 27). II Samuel 3 records David's brief elegy for Abner.

On the occasion of the transfer of the ark of the covenant to Jerusalem, a poem is inserted in the narrative with the heading, "Then on that day David delivered first this psalm to thank the Lord into the hand of Asaph and his brethren" (I Chron. 16:7). While it does not specifically state that David himself composed this psalm, this is implied. The first 15 verses of this psalm are the same as the first 15 verses of Psalm 105, the next 11 verses are similar to Psalm 96:1-13, and the last 3 verses are found also in Psalm 106:1, 47, 48.

B. *The Book of Psalms.* How many of the Psalms were written by David is a subject on which there is a considerable difference of opinion. Radical critics give him credit for none or only a few of them, whereas the more conservative the scholar is, the more Psalms he attributes to David. The headings of 73 of the Psalms, most of which are found in the first part of the book, ascribe their authorship to David, but it must be recognized that these headings are editorial additions and not part of the original inspired text. A few of these headings refer to the historical events in the life of David with which the psalm is connected. For example, Psalm 3 has this title: "A Psalm of David when he fled from Absalom." That the Psalms of David were intended for public worship is indicated by the fact that so many of them are addressed: "To the Chief Musician."

Of greatest influence in the consideration of the question of Davidic authorship of the Psalms is the ascription in the NT of such authorship in references to several of them. Referring to Psalm 110, which bears the title "A Psalm of David," Jesus plainly called David the author (Mark 12:36, 37; Luke 20: 42). Psalm 41, also ascribed to David by its heading, is referred to by Peter as Scripture which "the Holy Ghost by the mouth of David spake" (Acts 1:16). In his Pentecost sermon Peter ascribed Psalms 16 and 110 to David. Peter and John also speak of David as the author of Psalm 2 (Acts 4:25). Paul called David the author of Psalm 32 (Rom. 4:6, 7) and Psalm 69 (Rom. 11:9). The author of Hebrews, referring to Psalm 95, talked of God as "saying in David" what is mentioned in this psalm (Heb. 4:7). Significantly, Psalms 2 and 95 do not have headings referring to David. Therefore, it is quite possible that David wrote not less but more of the psalms than those specifically ascribed to him by the titles in the book of Psalms. The Psalms of David are powerful and have been a tremendous influence in the lives of God's people down through the ages. They come from the soul of a man who knew God in a very personal way and have been a blessing to millions of people.

V. Later References to David

A. *Old Testament References.* The tremendous influence of David is obvious from the many important references made to him in the remainder of Scripture. His great influence upon the life of his son Solomon becomes apparent when one reads the Scriptural account of the life of Solomon. Again and again Solomon spoke of "David my father" (I Kings 2:24; 3:6; 5:5, etc.). One of Solomon's greatest achievements, the building of the temple, was an event for which David had made complete preparations. The capital city, Jerusalem, had so completely been identified with David that it was often called "the city of David" (I Kings 9:24; 11:27; 11:43, etc.). The kings that followed were not only individuals in their own right, but more important, they were of "the house of David" (I Kings 12:19; 13:2; 14:8, etc.). It was "for David's sake" (I Kings 11:32; 15:4) that God had mercy on Judah. The goodness or evil of the kings that followed was often described in terms of their likeness to David (II Kings 14:3; 16:2). When men spoke of David in their prayers to God, they frequently called him "David thy servant" (II Chron. 6:15, 16, 17, 42).

Isaiah called Israel "the house of David" (7:2, 13) and the Lord "the God of David" (38:5). He predicted that the Messiah would be a shoot from the stump of Jesse, which was a way of referring to David (11:1). Among 15 references which he made to David, Jeremiah spoke frequently of "the throne of David" (22:2, 4, 30, etc.). Speaking through Ezekiel, on four occasions God called David "my servant." The prophets Hosea, Amos, and Zechariah also mentioned David.

B. *New Testament References.* Again and again in the gospel records Jesus is called "the son of David" with obvious Messianic implications (Mt. 1:1; 9:27;

12:23; 15:22, etc.). Before Jesus' birth, the angel announced to Mary that He would gain the throne "of his father David" (Luke 1:33). Jesus was born in Bethlehem because he was of the lineage of David. In His debate with the Pharisees a few days before the crucifixion, Jesus confounded them by asking for an explanation of how the Messiah could be both David's son and David's Lord (Mt. 22:42-45), reflecting on His own lineage.

In sermons recorded in the book of Acts, Peter (2:25, 34), Stephen (7:45), and Paul (13:22, 34, 36) all made references to David. Paul in his epistles described Jesus as being "of the seed of David" (Rom. 1:3; II Tim. 2:8). In the book of Revelation the Davidic origin of Jesus is also mentioned (5:5; 22:16).

C. *Traditions.* In the writings which incorporate Jewish traditions, David is frequently mentioned. The rabbinic paraphrases and commentaries on the OT add various details to the Biblical account. For example, the Targum of Jonathan claims that Goliath was the one who had killed Hophni and Phinehas, Eli's sons. The Aramaic Paraphrase of David's Last Words (Targum of II Sam. 23:1-7) interprets this passage as being definitely Messianic.

There are several references to David in the apocryphal books. Ecclus. 47:11 speaks of God as exalting David's horn forever. I Macc. 2:57 describes David as inheriting a kingdom forever because he was merciful. The 17th Psalm of Solomon calls the Messiah David's Son who will overthrow the heathen and usher in a rule of righteousness.

Josephus in his *Antiquities of the Jews* gave an extended account of the life of David which followed the Biblical account rather closely but added many details not found in Scripture. For example, he described David's crown which he wore continuously as one taken from the king of Ammon, weighing a talent of gold with a sardonyx stone in the middle. Josephus described in some detail the symptoms of the pestilence which came after David numbered the people. He also described the great wealth which supposedly was buried in the tomb of David. Josephus praised David by saying: "This man was of an excellent character, and was endowed with all the virtues that were desirable in a king." Of even higher praise is the description given in Scripture where Stephen quoted God as saying, "I have found David the son of Jesse, a man after mine own heart, which shall fulfill all my will" (Acts 13:22).

BIBLIOGRAPHY:

A. W. Blackwood, *Preaching from Samuel* (New York, 1946), 187-242.

R. A. Hasler, "Influence of David and the Psalms upon John Calvin's Life and Thought," *Hartford Quarterly* (Winter 1965), 5:7-18.

A. Maclaren, *The Life of David as Reflected in His Psalms* (London, 1884).

F. B. Meyer, *David: Shepherd, Psalmist, King* (New York, 1895).

G. Parmiter, *King David* (New York, 1961).

J. M. P. Smith, "The Character of King David," *JBL* (April 1933), 1 ff.

C. H. Spurgeon, *Sermons on Men of the Old Testament* (Grand Rapids, 1960), 164-178.

A. Whyte, *Bible Characters: Gideon to Absalom* (Edinburgh), 103-149.

HARRY BUIS

DAVID, SAINT (d. *c.* 601), patron saint of Wales. About his life it is virtually impossible to extricate truth from legend. Biographers, the earliest in the 11th century, describe him as being of noble birth. Stated on dubious authority as having been primate of S Wales, David (or Dewi) founded numerous churches within that area, and is credited with many miracles. Leader of his age's monastic revival, he is said to have founded an abbey of extremely ascetic rule. He is supposed also to have attended a synod called to suppress the Pelagian heresy and there to have been so eloquent that the supporters of Pelagius were silenced.

DAVIDSON, Andrew Bruce (1831-1902), Scottish OT scholar. Born into a poor Aberdeenshire family that in the Scots tradition made sacrifices for his education, Davidson graduated in Arts at Aberdeen (1849). After three years as a schoolmaster, during which he mastered Hebrew and several modern languages, Davidson entered New College, Edinburgh, the theological seminary of the Free Church of Scotland formed at the Disruption nine years earlier. Licensed as a preacher in 1856, he was subsequently assistant (1858) and then the successor (1863) to the famous "Rabbi" Duncan as professor of Hebrew and Old Testament. A lifelong bachelor of diffident temperament, Davidson proved himself a superb teacher. A pioneer in introducing historical methods of OT study in Scotland, Davidson taught his students to read the Bible with grammar and dictionary in hand rather than regard it merely as a source of proof texts to support views taught in the Department of Dogmatics. He was also an influential member of the OT revision committee (1870-84). Though he was conservative in theology, his moderating views and some of his methods led a few of his students to adopt and further positions contrary to Scripture. Davidson was the author of a number of Bible commentaries (in the "Cambridge Bible" series) and theological works, but is now best remembered for his *Introductory Hebrew Grammar* (1874), a text book to many generations of students. He also contributed extensively to the *Encyclopaedia Britannica* and Hastings' *Dictionary of the Bible*.

BIBLIOGRAPHY:

J. Strahan, *Andrew Bruce Davidson* (London, 1917).

JAMES DIXON DOUGLAS

DAVIES, Samuel (1723-1761), the father of Southern Presbyterianism. Born in Newcastle County, Delaware, he received his classical and theological education at the school of the Rev. Samuel Blair (Presbyterian) at Faggs Manor, Pennsylvania. He was licensed to preach by Newcastle Presbytery on February 19, 1747. He then settled in Hanover, Virginia, where he served with "glowing zeal and exemplary prudence." In three years he could count some 300 converts. On December 3, 1755, he convened the first meeting of Hanover Presbytery, the mother presbytery of the Presbyterian Church in the South. In 1759 he was called to the presidency of the College of New Jersey (later Princeton). He served there until his early death, leaving the college in as high a state of literary merit as it had possessed to that date.

He was a prince among early American preachers, the apostle to Virginia, and the father of Southern Presbyterianism. His influence was diffused throughout the area of Virginia and remained for generations after his passing. His preaching was of such eloquence as to appeal to the most learned, and of such simplicity as to reach the most ignorant. Three volumes of his sermons were published.

BIBLIOGRAPHY:

W. H. Foote, *Sketches of Virginia, Historical and Biographical* (Philadelphia, 1850).
W. Sprague, *Annals of the American Pulpit*, III (New York, 1858), 140 f.
H. A. White, *Southern Presbyterian Leaders* (New York, 1911).

MORTON H. SMITH

DAVIS, John D. (1854-1926), an American, Calvinistic, OT scholar. After having studied at the College of New Jersey, the University of Bonn, Princeton Theological Seminary, and the University of Leipzig, Davis held several positions in the OT Department at Princeton Theological Seminary. Calvinistic in his theology, he sought to lead his students to the traditional Christian position on the development of the religion of Israel. Noted for his knowledge of archaeology and Assyriology, his best-known work was his *Dictionary of the Bible* (1898), which underwent several revisions. It was later rewritten by H. S. Gehman and titled *The Westminster Dictionary of the Bible.*

Davis also wrote *Genesis and Semitic Tradition* (1894) as a result of years of study of cuneiform documents. He wrote discussions in *The Bible Student*, critical notes in the *Westminster Teacher*, an essay on "Persian Words and the Dating of Old Testament Documents" in *Old Testament and Semitic Studies*, and many articles in theological journals.

BIBLIOGRAPHY:

F. W. Loetscher, "John Davis," *PTR* 24 (1926), 529-567.

HARRY BUIS

DAY. The Biblical terms יוֹם (*yom*) and ἡμέρα (*hēmera*) possess a threefold meaning which parallels that of modern English, except that the third is wider in usage than today:

(1) *Daylight* (Gen. 1:5; Mt. 4:2), lasting approximately 12 hours (John 11:9). In the NT "the third hour" thus signifies about 9:00 A.M. (Mt. 20:3); the sixth hour, noon (vs. 5); and so on (except for possible Roman counting from midnight and noon in John 1:39; 4:6, 52). During OT times the concept of hours did not exist— שָׁעָה in Daniel 3:6, 4:19 (*hour*, AV) is better rendered *moment*—daylight was divided only into morning, noon, and evening (Ps. 55:17). Daylight came naturally to represent illumination (as opposed to "stumbling," John 11:9), rightness, and salvation. The appearance of faith is described as the dawning of day (II Pet. 1:19), and Christians are called "children of the day" (I Thess. 5:5). The ultimate New Jerusalem will have "no night there" (Rev. 21:25; 22:5).

(2) *Calendar days* (Gen. 1:8; Mt. 6:34), once literally "day and night" (Ex. 24:18; Num. 11:32), extending from morning to evening and then to the next morning (Gen. 19:34; cf. Mt. 28:1; Acts 4:3). With the Mosaic legislation of the Passover and other holidays that began at sunset (Ex. 12:18; 23:32); however, days came increasingly to be reckoned as "night and day" (Isa. 27:3), from an evening to the following evening. Only the sabbath day was named; others were simply numbered, e.g., "the first day of the week." In the NT Sunday, because of its rich Christian associations (John 20:1; Acts 2:1), came to be called "the Lord's day" (Rev. 1:10; *Arndt-G*, p. 459). (The parallel of the sabbath suggests God's creative days as normal, 24-hour periods, though possibly non-consecutive: literally *a* second day, etc., not *the* second day; cf. Ex. 20:11, "Remember the sabbath day . . . for *in respect to* [the Hebrew lacks the preposition "in"] six days the LORD made heaven and earth").

(3) *Periods*, in which a "day" marks off a given state or activity. These range from the indefinite, e.g., "the day of trouble," whenever that may be (Ps. 20:1), to the more specific, e.g., "the day of temptation in the wilderness . . . forty years long" (Ps. 95:8-10). The words in Genesis 2:4, ". . . in the day the LORD made earth and heaven," thus include the entire creative process and mean simply ". . . when He made . . ."; a man's "days" are his lifetime (Gen. 26:1); and "the last days" (e.g., in Gen. 49:1) are the end period under discussion, perhaps Messianic times (vs. 10) or perhaps earlier (vss. 7, 27). Similarly, "the day of the Lord" is any period in which God acts, whether for good or ill, e.g., the fall of Jerusalem in 586 B.C. (Zeph. 1:7-12), or the yet future coming of Christ (Zeph. 3:8-11).

See DAY OF ATONEMENT; DAY OF JUDGMENT; SABBATH.

BIBLIOGRAPHY:
Arndt-G, 346-349.
BDB, 398-401.
KB, 372-374.
MM, 280.
TWNT, II:945-956.
R. D. Culver, *Daniel and the Latter Days* (Westwood, N. J., 1954), 106-108.
J. D. Davis, *A Dictionary of the Bible* (Philadelphia, 1927), 152.
J. Finegan, *Handbook of Biblical Chronology* (Princeton, 1964), 7-15.
J. B. Payne, *Theology of the Older Testament* Grand Rapids, 1964), 134-136, 464-468.
G. Vos, *Biblical Theology, Old and New Testaments* (Grand Rapids, 1948), 313-314.

J. BARTON PAYNE

DAY, John (1522-1584), English printer. Day's family came from Dunwich in Suffolk. Day was one of the best known Elizabethan printers and worked closely with John Foxe (*Acts and Monuments*) as well as republishing works of such leading Reformation writers as William Tyndale and John Ponet. Documentary evidence is scarce, but he was almost certainly a Marian exile on the Continent. He was imprisoned in the Tower of London in 1553 for publishing "heretical" books. On his return from exile he established his press again in London. Although the importance of Day has been recognized, he has been little studied, and virtually the only accounts of him are in the *Dictionary of National Biography* and very briefly in C. Garrett, *The Marian Exiles*, Cambridge, 1938, reprinted 1966.

G. E. DUFFIELD

DAY OF ATONEMENT, the tenth day of the seventh month, Tishri. Leviticus 16 prescribes this day, but the following passages are also relevant: Ex. 30:10; Lev. 23:27-32; 25:9; and Num. 29:7-11. Hebrews 9 shows the fulfillment of this day in Christ. There are scholars today who refuse to see an original unity in Lev. 16. It is also claimed that the Day of Atonement came into being only after the Babylonian exile. This claim is based on the argument that the historical books of the OT do not mention its celebration. But it is always dangerous to argue from silence. Furthermore, it is not at all probable that the precepts for the Day of Atonement were drawn up during the Exile, for the temple was in ruins at that time and these precepts contain rules for the purification of the sanctuary. Nor are we dealing with a vision, as in Ezek. 40–48. No proper proof for a late origin of this observance has been given.

It is clear from Leviticus 16 that even the high priest was not allowed to enter the Holy of Holies at all times, but only once a year on this day, and then only with special ceremonies. He and his house needed atonement as well as the people of Israel and the sanctuary. The fasting prescribed for that day stressed the holiness of the Lord and the sinfulness of man, even of the people of the covenant and of the holiest persons among them. This day showed that the Day of Atonement at Golgotha was necessary.

The Jews still greatly honor the Day of Atonement and celebrate it in their synagogues. A section of the Mishnah is called Yomah ("the day"). For the Jews it is *the* day. (Other peoples of antiquity, e.g., the Babylonians, the Greeks, and the Romans, also knew of purification ceremonies.) It is necessary to consult Num. 29:7-11 as well as Lev. 16 to arrive at the total number of sacrifices brought on this day. There are at least 15 and, counting the goat for Azazel, 16: 12 burnt offerings (one bull, Num. 29:8; two rams, Lev. 16:3, 5; Num. 29:8; nine sheep, Num. 29:8, 11) and three sin offerings (one bull, Lev. 16:3; and two goats, Lev. 16:5; Num. 29:11). (If the ram mentioned in Num. 29:8 is counted separately, then there are 13 burnt offerings and, with the goat for Azazel counted as a sin offering, four sin offerings altogether.

The total would then be 17 offerings.)

The Day of Atonement was a perfect sabbath on which a holy meeting took place and all of the people fasted. On that day the high priest bathed himself and was not clothed in his beautiful high-priestly robes but in linen garments (Lev. 16:4). For himself and his house he took a young bull for a sin offering and a ram for a burnt offering. Two male goats were placed at the entrance of the tent of meeting and the lot was cast upon them: one for the LORD and one for Azazel. The goat assigned to the LORD served for a sin offering, but the goat for Azazel was presented alive before the LORD to consecrate it for the purpose described in Lev. 16:20-22, and after that it was sent to Azazel in the desert. There is a variety of translations for *Azazel* in Lev. 16: 8, 10, 26. There is reason for conceiving of *aza'zel* as a proper name; it is used in parallelism with "the LORD," which is also a proper name in Lev. 16:8. For this reason also we should not think of a place name but of the name of a being, a desert-demon (cf. Isa. 13:21; 34:14; Mt. 12:43; Luke 11:24; Rev. 18:2). In Lev. 16 no mention at all is made of making a sacrifice to a demon; rather, there is an element of revilement in sending him a goat symbolically laden with the sins of Israel. The idea is that sin belongs to the demon of the desert (cf. Zech. 5:5-11), who has correctly been thought of as Satan himself. But it is not certain what the name Aza'zel really means.

When the lots between the two goats had been cast, Aaron killed the bull as a sin offering for himself and his house. He took a censer full of fiery coals from the altar and two handfuls of sweet incense beaten small, and brought them within the veil. He put the incense on the coals before the Lord so that the cloud of incense would cover the mercy seat. Then he took some of the blood of the bull and sprinkled it with his finger on the mercy seat seven times and also in front of the mercy seat seven times. Then Aaron killed the goat for the sin offering and did with its blood as he had done with that of the bull. He also sprinkled the holy place and the horns of the altar of incense (Ex. 30: 10). After this, he placed the live goat before the altar of burnt offering and rested both his hands on its head, confessing over it all the iniquities of the people of Israel and all their transgressions, symbolically placing these on the goat's head. Then he had the goat taken to the desert by a man who was standing by for this purpose. This action symbolized the removal of sin before the eyes of the Israelites (cf. Ps. 103:12; Isa. 38:17; 43:25; 44:22; 53:6, 11, 12; Micah 7:19; John 1:29; II Cor. 5:21).

When Aaron had completed the act prescribed in Lev. 16:21, he went to the tent of meeting and took off the linen garments and left them there. He bathed himself, put on his official robes, and offered both rams in the court as burnt offerings to make atonement for himself and the people. The bull and the goat for the sin offering, whose blood was brought in to make atonement in the holy place, were carried outside the camp; their skin, flesh, and dung were burned with fire (cf. Heb. 13:11, 12). The person who did this, as well as the one who had led the living goat to the desert, had to wash his clothes and bathe himself.

The Day of Atonement is the only day of fasting prescribed by the law. The Yomah of the Mishnah contains this precept in VIII (1): "On the Day of Atonement it is forbidden to eat, to drink, to wash oneself, to anoint oneself, to wear sandals, and to have intercourse." It is thus the day of highest degree of fasting. However, there were exceptions. Children, pregnant women, and sick people did not fast on this day. According to the Jewish conception, fasting on the Day of Atonement has the power to abolish sin since it is a sign of inward repentance. According to this view, fasting is thus a meritorious work. In Lev. 23:27-32 the great emphasis fell on the duty to fast and to rest. But even here the idea of the sabbath is central.

The Jews have a day of preparation before the Day of Atonement. The Day of Atonement itself is celebrated in the synagogue in a service which lasts for the whole day. The evening of the day of preparation is called *Kol Nidrē* ("all vows"), from the opening words of the formulary read in the synagogues in which the congregation confesses its deep regret over the vows and oaths which it takes upon itself. Part of this confession reads: "Our vows are no vows, our oaths are no oaths." The question arises what one must think of this custom. Anti-Semitism, quite understandably, has cited these words of *Kol Nidrē* against the Jews. But this is unjustly done. For this is not a question of legal oaths or vows given to one's fellow men, but rather of acts to be done before God, especially vows of abstinence. *Kol Nidrē* is strictly personal. A man can say his vows thoughtlessly and easily forget them. In *Kol Nidrē* the Jew asks forgiveness for this sin. The vows are self-imposed and concern no one else. Only the congregation or its representatives may relieve one from such a vow.

W. H. GISPEN

DAY OF JUDGMENT, DAY OF THE LORD. The terms "day of judgment" and "day of the Lord" are often used interchangeably and usually refer to the last day of the present world, when God will vindicate Himself and His people and will judge the world. The term "Day of the Lord" (*Yom Yahweh*), however, is also used in a wider sense, referring to the day of worship (cf. Rev. 1:10).

OT Usage

The term "day," which occurs approximately 2,000 times in the OT, is in itself neutral, indicating the period of light or else a period of 24 hours. At times it has a meaning that transcends this normal usage. When applied to the activity of God "that day" can refer to the past (Gen. 15:18), the present (I Sam. 3:12), or the future (Isa. 17:4). It also eventually obtains a specific eschatological meaning, referring to the final activity of God in judgment and mercy (cf. Joel 3:18; Zeph. 3:16).

The word "judgment" also goes through a process of development in the OT. At first it is closely related to, if not identified with, Israel's redemption. Jehovah intervenes in history on behalf of His people to bring them deliverance (cf. Deut. 32:36; Isa. 1:27; 30:18; Jer. 30:11). The idea that God is judge is found in the oldest books of the OT, but especially in the Psalms (cf. Ps. 9:9, 19; 92:2; 96:10, 13; 98:9), where again the idea of judgment as bringing salvation to God's people is frequent (cf. Pss. 93. 95, 98). Eventually the emphasis shifts from judgments in the course of history to the one great day of judgment, when God shall pronounce final judgment. This day is called the "day of judgment" or the "day of the Lord." When Israel, in a false sense of security, begins to think that this day simply means vindication of the nation and destruction of its enemies (i.e., the Gentiles), the prophets raise their voice of protest. Amos cries out, "Woe to you who desire the day of the Lord!" (Amos 5:18—the first occurrence of the expression in Scripture); faithless and unbelieving members of Israel will also be punished (Amos 5:18 f.; Hos. 5:8; Isa. 2:10). Yet the day will mean salvation for God's true children (Amos 9:11 f.).

After the exile the picture becomes increasingly clear. Whereas for the 8th-century prophets, judgment is virtually limited to Israel and its closest neighbors, it is now seen as extended over the whole earth (cf. Zeph. 1:2; 2:4-15; Ezek. 32:18; 38–39 [Gog and Magog]; Zech. 14). In Daniel we see the process completed when we read of the Son of man, to whom is given dominion and glory and a kingdom by the Ancient of Days (Dan. 7:13, 14). In this prophecy we also read of a general resurrection of all men, both righteous and wicked (Dan. 12:2). At this stage the "day of judgment" has become so familiar that the prophets at times speak simply of "that day" (cf. Zeph. 1:15; Zech. 2:11; 9:16; Dan. 9:26; 11:27; 12:13; cf. Ezek. 7:6 f.). This "day" marks the end of the world and the beginning of a new order that is transhistorical (cf. Joel 3:15 ff.). It is clear that the day itself is related to history, a cosmic drama that takes place on earth. It also becomes increasingly clear that the Messiah plays a part in the drama. The eschatological Son of man in Dan. 7:13 f. is a Messianic figure, even though this may not have been recognized by the Jews of that time.

NT Usage

In the NT there is a rich variety of terms: day of judgment (II Pet. 2:9); day of the Lord (Acts 2:20; I Thess. 5:2); day of the Son of man (Luke 17:24 f.); day of the Lord Jesus (I Cor. 1:8); day of Christ (Phil. 1:6, 10); a day (Acts 17:31); that day (Mt. 7:22; II Tim. 1:12, 18); the great day (Jude 6; Rev. 6:17; 16:14); day of visitation (I Pet. 2:12), and day of wrath (Rom. 2:5). Terms like *parousia* (presence, coming), *epiphaneia* (appearing), and *apokalypsis* (revelation) are also used. Throughout the whole NT the day is associated with Jesus, the Messiah, who was sent by God and will come again to judge the living and the dead (as later creeds formulate it). In the NT the term "day of the Lord" is also used as an indication of the day of worship. This use is very apt, as it is the day on which the congregation remembers the resurrection of its Lord (Rev. 1:10) and at the same time in the Lord's supper proclaims His redeeming death until His coming again (cf. I Cor. 11:26).

From the very beginning the idea of a day of judgment plays a part in the proclamation. We find it as early as the preaching of John the Baptist (cf. Mt. 3:7-12). And in the early ministry of Jesus Himself the note of an *eschatological* judgment is clearly present (cf. Mt. 7:21 f.; 13:24 f., 36 f., etc.). The full picture in the NT, however, is rather complex. Not only is there eschatological judgment, but we also read of a *provisional* judgment, immediately after death (cf. Luke 16:19-31; 23:43; Phil. 1:21, 23; II Cor. 5:7, 8). This provisional judgment will be confirmed publicly in the final eschatological judgment. Furthermore, in some of the parables and especially in the writings of John we find what has been termed the idea of *realized eschatology*. John associates the idea of judgment with Christ's first coming, the Incarnation (cf. John 3:18, 19; 8:16; 9:39; 12:31; 15:22 f.). C. H. Dodd, J. Jeremias, and J. A. T. Robinson have strongly emphasized this present aspect of judgment. Robinson regards the "parousia" of Christ as a symbolical or mythological presentation of "what must happen, and is happening already, whenever the Christ comes in love and power, wherever the signs of His presence are to be traced, wherever the marks of His cross are to be seen. Judgment Day is a dramatized, idealized picture of every day" (*Jesus and His Coming*, London, 1957, p. 69). Although there undoubtedly is an element of truth in this view—believers do experience redemption here and now, while those who reject Jesus are "condemned already" (John 3:18)—yet all the Gospels, including that of John, speak of a final consummation as well, at which time the final judgment will take place (cf. John 5:28 f.; cf. also 6:39 ff.; 11:24; 12:28).

The final judgment, therefore, is much more than an "automatic working of history" or a rectilinear "evolutionary development" (Snaith). It is clearly associated with the *end of history*. It is "the day of Christ" (Phil. 1:10). The NT sees it as a cosmic, cataclysmic event, associated with the resurrection of the dead and the renewal of heaven and earth. Several images and pictures of a world-wide, even universal, scale are connected with it (cf. Mt. 24; Mark 13; I Thess. 4:16 f.; Rev. 20:11 ff.). On that day Jesus Christ will appear as the eschatological Son of man (Luke 17:24 f.) and He will judge the world, all men (Mt. 11:20 f.; Luke 12:17 f.; Rom. 2:12 f.), including believers (I Cor. 5:10). Even the angels are included (II Pet. 2:4; Jude 6).

No one knows the *length* of this "day." It will most likely be much longer than 24 hours. When we think of all that will happen (resurrection of the dead, judgment, consummation) it is quite natural to accept the idea that this will be a period of time, a "day of the *Lord*" determined by Him. Also, no one knows either *when* it will come. Here, too, we must say that it is "the day of the Lord"! It depends on His will. "But of that day and hour no one knows, not even the angels of heaven, nor the Son [i.e., in His incarnate state], but the Father only" (Mt. 24:36). The day will come as a thief in the night (I Thess. 5:2; cf. also II Thess. 3:11 f.; Acts 1:7). The NT congregation, however, is not frightened or depressed, but rather encouraged by this, for it is a fellowship that already lives in the light of Christ's day. "You are all sons of light and sons of the day; we are not of the night or of darkness. So then let us not sleep, as others do, but let us keep awake and be sober" (I Thess. 5:5, 6). The Heidelberg Catechism speaks of the comfort of this day: "That in all my sorrows and persecutions, with uplifted head I look for the very same Person who before has offered Himself for my sake to the tribunal of God and has removed all curse from me, to come as Judge from heaven" (Answer 52).

See ESCHATOLOGY; FUTURE STATE; JUDGMENT.

BIBLIOGRAPHY:
K. Dijk, *De Toekomst van Christus* (Kampen, 1953), 3 vols.
J. P. Martin, *The Last Judgment* (Grand Rapids, 1963).
S. Mathews, "Day of Judgment," *HDCG* I, (1918), 421-424.
L. Morris, *The Biblical Doctrine of Judgment* (London, 1960).
W. Strawson, *Jesus and the Future Life* (London, 1959).

KLAAS RUNIA

DAY'S JOURNEY, a length equal to the distance traversed by a traveler in one day. With this in mind one should shun modern attempts to equate the ancient "day's journey" with some exact modern distance. It would, however, be quite proper to recognize that the average day's journey might consist of a distance of some 10 to 25 miles.

In Ex. 3:18 Moses asks Pharaoh to allow the children of Israel to go "three days' journey into the wilderness." Elijah in I Kings 19:4, when fleeing from Jezebel, went from Beersheba "a day's journey into the wilderness."

An interesting usage of the expression is found in Jonah 3:3, 4, where Nineveh is described as "an exceeding great city of three days' journey," and it is then said that "Jonah began to enter into the city a day's journey." How far was this *day's journey* of Jonah? Note the following in connection with this question:

If Nineveh's being a great city of "three days' journey" refers to the city's circumference, then by simple mathematics its diameter would only be one day's journey. This, however, cannot be the case, for then Jonah *in his march of one day's journey* would have completely walked through the city. The narrative forbids this and shows rather that he "began to enter into the city a day's journey." That is, he walked one third of the city's diameter and found himself in the heart of the city, whereupon he preached. Thus Nineveh, it would appear, was a great city with a "three days' journey" diameter.

In 1845 Henry A. Layard discovered the walls of ruined Nineveh to be 7.5 miles in circumference, which makes the diameter of the city to average 2.4 miles. How does this compare with Jonah's Nineveh of the 9th(?) century B.C.? This walled Nineveh would at first seem to be neither three days' journey in diameter nor even three days' journey in circumference—yet by ancient standards it was truly a great city (Jericho 8 acres; Hazor 200 acres; Nineveh 1,800 acres within the walls).

Certainly the three days' journey cannot refer to Jonah's trek from the Mediterranean to Ninevah for this distance is some 400 miles. Most probably the answer lies in the fact that *either* a day's journey considered stops and conversation and was only about a mile in length, *or* Jonah refers to what we would today call "Greater Nineveh," of which the wall-enclosed dual mound area was only the center. If this latter is so, then the farms and military outposts surrounding walled Nineveh made a circle the diameter of which was some 30 to 80 miles.

See SABBATH DAY'S JOURNEY.

GARY G. COHEN

DEACON, DEACONESS. The term "deacon" occurs in the AV only in Phil. 1:1 and I Tim. 3:8, 13, whereas the Greek word διάκονος (*diakonos*) from which it is taken is found some thirty times and the cognate verb διακονέω (*diakoneō*) "to minister" and its related noun διακονία (*diakonia*) "ministry" occur nearly seventy times. The title "deacon" described one of the major orders of ministry in the church from apostolic times.

DERIVATION. In secular society, a διάκονος (*diakonos*) was a waiter, messenger, or servant, but in a pagan religious sense the word described certain temple or cultic functionaries. In the NT, the sense of "servant" occurs in Mt. 22:13 (royal servants) and I Thess. 2:2 (servant of God). The idea of service is characteristic of NT references, whether of a material nature (cf. Mark 1:13; John 2:5, 9; II Cor. 8:4) or in connection with the ministration of the Gospel (Col. 1:7, 23, 25).

ORIGIN OF OFFICE. The institution of the diaconate is usually related to the events mentioned in Acts 6:1-6, in which seven men were selected as assistants to the twelve apostles and given responsibility for distributing charitable gifts to the Hellenistic widows in Jerusalem. These men, however, were not designated "deacons"; instead, the verb διακονεῖν (*diakonein*) is used of their activities, translated as "serving tables" in the commonly accepted contemporary sense. In fact, the term "deacon" does not occur in Acts, and where one of the seven is mentioned he is described as an "evangelist," not a "deacon" (Acts 21:8). The idea of "table service" was thus consistent with the saying of Christ to the effect that He came to minister to others (cf. Mark 10:45, and particularly Luke 22:26-27). Christ is thus the supreme Deacon, the table-waiter of His church, and members in turn are encouraged to exhibit this type of service (cf. John 13:13-17).

THE NT DIACONATE. The reference to deacons in Phil. 1:1 is to those responsible for collecting and dispatching the offerings which Paul needed. It would thus describe aptly those with administrative and financial responsibilities in the church having the attributes of character that are listed in I Tim. 3: 6-14. The range of work of social service in the primitive church was thoroughly consistent with the idea of service inherent in the term "deacon." Elsewhere the term was used by Paul to describe his fellow evangelists (cf. I Thess. 3:2; Col. 1:7; 4:7) or his own ministry (I Cor. 3:5; Col. 1:23, etc.). As an exemplar of Christ's own service the diaconate is the basis of all ministry in the church.

DEACONESSES. In Rom. 16:1 the AV translates διάκονος (*diakonos*) as "servant," but "deaconess" would clearly be appropriate for Phoebe. The NT does not indicate such a ministerial order, though some have taken I Tim. 3:11 to refer to women. Post-apostolic references to deaconesses are frequent in the fourth and fifth centuries.

DEAD. See DEATH.

DEAD, BAPTISM FOR THE (I Cor. 15:29). In the history of the exegesis of this verse no one has yet been able to present a satisfactory solution. The following are some of the interpretations that have been offered of "being baptized on behalf of the dead":

(1) baptism on behalf of Christians who had died unbaptized;

(2) baptism on behalf of relatives or acquaintances who had died before the Gospel was preached in Corinth.

(3) baptism of unbelievers "because of" Christian relatives who had died so as to insure that they would see them again in the resurrection (so, for instance, J. Jeremias);

(4) baptism "on behalf of the dead" meaning "on the dead," i.e., baptism "above their graves" in order to witness in this manner to the resurrection of the dead (so, for instance, Luther);

(5) baptism understood as martyrdom;

(6) baptism as a result of conversion because of the testimony of martyrs;

(7) baptism as a result of conversion because of the testimony of the lives of some now dead;

(8) baptism on account of God's judgment of death upon disobedient Christians;

(9) baptism as indicating a burial in death with a view to the resurrection;

(10) baptism as indicating the peril of death of those who follow Christ;

(11) baptism with a view to and in expectation of the resurrection of the dead (cf. the symbolism of Rom. 6:3-5).

Many make use of this text to substantiate their view that Paul held a realistic *naturhafte* conception of the sacraments that he supposedly derived from the mystery religions. Nowhere is it clear, however, that the heathen religions had such a thing as being baptized on behalf of the dead. Paul does not give us his own view of what it is. It is certain, however, that he alludes to what clearly presupposed the resurrection of the body, without any indication that he disapproved.

DEAD, PRAYERS FOR THE. Prayer for the departed has been a subject hotly debated between evangelicals and those of a Roman or E tradition. The Roman case may be seen in summary form in Cross's *Oxford Dictionary of the Christian Church*, p. 378, where it is asserted dogmatically that such prayers have explicit scriptural sanction in II Macc. 12: 40-46 and that the practice in Christian times is closely connected with purgatory. Official RC statements may be found in the proceedings of the Council of Trent, Sessions 22 and 25. The case in Cross's dictionary is full of errors. With regard to Biblical evidence, the Apocrypha is not in the Jewish canon and is not accepted as canonical and doctrinally authoritative Scripture. The Reformers were not entirely of one mind in the standing they gave to it, but even in the Church of England, where it was retained "for example of life" (Article 6 of the 39 Articles), it was explicitly stated that it had no doctrinal standing. Then, when one looks at II Macc. 12: 46, the crucial verse, there is some doubt about the text, but also it is highly probable that Judas did not pray for the departed but sent some persons to make a sin-offering as a sign of penitence for the idolatrous practices of some of his soldiers, who had been killed in battle as a judgment of God.

The only serious attempt to argue from the NT for prayer for the departed comes from II Tim. 1:18, but the case rests on an assumption that Onesiphorus was dead, an assumption wholly without proof of any kind. Prayer for the dead is not found among the earliest Fathers—Clement, Ignatius, Justin Martyr, Polycarp—nor does the Shepherd of Hermas mention it. The attempts of Dean Luckock to establish it were abandoned when the inscriptions on which he relied were found to be either false or dated much too late. In his *After Death* he dated the crucial one at 282 B.C. to prove the Jewish practice, but subsequently it was proved to belong to the 8th century A.D.!

The assertion of the Cross dictionary of a close connection with purgatory is only partly true. Certainly Romans have traditionally believed that souls pass through purgatory before they reach the final beatific state, and that prayer from the living and masses for the dead can help them on their way. But the E churches pray for the dead without accepting the concept of purgatory. The early Reformers concentrated on the abuses caused by the exploitation of purgatory (e.g., Tetzel's indulgences), but as they worked out their theology they also came to see that a Biblical understanding of justification by faith alone left no place for purgatory or prayers for the departed. They drew the logical conclusion. If men are justified by faith, then they have no need of prayer after death, for they are already with Christ. If they are not justified in this life, the idea that somehow the prayers of those still living would change their status before God requires the doctrine of a second chance, which may be sentimentally attractive but which has no Biblical warrant. Prayer for the dead, whether related to purgatory or not, is a contradiction of justification by faith. Hence the condemnation of the practice in the third part of the Homily on Prayer (*The Homilies* are part of the Church of England's official formularies).

In England and elsewhere in places where English settlers and missionaries had penetrated, prayers for the dead became a battleground between evangelicals and ritualists. They had been in the 1549 Prayer Book, but were pointedly removed in the 1552 revision. But during the Boer War some senior Anglican dignitaries introduced (quite unlawfully) occasional services containing prayers for the dead. Then the terrible carnage of World War I accelerated the trend, and the practice became widespread among many whose theology would logically have denied the practice. The issue has appeared again in the liturgical revision of the Church of England. The laity insisted on prayers that could be construed either way and only accept the services concerned on the understanding that offensive parts would be removed and honorable agreement reached. The sentimental attractions of the practice have meant a number of other Protestant churches adopting prayers for the dead, usually without awareness of any theological implications. The best brief accounts are found in the article in *The Protestant Dictionary*, rev. 1933, and in C. H. H. Wright's *The Intermediate State and Prayers for the Dead*, 1900.

G. E. DUFFIELD

DEAD SEA, a salt water lake in the deepest spur of the Syrian rift (a sinking of the earth's crust) into which the River Jordan empties. The surface lies about 1,300 feet lower than the Mediterranean; and the bottom is another 1,300 feet below that, or 2,600 feet below sea-level. It is 47 miles in length and 9 to 10 miles wide. It is not possible to travel along the banks around the sea because the shore, except in the N and S, consists mainly of steep cliffs. As is well known, this sea has a particularly high salt content (six times higher than the ocean) as a result of heavy evaporation and lack of an outlet. The high salt content precludes all life in the water, hence the name "Dead Sea." This name, however, is not found in the Bible, but it can be traced to Jerome, who used it in a marginal note in his translation of the Bible (the Latin Vulgate). The Bible speaks of the "Salt Sea" (Gen. 14:3) or the "Sea of the Plain" (Deut. 3:17; Josh. 3:16) and a few times of "the Eastern Sea" (Ezek. 47:18; Joel 2:20), the latter in contrast to the Mediterranean Sea in the W. Josephus referred to it as the "Asphalt Lake," and the Arabs called it Bahr Lut, "the Sea of Lot." Besides many salines such as calcium chloride, potassium chloride, magnesium chloride, magnesium bromide, and sodium chloride, the Dead Sea also contains excellent asphalt (bitumen). Unclassified types of asphalt come from the depth of the sea and are driven by the wind to the shore, where they normally can be found. The asphalt at the bottom of the sea dates from the time before the destruction of Sodom and Gomorrah. Gen. 14:10 tells us that "the Valley of Siddim was full of asphalt pits," and adds that the inhabitants of these cities fell into these pits during their flight from the kings of the E. In addition, the Dead Sea contains an almost inexhaustible wealth of potash, which has been valued at not less than 1,200 million dollars.

On the SW shore of the sea lies the so-called Sodom Mountain (Jebel Usdum), which displays bright and striking shapes formed from salt, gypsum, lime, and chalk. Tourists are shown these "pillars of salt" as the remnants of Lot's wife (see Gen. 19:26). The cities of Sodom and Gomorrah, whose destruction is described in Genesis 19, are probably now lying in the S part of the Dead Sea between El Lisan ("The Tongue," a peninsula in the sea) and the Sebkha (a swampy marshland). The idea that the Dead Sea came into existence at the place where the famous cities were once located, and is therefore a sign of God's judgment and a monument to their destruction, finds no support in the Bible. The sea could very well have already existed in the time when God set these cities in flames for their wickedness. The latest theory posited about the destruction of Sodom and Gomorrah and the origin of the Dead Sea is that this all happened as a result of an atomic explosion caused by some astronauts from another planet (who in the narrative of Gen. 19 appear as angels). This theory must be rejected as phantasy, inasmuch as it fails to do justice to the narrative of the text itself, in which all of the emphasis falls on the declaration that God overthrew the cities (see Gen. 19:24-25). It is not impossible to suppose that God had accomplished the catastrophe in an indirect way, through an internal operation or working of elementary powers in the earth itself or by means of a tremendous earthquake timed to correspond with the moment when the measure of the cities' sin had become full. In agreement with this is the phenomenon Abraham viewed the day following the ominous disaster: "When he looked in the direction of Sodom and Gomorrah and the whole land of the plain, he beheld, and lo, the smoke of the earth went up as the smoke of the smelting furnace" (Gen. 19:28). During the earthquake of July 11, 1927, the people in the area of the Dead Sea viewed a similar phenomenon when thick clouds of smoke rose and darkened the air.

J. G. AALDERS

DEAD SEA SCROLLS. This designation is given to manuscripts found near the NW end of the Dead Sea in Palestine, principally at Qumran, Wadi el-Murabba'at and Khirbet el-Mird. In 1952 excavations were conducted at Khirbet Qumran, revealing an old building which had probably been the headquarters of a religious sect. Whether this was a sect of Essenes cannot perhaps be positively stated, but the evidence seems to favor such an identification. The mss discovered in the caves near Qumran probably came from a library of the Qumran group. There is evidence that they may have been copied out by those who lived at Qumran.

Discoveries

The first discovery seems to have been made in 1945 (some say 1947). The first scrolls taken, from what is now labelled Cave No. 1, found their way ultimately in part to the American Schools of Oriental Research and in part to the Hebrew University in Jerusalem. Some thirty-nine caves have been investigated, and some 4,000 fragments of mss have come to light. Over 400 separate scrolls have now been identified, about 100 of which are Biblical. All of the books of the OT, with the exception of Esther, have been identified.

Identity of the Scrolls Discovered

Of the scrolls discovered at Qumran the most significant from the standpoint of OT studies is the great roll of Isaiah. This consists of the entire book of Isaiah, with a few minor lacunae, written in fifty-four columns in a beautiful style of writing. Interesting marginal markings occur throughout the ms, the precise significance of which is not yet known. On the whole the text is in agreement with the Massoretic text. There are, however, divergences, and these divergences have been the subject of much discussion. This scroll is probably to be dated in the late first century B.C. It thus serves, inasmuch as it preserves the text in its entirety, to refute the position of Duhm, that the book of Isaiah did not acquire its present form until the first century B.C. The text is also of significance with respect to the question of the authorship of the prophecy. There is no major break between the close of chapter thirty-nine and the beginning of chapter forty. Chapter thirty-nine closes one line from the bottom of the column, and there remains on that line space for seven or eight letters. Chapter forty then begins on the last line of the column without any indentation. This clearly shows that no break was intended at this point. As is well known, it is the claim of modern negative criticism that with chapter forty we are no longer dealing with Isaiah's prophecies but with the work of a writer who lived long after the time of Isaiah and who is called the "Second" Isaiah. It is now that much more difficult to answer the question how, if there really was such a division as modern negative scholarship posits, the two portions were ever brought together.

A second ms of great significance is known as the Habakkuk Commentary. It consists of two chapters of Habakkuk with comments. These comments do not purport to expound the book of Habakkuk, but rather apply the text to events contemporary with the author. The comments begin with the word *pishro*, i.e., "its interpretation (is)." In these comments we are introduced to a Teacher of Righteousness to whom God revealed the secrets of the prophets. Whether this Teacher was actually the founder of the sect which lived at Qumran is difficult to say. His influence was short lived, for in the writings of Josephus, Pliny, and Philo, each of whom speaks of the Essenes, there is no mention of the Teacher of Righteousness. Numerous attempts have been made to identify this Teacher, but none yet seems to have compelled universal assent. Another figure which appears in the Habakkuk Commentary is the Wicked Priest, who rises up in enmity against the Teacher of Righteousness. Scholarship is also still engaged in the discussion of the identity of this figure.

Another document is the so-called Manual of Discipline. This consisted of two mss found in Cave No. 1 and which are now generally regarded as belonging together. Even a cursory glance at the ms reveals that it consists of rules and regulations which have to do with a group, such as that which lived at Qumran. The group followed the calendar of the book of Jubilees, held communal meals, and had ceremonial ablutions. It was a community in which they believed that they were fulfilling Messianic hopes, that they were the Servant of the Lord mentioned in Isaiah. They had a distinctive way of interpreting the Scriptures (cf. F. F. Bruce, *Biblical Exegesis in the Qumran Texts*, Grand Rapids, 1959).

The fourth document to come from Cave No. 1 is known now as a Genesis apocryphon. Before it was unrolled, it was believed to be the Book of Lamech, inasmuch as the name Lamech had been made out on it. Now, however, it has been unrolled and copied, and it appears to be an Aramaic expansion of parts of Genesis. It gives greater detail about some of the matters mentioned in Genesis, such as, e.g., the beauty of Sarah.

Three of the mss from Cave No. 1 found their way to the Hebrew University. One of these is another text of Isaiah, not as complete as the first but perhaps adhering more closely to the Massoretic text. Another is a collection of hymns in praise of God, and a third ms has come to be known as the "Wars of the Children of Light With the Children of Darkness." In this latter ms, as also in the Habakkuk Commentary, there is mention of the Kittim. There is a question whether this refers to the Romans or to the Greeks of the times of Antiochus Epiphanes.

The other caves are also yielding material. Of particular interest are the copper scrolls, which contain directions for the discovery of a buried treasure. The precise significance of these scrolls is yet a matter for conjecture.

From the caves at Murabba'at further mss were brought to light. Excavations began here in 1952. Of particular significance is yet another ms of Isaiah agreeing with the Massoretic text. Possibly the oldest of all the finds also comes from Murabba'at, a palimpsest. The later text consists of a list of names and numbers written in the archaic Hebrew alphabet dated in the 6th century B.C., whereas the older text is apparently a letter and is dated in the 8th century B.C. Many non-Biblical texts also were found in Murabba'at. Letters, purporting to be from ben Kosiba to an officer, constitute some of the most interesting discoveries to come from this place.

In 1953 excavations were also undertaken at Khirbet Mird. NT books, both in Greek and in Palestinian Aramaic, were found. Letters, written in Greek, Syriac, and Arabic, also came to light.

Significance of the Discoveries

At first it was believed that these discoveries would be of interest only to OT scholars, but it is now apparent that they are of great interest to those working in the NT field. Extravagant claims have been made, but patient research is rejecting most of them. It has been held, for example, that the Teacher of Righteousness was but a forerunner of Christ and that he set a pattern for Christ to follow. A careful comparison, however, shows a profound difference between the Teacher of Righteousness and the Person of the Lord Jesus. It has also been held that the Teacher of Righteousness was crucified, but there is no evidence for this. Then, too, it has been claimed that the Lord's supper originated from the Qumran communal meal, but evidence is causing this view to be abandoned. The same holds true for the doctrines taught in the mss. It is clear, for example, that there is no real forerunner here of the doctrine of justification by faith.

The Qumran sectaries were doubtless sincere and earnest men, who desired to fulfill the law and believed that their community was indeed fulfilling Messianic functions, in particular prophecies concerning the Servant of Isaiah. It may also be, too, that after the dispersion caused by the invasion of Vespatian in 68 B.C., with its destruction of the Qumran buildings, some of the members of this sect turned to the early church. The great significance of the Dead Sea Scrolls lies in the light which they are able to cast upon Judaism about the time of our Lord and before.

BIBLIOGRAPHY:

F. F. Bruce, *Second Thoughts on the Dead Sea Scrolls* (Grand Rapids, 1958).

M. Burrows, *The Dead Sea Scrolls* (New York, 1955).

M. Burrows, *More Light on the Dead Sea Scrolls* (New York, 1958).

F. R. Cross, *The Ancient Library of Qumran* (New York, 1958).

T. H. Gaster, *The Dead Sea Scriptures in English Translation* (New York, 1956).

W. S. LaSor, *Amazing Dead Sea Scrolls and the Christian Faith* (Chicago, 1957).

C. F. Pfeiffer, *The Dead Sea Scrolls* (Grand Rapids, 1957).

H. H. Rowley, *The Zadokite Fragments and the Dead Sea Scrolls* (Oxford, 1952).

K. Stendahl, *The Scrolls and the New Testament* (New York, 1957).

Y. Yadin, *The Message of the Scrolls* (New York, 1957).

EDWARD J. YOUNG

DEATH, NATURAL AND SPIRITUAL

I. Death as a Judgment

Death is the penalty exacted from Adam and his posterity because of his breaking the commandment in Eden (Rom. 5:12). Although Pelagius taught that man was mortal by nature so that he was subject to death even before the Fall, it is now generally agreed by Christians that, whatever means God may have had for moving man from a state of probation to a state of immutable bliss, death as we now know it is not natural or even inevitable. Death is a judgment, and that for sin (Ezek. 18:4; Rom. 6:23). But there are differences in opinion concerning Adam and his judgment.

When was the penalty exacted? Some believe that the grace of God intervened and so death did not occur until Adam had another chance in grace to secure eternal life (Wiley, *Christian Theology,* II, 93). Others, arguing a distinction between spiritual and physical aspects of death, believe that the penalty was meted out so that spiritual death was experienced immediately, and physical death came in due time and as a result of spiritual dying. On the whole, Scripture seems to be on the side of the latter view: "*In the day* that thou eatest thereof . . ." (Gen. 2:17).

What was the nature of the penalty? Some believe that death came as a result of a noxious condition of the fruit eaten—a sort of *ex opere operato* view of spiritual death. Others see death as a result of (1) the separation from God, who is the only source of life, and (2) the curse which God as the only Judge placed on man and on all physical creation. Again Scripture is on the side of the latter view. There is no hint in Scripture that the tree of the knowledge of good and evil was anything more than a symbol of probation and of disobedience (cf. Vos, *Biblical Theology*, p. 39).

What was the character of Adam's agency? Some believe that Adam is an example for all men, so that all who sin like him suffer his penalty (Pelagius). Others believe that Adam passed on by ordinary generation a nature weakened by sin but not in itself sinful, and that his posterity suffer death because inevitably they sin as he did (Wiley, *op. cit.*, 125). Others argue that all men were seminally in Adam, whose nature has been successively divided among the members of the race and so all men die because as a matter of fact all men have that very nature which sinned (Shedd, *Dogmatic Theology*, II, 30 f.). Finally, some teach that Adam represented all men in the Covenant of Works and, in virtue of that representation by which Adam's sin is reckoned to their account, all men die (C. Hodge, *Systematic Theology*, III, 192 f.; J. Murray, *The Imputation of Adam's Sin*). This last view is found in Romans 5:12 f., where Paul illustrates the immediate imputation of Christ's righteousness by drawing attention to the analogy between Adam and Christ.

Death then is God's judgment for sin, and God has decreed that sinful man will suffer separation from His loving care. This separation was symbolized by the expulsion from Eden and the placing of cherubim to guard the way to the tree of life. Terrifying though this prospect is, sin has so perverted man's sensibilities that he concurs in this separation and prefers it to grace (Rom. 2:5).

II. The Process of Inflicting the Penalty

The punishment is at the will of God the Judge (I John 5:16, 17). Thus, though all men are spiritually dead now (Eph. 2:1 f.), the enacting of the penalty of physical death is delayed. This is an act of grace and is in accordance with the glorious purposes of God. Final punishment is delayed pending the offer of the Gospel (II Pet. 3:9). When physical death comes, only judgment remains (Heb. 9:27). Eternal death is the judgment on those whose sins are unremitted (Rev. 20:12).

Similarly, the lifting of the penalty is at the pleasure of the Judge. Salvation from the penalty of sin is not an instantaneous, automatic, judicial process, for the satisfaction of Christ was not commercial in character (C. Hodge, *Systematic Theology*, II, 470 f., 487, 555). Deliverance from condemnation is immediate: the sinner "has passed from death unto life" (John 5:24). However, the full benefits of that redemption are not realized until the eternal state. Therefore believers die. But their death is no longer a judgment (John 11:25, 26); it is a joyous passing from the relative bliss of Christian living to the greater joy of God's presence (I Cor. 15:56; Phil. 1:23; II Tim. 4:6-8). Still, in all but a few cases of those who do not experience it (Gen. 5:24; I Thess. 4:13 f.), the unnatural experience of death is the prospect even of Christians. So Paul looked on death and the ensuing disembodied state as an experience less to be desired than translation or the resurrection. To be disembodied is to be "naked." Paul would much prefer to be "clothed upon" with the resurrection body (II Cor. 5:1 f.). Thus there is a progression in the Christian's bliss: this life is relatively good; to be with Christ is "far better"; to be with Christ in the resurrection body, joy inexpressible. This is the way that the Christian must view his dying (Ps. 116:15).

Though death is to be viewed as a judgment pronounced by God, there are also passages which indicate a certain hegemony of the Devil over death (e.g., Heb. 2:14, 15). If we distinguish between death as an "event," and death as a "state," the apparent conflict is resolved. Scripture uniformly places death as an event in the hands of God (Rom. 14:9; Rev. 1:18; in Luke 12:5, as L. Morris points out, "it is God, not the devil, who is meant," *The Wages of Sin*, p. 9). But Satan rules over the state of death, subject to the sovereign sway of God. "The devil, as the author of sin, has the power over death, its consequence" (Rom. 5:12). It is not as though he could inflict it at his pleasure, but death is his realm; he makes it subservient to his end (cf. John 8:44; I John 3:12; John 16:11; 14:30). "Death, as death, is no part of the Divine order" (Westcott, on Heb. 2:14).

III. Spiritual Death

In Rom. 8:5 f., Paul makes two categorical statements about death which amount to a definition: (1) "A carnal state of mind, which reveals itself in the desire and pursuit of carnal objects, is death. And by death is of course meant spiritual death, the absence and the opposite of spiritual life. It includes alienation from God, unholiness, and misery" (Hodge on Rom. 8:6). (2) Opposition to God is death. "This opposition on the part of the carnal mind is not casual, occasional, or in virtue of a mere purpose. It arises out of its very nature. It is not only not subject to the law of God, but *it cannot be*. It has no ability to change itself. Otherwise it would not be death. It is precisely because of this utter impotency of the carnal mind, or unrenewed heart, to change its own nature, that it involves the hopelessness which the word *death* implies" (Hodge on Rom. 8:7).

Spiritual death is thus anything but inactivity. In Eph. 2, Paul's characterization of unbelievers as dead involves (a) an activity more or less conscious that is responsive to demonic influences (vs. 2) and (b) a manner of life more or less deliberate which issues from concupiscence, so that man by nature is an object of divine wrath (vs. 3). To be dead involves a certain relationship toward God: the unbeliever is without God and His covenantal promises, and hence he has "no hope" (vss. 11, 12).

But the activity of the unbeliever is perverted at every point. His mind is "vain"; his understanding, "darkened"; his heart is "blind"; he is "past feeling" (Eph. 4:17-19). Spiritual death must not be viewed as merely a result of man's departure from God. Although man refused to have God in his knowledge (Rom. 1:28), God also refused man and gave him over to "uncleanness" (vs. 24), "vile affections" (vs. 26), and "a reprobate mind" (vs. 28).

The perversion brings a faulty judgment, for the unbeliever "treasures" wrath (Rom. 2:5), and is insulated against all warnings of judgment (Rom. 1:32). To be spiritually dead is to misunderstand the Gospel, and even to deem it foolishness (I Cor. 1–2).

IV. Physical Death

Death as an event is described in the Bible by a variety of terms and phrases: "gathering to the fathers," "sleep," "going down to Sheol," "going the way of all the earth," "laying down one's life," "giving up the spirit." Although Biblical writers sometimes content themselves with expressions which look on death as something natural (I Pet. 1:24, 25), more frequently it is viewed with horror, fear, and dismay (Ps. 55:4, 5;

90:6, 7; Heb. 2:15). Death is a judgment; sudden death, a calamity; early death could be a sign of God's extreme displeasure.

In death the vivifying principle of the organism ceases to function, and putrefying of the body begins (Jas. 2:26; John 11:39). This putrefaction ends in a full return of the chemical elements of the body to the earth itself (Gen. 3:19). Morris suggests that physical death comes naturally once the spiritual link with God is broken. "Is it too much to imagine that this closeness to God and this primacy over nature found expression in forces of a spiritual character which kept the natural tendency to bodily decay in check? The entrance of sin so radically altered the situation that fleshly dissolution could no longer be held at bay, and thus death became inevitable" (*op. cit.*, p. 14).

Sorrow at the time of physical death is never condemned in the Bible. But excessive and hopeless grief is not a Christian attitude because it is a tacit denial of the resurrection of believers (I Thess. 4:13 f.). Comfort for relatives and friends of those who die without Christ must be found in the promises of the Gospel (e.g., Isa. 61:1).

V. Eternal Death

The sinner who has never been released from death as a state and who experiences death as an event is subject to "the second death" (Rev. 2:11; 20:6, 14; 21:8). Jude speaks of some who in God's judgment are already "twice dead" (vs. 12), for to them "is reserved the blackness of darkness for ever" (vs. 13). This eternal death is one of conscious and unending suffering (Mt. 25:41 f.; Mark 9:47 f.; II Pet. 2:17). (See PUNISHMENT, EVERLASTING.)

VI. Figurative Uses of the Word

(1) Death is often personified. It is a king (Rom. 5:14 *et al.*), and has slaves (Rom. 6:17 *et al.*). It is an enemy of Christ and His people (I Cor. 15:26). It will be destroyed as a part of Christ's victory (II Tim. 1:10; Rev. 20:11, 12). In another vigorous figure, death is the child of sin and the grandchild of lust (Jas. 1:15; cf. *MM* on ἀποκυέω).

(2) Death is used of that which may produce it (II Kings 4:40).

(3) Frequently death is used to characterize dying to the law, to sin, and to the world (Rom. 6:1 f.; II Cor. 5:14).

(4) Death is sometimes used to describe any sort of inactivity, whether of sin as it lies latent (Rom. 7:8), of the unbeliever in his impotence before the law (Rom. 7:9), or of a church's inactivity in God's service (Rev. 3:1, 2). In some instances the inactivity may be due to weakness.

(5) Death may connote hopelessness, as when the father of the prodigal called his son "dead" to indicate a sense of alienation and debauchery almost beyond hope.

BIBLIOGRAPHY:

S. Babbage, *Man in Nature and in Grace* (Grand Rapids, 1957).
H. Bavinck, *Gereformeerde Dogmatiek* (Kampen; 4th ed., 1930).
A. De Bondt, *Dood en Opstanding in Het Oude Testament* (Kampen, 1938).
K. Dijk, *Tussen Sterven En Opstanding* (Kampen, 1951).
C. Hodge, *Systematic Thology* (Grand Rapids, 1946).
L. Morris, *The Wages of Sin* (London, 1954).
J. Mueller, *The Christian Doctrine of Sin* (Edinburgh, 1877).
W. G. T. Shedd, *Dogmatic Theology* (New York, 1889).
G. Vos, *Biblical Theology* (Grand Rapids, 1948).
H. O. Wiley, *Christian Theology* (Kansas City, 1945).

JOHN W. SANDERSON, JR.

DEBIR:

(1) A Palestinian city in the S hill-country, 13 miles SW of Hebron (Josh. 10:38-40; 11:21; 12:13; 15:13-17, 48-49; Judges 1:11). Originally it was

called Kiriath–sepher (Josh. 15:15; Judges 1:11) or Kiriath–sannah (Josh. 15:49). Excavations at Tel Beit Mirsim by Kyle and Albright (1926-32) uncovered ten periods of Debir's history, beginning late in the third millennium B.C. and extending almost 2,000 years. Under Canaanite rulers it attained high levels of civilization but was repeatedly destroyed and rebuilt.

Most Biblical references to Debir occur in the record of Joshua's S campaign. It suffered two Israelite sieges, one by Joshua-led forces (Josh. 10:38-40) and a subsequent recapture (implying Canaanite reoccupation) after Joshua's death by Othniel, Caleb's brother (Josh. 15:13-17; Judges 1: 9-13). Excavations in the conquest-period stratum support the accuracy of Joshua's report that Israel occupied Canaan by invasion, not by infiltration. After the conquest, arrangements for the patrimony of the priests assigned Debir to the Kohathites (Josh. 21:13-15; I Chron. 6:8).

Although unmentioned subsequently in Scripture, nearly 1,000 years of Debir's post-conquest history is illuminated by archaeology. Israelite Debir became a center of weaving and dyeing. The oldest known Israelite fortifications were erected there in David's time. It was destroyed by Shishak of Egypt about 926, partially demolished by Sennacherib (701), stripped of its defenses by Nebuchadnezzar (598), and razed soon afterward. Like many Palestinian cities destroyed at that time, it was never reoccupied.

(2) A place mentioned in Josh 15:17, which was on Judah's N boundary near the valley of Achor.

DEBORAH:

(1) The most famous woman of this name finds her place in the line of Israel's judges by the side of Barak. She was "a mother of Israel" (Judges 5:7) in the time of Jabin, the king of Canaan who heavily oppressed the people of God. The Israelites customarily came to her for spoken judgments where she was "seated"—in Ephraim, somewhere between Rama and Bethel (Judges 4:5). People considered her a prophetess, which indeed she was. She, in the name of the Lord, foretold to Barak the defeat of Sisera, Jabin's general, if he would march against him with ten thousand men out of the tribes of Naphtali and Zebulun. How powerful her personality was is evident in Barak's unwillingness to commit himself to battle against Sisera unless Deborah went with him. This she promised to do, but predicted at the same time that he would get no honor in the battle: the honor would be allotted to a woman, which later proved to be Jael, the wife of Heber the Kenite (Judges 4:17-22; also 5:24-27). Deborah gave Barak the signal for the battle, and, after a tremendous victory over Jabin and Sisera, they sang a song of praise together (Judges 5), ever since famous as the "Song of Deborah." This song is considered as one of the oldest compositions of Israel's poetry. It also presents great difficulty to translators because various words and expressions are not clear.

(2) The name Deborah was also given to the nurse of Rebekah (Gen. 35:8).

DEBORAH, SONG OF. This is the song in Judges 5, a poetical expression of the events narrated in prose in Judges 4. The historical data mentioned is essentially that already delineated, viz., the relation in time to Shamgar's rule (vs. 6), sin on the part of Israel (vs. 8), a period of oppression (vss. 6, 7), Deborah's leadership (vs. 7), her exhortation to Barak as the military leader (vs. 12), the battle participation of Zebulun and Naphtali (vs. 18), the battle on the plain near the Kishon River (vss.

19, 21), the victory achieved by Jehovah (vss. 4, 5, 20-23), and the death of Sisera at the hand of Jael, wife of Heber the Kenite (vss. 24-27).

The song adds little factual data but a great deal of poetic embellishment. Added information includes discussion of the relationship of other tribes to the battle and the specification that Taanach was the site of the battle.

Most expositors understand vs. 1 to attribute the authorship to Deborah, the prophetess and judge of Israel (cf. 4:4), and this is thought to be supported by the personal references (vss. 9, 13, 21). The song is indeed a hymn of nationalistic devotion and religious praise, such as one in her capacity would be expected to produce, and psychological considerations point to female authorship. Another view, not well substantiated, identifies "Deborah" as the city near Mt. Tabor mentioned in Josh. 19:12 and 21:28, rather than as the composer of the song.

It is generally agreed that the song is contemporaneous with the events described, the account of an eye-witness. W. F. Albright's dating as about 1125 is most generally accepted, dependent upon the failure of both Judges 4 and 5 to mention the city of Megiddo, the assumption being that so relatively large and influential city, had it been inhabited at the time, would not have gone unmentioned if a smaller place, Taanach, was named (vs. 19). Archaeological discovery indicates that Megiddo continued in ruins from about the middle of the 12th century for a period of half a millennium. This conclusion assumes a late dating for the Exodus in opposition to Biblical evidence, which points to it as taking place in the 15th century. G. E. Wright concedes that the evidence governing the dating of Judges 5 could be so interpreted as to point to a date other than Albright's. And Martin Noth (*The History of Israel,* New York, 1958, p. 151) states: "We have no evidence at all on which to assign a date to the victory over Sisera, even very roughly. . . ."

Judged from the standards of modern criticism, a document recognized by Biblical scholars as of relatively ancient composition might be expected to exhibit a somewhat crude form of religion, but such is not the case. The song manifests a high conception of God. Personal revenge and passion are lost sight of in the righteous acts of God in the deliverance of His people. Jehovah's sovereignty is not narrowly limited. Its universality is indicated by reference to its extension from Sinai to Edom to N Palestine, even though Edom was a separate nation with its own god, Qaus. Idolatry had been responsible for the oppression by the Canaanites (vs. 8). Verse 11 refers to "the people of the LORD" and vs. 31 to those who love the LORD. Verse 23 speaks of "the angel of the LORD," a phrase having deep, significant religious implications. God-consciousness is present throughout the poem.

Efforts have been made to press the song into a formal poetic mold with regular rhythm, lines, and stanzas. Many have tried to correct supposed textual corruptions by emending the text so that it might coincide with the structural pattern. However, Ewald's statement regarding Hebrew poetry ("On Hebrew Poetry," *Journal of Sacred Literature* 1 [1848], 321) says that in ancient Hebrew, rhythm was "still exclusively dependent upon the movement of their thoughts, their dance and progress, their pitch and harmony. . . . The number of the members, and then again the number of the syllables in every member, although not without limits, may yet just as the sense and the emotional mood require, so easily vary in almost every place in the course of the song." G. Gerleman ("The Song of Deborah in the

Light of Stylistics," *VT* [1951], 180) affirms that Judges 4 is characterized by "syntactic-logical" style as over against the spontaneous "artistic variant" style of the following chapter. This is seen as regards sentence structure, tenses, word order, and overall structure. Arabic verse forms would have demanded a rigid metrical and rhythmical scheme, but in Hebrew verse the composer could be like Deborah, impressionistic, free to emphasize emotion, color, and life at will, not bound narrowly by technical requirements of regularized poetic form.

The practice of conjectural emendation of the Hebrew text is very radical. One critic or another would to some extent alter the text of almost every verse. For instance, C. F. Burney would emend in some way two verses out of every three. Alterations are suggested on the ground of both internal and external considerations. However, the emendations of one scholar are discounted by others, and a sympathetic approach to the understanding of the Massoretic text generally results in meaningful interpretation.

BIBLIOGRAPHY:

P. R. Ackroyd, "Composition of the Song of Deborah," *VT* 2 (1952), 160-162.

W. F. Albright, "The Song of Deborah in the Light of Archaeology," *BASOR* 62 (1936), 26-31.

C. F. Burney, *The Book of Judges* (London, 2nd. ed., 1930).

P. Cassel, *Das Buch der Richter und Ruth* (Leipzig, 1887).

A. B. Davidson, "The Prophetess Deborah," *Expositor*, Third Series 5, 38-55.

G. Gerleman, "The Song of Deborah in the Light of Stylistics," *VT* 1 (1951), 168-180.

B. L. Goddard, "The Critic and Deborah's Song," *WThJ* 3 (1941), 93-112.

E. Grant, "Deborah's Oracle," *AJSLL* 36 (1920), 295-301.

O. Grether, "Das Deboralied. Eine metrische Rekonstruktion," *BFChrTh* 43:2 (1941).

P. Haupt, "Die Schlacht von Taanach," *BZAW* 27 (1914), 191-225.

C. F. Keil, *Joshua, Judges, Ruth* (Edinburgh, 1880).

W. Lotz, "Das Deboralied in verbesserter Textgestalt," *NKZ* 30 (1919), 191-202.

G. Margoliouth, "The Fifth Chapter of the Book of Judges," *Expositor*, Eighth Series 18 (1919), 207-33.

G. F. Moore, *The Book of Judges* (Leipzig, 1900).

G. F. Moore, *A Critical and Exegetical Commentary on Judges* (New York, 1910).

R. D. C. Robbins, "The Song of Deborah," *BS* 12 (1855), 597-641.

P. Ruben, "The Song of Deborah," *JQR* 10 (1898), 541-558.

E. Sellin, "Das Deboralied," *Festschrift Otto Procksch* (1934), 149-166.

I. W. Slotki, "The Song of Deborah," *JTS* 33 (1932), 341-354.

BURTON L. GODDARD

DEBTS. There is no trace of professional money-lenders in the early part of the Bible. What we find is borrowing in time of need, with interest-free repayment (Ex. 22:25), except in the case of foreigners (Deut. 23:20). The borrower left a redeemable pledge (Ex. 22:25-27). He might give land in a way equivalent to a mortgage, but even then if neither he nor some kinsman could pay off the loan, the land reverted to him in the year of jubilee (Lev. 25:25-28). A house in a city could not be sold on the same terms, but if treated as a mortgage it had to be redeemed within a year; otherwise the purchaser kept it in perpetuity (Lev. 25:29, 30). The interpretation of Deut. 15:1, 2 is uncertain, where after seven years the creditor has to release the loan.

Creditors later became harder. Isa. 24:2 probably refers to a class of professional money-lenders. A guarantor is warned that money-lenders will be merciless in case of default (Prov. 6:1-5; 11:15). The enslavement of families for debt, already practiced in Elisha's time (II Kings 4:1), nearly wrecked Nehemiah's project (Neh. 5:1-5).

Christ tells a parable of the generous creditor with two debtors (Luke 7:41, 42) and another of the creditor who releases his servant debtor, who in turn refuses to release his fellow servant (Mt. 18:23 ff.). The unjust steward

(Luke 16:1-12) is not concerned with money-lending, but with credit. Christ attacked commercialization in the temple precincts, including money-lending (Mt. 21:12, 13), but did not oppose simple investment of money at interest (Mt. 25:27).

The term "debt" is used of one aspect of sin in the Lord's Prayer (Mt. 6:12). Sinners have run up a bill which they cannot pay, and are lost unless someone pays it for them. Christ did this upon the cross, when He became a ransom for many (Mt. 20:28; II Tim. 2:6).

Up to the Reformation, Christians were not supposed to lend money at interest, and such lending was largely in the hands of Jews. After the Reformation, rates of interest were controlled by law.

See USURY.

J. S. WRIGHT

DECALOGUE. See COMMANDMENTS, TEN.

DECAPOLIS, "ten cities," the territory lying mainly SE of the Sea of Galilee, E of the Jordan (Mt. 4:25; Mark 5:20; 7:21). It originally comprised ten cities, leagued together for purposes of defense. They contained a strong Greek element and were liberated from Jewish authority by Pompey. Though recognized as an independent Hellenistic community, they were subject to the governor of Syria and liable to imperial taxation. Their religion was more Hellenic than Jewish. Only Scythopolis (Beth–shean) lay W of the Jordan. Those cities on the E were Gadara, Hippos, Pella, Gerasa, Dion, Philadelphia, Raphana, Kanatha, and Damascus. The confederacy name was retained when the league was enlarged.

BIBLIOGRAPHY:

T. R. Sampey, *HDCG* I (1906), 435-436.

G. A. Smith, *Historical Geography of the Holy Land* (London, 1895), 593 f.

WILLIAM J. CAMERON

DECIAN PERSECUTION. Decius was ruler of the Roman Empire from A.D. 249-251. He wished to revive old Roman customs and was of the opinion that the decline of the empire was due to the steady advance of Christianity and that the empire would flourish again only when Christianity was completely annihilated. Shortly after assuming the office of emperor he sent out a general edict requiring every citizen, wherever he lived, to take part in the heathen sacrifices. Each one was ordered to attend a sacrificial meal, or bring a libation, or burn incense to the gods. This was an attempt to induce the Christians to apostatize. The time was ripe for this, since the spiritual resistance of the Christians was weakened by the long preceding period of peace. According to the report of Cyprian, Bishop of Carthage, many yielded to these threats. Some brought the prescribed offerings (*sacrificati*), others bought an official certificate stating that they had participated in a sacrificial ceremony (*libellatici*). During this violent persecution, however, there were many who with great steadfastness professed their faith in Jesus Christ, refused to obey the edict, and consequently died martyrs' deaths.

BIBLIOGRAPHY:

P. Allard, *Histoire des persecutions pendant la premier moitie du troisieme siecle* (1905).

W. H. C. Frend, *Martyrdom and Persecution in the Early Church* (Oxford, 1965).

A. Hamman, *La geste du sang* (1953).

M. F. Schurmans, *Bloedgetuigen van Christus* (1940).

H. MULDER

DECREES OF GOD. See GOD, DECREES OF.

DECRETALS, FALSE, a collection of ecclesiastical regulations which purported to be the official decrees of popes and councils during the first seven centuries of the Christian era. Since Isidore Mercator was claimed as compiler, it was generally accepted for a time that the collection came from Isidore of Seville. They are sometimes known as the Pseudo-Isidorian Decretals. However, all attempts to identify Isidore have failed. Their place of origin was most likely in France since Frankish expressions and idiomatic Latin appear in them.

The work is a compilation consisting of sentences, phrases, and words taken from older writings, genuine and apocryphal. The author made alterations where it suited his purpose. This was necessary in order to give a 9th-century product the stamp of antiquity.

The contents are as follows: (1) preface, in which the author claims that he has been prompted by the bishops to make the collection, (2) letter from Aurelius, Bishop of Carthage, to Pope Damascus (366-384) asking for copies of papal decisions from Peter to Damascus, (3) the reply of Damascus, (4) sixty decretals from Clement (*c.* 96) to Miltiades (d. 314)—all forgeries, (5) the Donation of Constantine, according to which the emperor gave territories in Italy (including Rome) to Pope Silvester and his successors, (6) canons of councils and synods from Nicea (325) to Toledo (683), (7) decretals of 33 popes from Silvester to Gregory II, 40 of which were forgeries.

The purpose of these decretals was fourfold: (1) to promote the unity of the church by recognizing the authority of Rome, (2) to defend the rights of diocesan bishops against the tyranny of metropolitans, (3) to prevent civil powers exercising authority over bishops, and (4) to prevent secular tribunals from dealing with ecclesiastical cases.

These decretals were used by popes and scholars in the defense of the papacy for about five centuries. The forgery was proved in 1558.

ALEXANDER BARKLEY

DECRETUM HORRIBILE. Calvin (*Institutes*, III, xxiii, 7) refers to the decree of reprobation as a *decretum horribile*. Some interpret this to mean that even Calvin had qualms about his terrible Calvinism. Charles Wesley wrote two hymns lampooning this "horrible decree." However, Augustus Toplady (*Complete Works*, 1869, p. 274) gives the correct interpretation: "I would willingly imagine that Mr. Wesley is not so wretched a Latinist as to believe that he and his subaltern acted fairly in rendering the word *horribilis*, as it stands in the above connection, by the English adjective 'horrible.' Though there is a sameness of sound, there is no necessary sameness of signification in the two epithets. We have annexed a secondary idea to the English words 'horror' and 'horrible,' which the Latin *horror* and *horribilis* do not always import." After quoting Cicero, Virgil, and other Latin sources to prove his point, Toplady concludes, "Calvin therefore might well term God's adorable and inscrutable purpose respecting the fall of man *decretum horribile,* i.e., not a horrible, but an awful (one producing awe), a tremendous, and a venerable decree."

GORDON H. CLARK

DEDAN, DEDANITES. Dedan was a grandson of Abraham and Keturah (Gen. 25:3), whose descendants inhabited a territory in N Arabia. Around the time of the Captivity the dwellings of the Dedanites bordered those of the Edomites (Jer. 25:23; 49:8). In Ezekiel 25:13 it is prophesied that the judgment upon Edom shall extend from Teman (the farthest N) to Dedan (the southernmost border of the land). The present location of a city called Dedan is at the oases El–Elah and Khaibar in N Hijaz, ten degrees S of Taima and ten degrees N of Medina. In the genealogy of Genesis 10:7, there is a Dedan that appears as a Cushite or Ethiopian nation, which would point in the direction of S Arabia. However, it is questionable whether Cush is always synonymous with Ethiopia. In Genesis 2:13 the name Cush is mentioned in connection with the Tigris and Euphrates, a reference to Mesopotamia.

The Dedanites were powerful merchants in the ancient world (see Ezek. 27:15, 20; 38:13), of which Isaiah foretold that their caravans would have to lodge in the forest of Arabia because they would no longer be able to travel and draw water in safety (Isa. 21:13).

J. G. Aalders

DEDICATION, FEAST OF. The Feast of Dedication was instituted by Judas Maccabaeus to commemorate the purification of the Temple from the pollutions of Antiochus Epiphanes by the dedication of a new altar on December 25, 165 B.C. The festival lasted eight days, and its special feature was the illumination of private houses, from which its alternative name, "the Feast of Lights," is derived (I Macc. 4:36 ff.; II Macc. 10:6).

The reference to the Feast of the Dedication in John 10:22 is significant, since it shows the Pharisees asking in effect if Christ is to be a second Judas Maccabaeus, the Hammer of the Romans, as Judas had been of the Syrians: "If thou be the Christ, tell us plainly." Christ's answer, including His claim to unity with the Father, led to the Jews taking up stones to stone Him for blasphemy, perhaps using the stones of the old altar desecrated by Antiochus, which at the first celebration of the Feast of the Dedication had been hidden away in a corner of the Temple, till the Prophet should come and tell what was to be done with them. Modern Jews celebrate the Feast of Dedication as "Hanukkah."

Hugh J. Blair

DEFILEMENT AND PURIFICATION, CEREMONIAL. The OT lists the following as defiling: (1) eating unclean animals (Lev. 11; Deut. 14:3-20); (2) the birth of a child (Lev. 12); (3) leprosy (Lev. 13 and 14); (4) various discharges (Lev. 15); (5) contact with a corpse or a carcass (Lev. 11; Num. 19); and (6) booty taken from Gentiles (Num. 31:23, 24). All these passages contain precepts which the Lord gave to Israel during their desert journey. The people were prepared for these rules by commands such as are found in Ex. 19:10 and Ex. 30: 17-21. For the execution of these precepts compare Ex. 19:14, 15 and 38:8. Gen. 35:2 is also relevant.

The words most frequently used in Hebrew for *clean* and *unclean* are טָהוֹר (*tāhōr*) "gleaming" and טָמֵא (*tāmē*) "polluted." This distinction does not coincide with being bodily *clean* or *dirty*. Physical uncleanness may be a factor, but only a secondary one. For we are dealing here with the area of cultic legislation and in general with the sphere of religion. The unclean person could not participate in OT worship. He was required either to wait for a certain period of time or to cleanse himself, be cleansed, or be declared clean (cf. Lev. 11:24, 25, 28, 39, 40; 12:6-8; 13:6, 45, 46; 14:1-32; 15:5, 6, 13-15, 16,18; and also Ex. 19:10-15; Num. 19:7, 8, 10-22; 31:22-24; I Sam. 20:26; 21:4-6; Ezek. 44:25-27). Unclean objects were required to be cleansed or destroyed (cf. Lev. 13:47-49; 14:33-53; Num. 31:22-24).

The distinction between clean and unclean is not peculiar to Israel but appears also in other cultures. It has been related to the idea of taboo, the meaning of which is in dispute, but which signifies to some that an object is dangerous, forbidden, and fearful.

Some take the standpoint that when the people of Israel received the laws governing uncleanness they maintained ideas quite similar to those of the peoples that believed in taboo or totem. But it makes a difference whether we are dealing with Israel or Polynesia. For in God's laws and in all of His special revelation, the Lord explicitly opposed the remnants of pagan ideas still found in Israel (cf. Lev. 17:7). It is not a question here of adaptation but of a prohibition of customs derived from other cultures. In regard to the laws concerning cleanness and uncleanness, we may not forget that we are not dealing with something that already existed in the consciousness of the Israelites but with Divine Revelation presented through Moses and Aaron (cf. Lev. 11:1; 12:1; 13:1; 14:1, 33; 15:1). In this revelation the Lord took account of the mentality of Israel at that time. But the point of view which forms the background of the distinction between clean and unclean is quite different. This is evident in Lev. 11:44, 45; 19:2; 20:7, 26; cf. also Ex. 19:6; I Thess. 4:7; I Pet. 1:15, 16. Israel had to live as a holy nation, as the people of the Holy One. The Lord set it apart from other nations so that it might be His possession. By means of this Divine separation God planned to form for Himself a people cleansed from sin. The prophets made this very clear by alluding to these precepts when calling the people to purity of heart (cf. Isa. 1:16; Ezek. 36:25). Israel was forbidden the sin represented by this uncleanness and whatever might point to this uncleanness (cf. Lev. 15:31; Deut. 23:14). The Israelites might not defile the dwelling of the Most High which was in their midst (cf. Lev. 11:44; 16:16; Num. 19:13). It is very clear from this that uncleanness is of a cultic nature. We meet the same thought in Ex. 29:45, 46. The purpose of the deeds and laws of the Lord was that He might dwell among His people. This is the final goal of all the ways of the Lord (cf. Ezek. 48:35; Rev. 21:3), the fulfillment of the prophecy of Paradise (Gen. 3:8). The tabernacle was the foreshadowing and symbol of this dwelling of God with His people.

It is true that in the laws defining *clean* and *unclean* other motives also were a factor, but these were not primary. For example, some of the unclean animals, such as swine, were forbidden because they played a role in the worship of other deities. Here there was clearly a cultic motive. Again, animals were forbidden because they were detrimental to the health of people. The hygienic factor could thus play a role. Furthermore, there were animals which were inherently repulsive (serpents, reptiles). Then there was doubtless the connection with death: a bird of prey looks for dead and putrefying flesh; a woman giving birth suffers severe loss of blood; a leper is like the dead (Num. 12:12). Some of the precepts were arbitrary, so that the Jewish wise men were correct when they interpreted these as decrees of the King about which man must not ponder. This arbitrary element pointedly reveals the nature of subservience under the yoke of the law.

It is impossible to bring all of the precepts within a single point of view unless we take note of the fact that the Holy One Himself points His people to the necessity of being distinct from other nations through the avoidance and awareness of uncleanness which has entered the world through sin. For this reason, also, Christ—who takes the sin of the world upon Himself as the Lamb of God (John 1:29), who has broken down the dividing wall of partition (Eph. 2:14-16), who is the substance of the shadow (Col. 2:16-23)—this Christ spoke the profound word, "Not what goes into the mouth defiles a man, but what comes out of the mouth, that defiles a man" (Mt. 15:11; cf. also Acts 10:9-16; 15:29; Rom. 14:14-17; Heb.

9:9, 10). The Christian is thus always duty-bound to flee sin in all its forms (Jude 23). The totality of human life is subject to the Holy One, the God of the Covenant (I Cor. 10:31).

The ceremonial purifications symbolized the purifying power of the blood of Jesus Christ (I John 1:7). The ceremonies consisted of the washing of clothes (cf. Lev. 11:40) and the bringing of a burnt offering and a sin offering (cf. Lev. 12:6-8). For the leper who was to be purified, two clean, living birds had to be brought, along with cedar wood, scarlet, and hyssop (Lev. 14:4). One of the birds was killed in an earthen vessel over running water (Lev. 4:5). Then the living bird, the scarlet, and the cedar wood were to be dipped in the blood of the dead bird. The priest sprinkled the person to be cleansed from leprosy seven times and thus purified him. The living bird was set free in the open field (Lev. 14:6, 7). After this the leper had to wash his clothes, shave off all his hair, and bathe himself in water, and he would be pronounced clean. He could come into the camp, but had to dwell outside his tent for seven days (Lev. 14:8). In this first part of the ceremony of purification we discover the type of Christ, who was crucified so that we might be acquitted in the judgment of God. This first act represented the return of the one who was considered dead into the community of the living. For this reason this act was performed outside the camp. The second act, prescribed in Lev. 14:9-20, deals with the return into communion with God, with the re-admission to the tabernacle. A guilt offering, a sin offering, and a meal offering had to be brought. Purification measures were also prescribed in case the leprosy had spread to garments, leather utensils, and houses (Lev. 13:50-58; 14:34-53).

Washing and bathing were prescribed for discharges (Lev. 15). An earthen vessel touched by one with a discharge had to be broken; a vessel of wood had to be rinsed in water (Lev. 15:12). When the person with a discharge was cleansed, he counted seven days for his cleansing, washed his clothes, and bathed his body in running water, and he would be pronounced clean (Lev. 15:13). On the eighth day he had to take two turtle doves or two pigeons and come before the Lord at the door of the tent of meeting and give them to the priest. The priest would prepare them, one for a sin offering and the other for a burnt offering, and make atonement for him before the Lord for his discharge (Lev. 15:15). Intercourse also made one unclean. The man and the woman had to bathe themselves in water and be unclean until the evening (Lev. 15:18). The following section deals with the usual monthly uncleanness of women through menstruation. Lev. 15:25-30 discusses discharge as a feminine disease. Verses 28-30 prescribe the ceremonies a woman had to go through after her cure. Again, two turtle doves or two pigeons had to be brought as a sin offering and as a burnt offering.

Contact with the carcasses of clean as well as unclean animals defiled until the evening of the day (Lev. 11:24, 27, 31, 39), which was the time for washing and bathing. The same rules applied for one who ate the carcass of a clean animal (Lev. 11:25, 28, 40). An earthen vessel when unclean had to be broken (Lev. 11:33). Since it was not glazed, something of the defiling carcass which had fallen into it could easily remain in it, even if it were washed.

There were separate prescriptions for the purification of priests (cf. Lev. 21:1–22:16). Num. 5:2 teaches that a leper, one with a discharge, and anyone unclean because of contact with a corpse had to be sent out of the camp.

Num. 19 contains the precept about the water of impurity (cf. vs. 9) which had to be used whenever anyone touched the body or bones of a dead man or a grave (cf. vss. 11, 13, 16, 18). This water was also sprinkled on certain objects. In vss. 2-10 we read how the water was prepared and in vss. 11-21 how it was used. In the sections of the Mishnah entitled *Ohaloth* (*tents*) and *Para* (*cow*) there is a more detailed elaboration of the precepts of this chapter. These OT passages are relevant: Lev. 21:1; Num. 5:2; 6:9; 9:10; 31:19-24; Deut. 26:14; II Kings 23:13, 14; Ezek. 9:7; 44:25; Hos. 9:4; Hag. 2:13.

In Heb. 9:13, 14, the purifying power of the blood of Christ is placed above that of the blood of goats and bulls and the ashes of a heifer. The Scriptures thus clearly reveal that the precepts of purification of Num. 19 are fulfilled in Christ.

W. H. GISPEN

DEGREES, SONGS OF, a group of 15 Psalms (Ps. 120–134), each of which bears the title "A Song of Degrees," or "A Song of Ascents." Various views have been expressed as to the significance of the title. The following are the most important:

(1) The "going up" or "ascent" refers to the return from Babylon after the Exile. Appeal is made to Ezra 7:9, which speaks of "the going up from Babylon." However, it is impossible to reconcile the references to the temple in these Psalms to this period.

(2) The later Jewish interpretation claims that the "goings up" or "ascents" refer to the 15 steps which led from the Court of Israel to the Court of the Women in the second temple. On the first day of the Feast of the Tabernacles, the Levites stood with musical instruments on these steps. Delitzsch rejects this theory as void of historical basis.

(3) Gesenius advanced the explanation that the title is descriptive of a certain progressive movement in the thoughts expressed in the Psalms. A word or thought in one line is repeated or expounded in another. A serious objection to this view is that in several Psalms of the group this characteristic is not found.

(4) The most commonly accepted explanation is that these Psalms were sung by pilgrims as they journeyed "up" to Jerusalem for the observance of the appointed feasts. Since Jerusalem was located high in the hills, a traveller from any direction would have to go up to it.

(5) Another interpretation worthy of serious consideration is that of J. W. Thirtle. He relates the "degrees" to the "degrees" or "steps" of the sundial mentioned in the history of Hezekiah (II Kings 20:8-11; Isa. 38:8). He shows how these Psalms are connected with Hezekiah's times and experiences, and constitute a commentary upon some of the events of that period.

BIBLIOGRAPHY:

S. Cox, *The Pilgrim Psalms* (London, 1885).
J. W. Thirtle, *Old Testament Problems* (London, 1916).

ALEXANDER BARKLEY

DE GROOT, Hugo. See GROTIUS HUGO.

DEIFICATION. Deification, or apotheosis, generally refers to the pagan custom of regarding deceased emperors and certain others as gods. Fustel de Coulanges in *The Ancient City* (III, ch. 5) gives a series of cogent references from classical literature showing that the founder of a city came to be worshipped as a god; no city sent out a band of colonists without appointing a founder, who received heroic honors after death. John A. Wilson says, the "central doctrine of the Egyptian state in all its aspects, [was] the doctrine of the god-king" (*The Culture of Ancient Egypt*, p. 45). Wilson proposes a theory of origin in the security of Egypt's geographical position. "The gods of the larger cosmos did not need to hover over her, cautiously deputizing a mortal to rule on their behalf but retaining to themselves the functional elements of power and control. No; they could go confidently about their cosmic business because one of their number, the pharaoh, who was himself a god, carried the functions of power and control and resided in Egypt" (*op. cit.*, p. 45). Wilson thinks the dogma of the divinity of the king was a pragmatic, functional device to secure a peaceful rule. Cyrus H. Gordon (*Homer and Bible*, pp. 64-65) adduces parallels from the ancient E and classical literature to show the divinity of kings. Isa. 60:16 shows that the concept was used figuratively in Biblical literature.

An important point in any discussion of deification is the attitude of the church toward Jesus Christ. Was the attitude of the early church toward Jesus one of deification, the elevation of man to deity; or was it the reverence due to one who was in fact the eternal Son of God? J. G. Machen says, "H. J. Holtzmann (in *Protestantische Monatshefte*, IV, 1900, pp. 465 ff., and in *Christliche Welt*, XXIV, 1910, column 153) admitted that for the rapid apotheosis of Jesus as it is attested by the epistles of Paul he could cite no parallel in the religious history of the race" (*Origin of Paul's Religion*, p. 22, n.). Paul's testimony, as a pure monotheist, is given in I Cor. 8:5, 6. He believed he had good reason for regarding Jesus as "one Lord Jesus Christ by whom are all things. . . ." The worship of Jesus Christ is not the deification of a man; it is the worship due to the eternal Son, through whom all things were created.

Deification is occasionally used by Church Fathers to express the ultimate effect of Christ's work in saving men. Thus Athanasius (*Orat. de Incarn.*, LIV) writes: "Christ became man that we might be deified." This is a concept, however, which must be carefully distinguished from pagan notions of the deification of man or his absorption into deity. Athanasius is saying in effect that the purpose of Christ's humiliation was our exaltation and glorification.

WILBER B. WALLIS

DEISM. There are two meanings of the word deism. The more recent and increasingly common usage is one in which the word describes a special view of the relation of god to the world which he created. By this very statement deism is seen to be a kind of theism, since it recognizes, in contrast to atheism and agnosticism, that there is one god. This god, according to deism, is distinct from and above the world (in contrast to pantheism). In fact, he is not only distinct from the world, but he has not, after the creation, intervened in the world, which is a causally closed system proceeding on its way according to endemic natural laws. Unlike Biblical theism, deism has no doctrine of providence, understood as the active exercise of the Divine will in preserving and governing the creature at all times and in all places. Miracles, as ordinarily understood, are especially obnoxious in such a system.

In its historical reference, deism is a term used to describe a current of rationalistic thought in theology which had its primary representation and emphasis among English intellectuals of the late 17th and early 18th centuries. (The word deism first appeared about the middle of the 16th century in France.) The following are considered among the chief names of English deists: Lord Herbert of Cherbury (1583-1648), Charles Blount (1654-1693), Matthew Tindal (1657-1733), William Wollaston (1659-1724), Thomas Woolston (1669-1733), Junius Janus (or John) Toland (1670-1722), the third Earl of Shaftesbury (1671-1713), Viscount Bolingbroke (1678-1751), Anthony Collins (1676-1729), Thomas Morgan (?-1743), Thomas Chubb (1679-1747), and Peter Annet (1693-1769). (Note the short span in which all the men, except for Lord Cherbury, were born and wrote.)

These men differed rather widely in their personal beliefs. That on which they all agreed was that reason alone could establish the sufficiency and certainty of natural religion in distinction from all positive, historical religions. Some of them found this *Evangelium aeternum* in the Christian Scriptures as an underlying current by assuming a loose view of what was written, whereas others impugned and attacked the Scriptures as constituting a disservice to the truth. Lord Cherbury, the "father of deism," set forth five articles which later came to be accepted by most deists as the indefeasible ingredients of an adequate natural religion: (1) one supreme god exists; (2) all men are duty-bound to worship him; (3) divine worship consists in practical piety and motive of life; (4) all men should forsake their sins; (5) since the soul is immortal, men should prepare for an after-life in which rewards and punishments shall be measured out.

Increasingly this simplified version of religion appealed to those intellectuals who were weary with the controversy and divisions which had marred the course of the Reformation in England. These truths were put forward as constituting an expression of religious truth that escaped all party loyalties and might serve to unite the divers factions. The causes of deism, however, go deeper than mere practical considerations. Some of these causes were expressed by Francis Bacon (d. 1626), who was by no means a deist, though his writings express a vigorous rejection of the methods of scholastic theology and a plea to return to experience as the humble handmaid to truth. Thomas Hobbes (d. 1679), whom Thorschmidt has called the "grandfather of freethinkers in England," taught that all religious beliefs and cults were the product partly of the faculty of curiosity reflecting upon past experience, and partly of fear which had been shaped or hardened into "revelation" by the founders of states and the makers of law; in this way positive religions were developed. The philosophy of John Locke (d. 1704) proved a ready school for deists. According to him all knowledge, including that of religious and ethical concepts, was traced back to sensation and reflection, i.e., introspection; and the final norm of all truth, including revealed truth, was reason reflecting upon the data of sense perception.

Taking up with these ideas and seeking to restate religious truth in terms of what they believed to be the implications of the Copernican revolution in science, the deists enunciated several themes which came to play an important role in later religious modernism. These ideas have survived down to the present, so that it is of value to survey them here in their historical setting.

Edward Herbert (Lord Cherbury) attributed the loss of natural religion to the priestly class, which, out of selfish motives, had encrusted natural religion with their own doctrines and devices. Beginning, however, with Blount, the historico-critical examination of the OT takes on a shape which definitely anticipates later critical theory. He expanded Hobbes's attack on the Mosaic authorship of the Pentateuch, claimed that Copernicus' view of the universe could not be harmonized with Genesis, and rejected as sacrilegious the idea of Christ as mediator between God and man.

Shaftesbury made it plain that he laid little weight on the letter of Scripture. In a sense he anticipated Schleiermacher in his emphasis upon feeling as the root of religion in contrast to theology which "pays handsome compliments to the Deity" but generates little zeal, devotion, or warmth.

Toland, an Irishman, created a sensation when he published his work *Christianity Not Mysterious* (1696). Herein he applied Locke's method, but went beyond him in claiming that nothing which properly pertained to the Gospel was above reason, or in any way beyond the reach of reason. To establish this thesis, Toland attempted to show that in primitive Christianity there were no mysteries till the church began to appropriate Jewish levitical usages and feasts, together with the mysteries of heathen religions. Judging by the large literature of refutation and exposé which it inspired, Toland's work must be called a major document of deism. By order of the Irish parliament, the book was publicly burned by the executioner, and the author fled Dublin to escape prosecution. Some have observed that his view of early church history anticipated that of Johann Semler (d. 1791) and the Tübingen school. Toland invented the word "pantheism."

Collins, a personal friend of Locke, in 1713 anonymously published his *Discourse on Freethinking* (freethinker became a synonymn for deist), in which he pleaded the necessity for delivering the mind from the shackles of religious authority. He argued that the prophets of the OT, Jesus, and the early apostles were all freethinkers. In all ages the men with the greatest insight and virtue were freethinkers, according to Collins. Collins attacked as weak the use of prophecy to prove the truth of Christianity after the example of the later NT writers. This led to a discussion of the proof from miracles. Woolston in his *Discourses on the Miracles of Our Saviour* (1727-30) propounded the thesis that the miracle stories were to be understood allegorically and vehemently repudiated a literal view of miracles.

Morgan in his *Moral Philosopher* (1737) criticized the moral flavor of certain men and events in the OT and suggested the theory of accommodation of the truth by Jesus and the apostles to secure the hearing of their bigoted contemporaries.

The overall position of deism in relation to historical Christianity was best stated in Tindal's *The Gospel, a Republication of the Religion of Nature* (1730) and *Christianity as Old as the Creation* (1733), which came to be known as the "Deist Bible." Here Tindal argues that Christianity is a true religion insofar as it corresponds to natural religion. But since natural religion consists of the exercise of morality according to the will of God, as this will is discerned by reason, natural religion cannot be either increased or diminished by supernatural revelation. It is in itself complete.

Chubb, developing this theme, contended that Christianity is a way of life, not a doctrine, another deist emphasis which was to assume prominence in later religious liberalism. He also contrasted the teachings of Paul with those of Christ as reported in the Gospels. These opinions were set forth in his *True Gospel of Christ.*

In summary, all deists were more than suspicious of the concept of a "chosen people" and insisted on the possibility of the salvation of the heathen. They all rejected the doctrine of the Trinity and the imputed righteousness of Christ, and stressed the teachings of Christ rather than the teachings about Him. In attempting to reduce religion to a common denominator, they cut away all that was distinctive, peculiar, and individual in Christianity, and thus lost all intensity in religious life. Though deism repeatedly laid claim to the name Christian and fancied itself the opponent of superstition and priestcraft, yet it became a tea-table religion, a kind of mode in polite society, tapering off into skepticism and religious modernism. In France and Germany deism made its contribution to rationalism and naturalism. The greatest of the French deists was Voltaire, who lived in England for three years (1726-1729). In Germany, men like Eberhard, K. F. Bahrdt, Reimarus, and to a lesser degree Lessing and Semler promulgated views similar to those of the English deists. The revival movement, commonly associated with the beginnings of methodism, helped to stay the influence of deism in England, and to a lesser degree pietism rendered a similar service in Germany.

BIBLIOGRAPHY:
A. S. Farrar, *A Critical History of Free Thought* (1862), Bampton Lectures.
J. F. Hurst, *History of Rationalism* (New York, 1902).
G. B. Lechler, *Geschichte des Englisches Deismus* (1841).
J. Leland, *A View of the Principal Deistical Writers* (1837), 2 vols.
J. Orr, *English Deism, Its Roots and Its Fruits* (Grand Rapids, 1934).
D. B. Schlegel, *Shaftesbury and the French Deists* (Chapel Hill, N. C., 1956).
L. Stephen, *History of English Thought in the 18 Century* I (1876).

DEISSMANN, Gustaf Adolf (1866-1937), German theologian and philologist. Born at Langensheid, Nassau, and educated at Marburg and Tübingen, he became professor of NT at Heidelberg in 1897 and in 1908 accepted a similar appointment at Berlin. He travelled extensively in Greece, Asia Minor, and Egypt. He became keenly interested in the ecumenical movement, being a delegate at the Stockholm and Lausanne Conferences.

Deissmann did outstanding work in applying the knowledge of Hellenistic Greek derived from inscriptions and papyri to the interpretation of the Greek Bible. He was among the first to recognize the bearing of the light thrown by first-century non-literary *koinē* on the supposedly unparalleled peculiarities of NT Greek. Before his time these had commonly been attributed to Semitic influence. But the realization that the NT was written in the everyday language of the people brought about a revolution in the thinking of grammarians.

His writings include *Bibelstudien* (1895; Eng. tr., 1901); *Neue Bibelstudien* (1897; Eng. tr., 1901); *Licht von Osten* (1908); Eng. tr., 1910); *Paulus und religionsgeschichte Shizze* (1911; Eng. tr., 1912). Along with C. K. A. Bell, he edited a collection of Christological essays by German and English scholars, published in English in 1930 under the title *Mysterium Christi.*

BIBLIOGRAPHY:
Festgabe für Adolf Deissmann (Tübingen, 1927).
H. Lietzmann, *ZNW* 35(1936), 299 f.
J. Schmid, *LThK* (1959), 199.

WILLIAM J. CAMERON

DEKAR, "lancer," the father of one of Solomon's appointed officers whose task it was to supply the royal household's necessities for a month each year (I Kings 4:9). The AV transliterates the Hebrew term reading *Ben-deker.*

DELAIAH, "Jehovah has delivered," the name of five men of the OT:

(1) A descendant of David living in post-exilic times, at least eight generations after king Jehoiakim (I Chron. 3:24). The AV reads Dalaiah.

(2) A descendant of Aaron, chosen to serve the 23rd course of the sacrificial service in David's time (I Chron. 24:18).

(3) The ancestor of a family group who could not prove that their ancestry was in Israel (Ezra 2:60; Neh. 7:62).

(4) The father of Shemaiah, who, in fear of Sanballat, suggested that refuge be sought in the temple (Neh. 6:10).

(5) A prince who vainly interceded with king Jehoiakim not to burn the roll containing Jeremiah's prophecies (Jer. 36:12, 25).

DELILAH. The name is Semitic and means "devotee." It is possible that the name was linked with that of some god whose devotee the woman of this name (Judges 16) had become. She has generally been regarded as belonging to the Philistines, although this is not specifically stated. Contact between the Israelites and the inhabitants of Canaan resulted in Semitic names among the Philistines. Delilah was from "the valley of Sorek," which is the modern Wady Surar. A ruin about two miles from Zorah in the upper region of the wady still bears the name Surik. Some authorities hold the view that Delilah was Samson's wife, but there is no mention of marriage in the record. She apparently possessed certain attractive qualities, including an alert mind, persuasive speech, and tact. The Philistines recognized her abilities and were prepared to pay a high price for her help. By skillfully playing on the emotions of Samson, she obtained the information desired and thus brought about his discomfiture. The action of Delilah is typical of the subtle methods of Satan in his efforts to destroy the witness of the Lord's servants.

See SAMSON.

ALEXANDER BARKLEY

DELITZSCH, Franz (1813-1890), German evangelical OT scholar and exegete. Delitzsch was born in Leipzig, Germany. Present at his baptism as a godfather was a Jewish second-hand dealer Franz Julius Hirsch. This may account for the spread of the idea that Delitzsch was of Jewish descent, but Delitzsch himself labeled this notion a fairy tale. Of his boyhood little is known. He became, according to his own testimony, a rationalist, and was interested in the philosophy of Fichte. A fellow student, however, spoke often with him about his soul's salvation, and at last he became a believer.

Delitzsch immediately plunged himself into the study of the Semitic languages, studying the OT with Rosenmüller, Arabic with Fleischer and also with Furst. In 1842 he began his lectures at the university, offering a course five hours weekly on the prophecy of Isaiah. Later, he collaborated with C. F. Keil in the preparation of a thorough commentary on the OT.

A firm believer in the supernatural, Delitzsch sought in his writings to glorify the Supreme Author of the Scriptures. At the same time in a practical way, he endeavored to make the truth of the Scriptures known. His aim in life was to make the OT better known to Christians and the NT better known to Jews. In the accomplishment of this purpose he translated the NT into Hebrew, and with others, went to the Leipzig fairs to distribute testaments to the Jewish merchants who gathered there.

Toward the close of his life Delitzsch wavered somewhat in his attitude toward negative Biblical criticism. He never actually denied the Isaianic authorship of the prophecy of Isaiah, but he did hesitate to make a vigorous affirmation of belief in such authorship. At the same time he always maintained a high view of the Messianic prophecies, and without a doubt was one of Germany's greatest OT scholars. Delitzsch died on the anniversary of his baptism, March 4, 1890.

BIBLIOGRAPHY:

S. I. Curtiss, *Franz Delitzsch, A Memorial Tribute* (Edinburgh, 1891).
A. Kohler, *PRE*, sv.
F. Vigouroux, *DB*, sv.

EDWARD J. YOUNG

DELITZSCH, Friedrich (1850-1922), German orientalist. The son of Franz Delitzsch (1813-1890), Friedrich was born in 1850. This was the same year in which his father became professor of theology at Erlangen. Friedrich Delitzsch was educated at Leipzig, the university to which his father had moved in 1867, and later became professor of Semitic languages and Assyriology successively at Leipzig, Breslau, and Berlin. He was a prolific and erudite author of grammatical treatises, but became embroiled in controversy when in *Babel und Bibel* (1902) he denied the verbal inspiration of the OT, maintained that Semitic monotheism had evolved gradually and that the OT itself had been largely inspired by Babylonian myths and legends. These views, delivered as part of court lectures, were seen as a challenge to orthodoxy and received imperial condemnation. His conclusions were adopted by other scholars, but modern archaeological discoveries have discounted them.

DELUGE. See FLOOD.

DEMAS, Christian worker at Rome during Paul's imprisonment there (Philemon 24; Col. 4:14; II Tim. 4:10). His name is, perhaps, a shortened form of Demetrius. In Philemon 24 he is mentioned along with those described as "fellow-laborers"; in Colossians 4:14 no description accompanies his name; whereas in II Timothy 4:10 it is said that he had forsaken the apostle, "having loved this present world," and had gone to Thessalonica. It may have been that in view of Paul's impending trial he became afraid that if the apostle was condemned his close associates would also be in danger. Or it is possible that an opportunity of obtaining material gain had presented itself at the busy mercantile capital of Macedonia to which he may have belonged. The twofold occurrence of the name Demetrius among the names of politarchs at Thessalonica renders it possible that he attained to civic honors, but on the other hand the name was common there. If the Epistle to the Philippians was written from Rome, Phil. 2:20, 21 may contain an allusion to Demas. Whether he entirely renounced the Christian faith is not clear, but there appears to be no solid foundation for the tradition that he became a pagan priest. As early as the time of Epiphanius, however, he was regarded as an apostate, and in more recent times Bunyan's interpretation of his conduct in the *Pilgrim's Progress* has served to popularize this view. At all events, the final notice of him in Scripture remains to warn the worldly minded rather than to encourage the penitent.

BIBLIOGRAPHY:

J. B. Lightfoot, *Saint Paul's Epistles to the Colossians and Philemon* (London, 1876), 36, 242.

W. M. Ramsay, *St. Paul, The Traveller and Roman Citizen* (London, 1898; first ed., 1895), 358.

WILLIAM J. CAMERON

DE MEDICI, Catherine (1519-1589), Catherine of France, born in Florence, the daughter of Laurent II de Medici and Madeleine de la Tour d'Auvergne. She was the grand-niece of Pope Clement VII (Jules de Medici). Because of negotiations between Clement VII and King Francis I, she was married at the age of 14 to Henry, Duke of Orleans, who was to reign later under the name of Henry II. She had to bear the outrageous competition of Diane de Poitiers, the favorite of her husband. She had several sons, three of whom became king: François II, Charles IX, and Henry III. She also had two daughters, one of whom married Henry IV and is known as Queen "Margot," and the other married Philip II of Spain. At the death of Henry II, who was mortally wounded in a tournament, she exercised a profound influence on her son François II, who had married Marie Stuart, niece of the princes of Guise. The Chancellor at that time was Michel de l'Hospital, who favored the principle of toleration: "Let us do away," he said, "with these devilish words, Lutherans, Huguenots, Papists, which are names of parties, factions and seditions. Let us not change the name of Christian."

When François II died, Charles IX succeeded him at the age of ten. In 1565, Catherine, with her son, travelled through the various provinces of the kingdom. It is then that she had a meeting at Bayonne with the Duke of Alba, where it is reported the massacre of Saint Bartholomew's night was decided upon. In 1561 at the colloquy of Poissy, she had gathered the Catholic hierarchy and 12 Reformed pastors, and she seemed moved by the presentations made by Theodore Beza and by Peter Martyr Vermigli. By 1571, Coligny had gained a dominant influence over Charles IX, who called him his father. Catherine decided together with the princes of Guise to put him to death. In the first attempt on August 22 the admiral was merely wounded in the shoulder by Maurevert. Then Catherine succeeded by dint of insistent request to lead Charles IX to commit himself to massacre the admiral and Protestants. "Let them all be killed," he exclaimed, "lest any of them should survive and charge me with this crime." On August 24, 1572, on Saint Bartholomew's night, this massacre took place. In Paris alone more than 10,000 people were slaughtered. Charles IX died haunted by remorse for this even in his last moments on earth, and Henry succeeded him in 1574. His mother continued to exercise on him a pernicious influence. She died in 1589, 13 days after the assassination of the Duke of Guise. Above all things she had given herself to political intrigue and had sought power for herself and her sons without denying herself any means which could help to achieve this end. It is well known how she used the "flying squadron" of the female beauties of her court to influence those whom she wanted to recruit for her side. Her name is forever spotted with the responsibility for the massacre of St. Bartholomew's night.

JEAN CADIER

DEMETRIUS, "belonging to Demeter" (the Greek goddess of agriculture), the name of two persons in the NT:

(1) A disciple warmly commended by John (III John 12).

(2) A silversmith at Ephesus (Acts 19:24 f.). This craftsman appears to have been the leader of associated traders engaged in making miniature shrines of various materials for votaries to dedicate at the temple of Diana. Silver was the material favored by the wealthy. Vast numbers of such shrines were offered until the Gospel produced a sharp decline in demand, resulting in strong protest (Acts 19:28). An inscription found at Ephesus describes a certain Demetrius as temple-warden in A.D. 57.

DEMIURGE, a Greek term, literally meaning "craftsman," but in Greek, Christian, and gnostic thought also used for "Creator." Plato used it in his *Timaeus* (40C) and *Republic* (530A) for the inferior deities who form the world, according to the pattern of the eternal ideas. Greek theologians used it as a name for god as the creator of all things. The term became particularly prominent in some gnostic systems, especially those of Valentinus and Marcion. The system of Valentinus, which is known only in the developed form of his followers, was deeply influenced by the thought of Plato. The only real world is the world of god, the ideal or heavenly world (called the "Pleroma"). God dwells for countless ages alone with his thought, until he produces a pair of aeons, which in turn produce another pair, and so on. Sophia (wisdom), one of the lowest aeons, who was less perfect because of being so far removed in the long line of generation from the father of all, gave birth to the demiurge, who created the visible world. This demiurge was identified with the creator-god of the OT, who, because of his low origin, was imperfect, ignorant, even incapable of spiritual ideas. In Marcion's theology, which came later and abandons the fanciful system of aeons, the contrast between the God of the OT and the God of the NT is retained. The God of the OT is the Demiurge, the creator-god, who is capricious, cruel, and wicked. He is the God of the law as opposed to the God of Jesus Christ, who is the God of love and grace.

See GNOSTICISM.

KLAAS RUNIA

DEMONS, DEMONOLOGY. The Greek word δαίμων (*daimōn*) lacks any suggestion of the concept of Satan and of evil, and its use in the NT is in terms of Hebraic and OT concepts. Demons are, in Scripture, spiritual beings, "angels who kept not their first estate" (Jude 6). The term "angels" in this sense of fallen angels is several times applied to them (Mt. 25:41; Rev. 12:7, 9). Although powerful, they are still subject to the authority of Christ and His servants, however reluctantly (Luke 4:35; 9:1, 42). Their prince is Satan (Mt. 9:34; 12:24; Mark 3:22; Luke 11:15). Satan is given a variety of names in Scripture: he is called the destroyer, Abaddon in Hebrew, Apollyon in Greek, and the angel of the bottomless pit in Rev. 9:11; prince and god of this world, i.e., the ruler fallen men follow, in John 12:31 and II Cor. 4:4; prince of darkness, in Eph. 6:12; a roaring lion and an adversary, in I Pet. 5:8; a sinner from the beginning, in I John 3:8; Beelzebub in Mt. 12:24; accuser in Rev. 12:10; Belial in II Cor. 6:15; deceiver in Rev. 20:10; dragon in Rev. 12:3; murderer, liar, and father of lies in John 8:44; leviathan in Isa. 27:1; Lucifer in Isa. 14:12 (both the terms of leviathan and Lucifer are primarily applied to nations as examples of evil, not essentially to Satan); serpent in Gen. 3:1; Rev. 12:9; 20:2; Satan in Job 2:1; and tormentor in Mt. 18:34.

This assortment of designations says virtually all that Scripture has to say on demons and demonology. This silence is notable. The references to Satan are historical, not theoretical; Satan is mentioned only as he enters into history by tempting, possessing, or opposing men and Christ. Modernist scholars who state that the Biblical doctrine of Satan and demons comes from the Persian period make the assumption that all of the Biblical references to Satan and demons were added to the texts after that period. But Persian demonology is both dualistic and theoretical, non-historical, whereas Biblical demonology is always theistic in its framework of reference and always historical. The differences between Persian and Biblical demonology are thus basic, profound, and irreconcilable.

The Biblical evidence points to instances of possession, cases where men who were unregenerate and open to evil became so possessed by demons that their personalities and consciousnesses were taken over by the invader. Scripture specifically distinguishes demon possession from illness (Mt. 8:16); it is also distinguished from lunacy (Mt. 4:24). These and other passages make clear that there was a sharp awareness of the difference between demon possession and various mental ailments. Jesus clearly treated the cases of demon possession as a reality. The Incarnation brought God's redemptive history to focus on Palestine, and so the hostility of Satan brought demonic activity to focus at the same point in time, and we find more evidence of demon possession in the NT than at any other time.

Demonology has been extensively influenced by a wide variety of superstitions and pagan beliefs, so that many popular concepts of demons are derived in reality from non-Biblical sources and from art. The influence of artists on the thinking of W culture at this point has been enormous and deserves special study.

The doctrine of demonology in Scripture cannot be understood without reference to the central texts, the temptation of Eve and the temptation of Jesus. The serpent's temptation in Eden is important because the basic religion of demonism is clearly presented. First, God's absolute word is negated: "Yea, hath God said?" (Gen. 3:1), and "Ye shall not surely die" (Gen. 3:4). Instead of God's Word, another, better word for man is offered. Second, the promise is that "your eyes shall be opened" (Gen. 3:5). The revelatory, enlightening word is not God's Word but the creature's word. God's Word is made darkness, the creature's word light. Third, "ye shall be as gods (or God), knowing good and evil" (Gen. 3:5). The verb "knowing" here has the force of "determining." Man shall be his own god, determining good and evil for himself. Every man will become his own god or absolute, his own source of determination or predestination. Instead of the Divine decree and eternal counsel, man will establish his own fate and destiny.

This was the religion and philosophy of the temptation, hence it is the thesis of demonology, which is in essence also that of modern relativism, pragmatism, positivism, existentialism, Marxism, and other related philosophies. It may be added that the temptation gives us probably the first instance of animal possession, if "serpent" is the correct rendering here. The case of swine in Mt. 8: 28-34 gives us another instance of animal possession.

The second great revelation of the doctrine of demonology is the temptation of Jesus in the wilderness (Mt. 4: 1-11). The first temptation, "If thou be the Son of God, command that these stones be made bread" (vs. 3), came after forty days of fasting. Moses had fasted forty days before receiving the table of the law (Ex. 34:28; Deut. 9: 11); Jesus as the new and greater Moses came to re-establish man in every law-word of God and underwent the same preparation. The first temptation involved bread, a call to bring fulfillment to the people by means of miracles in the economic realm. Men want a solution to the economic problem; they desire independence from want, to live by bread without work or faith. Jesus' answer, citing Deut. 8:2, 3, was, "Man shall not live by bread alone, but by every word that proceedeth out of the mouth of God" (Mt. 4:4). Against a man's own word as the infallible guide, Jesus established the "every word" of God, the totality of Scripture, as man's only guide.

The second temptation of Jesus was to cast Himself down from the pinnacle of the temple (Mt. 4:5, 6). The temple was the symbol of the presence of God with His people. It called for a religion of sight, of demonstration. It echoed the demand of Israel at Masseh, "Is the Lord among us or not?" (Ex. 17:7). The demand of Satan was that God prove Himself to man, rather than man prove himself to God. Instead of faith by man in God, it was a demand for God to trust in man. Jesus answered, "It is written again, Thou shalt not tempt the Lord thy God" (Mt. 4:7), citing Deut. 6:16, translated by some as, "You shall not put God to test," or "You shall not put the Lord to the proof." The idea that man can be a judge over God was rejected.

The third temptation of Jesus was to receive all the kingdoms of the world on the condition that He fall down and worship Satan (Mt. 4:8, 9). This was a call to accept the principles of dualism, that God has the right to rule in His realm and that Satan has the right to rule in his. The counterpart of this today is the idea that man can hold on to autonomous human reason and at the same time honor God by "faith." It is the call to "salvation" while honoring and supporting the human world system, its reasonings and programs. Jesus' answer, citing Deut. 6:13, was, "Get thee hence, Satan: for it is written, Thou shalt worship the Lord thy God, and him only shalt thou serve" (Mt. 4:19).

The issue was thus God's every or total Word as against man's word. The doctrine of demons was thus the doctrine of the creature's word and will justified against God. Wherever man's word was advanced, there Satan's doctrine was present. This explains why, when Peter dissented with the necessity of the cross, Jesus called him Satan, saying, "Get thee behind me, Satan: thou art an offense unto me: for thou savourest not the things that be of God, but those that be of men" (Mt. 16:23). There is no ground whatsoever for speaking of Peter as Satan-possessed at this point. Rather, by opposing God's absolute Word with man's wishes, he had identified himself with Satan for the moment.

Two other appearances of Satan give evidences of his position. Satan asserted to God that man's entire being is always and inescapably egocentric. Man's motive is the value of his actions, and the actions of man are only motivated by self-preservation and self-salvation (Job 1:9-11; 2:6). The book of Job demonstrates Satan's misreading of man; Job's faith was true, although his understanding was defective. In Zechariah 2:1-5, Satan appears again as man's accuser, denying that God has a right to forgive sins, apparently insistent that man's self-righteousness is the only valid form of righteousness which should be permitted.

From these episodes, it is apparent that Satan's major manifestation and the most prevalent form of his presence is doctrinal. Every form of humanism, every undercutting in the slightest degree of the "every word" of God is thus demonic and represents the major form of demonic influence in human society.

It is significant that in the early church and for some centuries thereafter, major theologians and the Church Fathers denounced the popular forms of belief in demons as superstitious and false. There was an extensive reluctance to accept the reality of popular and pagan beliefs in witchcraft, and the general remedy offered was sound doctrine.

In popular belief, demons became more and more identified with pagan spirits and thus became playful imps and pranksters in popular opinion, tempting people to vices and enjoying man's discomfiture. Since many drunkards, gamblers, and whoremongers are converted, it was reasoned that demons, who were their tempters in these things, could also be converted. The problem was not seen as sin, the principle of lawlessness and autonomous independence of God, but as sins, particular offenses. In this case the conversion of demons was as logical as the conversion of man. As a result, some theologians, whose thinking was heavily infected by Greek thought, began to speak of the possibility and even necessity of Satan's conversion. Such opinions of the conversion of demons also occurred in the Talmud and in the Koran. These opinions found a place in literature much later. In Klopstock's *Messias*, the demon Abbadona repents and enters paradise. George Sand in *Consuelo* and Montanelli in *The Temptation* give us a redeemed Satan. Alfred de Vigny and Victor Hugo both planned poems with the same idea in mind. In modern theology, universalism has become an increasingly important theme. As a result, it is not surprising that this universal salvation is seen as including

Satan and his hosts. Thus, J. S. Whale, in *Victor and Victim* (1960), speaks of "the fulness of reconciliation in Christ" as one which "will include, not exclude the demonic powers. It means, as even Gregory of Nyssa argued in his *Oratio catechetica* (chapters XXII to XXVI), that Satan himself is finally saved."

Such opinions involve a serious misreading of Scripture as well as a misunderstanding of Satan's religious principle. Many non-Christian men and groups have not misunderstood and have instead worshipped him.

The thesis of the church, as it moved against the various witches' covens of the late medieval and Reformation and Counter-Reformation periods, was that these groups represented a Satan-worshipping conspiracy against the church. The prevalence of the Satanic Mass, a deliberate mockery of the sacrament of communion, certainly points to a widespread and self-conscious Satanism. The origin of the various Satanic cults is linked to Paulicianism, Catharism, and other forms of Manichaean and semi-Manichaean heresies. Rhodes states that "the god of the witches and sorcerers was the Cathar Satan." These cults were closely linked also to the ancient fertility cults, so that phallic worship was common to their activities. Jules Bois held that, instead of celebrating the fact that "the Word was made flesh," the Black Mass in effect celebrated the faith that "the flesh was made the Word," an excellent insight into the meaning of that Satanic ritual. The extensive Satanism of the late medieval and Reformation periods continued into the modern era. The court of Louis XIV had many Satanists In Rosicrucianism, Freemasonry, and related movements, the doctrines of Satanism were formalized and institutionalized.

Michelet characterized the Black Mass as the communion of revolt or of revolution. The theoretical background was the resurgence of Greek philosophy as Scholasticism, whereby the world of nature was separated from the world of grace, so that in effect miracles belonged to God but the rest of the world to nature, and, by default, to the prince of this world, Satan. As a result, demonology came to loom large in popular feelings and beliefs; devils were close and everywhere, and God remote. Hatred of Christianity led to a religious Satanism during the 13th century in particular.

Murray found evidences of the extensive use of the name Diana (the feminine of Janus or Dianus, the two-faced god) as the name of the female leader or deity of the witches of W Europe. Human sacrifice, often of children, was a part of many cults; and sexual rites were commonplace and a form of communion with the devil-god or goddess. The terms witch and devil were Christian descriptions of a pagan cult, but in hostility to Christianity the groups identified themselves with the Devil as an anti-Christian force. Murray found four forms of sacrifice among the cults: (1) a blood sacrifice of the witch's own blood; (2) the sacrifice of an animal; (3) the sacrifice of a human being, usually a child; and (4) the sacrifice of the god (Murray, *The Witch-Cult in Western Europe*, p. 152).

War was declared by the church in the 13th century against the revivals of paganism, defined as witchcraft and demon-worship. Some churchmen adhered to both paganism and the church for political reasons. Many of the pagans refused to call their god the Devil, whereas some others accepted that description. The old pagan cults became progressively more and more imitative of the church by aping it in mockery, and thus became increasingly sterile in becoming essentially a force for negation.

The Salem witchcraft trials, long held

to be an instance of superstition and injustice, have been re-examined by the non-Christian scholar, Chadwick Hansen. Hansen holds that witchcraft did exist at Salem, was extensively practiced, harmed its victims, and was a genuinely criminal offense. Many executed were probably innocent, but there were truly guilty persons. The clergy attempted to keep the trials within bounds, but popular reactions to the danger led to excesses. It was the clergy, not the public, which finally brought the trials to a halt.

The evidences for the reality of a movement in Europe, with premises radically anti-Christian and progressively demonic, are very extensive and cannot be more than barely indicated here. The principles of these cults and movements became, with the Enlightenment, less and less ritualistic and emotional and more and more rationalistic in nature. Various illuminist groups self-consciously modernized the older beliefs into secret societies aiming at man's total control over man, time, and history, but their beliefs passed steadily from the arena of the cults to that of philosophy and science.

BIBLIOGRAPHY:

M. Bessy, *A Pictorial History of Magic and the Supernatural* (London, 1964).
M. W. Fishwick, *Faust Revisited, Some Thoughts on Satan* (New York, 1963).
M. Garcon and J. Vinchon, *The Devil, an Historical Critical and Medical Study* (New York, 1930).
G. B. Gardiner, *Witchcraft Today* (New York, 1955).
A. Graf, *The Story of the Devil* (New York, 1931).
C. Hansen, *Witchcraft at Salem* (New York, 1969).
G. L. Kittredge, *Witchcraft in Old and New England* (New York, 1929).
K. Koch, *Between Christ and Satan* (Grand Rapids, 1961).
H. C. Lea, *Materials Toward A History of Witchcraft* (New York, 1938, 1957), 3 vols.
E. A. McDowell, *Son of Man and Suffering Servant* (Louisville, 1944).
J. Michelet, *Satanism and Witchcraft* (New York, 1939 reprint).
M. Motley, *Devils in Waiting* (New York, 1960).
M. A. Murray, *The God of the Witches* (London, n.d.).
M. A. Murray, *The Witch-Cult in Western Europe* (Oxford, 1921).
T. K. Österreich, *Possession, Demoniacal and Other* (New York, 1966, reprint).
H. T. F. Rhodes, *The Satanic Mass* (New York, 1955).
E. Rose, *A Razor for a Goat, Problems in the History of Witchcraft and Diabolism* (Toronto, 1962).
R. H. Robbins, *The Encyclopedia of Witchcraft and Demonology* (New York, 1959).
P. W. Sergeant, *Witches and Warlocks* (London, 1936).
M. Summers, *The Geography of Witchcraft* (London, 1927).
M. Summers, *The Vampire* (New York, 1960).
M. Summers, *The Werewolf* (New York, 1966).
M. F. Unger, *Biblical Demonology* (Chicago, 1952).
J. S. Whale, *Victor and Victim* (Cambridge, 1960).
C. Williams, *Witchcraft* (London, 1941).

ROUSAS JOHN RUSHDOONY

DEMON POSSESSION. Possession by demons (fallen angels, also called "unclean spirits") is set forth in the Scriptures as an actual phenomenon and not merely as a figure of speech. Possession is not, as has been alleged, a primitive explanation for madness, epilepsy, or other mysterious afflictions and diseases. The gospel writers, and notably Luke, who was a physician, were always careful to distinguish demon possession from sickness caused by disease or injury (cf. Luke 4:33-36, 40, 41; 6:17, 18; 9:1, 2; Mt. 4:23, 24; 10:1; Mark 1:32). Moreover, the recording of the entrance of the demons into a herd of swine at the permission of Christ is explicit evidence of the belief of the NT writers in the objectivity of demons and their power to possess not only human beings but animals as well.

Whereas demon possession is everywhere distinguished from illness and madness, it is nevertheless identified as one of several separate causes of both. Disease or injury (organic problems), sin, and demon possession are viewed Biblically as the three discrete causes of madness and illness. The symptoms of demon possession are closely related to those maladies that result from various convulsive and perceptual disorders. Matthew's words are especially interesting when he says, "they brought to him all who suffered from various ailments and pains—demoniacs, epileptics, and paralytics. And he healed them" (Mt. 4:24, Berkeley). According to this classification, demon possession is considered to be one among several possible sources of painful ailments. When a demon is cast out, the formerly possessed person, therefore, is said to be "healed" (cf. *supra*, Luke 8:2, etc.) or "in his right mind" (Mark 5:15). Symptoms of madness and illness due to demon possession include convulsions (Mark 9:18, 20, 26; cf. Berkeley trans.), self-injury (Luke 4:35; Mark 9:18, 22), bizarre behavior (Luke 8:27), isolation and withdrawal (Luke 8:27—demons are thought perhaps to have been called "unclean" because of their association with ceremonially unclean tombs), and deafness and dumbness (Mark 9:17-27). When Jesus was accused of possessing a demon He was at the same time declared to be insane (cf. John 7:20; 8:48 ff.; 10:20, 21; Mark 3:21, 22, 30). In our day, when we have begun to understand that the same perceptual symptoms may arise from the distortion of bodily chemistry by the use of hallucinogenic drugs, from significant sleep loss, or from bodily malfunctions, there should be no difficulty in believing that bizarre behavior may also result from other causes, including demon possession. Moreover, in a day in which the effects of hypnotism are so well known that its use has become a therapeutic and anesthetic technique, there should be no *a priori* arguments raised against the possibility of the control of one personality by another.

Far from being an occasional matter infrequently noted, demon possession is mentioned 52 times in the Gospels and in addition there are references to it in Acts. Why should this subject occupy so large a proportion of space? The earthly ministry of Jesus Christ prior to the cross to a large extent was concerned with the direct confrontation of Satan's kingdom. This confrontation was mainly manifested by Christ's exorcism of demons. The comments of the demons themselves, who regularly recognized Jesus as "the Son of God," indicate this; as does also their fear of His ministry as the beginning of the end of their kingdom (Mt. 8:29). Jesus Himself rejoices over the expulsion of demons by His disciples as the "fall of Satan" from "heaven" (Luke 10:17, 18) and directly relates the casting out of demons to the coming of the "kingdom (or empire) of God" and to the "binding" of Satan (Mt. 12:28, 29; Mark 3:20-27). Thus the frequent reference to demon possession in connection with Christ's ministry of exorcism is not incidental but central to the gospel writers' purpose. It is to be understood in eschatological terms as evidence of the Messianic identity of Jesus, who came not only to preach the kingdom (Mark 1:14, 15) but also to establish it (Mt. 28:18, 19; Acts 1:3).

Paul predicted that extensive demonic activity would characterize the last days of the NT era (I Tim. 4:1). Satan's rage would be intensified because he had been cast down upon the earth (Rev. 12:13). Significantly, at the end of the millennial era (which extends from the ascension of Christ to a point shortly prior to His second coming) Satan will be released to "deceive" the Gentiles again as he did throughout the OT era (cf. Rev. 20). During the present "times of the gentiles" the empire of God has been spreading (like a stone growing into a large mountain) throughout the world so that some from every tribe, tongue, and nation shall become part of that empire. Looking forward to these times, Zechariah predicted that the "unclean spirits" would be removed (Zech. 13:2). The present restraint that Paul declared would be imposed upon Satan (II Thess. 2:1-22; n.b. vss. 9-22) prohibits wholesale "deceit" by direct demonic activity. Yet Paul, with John (Rev. 20), predicted that this restraint will be lifted just before the return of Christ, thus bringing about another brief period of intensive demonic influence (cf. also Rev. 16:14 with II Thess. 2: 9-12 and Rev. 20:7-10). The eschatological timetable and the nature of the present millennial era adequately account for the failure of the modern church to encounter demon possession as a common daily contemporary phenomenon.

Christians have differed about the fact of demon possession today, and indeed some missionaries have cited instances of supposed possession. John L. Nevius in his classic, *Demon Possession* (recently republished), has set forth the most systematic statement of this position. Yet the book, like most of the accounts by individuals, is unsatisfying since it tends to accept pagan testimony and categories along with personal experience as the standard for determining what are cases of demon possession rather than applying Biblical criteria. An adequate study in terms of the Biblical data has not yet appeared.

Modern Pentecostalists and others have gone beyond Scripture in claiming to be able to distinguish a second phenomenon that they call demon *oppression* in distinction from demon *possession*. Demon oppression is said to represent a strong and even controlling demonic influence over Christians. In such cases prayer or even exorcism may be necessary as in cases of actual possession. In fact, while zealously distinguished from possession, the symptoms said to be connected with the phenomenon of oppression seem to be nearly identical. This distinct category takes its origin from Acts 10:38, where part of the work of Christ's ministry is described as "healing all that were oppressed by the devil." However, there is no warrant for supposing that this summary statement looking back upon Christ's ministry as a whole refers to anything other than the work of casting out demons about which the Gospels continually speak. It would be strange indeed for Luke to introduce a new activity of Christ's ministry in Acts about which he and all of the gospel writers were utterly silent. The fact that this is a general summary rather than an explicit statement about a specific and distinct sort of Satanic influence is clear from the use of the word "devil" rather than the word "demon." Here all of the individual cases of possession by specific demons are viewed collectively as the work of the evil one who stands behind them. The term καταδυναστέω (*katadunasteō*) means "to oppress, dominate or exploit," and may be applied aptly to the whole Satanic enterprise of demonic exploitation, domination, and control of possessed persons.

There is no Biblical reason to think that demonic possession (or oppression) can occur in the life of a Christian. The simultaneous presence of the Holy Spirit, who dwells within every true child of God, and an "unclean spirit" is impossible. This is clear from the utter antithesis of the two noted in Mark 3:20-30. Here also Jesus warns that it is unforgivable blasphemy to attribute the work of the Holy Spirit to a demon.

Pagan and Jewish ideas that demons were the shades or souls of departed wicked men (cf. Josephus, *The Wars of the Jews*, 7:6:3) must be rejected as foreign to Biblical teaching. However, the LXX uses the word demon to describe pagan gods, as also I Cor. 10:20, 21, and possibly I Tim. 4:1 also seem to do (cf. also Ps. 106:37, Berkeley).

The connection between pagan idolatry, demonic deception, and possession is not hard to see.

BIBLIOGRAPHY:
J. E. Adams, *The Time Is At Hand* (Nutley, N. J., 1970).
H. Farmer, *An Essay on the Demoniacs of the New Testament* (London, 1775).
J. L. Nevius, *Demon Possession* (Grand Rapids, 1968).

JAY E. ADAMS

DEMYTHOLOGIZATION. The thesis that in the Gospels the life of Jesus was mythologically rewritten in the light of OT prophecy was surveyed by D. F. Strauss in his *Life of Jesus*, I-II (1835-36; Eng. tr. 1846). It produced one of the most violent theological controversies of the 19th century. Then after the turn of the century Arthur Drews, *The Christ Myth* (Eng. tr. 1910), argued that the story of Christ was fictitious mythology.

But the modern plea for demythologization of the NT, made by Rudolf Bultmann (b. 1884) and his school, dates from 1941, when Bultmann privately circulated an essay on "New Testament and Mythology," which was subsequently published in *Kerygma and Myth*, I (1948; Eng. tr. 1953). It was elaborated in various later works, including *Primitive Christianity in Its Contemporary Setting* (Eng. tr. 1956) and *Jesus Christ and Mythology* (Eng. tr. 1960). At most, Bultmann appears to have been only indirectly influenced by Strauss and not at all by Drews. More important seems to have been the work of Johannes Weiss, *The Preaching of Jesus about the Kingdom of God* (1892). The latter showed that Jesus' teaching could not be reduced to liberal, altruistic spiritual ideas. The kingdom is eschatological. It transcends the historical order, and will be realized by the supernatural intervention of God. This raises the acute question of the importance and meaning of the NT for modern man.

In contrast with earlier liberals who contended that certain events (such as the virgin birth and the empty tomb) were mythical, Bultmann argues that virtually the whole thought-world of the NT writers is mythical. The three-deck view of the universe (heaven, earth, and hell), angels and demons, the Kingdom of God, redemption, salvation, resurrection, and judgment are all mythological concepts. These ideas derive mainly from two sources: Jewish apocalyptic (with its belief in the imminent end of the world, the two ages, and the Messiah) and pagan gnosticism (with its dualism of light and darkness, the powers of good and evil, and the heavenly redeemer). For Bultmann, myth is incompatible with the modern scientific view of the universe, in which everything is explained in terms of natural causes. Many beliefs and practices (such as sacramental conveyance of grace, atonement by sacrifice, and resurrection) are impossible for modern man.

However, the real purpose of myth, according to Bultmann, is not to present an objective picture of the universe, but to express man's understanding of himself in the world in which he lives, and to speak about the transcendent factors which affect human existence. But the objective, obsolete imagery of mythological language obscures its contemporary relevance. The task, therefore, of demythologization (German: *Entmythologisierung*) is not to eliminate the mythology of the NT, but to interpret it critically, and thus discover the essential message of the primitive Christian kerygma or proclamation.

When the process is carried out, the result, as Bultmann admits, has marked kinship with the existentialism of Martin Heidegger. It makes use of the existentialist categories of thought, although Bultmann insists its message of redemption is lacking in Heidegger. A distinction is drawn between human existence apart from faith (in which man is enslaved by material and selfish pursuits) and the "authentic" life of faith (based on unseen, intangible realities, in which man is delivered from the bondage of the past and the quest for visible security). Faith means "to open ourselves freely for the future" (*Kerygma and Myth*, I, 19). This is realized through the proclamation of the cross and resurrection of Christ. These are not to be understood in a literal or historical sense, for Bultmann is skeptical whether we can penetrate beyond the Easter faith of the first Christians. Nor does he believe in an abstract metaphysical atonement or the resuscitation of a corpse.

On the other hand, the cross and resurrection represent intangible realities. The preaching of them as the event of redemption challenges hearers to appropriate their significance—to be crucified to the world and lead the life of faith, liberated from care. There is no way of encountering Christ other than in this proclamation which presents man with the unique opportunity to understand himself.

Bultmann's demythologizing has been criticized as giving a gospel that is so reduced and attenuated that it is difficult to see why anyone should bother about Christianity any more, or why the first Christians were so moved by it. It raises the question of how the Biblical writers came to be so mistaken in their understanding of their faith. Bultmann has shifted its onus from its object, Jesus Christ and His historical work, to the subjective disposition of the believer when confronted by a certain message.

On the other hand, while Bultmann reserves the right to be skeptical about everything else, he stops short at the proclamation (or kerygma) of the cross and resurrection. This has prompted radical thinkers, such as Schubert Ogden and Fritz Buri, to question whether the idea of God should not also be demythologized, and whether the kerygma should not be "dekerygmatized." Bultmann, however, has refused to concede the point, and is content with reaffirming that, from a theological standpoint, the saving message is bound up with the proclamation of the cross and resurrection.

On historical and critical grounds scholars have questioned whether the NT was indebted to gnosticism in the way that Bultmann claims. The evidence suggests that one cannot speak of gnosticism in any developed sense in the NT era. The gnostic myths of a heavenly redeemer all belong to the post-Christian age, and the evidence indicates that they were borrowed from Christianity, and not vice versa.

Bultmann's historical skepticism is bound up with his skeptical form criticism. In his handling of data he is not infrequently guilty of what R. W. Hepburn has termed "the flight from the evidential." Thus he rejects I Cor. 15: 3-8 as evidence for the Resurrection, not explicitly on critical grounds, but because "that line of argument" is "fatal because it tries to adduce a proof for the kerygma" (*Kerygma and Myth*, I, p. 112). In removing the kerygma from all objective verification and falsification Bultmann removes it from the realm of truth. The NT writers themselves were, however, deeply concerned about the historical veracity of their testimony (cf. e.g., Luke 1:1-4; John 20:30 f.; Acts 3: 14 ff. I John 1:1 f.).

Bultmann has also been widely taken to task for confusing myth and metaphor. Because a man speaks of heaven, earth, and hell, it does not mean that he is committed to a literal, physical conception of the universe. G. B. Caird has suggested that the author of Revelation used mythical imagery with the insight of a political cartoonist. The question of the meaning of any given text or piece of imagery can be settled only by exegesis of the text concerned, and not by a wholesale, *a priori* hermeneutic. At this point Bultmann's understanding of myth is highly vulnerable. His definition is so wide as to embrace all pictorial, symbolical, and analogical religious language. "Mythology is the use of imagery to express the other worldly in terms of this world and the divine in terms of human life, the other side in terms of this side" (*Kerygma and Myth*, I, p. 10). On this basis, any Christian, theistic view is automatically ruled out. It also makes the task of demythologizing logically impossible, for religious language cannot be restated except in such terms as Bultmann has designated mythological.

Elsewhere, conscious of this difficulty, Bultmann has attempted to rescue the term "act of God" from the realm of the mythological, by designating it "analogical" (*op. cit.*, p. 196 f.). "Mythological thought regards the divine activity, whether in nature or in history, as an interference with the course of nature, history, or the life of the soul, a tearing of it asunder—a miracle, in fact." But, on the one hand, this second definition conflicts with the original one. And, on the other hand, it will be noticed that Bultmann has shifted his ground. Whereas the first definition was concerned only with the *form* of language and said nothing about its *content*, the second implies a fundamental, *a priori* rejection of the Christian, theistic view of God and the universe. (We leave aside the question of whether Bultmann here properly uses the word "miracle.")

Bultmann's own statements thus raise the question whether his use of the word "myth" is precise or consistent enough to be meaningful, and therefore whether the program of demythologization may properly be regarded as a scientific, critical enterprise. It also raises the deeper question of method of approach in theology and knowledge in general. Bultmann's prior, general world-view rules out *in advance* the Christian theistic interpretation of the Bible which the Biblical writers themselves hold. No matter what the evidence may be from Scripture, nothing is allowed to count against Bultmann's interpretation, because the decision to interpret it in a non-theistic sense has already been taken. But to adopt such a position not only calls in question the claim of Bultmann's approach to be taken seriously as critical, empirical investigation. It also rules itself out of court as Christian theology. For the latter can proceed only in faith and obedience to the Word of God, and not by deciding in advance the form and content of that Word.

See BULTMANN; FORM CRITICISM; HERMENEUTICS.

BIBLIOGRAPHY:

H. W. Bartsch, ed., *Kerygma and Myth*, I, 1953; II, 1962.
D. Cairns, *A Gospel without Myth?*, 1960.
F. Gogarten, *Demythologizing and History*, 1955.
R. W. Hepburn, "Demythologizing and the Problem of Validity" in A. Flew and A. MacIntyre, eds., *New Essays in Philosophical Theology*, 1955, 227-242.
P. E. Hughes, *Scripture and Myth*, 1956.
C. W. Kegley, ed., *The Theology of Rudolf Bultmann*, 1966.
J. Macquarrie, *An Existentialist Theology*, 1958.
J. Macquarrie, *The Scope of Demythologizing*, 1960.
A. Malet, *The Thought of Rudolf Bultmann*, 1969.
L. Malevez, *The Christian Message and Myth*, 1957.
T. F. O'Meara and D. M. Weisser, eds., *Rudolf Bultmann in Catholic Thought*, 1968.
G. Miegge, *Gospel and Myth in the Thought of Rudolf Bultmann*, 1960.
H. P. Owen, *Revelation and Existence*, 1957.
B. H. Throckmorton, *The New Testament and Mythology*, 1960.

COLIN BROWN

DENK (DENCK), Hans (*c.* 1500-1527), Anabaptist mystic. Denk studied at the universities of Ingolstadt and Basel, thus becoming thoroughly acquainted with humanism. He was appointed as an educator in Nüremberg

(1523), but his emphasis on mysticism caused sharp differences with the Lutherans, especially Osiander. Denk was tried and banished (1524), and then came into contact with the Anabaptists. In Augsburg, he was baptized by Hübmaier, and later became leader of the Anabaptists there when Hübmaier went to Nikolsburg. His ministry was very successful, but again Lutheran opposition compelled him to take up a life of wandering. During the course of his journeys, he came to Worms and there assisted Hätzer in the translation of the OT prophets. Three months before his death, he presided at the famous "Martyr Synod" in Augsburg, which commissioned him to go to the areas of Basel and Zurich. In Basel he held a series of discussions with Oecolampadius, which led Denk to modify his position to such an extent that he no longer regarded baptism upon profession of faith as necessary. He also rejected the Anabaptist prohibition of the oath. He regarded ecclesiastical institutions as unnecessary, perhaps even harmful. In doctrine he was anti-Trinitarian, denying the deity of Christ. What really mattered to him was a life of piety and mysticism, as expressed in the most noted of his numerous writings, *Von der waren Liebe*.

See ANABAPTISTS.

BIBLIOGRAPHY:

G. Baring, *Quellen zur Geschichte der Täufer, VI: Hans Denck* (Gütersloh, 1955).

G. Baring, "Hans Denck und Thomas Müntzer in Nürnberg," *Archiv für Reformationsgeschichte* 50 (1959), 145-182.

C. Boerlage, *Hans Denck* (Amsterdam, 1921).

A. Coutts, *Hans Denck (1495–1527): Humanist and Heretic* (Edinburgh, 1927).

H. Denk, *Schriften* (Gütersloh, 1955-56), 2 vols.

J. Kiwiet, "The Life of Hans Denck," *MQR,* 31 (1957), 227-259.

J. Kiwiet, "The Theology of Hans Denck," *MQR,* 32 (1958), 3-27.

O. E. Vittali, *Die Theologie des Wiedertäufers Hans Denck* (Offenburg, 1932).

F. L. Weis, *The Life, Teachings, and Works of Johannes Denck* (Pawtucket, R. I., 1925).

PETER J. KLASSEN

DENNEY, James (1856-1917), Scottish Free Church theologian. His writings combine penetrating thought with clarity of expression. His most important works deal with the Person of Christ and the Atonement. In doctrine he was generally conservative. Born at Greenock, he had a brilliant student career at Glasgow University and the College of the Free Church of Scotland at Glasgow. From 1886 to 1897 he was pastor of the East Free Church at Broughty Ferry. In 1897 he was elected professor of systematic theology at the College of the Free Church of Scotland at Glasgow and then appointed to the professorship of NT in 1899, becoming principal in 1915. He was actively interested in reunion with the Church of Scotland.

His works include articles on "The Epistles to the Thessalonians" (1892) and "The Second Epistle to the Corinthians" (1894), both in the *Expositor's Bible; Studies in Theology* (1895); "The Epistle to the Romans" in the *Expositor's Greek Testament* (1900); *The Death of Christ* (1902); *The Atonement and the Modern Mind; Jesus and the Gospel* (1908); and *The Christian Doctrine of Reconciliation* (1917).

BIBLIOGRAPHY:

J. Moffatt (ed.), *The Letters of Principal James Denney to his Family and Friends* (London, n.d.).

W. R. Nicoll (ed.), *The Letters of Principal James Denney to W. Robertson Nicoll, 1893–1917,* with an "appreciation" by W. R. Nicoll, xiii-xxvii; and "Memoirs of a Student," by J. A. Robertson, xxxi-xliii (London, 1920).

A. S. Peake, *DNB* (1912-1921), 153 f.

T. H. Walker, *Principal James Denney, D.D., A Memoir and Tribute* (London, 1918).

WILLIAM J. CAMERON

DEPRAVITY, the corruption of man's nature, resulting from sin and the Fall. The effects of the Fall (see FALL OF MAN) are called original sin, which includes original guilt and original pollution (see also SIN). Original corruption or pollution that is transmitted to the human race is called depravity. This depravity extends to all men without exception (Rom. 3:10-18). It is called *total depravity* (*q.v.*) because it affects every part of man's nature. It is an evidence of God's common grace (*q.v.*) that the evil potential of man's sin is restrained, so that the standards of decency, order, and justice, and restraint of wrongdoers have been preserved to a greater or lesser extent among men. In total depravity there is also a total inability of man to save himself or contribute in any way to his salvation.

Historically there have been theological positions that have erred fundamentally by distorting the doctrines of sin and depravity. Pelagianism and Socinianism deny all original sin. Arminianism (see REMONSTRANCE and WESLEYAN ARMINIANISM) and semi-Pelagianism typical of RC theology hold to a view of original sin that recognizes a kind of depravity but denies total depravity.

See FALL OF MAN; PELAGIUS, PELAGIANISM; REMONSTRANCE; SIN; TOTAL DEPRAVITY; WESLEYAN ARMINIANISM.

DEPRESSION, formerly known as *melancholia* (from the Greek meaning "black bile," a secretion that the ancient Greeks believed was the cause of gloominess, irascibility, and dejection). Depression is a condition characterized by a low mood, lack of zest and energy, self deprecation, and a dismal outlook on life. In serious depression, unpleasant chores are abandoned and there is little or no interest in going anywhere or doing anything. Insomnia and loss of appetite frequently leading to loss of weight (although some eat excessively) sometimes accompany such a state, and there is always the possibility of suicide.

While physical sickness or biochemical factors in some instances may cause depression (e.g., in *post partum* depressions), by far the most frequent source of depression is moral; the conscience "bears witness" to sinful transgressions and sinful ways of handling (or failing to handle) life's problems (cf. Rom. 2:15), triggering painful feelings of depression. Constant reference to depression of this sort occurs in the Scriptures, particularly in the Psalms (cf. esp. Ps. 32, 38, 51).

God's words to Cain, whose face was described as "downcast," point to the fundamental solution to depression: "If you do right, will it [your face] not be lifted up?" (Gen. 4:5-7. The AV misses the point with the translation "accepted." The more literal translation "lifted up" is correct.) The Psalms mentioned above show how repentance leading to confession, forgiveness, reconciliation, and restoration to a life of active faith bring relief from depression. Release from mourning and depression is intimately linked to the redemptive work of Christ (Isa. 61:3), and the state of being that should characterize the Christian is described in the NT as continued joy and peace (James 1:2; Phil. 4:4-9; Rom. 14:17).

At one time depression was considered to be a problem "which nothing but clear views of religion can possibly correct" (Crabb's *Synonyms*, New York, 1891, p. 307), but more recently it has become a subject of psychiatric treatment and speculation. Ministers have been wrong in abandoning depressed persons to the psychiatrists, because the answer to depression lies in the Scriptures rather than in the works of Skinner, Rogers, or Freud. A minister, working closely with a physician, affords the best approach available. The physician might uncover some of the infrequent cases of chemically caused depression and in very serious cases may help the pastor to engage in meaningful counseling by temporarily administering antidepressants (see *Competent to Counsel*).

The minister will be most successful with depressed and suicidal persons when he takes them seriously about their sin. Depressed persons as a rule will mention the true cause of the depression, though perhaps obliquely: "I guess I haven't been much of a mother" or "My family would be better off without me." Such statements should not be minimized. To deny such statements or try to switch the conversation to more positive thoughts does not comfort. A truly depressed person (not someone who uses self-deprecation to elicit praise) is expressing an honest evaluation, and it should be taken as such by the counselor: "Not to be a good mother is a serious matter; tell me some of the ways in which you have failed," or "I am sure that you have good reasons for so serious an evaluation; tell me how your life has become a detriment to your family. Your evaluation is probably correct but your solution (suicide, depression) is wrong." The rapidity with which such an approach elicits response is amazing. Solutions to the behavioral problems behind depression lie in repentance, confession, forgiveness, reconciliation, and then learning to handle life's problems God's way ("works appropriate to repentance").

BIBLIOGRAPHY:

J. E. Adams, *Competent to Counsel* (Nutley, N. J., 1970).

D. M. Lloyd-Jones, *Spiritual Depression* (Grand Rapids, 1965).

S. I. MicMillen, *None of These Diseases* (Westwood, 1963).

O. H. Mowrer, *The Crisis in Psychology and Religion* (Princeton, 1961).

JAY E. ADAMS

DEPUTY, in the OT, an officer inferior to a king or governor (I Kings 22:47). Among Assyrians, Babylonians, and Persians, deputies governed lesser districts and cities within satrapies. In the NT, the term is better rendered "proconsul" (RSV), the highest official in Roman senatorial provinces. Appointed for one year, proconsuls held virtually absolute military, judicial, and administrative authority. The NT mentions Sergius Paulus of Cyprus (Acts 13:7, 8, 12) and Gallio of Achaia (Acts 18:12). Acts 19:38 refers to the class as a whole and does not suggest the presence of more than one in the province of Asia.

DERBE, a city in Asia Minor and the terminus of Paul's first missionary journey (Acts 14:20, 21). Paul visited it again during the second missionary journey (Acts 16:1); and according to the generally accepted text, a certain Gaius belonging to it accompanied him to Jerusalem, probably in connection with the collection for the poor saints (Acts 20:4). Stephanus of Byzantium states that the name is derived from *delbeia,* the Lycaonian juniper. There is some doubt as to the site. Sterrett concluded in 1885 that it was situated in the neighborhood of the modern Zosta in S central Turkey. Ramsay, however, maintained that Gudelissin, three miles NW of Zosta, is the only possible site. Sterrett recognized that this place showed many traces of an ancient village or town but thought that they belonged to Christian times. Ramsay, on the other hand, held that excavation would disclose evidence of a very old city. Kirsopp Lake, while admitting the probability of the latter view, thought that the distance from Zoldera, the site of Lystra, might be too great. Derbe was ethnically and geographically Lycaonian, but politically it was included in the province of Galatia, where it had importance as a frontier fortress from A.D. 41 to A.D. 72. Claudius bestowed on it the title Claudio-Derbe. Its people, like those of Lystra, were bilingual. The Lycaonian language survived as a spoken language until the 6th century. Derbe remained in the province of Galatia until A.D. 135, when it became part of the triple province Cilicia-Isauria-Lycaonia. At a later date it was included in a separate province of Lycaonia. A bishop of Derbe attended the Council of Constantinople in 381. On the S Galatian theory, the church at Derbe was one of those addressed in Paul's Epistle to the Galatians.

BIBLIOGRAPHY:

K. Lake, "Paul's Route in Asia Minor," *The Beginnings of Christianity* (London, 1933), Pt. I, V, 227.

W. M. Ramsay, *The Cities of St. Paul* (London, 1907), 385-404.

J. Strahan, *HDAC* I (1915), 288-289.

WILLIAM J. CAMERON

DESCARTES, René (1596-1650), French mathematician and philosopher. Born in the village of La Haye in Touraine, in 1606 he entered the Jesuit College of La Flèche, where he studied the liberal arts and philosophy. In his *Discourse on Method*, he states that he also perused all the books of occult and rarefied knowledge which happened to fall into his hands. Dissatisfied with the state of knowledge in his time, Descartes turned to the study of "the book of the world" and of his own nature, resolving to employ all the resources of his mind to choose the paths he ought to follow. In 1618 he joined the army of Prince Maurice of Nassau, where he met Isaac Beeckman, a mathematical physicist whom he came to cherish as the "promotor and first author" of his studies (Letter of Descartes to Beeckman, April 23, 1619). On November 10, 1619, he had dreams, ascribed by him to the "Spirit of Truth," confirming his resolution to accept as true only what he found indubitably certain and to pursue a rigorously analytical procedure in the search for truth. During the next decade, he composed his *Rules for the Direction of the Mind*, an unfinished work published posthumously in 1701. In 1628 he settled in Holland, where he enjoyed solitude and leisure to work out his philosophical system and to engage in scientific research. His invention of analytical geometry marked a milestone in the history of mathematics. In 1637, together with his *Geometry* and two other scientific treatises, Descartes published his *Discourse on Method*, in which he sketched his philosophical principles and his scientific aspirations. The philosophical system is more fully developed in the *Meditations on First Philosophy* (1641) with objections and replies, and in the *Principles of Philosophy* (1644), and the psychology involved in these views found its most mature formulation in *The Passions of the Soul* (1649). Descartes died in Sweden, where he had gone in response to an invitation from Queen Christina.

I. DESCARTES' VIEW OF GOD AND THE SOUL

Augustine had expressed a desire to know only God and the soul, and Calvin's *Institutes* opens by identifying true and substantial wisdom with the knowledge of God and of ourselves. Whereas Cartesian philosophy reflects the Augustinian preoccupation with the soul and God as primary objects of knowledge, it deviates from Augustinianism by finding its starting point in doubt rather than faith and in aiming at the construction of a scientific view of the world.

Doubt is employed methodically by Descartes as a means of exposing all inadequate foundations of knowledge and of disclosing a foundation that can withstand all criticism. From the occasional deceptiveness of sense perception, Descartes concludes that the senses cannot be trusted as infallible witnesses in anything. The difficulty of formulating a criterion to distinguish waking from dream states casts doubt upon the reality of the external world. Even mathematical truths become uncertain if God should be willing for us to be deceived when "some malignant genius exceedingly powerful and cunning has devoted all his powers" to deceive us. Following a line of thought first proposed by Augustine, Descartes finds one initial certainty about which the mind cannot be mistaken: "I think, therefore, I am." An evil genius cannot make me think that I am thinking if I am not really thinking, nor can he deceive me into supposing that I exist if I do not really exist. I know then that I am a thinking thing and thus that my soul exists entirely distinct from the body, the existence of which remains doubtful. Consciousness and its internal objects alone are granted immediate certainty, even though certain self-evident truths of a universal nature are employed from the outset. The next step in the argument is the demonstration of the Existence of God. Descartes adopts two distinct types of procedure, one employing the principle of causality, the other restricting itself to the rational law of noncontradiction. Ideas are modifications of the human mind, capable of representing real beings. To ideas a degree of objective reality may be ascribed corresponding to the formal or actual reality of the beings they represent. It is also a dictate of the natural light of reason that the cause of an idea must be at least as real as that which the idea represents. Now the human mind possesses the idea of God, "a substance that is infinite, immutable, independent, all-knowing, all powerful, and by which I myself and everything else, if any such other beings there be, have been created" (*Meditation*, III). The idea of such an infinite substance cannot have originated from myself, for I am finite and thus less real than an infinite being. The idea of the infinite is not the product of mere negation of the finite. I could not recognize myself to be finite except by way of contrast with the infinite. The idea of God must be innate in the human mind and placed there by none less and thus none other than God Himself. This Cartesian form of causal proof differs from the cosmological proofs of Aristotle and Aquinas in that it does not proceed from any observed fact of nature but from the idea of the infinite Being.

For Descartes the Existence of God is more certain than the existence of nature, and hence it is the basis of a well-grounded belief in the reality of the external world. Nevertheless, for the sake of those who cannot follow the above proof, Descartes formulates and demonstrates "in a way more easily grasped an identical conclusion, from the fact that the mind possessing that idea cannot be self-derived" (*Reply to Objections*, II). Since I cannot give myself the perfections I lack, I cannot preserve myself in existence, for perfections are attributes whereas I am a substance. The Being that preserves me must contain in Himself formally or eminently all the perfections that are in me as well as those which I lack and which are contained in the idea of God.

The existence of God as the perfect Being that has created me provides me a guarantee that what I clearly and distinctly perceive must be true, and that the natural light of reason is therefore trustworthy. A logical circle appears in Descartes' argument at this point. Appeal has been made to the natural light or intuition of self-evident principles to develop the proof of the Existence of God. Now the natural light itself is vindicated on the basis of God's veracity. Another, though closely related, discrepancy in the argument is that the "cogito" ("I know") was established as the one indubitable initial certitude, whereas the causal proof brings to light that "there is manifestly more reality in the infinite substance than in the finite substance, and my awareness of the infinite must therefore be in some way prior to my awareness of the finite, that is to say, my awareness of God must be prior to that of myself" (*Meditation*, III).

Descartes also takes the ontological proof of the existence of God to have the same character and validity as a geometrical demonstration. As the equality of its angles to two right angles is comprised in the idea of a triangle, so existence is included in the idea of a perfect Being and "in consequence it is at least as certain that God who is this perfect Being, is or exists, as any demonstration of geometry can possibly be" (*Discourse on Method*, Part IV).

However, the veracity of God guarantees some basis of truth for all our ideas. Descartes thus finds a ground for our conviction that material things exist. The essence of matter is extension, and that of mind is thought. The mind and the body are thus two distinct substances. Nevertheless, they can interact, for in sensation the soul is affected by bodily changes and in volition the mind acts upon the body, directing its movements. Apart from the mind, the human body is a machine subject to natural laws. Animals are merely automata, devoid of consciousness.

Descartes' philosophy is rationalistic; it finds the basis of knowledge in human reason rather than in sense perception. The criterion of truth is found to be clear and distinct perception of ideas and their relations. The reality of the external world becomes a problem resolved only by an appeal to the goodness of God. Even mathematical truths are dependent for their validity on the will of God.

II. The Influence of Descartes on Christian Thought

A. *The Cartesian Controversy in the Netherlands.* In 1641 at the University of Utrecht a controversy broke out between Gisbertus Voetius, the eminent Reformed theologian, and Johannes Regius (Leroy) of the medical faculty, an enthusiastic disciple of Descartes. Regius proposed the thesis that the union of mind and body gives rise to a being *per accidens* and not *per se*. Descartes himself was displeased with this thesis, and Voetius argued that since Christ, the God-man, is a unity *per se* though composed of two natures or complete substances, so much more must the union between the human soul and body be substantial and *per se*, since body and soul are not as different nor as complete substances as Divinity and humanity (*Disputationes selectae*, I, 878). The Scholastic-Aristotelian philosophy defended by Voetius triumphed at Utrecht over the Cartesian innovations proposed by Regius. Voetius continued the controversy by attacking Descartes directly, seeking support from the Parisian monk Mersenne, who gave him the disappointing reply that Descartes was in agreement with Plato and Aristotle, properly understood, and would be supported by Augustine without the least reservation. Voetius and his supporters, including his son Paul and his pupil Martinus Schoock, charged Descartes with implicit or secret atheism, laying stress upon the method of universal doubt and the rejection of the proof of God's Existence from His works. (Voetius, *Disp. Sel.*, II, 114-135, 135-149, 149-166, 166-226, contains four disputations held in 1639.) Descartes defended himself in a lengthy epistle directed to Voetius in 1643, in which he accused Voetius of having written a polemic treatise, *Admiranda Methodus Novae Philosophiae Renati des Cartes*, a work that appears to have been from the pen of Schoock, possibly aided by Voetius. At the University of Leiden, Abraham Heidanus, professor of theology, defended Cartesianism and deviated from the orthodox Reformed doctrine on Cocceian lines, particularly on the question of the sabbath.

B. *The Christian Philosophy of Malebranche.* The philosophy of Nicolas Malebranche may be understood as an attempt to develop a Christian philosophy on a Cartesian basis. In the "avertissement" to his *Conversations chrétiennes,* he states that he speaks to modern philosophers the language they understand and follows the principles they receive, just as Thomas Aquinas used the sentiments of Aristotle, and Augustine used those of Plato. In Malebranche's mind, however, the principles of Descartes are transformed and a doctrine is expounded that resembles the Augustinian vision of reality in terms of eternal Ideas. For Malebranche, ideas, unlike perceptions, are not modifications of the human mind, but objects that enjoy an eternal and necessary being in the mind of God. Thus we see all things in God, with whom alone our mind is immediately united. Even material things are seen as modifications of the eternal idea of intelligible extension. Created bodies as such are invisible, but the ideas that represent them in the Divine Mind are the immediate objects of our perception. This theory of knowledge, known as Ontologism, is closely associated with the theory of Occasionalism developed by Malebranche on the basis of inferences drawn from Cartesian principles by La Forge, Cordemoy, and Geulinex. The body, being naturally inert, is incapable of causal activity. Mind and body, as substances with nothing in common, cannot act on one another. God is the one real cause of all movements in the world of matter, and of perceptions and feelings in the realm of spirit. Since God acts according to perfect rules of order, there are regular sequences of bodily and mental events, particularly in the experiences of sense perception and voluntary action. An act of will is an occasional cause of God's producing a bodily movement, as the stimulation of a sense organ, or rather a subsequent motion of the animal spirits in the brain, serves as the occasional cause for the production of a sensation. Thus, the Cartesian problem of interaction of mind and body is solved. The problem of evil is resolved by the idea that God always acts by the simplest ways, using a small number of natural laws to produce a large number of admirable works. The ultimate conquest of evil, as of finitude itself, is the Incarnation of the Son of God, who alone gives value to finite being and brings redemption to a fallen world.

See APOLOGETICS; ATHEISM; GOD, EXISTENCE OF; PHILOSOPHY; SOUL.

BIBLIOGRAPHY:

R. Descartes, *Philosophical Works,* ed. Haldane and Ross (Cambridge, 1934), 2 vols.

R. Descartes, *Philosophical Writings,* selected and translated by N. K. Smith (New York, 1958).

E. Gilson, *Études sur le rôle de la pensée Médiévale dans la formation du système Cartésien* (Paris, 1951).

M. Guerolt, *Malebranche: II, Les cinq abîmes de la providence* (Paris, 1949).

N. Malebranche, *Oeuvres complètes,* vols. 4, 5, 10, 15, 16, 17/1, 18, 19 (Paris, 1958–).

G. Voetius, "De Atheismo," *Selectarum Disputationum Theologicarum,* Part I, Disp. 9-12 (Utrecht, 1648).

WILLIAM YOUNG

DESCENT OF CHRIST INTO HELL, THE. The expression "[He] descended into hell" (Latin: *descendit ad inferna* or *inferos*) occurs in the so-called Apostles' and Athanasian Creeds, but not in the Nicene Creed. As a credal article, it is comparatively late. It was not in the Old Roman Creed (the earlier and briefer form of the Apostles' Creed which dates from the second century). Its first appearance in a creed was in the Fourth Formula of Sirmium (359), which affirmed (alluding to Job 38:17) that the Lord "died, and descended to the un-

The Creeds

derworld." Other Arian creeds (Nicé, 359, and Constantinople, 360) contained similar statements. The first orthodox creed to contain it was the Aquileian Creed of Rufinus (*c.* 345-410). It gradually found acceptance in the W church and was incorporated in the Apostles' Creed. Although it had significance in E Christian thought, it did not become a clause in the official creeds of the church in the E.

The beliefs of the early church about Christ's descent into hell were bound up with particular interpretations of certain Biblical passages. Cyprian believed that Jesus Himself had hinted at it in His prophecy that the Son of man would spend three days and three nights in the heart of the earth (Mt. 12:39 f.; cf. Cyprian, *Testim.*, II, 25). Rom. 10:7 ("Who will descend into the abyss?—that is, to bring Christ up from the dead"), Eph. 4:9 (the victorious descent liberating captives from "the lower parts of the earth"), and Col. 1:18 ("the first born of the dead") were also taken to refer to a visit of Christ to the departed.

Scripture

Other crucial statements included the pronouncements of Peter about Christ: "For thou wilt not abandon my soul to Hades, nor let thy Holy One see corruption" (Acts 2:27, quoting Ps. 16:10); Christ "being put to death in the flesh but made alive in the spirit; in which he went and preached to the spirits in prison" (I Pet. 3:18 f.); "For this is why the gospel was preached even to the dead, that though judged in the flesh like men, they might live in the spirit like God" (I Pet. 4:6). John 5:25, 28 was also taken as a prophecy of the descent: "Truly, truly, I say to you, the hour is coming, and now is, when the dead will hear the voice of the Son of God, and those who hear will live. . . . Do not marvel at this; for the hour is coming when all who are in the tombs will hear his voice."

Interpretation and Significance

The descent figured in early Christian teaching from Ignatius of Antioch onward (*Magnesians*, 9). Tertullian expressed the belief that all souls descended into Hades on death, and that Christ satisfied the law "by undergoing the form of human death in the underworld and did not ascend aloft to heaven until he had gone down to the regions beneath the earth" (*De anima*, 55). In the second century two broad, though not always distinct, lines of interpretation began to emerge which attempted to explain the nature and purpose of the descent. According to one, Christ's activity consisted in preaching (Justin, *Dialogue*, 72; Irenaeus *Adversus haereses*, III, xx, 4; IV, xxii, 1; *Epideixis*, 78; Origen, *Contra Celsum*, ii, 43; Hippolytus, *De Christo et anti-Christo*, 45). According to the other, Christ visited Hades to liberate the spirits of the OT saints. The thought was elaborated into a victorious combat with the devil in the underworld (Rufinus, *Commentarius in symbolum Apostolorum*, 16 f.) and the liberation of pious pagans. The latter view was condemned by Augustine as heretical (*De haerisibus ad Quodvultdeum*, 79).

Various motives have been suggested for the inclusion of the clause in the Apostles' Creed, such as the desire to counter Apollinarianism or Docetism, or to further belief in purgatory or universalism. However, the only unanimity that may be deduced from the pronouncements of early writers is the belief that Christ truly died, that He entered fully into the experience of death, and that this was part of His saving work. Significantly, the creed itself merely makes the assertion without any explanation.

In the Middle Ages, Thomas Aquinas held that Christ visited all in hell, but that only those who were already united with Him in His passion were saved (*Summa Theologiae*, III, Q. 52). Not all who were in purgatory were immediately set free, but only those who were sufficiently purified at the time.

The Reformers and their successors were generally cautious in their statements about the descent. Article III of the *Thirty-Nine Articles of the Church of England* (1571) simply states: "As Christ died for us, and was buried, so also is it to be believed, that He went down into Hell." Calvin's *Catechism of the Church of Geneva*, in 1542 (Questions 65, 66) explained that the descent of Christ meant not only natural death, the separation of the body and soul, but that Christ's soul was gripped by the fearful agonies which Peter calls the pains of death (Acts 2:24). This was necessary to make satisfaction to God in the name of sinners. It was requisite that His conscience should be tormented by such agony, as if He were forsaken by God, even as if God were hostile to Him. It was in this agony that he cried: "My God, my God, why hast thou forsaken me?" (Mt. 27:46; Mark 15:34; cf. Ps. 22:1). Calvin elaborated this view in his *Institutes of the Christian Religion*, II, xvi, 8-12. He noted that the clause was accepted only comparatively late in the creed and that it is liable to misunderstanding, that nevertheless it is an important article of faith. Calvin rejected the later patristic interpretations and explained the preaching of Christ to the spirits in prison (I Pet. 3:19) as an awareness of Christ's death by the dead.

The *Confession of Augsburg* (1530), which was drawn up as a statement of Lutheran faith, was content merely to affirm the descent into hell in its Article III on the Son of God. Later Lutheran theologians attempted various explanations as to whether Christ had visited hell literally, whether He went in body or soul, and whether the doctrine refers to the suffering or victory of Christ. The *Formula of Concord, Epitome* IX (1577) attempted a mediating position, insisting that the doctrine could not be comprehended by reason or the senses. It was enough to believe and know that Christ visited hell and destroyed it for the faithful, rescuing them from the power of the devil and eternal damnation. How this was accomplished will only be known in glory.

The British Puritan statements of faith were even more cautious than Calvin. The *Westminster Confession* (1647) stated that after death Christ "was buried, and remained under the power of death, yet saw no corruption" (Chapter VIII, cf. Acts 2:23 f., 27; 13:37; Rom. 6:9). *The Larger Catechism* (1648) amplified the thought slightly: "Christ's humiliation after His death consisted in His being buried, and continuing in the state of the dead, and under the power of death till the third day; which hath been otherwise expressed in these words, *He descended into hell*" (Question 50, cf. I Cor. 15:3 f.; Ps. 16:10; Acts 2:24 ff.; Rom. 6:9; Mt. 12:40).

The contemporary RC theologian, Karl Rahner, has attempted an interpretation which cuts right across traditional Catholic teaching about the descent. It was not a saving act on behalf of those who lived before Christ; rather it established "an open, real-ontological relationship to the world in its oneness." Against this it may be observed that the Biblical passages cited above give Christ's dead state a saving significance and also suggest that there is an important difference between Christ's state and that of the lost: He was not abandoned to Hades, and His flesh did not see corruption (cf. Acts 2:31).

The idea of a continued but victorious conflict with Satan in Hades is not warranted by Scripture. Christ's death is the ground of salvation. The fact that Christ entered fully into man's plight, bearing the consequences of man's sin to the uttermost, enables Him to release the dead from the power of death. The more imaginative views of the descent into hell turn upon certain interpretations of I Peter 3:19 and 4:6. These passages may, however, mean no more than that Christ proclaimed His finished work to the dead. An alternative view is that they do not refer to the descent at all, but that they indicate the pre-incarnate revelation of Christ in OT times, comparable with I Cor. 10:4.

BIBLIOGRAPHY:
J. H. Crehan, "Descent into Hell," *A Dictionary of Catholic Theology*, ed. H. F. Davis *et al.*, II (1967), 163-166.
J. N. D. Kelly, *Early Christian Creeds* (1950), 378-383.
J. A. MacCulloch, *The Harrowing of Hell* (1930).
K. Rahner, *On the Theology of Death* (1960).
E. G. Selwyn, *The First Epistle of St. Peter* (1946).

COLIN BROWN

DESERT, sometimes translated "wilderness," used variously for a number of OT and NT terms:

(1) מִדְבָּר, *midhbar*, ἔρημος, *eremos*, (and ἐρημία) designate "pasture" and are used for the vast wilderness of Sinai (Ex. 4:27) and Arabia (I Kings 9:18) which is barren in summer, and for the wilderness of Judah (I Sam. 17:28) which is the bleak, rugged area W of the Dead Sea. Both are the lands of nomads moving about to find pasture. These terms are also applied to waste lands near settled areas which provide fine pasture in spring but which are dusty and dry in summer. Generally, they are called by the name of the contiguous village (I Sam. 23:15).

(2) עֲרָבָה, *arabah*, designates "parched" and is used for arid areas generally or, with the article in the historical books, refers particularly to the valley plain from Tiberias to the Gulf of Aqabah, which is generally hot and subject to drought (Deut. 1:7).

(3) יְשִׁימוֹן, *yeshīmōn,* designates "wasteland" and is used, with the article, in the historical books for the wastes on either side of the Dead Sea (Num. 21:23). Without the article, it is used for large uncultivated areas (I Sam. 23:19), especially the peninsula of Arabia, in which the Israelites wandered (Num. 21:20).

(4) חָרְבָּה, *chorbah,* designates any dry (Isa. 48:21) or desolate (Lev. 26:31) region, especially ruins (Job 3:14) or any area laid waste by man (Ezra 9:9).

Desert, or wilderness, is also symbolic of loneliness (Job 38:26) and unfruitfulness (Isa. 32:15).

One must not visualize deserts of Scripture then as necessarily arid, sandy plains like the Sahara. Desert areas familiar to the Israelites were often floored rather by rough and porous rocks which, with long summer droughts, led to a paucity of permanent streams. But most desert areas were sensitive to changes in rainfall of a short- or long-term nature and often had wells, oases, verdant *wadis*, and sparse, seasonal grass cover to perhaps a greater degree than at present.

BIBLIOGRAPHY:
D. Baly, *The Geography of the Bible* (New York, 1957).
M. Evenari and D. Keller, "Ancient Masters of the Desert," *Sci. Amer.* 194 (Apr. 1956), 44-50.
N. Glueck, *Rivers in the Desert* (New York, 1959).
W. C. Lowdermilk, "The Reclamation of Man-Made Desert," *Sci. Amer.* 202 (Mar. 1960), 55-63.

THOMAS H. LEITH

DES GALLARS, Nicolas (1520-1584), French Reformer.

Nicolas Des Gallars, Lord of Saules, while still a young man, went to Geneva in order to receive instruction from Calvin. He became such a devoted disciple that he liked to call him "his father." In 1544 he began his pastoral ministry in

Geneva. In 1557 he went to Paris to replace the pastor François de Morel, who had been obliged to flee because of persecution. Des Gallars too was obliged to leave in 1558 and was replaced by Jean Macard. He then returned to Geneva, where he had left his wife and children. In 1560 he went to London with letters of recommendation from Calvin. There, at the beginning of Queen Elizabeth's reign, it was possible to reorganize the church of the French refugees who had been scattered under Mary Tudor. Des Gallars was notably successful in this work in spite of painful contentions with his colleague, Pierre Alexandre. In 1561 he was designated as one of 12 pastors who represented the Reformed churches at the colloquy of Poissy, gathered by the regent queen, Catherine de Medici. At the side of Theodore Beza, he played an important part in this conference. He sent a daily report of the proceedings to Throckmorton, bishop of London, and also to Calvin. After this, he did not go back to London, but settled for a while in Geneva. In 1563 we find him as pastor in Orleans. He was elected moderator of the fifth National Synod (Paris, 1565) and secretary of the seventh National Synod (La Rochelle, 1571). It is this latter synod, at which Theodore Beza presided, which provided the final draft of the confession of faith of the Reformed churches first proposed at the first synod of Paris (1559). Jeanne d'Albret attended this Synod of La Rochelle, signed the confession of faith on behalf of the church of Béarn, and retained Des Gallars as her pastor. The following year she died in Paris, but Des Gallars remained in the Béarn province. He followed Pierre Viret first in the academy of Orthez and later of Lescar. He lived in Pau, in the very lodgings of Viret. He continued teaching in the academy until 1584, the probable date of his death.

Des Gallars, whose Latinized name was Gallasius, was one of the most remarkable co-laborers of Calvin in his pastoral connection in Geneva, 1544-57, and also as his secretary. He translated into Latin several treatises of Calvin: *The Treatise on the Lord's Supper* (1545); *The Treatise on Relics* (1548); *The Treatise Against the Anabaptists,* and Calvin's commentaries on Isaiah and Exodus. He also published the works of Irenaeus with numerous footnotes. He was a fellow-worker of Theodore Beza in the publication of Calvin's small treatises and in writing *The Ecclesiastical History of the Reformed Churches of France.* He was therefore, at the side of the Reformers, a friend, a valuable helper, and a faithful secretary. We possess some 30 letters which Calvin addressed to him; they manifest a deep affection and a complete trust.

JEAN CADIER

DETERMINISM. Emotive use of language is reflected in dictionary definitions of determinism which import negative implications into the meaning of the term. Moreover, the word is not employed consistently in theological, scientific, and philosophical discussions. In the present discussion "determinism" will be understood as the doctrine of metaphysical necessity, which Jonathan Edwards defines as a full, fixed, and certain connection between the subject and predicate of a proposition. Determinism is the theory that every true proposition is necessary in this metaphysical sense. Propositions asserting the occurrence of contingent events are not logically necessary, but may express metaphysical necessity either if they relate a past event, which obviously is unalterable, or an event causally connected with past events. In this sense determinism holds all events, including acts of will, to be necessary.

Arguments in favor of determinism

have been marshalled by scientists, philosophers, and theologians representing divergent and even irreconcilable points of view. Psychologists have argued that all human behavior may be explained, if not in principle predicted, by the laws of association, conditioned reflexes, or unconscious motives. Sociologists have asserted that the individual is simply the product of his social environment, although biologists have sometimes stressed the effects of heredity. Mechanists assert that the laws of motion in principle explain fully the most complex of cultural phenomena, whereas Marxists teach an economic determinism in history. All forms of scientific determinism are thus one-sided attempts to reduce the wealth of creation to some one or few of its aspects. Philosophical determinism, on the contrary, adduces purely logical arguments to defend the abstract thesis of metaphysical necessity. Thus Edwards refutes the Arminian doctrine of the will's self-determining power by reduction to the absurdity of a prior act of will determining the will's first act and establishes determinism by a general consideration of the principle of causality. Theological argument for determinism, while incompatible with merely scientific, may provide a transcendent ground for purely philosophical determinism by seeing the omniscience and omnipotence of the sovereign Creator as the origin of both logical necessity and factual contingency in the created order. Divine omnipotence can no more be frustrated or assisted than Divine omniscience surprised or disappointed.

The burning question which arises is whether determinism is compatible with human responsibility. Indeterminists commonly argue for "free will" on the Pelagian principle that ability limits obligation, or in Kant's language, "If I ought, I can." Augustine's prayer, "Command what You will, and give what You command," is the reply of the gracious heart. The most powerful philosophical arguments ever penned on this point may be studied in Part III of Edwards' unsurpassed masterpiece on the will. In God Himself and in the human nature of Christ, moral character and moral necessity coincide. Those judicially abandoned to sin are not excused by their inability to avoid sin. Responsibility, while inconsistent with natural inability, is compatible with moral inability or necessity. Indeterminism rather than determinism destroys moral responsibility, for chance occurrences have no moral character. The seeming inconsistency of determinism with responsibility arises from linguistic confusion, the failure to distinguish ordinary uses of "must," "can't help it," "could have done," etc., from the philosophical usage of "necessary," "inevitable," "inability," and related expressions.

While Edwards' theory may not be identified with the doctrines of the Stoics, Hobbes, or Spinoza, it has some affinities with Leibniz. The doctrine of identity of indiscernibles is appealed to as a ground for regarding the Divine will as necessarily determined by sufficient reasons. This speculation, however, is not entailed by the stringent logical analysis of the earlier argument.

Determinism should be regarded as a strictly philosophical issue to be settled by methods of logical or linguistic analysis. While the assertion of it can be a confirmation of the Scriptural teaching of the all-embracing counsel of God, it has not been adopted by all theologians who are unreservedly loyal to the doctrine of free and sovereign grace. "Rabbi" Duncan found the determinism of Edwards uncongenial: "I dissent from Jonathan Edwards' doctrine, because he hazards a speculation on will *qua* will, and therefore in reference to all will, Divine and human. It is fatal to establish a necessary chain throughout every will in the universe. The Divine acts are free.

They are necesary, I maintain, *qua* moral, though free *qua* will. But I am a determinist as much as Edwards" (*Colloquia Peripatetica*, Edinburgh, 1879, p. 29).

See ARMINIUS; AUGUSTINE; EDWARDS; KANT; PELAGIUS; PREDESTINATION; SPINOZA; STOICS.

BIBLIOGRAPHY:

J. Calvin, *De Libero Arbitrio Tractatus* (Geeva, 1576).

W. Cunningham, *The Reformers and the Theology of the Reformation* (Edinburgh, 2nd ed., 1866).

J. Duncan, *Colloquia Peripatetica* (Edinburgh and London, 6th ed., 1905).

J. Edwards, *A Careful and Strict Enquiry into the Modern Prevailing Notions of that Freedom of Will which is supposed to be Essential to Moral Agency, Virtue and Vice, Reward and Punishment, Praise and Blame* (Boston, 1754).

W. Geesink, *Van 's Heeren Ordinantien* (Kampen, 1925), I.

M. Luther, *The Bondage of the Will* (London, 1931).

D. Stewart, *The Philosophy of the Active and Moral Powers of Man*, Book II, Chap. VI (Edinburgh, London, 1828).

A. M. Toplady, *The Scheme of Christian and Philosophical Necessity Asserted* (London, 1775).

WILLIAM YOUNG

DEUEL, "Invocation of God," the father of Eliasaph, a renowned prince of the tribe of Gad, who had various functions in the camp in the wilderness (Num. 1:14; 7:42, 47; 10:20). In Num. 2:14 Deuel is Reuel, the Hebrew "d" having been misread as "r."

See ELIASAPH; REUEL.

DEUTERONOMY, the fifth book of the Pentateuch, bearing in Hebrew the title, "These are the words" אֵלֶּה הַדְּבָרִים (*ēlleh haddabarîm*). The name Deuteronomy comes from the LXX rendering of Deut. 17:18 as "this second law" (*τό δευτερονόμιον τοῦτο*). The Vulgate likewise rendered, "deuteronomium," but these are not accurate renderings of the passage, which should be read, "a copy of this law." Among the Jews the work came to be designated "The repetition of the law," or simply, "repetition."

Deuteronomy was written by Moses (with the exception of the account of his death) and forms a suitable completion to the Pentateuch. Together with the first four books, it comprises that portion of Scripture known as the Law. The books which belong to the Law were written by the human founder of the OT economy, Moses. To this, attestation is given by those passages in the book itself which speak of Moses as writing or speaking. In Deut. 31:9 we read, "And Moses wrote this law and gave it unto the priests the sons of Levi, which bare the ark of the covenant of the LORD, and unto all the elders of Israel," and in vs. 24, "And it came to pass, when Moses had finished writing the words of this law in a book, until they were finished. . . ." Here are two explicit statements to the effect that Moses wrote "this law." In Deuteronomy 31:22 there is an attestation of Mosaic authorship to the song, "And Moses wrote this song in that day, and he taught it the children of Israel." Of particular significance also is testimony such as the following. "These are the words which Moses spake unto all Israel" (Deut. 1:1), "On this side Jordan, in the land of Moab, began Moses to declare this law, saying," (Deut. 1:5), "And the Lord spake unto me, saying," (Deut. 2:2). If one will read carefully through Deuteronomy he will note many passages in which Moses claims to be speaking or delivering the message which God has given unto him. The testimony of the book itself, therefore, is clear on the question of authorship.

Authorship

The NT also attests Mosaic authorship, for Christ spoke of the Law of Moses. We may note but one example, "And beginning at Moses and all the prophets, etc." (Luke 24:27). Compare also Mt. 19:8; Mark 10:5; Mt. 8:4; Mark 1:44; 7:10; 12:26; Luke 5:14; 20:37; 16:31; John 5:47; 7:19. Whereas none of these passages mentions Deuteronomy by name, nevertheless by phrases such as "Moses wrote," "the Law of Moses," etc., reference is clearly made to the Pentateuch, of which Deuteronomy is an integral part. In this connection it may also be noted that Christ refuted the tempter by quoting from the book of Deuteronomy.

In addition to the witness of Scripture, it must be noted that Deuteronomy forms a fitting close to the first four books of the Pentateuch. It sums up the law and applies it to the nation about to enter the land of promise. In Deuteronomy the covenant is renewed, and the book in its formal structure follows the form of the suzerainty treaties of the Mosaic age. This identification, to which we shall later advert, has been first fully recognized by Meredith G. Kline, and constitutes a strong argument for the early date of Deuteronomy. Indeed, if the book, in a formal sense, parallels those suzerainty treaties which come from this early date, it is difficult to explain this form on the supposition that the book was composed at a much later time.

Despite the clear evidences for Mosaic authorship, however, the predominant view of negative criticism is that the book is not Mosaic.

The Position of Negative Criticism

In 1805 De Wette in his doctoral dissertation claimed that the book of Deuteronomy had been written at the time of Josiah and was the book discovered in the temple. He believed that Deuteronomy was presupposed by the other books of the Pentateuch. This position became the heart of the later view of the Pentateuch espoused by Julius Wellhausen. Deuteronomy was thought not to have been written by Moses, but to have been composed at the time of Josiah, and its discovery was responsible for the Josianic reform. According to this view, Deuteronomy demanded centrality of the cultus in distinction from the previously existing practices which supposedly permitted worship at any sanctuary whatever.

As time passed this view was unable to maintain itself, for its inherent weaknesses made themselves manifest. More and more it became apparent that Deuteronomy was not in conflict with the earlier books of the Law, nor was it presupposed by them. More careful reading of Deuteronomy also showed that the purpose of the book was not merely to teach a centrality of the cult at Jerusalem. Josiah's reformation did not concern itself primarily with the centralization of the cult but rather with its purity and with the extirpation of idolatry.

In more recent times attempts have been made to date Deuteronomy earlier and to find for it a N provenience. Others have sought a later exilic or post-exilic date. The discovery of fragments of Deuteronomy in the Dead Sea caves is likely to rule out any serious acceptance of a post-exilic date for the work.

The purpose of the book can best be understood by a consideration of its analysis and a comparison with the suzerainty treaties of the Hittites.

Analysis

We may then analyze as follows: Preamble (1:1-5); Historical Introduction (1:6–4:49); The Commandments of God (chapters 5–26); Curses and Blessings (chapters 27–30); and Arrangements for the Continuation of the Covenant (chapters 31–34).

The introductory words, "These are the words," in themselves identify the work as a covenant document. It is the Lord who gives the covenant and Moses who mediates it. The first five verses compare closely in form to the prologues of suzerainty treaties. In the renewal of these treaties or covenants the historical situation is reviewed, and this is precisely what we have in Deuteronomy, chapters 1–4. Instead, therefore, of finding difficulty with chapters 1–4 (and also 5–11)—for some negative criticism has maintained that one or the other of these sections is superfluous—we now see that they fit well together. The large section, chapters 5–26, corresponds roughly with the stipulations or conditions which are laid down in the historical treaties. Chapters 27–30, which speak of blessing and cursing, likewise have their counterparts. Chapters 31–34 are concerned with the continuity of the covenant. We note the enlisting of witnesses and the direction for the deposit of the law in the sanctuary. Here again, there is formal parallel with treaty arrangements.

This brief sketch gives an idea of the formal nature of the book. It is not, therefore, to be regarded as a product of the Josianic age or of any age other than that of Moses. It is a treaty which serves the purpose of renewing and strengthening the covenant made by the Lord with Israel at Sinai, and serving to prepare the nation for its entrance into the land of promise. With this wide analysis serving as a background, we may look more closely at the content of the book.

PROLOGUE (1:1-5)

The introductory words, even though paralleling the introduction of Hittite suzerainty treaties, also serve to connect the book with what precedes (cf. Num. 36:13). Note the emphasis upon history and detail. The message of God was revealed to Moses at a definite time and place.

HISTORICAL INTRODUCTION (1:6–4:49)

Summary of events up to Kadesh (1:6-46). In this summary we may note the prominence of Moses the servant of the Lord. The discourse mentions the appointment of the judges, for the nation had grown and was becoming large. Thus, there appears to be a reminder of the promise made to Abraham that his seed should become numerous. That promise was being fulfilled. After recounting the departure from Horeb Moses speaks of the rebellion of the people against the command of the Lord to enter the land and to possess it. "Ye would not," is the charge which Moses must bring against the people (1:26). Therefore that generation was not permitted to enter the promised land. "So ye abode in Kadesh many days, according unto the days that ye abode there" (1:46).

The conquest of the land E of the Jordan (2:1–3:29). In preparation for the allotment of the land to the two and one half tribes Moses continues his discourse after the conquest of the land E of the Jordan River.

The goodness of God in giving the Law to the nation (4:1-43). It is the Law which is their precious and prized possession, and which they are to obey with the whole heart. God did not so bless other nations. What distinguishes Israel is the possession of this Law, from which they are not to depart either to the right hand or to the left.

In this brief section we may notice a shift between the first and the second person pronouns. The reason for this at this point appears to be that the Lord has in mind both the nation and the individual. It is also true that at times He may address the nation as an individual.

The section is of particular significance in that it shows the distinctiveness of Israel in the midst of the nations. The religion of Israel and her entire life are distinct and separate from those of the world about. Israel is the people of God to whom the Law has been entrusted.

The cities of refuge (4:41-49). The cities of refuge were set apart by Moses for the safety and security of the man who had murdered unwittingly. In this act the mercy of God is shown. No other nation of antiquity had made such a provision.

The Commandments of God (5:1–26:19)

This section comprises Moses' second discourse. It forms the heart of the book. We may analyze it as follows:

Expanded exposition of the Ten Commandments (5:1–11:33). By way of introduction Moses reminds the people that the covenant had been made with them. Many who now heard his voice had been alive at the giving of the Law at Sinai. These introductory words are followed by a repetition of the Ten Commandments. There are minor verbal variants in the commandments from the form in which they appear in Exodus 20. At this point Moses evidently believed that these variants would be necessary and more appropriate for the good of the people than a mere verbatim repetition of what had already been given. The most significant change from Exodus 20 is the reason annexed to the fourth commandment. In Deuteronomy the reason for obedience to the fourth commandment is that the nation was a bondslave in Egypt and had been delivered. This is not at all in conflict with the reason given in Exodus 20 (namely, an appeal to the creation), but simply an addition to it. Here the sabbath is definitely connected with redemption.

The exposition of the Ten Commandments proper begins at Deut. 6:4, with the command: "Hear, O Israel; the LORD our God is one LORD." This is the great and majestic declaration of monotheism, upon which the entire revelation to Israel is founded. It is not, however, a mere abstract conception, for immediately there follows the command to love this LORD. Thus, in the fullest sense a true and genuine monotheism is presented. The one LORD has absolute claim over the entirety of being of His people. Furthermore, there devolves upon His people the duty of teaching this truth and the great truth of redemption to their children, and this teaching is to be of such a nature that it will be exemplified in the entirety of the lives of the people.

True worship of the Lord involves not merely the proper recognition that God is. There is also a negative aspect. If one is truly to worship the Lord, he must also turn aside from all kinds of idolatry. There follow, therefore (chapter seven), commands to eradicate the Canaanites from the land. It should be noted that this command would be practically devoid of meaning if Deuteronomy were written at a time long after the Canaanites had disappeared. It is, however, full of meaning, if uttered by Moses to the Israelites just before they are ready to enter the land of promise.

Even if the Canaanites are eliminated, there is also the need for other warnings, for the temptations to meet the Israelites in the promised land will still be many. Hence, in chapter eight Moses warns the people not to forget the Lord and what He has done for them. Should they forget Him, for one reason or another, they would certainly perish.

In chapters nine and ten Moses seeks to turn the nation aside from confidence in its own goodness and righteousness by calling to their mind the various rebellions in which they had already taken part. In particular, he calls to mind the sin at Horeb (the golden calf) when he was in the mountain receiving the Law. In briefer fashion he mentions other rebellions—Taberah, Massah, Kibroth-hattaavah, and the refusal to enter the promised land. The whole may be summed up in the words, "Ye have been rebellious against the LORD from the day that I knew you" (9:24). Moses then recounts God's mercy in permitting him to have again the two tables of the Law and he further exhorts the nation to obedience. This is continued throughout chapter eleven. Obedience to God's Law will result in blessing, but disobedience thereto will bring upon the people a curse.

An exposition of principal laws (12:1–26:19). The twelfth chapter is of unusual interest, for about it much discussion has revolved. The negative critical school influenced by Graf, Kuenen, and Wellhausen maintained that the chapter taught that there was to be one place of worship, namely Jerusalem, and that this chapter had been composed for the express purpose of bringing about a centralization of worship. But is this the teaching of the chapter? Hitherto the people had worshipped at the tabernacle, which had been carried with them in their wanderings in the wilderness. When, however, the people enter Palestine, will the tabernacle still be carried about among them or will it be located in one permanent place? In answer to these questions we are taught that idolatry must be exterminated from the land, and that the people are to worship where the Lord chooses. This, of course, would be the place where the tabernacle is to be found. We are not told where this place is, and it is not to be determined until the Lord gives rest to the people from their enemies all about. If the purpose of the book were simply to establish immediately a central sanctuary, it is strange that the Lord asserts that only after rest is given from the enemies about will the location be settled upon. So the negative view has missed the point of what is taught in this chapter.

There is, of course, the ever-present temptation to idolatry. Nevertheless, idolatry is so great a sin that there must be constant warning against it. In chapter thirteen Moses warns the nation against the false prophet who may lead it into idolatry. Even if such a prophet performs a sign or wonder, the people are not to follow him if he speaks in the name of other gods. God may test the nation to discover whether it loves Him with all the heart. In moving language of great depth and beauty Moses depicts the duty of the people to love and fear the God who is doing so much for them.

It is stressed as being of particular importance (chapter fourteen) to avoid the customs of the Canaanites. Instead certain laws for the benefit of slaves and the poor (chapter fifteen) are stressed. In chapter sixteen the three annual festivals are given, and in chapter seventeen preparation is made for a future king. All of this is in preparation for the entrance into Canaan. Yet the prescriptions given here do not conflict with the attitude of Samuel, who regarded the request for a king as tantamount to a rejection of the Lord Himself.

One of the most significant chapters in the entire book is chapter eighteen, in which the law of the prophet is given. Israel is told that when she enters the land of promise she will find there abominable practices. Nine of them are listed: human methods of obtaining information concerning the future and other matters. Israel is told that she is not to learn to do according to these abominations of the nations who inhabit Canaan. The practices listed have largely been confirmed by archaeological discoveries. Among them is passing one's son or daughter through the fire, soothsaying, and spiritualism. These are condemned, and those who practice such things are said to be abominations to the Lord.

In distinction from these practices and false methods of obtaining information, God will give to Israel a true method, namely, the institution of prophecy. It is a statement of the Divine authorization for prophecy and the prophetic office.

It is to be noted that the office of prophet in Israel is not to be compared with that of the soothsayers and diviners of the ancient world generally. Such groups often formed bands to which there were rites of initiation. The prophet of Israel, on the other hand, was a man raised up of God who spoke the words which God gave to him.

The office of prophet was personal, and not hereditary. In Israel the prophet is compared with Moses, that is, just as Moses was a mediator between God and the nation so will the prophet be. As at Sinai, the nation could not bear to see the great theophany and pleaded for Moses to speak to it, so the prophet will speak to the nation on behalf of God. It is in this sense that the prophet is said to be like Moses.

Moreover, the prophet is to be an Israelite, and to be raised up of God. If he be not raised up of God, he will be a false prophet. His function is not to perform mysterious rites, but to speak the Word of the Lord. In Deut. 18:18 we are expressly told that God will place His words in the mouth of the prophet, and the prophet will speak forth that which God commands him. Thus, it is seen that a true prophet is an accredited spokesman for God and this is his primary function. The words which he speaks are not his own; they are not even his own outworking of a fundamental message which God has given to him. The words which he speaks are to be the identical words which God has revealed to him, words which God has placed in his mouth. To hear the prophet then is to hear God.

The word which Moses uses for "prophet" is in the singular, and the reason for this is that the great Prophet whom God would raise up is one Person, the Lord Jesus Christ. He alone is the true Prophet who is like Moses. At the same time there is a lower, secondary reference to the institution of prophecy as such. This is shown by the fact that a comparison is made between true and false prophets. It would be impossible for the nation to distinguish between those who truly spoke forth the Word of God and those who did not if the reference here was only to Christ.

The chapter closes therefore with helpful information on how one was to distinguish between the true and the false prophet. First, if a prophet spoke in the name of the Lord and the prophecy was not fulfilled, it was clear that he was not a true prophet. In the case of Messianic prophecies, when neither the speaker nor those who heard his words would live to see the fulfillment, we may suppose that the prophet would be accredited by his local and daily messages. We find that true prophets gave short-term as well as distant prophecies, so that this could be true. When a prophet spoke on many matters, these were fulfilled so that people would know that he was a man sent from God and that they could therefore give their credence to those messages which dealt with long-distant times.

Another criterion was the name of the God in which the prophet spoke. A true messenger would utter his words in the Name of the Lord, but a false prophet might speak in the name of other gods. This was a sure criterion: a man who spoke in the name of other gods was not to be listened to. Thus, Deuteronomy gives practical help on how true prophets were to be distinguished from the false.

Chapter nineteen again reminds the nation that God will give them the land into which they are to come. It thus sets forth the true account of the conquest, namely, that the land was not taken by the superior power of Israel, but rather that the Lord Himself would cut off the nations which stood in the way of Israel's entrance into the land. After the

Lord has given the land to the nation, three cities of refuge are to be set apart. E of the Jordan three cities had already been assigned and these three had been mentioned by name. The present passage now takes up three more, already mentioned in Numbers 35:14. That these latter three are not named is evidence that the land had not yet been taken. Had Deuteronomy been written after the conquest of the land, we might have expected that the cities would be mentioned by name. Certain laws follow which have to do with a prohibition against the removing of landmarks. Inasmuch as the landmark determined the inheritance of each Israelite, its removal would be a serious offense. Useful information concerning the practice of witnessing against a person accused of crime is also given. One witness will not be sufficient to condemn a man; his criminality must be established at the mouth of two or three witnesses.

Chapters twenty through twenty-six contain various laws for the welfare of the nation. Of particular interest is the confession which the Israelite is to make when he brings the firstfruits before the Lord (26:5 ff.). In this confession acknowledgment is made of the early history of the nation, of its growth in Egypt, and of the mighty deliverance from it. The offering is therefore connected with an acknowledgment of redemption from Egypt. From small insignificant beginnings, "An Aramean ready to perish was my father," to a great and mighty nation, such had been the course of the nation's history. And that the nation had enjoyed such a course of history was due to the goodness of God.

The Renewal of the Covenant — Cursings and Blessings (27:1–30:29)

The summary of the people's attitude is expressed in the command, "Keep all the commandments which I command you this day" (Deut. 27:1). It is perfect obedience which should characterize the attitude of the nation toward the law of God. That there may be such obedience, the law is to be set up as a witness, written on the plaster which covers the stones that will form the altar. This is the standard of obedience, and the altar of sacrifice is the symbol that man has disobeyed. Thus these two significant symbols are brought together, the law and the altar. The whole of man's sin is thus ever before his eyes, for it is the sacrifice of Christ alone which removes from man the reminder of sin.

Disobedience to the law will bring the curse, and in actual history this curse was fulfilled when the nation turned aside from God to idolatry. The exile finally came and brought an end to the theocracy. Chapter 27 is filled with the curses that are to be pronounced upon the disobedient. On the other hand, if the nation is obedient blessing will follow, and a number of these blessings are listed in chapter 28. After enumerating the blessings Moses adds additional curses. There is thus a greater emphasis upon cursing than upon blessing. In all, twelve curses are mentioned but only six blessings. The reason is that the people had a tendency to disobey, and needed to be reminded of the seriousness of disobedience.

Chapters twenty-nine and thirty constitute a renewed declaration of the covenant already made at Horeb. The heart of these chapters is found in the words, "See, I have set before thee this day life and good, and death and evil" (30:15). Obedience to the law is life and good, disobedience to it is death and evil.

Arrangements for the Continuation of the Covenant (31:1–34:12)

Preparations are made for entrance into the land of promise. Joshua is set apart as the leader who is to bring the nation into Canaan. The statement is then made that Moses wrote this law and delivered it to the priests giving the charge that once every seven years the Law was to be read.

Of particular interest and significance is the great final song of Moses. He appeals to the heavens and the earth, for they had witnessed the formation of the people into a nation. Moses' purpose in this song is to ascribe greatness to his God. We may analyze the song briefly as follows: In vss. 1-6 Moses seeks to speak forth words of truth and to glorify God who has done so much for Israel. Verses 7-14 contain an appeal to the great acts which God has performed in former times, in particular to the election and exaltation of Jacob. This is followed (vss. 15-52) by the thought that despite all that God has done for her, Israel turned aside from God in rebellion and followed after idolatry. Israel's sin is great, and certain punishing judgment will come upon her.

The thought of the song is really continued in chapter 33, where mention is made of each of the tribes. Lastly, in the thirty-fourth chapter the account of Moses' death is given and a statement made of his uniqueness in the OT economy (vs. 10). The question arises whether Moses was the author of this chapter. In past times some (e.g., Philo and Josephus) believed that Moses wrote this account of his own death. It is not necessary, however, to maintain that position. It is quite possible that vss. 5 ff. were written by Joshua or someone else under Divine inspiration and so are legitimately regarded as a part of the book. The claim for Mosaic authorship of the Pentateuch does not require that Moses necessarily wrote every single word of it, but only that he was the primary author. This may be held because its essential author is God Himself. We may, therefore, assume that this account of Moses' death was written by some inspired penman other than Moses and yet that it is truly a part of Scripture.

The last chapter forms a fitting conclusion to this great final book of the Pentateuch. Throughout the book the holiness of the sovereign God is manifested and made prominent. The nation is instructed in the will of the Lord, especially with respect to the heinousness of idolatry. It knows that it will meet with enemies, and with those who would tempt it to turn from the commands of the Lord. But accompanying it will be the Lord Himself, to watch and guard it in all the ways that it must go.

BIBLIOGRAPHY:

A. Bentzen, *Die josianisch Reform* (Copenhagen, 1926).
J. B. Griffiths, *The Problem of Deuteronomy* (London, 1911).
J. H. Hospers, *De numerus-wisseling in het boek Deuteronomiums* (1947).
R. H. Kennett, *Deuteronomy and the Decalogue* (Cambridge, 1920).
M. G. Klein, "Dynastic Covenant," *WThJ* 23 (1960), 1-15.
W. Möller, *Rückbeziehungen des 5. Buches Mosis auf die vier ersten Bücher* (1925).
T. Oestreicher, *Das Deuteronomische Grundgesetz* (1923).
J. Reider, *Deuteronomy With Commentary* (Philadelphia, 1937).
J. Ridderbos, *Het boek Deuteronomium* (Kampen, 1950-51).
W. Staerk, *Das Problem des Deuteronomiums* (Gütersloh, 1924).
G. von Rad, *Das Gottesvolk im Deuteronomium* (Stuttgart, 1929).
G. von Rad, *Studies in Deuteronomy* (Chicago, 1953).
A. C. Welch, *The Code of Deuteronomy* (London, 1924).
A. C. Welch, *Deuteronomy, The Framework to the Code* (London, 1932).
H. Wiener, *The Main Problem of Deuteronomy* (Oberlin, 1920).
E. J. Young, *Introduction to the Old Testament* (Grand Rapids, 1958), 101-114; 157-58.
E. J. Young, *My Servants the Prophets* (Grand Rapids, 1952), 13-37.
A. Zahn, *Das Deuteronomium* (Gütersloh, 1890).

EDWARD J. YOUNG

DÉVAY, Mátyás Biró (*c.* 1500-1545), Hungarian Reformer. After a few years of study at Cracow, Dévay was active as a Roman Catholic priest in Hungary. However, he was gradually won over to the principles of the Reformation. In 1529 he went to Wittenberg, where he studied in close contact with Luther. In 1531 he returned to his native land and labored in the Hungarian capital of Ofen (Buda), as well as other places, in the spirit of Luther, so that he could rightly be called the Hungarian Luther. He was imprisoned several times but later worked under the protection of Count Nádasdy and other influential persons in W. Hungary. In 1536 and 1537 he stayed with his friend Veit Dietrich in Nüremberg for the publication of his polemic writings. At Wittenberg again he experienced Melanchthon's influence. Upon his return to his fatherland he worked with Johan Sylvester (Erdösi) in the interest of schools and of a printing shop which they established. Among his publications was a short dogmatics or catechism. Because of the advance of the Turks he again had to flee to Wittenberg in 1541. It is not certain whether or not he also went to Switzerland during this period. But when he could again resume his activities, especially at Debrecen, it appeared that he was closer to the Swiss Reformers in his view of the Lord's supper and was opposed by Luther in 1544.

BIBLIOGRAPHY:

H. J. Grimm, *The Reformation Era 1500–1650* (New York, 1955).

G. Loesche, *Luther, Melanchthon und Calvin in Oesterreich-Ungarn* (Tübingen, 1909).

I. Révész, *D. B. M. tanitasai* (Klausenburg, 1915).

K. Révész, in *P.R.E.* IV (3rd ed., 1898), 595-598.

D. NAUTA

DEVIL, THE. See SATAN.

DEVOTIO MODERNA. The *Devotio Moderna* (Latin for Modern Devotion) is the name of a revival movement within the medieval church in the second half of the 14th century. It began with the conversion of Geert Groote (1340-84), a promising young theologian in the Netherlands who, probably in 1377, suddenly turned to a life of dedicated asceticism. He relinquished all his benefices and made his house available to pious women. After a stay of a few years in a monastery, he became an itinerant preacher, calling people to repentance and an ascetic life, and denouncing abuses in the clergy (simony, living in concubinage, etc.). His friend Floris Radewijnsz, who shared his views, established a community for men, first at Deventer, later on also in other places. The "Sisters of the Common Life" devoted much of their time to prayer and meditation, particularly on the passion of the Lord, and supported themselves by working in or outside their communities. The "Brethren of the Common Life" attended to the pastoral care of the people in their neighborhood and established boarding houses for students in the schools attached to the monasteries. By their pious walk of life they deeply influenced many young people, and their impact was felt not only in the Netherlands but also in Germany, where they also established their fraternities.

In 1387, probably against the intentions of Groote, who emphasized the need for an ascetic life *in* the world, a monastery of Augustinian Canons was established by six of Groote's disciples at Windesheim, near Zwolle, Holland. Under their second great prior, John Vos, they formed with three other Dutch monasteries the "Congregation of Windesheim." By the end of the 15th century, the Congregation embraced nearly 100 monasteries, in the Netherlands, Germany, and Switzerland. They included important writers and scholars, such as Thomas à Kempis (the author of *The Imitation of Christ*) and Gabriel Biel (one of the last great scholastic thinkers). Yet on the whole their emphasis was on pastoral care and a life of ascetic devotion rather than on scholarship. This was one of the reasons why the humanists (e.g., Erasmus) turned away from them.

The monasteries of the Congregation of Windesheim (as well as the monasteries for women, e.g., in Diepenveen) contributed much to the reform of monastic life in the 15th century. By their preaching in the vernacular and their exemplary lives, they deeply influenced the religious and moral life of the common people, not only in the areas around their monasteries but also far beyond. Although they cannot be called forerunners of the Reformation—in their theology they were true "Catholics"—they did prepare the soil in which afterwards the seed of the Reformation took root. As such they are of great significance for the period which marked the transition from the Middle Ages to the Reformation. During the Reformation the Dutch houses and monasteries were closed down and abandoned. A number of the Brethren and Sisters joined the Reformation. In other countries the Congregation continued until the French Revolution.

Bibliography:

J. G. R. Acquoy, *Het klooster te Windesheim en zijn invloed* (Utrecht, 1875-80), 3 vols.

J. Dols, *Bibliografie der Moderne Devotie* (Nijmegen, 1941).

A. Hyma, *The Christian Renaissance*, History of the "Devotio Moderna" (New York, 1925).

E. F. Jacob, "Gerard Groote and the beginning of the 'New Devotion' in the Low Countries," in *JEH*, III (1952), 40-57.

W. J. Kuhler, *Joh. Brinckerinck en zijn klooster te Diepenveen* (Rotterdam, 1908).

R. R. Post, *De Moderne Devotie* (Amsterdam, 1940).

J. Van Ginneken, S.J., *Geert Groote's levensbeeld naar de oudste gegevens bewerkt* (Amsterdam, 1942).

Klaas Runia

DEW, the water left from moist sea breezes during cool nights. In the Bible it is frequently copious (Judges 6:38), especially during the summer drought. It makes a substantial and vital contribution to Palestinian ecology and thus is a major aspect of God's bounty in Scripture (Gen. 27:28, 39; Deut. 33:13, 28; Isa. 18:4; Zech. 8:12). In the wilderness the manna which God sent fell with the dew (Ex. 16:13f.; Num. 11:9).

Dew is symbolic of God's blessing (Job 29:19; Ps. 133:3) and representative of vitality (Song of S. 5:2; Isa. 26:19). Dew is in the hands of the Lord (Job 38:28; Prov. 3:20), and its withdrawal in judgment is disastrous (II Sam. 1:21; I Kings 17:1; Hag. 1:10). In the Messiah God's people are, like the dew, the instrumentality and manifestation of divine power and refreshing (Ps. 110:3; Mic. 5:7). The word of God similarly comes from heaven to nourish with a gentle but invincible efficacy (Deut. 32:2).

The fleeting nature of dew, soon to perish in the heat of the day, also made it an apt figure in Hosea for Israel's inconstancy (Hos. 6:4) and jeopardy (Hos. 13:3). Yet because it comes again on another day after dissipating, the Lord declares that He will Himself be unto His people as the dew (Hos. 14:5), reviving and sustaining their life by a grace not once given, but daily renewed.

Joseph P. Duggan

DEWEY, John (1859-1952), American philosopher and educator. Born in Burlington, Vermont, Dewey's professional teaching career centered in the Universities of Michigan, Chicago, and Columbia, though as a lecturer and author he was internationally influential. Sharing with W. James and F. Schiller the claim to have originated the philosophy of pragmatism, he also achieved the most comprehensive and articulate formulation of that point of view. He was also singular in achieving major influence in areas of educational, social, and legal reform. The tribute, "one of the greatest of living Americans," given to him in 1939 cannot be easily questioned, even if his influence finally should be construed to be less.

For John Dewey, pragmatism was essentially a movement of "reform." Traditional philosophy must be reconstructed to get rid of its preoccupation with abstraction and certainty, and reconstructed philosophy must become the medium for resolving the conflict between "man's beliefs about the world in which he lives and his beliefs about the values and purposes that should direct his conduct" (see Dewey's essay, "Experience, Knowledge and Value," in *Philosophy of John Dewey*, ed. P. Schilpp, New York, 1951, 2nd ed., p. 533).

The import of this second proposal can best be illustrated here by Dewey's evaluation of religion. Strangely enough, John Dewey emphasized the historical character of every religion. There cannot be universal religion because each religion is an exclusive commitment to belief in a superior Being and to an institutional embodiment (ethical and cultic). Recognizing the historical character of every religion enables us to distinguish clearly the important human needs which produce religions and the accidental historical form which each religion develops. Taken collectively, religions have successfully created goals, unified human interests, and negated selfishness. They have failed in the measure that they have immorally hypostatized their ideals or refused to admit the legitimacy of other interests or of the change of ideals. Thus Dewey sides with "Fundamentalism" against "Modernism" in recognizing that Christianity and science are in mortal conflict. He repudiates the parochialism of fundamentalism (science has created "new methods of inquiry and reflection") and its immoral escape into a vacuous supernaturalism. "The assumption that these objects of religion exist already in some realm of Being seems to add nothing to their force, while it weakens their claim over us as ideals, insofar as it bases that claim upon matters that are intellectually dubious" (Dewey, *A Common Faith,* New Haven, 1934, p. 41).

Traditional philosophy must undergo the same manner of reformation. Though the mental operations of knowing and reasoning are necessarily abstract, like every other human action they become meaningful only to the extent that they are related to the problems of life. Similarly, the "truth" to which these mental activities aspire can be measured only by the success with which the ideas terminate the problem out of which they arose. Philosophy as thus reconstructed repudiates systems or even quests for truth. Its distinctive role is to provide critical assessment and application of religious and poetic ideals to life in the same way that science realizes the inventor's dreams in material areas. Nevertheless, philosophy also happens surreptitiously to be the "general logic of experience" through which all experience is most fruitfully interrelated and valued (S. Ratner, "Dewey's Conception of Philosophy," ed. P. Schilpp, *op. cit.*, p. 71 ff.). Major criticism of Dewey has arisen to question his formulation of the method of inquiry as well as to debate his theory of truth.

Pragmatism as "intelligently conducted doing" receives its final justification in a theory of human behavior. Any interest which motivates to action is good, *insofar* as it does so. Within the general pattern of responses, however, those which "set free and develop the capacities of human nature without respect to race, sex, class, or economic status" provide the decisive norm of activity. Thus a freely creating, self-correcting, and self-respecting society is its own end and the assumption upon which it builds, i.e., that man is basically morally good and wise, seems quite obvious (J. Dewey, *Reconstruction in Philosophy*, Boston, 1948; cf. pp. 186, 195).

It can be readily observed that Dewey proposes a radical reform, in important ways antagonistic to Christianity. As a social program, it denies that pervasive capacity of man for cruelty and stubbornness even to the point of self-destruction. As a theory of culture, it explains religion as a psycho-sociological product of secondary importance. This not only denies the historical authenticity of Scripture as God's revelation, but questions the very meaning and possibility of such a revelation.

BIBLIOGRAPHY:
G. Clark, *Dewey* (Philadelphia, 1960).
J. Dewey, *A Common Faith* (New Haven, 1944).
J. Dewey, *Experience and Nature* (Chicago, 1925).
S. Hook, et al., *John Dewey* (New York, 1950).
P. Schilpp, ed., *Philosophy of John Dewey* (New York, 1951).

HAROLD J. FRANZ

DIADEM. Although in modern usage diadem and crown are interchangeable, the ancients drew a clear distinction between them. The crown was a garland of flowers, leaves, or leaf-like gold, symbolizing victory or exaltation, but never royalty. Originally, the diadem was simply an Oriental headpiece to bind the hair, consisting of a cloth band, about two inches wide, and tied at the back. Later it became more ornamental and was adopted by monarchs as an emblem of sovereignty, royal diadems being distinguished by their color, studded jewels, or pendants of gold or rare gems. The diadem is mentioned only twice in the OT (Isa. 28:5; 62:3). In two other places where the AV gives "diadem" (Job 29:14; Ezek. 21:26), the RSV "turban" is preferable.

In the NT, diadem (AV crown) is the correct rendering in three places, where it is symbolic of power to rule: the diadem of the red dragon (Rev. 12:3), the diadem of the beast (Rev. 13:1), and the many diadems of the imperial Christ riding forth on His white charger to smite the nations (Rev. 19:12).

See CROWN.

RICHARD ALLEN BODEY

DIAL, a simple instrument with an indicator or gnomon that casts a shadow upon a surface, thus pointing out the hours. References are found in II Kings 20:11 and Isa. 38:8. The Hebrew word is simply *ma'alôt*, "a going up"; Greek *bathmos*, "a step." The word occurs also in the titles of Psalms 120–134, where the meaning is "degrees." The dial was in use in ancient times as early as the 8th century B.C. The OT reference is to the sundial of Ahaz, which possibly had graduated lines called degrees or steps. If the word means "steps" it might refer to a flight of steps leading to the royal palace of Ahaz, on the top of which was placed a gnomon in the form of an obelisk. The steps then served to measure the shadow of the sun thrown upon them. Or it might refer to a massive structure towering into the sky that would serve the double purpose of an observatory and a dial. King Ahaz copied one he saw in Babylon. It is well known that the Greeks learned from the Babylonians, who excelled in the science of astronomy. Herodotus states, "the Greeks learned from the Babylonians the dial, and the gnomon, and the division of the day into twelve (parts) hours" (*Eut.*, 109).

The question arises as to how to explain the recession of the shadow ten degrees on the dial of Ahaz. It is written that it was a "sign" of the Lord in the above references. The least that can be inferred is that it was an extraordinary wonder performed by the hand of Almighty God in the sight of the Jewish people, recorded to strengthen the faith of the worshippers of the God of Israel in all the ages. However, it is not necessary to understand the event as consisting in a reversing of the earth's diurnal rotation. It could refer to a wonder limited to the land of Judea (II Chronicles 32:31).

DAVID FREEMAN

DIALECTICAL THEOLOGY. According to the German philosopher G. W. F. Hegel (1770-1831), the movement of thought—the spirit as movement and development—can move toward the superior category of *synthesis* only by uniting inseparably two contradictories: the *thesis* and the *antithesis*. This is the Hegelian dialectic.

In a lecture entitled "The Word of God, task for theology," delivered in October, 1922, at Egersburg, at the conference of the "Freuden der Christlichen Welt," Karl Barth described the three paths that the theologian can follow: the dogmatic path, the critical path, and the dialectical path. Whereas the *dogmatic* (orthodox) theologian asks a man to believe without human rationale, and whereas the *critical* (idealist, mystical) theologian invites a man to abase himself before a God who is unqualified Being, the *dialectical* theologian leaves God as a synthesis, allowing Him the freedom and the prerogative to effect, or rather to be, Himself. He expounds at once both the thesis and the antithesis, the YES and the NO, stating that neither the affirmation (dogma) nor the negation (concept of unqualified Being) represents the ultimate reality.

In the years that followed the First World War, dialectical theology rallied around Karl Barth and the review *Zwischen den Zeiten*. It made vigorous progress, particularly in Germany with Gogarten and Bultmann and in Switzerland with Brunner.

According to dialectical theology, the inevitable paradox is that (1) when speaking of God, the theologian as a sinner cannot affirm without denying, and (2) when speaking of God, the theologian as a believer cannot deny without affirming.

The dialectical theologian's hope is *eschatological* in the sense that, "beyond every this-side-of and every beyond" (Barth), beyond every affirmation and every negation, he awaits the unforseeable and final revelation of God. In faith, "man is what he is not, he knows what he does not know, he does what he cannot do" (Barth). "To have faith (to have it really, in fact) means to be someone who is waiting, because what faith has (what it has really, in fact) is the promise of what it does not have now. *Verbum solum habemus*" (Brunner).

After Hegel and before the rise of dialectical theology, the Danish philosopher Søren Kierkegaard (1813-1855), came on the scene. He actually represents another strand in dialectical theology. From Hegel, his master and adversary, Kierkegaard took over the dialectic of thesis and antithesis. What he rejected, with passionate determination, was the synthesis, called by Kierkegaard sometimes the "system," sometimes the "mediation." In place of the synthesis which weakens and in the last resort annuls the truth of the thesis and of the antithesis, the Danish thinker intrepidly maintains the "paradox" which unites the "contradictories" in the "absurdity" of faith.

For Kierkegaard, every synthesis, in trying to explain and unify the thesis and the antithesis, suppresses the truth. To the homogeneity of the Hegelian relation, Kierkegaard opposes the heterogeneity of the relation of paradox. Where the "system" blurs the terms that it seeks to "mediate," "paradox" carries these terms to the extremity of their sense and their capacity. To the intemporal world of abstract and mediating thought, Kierkegaard opposes the existential world of trembling and despair, faith and hope. To Hegelian rationalism, Kierkegaard opposes the risk and the irrational leap of faith.

Dialectical theology appears to effect an unacknowledged synthesis of the irrationalism of Kierkegaard and the rationalism of Hegel. This is a synthesis, however, in which the proportions of irrationalism and rationalism vary from one theologian to another.

This synthesis can be seen, for example, in the doctrine of Holy Scripture. Orthodox evangelical theologians have always held *both* that Holy Scripture is a book of men who wrote in different ways and at different periods, *and* that it is the Word of God. They did not develop this doctrine of Scripture out of an irrational love of paradox or in the search for thesis and antithesis; they developed it in order to follow faithfully what Scripture tells of itself. The affirmation, which is itself Scriptural, of the (organic and plenary) inspiration of Scripture expresses and in a certain sense "explains" how Scripture is at once the Word of God and human words. Again, it is not from a rational taste for "system," nor by searching for a synthesis, that orthodox evangelical theologians teach the (organic and plenary) inspiration of Scripture, but in order to follow faithfully what Scripture says. It is clear that this doctrine leads to questions and encounters difficulties (questions and difficulties which are inherent in our situation of men who are at once believers, sinners, and "pilgrims") that cannot and must not be brushed away either by a "mediating" rationalism or by an irrationalism that takes the risk of "absurdity." But a thousand difficulties do not make one doubt, and faith, provided by God Himself, holds on and perseveres. Orthodox evangelical theology, striving in the course of centuries to assimilate progressively the whole of the revealed datum, takes care to preserve side by side, not indeed "antinomies" or "contradictories" (which would be untenable, even by someone who upheld "paradox" as against "synthesis"), but "complementaries" or "opposites" which lean against one another; it joins them together by *et tamen* (and yet).

The dialectical theologians, on the other hand, propose a much different doctrine of Holy Scripture. In rationalist style they affirm that since Holy Scripture is a human book, written by various men at various periods (facts that no one denies), *therefore* it necessarily contains errors and contradictions. In *irrationalist* style, on the other hand, they declare that this book, though "vulnerable and fallible in its religious and theological structures" (Barth), becomes nevertheless the Word of God. Dialectical theology affirms simultaneously a proposition and its contrary, as if one could marry together water and fire ("the Bible *is* the Word of God," and also "the Bible is *not* the Word of God"). Or alternatively, putting out the fire with the water or evaporating the water with the fire, it eliminates one "complementary" and preserves only the other one, treating these "complementaries" as if they were "antinomies" or "contradictories" ("the Bible, being a human book, is not Revelation, but only a fallible witness to Revelation"). Oscillating in this way between irrationalism and rationalism at its pleasure, dialectical theology becomes more and more diversified, and finally founders in the subjectivism in which everyone takes or leaves whatever he likes of Scripture.

It is true that in many pages of his monumental *Kirchliche Dogmatik*, Barth let himself be led by Holy Scripture and by the central motif of Scripture—Creation, Fall, Redemption—rather than by the motif of dialectic; but this does not alter the fact that the dialectical path, which is defined by Barth as the true path for theological endeavor, leads him away from the only royal road for theology, the path where Scripture *alone* and *the whole* of Scripture leads. And, following the dialectical path, Barth's followers, once freed from what their master still maintained, deviate further and further from the Revelation of the Christ of Scripture and of the Scripture of Christ.

Karl Barth, Emil Brunner, and Reinhold Niebuhr have sometimes been identified as "new orthodoxy." In the 1930's and 1940's, because they emphasized that men, plunged in sin and separated from God, could be saved only by the sovereign grace of God in Jesus Christ through the work of the Holy Spirit, it was hoped that the "theology of crisis," as it was then called, amounted to a renewal of orthodoxy. But unhappily for Protestantism and for Christianity, it amounted rather to a *new modernism.* The fruits of dialectical theology have indeed shown that the tree was not good and that a new orthodoxy—that is, true evangelical theology—must be sought and found elsewhere.

PIERRE COURTHIAL

DIANA OF THE EPHESIANS. The goddess Diana whose worship centered in Ephesus was a nature divinity of Asiatic conception. She was of the same general type as goddesses like Cybele and Astarte. Representations that have come down to us conceive her, however grotesquely, as the mother-principle of nature, embodying reproductive and sustaining power. The Greeks who settled in Ephesus associated her with their own Artemis, whom the Romans identified with their own Diana.

The image of Diana (Artemis) at the temple near Ephesus, like other images in ancient times, was claimed to have fallen from heaven (Acts 19:35). Also, the famous temple of the Hellenistic period was regarded as one of the seven wonders of the world. The sun in all his course, it was said, saw nothing more magnificent than the temple of Diana. Situated over a mile from the city proper, it rose from a platform about 425 feet long and about 240 feet wide. The temple itself measured about 342 feet in length and 164 feet in width. Its 100 marble columns and the white marble tiles on its roof helped make its exterior brilliant. Its interior was adorned with painting and sculpture and was embellished with gold. The work of Phidias, Praxiteles, Scopas, Parrhasius, and Apelles contributed to its artistic excellence.

The worship of Diana was by no means confined to the temple at Ephesus. Demetrius the silversmith, a maker of silver shrines of Artemis, could say that all Asia and the world worshiped her (Acts 19:27). Great numbers of pilgrims came to Ephesus; devotees kept miniature shrines in their homes and even placed them in graves. Traces of her veneration have been found not only in Asia Minor, but also in Greece, Italy, the Crimea, France, and Spain. To many people in many places she was "Great Artemis," the "Queen of Ephesus."

Many priests, priestesses, and others performed the temple service at Ephesus with orgiastic rites, a defilement of the cult being ceremonial prostitution.

When Paul was in Ephesus he wrote to the Corinthians: "As concerning therefore the eating of those things that are offered in sacrifice unto idols, we know that an idol is nothing in the world, and that there is none other God but one" (I Cor. 8:4). Demetrius the silversmith aroused craftsmen who profited from the Diana-cult by declaring that their craft and the magnificence of Diana were threatened by the success of Paul's doctrine that "they be no gods, which are made with hands" (Acts 19:26). A large commotion was consequently produced, and there was much invoking of

"Great Diana of the Ephesians." Today the site of the temple of this "Great Diana," this "greatest god," and the "Queen of Ephesus" is covered by a stagnant pond.

BIBLIOGRAPHY:
J. Finegan, *Light from the Ancient Past* (Princeton, 1946), 265-269.
W. M. Ramsay, *The Church in the Roman Empire before A.D. 170* (New York, c. 1893), 112-145.
W. M. Ramsay, "Diana of the Ephesians," *HDB* I, (1902), 605-606.
W. M. Ramsay, *The Letters to the Seven Churches of Asia* (New York, 1905), 210-236.
L. Schmitz, "Artemis," and "Diana," *Dictionary of Greek and Roman Biography and Mythology* I, W. Smith, ed. (1869), 375-376, 1000.
A. Souter, "Diana," *HDAC* I (1916), 295-296.
W. J. Woodhouse, "Diana," *EB* I (1899), 1098-1099.

JOHN H. SKILTON

DIASPORA. See DISPERSION OF THE JEWS.

DIATESSARON, a harmony of the four Gospels in the form of a continuous narrative, compiled about 170. The author, Tatian, a Syrian, was a convert of Justin Martyr. The book is a significant witness to the authority of the four Gospels at the time of its compilation. The language of the original is uncertain. The Greek title usually applied to the work and the small fragment of a Greek edition found at Dura Europos in 1933 do not provide conclusive evidence. The Diatessaron was widely circulated in Syriac and became the accepted text of the Gospels in the Syrian churches until the 5th century.

Parts of the Diatessaron are known through quotations in works of the early Syrian Fathers and various versions. An Armenian version of a 4th-century commentary by Ephraem Syrus was published in 1836. A Latin translation of this version, based on two mss., was issued in 1876. From this translation and quotations in the Homilies of Aphraates, Zahn reconstructed the outline of the harmony and prepared a provisional reproduction of a part of its text. In 1957 a 5th- or 6th-century ms., containing about three fifths of Ephraem's commentary in the original Syriac, was identified by Sir Chester Beatty and was published, with a Latin translation, by Louis Leloir in 1963.

The Latin Codex Fuldensis, written between 541 and 546, includes the Gospels arranged in a single narrative in imitation of the Diatessaron. The order agrees with Zahn's conjecture but the text is assimilated to Jerome's Vulgate. An Arabic version of Tatian's work, based on two late mss. and published in 1888, is a valuable witness to its general characteristics. However, the text is assimilated to the Peshitta, although the available evidence indicates that Tatian's Syriac text was the Old Syriac corrected by Western Greek.

The harmony began with the opening words of John's Gospel and omitted the genealogies. During the 5th century there was a switch from the Diatessaron to the Peshitta, which included each of the four Gospels, in separate form. Theodoret, bishop of Cyrrhus (423-457), condemned the Diatessaron on account of its omissions and removed two hundred copies from circulation; but among Nestorians it was in use until the 14th century.

BIBLIOGRAPHY:
HDB, Extra Vol. 4 (New York, 1909), 451-461.
L. Leloir, *Ephrem de Nisibe, Commentaire de L'Evangile Concordant ou Diatessaron* (Paris, 1966).
B. M. Metzger, *Text of the New Testament* (Oxford, 1964), 89-92.
J. Quaesten, *Patrology*, 1 (Utrecht, 1950), 225-228, lists recent literature.

WILLIAM J. CAMERON

DIAZ, Juan, or Diazius, John (*c.* 1510-1546), Spanish Protestant martyr. A native of Cuenca, Spain, Diaz came to Paris in 1532, where he studied Greek and Hebrew in the humanistic fashion. He was associated with Guillaume Budé (Budaeus) and became a friend of Budé's son Matthias, Jean Crespin, Claude de Senarclens, and others. His compatriot Jaime (Diego) de Enzinas (brother of Francesco, also called Dryander) seems to have been the means for winning him for the cause of the Reformation.

After several of his friends had already preceded him, Diaz went to Geneva in 1545. There he lived for three months at the home of Nic. des Gallars and also came into contact with Calvin. From his subsequent correspondence, it is evident that he considered Calvin as his teacher.

In the same year Diaz left for Strasbourg via Lausanne, Neuchâtel, and Basel. At Strasbourg he joined the French church by public profession. With Bucer he became a delegate to the religious discussions at Regensburg. Pedro Malvenda, chaplain and trusted adviser of the emperor, was the leader of the RC group. Malvenda, who had personally known Diaz at Paris, was surprised at his presence on the side of the Protestants. He tried to force him to recant but did so in vain. When Diaz' brother Alfonso, who was a lawyer at the papal court of justice in Rome, heard about his attitude, he set out for Regensburg. Meanwhile, Diaz had left for the neighboring city of Neuburg to supervise the printing of a writing of Bucer against Latomus. But Alfonso managed to find him there and did his utmost to persuade Diaz to return to the RC Church. When this failed, he cunningly instigated his murder on March 27, 1546. The murderers were arrested at Innsbrück but were freed again after a short time. Afterwards, Alfonso committed suicide at Trent (1551).

This murder caused great alarm among the Protestants. Diaz' friend Claude de Senarclens, with the aid of Enzinas, published the story of his death at Basel in 1546. Bucer provided a preface.

Only one published work of Diaz is known, published shortly before his death. It is a short summary of the Christian faith, wholly in the spirit of Calvin.

BIBLIOGRAPHY:

Historia vera de morte sancti viri Joannis Diazii Hispani, quem eius frater germanus Alphonsus Diazius . . . nefarie interfecit, per Claudium Senarcleum (Basel, 1546); Spanish translation by Usoz (Madrid, 1865).

M. Bataillon, *Erasme et l'Espagne* (Paris, 1937), 551 f.

E. Boehmer, *Spanish Reformers of Two Centuries from 1520,* I (London, 1874), 185-216.

J. Bonnet, *Récits du seizième siècle,* 177-241; German edition by F. Merschmann (Berlin, 1864), 139-190.

J. Crespin, *Histoire des Martyrs,* Ed. nouvelle par D. Benoit, I (Toulouse, 1885), 468-487.

H. Eells, *Martin Bucer* (New Haven, 1931), *passim.*

H. Jedin, *Geschichte des Konzils von Trient* II (Freiburg, 1957), 177.

M. M. Pelarjo, *Historia de los heterodoxos españoles* II (Madrid, 1878), 207-218; 732-743.

F. Roth, *Zur Verhaftung und zu dem Prozess des Doktors Alphonso Diaz,* in: *Archiv fuer Reformationsgeschichte* VIII (1910), 413-438.

M. F. van Lennep, *De Hervorming in Spanje in de zestiende eeuw* (Haarlem, 1901), 320-335.

D. NAUTA

DIBELIUS, Martin Franz (1883-1947), German NT scholar. Educated at Neufchatel, Leipzig, Tübingen, and Berlin, Dibelius succeeded Johannes Weiss as professor of NT exegesis and criticism at Heidelberg in 1915, and held this post until his death. He was a pupil of Gunkel and Harnack. Gunkel had been a leader in laying the groundwork of what became, under Dibelius, Schmidt, and Bultmann, form criticism. Dibelius described his approach to the NT in *A Fresh Approach to the New Testament and Early Christian Literature.* It is recognized that he elaborated principles of form criticism which had been expounded by Weiss.

Basic to Dibelius' conception, and to form criticism generally, is the idea that the gospel stories are to be treated as separate bits of tradition embedded in a chronological and geographic framework which does not reflect the actual sequence of events and teaching in Jesus' ministry. The "form" of the present narrative was shaped by the life and interests of the church. It is implied in this representation that the present form of the Gospels arose subsequent to the shaping of the individual stories; because of the shaping in the oral tradition and later editorial revision, the chronological and geographical outline of Jesus' life is very unreliable. The skepticism latent in form criticism is best seen in the yet more radical demythologizing of Rudolph Bultmann.

Dibelius' work must share the fundamental weaknesses of form criticism—principally, the deprecation of the accuracy with which the witness concerning Jesus was transmitted. He laid great emphasis on the sermon as the means of transmitting the Lord's words. His attitude toward the gospel tradition is felt to be more conservative than most members of the *Religionsgeschichte* school.

WILBER B. WALLIS

DIBLAH (Diblatha, LXX), a place mentioned only in Ezek. 6:14. But such a place is entirely unknown. Whereas the Hebrew *d* can easily be mistaken for *r*, it is possible that Riblah was the place referred to in the original ms. The RSV and the BV read Riblah.

See RIBLAH.

DIBLAIM, "two cakes," the father of the adulteress Gomer, whom Hosea took when he was commanded to take a wife of whoredoms. Diblaim's daughter was representative of the N kingdom's relationship to the Lord (Hos. 1:3).

See GOMER.

DIBON:

(1) The modern Dhiban, a city of central Moab about four miles N of the Arnon River along the ancient N-S road. At the time of Israel's wilderness journey, the Amorites under Sihon seized the Moabite lands N of the Arnon including Dibon (Num. 21:30). After the Israelites bypassed the Edomite and Moabite kingdoms, it was the first city occupied. They called it Dibon-gad (Num. 33:45, 46), reflecting that it was first assigned to the tribe of Gad (Num. 32:3, 34) but then later to Reuben (Josh. 13:17). The populace of Dibon, like the rest of N Moab, however, remained predominantly Moabite despite this and subsequent Israelitish subjugation of the area.

Mesha, who threw off the yoke of Israel's Omride dynasty, described himself as a Dibonite and apparently made his capital at Dibon. There he erected the Moabite Stone, citing on it the loyalty of the Dibonites and stressing the building of Qorchah, which is most probably located in, or adjacent to, Dibon (see A. H. van Zyl, *The Moabites*, Leiden, 1960, pp. 78-80). Dibon continued as one of Moab's prominent cities, being named in the judgments pronounced by Isaiah (Isa. 15:2) and Jeremiah (Jer. 48:18, 22). In Isa. 15:9 the name is altered to Dimon to make more forceful the connection with the blood (Hebrew root, dm) which was to characterize its fate. A similar intentional change of the name is possible, but by no means certain, in the Madmen of Jer. 48:2.

(2) An unidentified town of Judah listed in Neh. 11:25 among those occupied after the return from exile. Its identity with Dimonah (Josh. 15:22) has been frequently suggested.

DIBRI, a man of the tribe of Dan, grandfather of a blasphemer stoned to death (Lev. 24:10). Dibri's daughter

Shelomith, mother of the one stoned, was married to an Egyptian.

See SHELOMITH; BLASPHEMY.

DICK, John (1764-1833), Scottish preacher and theologian. He was born in Aberdeen, Scotland, where his father, Alexander Dick, was a Secession minister. John followed his father into the ministry of the Secession Church and, while studying under John Brown of Haddington, developed a deep interest in theology. In 1786 he became minister at Slateford, Edinburgh, and in 1801 he was called to the mother-church of the Secession in Glasgow, which became known as the Greyfriars Church. From 1820 he also served as professor of theology to the Associate Synod.

At a time when creed-subscription was agitating the Secession Church, Dick preached and published a mediating sermon entitled *Confessions of Faith Shown to Be Necessary*. But the Old Light section thought it too concessive to those who desired to relax subscription of the Confession of Faith, and they wrote against it. Dick's publications also included *Lectures on the Acts of the Apostles*, an *Essay on Inspiration*, and posthumously published *Lectures in Theology*.

BIBLIOGRAPHY:

A. C. Dick, *Memoir* of John Dick prefixed to Dick's *Lectures in Theology*.

Dictionary of National Biography, vol. xv.

J. McKerrow, *History of the Secession Church*.

R. Small, *History of the Congregations of the United Presbyterian Church*.

G. N. M. COLLINS

DICKINSON, Jonathan (1688-1747), Presbyterian theologian and educator. Dickinson was born at Hatfield, Massachusetts, graduated from Yale College (1706), studied theology, and was ordained pastor of the church at Elizabeth Town, New Jersey (1709), which he served for almost 40 years. He was able to persuade his Congregational church to join the Presbytery of Philadelphia in 1717. One of the ablest colonial Presbyterian ministers, he was also a practicing physician. Although he was a strong Calvinist and defended Presbyterianism with great vigor, he was opposed to rigid confessionalism as a test of orthodoxy, preferring instead strict examination of candidates and strict church discipline. He helped to compose the differences between the factions of the Synod of Philadelphia by supporting the compromise Adopting Act (1729), which required candidates for ordination to accept the Westminster standards "as being in all the essential and necessary articles, good forms of sound words and systems of Christian doctrine, and do also adopt the said Confession and Catechisms as the confession of our faith." He was a strong opponent of deism and Arminianism, and an outstanding advocate of the Calvinistic revivalism of the Great Awakening. After the expulsion of the New Side evangelists from the Synod, he played a leading role in the formation of the Synod of New York (1745), of which he was elected moderator. Through his efforts the charter of the College of New Jersey was granted (1746). He was elected the first president of this school, which was opened in his home in 1747. Before the college could be moved to Princeton, he died, on October 7, 1747. In Sprague's *Annals* is found this testimony: "It may be doubted whether, with the single exception of the elder Edwards, Calvinism has ever found an abler or more efficient champion in this country, than Jonathan Dickinson." His most famous work was a defense of the five points of Calvinism, *The True Scripture-Doctrine Concerning Some Important Points of Christian Faith* (Boston, 1741). Other publications include: *Defence of Presbyterian Ordination* (Boston, 1724), *The Reasonableness of Christianity* (Boston, 1732), *The Scripture-Bishop, or the Divine*

Right of Presbyterian Ordination and Government (Boston, 1732), *The Reasonableness of Nonconformity to the Church of England* (Boston, 1738), *Danger of Schisms and Contentions with Respect to the Ministry and Ordinances of the Gospel* (New York, 1739), *A Display of God's Special Grace* (Boston, 1742), *The Nature and Necessity of Regeneration* (New York, 1743), *Familiar Letters to a Gentleman, Upon a Variety of Seasonable and Important Subjects in Religion* (Boston, 1745), and *Brief Illustration and Confirmation of the Divine Right of Infant Baptism* (Boston, 1746). An edition of his *Sermons and Tracts* was published in Edinburgh (1793). The Princeton University Library has a collection of his papers.

BIBLIOGRAPHY:
DAB V, 301 f.
H. C. Cameron, *Jonathan Dickinson and the College of New Jersey* (Princeton, 1880).
J. Maclean, *History of the College of New Jersey* (Philadelphia, 1877).
W. B. Sprague, *Annals of the American Pulpit*, III (New York, 1858), 14-18.
L. J. Trinterud, *A Bibliography of American Presbyterianism During the Colonial Period* (Philadelphia, 1968).

ALBERT H. FREUNDT, JR.

DICKSON, David (*c.* 1583-1663), Scottish theologian. He was born in Glasgow, the son of a prosperous merchant. Upon graduating from Glasgow University, he was appointed professor of philosophy there and continued in that appointment for eight years. In 1618 he became minister of the Ayrshire parish of Irvine, where he served for 23 years. His opposition to episcopacy led to his being "banished" for a time to Turriff, in Aberdeenshire, but he was later permitted to return to Irvine. On his resuming his ministry there, the parish was visited with a spiritual quickening which continued for five years. As a preacher he aimed at the utmost simplicity and his influence was unusually widespread.

Dickson was a prominent member of the famous Glasgow Assembly of 1638 which abolished episcopacy. He was with the Covenanting army at Dunse Law in the following year, and in that same year he was elected moderator of the General Assembly. He had a large share in the drawing up of the *Directory for Public Worship* and collaborated with James Durham in the production of *The Sum of Saving Knowledge*. In 1640 he was appointed to the new chair of divinity in Glasgow University, where he continued until 1650, when he moved to a similar chair in Edinburgh University. At the Restoration of Charles II he declined to take the Oath of Supremacy, and was therefore ejected from his chair (1662). The hardships which he subsequently endured and his grief over the bitter strife between Resolutioners and Protesters in the church undermined his health, and he died the following year.

Dickson aimed at providing a series of Commentaries on Holy Scripture. It is to his initiative that we are indebted for such commentaries as Hutchison on Job, the Minor Prophets, and the Gospel of John; Ferguson on the Epistles; and Durham on the Song of Solomon and Revelation. His own *Commentary on the Psalms* is well known, and in addition he wrote *A Treatise on the Promises, An Explanation of Hebrews, A Brief Exposition of Matthew,* and *Therapeutica Sacra*, his most notable work. His sacred songs, sung "to the common tunes of the Psalms," acquired considerable popularity among the country people.

BIBLIOGRAPHY:
R. Baillie, *Letters and Journals.*
J. Balfour, *Annals.*
W. G. Blaikie, *The Preachers of Scotland.*
D. Calderwood, *History of the Kirk of Scotland*, Vol. VII.
Chambers, *Lives of Eminent Scotsmen*, Vol. I.
Dictionary of National Biography, Vol. V.
D. Dickson, *Memoir* prefixed to *Select Writings of Dickson*, Vol. I.

J. Howie, *The Scots Worthies.*
A. Smellie, *Men of the Covenant.*
Spalding, *Memorials of the Troubles.*
W. M. Taylor, *The Scottish Pulpit.*
J. Walker, *Scottish Theology and Theologians.*
R. Wodrow, *Select Biographies.*
R. Wodrow, *History of the Sufferings of the Church of Scotland.*

G. N. M. Collins

DIDACHE, a short anonymous book of Christian instruction well known in the early church. Clement of Alexandria appears to cite it as Scripture. Origen seems to have doubts about its canonicity, at one time accepting it and at another excluding it. Eusebius lists it as spurious, but Athanasius commends it as private reading for catechumens. Until the late 19th century its precise form and contents were unknown, although a common source was believed to lie behind such works as theApostolic Canons and the Apostolic Constitutions. But in 1883 Bryennios, metropolitan of Nicomedia, issued an edition of an 11th-century ms. which he had discovered in the Convent of the Holy Sepulchre at Constantinople and which subsequently came to be known as the Jerusalem ms. Shortly afterwards two other sources became available, a 10th-century Latin fragment traced by Gebhart in 1884, and an 11th-century Latin ms., coextensive with the first six chapters only, published by Schlecht in 1900.

The work consists of two parts of six and ten chapters respectively. The first part contains pre-baptismal instruction. It describes the Way of Life as loving God and one's neighbor, guarding against sin in its obvious and more subtle forms, and fulfilling Christian obligations in home and church. Then the Way of Death is indicated by listing particular sins, and warning is given that the Way of Life must be followed as far as possible. Regarding food, it is laid down that what has been offered to idols should be avoided. The second division includes guidance on the manner of baptism, fasting, prayer, the common meal, and the Lord's supper. There follows advice as to the reception of visiting apostles and on relations with itinerant or settled prophets. Mention is also made of local bishops and deacons, and the concluding chapter exhorts to watchfulness in view of the trials and dangers of the last days. The author quotes from the OT and Matthew, and has a number of reminiscences of other parts of Scripture. Certain passages suggest the language of the fourth Gospel and some point to familiarity with I Corinthians.

There is a marked Jewish flavor about the first part, which has led to the conjecture that it depends on a Jewish proselyte catechism, and C. Taylor draws attention to many parallels with Jewish teaching (*The Teaching of the Twelve Apostles with Illustrations from the Talmud*, Cambridge, 1886). This view seemed to be strengthened when it was found that the Latin ms had only the first six chapters and a conclusion not found elsewhere, and that certain other works had in common with the Didache only matter found in the first part. But it is not necessary to assume that the original form of the Didache consisted of no more than six chapters, to which the remaining chapters in the Jerusalem ms. were later added. Even if the first division is modelled on a Jewish catechism, that document may have contained also guidance about circumcision and ritual, for which a Christian writer would naturally substitute teaching appropriate to persons of his own faith. Possibly the passage 1,3–11,1, omitted in the Latin version and having no parallels in Barnabas, may have been added by a later hand; but, this apart, there appears to be no cogent reason for not accepting the Jerusalem ms. as representing substantially the original form of the Didache. Dependent writers would use no more of it than suited their immediate purpose.

However, keen debate has taken place

as to the relation between the Didache and the Epistle of Barnabas, some scholars strongly maintaining that Barnabas is earlier, and others confidently affirming the priority of the Didache. Of more recent writers on the subject, F. E. Vokes champions the former opinion, but J. Quaesten believes it cannot be conclusively established and J. A. Kleist rejects it. Among works which undoubtedly used the Didache the most obvious debtor is the Apostolic Canons, a 3rd- or 4th-century work that originated in Egypt. Here the first part is distributed among twelve apostles, each of whom speaks in turn. The seventh Book of the Apostolic Constitutions, written in Syria in the late 4th century, is another which owes much to the Didache but adapts borrowed matter to the conditions of a later age.

The Didache has been assigned to dates ranging from the last quarter of the 1st century to the first third of the 3rd century. Those who reject the priority of Barnabas and Montanist origin tend to favor, with J. B. Lightfoot, a date about the end of the 1st century or the beginning of the 2nd century. The place of origin was either Egypt or Syria, perhaps more probably the latter.

If the earlier dating is preferred, the Didache has the value of supplying a gap in our knowledge of the worship, doctrine, and ministry of the church in the transitional period between the apostolic age and the 2nd century. It is unlikely that it was written to promote or to oppose any particular heresy. The church life reflected is early but a little removed from apostolic times. Presbyters are not mentioned as distinct from bishops. Prophets are prominent, but the office is being abused. Fasting is a regular practice, and baptism by sprinkling is valid when water is not plentiful. The book purports to represent the teaching of the apostles, and it may well be the earliest specimen of a Christian catechism outside the NT.

Bibliography:

DACL, IV (Paris, 1921), cols. 747-770.
HDB, Extra Vol. (New York, 1909), 434-451.
HDAC, I (New York, 1915), 296-302.
R. H. Connolly, "The Didache in relation to the Epistle of Barnabas," *JTS*, XXXIII (1932), 227-235.
J. R. Harris, *The Teaching of the Twelve Apostles* (London, 1887).
Hitchcock and Brown, *The Teaching of the Twelve Apostles* (London, 1885).
J. A. Kleist, "The Didache," *Ancient Christian Writers*, VI (London, 1948).
J. B. Lightfoot, *The Apostolic Fathers*, ed., J. R. Harmer (London, 1898), 1, 390-391.
J. Quaesten, *Patrology*, I (Utrecht, 1950), 29-39.
F. E. Vokes, *The Riddle of the Didache*, etc. (London, 1938).

William J. Cameron

DIDASCALIA APOSTOLORUM ("Teaching of the Apostles"), a Church Order of the early 3rd century, deriving its name from the Greek word for teaching. It was probably written originally in Syria in the Greek language. The earliest extant mss are two recensions in Syriac, the first of which was partly translated by Bickell in 1843. This version is divided into 26 or 27 chapters. The writer of the *Didascalia* made use of the much more famous *Didache*, as well as the *Pericope Adulterae* (John 7:53–8:11), the Epistles of Ignatius, and other early Christian writings. In turn, the first six books of the *Apostolic Constitutions* consist of an enlarged form of the *Didascalia*. Fragments of about one third of the contents of the *Didascalia* are also extant in a Latin translation. There are also a Coptic version and two recensions in Arabic. Part of the Arabic version is quite similar to the *Testament of our Lord*. The earliest mention of the work was by Epiphanius, who considered it to be apostolic, as indeed it claims to be.

Although it is a Church Order, it is written with considerable warmth, and has a strongly ethical emphasis. The first section deals with the ideal conduct of all Christians. The next deals with the duties of pastors and bishops, especially on the matter of discipline. It advocates kindly treatment in restoring penitents to the church. The next section deals with the ministry of those officially designated as widows. The remaining sections deal with the treatment of orphans, almsgiving, confessors, martyrs, the resurrection and the judgment, heresy, and schism.

BIBLIOGRAPHY:

J. V. Bartlet, *Church-Life and Church-Order* (Oxford, 1943).

J. V. Bartlet, "Fragments of the Didascalia Apostolorum," *JTS* 18 (1916-17), 301-9.

J. W. Bickell, *Geschichte des Kirchenrechts* (Giessen, 1843), 148-159.

C. K. J. Bunsen, "Didascalia purior," *Analecta Ante-Nicaena* (London, 1854).

J. Chapman, "Didascalia Apostolorum," *CE* (New York, 1908), IV, 781-2.

R. H. Connolly, *Didascalia Apostolorum* (Oxford, 1929).

F. X. Funk, *Didascalia et Constitutiones Apostolorum* (Paderborn, 1905), 2 vols.

F. X. Funk, *Kirchengesh. Abhandlungen* (Paderborn, 1907).

F. X. Funk, "La date de la Didascalie des Apôtres," *RHE* (Oct. 1891).

P. Galtier, "La Date de la Didascalie des Apôtres," *RHE* 42 (1947), 315-51.

M. D. Gibson, *The Didascalia Apostolorum in Syriac* (London, 1903).

J. M. Harden, *The Ethiopic Didascalia* (London, 1920).

E. Hauler, *Didascalia Apostolorum fragmenta veronensia latina* (Leipzig, 1900).

K. E. Kirk, *The Apostolic Ministry* (London, 1946), 308-11.

P. A. Lagarde, *Didascalia apostolorum syriace* (Leipzig, 1854).

J. Quasten, *Patrology* (Utrecht, 1953), II, 147-52.

HARRY BUIS

DIDYMUS OF ALEXANDRIA (*c.* 311-396), called Didymus the Blind. He became blind while very young, but by great diligence Didymus mastered "Dialectics and even geometry," as Jerome relates (*Lives of Illustrious Men*, ch. 109). Because of his unusual command of Scripture and wide learning, he was placed by Athanasius at the head of the catechetical school in Alexandria, where Pantaenus and Clement had served. He was the author of many commentaries (*ibid.*). Of special interest is his influence in teaching and doctrine. He is known as a defender of Origen, but Bright (*Dictionary of Christian Biography*, I, 828) says: "In his extant writings there is no assertion of Origenian views as to the pre-existence of souls, and he affirms, more than once, the endless nature of future punishment; but he seems to have believed that some of the fallen angels occupied a midway position between angels and demons, and would ultimately be forgiven." Though he is not named, he is supposed to have been anathematized by the Fifth General Council. Probably the anathema against Origen was construed to include others more or less identified with him. Didymus' work *On the Holy Spirit* was a polemic against Macedonianism. In his commentary on I Peter he shows a dislike for chiliasm. At one time he said II Peter was not in the canon, but later admitted it as genuine. *Against the Manichaeans* disproves the existence of brute, unoriginated principles and establishes the reality of free will and responsibility. At one place, according to Bright (*ibid.*), he invokes the archangels and expresses his belief in the intercession of the saints.

WILBER B. WALLIS

DIETRICH, Veit (1506-1549), German Reformer. A native of Nuremberg, Dietrich studied at the University of Wittenberg and came under the influence of Melanchthon and Luther, several of whose works he edited and translated from Latin into German. He was one of the regular table companions of Luther and served as his personal secretary. He accompanied Luther to the Marburg Colloquy (1529) and the Augsburg Diet (1530). He participated in the Colloquy of Regensburg (1546). After a disagreement with Luther in

1535 he became the pastor at St. Sebald's Church in Nuremberg, where he repeatedly collided with Osiander, whom he considered too popish. His importance lies in his reformation of the liturgy for the developing Lutheran Church. His scheme of worship remained in force in Nuremberg for over two centuries. He objected to Roman practices such as private confession and the elevation of the elements of the Lord's supper. He was forced to resign his pastorate when he objected to the emperor's intention to re-introduce the Catholic religion (1547), and died shortly after Nüremberg bowed to the Augsburg Interim (1549). He left behind a collection of Luther's table talk, lectures, sermons, and letters. Of his own works the most popular were *Summaria über das Alte Testament* (Wittenberg, 1541) and *Summaria über die ganze Bibel* (1545).

BIBLIOGRAPHY:
RGG II, 195.
O. Dietz, *Die Evangelien-kollekten des Veit Dietrich* (Leipzig, 1930).
A. Freitag, "Veit Dietrichs Anteil an der Lutherüberlieferung," *Lutherstudien* (1917), 170-202.
G. T. Strobel, *Nachricht von dem Leben und den Schriften Veit Dietrichs* (Nuremberg, 1772).
W. G. Tillmanns, *The World and Men Around Luther* (Minneapolis, 1959).

ALBERT H. FREUNDT, JR.

DIKLAH, a derivative from the word *dekel*, meaning date tree. The name Diklah is thought to refer to an Arabian date-raising area. In Scripture Diklah is mentioned as the name of one of Joktan's sons (Gen. 10:27; I Chron. 1:21).

DILEAN (Dilan, RV), a S city allotted to Judah (Josh. 15:38), located in the Shephelah (lowlands). Grollenberg suggests that today it is named Tell en-Najileh (L. H. Grollenberg, *The Atlas of the Bible*, Melbourne, 1957, Map 13, p. 147).

DIMNAH, "dung," a city with suburbs given to the Levites within the Zebulun area (Josh. 21:34, 35). Some scholars identify Dimnah with Rimmon, explaining it as a scribal error. Though Dimnah's location is entirely unknown today, the likelihood of a scribal error is small.

DINAH, one of Jacob's daughters. Jacob evidently had several daughters (Gen. 37:35; 46:7), but Dinah is the only one whose name is known. She was born to Leah in Haran (Gen. 30:21) and was apparently her only daughter (Gen. 46:15). The only details known about her, besides her birth and her migration to Egypt with her family, are given in Gen. 34. This relates her seduction by Shechem ben Hamor, a Hivite (Hurrian, see LXX) prince of Shechem. The indignant reaction of her family points to the high moral standards of the patriarchs in contrast with the contemporary inhabitants of Canaan, even though the deceitfulness and violence of the revenge taken by her brothers, Simeon and Levi, are not to be condoned (Gen. 49:5). Their proposition of circumcision for the Shechemites is evidence of its early general practice.

The suggestion has often been made that Gen. 34 is composed of several traditions in which Dinah is merely an eponym, standing for a shadowy Israelite tribe that figures in the struggle of other tribes for central Palestine, but otherwise unknown. However, the story may be taken as it stands. Although it is true that the negotiations of the Israelites with Hamor and Shechem have political features, there is nothing to prevent all characters being identified as individuals. The proposal of Cheyne that Dinah's death was recorded in the original text of Gen. 35:8 is baseless. No convincing etymological connection of the name Dinah with "judgment" has yet been made.

BIBLIOGRAPHY:
E. Nielsen, *Shechem: A Traditio-Historical Investigation* (Copenhagen, 2nd ed., 1959).
FRANCIS I. ANDERSEN

DINHABAH, Edom's royal city in the days of King Bela, son of Beor (Gen. 36:32; I Chron. 1:43). Its exact location is unknown today.

DIOCESE, the district administered by a bishop. This has been the fixed meaning since the 9th century. Before that period the word used for a bishop's district seems to have been *parochia.* Long used in the Roman Empire, *diocese* came, in the time of Diocletian (early in the 4th century), to mean one of the 12 major divisions of the empire. In the Christian empire the ecclesiastical diocese or *parochia* often coincided with the civil district. In E Christendom *parochia* is still used for the bishop's area of administration; but *diocese* is used for a larger or *patriarchal* area, which in the W is called a *province.*

A diocese is a unit with a see-town, from which it usually takes its name, e.g., Canterbury, Armagh, and Lyons. In new areas of episcopal churches the name of a diocese may be the name of the area itself rather than the name of the see-town. A diocese may be divided into archdeaconries and rural deaneries. A bishop may appoint vicars-general and assign them to some important powers of administration. Diocesan courts exist, and diocesan synods and conferences of diocesan clergy may be held.

DIOCLETIAN (245-313), Roman emperor. A native of Salona, in Dalmatia, and of humble birth, he was made emperor of Rome by the army in 284. At first he was a wise and heroic ruler and defeated Carinius in Moesia (286) and conquered the Allemanni. Because of dangers to the empire, he associated Maximian with himself as "Augustus" of the W, while he personally ruled the E from Nicomedia, with Galerius helping him as "Caesar." Constantius Chlorus assisted Maximian in the W as "Caesar" and ruled Britain, Gaul, and Spain. This arrangement led to great successes against the barbarians, who were becoming a peril.

Diocletian was beloved by his subjects and, in spite of much pressure, did not persecute the Christians for 18 years, realizing that they were now powerful even in the army. In the palace and in the state, Christians were in the highest posts, some being governors of provinces, and even Diocletian's wife and daughter were Christians. After 40 years of peace the church was strong numerically and splendid edifices for worship were built in most cities. In the army, however, many Christians suffered grievously under military discipline for not participating in the pagan practices of the legions. The chief blame for the persecution which began in 303, under Diocletian, must be attached to his colleague Galerius, who along with others persuaded the aging emperor to begin what was the worst of all the persecutions. The first edict ordered the destruction of places of worship and sacred books, and ordained that Christians be dispossessed of all honors and dignities, and be liable to cruel torture. The prefect and the soldiers, on entering the magnificent church at Nicomedia, were amazed to find no figure of the Deity. The furniture and communion vessels were pillaged and the building razed. When there was opposition to such proceedings, men were seized, tortured, and sometimes burned alive.

A second edict ordered the arrest of all officials of the church, and the prisons were crammed full of bishops, presbyters, deacons, and others, until there was no room for criminals. Where Diocletian ruled directly, the measures were somewhat mild; but in Syria, under Galerius, scourging, torture, and death were inflicted on Christians for attending worship and for refusing to surrender the Scriptures.

In 305 Diocletian and Maximian abdicated the throne. The former retired to his birthplace, where he died in peace in 313. Constantius, who then became emperor, ended the persecution in the W, but it continued in the E for another ten years.

BIBLIOGRAPHY:

P. Allard, *La Persécution de Dioclétian et le Triomphe de l'Église* (Paris, 1890).

Eusebius of Caesarea, *Ecclesiastical History*, trans. by A. C. McGiffert in *Nicene and Post Nicene Fathers* (1890), VIII.

E. Gibbon, *The Decline and Fall of the Roman Empire*, ed. by J. B. Bury (London, 1908), Chapters XIII, XVI, XVII.

A. J. Mason, *The Persecution of Diocletian* (Cambridge, 1876).

H. M. Gwatkin, *Early Church History* (London, 1909), II, 323-339.

B. J. Kidd, *History of the Church* (Oxford, 1922), Vol. I, Chapter XIII.

V. Schultze, in Herzog—Hauck's Realencyklopädie (1898), IV, sv.

A. M. RENWICK

DIODATI, Giovanni (1576-1649), Calvinist theologian. Born in Geneva of an Italian Protestant refugee family, he became Hebrew professor (1597) and pastor (1608) there before succeeding Beza as professor of theology (1609), which was a post he held till his death. He was also Genevese representative at the Synod of Dort. Diodati's Italian translation of the Bible appeared in 1607, a revised edition with notes in 1641. This version is still commonly used by Italian Protestants. Of great accuracy and lucidity, it nevertheless displays also his own theological tendencies. He produced also a French translation of the Bible in 1644.

DIODORUS (*c*. 330-*c*. 390), bishop of Tarsus. Diodorus founded the later school of Antioch and was one of the champions of orthodoxy against Arianism. Probably born at Antioch, he received a liberal education at Athens and later became a disciple of Eusebius of Emesa. Returning to Antioch, he held secret services at night (prior to his ordination) because the bishop of the city, Leontius, was an Arian. When the succeeding and orthodox bishop, Meletius, was forced to flee to Armenia, Diodorus took charge of the situation. When Julian the Apostate tried to make Antioch a center for the revival of paganism, Diodorus attacked him both in sermons and in writings. Later, the Arian Valens forbade the orthodox to meet in the city, so Diodorus gathered his people in a church outside the walls. Being forced from this edifice, he gathered worshipers in whatever places he could. He served as presbyter in the city, but in 372 was forced to flee and join Meletius in exile in Armenia. There he came under the influence of Basil the Great.

In 378, having returned from exile, Diodorus became bishop of Tarsus. He participated in the Council of Antioch (379) and that of Constantinople (381), continuing to exert his influence on behalf of the Nicene faith. By decree of Emperor Theodosius (381), communion with Diodorus and several other E ecclesiastical leaders became a test of orthodoxy. Upon the death of Meletius, Diodorus helped in the appointment of his friend Flavian as bishop of Antioch, an act which brought him into extreme disfavor with the bishops of the W. Diodorus is also noted for being a forerunner in the development of a historico-grammatical form of exegesis in contrast to the allegorizing methods which prevailed in his day. However, sometimes he had a tendency to over-rationalistic explanations.

In opposing Apollinarianism, he tended to go to the opposite extreme and thus became the forerunner of the Nestorian heresy. His attempt to solve the problem of the two natures of Christ led him to a position where he thought that the

Logos resided in the man Jesus as in a temple or a garment. For him, the union of the two natures was external and moral rather than substantial. The son of David was conceived by Mary, but the Logos of God was not. In effect, he divided Christ into two persons, rather than affirming one person with two natures. As a result, after his death, Cyril of Alexandria and later Flavian III of Antioch sought his condemnation. These attacks led the Nestorians to hold him in high esteem.

Most of the writings of Diodorus were lost as a result of this suspicion of heresy. He had written commentaries on most of the books of the Bible. His many polemical works included writings against Plato, Aristotle, Sabellius, Photinus, Marcellus, the Manichaeans, the Eunomians, and the Apollinarians. Photius gives an elaborate summary of his writings. One of his best-known works was *Contra Fatum.* Theodore of Mopsuestia, Theodoret, and Chrysostom were among his pupils. Diodorus placed a strong emphasis upon rigid monasticism and lived such an extremely ascetic life that Chrysostom called him a "living martyr."

Bibliography:

MPG XXXIII, 1545-1627.

B. Altaner, *Patrologie* (Freiburg, 2nd ed., 1950).

R. Ceillier, *Histoire Generale des auteurs sacres et ecclesiastiques* (Paris, 1863-5), V, 586 ff.

J. Chapman, "Diodorus," *CE* II (1909), 8.

J. A. Fabricius, *Bibliotheca Graeca* (Hamburg, 1705-1728), IX, 277-282.

P. Godet, *DThC* IV (1911), cols. 1363-6.

A. Harnack, "Diodor von Tarsus," *TU* (1901), N.F. VI, 4.

A. Harnack, "Diodorus," *SHERK* III, 435-6.

P. Sherwood, *EC* IV (1950), cols. 1657-60.

Socrates, "Hist. eccl.," vi, 3, *The Nicene and Post-Nicene Fathers,* 2nd series (New York, 1890-1900), II.

S. H. Sozomen, "Hist. eccl.," viii, 2, *The Nicene and Post-Nicene Fathers,* 2nd series (New York, 1890-1900), II.

Theodoret, "Hist. eccl.," iv, 22-24, *The Nicene and Post-Nicene Fathers* (New York, 1890-1900), III

C. H. Turner, "Patristic Commentaries," *HDB* extra volume (1904), 500-501.

E. Venables, "Diodorus," *DCB* I (1877), 836-40.

HARRY BUIS

DIOGNETUS, The Epistle to, an anonymous letter addressed to Diognetus, generally dated in the second or early 3rd century. The only ms, dating from the 13th or 14th century, was kept at Strasbourg, where it was destroyed by war in 1870. However, prior to its destruction, several copies were made by H. Stephanus (Paris, 1592) and others. Lightfoot called it "the noblest of early Christian writings." It gives indication of both Pauline and Johannine influences. At first it was mistakenly attributed to Justin Martyr. Though the authorship is unknown, considerable evidence favors Asia Minor as its origin. The letter consists of 12 chapters, the last two of which seem to have been appended from another document.

The purpose of the letter was apologetic. The writer describes the superiority of Christianity over pagan idolatry and the religion of the Jews. He claims that the Christian faith is not the result of the discovery of man but that it is a revelation sent by God through His Son, whom he describes as "the Designer and Maker of the universe himself." The author of the last two chapters claims to have been "a disciple of the apostles."

Bibliography:

B. Altaner, *Patrologie* (Freiburg, 2nd ed., 1950).

J. A. Kleist, *Ancient Christian Writers,* vol. 6 (Westminster, Maryland, 1948), 125-147, 210-221.

J. B. Lightfoot, *Apostolic Fathers,* 5 vols. (1886-1890).

C. C. Richardson, *Early Christian Fathers* (Philadelphia, 1953), 205-224.

HARRY BUIS

DIONYSIUS ("THE GREAT") OF ALEXANDRIA (d. *c.* 264), a notable scholar and leader of the early church. He was a pupil of Origen, succeeded Hereclas as head of the Catechetical School at Alexandria (232), became bishop of Alexandria (247), and suffered banishment in the Decian persecution (250) and again in the Valerian persecution (257). He engaged in many controversies. He argued for readmission of the lapsed into the church and against the rebaptism of heretics. Opposing Sabellianism, he was accused of tritheism; but Athanasius defended him. His exegetical skill was widely recognized, and he is remembered today mainly on account of his critical view of the authorship of the Apocalypse. While holding that it was the work of a holy man, he believed that it could not have been written by the same person as the writer of the Fourth Gospel, which he attributed to the Apostle John, because the styles were so dissimilar.

BIBLIOGRAPHY:
DHGE XIV, 248-253.
MPG X, 1233-1344, 1575-1602.
O. Bardenhewer, *Geschichte der Altkirchlichen Literatur* (Freiburg, 1903-1924), II, 167-191.
J. Chapman, *CE*, s.v.
F. Dittrich, *Dionysius der Grosse von Alexandrien* (Freiburg, 1867).
C. L. Feltoe, *Critical Edition*, Cambridge Patristic Texts (Cambridge, 1904).
P. S. Miller, *Studies in Dionysius the Great* (Erlangen, 1933).
M. Pellegrino, *EC*[12] (Rome, 1949-1954), IV, col. 1661-1662.
B. F. Westcott, *DCB*[4] (London, 1877), I, 850-852.

WILLIAM J. CAMERON

DIONYSIUS THE AREOPAGITE, an Athenian convert of the Apostle Paul. The only mention of this Dionysius is in Acts 17:34. Eusebius claims that Dionysius of Corinth names Dionysius the Areopagite as the first bishop of Athens. Suidas gives a fuller account of his life, and Aristides the Apologist says that he was martyred at Athens. Mystical writings which were written no earlier than the 5th century were falsely attributed to him and had a strong influence on the thought of Christians during the Middle Ages.

BIBLIOGRAPHY:
N. Bonwetsch, "Dionysius the Areopagite," *SHERK* III, 438-440.
Eusebius, *Nicene and Post Nicene Fathers* (New York, 1890), I, 137, 138, 200.
J. Stiglmayr, "Dionysius the Pseudo-Areopagite," *CE* (New York, 1908), V, 13-18.
B. F. Westcott, *Essays in the History of Religious Thought in the West* (London, 1891), 142-193.

HARRY BUIS

DIONYSIUS EXIGUUS, 6th century Scythian monk and scholar. The name "Exiguus" means "little" and refers either to stature or to humility. He brought Greek learning to Rome by assembling a collection of important canons (laws), in two recensions, and a collection of decretals. Both of these were used extensively at Rome. He also continued the Easter Table of Cyril of Alexandria and thus introduced the E computation into the W church, where it gradually became the accepted method for calculations of the date of Easter. In these computations, Dionysius began dating the years from the Incarnation of Christ. However, he set the birth of Christ at 753 A.U.C. (years after the traditional founding of Rome), thereby introducing an error of several years which continues in our present system. Dionysius also translated some of the writings of the scholars of the E church.

BIBLIOGRAPHY:
MPL 67 (Paris, 1844-64), 9-520.
H. Achelis, "Dionysius Exiguus," *The New Schaff-Herzog Religious Encyclopedia* III, 441, 442.
M. A. Cassiodorus, *Institutiones divinarum et saecularium litterarum*, Vol. I, chapter 23.
B. Krusch, "Dionysius Exiguus, der Begrunder der Christlichen Ara," *Studien zur Christlich mittelalterlichen Chronologie* (Berlin, 1938).
F. Maassen, *Geschichte der Quellen und der Literatur des kanonischen Rechts* (Graz, 1870), I, 130-136, 422-440, 960-965.
R. Oudin, *Commentarius de scriptoribus ecclesiae antiquis* (Leipzig, 1722), I, 1405 ff.
F. Ruhl, *Chronologie* (Berlin, 1897), 129 ff.
W. Smith and H. Wace, *Dictionary of Christian Biography* (Boston, 1877-87), I, 853, 854.
A. Strewe, *Die Canonensammlung des Diony-*

sius Exiguus in der ersten Redaktion (1931).
C. H. Turner, *Ecclesiae occidentalis monumenta* (Oxford, 1899), Vol. I.
H. Wurm, *Studien und Texte sur Dekretalensammlung des Dionysius Exiguus* (1939).

HARRY BUIS

DIONYSIUS THE PSEUDO-AREOPAGITE, a mystic of the late 5th century who used the name of Paul's convert of Acts 17:34 (Dionysius the Areopagite). The approximate date is determined by the fact that in the works of this pseudo-Dionysius, *Mystical Theology* and *Divine Names,* he paraphrases material from the Neoplatonic philosopher Proclus (A.D. 410-485) and shows a knowledge of the *Henotikon* of Emperor Zeno (A.D. 482). Neoplatonism mainly held two theses, that God is unknowable and evil is not a reality. The *Henotikon* was an edict attempting to unify divergent Christian factions.

Two quotations will give a sample of his mysticism:

Mystic Theology 1:1: "Triad supernal, both super-God and super-good, Guardian of the theosophy of Christian men, direct us aright to the super-unknown and super-brilliant and highest summit of the mystic oracles, where the simple and absolute and changeless mysteries of theology lie hidden within the superluminous gloom of the silence, revealing hidden things, which in its deepest darkness shines above the most super-brilliant, and in the altogether impalpable and invisible fills to overflowing the eyeless minds with glories of surpassing beauty."

Divine Names 2:10: "Deity of our Lord Jesus, the cause and completing of all, which preserves the parts concordant with the whole, and is neither part nor whole, as embracing in itself everything both whole and part, and being above and before, perfect indeed in the imperfect as source of perfection, but imperfect in the perfect as super-perfect and preperfect, form producing form in things without form as the source of form, formless in the forms as above form, essence penetrating without stain the essences throughout, and super-essential, exalted above every essence, setting bounds to all principalities and orders, and established in every principality and order."

Because of the ignorance of the Dark Ages and the decadent state of Christianity, these books were accepted as genuine writings of the original Dionysius. Since he was assumed to echo the thought of the Apostle Paul, a considerable amount of Neoplatonic paganism was thus introduced into the thought of the church. In the later Middle Ages John Scotus Eriugena (810-877) reinforced the Neoplatonic influence by translating the pseudo-Dionysius into Latin and commenting on it. Even Thomas Aquinas (1224-1274) was deceived, wrote a commentary, and adopted some Neoplatonic ideas along with his general Aristotelianism.

See MYSTICISM; NEGATIVE THEOLOGY.

GORDON H. CLARK

DIONYSIUS OF ROME (d. 268), bishop of Rome from 259 to 268. Dionysius' most important contribution to theology was his pronouncement concerning the doctrine of the person of Christ. Dionysius of Alexandria, in writing against Sabellianism, moved too far in the opposite direction. As a result, Christians in Alexandria brought charges against him to Dionysius of Rome. The latter made a statement in which on the one hand he attacked Sabellianism and on the other he condemned the extremes of anti-Sabellianism. Earlier, Dionysius had taken part in a controversy concerning heretical baptism, and later he sent a noted letter of sympathy to the church of Caesarea, which suffered from the attack of the Goths upon Cappadocia.

BIBLIOGRAPHY:

O. Bardenhewer, *Geschichte der Altkirchlichen Litteratur* (Freiburg, 1902), II, 581, 582.
A. Bower, *History of the Popes* (London, 1748), I, 35-37.
I. A. Dorner, *History of the Development of the Doctrine of the Person of Christ* (Edinburgh, 1861-63), II, 182 ff.
H. Hagemann, "Das Lehrschreiben des Papstes Dionysius," *Die romische Kirche und ihr Einflutz* (Freiburg, 1864), 432-453.
J. P. Migne, *Patrologiae cursus completus*

series Latina (Paris, 1844-64), V, 99-136.
J. A. W. Neander, *Christian Church* I, 606-610.
P. Schaff, *History of the Christian Church* (New York, 1911), II, 570-571.

HARRY BUIS

DIOSCURI, the twin stars of the Zodiac constellation Gemini. There is only one mention of the Dioscuri in the Bible, Acts 28:11. Here the translators of the AV did not transliterate the Greek word, but gave instead the names of the twin stars thus represented, i.e., "Castor and Pollux." These bright stars could be seen overhead by sailors in Mediterranean waters throughout much of the year.

In mythology the Dioscuri were the twin sons of the god Zeus and the goddess Leda. Castor was famed as a tamer of horses and Pollux as the master of boxers. Thus these brave and agile twin sons became the patron and tutelary gods of youths. They also came to be the patrons of sailors. Sailors were to call upon them in times of storm, and, upon deliverance, sacrifice a lamb to them.

The Alexandrian vessel in which Paul and Luke sailed from Malta (Melita) to Rome (actually disembarking at Puteoli, which is 100 miles S of Rome) had the Dioscuri for its sign. The faces of these Dioscuri twins may have been carved upon the wooden prow of the ship.

GARY G. COHEN

DIOTREPHES (nursling of Zeus), an unattractive, ambitious man, mentioned only in III John 9. His name may indicate connection with the aristocracy. He loved taking the lead in the congregation, where he probably held office. He objected to providing hospitality for certain itinerant preachers whom John highly commended, and aimed at the excommunication of all who made them welcome. Moreover, he spoke spitefully among the people about John himself. Although the epistle does not charge him with heresy, it warns that John will call him to account for his presumptuous, malicious, and high-handed behavior, and that his evil example should not be followed.

WILLIAM J. CAMERON

DIPHATH, son of Gomer and grandson of Japheth, third son of Noah (I Chron. 1:6, ARV). In the corresponding genealogy in Gen. 10:3 he is called Riphath. The AV has Riphath in both passages.

See RIPHATH.

DISCIPLE. The term "disciple" comes from the Latin *discipulus*, in turn derived from the verb *discere*, "to learn." A disciple is therefore a pupil, as distinguished from his teacher. But equally essential to the word is the element of adherence, conformity of life to the doctrine learned. The Greek μαθητής (*mathētēs*) has the same meaning.

In the Scriptures the word is found almost exclusively in the NT, appearing but once in the OT (Isa. 8:16). Following rabbinical and Greek usage, the NT designates by this term the adherents of John the Baptist (Mark 2:18), of the Pharisees (Mt. 22:16), and most frequently of Jesus, who chose it as the first name for His followers (Mt. 26:18). Although found more than 250 times, it is confined to the Gospels and Acts. In the Gospels it has a double significance, referring (1) to the large company of Jesus' followers in general (Luke 19:37) and (2) to the twelve apostles in particular (Mt. 10:1). In Acts, however, it is simply synonymous with Christian (Acts 11:26). In Acts, too, we note the transition from disciple (30 times) to the common apostolic designations of "saint" (four times) and "brethren" (about 32 times, not including addresses, and mostly in the latter half of the book). As the departure of Jesus receded further into the past, the Christian's calling to sainthood and his relationship with the brotherhood came into greater prominence; hence, the transition.

Outside of Christianity the disciple's faith and devotion were directed not to the person of his teacher, but to a tradition. By way of contrast, the Christian's first allegiance is to the Person of Christ (Mark 2:14) and then consequently to the Master's doctrine (John 8:31). The term itself, however, does not necessarily imply a regenerate character but is employed comprehensively to include all who sustained any external relationship to Christ (John 6:66, also the numbering of Judas among the Twelve).

BIBLIOGRAPHY:

A. B. Bruce, *The Training of the Twelve* (New York; 3rd ed., n.d.).

G. P. Gould, "Disciple," *HDCG* I (New York, 1911), 457-459.

J. G. Greenough, *The Apostles of Our Lord* (London, 1904).

H. Latham, *Pastor Pastorum* (Cambridge, 1891), 228-310.

A. Plummer, "Disciple," *HDAC* I (New York, 1916), 302-303.

RICHARD A. BODEY

In spite of its broad general usage and the fact that the word "disciple" occurs only in the Gospels and Acts, discipleship has a very important place in Christian teaching. It is found in the Lord's last words to His apostles (Mt. 28:19-20), and hence to the church to the end of the age (vs. 20). The charge that the Lord Jesus Christ left was to make disciples. In evangelism this means that the Lord is not pleased with mere converts, even if they are believed to be true converts. In church order and discipline it means that baptism, which is given as a step of discipleship, cannot be thought to be a secondary matter. It also means that in baptism the Lord is not pleased with a mere profession, even a valid testimony to a real Christian experience. In Christian education it means that the Lord is not pleased with mere knowledge, even if it is doctrinally correct, but is looking for the church to get its people to apply their knowledge, to know Him by the experience of following in His steps (I Pet. 2:21).

DISCIPLES OF CHRIST, a group of churches related to or derived from an early 19th-century movement that sought to break away from the denominationalism, which, it was held, had fragmented the body of believers. Instead of seeking to improve the denominational system, the leaders of this movement sought to restore in their worship, organization, and life the pattern of NT Christianity by going back beyond all the innovations and departures of the centuries to the authority of Christ Himself. They accepted Jesus Christ as the Son of God, the Savior of the world, and Lord. The central message of the faith they proclaimed was His Divine Sonship, His crucifixion that men might have eternal life, His resurrection, His headship of His church, and His Second Coming. They believed the Bible to be inspired of God, that the OT was "a tutor to bring us to Christ" (Gal. 3:24), and that we are only under the NT, which contains the final and complete revelation from God to man (John 16:13; II Tim. 3:16, 17; Jude 3).

The sermon by Peter on the Day of Pentecost converted 3,000 who believed that Jesus Christ was the Son of God and Savior, repented of their sins, confessed their faith in Him as Lord, and showed their obedience and submission to Him by being buried with Him in baptism for the remission of sins. They proclaimed that the same message accepted in the same way will make Christians in this century or any age.

Following the apostolic church, where the organization was kept at a minimum, they shunned a central organization or headquarters. Each local congregation was self-governing or autonomous, but sought to be united with other groups of believers in fellowship and love. Congregations cooperated as they chose in mission work and benevolence.

The Restoration Movement

Beginning in 1740 there swept through the American colonies a religious revival known as the "Great Awakening," with such men as Jonathan Edwards and George Whitefield as leaders. But at the end of that century there seemed to be a general unconcern for religion and a growth of skepticism. Perhaps this extreme condition contributed to the extreme reaction that followed in the "Second Awakening," or the "Great Revival of the West" of 1800. People on the frontier, who had not heard a preacher often, and many of whom had read little if any of the Bible, responded to the revival method of evangelism, which has been called uniquely American. This awakening was the forerunner of the restoration movement. Barton W. Stone was a leader of one of the main streams of the restoration movement. As early as 1798, when asked to receive the Confession of Faith he replied that he would accept it as far as he thought it was consistent with the Bible. In 1802 he was suspended from the Presbyterian Church and united with four other preachers to form the Springfield Presbytery. In their charter they agreed to give up all man-made creeds and party names and accept the name "Christian." Within a year even this organization was dissolved by a curious document entitled "The Last Will and Testament of the Springfield Presbytery." It declared for the right of self-government for each congregation, insisted on the Bible as the only "sure guide to heaven," and protested against the divisions and party spirit among professing Christians (W. W. Jennings, *Origin and Early History of the Disciples of Christ*, p. 66). Thus, without any denominational connections, Stone continued to preach what he was convinced was undenominational Christianity, gathering to his standard thousands of followers in Kentucky and nearby states. Nearly 30,000 people responded to his message.

Although Stone led the earliest large restoration movement to try to re-establish NT Christianity, his was not the only stream of this action. There was widespread sentiment, especially on the frontier, for the renunciation of human creeds in favor of the Bible as the only guide in faith and practice, interpreted by the individual conscience (A. T. De Groot, *The Grounds of Division Among the Churches of Christ*, p. 11; D. E. Walker, in *Adventuring for Christian Unity*, p. 87, states that there were "six streams of Christian action . . . in origin quite distinct" which contributed to the Disciples and Churches of Christ today).

In point of time, probably the first sizeable group was among the Methodists of North Carolina. They were led by a frontier preacher named James O' Kelly. In 1792 he led a minority against the Methodist Conference of Manchester, Virginia. He writes that he took a NT in his hand and said, "Brethren, hearken unto me, put away all other books and forms and let this be the only criterion, and that will satisfy me" (W. F. Mac Clenny, *The Life of Reverend James O'Kelly*, p. 91). The next year he withdrew with several other preachers, forming the "Republican Methodist Church," with about 1,000 members. The name signifies their belief in the republican rather than the episcopal form of church government. But this name was later dropped because they preferred to be called simply Christians.

In 1809 these people in North Carolina and Virginia discovered a similar group in New England. Nine years before, Abner Jones, a Baptist in Vermont, had become concerned about "sectarian names and human creeds" (A. H. Newman, *A History of the Baptist Churches in the United States*, p. 502). In 1802, Elias Smith, a Baptist preacher in New Hampshire, adopted the same views and the two groups were united in 1811. In spite of the difficulties of travel and communication, by 1820 these two groups were generally united in purpose and name with the Christian action under Barton W. Stone. Thus before the days of the outstanding leadership of Thomas and Alexander Campbell, Stone was the leader of what has been estimated at some 50,000 people.

In addition to the main currents which later joined with the Campbells, there were two other sources: the Indiana Free Baptist churches and the Scotch Baptists of the North Atlantic States. In 1813 an association of Free Baptist Churches was formed, which soon dropped the name Baptist and adopted the Bible as their only creed. The following year they dissolved the association and later united with some of Stone's and Campbell's followers (Walker, *op. cit.*, p. 19).

This is typical of the procedure often repeated in Kentucky, Indiana, Virginia, and North Carolina. Alexander Campbell acknowledged priority of an association of Baptist churches in his state, which proclaimed restoration ideals in 1805 ("History," *Millennial Harbinger*, 1831, p. 101). The church that claims to be the oldest congregation of the movement in continuous existence, traces its origin to the Scotch Baptists. This church in New York City was organized in 1810 after the order of independent Scotch Baptist congregations, which held essentially the restoration concept and which had been influenced by John Glas and his son-in-law, Robert Sandeman, around 1730. Several other congregations in the E sprang from the same root and later swelled the growth of the restoration tide.

The Campbells

This brief account of these various distinct movements toward a common goal emphasizes the receptive attitude of a large body of believers to the teaching and leadership of the Campbells. "Thomas Campbell and his son, Alexander, capitalized on the labors of these epidisciples, rallied their scattered forces, publicized their principles by the press, and debates, and great preaching, breathed into their proudly independent churches the spiritual bonds of a kindred purpose, and multiplied their number," so they have become the largest religious group indigenous to America (DeGroot, *op. cit.*, p. 48). Alexander Campbell made two major contributions to the restoration movement. He provided promotional leadership, and he led the way in advocating that a higher value be placed on the NT at a time when most were insisting that every book of the Bible was of equal value.

Thomas Campbell, Alexander's father, born 1763, was minister of the Anti-Burgher Seceder Presbyterian Church at Ahorey, N Ireland. As early as 1804 he was promoting a unity movement between the Burgher and Anti-Burgher branches of his church. He also came in contact with such evangelists as Rowland Hill and James Haldane and joined the Evangelical Society, which was an outgrowth of the work of Whitefield and Wesley and promoted by the Haldanes. In 1807 Thomas Campbell came to America for his health. His family started out to join him in the next year, but because of a shipwreck they spent the winter in Glasgow, where Alexander studied in the University.

When the family arrived in America they found that Thomas Campbell was already well on the way to revolting against denominationalism. He had been officially censured by the Presbyterian church for partaking of the Seceder communion service. Through the force of his personal influence in Washington and Allegheny counties of W Pennsylvania, he continued to preach to large crowds. At the home of Abraham Altars he and a number of friends organized the Christian Association of Washington, August 17, 1809 (Jennings, *op. cit.*, p. 117). For this group Thomas Campbell prepared what has been called the "magna charta" of the restoration movement, his *Declaration and Address.* This was on the press when his son, Alexander, arrived in America. He had been thinking along the same lines and immediately joined his father in their lifelong crusade for the principles that were enunciated in this address.

The introductory paragraph plainly stated that the Washington society did "by no means consider itself a church . . . nor the members as at all associated for the peculiar purposes of church associations; but merely as voluntary advocates of Church reformation." The principal plea was for unity among all Christians, and the principal premise was that the NT contained the "blue prints and specifications" of the one church. The rule for the society which Mr. Campbell had already proposed was: "Where the Scriptures speak, we speak; and where the Scriptures are silent, we are silent." This became the watchword for the restoration movement.

Growth of Independency

Upon his father's advice, Alexander began an intensive program of Bible study for six months during the winter of 1810. On July 15, 1810, he preached his first sermon, and from that time on his services were often in demand. It is interesting to note that he had determined to take no remuneration for preaching, and throughout a half century of preaching he followed this rule rigidly. A petition was made to the Presbyterian synod of Pittsburgh to admit Thomas Campbell into their communion. The petition was denied. This resulted in the first separate organization of these reform-minded Presbyterians as a church. At Brush Run, Pennsylvania, on May 4, 1811, 29 members, led by the Campbells, organized as an independent church. Following a careful study of the NT in regard to baptism, Thomas and Alexander Campbell, their wives, and three others were immersed by a Baptist preacher on a simple confession of faith in Christ. The result was that Brush Run church became a Baptist church, joining the Redstone Baptist Association. Ten years later, through some opposition to Campbell's teaching by the Redstone group, the Brush Run church entered the Mahoning Association (Abbott, *op. cit.*, p. 12).

In 1823 Alexander Campbell enlarged his agitation for reform through the pages of a new periodical, *The Christian Baptist.* He vigorously attacked all man-made innovations in the churches. His plea was for a restoration of an ideal NT church based on the Bible as the only rule of faith and practice. It was in these years that he became the spiritual progenitor of the present-day Disciples of Christ. By 1827 it was obvious that the Baptists were dividing over the teachings of Campbell. Individual churches such as those in Frankfort, Kentucky, and Nashville, Tennessee, repudiated their creeds and set out on a policy of restoring the "ancient order" of NT practice. Whole associations of Baptist churches, such as the Mahoning Association, were so permeated by Campbell's teaching that they dissolved their association, as the Springfield Presbytery had done under Stone's influence (Garrison, *op. cit.*, p. 128).

By 1830 the break with the Baptist fellowship was complete, and in 1832 the followers of Campbell and of Stone united. Following this union the movement grew tremendously to perhaps 350,000 in 1870. The name of Campbell's paper had been changed to *Millennial Harbinger*, and from 1830 to 1870 was the backbone of the movement's literature.

It is significant that the movement continued to grow in the decade of the Civil War. From the census in 1860 it appears that their strength was well divided between the sections, the North having some 1,241 churches and the South, 829. Ranking seventh in size of churches at that time and growing more rapidly than any, this young denomination was presented with the serious problem of unity in the midst of the Civil War. The solution was found in the distinction between faith and opinion. Although most of the papers were pacifistic, the rank and file of the membership took up arms as a matter of religious opinion, leaving others the right to a different opinion as to which side they chose, or as to whether they wished to fight at all. Thus, although there were some loyalty resolutions passed by the N churches, the Christians were not divided and emerged from the war with a threefold increase of their 1850 membership.

Division

Although unity could be maintained in the face of political disunity, division finally came over what were considered matters of faith by some and opinion by others. The result was a separation of the Churches of Christ from the Disciples, or Christian Churches. Alexander Campbell had promoted two fundamental principles: the union of all Christians and the NT as the only true basis for such a union. The Disciples chose to emphasize the first of these principles, saying less and less about the second. The Churches of Christ chose to emphasize the second principle, making the desirability of a union of all believers secondary.

The controversy centered in matters of inter-congregational cooperation through a missionary society and in the use of instrumental music in church worship. The Churches of Christ held that missionary work should be done under the supervision of the local church with other congregations cooperating if they desired to do so. They contended that a formal missionary society apart from the local congregation was un-Scriptural.

In 1968, the name "Churches of Christ (Disciples of Christ)" was changed to "The Christian Church (Disciples of Christ)."

See CAMPBELL, ALEXANDER.

DISCIPLINE, ECCLESIASTICAL

Its Nature

Ecclesiastical discipline is the censure by the church's office-bearers of those members who have committed some grave sin and are unrepentant. This discipline differs from civil punishment in that it is of a *spiritual* nature and is executed by spiritual means only (warning, admonition, censure, excommunication). Its fundamental principle is not the vindication of justice or retribution, but the correction and salvation of the sinner. Its purpose is threefold: (1) to prevent the blasphemy of God's name by the world; (2) to safeguard the church itself against the bad influence of the unfaithful; (3) to move the sinner to repentance (Calvin).

Its Foundation in Scripture

It is based on clear NT teaching: (a) *General* statements. Christ gave the power of the keys to His church (Mt. 16:19—Peter; Mt. 18:18—the whole congregation). After the resurrection He gave to His apostles the power to forgive or retain sins (John 20:23). These statements are the general scriptural foundation of ecclesiastical discipline. (b) *Specific* passages.

Paul commands excommunication (I Cor. 5:2, 13) and re-admission (II Cor. 2:7) of sinners in Corinth (cf. also Rom. 16:17, 18; I Thess. 5:14; I Tim. 5:1, 2; Rev. 2:20). In some passages the congregation is told not to have any fellowship with heretics and such as have forsaken the Lord (cf. Tit. 3:10, 11; II John 10; Rev. 2:14-16).

Its History

In the ancient church, discipline was taken very seriously. Gross sinners were not only barred from the Lord's table, but sometimes even deprived of such benefits of external worship as public prayer. More than once even emperors were denied communion (Maximus and Theodosius the Great, both by Ambrose). During the Middle Ages discipline increasingly became a political weapon and thus was externalized. It was extended, not only to persons, but to impersonal objects as well (buildings, lands, books, etc.); not only to persons in the church, but also outside the church; not only to individuals, but also to whole regions or even countries; not only to the living, but also to the dead (heretics, false teachers, etc.). The Reformers rejected this externalization and returned to a spiritual, scriptural discipline. Luther emphasized it more than once in his writings. Unfortunately, the Lutheran churches on the whole have been rather lax in their disciplinary practice, largely because of their concept of the "national church." Calvin strongly emphasized it, although he refused to make it one of the marks of the true church. In the churches that followed him, discipline became one of the main characteristics, even to the extent that it was seen as an indispensable mark of the church. Reformed and Presbyterian churches in France, the Netherlands, Hungary, and Scotland all practiced ecclesiastical discipline. Unfortunately, since the 18th century, it has increasingly fallen into disuse in the larger denominations.

Its Practice

The objects of discipline are those members of the church who have committed censurable sin. Those outside the church are outside its "jurisdiction" (cf. I Cor. 5:12, 13), but *in* the church all—rich and poor alike—are subject to discipline. Usually a distinction is made between discipline of ordinary members and office-bearers. As to the latter, great caution is required (cf. I Tim. 5:19, 20), but if they commit censurable sin, they should be disciplined, not only as believers but as office-bearers as well. The old Church Order of Dort (1619) describes such sin in a general way as "any public, gross sin which is a disgrace or worthy of punishment by the authorities" (art. 79) and specifies it in the next article as "false doctrine or heresy, public schism, public blasphemy . . . perjury, adultery, fornication, theft, acts of violence, habitual drunkenness, etc." The censure of office-bearers consists of suspension and/or deposition from office.

As to the discipline of church members, two kinds of offenses are distinguished: ungodly conduct and doctrinal error. Both are clearly condemned by Scripture. As to the former, see Acts 5:1-11; 8:18 f.; I Cor. 1:1 f.; 6:9, 10; Gal. 5:19 f.; Eph. 3:3 f.; Heb. 13:4; Rev. 21:8. As to the latter, see Mt. 7:15; Acts 20:28 f.; Rom. 16:17, 18; I Cor. 15:12 f.; Gal. 1:8, 9; I Tim. 1:18 f.; II Tim. 2:16 f.; I John 2:22; 4:2, 3; II John 7 f. A sin becomes censurable only when it gives offense, either by its public nature or by the unrepentant attitude of the sinner.

With the exception of public offenses, all discipline should start on the personal level, in accordance with the rule of Mt. 18:15-17. In fact, all official discipline should be rooted in the mutual discipline of the members of the congregation (cf. Rom. 15:14; I Thess. 5:11; Heb. 3:12, 13). When the sinner refuses to listen to personal admonition or when his sin is of a public nature, the office-bearers have to exercise the official censure (cf. I Cor. 5:1, 3; cf. also Acts 5: 1 f.; Gal. 2:11 f.). This will often start with admonition and suspension from the Lord's table. If the sinner persists in his sin, other, more or less public, steps are taken, leading to his final excommunication from the congregation. Genuine repentance, however, always means the end of all public discipline. After genuine repentance, even the excommunicated sinner is re-admitted to the fellowship of the church. As stated above, the aim of discipline is not to punish but to save. Therefore discipline should always be exercised in a spirit of Christian love (cf. I Cor. 13:4-7).

See also EXCOMMUNICATION.

BIBLIOGRAPHY:

R. Bohren, *Das Problem der Kirchenzucht im neuen Testament* (Zurich, 1952).

J. T. Cox, *Practice and Procedure in the Church of Scotland* (Edinburgh, 1969).

M. Monsma, *The New Revised Church Order Commentary* (Grand Rapids, 1967), 288-333.

W. Wolf, *Ordnung der Kirche* (Frankfurt am Main, 1961).

KLAAS RUNIA

DISEASE. See SICKNESS.

DISEASES OF THE BIBLE. The afflictions mentioned in the Bible seem mostly to have been familiar ailments in antiquity. However, the descriptions are empirical; and this, along with poor translation and archaic nomenclature, has made for confusion in understanding them. The medical emphasis of the Pentateuch was upon prevention, and its precepts for the control of communicable diseases agree remarkably with modern hygienic concepts.

a. Diseases with Cutaneous Symptoms

Prominent among these was *tsara'ath* (AV, "leprosy"), for which the diagnostic procedures were given in Lev. 13. Precisely what the disease was is uncertain, and it could comprise a grouping of cutaneous ailments including leprosy, syphilis, smallpox, and skin cancer. Some forms of *tsara'ath* did not require such strict medical surveillance as true leprosy, and may have included such fungus infections as favus, tinea, and actinomycosis. There is no doubt that clinical leprosy (Hansen's disease) was included among those envisaged in Lev. 13. The "botch of Egypt" (Deut. 28:27) was perhaps syphilis (cf. Num. 25:9), whereas the early and late forms of gonorrhea seem referred to in Lev. 22:4 and Prov. 7:22, 23 respectively. The disease that afflicted Job is uncertain. Hezekiah's boil was either a furuncle or a carbuncle (II Kings 20:7), whereas the "boil" of Ex. 9:9 was most probably anthrax. The "itch" referred to in Deut. 28:27 was scabies. *Tsara'ath* diseases not requiring isolation included acne, eczema, impetigo, and psoriasis.

b. Diseases with Internal Symptoms

Bubonic plague can be diagnosed with certainty in I Sam. 5, being common in the Orient. Spinal tuberculosis is mentioned in Lev. 21:20, and the febrile condition of Lev. 26:16, Deut. 28:22, and Mt. 8:14-16 was probably malaria. Dysentery seems to be indicated in Acts 28:8, perhaps accompanied by malarial fever.

c. Worm Infestations

Ascariasis or roundworm infestation was probably responsible for the death of Herod Agrippa I (Acts 12:21-23), producing intestinal obstruction.

d. Eye Diseases

Ophthalmia was very common in antiquity, frequently resulting in early blindness. Paul's affliction may have been chronic trachoma (Gal. 4:13; II

Cor. 12:7), but should be distinguished from the amaurosis of Acts 9:8, which was temporary.

e. Nervous and Mental Diseases

The principles of modern psychosomatic medicine, which recognize the interrelationship of emotional changes and bodily states, are anticipated in Scripture (cf. Prov. 17:22). Neurasthenia seems indicated in I Kings 19:4 and Phil. 2:25-30, where the pressures of life are clearly recognized. Also idiopathic epilepsy is described in Mt. 17:14-18. Demon-possession should be distinguished from mental illness. Though some cases could be interpreted as mental illness, the behavior in other cases does not fit any known type. This shows that a phenomenon is involved that is not recognized in present-day medicine.

f. Miscellaneous Diseases

These include hemorrhagia (Luke 8:43-44), perhaps resulting from a uterine fibroid; dropsy (Luke 14:2), which is itself symptomatic of disease elsewhere; spondylitis deformans (Luke 13:11-13); deaf-mutism (Mark 7:32-35); and spinal tuberculosis (Lev. 21:20), though the latter may be true cretinism. Unspecified illnesses are mentioned in I Kings 14:17; II Kings 13:14; Ezek. 24:16; and II Tim. 4:20. Treatment other than that of an empirical clinical nature included prayer by the elders of the church and the anointing of the sufferer, as prescribed in James 5:13-20.

DISPENSATION:

(1) A relaxation of a law or canon of the church in special circumstances. If exception to a rule is permitted and licit, it must be made by lawful authority and after enquiry into the circumstances. Dispensations may exempt from the duty of complying with a rule, or an obligation such as an oath. In the RC Church the pope (or in minor issues a diocesan bishop) may grant license to do what is forbidden, or to omit to do what is enjoined by ecclesiastical rules. It is assumed that the pope (and his delegates) can vary the application of the church's laws. Marriage regulations provide the commonest field for dispensations. In non-RC churches the only dispensation likely to affect ordinary members is the church license for a marriage. This is a procedure which dispenses with the necessity of having Banns of Marriage called on successive Sundays in the church service. The RC practice now reserves dispensations to the Congregation of Rites in Rome (Constitution *Sapienti Consilio*, 1908).

Indulgence is a term sometimes used for the relaxations of church law; these are correctly called dispensations. *Indult* is an obsolete term signifying a permission given by the pope to authorize something to be done which is not sanctioned by the common law of the church. It is claimed that the church cannot suspend the *jus naturale* or the *jus divinum*. This involves many problems of definition of the extent of the natural law and the degree of immutability attaching to what we describe as Divine law. For example, the commandment, "Thou shalt not kill," has to be harmonized with the concept of a just war.

(2) In the Bible, from the Greek word οἰκονομία (*oikonomia*) "economy," an arrangement or management. It may refer to a management, administration, or stewardship entrusted to someone ("stewardship," Luke 16:2-4, AV; "dispensation," Eph. 3:2, AV; and Col. 1:25, AV), or to a plan, arrangement, or "economy" appointed (administered) by God (Eph. 1:10). In this latter sense it has been used to refer to one of the arrangements by which God has made Himself known or related Himself to men during various periods throughout history. Thus, the Gospel dispensation may be distinguished from

the Mosaic dispensation, and these may be distinguished from previous arrangements by which God "dispensed" knowledge and grace from Himself. In itself the term "dispensation" has nothing to do with dispensationalism (*q.v.*), for all recognize that there are different dispensations within Biblical history. Dispensationalists, however, believe that there are greater differences of theological significance than do others.

DISPENSATIONALISM, the name usually given to a form of premillennialism that had its beginnings as a system of theology in England and Ireland about 1830.

I. Origin

It is important to note the situation out of which this movement arose. There was a widespread feeling that the Christian church was worldly, with little concern for heavenly things. Therefore, there was an emphasis placed on the heavenly character of the church. It was believed that true Christians might gather around the Word and break bread together without any ecclesiastical direction or authorization, independent of the established church and ecclesiastical orders. Thus, a distinction was drawn early between the professing church—with its worldly arrangements, notably the distinction between people and clergy that is contrary to Scripture since all believers are priests—and the "assembly," consisting of the "called out" body of believers who recognized only the headship of Christ, their union with Him, and their any-moment expectation of His coming. The second emphasis was on the Second Coming of Christ, with special stress on its imminence, in oppposition to the then widely held Whitbyan postmillennialism. These were the early Brethren, later called Plymouth Brethren by their critics because one of their earliest Assemblies was in Plymouth, England (see BRETHREN, PLYMOUTH). Their most prominent leader was J. N. Darby (*q.v.*).

Dispensationalism is an outgrowth of this movement, but differs from it in an important respect: it does not hold to the anti-ecclesiasticism of the Brethren—their stigmatizing of all denominations of the visible, professing church as "sects" and their strict, even inquisitorial, discipline. But its prophetic teachings became very popular and found wide acceptance in the existing denominations, especially in Canada and the United States. Among the leaders may be mentioned J. H. Brookes, W. E. Blackstone, C. I. Scofield, H. A. Ironside, I. M. Haldeman, L. S. Chafer, and A. C. Gaebelein. The name "dispensationalism" comes from the fact that they all divide human history into a series of dispensations, "during which man is tested in respect to some specific revelation of the will of God" (Scofield Reference Bible, p. 5). The tendency is to stress the specific dealings of God with man in each dispensation in such a way that, instead of representing relative emphases, the differences become radical and even exclusive.

II. Teachings

Basic to the entire system are (1) grammatico-historical interpretation of all of Scripture including prophecy, (2) the program of God beyond His work of personal redemption, and (3) the distinctive doctrine of the church. Although the first two principles are of primary importance, a general characterization of the system may be understood more easily by discussing its distinctive doctrine of the church.

A. The Church

1. *The church a heavenly body.* A characteristic of dispensational teaching is its tendency to draw sharp distinctions. Dispensationalists assert the heav-

enly nature of the church in order to distinguish it sharply from Israel as an earthly nation. The OT speaks of Israel as an earthly people and of the future of Israel usually in national, earthly, and this-worldly terms, whereas the nature and destiny of the church is described as heavenly (II Cor. 5:1; Eph. 1:3; 2:6; Phil. 3:20; Col. 1:5; I Thess. 1:10). Chafer says, "The covenants and destinies of Israel are all earthly; the covenants and destinies of the Church are all heavenly."

The contrast between Israel as an earthly nation and the church as a heavenly body does not mean that there is no relation whatever between Israel and the church. The relationship, however, is one of type and fulfillment, *not* of identity, or predecessor and successor. This distinction is important for the interpretation of prophecy. If the church is a successor to Israel, then the OT prophecies of the future must be fulfilled in her; if the church, on the other hand, is a fulfillment of Israel as a type, this leaves open the possibility that there may yet be prophecies to be fulfilled in Israel as a continuation of the earthly people. It may be objected that types pass away when fulfillment has come. The priesthood and sacrifices of the OT were types fulfilled in Christ so that when Christ came, the types were taken away (Heb. 10:9). But not all types must necessarily pass away. Israel may continue as an earthly people, even though individual Jews find Christ spiritually.

However, it is objected that the NT expressly identifies OT Israel and the NT church (Rom. 4; Gal. 3:7-14; 6:15-16; Eph. 2:11-19; I Pet. 2:9-10). The NT church, then, is the heir and successor of Israel, the OT church. It is true that within the church of the NT the distinction between Jew and Gentile has disappeared (Eph. 2:14-22). But this does not make the NT church heir and successor of Israel. Dispensationalists note that none of the above Scriptures indicate what is claimed. That there is no barrier between Jew and Gentile is understood as applying to spiritual realities and fellowship, which do not necessarily wipe away all earthly ties.

2. *The church as mystery.* Ephesians 3 speaks of " the mystery of Christ" (vs. 4) and describes it as a mystery "which in other ages was not made known unto the sons of men. . . ." These words might easily be taken to mean that the church was entirely unknown to the OT prophets, and dispensationalists believe that such was the case. The mystery is that the Gentiles should be fellow heirs, and of the same body, and partakers of God's promise in Christ (vs. 6). Dispensationalists take this body to refer to the church apart from Israel. In other words, the salvation of the Gentiles was not a mystery. That was included in the prophecies of the OT. The mystery was the complete equality of Gentile and Jew in the NT church.

Since prophecies concerning Israel as an earthly nation have not been fulfilled, dispensationalists have concluded that there will be a future fulfillment. (Since the prophecies concerning Israel have not been fulfilled to Israel as an earthly nation, nondispensationalists conclude that they are or will be fulfilled in a spiritual Israel.) For a future fulfillment to be possible, a gap of time must occur in many OT prophecies. That the church is not in view in OT prophecies is thought to harmonize with the need for this gap of time. The gap, then, has been understood to consist of the church age. The most outstanding example of this type of interpretation is the seventy-week prophecy of Daniel (Dan. 9:24-27). Traditional interpretation puts all 70 weeks in past history. Dispensationalists, however, place a gap as a hidden parenthesis embracing the entire church age between the 69th and 70th weeks. The 70th week is placed in the future immediately following the rapture or catching up of the church to meet Christ in the air (I Thess. 4:16-17). A distinctive aspect of the dispensationalist view of the future concerns this rapture of the church. The 70th week of Daniel is identified with the events of the book of Revelation describing the Great Tribulation. Because of the dispensational significance of the church age and the idea that the parenthesis of the seventy-week prophecy is identical with the church age, it follows that the end of the church age, and hence the rapture, occurs immediately *before* the seven-year period of the Great Tribulation. Dispensationalists, therefore, always hold to a pre-Tribulation rapture. In fact, this frequently is a touchstone of dispensational orthodoxy. Generally a person who thinks through the problem in terms of Scripture cannot hold conscientiously to pre-Tribulationism unless he holds to *both* grammatico-historical interpretation of prophecy *and* the dispensational view of the church.

The interpretation given above for the seventy-week prophecy follows the grammatico-historical method. The only possible alternative is to interpret the prophecy ecclesiologically, i.e., by transferring references to the Jewish people and institutions symbolically to the church. This conflicts, however, with the dispensationalist view of the church. The objection that writers of the NT in fact do this very thing is explained in terms of types. According to this idea, a prophecy, in addition to having a future earthly fulfillment literally, may have a present typical fulfillment spiritually.

B. Grammatico-historical Interpretation

1. *Progressive revelation.* Critics accuse dispensationalists of making the OT control the NT in the matter of interpretation. By interpreting the OT prophecies literally, they say, dispensationalists are doing what the NT faults the Jews for doing. The Jews were looking for an earthly fulfillment of OT prophecies, but Jesus in effect repudiated that view when He said, "My kingdom is not of this world." Dispensationalists believe that words like these have been misunderstood.

They claim to hold to strict progressive revelation. They interpret prophecy the way they do because they believe that is the only way to do justice to both NT and OT revelation. Strict progressive revelation means that believers of each dispensation and period were given intelligible revelation, so that their understanding of it should be in harmony both with what was revealed earlier and with what was to be revealed later; and that this revelation is progressive, so that what is revealed later, in addition to revealing new truths, added to their understanding of what was given earlier. But because later revelation is in harmony with what was to be understood earlier, no reinterpretation of earlier revelation is necessary. This is why believers today are to interpret OT prophecies in terms of OT revelation, not reinterpreting it as nondispensationalists do. They say that if this view of progressive revelation is not true, then God must be charged with giving revelation in earlier times that necessarily led to false understanding, which cannot be true. This is the reason dispensationalists insist on an understanding of Biblical history and prophecy which preserves grammatico-historical interpretation throughout all Scriptures. Dispensationalists say, then, that OT prophecies ought to have a true, even if an incomplete, sense to those to whom it was delivered in OT times, and that only a grammatico-historical interpretation of prophecy gives such a sense. Furthermore, if it was true to them in OT times, then that same sense should be true today, when taken in historical perspective.

There is room for more debate on this point, and the matter is crucial, since critics note that Scripture speaks of a blinding and a lack of understanding of what was prophesied.

However, dispensationalists keep their cake and eat it too, through what they believe is the only proper use of typology. There are prophecies to be fulfilled literally, which also have a typical fulfillment that can be discerned only through study of the NT. The typical fulfillment could in no way have been known to the OT prophets from their own prophecies, because they lacked vital knowledge of the distinctive arrangements of the church dispensation.

2. *The double application of Scripture.* An objection is made that the apostles within the church actually apply OT prophecy as being fulfilled in the church, rather than being fulfilled literally in a future earthly kingdom. Dispensationalists do not believe this to be an insuperable objection. In the first place, they point out that most fulfilled prophecies have been fulfilled literally, in exactly the same way as they interpret prophecy. But they will say that passages—such as Peter's discourse in Acts 2, where he refers to Joel, Ps. 16, and Ps. 110, and James's reference to Amos 9:11-12 in Acts 15—do not refute their position because there are aspects of the future age in common with the church age. The primary fulfillment is maintained as being yet in the future.

Examples of this double application are found in the concepts of the kingdom and the new covenant. These are said to have primary fulfillment in future Israel. But it is clear that there is an application of both to the church. This, they say, does not automatically rule them out for the future, because the Lord of the church is to rule over Israel and the world in the earthly kingdom. Also, the One who died on the cross for Israel, shed His blood of the new covenant for the church.

C. God's Cosmic Program

1. *Charges of distorting God's work of salvation.* Because dispensationalists find different arrangements regarding salvation in different dispensations, critics have often charged them with contradicting Scripture and perpetrating radical, monstrous doctrines. Dispensationalists make a more serious charge in reply against their critics: that nondispensationalists deny the reality of OT revelation. They charge their critics with wrongly importing NT concepts into the OT and claiming for OT believers an understanding in conflict with what is revealed. They do this on a supposed continuity between the two testaments. After justifying this continuity, they turn around and do the opposite, erring in important matters concerning salvation in the NT. The critics, it is claimed, reestablish Jewish legalism, detrimental to a proper understanding of the Gospel and to the serious harm of those who come under their teaching. However, dispensationalists defend themselves concerning their own teaching by showing how their critics misstate their positions. (Also, critics seem prone to attack secondary matters upon which dispensationalists largely disagree.) Critics continue to say that dispensationalists believe that in the OT people were saved by works, in spite of repeated explanations to the contrary, and that in the millennium Jews and Gentiles will be saved apart from the cross of Christ, in spite of vigorous denials.

2. *God's program beyond his work of personal redemption.* One reason dispensationalists give for the way critics mistake their positions is the critics' truncation of the total program of God to glorify Himself in the world. Critics assume that everything can be subsumed under the categories of Creation, Fall,

and Redemption. But this is not the case. Nevertheless, it is thought to detract from Redemption by the cross of Christ to have an earthly Jewish kingdom in the future. Dispensationalists say that this is an arbitrary limitation upon the sovereignty of God. He is able to provide such a future kingdom in harmony with the cross of Christ, even though the details may not be clear to Christians at present. However, details of the kingdom, according to dispensationalist interpretation of OT prophecies, include a new Jewish temple and a priesthood offering animal sacrifices within it, receiving the blessing of God (Ezek. 40–46). Dispensationalists explain Paul's admonition against "turning again to the weak and beggarly elements" (Gal. 4:9) as applying only to the church dispensation.

The main thrust of the future millennium is not salvation, though that will be necessary, but the universal earthly reign of Christ before the final conflict and consummation. Dispensationalists (along with other premillennialists) believe that Scripture requires this kind of a future rule by such statements as "He shall rule them with a rod of iron" (Rev. 19:15). These statements cannot refer to the past or present, and they cannot refer to the future eternal state. So they most reasonably refer to a millennium. In this, God glorifies Himself in an overt, inflexible rule of Christ apart from the categories of Creation, Fall, and Redemption.

III. Conclusion

Dispensationalism is basically an approach to theology. Its foundational principles are (1) grammatico-historical interpretation applied to all Scripture, (2) recognition of God's program beyond creation, fall, and redemption, and (3) a sharp distinction between Israel and the NT church. The first of these leads to futuristic eschatology, a future Great Tribulation and a gap of time in OT prophecies. The second coupled with the first leads to premillennialism and the distinction of various dispensations apart from, but in harmony with, God's work of personal redemption. And the third principle in conjunction with the others leads to the concept of a future Jewish kingdom and the interpretation of the prophetic gap of time as the church age, ending in a pre-Tribulation rapture of the church.

Many nondispensationalists hold to the first two of these principles. It is the third principle that brings about the strongest cleavage and results in dispensationalism as such. The sharp distinction between Israel and the NT church further defines the separation between the various dispensations and requires a more strictly literal interpretation of prophecy. The dispensationalist's most difficult task is to maintain this sharp distinction in the face of conclusions he is forced to take in interpreting prophecy, such as leading him to assert that the future order will involve a gross, external ritual that is out of character with the fullness of the Spirit which will occur (Ezek. 40:1–48:35). Dispensationalists look on these as memorials in retrospect, believing that somehow they will yet occur; and they hold strongly that their position is that of Scripture.

DISPERSION OF THE JEWS (DIASPORA). The Dispersion of the Jews denotes the Jews who were removed from Palestine and scattered among the nations. The Greek noun *diaspora* (διασπορά), means a scattering or dispersion.

The term *Dispersion* occurs only three times in the NT, as follows: "Will he go unto the *Dispersion* among the Greeks, and teach the Greeks?" (John 7:35). "James, a servant of God and of the Lord Jesus Christ, to the twelve tribes which are of the *Dispersion*, greeting" (James 1:1). "Peter, an apostle of Jesus Christ, to the elect who are sojourners of the *Dispersion* in Pontus, Galatia, Cappadocia, Asia, and Bithynia" (I Pet. 1:1). Both James and Peter, whose ministries were primarily directed to Jews who had become Christians, seem to use *Dispersion* when addressing the now-scattered believers in Christ.

The Origins of the Dispersion

In 722 B.C. the Assyrians under Shalmaneser V came from the NE and carried away the N Kingdom of Israel (the Ten Tribes) into captivity. Thus the Dispersion began as Abraham's children were scattered to the four winds for their sins as Moses had long before prophesied (Deut. 28:25, 37, 41, 63-65, 68). The Assyrians practiced a policy of population manipulation in order to prevent rebellion from those they had conquered. They thus shifted and transplanted whole portions of their Israelite captives—scattering them like seed.

In 605 B.C. the Babylonians under Nebuchadnezzar came from the E and began to take away the remaining S Kingdom of Judah. They came again in 597 B.C. and in 586 B.C., destroying Jerusalem and the Solomonic Temple in this last and most thorough incursion. Thus by the Assyrian and Babylonian conquests and their subsequent aftermath Israel was scattered into Asia, Europe, and Africa. Tribal land holdings disappeared and the name "Jew" began to be applied not only to those of the tribe of Judah, but to all in Israel. Thus the Apostle Paul calls himself both a Jew and an Israelite (Acts 22:3; Rom. 11:1; II Cor. 11:22).

The Dispersion remained among the nations despite the subsequent resurgences of the nation Israel. In the 5th century B.C. under Ezra and Nehemiah only a small fraction of the deported nation returned to Palestine (Neh. 7:66-67; Ezra 2:64-65). By Christ's time there still was a substantial portion of the Jews outside of Israel (John 7:35), and at Pentecost in A.D. 30 there were Jews visiting Jerusalem "from every nation under heaven" (Acts 2:5-11).

Diaspora in Egypt

Jeremiah (Jer. 44) shows that there were Jews dwelling in Egypt at the time of Nebuchadnezzar's attacks (605-586 B.C.). Papyri discovered in 1904 at Aswan (Assouan), at Syene, in Upper Egypt, showed that a Jewish colony existed there in 470 B.C. In 1905-06, the nearby Elephantine Papyri were discovered, showing that a Jewish colony and temple were located there. One papyrus is addressed in 408 B.C. to Bagohi, the Persian governor of Judah (see Josephus, *Ant.* XI, vii, 7).

In 250 B.C. the translation of the OT into Greek, the Septuagint, was made in Egypt—so great was the rabbinical Jewish population there in N Africa at the time. And by the time of Christ the Jewish settlement at Alexandria with Philo as its famed spokesman occupied two-fifths of the city.

Roman Dispersions and After

In A.D. 70 under Vespasian and Titus the Romans quelled the First Jewish Revolt, leaving almost a million dead from famine and disease, and transporting another 100,000 to Rome. The Triumphal Arch of Titus, which can still be seen in Rome, commemorates this victory. By the end of the Second Jewish Revolt—the Bar Kochvah Revolt—*c.* A.D. 132-135, the Roman Emperor Hadrian forbade any Jew to approach within 10 miles of Jerusalem under pain of death, thus completing the ancient dispersions.

The Dispersion of the Jews meant further and further scattering during the Middle Ages as France, England, and Spain expelled the Jews from their countries. The papal, the Crusader, the Russian, and the Nazi persecutions further dispersed them. Even today, with the state of Israel again restored since 1948, Jews of the Dispersion are yet found in virtually all the nations of the world.

A theory concerning the Dispersion of the Jews is the British-Israelite teaching popularized by Herbert and Garner Ted Armstrong of Pasadena, Calif. Orthodox Bible scholars and historians from many denominations reject this hypothesis as both un-Scriptural and unhistorical. It advances the idea that when the N Ten Tribes were conquered by Assyria in 722 B.C. they were not further dispersed, but remained as one unit, migrated across N Europe, and 1,500 years later ended up in England under the name, British. By this theory all of God's end-time prophecies of the blessing and restoration of Israel are transferred to the Anglo-Saxon line. Today's Jews are declared not to be real Israelites, and thus they are not entitled to Israel's promises or blessings. This—though the advocates of the theory may not intend it to be so—frees the consciences of many who hate the Jews. The fact that Paul the apostle refers to himself both as a Jew and as an Israelite (Acts 22:3; Rom. 11:1; II Cor. 11:22) should cause any sincere Christian to pause before assenting to a theory that sees British-Israel blessed and the end-time Jews left barren of their restoration prophecies (Zech. 12:10; Rom. 11:26).

The British Israelite Myth

The Dispersion of the Jews will not continue forever. Ezekiel 37, 38, and 39 speak of a regathering, as does Zech. 8:20-23; 12:10 ff.; 13:1 ff.; 14:16 ff. And Jeremiah 16:14-15 declares, "Therefore, behold, the days come, saith Jehovah, that it shall no more be said, As Jehovah liveth, that brought up the children of Israel out of the land of Egypt; but, as Jehovah liveth, that brought up the children of Israel from the land of the north, and from all the countries whither he had driven them. . . ." It will be in the end time after much tribulation (Rev. 12). Although these are admittedly difficult passages to interpret, certainly no amount of historical or exegetical effort can honestly point to their having been already fulfilled at any time—post-captivity, Maccabean, or in the Christian era. Some day, however, they will find fulfillment; the Dispersion will be no more, as Israel and the Jews turn to Christ.

The End of the *Diaspora*

GARY G. COHEN

DISRUPTION, THE, a division in the Church of Scotland in 1843, when 451 of its 1,203 ministers left to form the Free Church of Scotland. During the previous "Ten Years' Conflict," many had felt that an established church was inherently subordinate to the state, betraying principles upheld at great cost by their ancestors. Others denied the allegation of Erastianism although admitting that, if substantiated, it would be a fatal defect. This was no clear-cut evangelical-moderate division; some evangelicals held that even an established church might remain "as spiritual, as holy, as independent as before." In 1834 the matter was put to the test over the question of lay patronage. The evangelicals revived an old ecclesiastical ordinance which said that "no minister be intruded on any congregation contrary to the will of the people." The proposed Veto Act stated that all who did not actively oppose the patron's choice of parish minister would be regarded as in favor. The time was not considered opportune to press Parliament to abolish patronage.

Civil Court Decisions

Two notorious cases soon followed. At Auchterarder the presentee was rejected by a 286-2 majority. He appealed to the civil court, which finally decreed that congregational views were not enough to refuse settlement and ordered the presbytery to proceed. At Marnoch the presentee was so unacceptable that only the innkeeper voted for him. The presentee appealed, and in March, 1838, the Court of Session by an 8-5 majority ordered that he be "admitted and received." This was tantamount to ordering the man's ordination, which spiritual function the Kirk had always jealously guarded as its own prerogative. An appeal to the House of Lords was curtly dismissed. Feeling ran high; this was the bicentenary year of the National Covenant, which had resisted the Crown's interference in the Kirk's affairs.

Meanwhile, there was trouble also in another area. In 1834 the General Assembly, concerned to encourage church extension, passed the Chapels' Act, which upgraded chapels-of-ease to the status of parish churches and gave their ministers a seat in the local presbytery. In 1839, after developments in an Ayrshire parish, the civil authority declared the Act invalid. Moreover, all decisions by presbyteries in which chapel ministers had sat were likewise illegal. On the latter technicality, two ministers deposed for scandalous behavior obtained reinstatement.

With presbyteries and parishes bewildered by civil interdicts and ecclesiastical penalties in stark confrontation, the 1842 Assembly for the first time declared itself to be against patronage and pressed for its abolition. It pointed to the 1690 Act, which had abolished in Scotland the royal supremacy over the church in spiritual and ecclesiastical matters. This "Claim of Right" was overwhelmingly rejected by the House of Commons in March, 1843.

The Kirk was divided. In appointing members to the 1843 Assembly, the choice of some presbyteries was dictated by fear that a Non-Intrusionist majority (the party of evangelical leader Thomas Chalmers) would end establishment and depose dissentients. In addition, a small middle party ("The Forty"), concerned with the damage done to the church's work by continued strife, withheld its support from Chalmers.

A Historic Occasion

May 18, 1843, was the fateful day in St. Andrew's Church, Edinburgh. After prayer Dr. David Welsh, the retiring moderator, instead of constituting the Assembly, read a protest signed by 190 commissioners, outlining the various encroachments upon the church's rights and liberties. Although patronage was the original complaint, the claim to complete spiritual independence was the ultimate ground of secession. Dr. Welsh then laid the protest on the table, bowed to the Queen's Commissioner, and left the church, followed by Chalmers, R. S. Candlish, and many others. Lord Cockburn recounts that when the procession left St. Andrew's Church, "and people saw that principle had really triumphed over interest, (Welsh) and his followers were received with the loudest acclamations." They made their way to the Canonmills, where a hall had been prepared, and there constituted the Free General Assembly, with Chalmers as moderator. The ministers, who had relinquished stipend and rights, were in most cases followed by their congregations. The Church of Scotland lost about one third of its membership, including representatives of every class. Exclaimed Lord Jeffrey: "I'm proud of my country; there is not another country upon earth where such a deed could have been done."

Patronage was abolished in the Church of Scotland in 1874, and congregations were given the right to elect their own ministers. After sundry unions, 95 percent of Scottish Presbyterians are once again within the Church of Scotland, established yet free. Among the four remaining smaller bodies is a remnant of the original Free Church of Scotland.

See SCOTLAND, CHURCH OF; CHALMERS, THOMAS; FREE CHURCH OF SCOTLAND.

BIBLIOGRAPHY:

T. Brown, *Annals of the Disruption* (Edinburgh, 1893).
J. Bryce, *Ten Years of the Church of Scotland, 1833-1843* (Edinburgh, 1850).
J. Burleigh, *A Church History of Scotland* (London, 1960), p. 334 ff.
J. Cunningham, *The Church History of Scotland* (Edinburgh, 1882, Vol. 2).
G. Henderson, *The Claims of the Church of Scotland* (London, 1951), p. 106 ff.
G. Ryley and J. McCandlish, *Scotland's Free Church* (London, 1893).

JAMES DIXON DOUGLAS

DISSENTERS. Dissenters, as a term with religious significance, owes its origin to the five dissenting brethren who opposed the presbyterian majority in the Westminster Assembly and upheld a freer church order of a congregational type. In the 18th century, Dissenting Deputies were chosen to further the interests of the three denominations—Congregational, Presbyterian, and Baptist. The term *dissenters*, however, came to be applied to all Protestants who are communicant members of churches other than the Church of England, though it was superseded in the 19th century by the term *Nonconformists* and in the 20th century by *Free Churchmen.*

The earliest dissenters objected to the Elizabethan settlement, though many did not desire separation from it. Seventeenth-century dissenters were usually congregationalist (or baptist) in outlook, and from the middle of the century the Quakers increased the variety among dissenters. The Act of Uniformity (1662) made the perpetuation of forms of dissent almost inevitable. Some scholars view this act as the formal origin of dissent. The Toleration Act (1689) ended the persecution of dissenters but left them under grave political and social disabilities which were not removed until the 19th century.

Methodists are usually reckoned to be among the dissenters, though they do not share all of the characteristics of dissent. These include hostility to state control and the idea of an established church, dislike of ecclesiastical hierarchy, distaste for ritualistic or formalistic worship, and advocacy of freer and more spontaneous expressions of church life, arising from the idea of the crown rights of the Redeemer in His church.

BIBLIOGRAPHY:

D. Bogue and J. Bennett, *History of Dissenters 1688–1808* (London, 1808-1812), 4 vols.
C. Burrage, *The Early English Dissenters* (Cambridge, 1912), 2 vols.
H. W. Clark, *History of English Nonconformity* (London, 1911-1913), 2 vols.
J. H. Colligan, *Eighteenth Century Nonconformity* (London, 1915).
D. Coomer, *English Dissent under the Early Hanoverians* (London, 1946).
G. H. Curteis, *Dissent in its Relation to the Church of England* (London, 1872).
H. Davies, *The English Free Churches* (Oxford, 1952).
C. S. Horne, *Nonconformity in the XIXth Century* (London, 1905).
C. S. Horne, *A Popular History of the Free Churches* (London, 1903).
A. Lincoln, *Some Political and Social Ideas of English Dissent 1763–1800* (Cambridge, 1938).
E. A. Payne, *The Free Church Tradition in the Life of England* (London, 1944).
T. Price, *The History of Protestant Nonconformity in England* (London, 1836), 2 vols.
E. Routley, *English Religious Dissent* (Cambridge, 1960).
H. S. Skeats and C. H. Miall, *History of the Free Churches of England* (London, 1891).
J. J. Tayler, *A Retrospect of the Religious Life of England* (London, 1845; 2nd ed., 1876).
J. Toulmin, *Historical view of the state of Dissenters in England* (London, 1814).
H. Townsend, *The Claims of the Free Churches* (London, 1949).
R. Vaughan, *English Nonconformity* (London, 1862).
W. Wilson, *The History and Antiquities of Dissenting Churches and Meeting Houses in London, Westminster and Southwark* (London, 1808), 4 vols.

H. H. ROWDON

DIVES, a word that means "rich" (Latin) and the traditional name given to the rich man in the story of Luke 16:19-31. Commentators differ over whether this is a parable or a factual story. The story shows that in Hades (not here, Gehenna), the state of existence between death and resurrection, there is already an impassable gulf between saved and lost.

J. S. Wright

DIVINATION, the attempt to discover present and future events by magical methods. Divination is denounced in the Law (Lev. 19:26), in the History (II Kings 17:17; 21:6), and in the Prophets (Ezek. 13:6; Zech. 10:2). In Ezek. 21:21 three methods are mentioned: (1) rhabdomancy, throwing arrows or sticks or bones in the air, and noting the pattern in which they fall—a method still used by witchdoctors, (2) consulting teraphim, or images, as in Zech. 10:2, and (3) hepatoscopy, examination of markings on the liver of a sacrifice.

Other passages condemn necromancy, the consulting of departed spirits (Deut. 18:11; Isa. 8:19, 20). Joseph is said to have practiced hydromancy, or divination through gazing into a bowl of water (cf. crystal gazing), but both references (Gen. 44:5, 15) are a part of the general deception that Joseph and his steward were practicing on his brothers, not hydromancy.

In Acts 16:16 a girl has a spirit of divination, probably equivalent to the control spirit of a medium, and Paul casts it out in the name of Jesus Christ.

Since diviners were asked to decide matters, the term "divination" could be used metaphorically of the decision of a king for his subjects who consult him on legal matters (Prov. 16:10).

See Dreams; Lots, Casting of; Teraphim.

DIVORCE

OUTLINE

I. Meaning of Term
II. Old Testament Provision
III. Teaching of Christ
IV. Pauline Teaching
V. Practical Lessons

Divorce refers to the dissolution of the marital bond. Spouses may be separated from each other and marital relations suspended for a longer or shorter period, unlawfully by perversity on the part of one or both, or unavoidably by circumstances of providence over which the spouses do not exercise control. But the term "divorce" should be used only when the action or status denoted thereby has in view the dissolution of the marriage tie that previously existed between living persons. The death of one partner dissolves marriage, but this dissolution is not that of divorce.

I. Meaning of Term

Annulment is not to be equated with divorce. The former takes place when the *alleged* marriage of a man and a woman is declared to be null and void for proper cause. Confusion arises when these are not distinguished. Neither annulment nor divorce is to be identified with the breaking of an engagement to marry, however culpable the latter may be in certain cases.

II. Old Testament Provision

Deut. 24:1-4 enunciates the OT law governing divorce. It should be noted, however, that this passage does not make divorce on the part of the husband mandatory in the circumstance mentioned in verse 1. Neither does it authorize divorce. Verses 1-3 are the protasis and verse 4 is the apodosis. The effect of this construction is that *if* a man puts away his wife and she marries another, the former may not under any conditions take her again to be his wife. This is the *law* which the passage establishes. Divorce was permitted under the Mosaic economy in the event that a man found some unclean thing in his wife, but this permission did not abrogate the original obligation inherent in the marital bond according to Gen. 2:23, 24. We have good reason to believe that this divorce was practiced (cf. Lev. 21:7, 14; 22:13; Num. 30: 9[10]; Deut. 22:19, 20; Isa. 50:1; Jer. 3:1; Ezek. 44:22). But we have allusion to the abiding sanctity of the original institution in Mal. 2:14-16 and the express indictment by our Lord of the perversity in deference to which this permission was granted by Moses (Mt. 19:8; Mark 10:5). The unclean thing for which a man was permitted to put away his wife was not adultery. Other provisions were made for this sin (Lev. 20:10; Deut. 22:13-27). But neither may we regard it as a trivial offense.

III. Teaching of Christ

The teaching of our Lord is found in Matthew 5:31, 32; 19:3-10; Mark 10:2-12; and Luke 16:18. In Mt. 5: 31 there is allusion to Deut. 24:1-4, but the form of this verse implies no more than that *if* a man put away his wife it was necessary to give her a bill of divorcement. In verse 32 Jesus expressly forbids divorce for any other reason than the act of sexual infidelity. Here at the outset He, in the exercise of His authority, abrogates the permission provided for in Deut. 24:1-4 and institutes the right of a man to put away his wife for adultery. This one exception accentuates the wrong of putting away for any other cause. Nothing is said in this text respecting the subsequent marital rights of the husband who divorces his wife for just cause, nor is it implied that he is under obligation to sever the bond of marriage with his unfaithful spouse.

The assumption of this passage is that the woman put away for any other cause than adultery is still the spouse of the man who put her away, and it is for this reason that sexual relations with another man is adultery on her part and on the part of the man who is her accomplice in these relations—she is made an adulteress and he commits adultery.

There is no reflection in this passage upon the adulterous character of subsequent remarriage on the part of the woman divorced for adultery. It is the woman divorced for another cause, and therefore an unlawful one, who is made to be an adulteress when she marries another; it is what follows upon illicit divorce that is in view in the latter part of verse 32.

Matthew 19:9 is distinctive in Jesus' recorded teaching. The unique feature of this text is that we not only find the exception for which a man may put away his wife, namely fornication, but also the right of remarriage for the man who divorces his wife for that very reason. It is maintained, particularly by the Church of Rome, that the right of remarriage is not implicit in this text; that, although a man may "divorce" his wife for the cause of adultery, yet the divorce is not of such a character that he is at liberty to remarry. This interpretation is not tenable on the basis of the text. It should be noted that if the words "except for fornication" do not apply to the committing of adultery in the event of remarriage, then the verse does not make good sense. Besides, divorce without dissolution of the marriage bond is contrary to the marital ethic which the Scripture throughout propounds, and if divorce implies dissolution of the marital bond, there is no reason why another marriage may not be contracted.

The fornication referred to in Mt. 5:32 and 19:9 cannot be restricted to pre-nuptial unchastity for which a man may break a betrothal. In the preceding context of both passages reference is made to the provisions of Deut. 24: 1-4, where the wife in question cannot be regarded as merely a betrothed woman. Hence the relationship expressed by the word "wife" in our Lord's teaching must be of the same character as that contemplated in Deut. 24:1-4. Otherwise the subject of discourse would have been abruptly changed and Jesus' deliverance would cease to be relevant to the question at issue. Furthermore, it is not feasible to confine the term "fornication" to extra-marital intercourse.

The difficulty of harmonizing Mt. 19:9 with Mark 10:11 and Luke 16:18 has been the strongest argument against the interpretation of Mt. 19:9 given above. In the latter two passages there is no exception to the wrong of putting away and remarriage—"whoever puts away his wife and marries another commits adultery against her" (Mark 10:11).

It is not, however, impossible to find all three passages compatible with one another without abandoning the plain import of Mt. 19:9. It must be observed, first of all, that in Mark and Luke no reference is made to the right of putting away for adultery; there is no exceptive clause in either account. But the exception is clearly established in Mt. 5:32 and 19:9. Without denying the genuineness of the exception so clearly stated in both these passages we are compelled to recognize the difference in this respect. The difference, however, does not prove that the exception stated in Matthew is not an authentic report of our Lord's teaching. It means only that Matthew records something additional which Mark and Luke, for a reason to be mentioned presently, did not find it necessary to include. Firstly, since Mark and Luke did not refer to the one exception for which a man might properly dismiss his wife, in the nature of the case they could not allude to the right of remarriage in such an event. Secondly, in Mt. 5:32; 19:9; and Mark 10:11 the main interest in Jesus' teaching is the abrogation of the Mosaic permission (Deut. 24:1-4). It is not the exception to the right of putting away that bears the emphasis but the prohibition of every other reason. In Mark 10:2-11 this is as patent as in Mt. 5:32 and 19:3-9. Mark focuses all his attention on this consideration. (The Lucan passage, though it lacks the broader context reported in Matthew and Mark, does the same.) It is in that light that Mark 10:11 is to be understood. But Matthew in both passages, without any less stress upon the abrogation of Deut. 24:1-4, includes the one legitimate exception to the wrong of putting away, which our Lord in the exercise of His own authority instituted, an exception which only accentuates the annulment of the Mosaic provision.

Mark 10:12 introduces another aspect of our Lord's teaching not reflected on elsewhere—"And if a woman shall put away her husband, and be married to another, she commits adultery." It has respect to what we may rightfully infer are the rights of the woman. This verse is, of course, prohibitive and denies to the woman what is denied to the man in verse 11, namely, the right to put away and remarry. But, since the exception must be regarded as authentic teaching of our Lord, then we should have to conclude that a wife also is granted the right to divorce a husband for the cause of adultery on his part.

In Paul's epistles there are two passages relevant to divorce, Rom. 7:1-3 and I Cor. 7:10-15. In the former Paul

IV. Pauline Teaching

enunciates the binding law of marriage, that the obligation to conjugal fidelity continues throughout the whole of life. There is no exception to such an obligation as it bears upon both spouses. Rom. 7:1-3 must not be interpreted, however, as excluding the possibility of dissolving a marriage when, due to infidelity on the part of one spouse, the innocent partner is so wronged that divorce may be the proper or necessary recourse. It would have been extraneous to the purpose the apostle had in mind here to take into account what would be legitimate under such abnormal circumstances. Paul deals elsewhere with situations which could not be introduced at Rom. 7:1-3 but which do arise in the complexity of life. This is the interest of I Cor. 7:10-15.

The sharp distinction between the circumstance dealt with in verses 10-11 and that in view in verses 12-15 is to be observed. This is marked by the contrasts. (1) In the former, Paul appeals to the teaching of our Lord and reiterates what had been Christ's own injunction; in the latter, he propounds in the exercise of apostolic authority something that did not fall within the scope of Jesus' teaching—"not I but the Lord" (vs. 10), "I, not the Lord" (vs. 12). (2) In the former, he enjoins that if separation has taken place the spouses are to be reconciled to each other but in any case not to marry another; in the latter there are no such injunctions. (3) In the former, by obvious implication, he is dealing with partners in marriage both of whom are professing believers; in the latter, one of the spouses is an unbeliever and the other a believer. (4) In the former, he gives a solemn charge that the wife is not to depart from her husband and that the husband is not to dismiss his wife; in the latter, though the believer is charged not to put away the unbeliever, the course of action to be followed by the believer in the event of desertion is prescribed.

The question on which judgment is acutely divided is the force of the statement, "the brother or the sister is not bound in such cases" (vs. 15). Some regard this as freedom for the believing spouse to dissolve the bond of marriage, others as freedom to separate without dissolution. There is much to be said in favor of the latter view. One of the most potent considerations in its support is that desertion on the part of an unbeliever, if it were regarded as a cause for dissolution, would institute another legitimate ground for divorce when our Lord Himself sanctioned only one ground.

This argument, however, is not conclusive for two reasons. (1) Jesus was dealing with the one ground for which a man might *put away* his wife; Paul is dealing with a different case, that of wilful *desertion* on the part of an unbeliever and not with a case of *putting away*. (2) Paul makes clear in verse 12 that he is dealing with a situation that did not come within the purview of our Lord's teaching. These facts should caution us against the conclusion that the other view would contradict our Lord's teaching.

In support of the inference that verse 15b contemplates dissolution of the marriage bond the following considerations may be pleaded. (1) There is the striking difference between the injunctions Paul gives and the terms he uses in verse 11 and those in verse 15. The separation posited in verse 11 is nothing more than from bed and board, and Paul strictly enjoins that as long as it lasts it may not be more; there must be left open the possibility of reconciliation. If no more than separation from bed and board is in view in verse 15, we would expect Paul to say something similar. If dissolution is not provided for, we should expect, at least, the same kind of reminder to remain unmarried. This is what we do not find, and the omission is significant. And not only is there this omission but we also find what points in the opposite direction, "let him [or her] depart," an expression with terseness and finality that carries the force of "be gone." The summariness of this imperative requires more than mere separation from bed and board. (2) The term "is not bound" is one of sufficient strength to denote dissolution, that is, freedom from the bond of marriage. In verses 27 and 39 and in Rom. 7:2 Paul uses a similar term to express the bond of marriage. The negative would indicate the loosing of this bond. Here he uses, if anything, a stronger term, and the negative "is not bound" would most naturally refer to release from the bond of marriage.

The situation envisioned in this passage must be strictly borne in mind. It is one in which a believer is wilfully deserted by an unbeliever, and the provisions must not be extended beyond that circumstance. Verses 10 and 11 underline that restriction, for in the case viewed in these earlier verses no such liberty is granted. It is the wilfulness and wantonness of the unbeliever that alone explain and vindicate the liberty bestowed upon the believer, and it is indefensible to extend this liberty to cases that do not fall into this category.

V. Practical Lessons

The law of God, as enunciated in Gen. 2:23, 24 and applied throughout Scripture (cf. Mt. 19:5-8; Mark 10: 5-9; Eph. 5:31) is that marriage is a lifelong bond by which the spouses become one flesh. It is a bond divinely instituted and sanctioned and may not be dissolved at the will of man. There are many desecrations of this holy estate. But so sacred is the union effected in marriage that no desecration is as grievous as the dissolution of it or the commission of an offense which gives ground for dissolution.

The Scripture does instance two offenses against the sanctity of marriage which warrant dissolution, adultery and wilful desertion of a believer by an unbeliever. The intrinsic gravity of these offenses against the nature of marriage must be duly appreciated, and God's Word allows for no other ground of divorce. The laxity which ignores or spurns God's institution spells disaster and destroys the basis of moral order. The family is the most elementary social unit, and when its sanctity is desecrated the whole social order crumbles.

The obligations attaching to the marital bond must also be properly assessed as they pertain to divorce. If divorce for the offenses mentioned is of Divine warrant, anything less than dissolution of the bond of marriage would be a travesty of the Biblical ethic as it pertains to marriage. To suppose the legitimacy of separation from bed and board while the bond of marriage is undissolved is an expedient of human invention that violates the basic demands of the marital relation. For where the bond is inviolate all the obligations incident to that bond are also inviolate. If divorce is a Divine institution, it can only be the divorce of dissolution. The one basis upon which the obligations can be terminated is that the bond itself no longer exists. A divorce that is not absolute is an anomaly that becomes a travesty of the nature of marriage.

Bibliography:

F. A. Adams, *Divorce . . . What Did the Lord say about it?* (Norwich, 1950).
F. A. Adams, *'Except it be for . . .' What?* (Norwich, n.d.).
R. H. Charles, *The Teaching of the New Testament on Divorce* (London, 1921).
F. L. Cirlot, *Christ and Divorce* (Lexington, 1945).
A. Devine, *The Law of Christian Marriage* (New York, 1908).
C. Gore, *The Question of Divorce* (London, 1911).
C. Gore and G. H. Box, *Divorce in the New Testament* (London, 1921).
J. Murray, *Divorce* (Philadelphia, 1953).

John Murray

DIZAHAB, one of the places named in Deut. 1:1. It was in the land of Moab, but the exact location is not known.

DOCETISM, a Christological heresy in the early church.

According to the most primitive form of docetism, the Son of God adopted only a phantasmal body (Greek *dokein,* to seem). More often, however, it revealed itself in a more subtle derogation from Christ's true humanity. The NT opposes this heresy but does not give any concrete description of it. Generally, it is not so much of a formulated and unified doctrine as an attitude that infected several heretical systems, particularly in the post-apostolic age. Docetism was found particularly in Marcion and the gnostics. Marcion taught that God is present in Jesus Christ to redeem the world, but He is not the Creator of the world. He is the God of the NT, who, essentially strange to this creation, cannot share in evil flesh but at best can adopt a phantom body. Marcion himself believed that in this body Christ did feel, act, and suffer as a man, but gnosticism as a whole went much further and actually denied the real suffering and death of Christ. Most of the various gnostic systems taught that from the spiritual world one of the aeons, the Divine Christ, descended and united himself for a time with the historical Jesus (whose body was usually seen as formed of "psychic" substance). According to Cerinthus the union of the Divine Christ with the earthly Jesus took place at the baptism in Jordan, and the Christ left Jesus before the crucifixion in order to fly to heaven. According to others there was a real Incarnation, but shortly before the crucifixion a substitution took place; not Jesus, but Simon of Cyrene or Judas Iscariot was crucified. The basic background of all these forms of docetism is the dualism between spirit and matter and the idea of divine impassibility. Therefore they have no place for the real corporeality of Christ or for His crucifixion and death, and this is their great offense! The effect of these doctrines is to discard the whole history of salvation and replace it with the eternal idea of redemption (salvation through mere knowledge).

In the following centuries docetism manifested itself in new forms, e.g., in the teachings of Apollinaris, monophysitism, and monotheletism. Some medieval sects also showed docetic tendencies. Later some of the anabaptists taught that Christ brought His humanity from heaven (Melchior Hoffmann, Menno Simons). RC Christology has a touch of docetism in its view of Christ's knowledge, fear, faith, and hope. Finally, liberal Christologies of the 19th and 20th centuries have revived docetism in their distinction between the historical Jesus and the ideal Christ.

The whole NT is distinctly anti-docetic. This is most obvious in the Johannine Epistles (cf. I John 1:1-3; 4:1-3; 5:6; II John 7) and John's Gospel (especially John 1:14: "the Word became flesh" (cf. John 19:37; 20:27). But it is also found in Paul's Epistles (cf. Rom. 8:3; I Cor. 1:18; Gal. 4:4: "born of a woman"; 5:11; Phil. 2:7); Hebrews (Heb. 2:14, 17, 18; 4:15), and the Synoptic Gospels (Luke 2:52; 22:43; 24:38, 39).

See Marcion; Gnosticism.

Bibliography:

K. Adam, *Christus unser Bruder* (1929).
G. Bareille, *DThC,* s.v.
G. C. Berkouwer, *The Person of Christ* (Grand Rapids, 1954), 195-238.
O. Cullmann, *Christ and Time* (London, 1957), 125-130.
A. Fortescue, *HERE* IV (1832-35), s.v.
A. VonHarnack, *Marcion, Das Evangelium vom fremden Gott* (1924).
H. A. Wolfson, *The Philosophy of the Church Fathers* (Cambridge, Mass., 1956), 518 f., 552 ff., 587 ff.

Klaas Runia

DODAI. See Dodo.

DODANIM ("leaders"), a son of Javan, grandson of Japheth (Gen. 10:4). Since the LXX and a few copies of the Hebrew text have *Rodanim* here and since most copies have this in the corresponding passage (I Chron. 1:7), many identify his descendants not with the Ionians (Javan), but with the inhabitants of Rhodes. The basis for this is the ease in confusing the Hebrew letters ד ("d") and ר ("r"), assuming an error in the copying of manuscripts.

DODAVAH (also written Dodavahu), "loved of Jehovah," an inhabitant of Mareshah, father of Eliezer the prophet who correctly prophesied against Jehosaphat after the Divinely disapproved alliance with Ahaziah had been made (II Chron. 30:37).

DODD, Charles Harold (1884–), British NT scholar and theologian. Educated at University College, Oxford, and Berlin, Dodd was ordained to the Congregational ministry in 1912. He became NT lecturer at Mansfield College, Oxford, in 1915; Rylands professor at Manchester in 1930; Norris-Hulse professor of divinity at Cambridge in 1935, retiring in 1949; and General Director of the New Translation of the Bible in 1950. Representative works include *The Authority of the Bible*, 1929; *The Apostolic Preaching and Its Developments,* 1936; *The Bible Today*, 1946; and *The Interpretation of the Fourth Gospel,* 1953.

In his writings Dodd gained much attention from his eschatological view, which he called "realized eschatology." The kingdom of God came in the events of Jesus' life, death, and resurrection. In the *kerygma* (apostolic preaching) there is no valid reference to a future coming of Jesus. He said, "It is impossible to think of Doomsday as a coming event in history. . . . Doomsday is followed by the 'new heavens and new earth,' 'the restoration of all things.' Here we are in a realm very far removed from this order of space and time" (*The Bible Today*, 115, 117).

Dodd tried to support his position in *The Apostolic Preaching and Its Developments.* The *kerygma* was shown to be set within one or the other of two eschatological frameworks: the present work of the Holy Spirit or the apocalyptic coming of Christ. Dodd rejected the latter as mistaken and claimed that the former represents the true prophetic spirit. In this way, Dodd, as a modern theologian, made the supernatural in eschatology to be innocuous.

WILBER B. WALLIS

DODDRIDGE, Philip (1702-1751), nonconformist preacher and hymnwriter. Doddridge was born in London, England, the son of an oil merchant who had been driven from Bohemia by religious persecution. In his boyhood his mother, a devout Christian, gave him a thorough religious training. Declining an offer for education in the Anglican Church, he went to the nonconformist school in Kibworth and became a Congregationalist pastor at the age of 21. In 1729, when only 27, he was recognized as a rising young preacher and was called to head a newly established nonconformist seminary at Market Harborough. In the same year he accepted a call from a congregation in Northampton, where he labored as a pastor along with his seminary responsibilities for the next 22 years.

Some 200 young men (mostly Dissenters) were trained for the ministry under his tutelage. He was compelled by tuberculosis to give up his work in 1750. A friend and supporter of George Whitefield, Doddridge, as a staunch Calvinist with a catholic spirit, gained the confidence of the Countess of Huntingdon (Whitefield's patroness), who made it possible for him to go to Portugal for his health. "I can as well go to heaven from Lisbon," he told her, "as from my own study in Northampton." He died in Lisbon and was buried near the novelist Henry Fielding in the English cemetery there.

In connection with his youthful interest in founding a nonconformist academy prior to his call to Northampton, he visited Isaac Watts, with whom he became a close friend and at whose flame, to use his own words, he "kindled his torch." He followed the example of Watts in writing hymns to go with his sermons. Their posthumous publication is the chief reason for his fame. Of the several hundred hymns which he wrote, a dozen or so are still sung. Perhaps the best-known is "Awake My Soul, Stretch Every Nerve," which was written in 1755 to conclude a sermon on the text Philippians 3:12-14. In this hymn we see Doddridge at his best. The poet uses, in places almost paraphrases, the Scripture and captures its spirit in true poetic beauty.

BIBLIOGRAPHY:

J. Boyd, *Memoir of the Life, Character and Writings of Philip Doddridge* (New York, 1860).

P. Doddridge, *The Rise and Progress of Religion in the Soul* (London, New York, 1849).

J. D. Humphreys, *Correspondence and Diary* (London, 1829), 5 vols. Compiled by Doddridge's grandson.

G. Nuttall (ed.), *Philip Doddridge, His Contribution to English Religion* (London, 1951).

J. Orton, *Memoirs* (1776).

K. L. Parry, *Companion to Congregational Praise.*

C. Stanford, *Philip Doddridge* (London, 1880).

T. Stedman, *Letters To and From Dr. Doddridge* (1790).

DODO, also written **Dodai,** "beloved." It seems to be related to the Akkadian, *Dudu.*

(1) A man of Issachar and grandfather of Tola, one of the Judges (Judges 10:1).

(2) A commander of a division in the army of King David (I Chron. 27:4). He was an Ahohite and the father of Eleazar, one of David's mighty men (II Sam. 23:24; I Chron. 11:26).

(3) A Bethlehemite, the father of Elhanan, one of David's mighty men (II Sam. 23:24; I Chron. 11:26).

DODS, Marcus (1834-1909), Scottish theologian and Bible scholar. Educated in Edinburgh, Dods became minister of Renfield Free Church, Glasgow, in 1864. He was elected professor of NT exegesis in New College, Edinburgh, in 1889, and succeeded Robert Rainey as principal in 1907.

Dods had wide learning and notable literary gifts. Outstanding among his productions are his translation of Augustine's *City of God*; *Genesis* and *I Corinthians* in the *Expositor's Bible*; and *John* in the *Expositor's Greek Testament.* He was a contributor to the *Encyclopaedia Britannica,* ninth edition, and to Hasting's *Dictionary of the Bible.*

One of his last productions was the Bross Lectures of 1904, *The Bible, Its Origin and Nature.* Here he gave a full statement of his view of inspiration. The inspiration of Scripture was the focal point of naturalistic unbelief in the 19th and early 20th centuries. One of the citadels attacked was New College, founded by zeal of the separating Free Church under Thomas Chalmers in 1843. The attack on the Scripture was signalized by Robertson Smith's articles in the ninth edition of the *Encyclopaedia Britannica.* Influential men such as A. B. Davidson, A. B. Bruce, Henry Drummond, and George Adam Smith were affected, as was Dods. His views of Scripture were challenged in 1890, but he had been made professor of NT exegesis in the previous year and the charges were dropped. Meanwhile, Robert Rainey, principal of New College from 1874 to 1907, was responsible for the Declaratory Act of 1892 which relaxed stringency of subscription to the Confession of Faith.

Against such a background Dods' book appeared in 1904. The reaction of alert and discerning conservative opinion can be seen in B. B. Warfield's review (*Critical Reviews,* pp. 118-127). One point of weakness in Dods' position was his conception that inspiration was personal rather than graphic; that the *writers*, not the books, were inspired. Says Warfield, ". . . we hope we have made it clear that the fountain of Dr. Dods' inadequate conception of Scripture as the documentation of God's revelation of Himself for salvation, lies in his inadequate conception of the modes of the Divine operation in the world—in a word, is his chariness with regard to the supernatural . . ." (*ibid.*, p. 124).

Though Dods was unduly concessive, Warfield could say, "We rejoice that Dr. Dods would preserve to us at least a supernatural Redeemer, even if he draws back before too supernatural a Bible" (*ibid.*, p. 127).

WILBER B. WALLIS

DOEG, an Edomite, chief herdsman of Saul. In I Sam. 21:7 he was at Nob for some ritual purpose when David was helped by the high priest, Ahimelech. He betrayed Ahimelech and his fellow priests to Saul (22:9, 10) and massacred them when Saul's followers refused to do this at Saul's command. His name is in the title of Ps. 52.

DOGMA, the authoritative formulation of the Biblical message by the church, under the guidance of the Holy Spirit.

THE TERM. The word is derived from the Greek verb δοκέω meaning "to seem, to seem good, to decree," hence, the literal meaning, "opinion, decree, ordinance." It is used in this way in the NT for the decrees of the magistrates (Luke 2:1; Acts 17:7; cf. LXX, Esther 3:9; Dan. 2:13; 6:16); the ordinances of the OT covenant (Col. 2:14; Eph. 2:15); and the decrees of the Council of Jerusalem (Acts 16:4; cf. 15:28, "It seemed good to the Holy Ghost and to us. . . ."). In pagan philosophy the term also acquired the meaning of an established truth, and subsequently that of a doctrinal statement of a teacher or school. This usage was introduced first into the Christian church and theology as a synonym for distinctive Christian truths by Ignatius of Antioch; yet it was not until the 16th century that it was generally accepted.

ORIGIN AND DEVELOPMENT. The NT itself does not contain creeds, confessions, or formulas of faith in the proper sense of these terms. There is, however, a common body of doctrine, definite in outline and considered as the possession of the whole church. There are also traces that this body of teaching was beginning to crystallize into more or less conventional patterns and forms. Three forms may be distinguished as existing side by side. The first form is the one-clause Christological affirmation, such as "Jesus is Lord" (Rom. 10:9; I Cor. 12:3); "Jesus is the Christ" (I John 2:22); or "Jesus is the Son of God" (I John 4:15; Heb. 4:14). The second form is the semiformal confession of a bi-partite structure based on the parallel ideas of God the Father and Jesus Christ His Son (e.g., Rom. 4:24; 8:11; I Cor. 8:6; II Cor. 4:4; Gal. 1:1; I Tim. 6:13 f.; II Tim. 4:1). The third form is the Trinitarian affirmation (e.g., II Cor. 13:14; Mt. 28:19; Eph. 4:4-6). Gradually these more or less loose forms developed into fixed formulas and creeds. Several factors seem to have been operative in this process. O. Cullmann (*The Earliest Christian Confessions*) distinguishes five factors: (1) baptism and catechumenism (later on resulting, for example, in the Apostles' Creed); (2) regular worship: liturgy and preaching (e.g., the *Te Deum*); (3) exorcism; (4) persecution; and (5) polemic against heretics (e.g., the Nicene Creed and the Formula of Chalcedon). This means that "Dogma is an exceedingly complicated historical structure. It has in its various constituent parts, constructed as they have been in the face of multifarious forms of opposition and under the inspiration of many practical (ethical and devotional) impulses and external (political and canonical) occasions, received the impress of different theological tendencies" (Seeberg).

In the course of the centuries several conceptions of dogma have developed.

ROMAN CATHOLIC CHURCH. The prevailing conception in the RC Church is that a dogma is a truth formally revealed by God and defined by the church, either solemnly (i.e., by a decision of the pope *ex cathedra* or of a church council) or ordinarily (i.e., by the fact that it is generally taught in the church without opposition) (cf. Vatican Council, Denzinger, *Enchiridion Symbolorum,* 1792). Generally the RC conception is one-sidedly intellectual (cf. Vatican Council: "we believe the 'matters' revealed by God to be true," Denzinger, 1789), and continues to be so, in spite of the criticism of the so-called "théologie nouvelle" since 1930. Further, although it does appeal to revelation, this revelation is found in two sources, namely, Holy Scripture and tradition. Hence, many new dogmas have been proclaimed that have no warrant in God's written Word (e.g., the immaculate conception, 1854, and assumption, 1950, of Mary). Because there was an urgent need of an authority capable of delimiting and defining this living tradition, the teaching office of the church was gradually included among the criteria of tradition, first in the form of an infallible council and later on in that of papal infallibility (Vatican Council, 1870). The infallible guidance by the Holy Spirit, promised to the apostles (John 14 and 16), is thereby claimed as the permanent possession of the church. Besides, the church itself is seen as the extension of Incarnation; i.e., in the church Christ Himself lives on in a mystical way. The consequences for the conception of dogma were tremendous. Dogma, pronounced by the infallible council and (or) pope, are infallible and therefore unalterable. "Dogma is eternal as God's Word, as God Himself is eternal. The Church speaks with the same firm conviction with which Christ, and afterwards the apostles, proclaimed the doctrine of the Gospel. She speaks, as her Founder, as one having authority" (Van Doornik). The "relation" between dogma and Scripture has been replaced by "identity."

THE ORTHODOX OR EASTERN CHURCH. Essentially the Orthodox Church is of a structure similar to the RC Church. It also accepts tradition as a source of revelation besides Scripture, considers the church to be the extension of the Incarnation of Christ, and regards the decisions of the first seven ecumenical councils as infallible and absolutely binding. Yet there are also decisive differences. Contrary to the RC conception of the church, which is first of all legal, the Orthodox Church sees the church most of all as a mystical, spiritual fellowship. There is no place for papal primacy, nor for papal infallibility *ex sese.* Yet the Orthodox Church also accepts the infallibility of the church, which operates through the church as a whole, the "sobornost," embracing all the members from the patriarch to the common laborer. Even the general council is not infallible in itself, but its decrees are only recognized as such when they have been accepted by the church as a whole.

THE REFORMATION. The churches of the Reformation, following Luther and Calvin, utterly rejected all infallibility of church and dogma. They indeed accepted the three ancient creeds (Apostles', Nicene, and Athanasian) and the decision of Chalcedon, but this was not because of their infallible character. It was because of their conformity with Holy Scripture (cf. *French Confession of Faith*, art. 5). Holy Scripture, being the Word of God, is the only infallible rule of faith and life. All traditions, however venerable, are subject to this rule. All dogmas, however ancient and cherished, are fallible and subject to correction by Scripture. "If anything shall be found wanting in this Confession, we are ready, God willing, to set forth further truth in harmony with the Scriptures" (Conclusion of the Augsburg Confession; cf. Preface to the Scotch Confession of 1560; the Belgic Confession, art. 8; and the Westminster Confession, xxxi, 4). Within the framework of this subjection to Scripture, however, dogma has a definite authority. Every church member must accept it unless he can prove it to be contrary to Holy Scripture.

The Reformation, in its Lutheran, Calvinistic, and Anglican forms, produced many new confessions in order to profess anew the orthodox faith over against the heresies of the RC Church and the sectarians of the day. Never before nor afterward has there been such a flow of well-written confessions. Unfortunately, in the 17th century scholastic theology began to penetrate into the confessions (noticeable in the Westminster Formularies; very obvious in the Helvetic Consensus Formula of 1675), undermining the real authority of dogma.

LIBERAL ATTITUDE. The origins of the liberal attitude are found in the early 17th century, when the Socinians rejected all binding authority of the confessions and the Arminians refused all legal assent in the form of subscription. The latter limited the authority of dogma to the main points of Christian doctrine and required freedom of interpretation on all other points. The natural consequence of these views is the modernistic position that confessions are not authoritatively binding, but subject to personal interpretation. Usually this interpretation is determined by the prevailing world view. The result is a boundless subjectivism, individualism, and relativism. In most of the larger denominations throughout the world this is the actual situation. In Reformed or Presbyterian churches it is often promoted by so-called Declaratory Statements.

NEO-ORTHODOX POSITION. In recent years, mainly under the influence of Karl Barth, the value and significance of dogma are again much more widely recognized. Yet the Barthian view itself is highly unsatisfactory. Confessions have only a spiritual authority; they are a first commentary on Scripture and then indicate the direction we must take. However, we are not bound by the detailed statements. This whole conception is built upon the false contrast between spiritual authority and codification by church law. The inevitable result is that dogma is subject to a continuous process of individual or collective reinterpretation.

DOGMA AND SCRIPTURE. The correct view is that of the Reformers. The basis and source of dogma is Holy Scripture, the infallible Word of God. "The Word of God establishes the articles of faith and further no one may go, not even an angel" (Luther, *Articles of Smalkald,* II, 2). "The whole counsel of God concerning all things necessary for his own glory, man's salvation, faith, and life, is either expressly set down in Scripture, or by good and necessary consequence may be deduced from Scripture: unto which nothing at any time is to be added, whether by new revelations of the Spirit, or traditions of men" (Westminster Confession, I, 6). The authority of dogma therefore, is derivative and relative. The older Protestant theologians used to express it thus: Scripture is *norma normans* (i.e., it measures all things, itself being measured by nothing); dogma is *normans normata* (i.e., it is normative only because and in as far as it is in agreement with Scripture). Dogma cannot make any claim to infallibility, but is continually to be compared with Scripture and therefore alterable. In fact, several Protestant confessions have been altered in the course of the centuries, either by replacing certain statements (e.g., Belgic Confession, art. 36, by several Reformed churches) or by an explanatory preface (Westminster Confession, by several Presbyterian churches).

DOGMA AND THE CHURCH. The task of the church in the formation of dogma, although important, is yet secondary and subordinate. She has only the formal task of deriving dogma from Holy Scripture in obedient reflection and reproduction, praying for and trusting in the guidance of the Holy Spirit. In His Word God Himself calls her, as the pillar and ground of the truth (I Tim. 3:15), to hold fast to the sound doctrine (I Tim. 6:20; II Tim. 1:13, 14; Titus 1:9, 13; cf. I Tim. 4:6; II Tim. 4:3; Jude 3), and to prove the spirits whether they are of God (I John 4:1). At the same time He promises the guidance of His Spirit (cf. John 16:13-15). This promise, however, is not an automatic guarantee but can be claimed only in correlation with an absolute subjection to Holy Scripture (cf. John 15:7, 10). The reliability of the church's speaking, therefore, does not depend on her own authority but is wholly determined by the conformity of her speaking with Holy Scripture. Materially, dogma derives its authority from Holy Scripture; only formally does it derive it from the church. The church's power here is "not sovereign and legislative, but only administering and declaratory" (H. Bavinck).

SUBSCRIPTION. On the other hand, the church is fully entitled, even obliged, to maintain the authority of dogma. Since her task is to speak the Word of God, she has to require adherence to dogma from all her members and office-bearers, in particular the ministers. She may never leave the interpretation of the Word of God, or of dogma, to the arbitrary choice of the individual preacher, but must watch to see that the flock does not receive stones instead of bread (cf. II John 10; Titus 3:10, 11; Rev. 2:14, 15, 20; Jude 3; I Tim. 3:15; 6:20; Gal. 1:8). The Reformation churches, therefore, soon required confessional subscription to their confessions from all the office-bearers. Such a subscription does not mean a legalization of dogma at the expense of its spiritual character, but it means that spiritual authority is taken seriously. By the subscription, the office-bearer declares of his own free will: I accept this confession as my own, because (*quia*) I believe it to be the true expression of the Biblical message. If later on objections arise against any part of dogma, a gravamen shall be lodged with the proper ecclesiastical assemblies or authorities.

The popular distinction today between a confessional (meaning legalistic) and a confessing (meaning spiritual) church is utterly false. The only truly confessing church is also a truly confessional church. Of course, the confessional church has to guard continually against the dangers of traditionalism, confessionalism, and dogmatism; yet these dangers do not annul, but rather underline the apostolic admonition: "Contend earnestly for the faith which was once for all delivered unto the saints" (Jude 3).

See CATHEDRA; CONFESSIONS AND CREEDS; CONFESSIONALISM; DOGMATISM; INFALLIBILITY OF POPE; TRADITION.

BIBLIOGRAPHY:

K. Barth, *Church Dogmatics* (Edinburgh, 1936 fl.), Vol. I, 1 and Vol. I, 2 (esp. 585-660).

L. Berkhof, *Introductory Volume to Systematic Theology* (Grand Rapids, 1932), 18-39.

G. C. Berkouwer, *De Strijd om het Rooms Katholieke Dogma* (Kampen, n.d.).

H. Bouman, "Die reine Lehre bei Luther und in den Bekenntnisschriften," *Lutherische Runblicke* 6 (1958), 88-101.

E. Brunner, *The Christian Doctrine of God* (London, 1949; 3rd ed., 1958), 3-116.
O. Cullmann, *The Earliest Christian Confessions* (London, 1949).
G. Gloege, "Dogma," *RGG* II (1958), 221-225.
V. Hepp, *De Waarde van het Dogma* (1920).
J. N. D. Kelly, *Early Christian Creeds* (London, 1960).
J. Koopmans, *Het oudkerkelijk dogma in de reformatie, bepaaldelijk bij Calvijn* (Wageningen, 1938). German ed., *Das altkirchliche Dogma in der Reformation* (Beihefte zur EvTh, Munich, 1955).
F. Loofs, *Leitfaden zum Studium der Dogmengeschichte* (1889; latest ed. 3 vols, 1950-1958).
W. Masselink, *General Revelation and Common Grace* (Grand Rapids, 1953), 28-66.
G. E. Meuleman, *De ontwikkeling van het Dogma in de Rooms Katholieke Theologie* (Kampen, 1951).
W. P. Paterson, *The Rule of Faith* (London, 1912; 5th ed., 1933).
A. D. R. Polman, *Onze Nederlandse Geloofsbelijdenis* (Franeker, n.d.), 9-103.
K. Runia, "The Authority of the Confession, The Barthian and the Reformed View," *RTR* 18 (1959), 6-20.
M. J. Scheeben, *Handbuch der katholischen Dogmatik* (Freiburg, 3rd ed., 1933), Vol. I.
H. Schokking, *De leertucht in de Gereformeerde Kerk tusschen 1570 en 1620* (Amsterdam, 1902).
E. Stauffer, *New Testament Theology* (London, 1955), 235 ff., 338 f.
A. Stewart, *Creeds and Churches* (London, 1916).

KLAAS RUNIA

DOGMATISM, not only a simple overestimation of the authority of dogma, but also that attitude of mind that regards dogma, either of science or of the church, as absolute and beyond any criticism. Dogmatism fully ignores the human factors which contributed to the fixation of the dogmas and therefore deems all revision not only unnecessary, but even impermissible.

In the church and in theology dogmatism means that dogma (which is the authoritative formulation of the Biblical message by the church, under the guidance of the Spirit) is equated with Holy Scripture itself. Reflection on and reproduction of the Scriptural revelation is identified with the Scriptural revelation itself. The formulation of the truth by the church is seen as identical with the truth itself.

The classic example of dogmatism is the RC conception of dogma. The *Syllabus Errorum* (1864) condemned the opinion of those who say "that the Roman Pontiffs . . . have even committed errors in defining matters of faith and morals" (Denzinger, 1723). Since 1870 (Vatican Council I), the official doctrine is that the pope, when he speaks *ex cathedra* (i.e., when, with his supreme apostolic authority, he defines a doctrine concerning faith and morals), is endowed with infallibility. Therefore such definitions are irreformable (Denzinger, 1839). One RC theologian says: "There is equivalence, basic identity between revelation and dogma." No wonder that any deviation from dogma or criticism of it is struck by the anathema. The results are disastrous. Dogma fully rules over exegesis. Scripture, the dynamic and infallible Word of God, is silenced by the superstructure of dogma, though the latter is a human and therefore fallible formulation of the truth.

Dogmatism is a permanent danger for all theology and religion, Protestant no less than RC. Basically, it is the result of human pride, which completely forgets the limitation and sinfulness of all human speaking and thinking.

See CONFESSIONALISM; DOGMA.

KLAAS RUNIA

DOLEANTIE, the second secession from the Dutch Reformed (state) Church (Hervormde Kerk) in the 19th century. The first one (1834), under the leadership of Hendrik de Cock and H. P. Scholte (after 1847 a minister in the United States), was called the "Afscheiding" ("Separation") and differed from the Doleantie not in principle, but in its more individualistic method of separation from the original church. This "Afscheiding" resulted in the founding of the Christian Reformed Church in the Netherlands; and members of this church, in turn, founded the Christian Reformed Church in America. After this first secession, many believers in the state church continued their fight against increasing liberalism by demanding strict maintenance of the creeds of the church (the Belgic Confession, the Heidelberg Catechism, and the Canons of Dort). Their first leader was the Calvinist statesman and historian Groen Van Prinsterer, who strove to restore the purity of the church, led the movement for Christian schools, and founded the Dutch Christian political party (Anti-Revolutionaire Partij). His successor in all these activities was Abraham Kuyper, also a statesman (prime-minister of the Netherlands in the beginning of the 20th century) but above all a great theologian, who revived the principles of the Reformation and applied them to the situation of his own time. He became the leader and organizer of the Doleantie of 1886. The term *Doleantie* means "complaining," that the believers who took part in this movement complained (were doleful) of the situation in the church. The Doleantie had its center in Amsterdam, where Kuyper had founded the Free University in 1880. The majority of the consistory (classis) there wanted to follow him in his attempts to liberate the church from the yoke of the liberal-minded synod. After many vicissitudes 75 members of the Amsterdam consistory were suspended and thereafter deposed from their office by synod. The consistory then broke with the synodical organization of the established church, readopted the old Church Order of Dort, and took the name "Dutch Reformed Church" (Nederduitsche Gereformeerde Kerk) with the addition of "Dolerend." In several other places other consistories followed their example, and these "Dolerende kerken" merged with the Christian Reformed Church (which had resulted from the "Afscheiding") under the name "Reformed [Gereformeerde] Churches in the Netherlands" (1892). The church polity of the Doleantie is marked by its stress on the strict maintenance of the creeds and relative autonomy of the local church.

Bibliography:

J. C. van der Does, *De Doleantie in haar wording en beginperiode* (n.d.).

K. Dijk, *De Reformatie van '86* (Kampen, 1936).

D. H. Kromminga, *The Christian Reformed Tradition* (Grand Rapids, 1943), 85-89, 111-116.

L. Praamsma, *Het Dwaze Gods* (Wageningen, 1954).

J. C. Rullmann, *De Doleantie* (Kampen, 1929).

J. C. Rullmann, *De strijd voor Kerkherstel* (Kampen, 1928).

W. Volger, *Om de vrijheid van de Kerk* (Kampen, 1954).

W. J. de Wilde, *Geschiedenis van Afscheiding en Doleantie* (n.d.).

Louis Praamsma

DÖLLINGER, John Joseph Ignatius von (1799-1890), a Roman Catholic historian. One of the outstanding church historians of his day, Döllinger became a leading scholar in the Old Catholic movement. Born in Bamberg, Bavaria, he first studied history and the natural sciences, and later theology, at Wurzburg. After studying law for a time at the request of his father, he continued studying theology at Bamberg, and was ordained as a priest in 1822. After brief service as chaplain to Marktscheinfeld, he became professor of church history at Aschaffenburg. There, in 1826, he published his first treatise, a treatise on the Eucharist in the first three centuries. The work was so outstanding that he was given a doctorate of theology. That same year he began to teach church history at the University of Munich, and about a decade later he became chief librarian and a member of the Academy of Sciences. In the meantime, he had begun publishing the first of many volumes which he wrote in the field of ecclesiastical history.

Although he was at first considered an Ultramontane, his careful studies and broad contacts led him to views which were bitterly opposed by the Jesuits. He took the position that the immaculate conception was a matter on which the church should permit differences of opinion. He proposed the idea of a national German Catholic Church, free from the state but in full communion with Rome. The Jesuits insisted on the absolute necessity of the Papal State, and when Döllinger delivered a lecture on the possible fall of this state, a bitter controversy ensued between the Jesuits and the theologians of Germany.

Prior to the Vatican Council (1870), when it became known that the purpose of that council would be to declare the infallibility of the pope, Döllinger wrote a series of articles in Augsburg's *Allgemeine Zeitung* under the name of Janus. He was suspected of being the author of these and of a number of other articles which opposed the aims of the papacy. He did not attend the council, and the minority group in the council, which opposed infallibility, asked him to discontinue writing on the subject. After infallibility was declared an article of faith, Döllinger was asked to accept it publicly, and when he refused he was excommunicated by Archbishop Scherr in 1871. He still regarded himself as a Roman Catholic, however. He became increasingly interested in the union of all Christian groups. Associating with the Old Catholic movement, he gave a series of seven lectures on the subject of reunion. He served as head of the University of Munich, and continued to write many important works on various aspects of church history. In his old age, Döllinger's views toward Luther and the Reformation changed considerably. His research and his own treatment at the hands of the RC Church enabled him to come to a greater appreciation of the Reformation. He continued to be very active until his death at the age of 90.

Bibliography:

J. Acton, "Döllinger's Historical Work," *The English Historical Review* V (1890), 723.

P. M. Baumgarten, "Döllinger," *CE* V (New York, 1908), V, 94-99.

J. B. Bury, *History of the Papacy in the 19th Century* (London, 1930), 62-64, 71-76, 97-113.

J. Döllinger, *Declarations and Letters on the Vatican Decrees* (Edinburgh, 1891).

J. Döllinger, *Der Papsttum* (Munich, 1892).

J. Döllinger, *Einige Worte über die Unfehlbarkeits adresse* (Munich, 1870).

J. Döllinger, *Erklarung an den Erzbishof von Munchen-Freising* (Munich), 1871).

J. Döllinger, *Erwagunger fur die Bishofe des Consiliums über die Frage der papstlichen Unfehlbarkeit* (Munich, 1869).

J. Döllinger, *The First Age of Christianity and the Church* (London, 1906).

J. Döllinger, *The Gentile and the Jew in the Courts of the Temple of Christ* (London, 1862).

J. Döllinger, *Hippolitus and Callistus* (Edinburgh, 1876).

J. Döllinger, *Kleinere Schriften* (Stuttgart, 1890).

J. Döllinger, *Lectures on the Reunion of the Churches* (New York, 1872).

J. Döllinger, *Lehrbuch der Kirchengeschichte* (Regensburg, 1843).

J. Döllinger, *Die Reformation* (Regensburg, 1845-8).

J. Friedrich, *Ignaz von Dollinger* (Munich, 1899-1901).

L. von Kobell, *Döllinger's Conversations* (London, 1892).

S. Lösch, *Döllinger und Frankreich* (Munich, 1955).

E. Michael, *Döllinger, Ein Charakterbild* (Innsbruck, 1894).

S. J. Tonsor, "Lord Acton on Döllinger's Historical Theology," *Journal of the History of Ideas* 20 (1959), 329-352.

Harry Buis

DOMINIC, SAINT (1170-1221), founder of the monastic Order of Preachers. Dominic was a Castilian who began his studies at Palencia at the age of fourteen. In 1191 he is said to have sold all his possessions, even his books, in order to help the poor during a famine. He became a canon in his native diocese of Osma in 1199, where the bishop, Martin de Bazan (1190-1201), had established a strict discipline among his canons following the rule of St. Augustine. Dominic then took charge of this community until 1203, when he left to accompany Diego on a preaching tour against the Albigensians in Languedoc. For these missionary journeys he voluntarily adopted poverty and gathered a band of like-minded men about him. In 1206 they opened at Prouille a home, under the care of several missionary friars, for women in danger of this heresy.

The official Albigensian crusade which began in 1208 under Innocent III found Dominic at the center, and in 1214 the castle of Casseneuil was put at his disposal by Count Simon IV of Montfort, whereupon he founded an order chiefly for the conversion of the Albigensians. In 1215 he attended the Fourth Lateran Council and petitioned for the establishment of an order of preachers, subject only to the papacy. Recognition came from the bishop of Toulouse and papal approval followed on condition that an existing rule be adopted since the creation of new orders was forbidden by the Council. The Augustinian rule was chosen, because its scope would allow for any kind of organization, and then supplemented by several customs, mostly borrowed from Prémontré, which really created a new order of friars.

The order was confirmed in 1216 by Honorius III, and Dominic's subsequent years were spent journeying through Italy, Spain, and France establishing monastic houses, as well as sending friars abroad especially to the university cities of Paris and Bologna. In 1220 he visited the first General Chapter at Bologna, at which time he insisted on the vow of poverty for the order, which also applied to the nuns. He journeyed to Hungary to preach in 1221 but fell ill and returned to Bologna, where he died. He was canonized in 1234 and given August 4th as a feast day. Austere and of great sanctity, he was less popular than his contemporary, Francis of Assisi. His only concern was to win souls from error through preaching true doctrine, and he refused a bishopric three times.

Dominic and Francis had similar if not equal visions, and the more methodical approach of the former was the result of the trail-blazing of the latter. Nearly the only words of Dominic remaining are those from his equally Franciscan Testament: "Caritatem habete, humilitatem servate, paupertatem voluntariam possedete" ("Hold to charity, preserve humility, possess voluntary poverty").

See DOMINICANS.

BIBLIOGRAPHY:

M. H. Vicaire, *Vie de St. Dominique* (Paris, 1957), 2 vols.

B. Jarrett, *The Life of St. Dominic* (London, 1924).

CHARLES GREENWOOD THORNE, JR.

DOMINICANS. The Order of Preachers (Dominicans) was founded (1216) for preaching and study and was therefore the first religious community to emphasize intellectual concern. Known as Black Friars in England and Jacobins in France, their founder was St. Dominic. The order was to practice both individual and corporate poverty, like the Franciscans. There were to be no possessions except for their houses and churches, and they were to live by begging. Thus the term "mendicant" was applied to them. The order spread rapidly through Europe and Asia, but in the later Middle Ages the discipline was relaxed when in 1465 Sixtus IV revoked the law of corporate poverty and permitted property and permanent income. Their chief interest was education, every house a center of teaching, and they established houses in most university towns. They provided many leaders: Albertus Magnus and Thomas Aquinas were chiefly responsible for the adaptation of Aristotelianism to Christian thought.

The Dominicans were highly organized and the popes used them for preaching the crusades, collecting monetary levies, and carrying out diplomatic missions. Also, the Inquisition was constantly staffed by their members, making them the watch-dogs of orthodoxy (*Domini canes*). With their great missionary zeal, in the age of exploration they followed closely along the paths of the Portuguese and Spanish in the E and W hemispheres. With the appearance of the Jesuits and the rise of other Counter-Reformation orders, the Dominicans were somewhat overshadowed, but they never lost their original characteristics as champions of learning and orthodoxy. Like the Franciscans, they had a Second and a Third Order attached to them, consisting of religious and secular nuns respectively. Both orders of friars surpassed their secular rivals in the universities.

The Dominicans were distinguished for their learning and industry and the Franciscans for their ideas. Both orders elevated preaching, and their churches were built around the pulpit rather than the liturgy. In emphasis, the Dominicans preferred stories of great men of the past, and the Franciscans the homely things of daily life. Both Dominicans and Franciscans had missions to the infidel, as well as feeding the faithful and correcting the heretic through preaching.

See DOMINIC, SAINT.

BIBLIOGRAPHY:

R. F. Bennett, *The Early Dominicans* (Cambridge, 1937).

G. R. Galbraith, *The Constitution of the Dominican Order, 1216–1360* (Manchester, 1925).

CHARLES GREENWOOD THORNE, JR.

DOMITIAN (A.D. 51-96), Roman emperor and persecutor of Christians. Titus Flavius Domitianus was the younger son of the military general and emperor Vespasian, who ruled A.D. 69-79. At the death of Vespasian, Titus, the older brother who had conquered Jerusalem in A.D. 69-70, became emperor. On his death (81) Domitian became the emperor and ruled for a decade and a half (81-96).

Domitian is described as both cruel and autocratic. Such Roman writers as Tacitus, Suetonius, and Pliny the Younger describe a ruler attempting to escape from the power of the Senate, which wished to limit and control his policy of property confiscation that he pursued to raise money for his military expeditions.

During his reign Domitian restored those parts of Rome devastated by the Great Fire of A.D. 79; he put down the Rhineland revolt of Saturninus; and he waged three indecisive frontier wars against Decebalus and the Dacians of the Teutonic Danube region. Domitian also is credited with conquering all of Britain. In the year A.D. 90 Domitian banished all philosophers from Italy, including the stoic, Epictetus.

Following Nero's persecution of A.D. 64-68, Domitian in A.D. 95-96 conducted the first of ten imperial post-Neronian persecutions, which extended into the beginning of the 4th century. He systematically attempted to eliminate Christians on the ground that they were atheists, that is, they would neither acknowledge nor give homage to the gods of Rome. Christians refused to worship the emperor, who had assumed the new title of *Dominus et Deus* ("Lord and God")—a title for which the older Romans who remembered the Republic hated Domitian.

Irenaeus (*c.* 130-*c.* 200), the student of Polycarp, who in turn was the companion of the Apostle John, wrote that John saw the Apocalypse "towards the end of Domitian's reign." This would place the apostle's exile on the island of Patmos in A.D. 96 (Rev. 1:9) and it would thus date the book of Revelation at that time.

Assassination in A.D. 96 ended the rule and persecution of the "Insane Tyrant" Domitian, and it ushered in the reign of Nerva and the Antinines—Rome's five good emperors—which some have called the "Golden Age of Rome."

DOMITILLA, Flavia (*c.* 100), early Christian martyr. Her consul husband, Titus Flavius Clemens, the Emperor Domitian's cousin, was put to death, perhaps for professing Christianity. His wife, also of noble birth, was first banished, later killed. On her property was a Christian burial place, traces of which still remain. Records are fragmentary: there may have been two of this name—the Flavia Domitilla mentioned above, and her niece by marriage.

DONATION OF CONSTANTINE, a document incorporated in the Pseudo-Isidorian Decretals (see DECRETALS, FALSE) which, according to most authorities, appeared about A.D. 750, apparently as part of the negotiations which led to the crowning of Pepin the Great as king of the Franks in 756. These Decretals contained genuine letters of the popes and decisions of church councils along with many spurious documents. The Donation of Constantine claims to have had its origin in the reign of Emperor Constantine early in the 4th century, and describes the miraculous healing of Constantine from leprosy by Pope Sylvester I. As an expression of his gratitude for this remarkable recovery, Constantine, according to this document, gave to Sylvester and his successors "the city of Rome and all the provinces, districts and cities of Italy and of the western regions" as their political domain and, in addition, the primacy over the other metropolitan sees (Antioch, Constantinople, Alexandria, Jerusalem). The document thus became an important factor in fashioning papal policy throughout the Middle Ages and beyond into more modern times.

Nicholas of Cusa in 1433 and Lorenzo Valla in 1440, working independently of each other, declared the document to be spurious on the basis of the historical issues involved and the differences between the Latin of the document and that used in the 4th century.

BIBLIOGRAPHY:

W. Barry, *The Papal Monarchy* (New York, 1902), 590-1303.

E. H. Davenport, *The False Decretals* (Oxford, 1916).

L. Duchesne, *The Beginnings of the Temporal Sovereignty of the Popes* (London, 1908).

K. F. Morrison, *The Two Kingdoms; Ecclesiology in Carolingian Political Thought* (Princeton, 1964).

W. Ullmann, *The Growth of Papal Government in the Middle Ages* (London, 2nd ed., 1962).

C. GREGG SINGER

DONATISTS, a schismatic group which originated in N Africa in the early part of the 4th century and seriously threatened the unity of the early church. Like the Novatian movement of 50 years earlier, this group was concerned with both the nature and the purity of the church. From the time of Cyprian on, there had been in the church in N Africa a strong element which believed that the validity of all ministerial acts depended on the pure character of the clergy who performed them. Unworthy ministers could not perform them in a truly Biblical manner. The Donatist controversy was specifically concerned with the problem of how to treat those who had lapsed from the faith during the persecution under Diocletian and who had surrendered copies of the Scriptures to the Roman officials. They felt that those who were guilty were no longer worthy to hold ecclesiastical office for they threatened the unity of the church. The issue came to a head in 311 when the moderate Mensurius, bishop of Carthage, died, and the majority of the clergy and people elected as his successor Caecilian, an archdeacon, who was immediately consecrated by the African bishops. Thereupon the stricter party charged that Caecilian had received ordination from one who was in mortal sin because he had surrendered copies of the Scriptures to Roman officials during the persecution. A group of Numidian bishops refused to recognize his election and summoned him to Carthage to explain his actions. Caecilian in turn refused to recognize their authority, and they accordingly deposed him from his office. These 70 bishops then chose Majorinus to succeed him. Majorinus died in 315, and he was then succeeded by Donatus, bishop of Numidia. The result of this action was a serious split in the N African church. The Donatists (for the movement now assumed the name of its new leader) now appealed to Constantine to settle the issues. The emperor agreed to make a decision because this controversy threatened the peace of the very institution which he had intended to use as a means for achieving peace and unity in his strife-torn empire. He directed Bishop Melchiades (Miltiades) of Rome and five Gallican bishops to hear the appeal of the Donatists. Their decision, given in 313, was in favor of Caecilian and against Majorinus and Donatus; Caecilian was declared to be the legitimate bishop of Carthage. This controversy caused Constantine to devise a method for settling such disputes, and in 314 he called the Council of Arles, which declared that the Donatists were in error and asserted that ordination was valid even if performed by unworthy clergy and that heretical baptism was valid if it was performed according to the Trinitarian formula.

In 321 the Donatists declared that they would no longer have fellowship with Caecilian because of the persecution to which they had been subjected through the policy of Constantine. About this same time the emperor restored full religious liberty to the Donatists, and by 331 they had nearly 300 bishops. Constans, the successor to Constantine, however, resorted to violent measures against them, and in 347 a more sustained persecution broke out. However, in 361 Julian the Apostate revoked all previous decisions and restrictions against them.

The Donatist party remained strong during the remainder of the 4th century. Its contention that it was the true church because of its purity had a strong appeal in an age in which the church was being torn asunder by the Arian heresy and in which it was becoming increasingly submissive to political forces which threatened its purity.

About A.D. 400 the controversy took a new turn with the appearance of Augustine on the scene in Carthage. There is some evidence that by this time the movement was also becoming somewhat Pelagian in its theology, and this development was sure to attract the attention of the great opponent of Pelagius. In 403 Augustine worked out a plan for their restoration. At this point it was his intention to combat the Donatist schism with instruction and persuasion rather than with force. Augustine persuaded the emperor, Honorius, to call a council at Carthage in 403 to which all the bishops of N Africa were invited. Here a plan was presented by which ten bishops were to be chosen by both groups to discuss the issue and reach an agreement. This attempt failed. Another council in 404 at Carthage was called for drastic action against the schismatics, but Augustine opposed the use of force. In 411 Honorius called another conference, at which Marcellinus, a friend of Augustine, presided. It was composed of 279 Donatists and 286 Catholic bishops. Augustine, in preaching the opening sermon, called for the manifestation of love toward those guilty of schism. Marcellinus decided the issues in favor of the Catholic party and the result was a series of more stringent laws against the Donatists. Their clergy were to be banished, and in 415 they were forbidden to hold religious services on pain of death. The conquest of N Africa by the Vandals a few years later brought great devastation to the church and a practical end to the controversy.

Donatism was another expression of a basic difference within the Christian community over the nature of the church. The Donatists went to one extreme in their insistence that only a church with a pure ministry is the true church and that any church which tolerated any degree of impurity ceases to be a part of the body of Christ. The Catholic party was equally in error in its extreme contention that there is no salvation outside of the true church. Both parties to the controversy failed to discern the Biblical doctrine of the distinction between the visible and invisible churches. It was at this point that Augustine made his great contribution to the doctrine of the church. Modern separatism is the contemporary expression of this age-old difference of opinion, and the only true solution to the problem is the Augustinian-Calvinistic distinction between the visible and invisible churches.

See DIOCLETIAN.

BIBLIOGRAPHY:

D. Benedict, *History of the Donatists* (Providence, 1875).

B. J. Kidd, *A History of the Christian Church to A.D. 461* (Oxford, 1922), 3 vols.

W. H. C. Frend, *The Donatist Church: A Movement of Protesting Roman North Africa* (Oxford, 1952).

P. Schaff, *History of the Christian Church* (Grand Rapids, 1952 reprint), 8 vols.

DONNE, John (1571/2-1631), Anglican poet and clergyman. Donne's father, a prosperous London merchant, died in 1576. His mother, a relative of Sir Thomas More, raised him as a Roman Catholic. After six years at Oxford and Cambridge, taking no degree, he began legal studies in London in 1591. He read widely, travelled abroad (1594-7), wrote love poetry and witty prose exercises (*Paradoxes and Problems*), and gained a reputation for wit and fashion.

Elopement with his employer's niece in 1601 cost him a promising position. The ensuing years were troubled by poverty, illness, the closing of his career, and growing family responsibilities. Donne probably turned to Anglicanism in the late 1590's, but from this period of frustration came both the leisure and the motive for a deepening spiritual experience. About 1605-07 he aided Bishop Thomas Morton in polemics against Rome, but refused clerical preferment. Most of the *Holy Sonnets* date from this period; so does *Biathanatos*, which in its discussion of suicide reflects both his despair and his growing theological interest. Theological implications of the Copernican revolution appear in *The First Anniversary* (1611). Donne's struggle to know his vocation is reflected in *Essays in Divinity*.

His ordination in 1615 was the climax of his journey from Rome. Upon his wife's death two years later, he turned entirely to his vocation as minister, becoming dean of St. Paul's in 1621. A few of his sermons were published during his lifetime, some 163 more after his death.

The best of his religious poetry shows an intensity of spiritual experience and a familiarity with the contemplative tradition, traits seen also in *Devotions upon Emergent Occasions*, written during a serious illness in 1623-4. His style is vigorous, and his far-ranging mind brings to the service of Christian poetry images from a wide variety of experience. He follows the Spanish mystics in describing religious experience in the language of love poetry; thus the erotic pieces of his youth and the religious verse are continuous. The wit, erudition, and love of paradox seen in Donne's poetry are prominent also in his sermons. He displays as well a tough-mindedness bordering on skepticism.

BIBLIOGRAPHY:
J. Bennett, *Four Metaphysical Poets* (Cambridge; rev. ed., 1953).
L. I. Bredvold, "The Religious Thought of Donne in Relation to Medieval and Later Traditions," *Studies of Shakespeare, Milton, and Donne*, University of Michigan Publications: Language and Literature, I (New York, 1925).
C. M. Coffin, *John Donne and the New Philosophy* (New York, 1937).
J. Donne, *Devotions*, J. Sparrow, ed. (Cambridge, 1923).
J. Donne, *Divine Poems*, H. Gardner, ed. (Oxford, 1952).
J. Donne, *Essays in Divinity*, E. Simpson, ed. (Oxford, 1952).
J. Donne, *Poems*, H. Grierson, ed. (Oxford, 1912), 2 vols.
J. Donne, *Sermons*, G. Potter and E. Simpson, eds. (Berkeley and Los Angeles, 1953–), 10 vols.
E. Gosse, *The Life and Letters of John Donne* (London and New York, 1899), 2 vols.
I. Husain, *The Dogmatic and Mystical Theology of John Donne* (London, 1938).
L. Martz, *The Poetry of Meditation* (New Haven, 1954).
R. Sencourt, *Outflying Philosophy* (Hildesheim, 1924).
E. Simpson, *A Study of the Prose Works of John Donne* (Oxford; 2nd ed., 1948).
I. Walton, *The Life of John Donne* (London, 1658).
H. White, "Donne and the Psychology of Spiritual Effort," in R. F. Jones *et al.*, *The Seventeenth Century: Studies in the History of English Thought and Literature from Bacon to Pope* (Stanford, 1951).
M. Wiley, *The Subtle Knot* (Cambridge, Mass., 1952).

CHARLES A. HUTTAR

DONUM SUPERADDITUM, a term used by Rome to describe what is thought to be a supernatural addition granted to man at the time of his creation. Two ideas stand in back of this thought: the eternal destiny of man (his deification and mystical fusion with God) and the meritoriousness of good works. In order to be a supernatural addition granted to Adam had to be granted, over and above his natural endowments, a gracious elevation which would bring the stated goal within his reach. Some (such as Thomas Aquinas) considered this elevation to be coincident with the original righteousness granted to man; others felt that it had to be distinguished from original righteousness either logically or temporally. In any case, according to this concept, man as such, with his purely natural possibilities, must be distinguished from the man who has been endowed with supernatural grace. In other words, this grace does not belong to man's nature. Consequently, when he loses it as a result of sin, he only falls back upon his natural state. The encyclical *Humani Generis* (1950), more or less in opposition to the so-called "théologie nouvelle," still expressly maintains this doctrine by stating that God could have created reasonable beings without a calling to eternal life.

The Reformation saw here both a denial of the high nobility which belongs to man by virtue of his creation and also a necessary weakening of the confession of original sin, since, with Rome, a certain natural soundness and integrity remain after the loss of the supernaturally added image of God. In opposition to this doctrine, the Reformation confesses, on the basis of the Holy Scriptures, the total depravity of fallen man.

See DEPRAVITY; FALL OF MAN; IMAGE OF GOD.

Y. FEENSTRA

DOOLITTLE, Thomas (1632-1707), Puritan minister and schoolmaster. Born at Kidderminster and converted there through hearing Richard Baxter preach the sermons later published as *The Saints' Everlasting Rest*, Doolittle went to Pembroke Hall, Cambridge, in 1649 to study for the ministry. After graduating he became pastor of St. Alphage,

London Wall, in 1653. He received Presbyterian ordination. Upon ejection in 1662, he opened a successful boarding-school, the Pioneer Nonconformist Academy, which continued in various premises in and around London until 1687. The younger Calamy and Matthew Henry were among his pupils. In 1666, after the plague and fire had driven many clergy of the established church away from London, Doolittle risked arrest by holding public services in a wooden shack in Bunhill Fields. Later, he built a permanent meeting-house for his congregation in Mugwell (Monkwell) Street; he was temporarily dispossessed of it but resumed his ministry there in 1689. Ecclesiastically, he was one of Baxter's "mere nonconformists." He was a good educator and catechist, and a useful preacher, but his published sermons are conventional and discursive rather than deep or thought-provoking.

BIBLIOGRAPHY:
A. Gordon, *DNB*, s.v.
A. G. Matthews (ed.), *Calamy Revised* (London, 1934), s.v.
F. J. Powicke, *Life of the Revd. Richard Baxter* (London, 1924), 155.

DOOR, DOORKEEPER. Private houses and rooms had doors in the normal way (e.g., Mt. 6:6; Luke 11:7). They might have bolts or locks and keys (Judges 3:25; II Sam. 13:17, 18). City gates and larger houses were guarded by doorkeepers or (AV) porters (II Sam. 18:26; Mark 13:34; John 18:16). Levites were doorkeepers in the temple (I Chron. 9:17, 18), and one of them says that he would rather be a doorkeeper in the temple than to enjoy the riches of the wicked (Ps. 84:10).

A door is used metaphorically of Christ as the entrance to life (John 10:7, 9); of opportunity (I Cor. 16:9; Col. 4:3; Rev. 3:8); of the barring of the life to Christ (Rev. 3:20); and of exclusion (Mt. 25:10; Luke 13:25).

DOOYEWEERD, Herman (b. October 7, 1894), Dutch jurist-philosopher. The author of numerous historical and systematic works in law, Herman Dooyeweerd is best known internationally as the principal founder and systematician of the philosophy of the Cosmonomic Idea (*Wijsbegeerte der Witsidee*), a critical and constructive system of philosophy animated and directed by basic Biblical principles.

LIFE

Born in Amsterdam to parents participant in the separatist movement of grievance (see DOLEANTIE) against modernism in the state (*Hervormde*) church, he was nurtured in home and at school on neo-Calvinist teaching.

As a student at the Free University of Amsterdam, Dooyeweerd initially preferred music and literature to the study of Groen van Prinsterer's social principles, which he found lacking in satisfactory philosophic depth. Upon promotion to the doctorate with his study of the Dutch Ministerial Cabinet, he began work as a legal assistant in the Department of Labor, researching the sources of law and preparing various departmental projects. After a few years he accepted the adjunct directorship of the Abraham Kuyper foundation with the stipulation that he should attempt a philosophical articulation of Reformed social and political principles. At that time he began to contribute articles regularly to journals and newspapers of the Reformed political party (*Anti-Revolutionaire Partij*).

In 1926 he assumed the chair of legal philosophy, systematic jurisprudence, and early Dutch law at the Free University, in which he served until he retired in 1965. The first decade of his tenure was a time of systematic development of the philosophy of the cosmonomic idea in collaborative fellowship with his brother-in-law, the *classicus*

D. H. Th. Vollenhoven, and with a growing circle of younger scholars.

Dooyeweerd believed that their efforts were linked to Kuyper's cultural principle of sphere-sovereignty. They were viewed by some, however (notably Reformed theologian Valentinus Hepp), as a threat to the theological purity of the movement based on Kuyper's theology. This episode and a later controversy and schism over the views of Klaas Schilder are reflected in Dooyeweerd's frequent strictures against scholasticism and in his continued insistence on a sharp distinction between basic, dynamic religious principles that are central to any comprehensive theoretical view, and theological reflection, which he confines to an analysis and synthesis of the data of faith, a particular mode of experience and "law-sphere" of finite reality.

BASIC PHILOSOPHICAL VIEWS

The major statement of the philosophical movement begun by Dooyeweerd is his own large work, *The Philosophy of the Law-Idea* (*De Wijsbegeerte der Wetsidee*), first published in Dutch in 1935 and later revised and extended in a three-volume English title, *A New Critique of Theoretical Thought*, appearing in 1953. This work, suffering from uneven translation, studded with neologisms and idiosyncratically used familiar terms, constitutes nevertheless the *summa* of this philosophy from which all other works take their point of departure. Some 2,000 pages in length, the *New Critique* offers not only a criticism but, in several formulations scattered throughout, a basic ontology and epistemology from which Dooyeweerd addresses numerous philosophic problems in the various sciences. Furthermore, its startling claim to be a *Christian* philosophy, not, like Thomism, a synthesis of Christian dogma and philosophy, underscores its distinctiveness.

It has been Dooyeweerd's life-long contention that the Biblical groundmotive summarily described by him in the themes of "creation, fall into sin, and redemption by Jesus Christ in the communion of the Holy Ghost" has a radical, salutary, revolutionary, and reformatory effect on our entire philosophic view of man and his experiential world. Kuyper first broke through the hegemony of the scholastic, dualistic world view of nature and grace, particularly in his rediscovery of God's revelation concerning the heart, man's religious center, from which sin proceeds and in which new birth occurs. Thus reason (and, in principle, all of man's faculties) is de-throned from the privileged role accorded it in scholastic thought. Dooyeweerd's philosophic work represents an attempt (1) to analyze the course of philosophy in terms of prevailing religious-ground-motives which variously animate at the heart-level the theoretical enterprise; (2) to criticize the *structure* of theoretical thought from this new perspective; and (3) to develop a constructive philosophic system centrally impelled by vital Biblical truth in its major themes.

On its critical side, Dooyeweerd's philosophy attempts to subject all philosophic systems and rational endeavors to a radical "transcendental critique," thus extending Kant's method of seeking the pre-conditions of various branches of science (e.g., the natural sciences, metaphysics), to theoretical thought as such. Historically this critique ranges over the entire course of W philosophy challenging the dogmatic assumption of autonomy, or religiously neutral independence of revelation, which in various forms appears in every major period of thought. In constructive philosophy this declaration of autonomy manifests itself in the guidance of theory by fundamental motives which frame the possibilities of world and life interpretation within the limits of the cosmos or of human experience. In the case of medieval thought, this was done within an unstable synthesis of immanence thought with the transcendence standpoint of Christian theism. Ancient Hellenic thought, on the other hand, labored within a dualistic world-view, polarized into permanent form and flowing matter. Then, after the emergence of Christianity, the church fathers and medieval doctors tried to synthesize nature conceived in terms of Graeco-Roman science, with grace, or revelational truth. The modern era, stemming from the Renaissance, has vacillated between the two postulates of nature and freedom. Although in each case primacy is variously given to one pole of thought in preference to the other, the latter takes its toll in the form of the inevitably dialectical character of all philosophic systems other than theism, impelled as they are by basically apostate guiding schemata such as those mentioned above.

Dooyeweerd's analysis of the greater number of occidental philosophies uncovers a basic proneness among them to absolutize some aspect of the cosmos or of human experience as the interpretative key to all understanding, an error which actually has pre-theoretical roots in a communal, religious, idolatrous penchant for importing some creaturely entity with God-like powers, and this cannot, in practice or in theory, be done.

By "theoretical thought" Dooyeweerd means the sciences in general, including what Anglo-Saxons would call the normative disciplines. In all its modal varieties, theoretical thought manifests for Dooyeweerd an antithetical relationship between the subject's analytic (or logical) function and the object (*Gegenstand*) under theoretical scrutiny. This relationship sharply distinguishes theory from the naive, everyday pre-scientific experience of temporal reality. Naive, ordinary experience is in immediate contact with the whole structures and concrete events of the world, and forms its conceptions of this concretely given medley of things and events. Theoretical abstraction, on the other hand, selects from the natural inter-connectedness of all given concrete reality a special field of investigation, setting apart by analysis each special "nuclear" meaning from other meaning-aspects of the cosmos.

In the above Dooyeweerd assumes an intentional structure to consciousness; it is not merely an inner state, but refers always to some object. Conceptuality, either at the everyday "naive" level or in the special case of theory, is a selective activity of concentrating on properties. But in the case of theorizing, properties are distinguished apart from their actual inherence in the medley of concrete things and events, and are conjoined in what Dooyeweerd calls "logical simultaneity."

A further assumption is the objective existence of the references of consciousness in the case not only of things but also of abstracted properties, and even the common realms of properties and laws which he variously calls "modalities," "modal aspects," "law-spheres," indicating such categories as physical, biological, psychological, etc. Delineation of these aspects is difficult, and Dooyeweerd has sometimes altered his arrangement of the modalities and, correspondingly, his order of the sciences. Furthermore, some of his collaborators have challenged the propriety of several aspects recognized by him. He nowhere advances formal proof for the "reality" of things, events, or aspects, but seems to assume it in general agreement with common sense and the Biblical doctrine of creation.

The character of theoretical thought in general is determined by the pre-scientific answers given to three basic transcendental questions concerning the world, the self, and the origin-God.

These answers are decisively influenced in turn by pre-theoretical forces disposing a thinker culturally and inwardly in his religious "ego," his selfhood, or in Biblical terms, "the heart." The theoretical "issue" proceeding ultimately from this basic dispositional force is the thinker's formulation of the idea of cosmic law, which is further determinative for subsequent, more special theoretical conceptions. Thus Dooyeweerd's analysis of theoretical thought agrees with his critical interpretation of the religious bases of W philosophy. Furthermore, it becomes apparent that general theory is radically pre-set by the informal commitments of a man's society and culture, interpreting life and the universe ultimately out of the religious depths of his heart.

Although the philosophy of the cosmonomic idea is avowedly anti-metaphysical in the sense of rejecting all theoretical speculations about "ultimate reality," nevertheless, in agreement with the dynamic religious fundamentals of the system, certain broad general doctrines emerge concerning the created world, or "temporal reality," as Dooyeweerd characteristically calls it.

The most fundamental and comprehensive determination of all creaturely reality is time, which is described as analyzable into order (nothing is born old) and duration. Only God and man in his religions transcend time. All creaturely reality shows in time its reference to its origin. The temporal structures, or laws, are in inextricable correlation with subjects. The reduction of either side of the correlation leads to rationalism (stressing the law side) or to irrationalism, frequently of an individualistic kind. Also, in time, the various modal aspects of meaning are irreducible to any one, nor are they causal one of the other, yet all are inseparable. Each aspect remains "sovereign," i.e., retains its peculiar perspective within its sphere, even as the separate hues of the color spectrum are disclosed as originating from white light.

Furthermore, somewhat reminiscent of a Leibnizian monad, each aspect reflects the full diversity of meaning in its own special way. Although the modalities (number, space, motion, energy, life, the psychical, analysis, history, language, social relations, economics, harmony—the aesthetic, legal retribution, love—ethics, and faith) are disclosed only through theoretical analysis and are not concrete, yet they do objectively exist.

EVALUATION

Dooyeweerd's work has attracted attention internationally. While sometimes criticized for its alleged "messianic" ambitions or its vagueness, it has nonetheless won increasing respect in a variety of ways, particularly as a critical instrument unmasking the tacit pre-theoretical dogmatic assumptions lurking beneath self-styled neutral, empiricist philosophies. Although in 1962 a philosophy conference at Wheaton College, Illinois, was dedicated to the study of his thought, his philosophy's imposing mass and Teutonic lingual form have hindered its accessibility in the Anglo-American world. The *New Critique* still awaits its crisp, American exposition. Nevertheless, his fame has spread by virtue of his lectures in Europe, Africa, and North America. Furthermore, Dooyeweerd, the Christian philosopher, has become a focus of serious study in a number of doctoral dissertations and monographs.

Since his retirement Dooyeweerd has published relatively little but has busied himself refining and completing his as yet unpublished *Encyclopedia of the Science of Law*, which combines both his philosophic and juridical knowledge in their maturity. In 1970 he returned again to America to receive an honorary doctorate of letters from Gordon College, Massachusetts.

BIBLIOGRAPHY:

Works by Dooyeweerd (philosophical works available in English):

Articles

"Christianity, Humanism, and the European Future," *Delta* (Winter, 1960), 39-41.

"The Contest about the Concept of Sovereignty in Modern Jurisprudence and Political Science," *Free University Quarterly* (1st year), 85-106.

"The Secularization of Science," *International Reformed Bulletin*, 9th year (July, 1966), 2-17.

"What is Man?" *International Reformed Bulletin*, 3rd year (No. 6), 4-16.

Books

In the Twilight of Western Thought. Studies in the Pretended Autonomy of Philosophic Thought (Philadelphia, 1960).

A New Critique of Theoretical Thought (Philadelphia, 1954-1957), 4 vols.

Transcendental Problems of Philosophic Thought. An Inquiry Into the Transcendental Conditions of Philosophy (Grand Rapids, 1948).

Works on Dooyeweerd (expository and critical):

V. Brummer, *Transcendental Criticism and Christian Philosophy* (Franeker, the Netherlands, 1961).

R. Clouser, *Empirical Pluralism*, An Essay in the Philosophy of Herman Dooyeweerd (dissertation, University of Pennsylvania, unpublished, 1970).

A. Holmes, *Christian Philosophy in the 20th Century* (Nutley, N. J., 1969).

M. Fr. J. Marlet, *Grundlinien der Kalvinistischen "Philosophie der Gèsetzesidee" Als Christlicher Tranzendental Philosophie* (München, 1954).

E. L. H. Taylor, *The Christian Philosophy of Law, Politics and the State.* A Study of the Political and Legal Thought of Herman Dooyeweerd (Philadelphia, 1966).

W. Young, "Herman Dooyeweerd," P. E. Hughes, ed., *Creative Minds in Contemporary Theology* (Grand Rapids, 1966), ch. 9.

T. GRADY SPIRES

DOPHKAH, a place in the desert where the Israelites encamped after leaving the wilderness of Sin (Num. 33:12, 13). The name is derived from a verb meaning "to drive (sheep) too quickly."

DOR, a port about twelve miles S of Carmel, whose king fought with Jabin against Joshua (Josh. 11:2; 12:23). It remained in Phoenician hands (Judges 1:27), however, until the early 12th century B.C., when the Peoples of the Sea, having been repulsed from Egypt, descended on the Palestinian coast. The Tjeker, a group closely associated with the Philistines, occupied the N and Dor, to which Wen-Amon recorded a visit (*ANET*, 25 ff.).

With David it passed into Israelite hands and Solomon's appointment of one of his sons-in-law as governor (I Kings 4:11) was doubtless to strengthen Israel's tenuous control in opposition to both Philistine and Phoenician interests. Although Dor served as a chief port, it never played a vital role in the economic life of Israel, whose Mediterranean commerce was principally through Phoenician intermediaries.

Tiglath-pileser established Du'ru as a province separate from Samaria about 733 B.C. and in the Persian period it was subject to the control of Sidon, whose prince Eshmunazar refers to Dor as one of "the mighty lands of Dagon" which had been given to him, implying that as late as the 5th century, Philistine influence was still powerful there. With the founding of Caesarea in 10 B.C., about nine miles S, Dor rapidly passed into oblivion.

DORCAS, a Christian woman in Joppa (Acts 9:36, 40). The miraculous restoration to life of Dorcas is the second of three incidents linked together in the missionary activity of Peter beyond Jerusalem. Peter's missionary activity helps to explain and illustrate the progress of the church, first in the healing of Aeneas at Lydda, then in the restoration of Dorcas, or Tabitha, at nearby Joppa, and finally in the extended and important narrative of the conversion and reception of Cornelius into the church.

The raising of Dorcas is one of the miracles done through the apostles to show their distinctive office of teaching and leadership in the church (cf. Acts 2:43; 5:12; 8:18).

DORNER, Isaak August (1809-1884), German theologian. Dorner was a mediating theologian who sought to combine historical objectivity, Schleiermachian experientialism, and Hegelian idealism. He was educated at Tübingen just after rationalist forces had supplanted the older supernaturalism, and he later taught at several German universities. According to Dorner, religious certainty rests not in the authority of God revealed in Scripture, but in a union of the subject and object of religious knowledge, and it must develop speculatively into scientific knowledge. Instead of beginning with the basic Biblical distinction between God and the creation, Dorner begins with the Incarnation, the essential feature of which is the unity of the Divine and human. God objectifies Himself in the Incarnation, which is the completion of creation. The God-man is necessitated by the Divine idea and the being of man, and He is only secondarily brought into connection with the need for redemption. The Trinity is not three Persons, one God, but three modes of being, all aspects of one personality arising out of the ethical constitution of God. Consequently, the Incarnation does not mean that the Second Person of the Trinity takes upon himself a human nature, but that a self-imparting Logos aspect of God is gradually united with the human person.

Dorner was also interested in church polity and pressed for a national German church to incorporate both rationalist-modernist elements and confessionalism on a minimal basis of union.

BIBLIOGRAPHY:

K. Barth, *Die protestantische Theologie im 19. Jahrhunderd* (Zurich, 1947).

H. Benckert, "Isaak August Dorners 'Pisteologie,'" *ZThK* 14 (1933), 257-276.

I. Bobertag, *Isaak August Dorner* (Guetersloh, 1906).

A. Dorner, "Dorner: Isaak August D.," *Allgemeine Deutsche Biographie* XLVIII (1904), 37-47.

"Dorner's Christology," *The Biblical Repertory and Princeton Review* 22 (1860), 101, 117.

Fr. H. R. von Frank, *Geschichte und Kritik der neueren Theologie* (Leipzig, 4th ed., 1908).

R. H. Gruetzmacher, *Textbuch zur deutschen systematischen Theologie und ihrer Geschichte vom 16. bis 20. Jahrhundert* (Guetersloh, 1955), I, 156-160.

G. S. Hall, tr., "Outlines of Dr. J. A. Dorner's System of Theology," *The Presbyterian Quarterly and Princeton Review* n.s. 1 (1872), 720-747.

E. Hirsch, *Geschichte der neuern Evangelischen Theologie* (Guetersloh, 1954), V.

O. Kirn, "Dorner, Isaak August," *RE*³ IV (1898), 802-807.

O. Pfleiderer, *Die Entwicklung der Protestantischen Theologie in Deutschland seit Kant und in Grossbritannien seit 1825* Freiberg i. B., 1891).

D. W. Simon, "Isaac August Dorner," *The Presbyterian Review* 8 (1887), 569-616.

NORMAN SHEPHERD

DORT, THE SYNOD OF. The Synod of Dort (1618-19) is well known because it dealt with Arminianism and rejected it as contrary to Scripture and to the confessional position of the Reformed Church. The Arminian controversy was the most important of the controversies which took place within the Reformed Church. It corresponds to the Pelagian controversy in the early church, involving the problem of the relation of Divine sovereignty and human responsibility. Calvinism represented consistent, logical, conservative orthodoxy; Arminianism represented an elastic, progressive, changing liberalism (P. Schaff, *Creeds of Christendom* I, 509-10).

Background

In 1603 James Arminius (a latinization of his Dutch name Jakob Hermandszoon) was appointed professor of theology in the University of Leyden. Having studied at Leyden and at Geneva under Beza, he was already under suspicion during his ministry in Amsterdam, in particular concerning his exposition of Romans 7, his rejection of the Reformed doctrine of reprobation, and his modification of the doctrine of original sin. From the beginning, his colleague at

Leyden, Franciscus Gomarus, distrusted his orthodoxy. Soon a conflict arose, which in a short time spread over all of Holland. During the conflict Arminius himself died in 1609, but his followers, in particular Episcopius and Uyttenbogaert, continued the battle and soon organized themselves into a party. In 1610 the Arminians met secretly in Gouda and drafted the *Remonstrance*, to be handed to the government. After a rejection of five Calvinist propositions, there followed five positive articles, teaching the following points: (1) conditional election (i.e., on the basis of foreseen faith); (2) universal atonement (i.e., Christ died for all men, though only believers will be saved); (3) the necessity of regeneration; (4) resistible grace; (5) uncertainty of perseverance.

In 1611 the Calvinists also met and drafted a *Counter-remonstrance*. Various conferences of the two parties led to no result. When the government, under the leadership of John Van Oldebarnveldt, openly began to support the Arminians, who were Erastians in their polity, Prince Maurice of Orange intervened, imprisoned some of the government leaders, and opened the way for a national synod.

The synod was convened by Parliament (at a cost of 100,000 guilders) and met on Nov. 13, 1618. It was composed of three groups: (1) delegates from the Dutch churches and universities (56 ministers and elders, and five professors); (2) foreign delegates (a total of 26 people from England, the Palatinate, Hesse, Bremen, Emden, Nassau, and several city churches in Switzerland); (3) political commissioners (18 in number, who were not members of synod, but supervised the proceedings and were required to report back to Parliament). The president of the august meeting was John Bogerman. The other members of the moderamen were Hommius, Damman, Faukelius, and Rolandus. Apart from the Arminian controversy, the synod made decisions on other important matters, such as the translation of the Bible (resulting in the Bible of 1637, the Dutch equivalent of the Luther Bible and the King James Version), preaching and catechizing, baptism of the children of non-Reformed parents, training for the ministry, the printing of religious books, and the revision of the church order (resulting in the Church Order of Dort).

Proceedings

The main business of the synod, however, was the Arminian controversy. Thirteen Remonstrants were summoned before synod. Officials were very unsatisfied with the Remonstrants' statements of their own positions and dismissed them with charges of deception. After this dismissal it was agreed that all delegations were to summarize the doctrines of the Arminians from their writings and to formulate their own views of these doctrines. When these *judicia* were handed in, there appeared to be a remarkable amount of agreement. They themselves agreed together on the following points: (1) they all formulated their own view in an infralapsarian manner; (2) they all rejected the idea of "foreseen faith"; (3) concerning reprobation, they all formulated it in the negative sense of "passing by"; (4) they all rejected the doctrines of the Arminians. A committee of six members, three foreign and three Dutch delegates, drafted a positive statement on the five major points of doctrine, followed by an explicit rejection of the Arminian errors. The five major points were (1) unconditional election; (2) limited atonement (Christ died for the elect only); (3) the total depravity of man; (4) the absolute need of regeneration by the irresistible grace of the Spirit; and (5) the final perseverance of the saints. After a few small alterations, the "canons" were signed by all members of the synod, on April 23, 1619.

After the synod, many Remonstrant ministers in Holland refused to sign the Canons of Dort, resulting in the deposition of some 200 of them. Many fled and went abroad but returned during the reign of Prince Frederic Henry and established their own Arminian churches. Always remaining a rather small denomination, they gradually became the most liberal church in the Netherlands.

Evaluations of the synod have been and still are widely divergent, depending on one's theological position. Arminians have called it "the persecuting Synod of Dort." Reformed theologians have eulogized it it the most glowing terms. It is evident that the Synod of Dort was of the utmost importance for the whole development of the Reformed Church and of Reformed theology. The Arminian issue was not peripheral, but concerned the very heart of the Christian faith. The question was whether salvation is fully God's work or whether man makes his own contribution, in the form of his act of faith. By rejecting the idea of mere foreseen faith the Synod of Dort upheld the sovereignty and gratuity of Divine grace.

Importance

See ARMINIUS; REMONSTRANCE; CONTRA-REMONSTRANTS; CONFESSIONS AND CREEDS.

BIBLIOGRAPHY:

G. Brandt, *History of the Reformation in and about the Low Countries* (London, 1720-1723), 4 vols.

C. A. Briggs, *Theological Symbolics* (Edinburgh, 1914).

W. Cunningham, *Historical Theology* (London, 1960), II, 371-513.

P. Y. De Jong, ed., *Crisis in the Reformed Churches* (Grand Rapids, 1968).

J. R. De Witt, "The Synod of Dort," *The Banner of Truth* (London, December, 1968), No. 63.

K. Dijk, *De strijd over Infra- en Supralapsarisme in de Gereformeerde Kerken van Nederland* (Kampen, 1912).

K. Doornbos, *De Synode van Dordrecht. getoetst aan het recht der kerk* (Amsterdam, 1967).

P. Geyl, *The Netherlands in the Seventeenth Century*, Vol. I (New York, 1961).

B. Glasius, *Geschiedenis der Nationale Synode in 1618 en 1619 gehouden te Dordrecht* (Leyden, 1860-61), 2 vols.

M. Graf, *Beitrage zur Kenntnis der Geschichte der Synode von Dordrecht* (Basel, 1825).

H. Kaajan, *De Groote Synode van Dordrecht in 1618–1619* (Rotterdam, 1918).

H. Kaajan, *De Pro-Acta der Dordtsche Synode* (Amsterdam, 1914).

H. H. Kuyper, *De Post-Acta* (Amsterdam, 1899).

J. L. Motleg, *The Rise of the Dutch Republic* (London, 1856), 3 vols.

P. Schaff, *The Creeds of Christendom* (New York, 1907), I, 508-523.

T. Scott, *The Articles of the Synod of Dort: with a History of Events which made way for that Synod*, etc. (London, 1818).

J. Uytenbogaert, *Kerckelijke Historie* (Amsterdam, 1646), 3 vols.

L. Wagenar, *Van Strijd en Overwinning* (Utrecht, 1909).

KLAAS RUNIA

DOSITHEUS:

(1) A Judaeo-gnostic heretic of the second century from Samaria about whom very little is known. According to Hegesippus, as quoted by Eusebius, he was a founder of one of the original sects in Palestine. Origen mentions him several times and claims that he posed as the Messiah foretold in Deut. 18:18, and insisted on a strict observance of the sabbath. The Clementine Recognitions (211-231) regard him as first a disciple and later the teacher of Simon Magus. Dositheus' followers (Dositheans) were only a small body and survived until the 10th century.

(2) A bishop (1641-1707), Patriarch of Jerusalem.

DOSKER, Henry Elias (1855-1926), Dutch Reformed theologian. He was born at Bunschoten, Netherlands. After immigrating to the United States, he studied at Hope College, Holland, Michigan (A.B., 1876; M.A., 1879) and New Brunswick Theological Seminary, New Jersey, and graduated from Mc-

Cormick Theological Seminary, Chicago (1879). He received honorary doctorates from Rutgers (1894), Central University of Kentucky (1905), and Hope College (1926). He was pastor of the Ebenezer Church, Holland, Michigan (1879-1882); pastor, Grand Haven, Michigan (1882-1886); instructor in historical theology, Western Theological Seminary (1884-1888); pastor of Third Church, Holland, Michigan (1889-1894); and professor of church history, first at Western (1894-1903), and later at Louisville Presbyterian Theological Seminary, Kentucky, from 1903 until his death there, December 23, 1926. He was a firm Dutch Calvinist, first in the Reformed Church in America and afterwards in the Presbyterian Church, U.S.A. He edited the Hope College magazine (1894-1903), was associate editor of the *Presbyterian and Reformed Review* (1898-1902), and after 1903 an editorial contributor to the *Christian Observer.* He wrote *De Zondagschool* (Kampen, 1882), *Levensschets van Dr. A. C. Van Raalte* (1893), *Topical Outline Studies in Ecclesiastical History* (Milwaukee, 1901; rev. Louisville, 1913), *The Early Dutch Anabaptists* (New York, 1910), *Recent Sources of Information on the Anabaptists in the Netherlands* (New York, 1917), *The Dutch Anabaptists* (Philadelphia, 1921), and numerous articles in periodicals and journals.

BIBLIOGRAPHY:

SHERK, III, 495 f.

P. N. Vandenberge, ed., *Historical Directory of the Reformed Church in America, 1628-1965* (New Brunswick, N. J., 1966).

J. M. Vander Meulen, "A Sketch of the Life of Rev. Henry Elias Dosker," *Union Seminary Review*, 38, iii (1927), 245-253.

ALBERT H. FREUNDT, JR.

DOSTOIEVSKY, Fyodor Mikhaylovich (1821-1881), Russian novelist and journalist. Dostoievsky was educated in Moscow and at the school of military engineers in Leningrad (then St. Petersburg). In 1841 he received a commission in the army; but three years later he left the army to devote himself to literature. The publication in 1846 of his first novel, *Poor Folk*, was an event marking the arrival of a new literary age in Russia. Dostoievsky came to be regarded as the most promising of the young Russian novelists. His early works show the influence of Gogol and to a lesser extent of Balzac. They manifest great sympathy for the humiliated and the downtrodden.

A wave of political reaction brought about the arrest of Dostoievsky on April 23, 1849, because of his association with a group which under the leadership of Petrashenski met to study the French socialists and to discuss social and political reform. By way of intimidation, Dostoievsky and others were condemned to death, and they were reprieved at the last moment before execution. Dostoievsky was sent to the penal colony of Omsk, where he spent four years. This imprisonment worked profoundly on him. During it he evolved his notion of Christianity, which tied the worship of Christ together intimately with what he thought was the deep-seated reverence for Him among the simple Russian folk. In 1854 Dostoievsky was released, and in 1859 was amnestied and allowed to live in the capital. By 1856 he had been able to resume his literary work.

Upon his return to Leningrad, Dostoievsky continued to publish novels and to engage in journalism. In the latter, he attempted to steer between the conservatives and the free-thinkers, and to advocate a democratic and Christian nationalism. This position was influenced heavily by the so-called slavophils, who looked to the simple Russian folk as the source of exalted spiritual values.

In 1864 Dostoievsky published *Letters from the Underworld*, which marked a turning point in his labors, beginning the series of great novels for which he is famous. Well-known novels belonging to this period are *Crime and Punishment* (1866), *The Idiot* (1868-1869), *The Possessed* (original title, *The Demons*) (1880), and his most mature novel, *The Brothers Karamazov* (1880).

Dostoievsky had many difficult times, personally and financially; but during his later years he became influential as a journalist and had rather favorable circumstances. His fame reached its high point in 1880, after his address at the unveiling of the Pushkin Memorial. At his death on January 28,1881, his funeral was accompanied by an inspiring public demonstration.

Dostoievsky's major theme was "life," which he defended against the titanism of Byron. For Dostoievsky, Byronism strangled life in a demoniacally inspired selfishness. This selfish willfulness he embodied in the figure of the Grand Inquisitor, who wished to put Christ to death again because He had refused worldly power in favor of the life of love. Indeed, when Dostoievsky speaks of life normatively, it is the new life in Christ which he has in mind. Nevertheless, he uses the term "life" in a too broad and undefined way, often scarcely distinguishing it from the conception of life found in paganism. Bohatec presents Dostoievsky as a life-philosopher, whose thoughts approximate those of the ancient myths of life as well as those of the Gospel of Christ.

Many of Dostoievsky's ideas parallel those of the slavophil thinker Solovyev, and more remotely those of late German Idealism. Dostoievsky regarded himself, too, as a slavophil. For him the calling of the simple Russian folk was to express its love for Christ and to extend the bounds of its influence for the sake of the kingdom of the new life of love in Christ.

Bibliography:

The Novels of Fyodor Dostoevsky, tr. Constance Garnett (London, 1916-1927), 12 vols.

Dostoyevsky Portrayed by His Wife, The Diary and Reminiscences of Mme. Dostoyevsky, tr. S. S. Koteliansky (London, 1926).

N. Berdyaev, *Dostoievsky: An Interpretation by Nicolas Berdyaev*, tr. Donald Attwater (New York, 1934).

N. Berdyaev, *The Russian Idea* (New York, 1948).

J. Bohatec, *Der Imperialismusgedanke und die Lebensphilosophie Dostojewskijs* (Graz-Köln, 1951).

A. Gide, *Dostoevsky*, new ed., reset (Norfolk, Conn., 1949).

R. Guardini, *Der Mensch und der Glaube: Versuche über die religiöse Existenz in Dostojewskijs grossen Romanen* (Leipzig, 1933).

V. Ivanov, *Freedom and the Tragic Life: A Study in Dostoevsky*, tr. Norman Cameron (New York, 1957).

S. J. Popma, "Dostojewski," *Denkers van deze tijd*, II (Franeker, n.d.), 69-129.

Robert D. Knudsen

DOTHAN, a town about nine miles NE of Samaria in a valley traversed by the main caravan route between Damascus and Egypt. It is strategically located in the pass leading from the Plain of Esdraelon to the mountains of Ephraim (Samaria).

At Dothan, Joseph found his brothers pasturing their flocks. In their jealousy they cast him into a nearby pit and subsequently sold him to passing Midianites (Gen. 37:17-28). The Egyptian empire-builder Thutmose III (*c.* 1490-1435 B.C.) lists Dothan among the places he captured during the course of his campaigns into Palestine.

The prophet Elisha was besieged by a band of Syrians (Aramaeans) at Dothan. The army was smitten with blindness and the prophet directed them to Samaria, where their sight was restored and they were sent home without further punishment (II Kings 6:8-23).

Excavations have been conducted at Dothan by Joseph P. Free since 1953. Discoveries include pottery from the Middle Bronze Age, attesting the existence of a city there during the Patriarchal Age.

BIBLIOGRAPHY:
J. P. Free, *BA* 19 (1956), 43-48.

DOUBLE PROCESSION OF THE HOLY SPIRIT. See FILIOQUE.

DOUKHOBORS (DUKHOBORS), a Russian sect. The name means "Spirit Wrestlers." They were persecuted both because of their "spiritual" anti-state attitudes and also because of the depravity of some of their "spirit-led" groups. Tolstoy and British Quakers assisted their emigration to Canada in 1899, and on the whole they have become integrated into community life, though with an ascetic slant. One group, the Sons of Freedom, have shown their contempt for material things by burning and destroying property. The sect rejects the Bible as authoritative, believing in man as "the living book," capable of receiving direct divine guidance. They reject the deity of Christ, but many expected His return in 1902.

DOUMERGUE, Emile (1844-1937), Calvin scholar. Professor of church history in the theological seminary of Montauban (1880-1919), Doumergue specialized in the scholarly study of John Calvin. His purpose was to refute the calumnies which from the beginning were spread by RC controversialists, and to show the up-to-dateness of the theological and ecclesiastical thought of Calvin. In this he was eminently successful. He published seven large volumes under the title *Jean Calvin, les hommes et les choses de son temps* (*John Calvin, the Men and the Things of His Time*) (1899-1927) and another work *Iconographie calvinienne* (*Calvinistic Iconography*) (1909) which brought together and discussed the portraits and representations of Calvin by artists and others. This whole work is replete with the presentation of historical facts, with theological discussions and with an appraisal of the views of many scholars. Doumergue also wrote a painstaking description of the local background of cities where Calvin's activity took place, especially Geneva (Vol. III). Critics have sometimes objected to Doumergue's admiration for Calvin and have spoken of a "Calvinistic hagiography." This accusation is not justified. Doumergue had to contend against a powerful stream of false charges and harsh judgments. He needed to bring to the fore the facts and the texts in order to show the great accomplishments of Calvin and his world-wide influence.

Doumergue also wrote a volume concerning the use of Psalms in the Huguenot church. He was a keen journalist who wrote incisive articles every week in the weekly *Le Christianisme au XXe siècle* (*Christianity in the 20th Century*) and in the review *Foi et Vie* (*Faith and Life*) edited by his brother Paul Doumergue. These articles wielded a great influence on the life of French Protestantism. He maintained in them the traditional stance of the defenders of the evangelical faith, what was called orthodoxy at the end of the 19th century. He was an indefatigable worker until an advanced age and adhered all his life to the line of Calvinistic thought to which he had made his early commitment. One might also mention his books on *Reformed Piety According to Calvin* (1909) and *The Character of Calvin* (1941), as well as very numerous addresses on Reformed thought, art, and history.

BIBLIOGRAPHY:
J. Pannier, "Le doyen Doumergue," *Bulletin de la Société de l'Histoire du Protestantisme Français* LXXXVI (1937), 86-89.
E. Doumergue, "Calvin, An Epigone of the Middle Ages, or An Initiator of Modern Times?" *Princeton Theological Review* VII (1909), 52-104.
E. Doumergue, "Music in the Work of Calvin," *Princeton Theological Review* VII (1909), 529-552.

JEAN CADIER

DOVE (as a symbol), one of the oldest and most common Christian symbols found in both literature and art. It has numerous but related meanings. The Biblical usage of the figure to describe the Holy Spirit's descent upon Christ at His baptism explains the use of the dove as the symbol of the Third Person, either alone, in combination with other Persons of the Trinity, or in representations of Biblical events, as the annunciation and Pentecost. Doves may represent the seven gifts of the Spirit (after Isa. 11:2, Vulg.), other Christian virtues, and the work of the Spirit in inspiration and illumination. They may also represent believers baptized with the Spirit (see also Mt. 10:16), and especially their souls leaving the body at death, as frequently in the Roman catacombs. The dove is also a symbol of Christ, after Song of S. 5:2 (the bride), or Lev. 12:1-8 (sacrificial doves), or Gen. 8:11 (the dove bringing news of peace to the ark, conceived of as the church). The dove has become the symbol for peace in general.

Bibliography:
J. P. Kirsch, "Colombe," *DACL* (1948), vol. III, part II, 2198-2231.
W. Stengel, *Das Taubensymbol des Hl. Geistes* (Strasbourg, 1904).
F. Suehling, *Die Taube als Religioeses Symbol im Christlichen Alterum* (*Römische Quartalschrift*, Supplement 24), 1930.

DOWNAME, John (d. 1652), Puritan practical theologian. A son of Bishop Downame of Chester, John Downame was educated at Christ's College, Cambridge. He ministered at St. Olave's, Jersey (1599-1601), St. Margaret's, Lothbury, London (1601-1618), and Allhallows the Great, Thomas Street, London, from 1630. In 1643 he became licenser of theological books for the press.

Downame stands with Perkins, Greenham, and Richard Rogers as one of the architects of the Puritan theology of godliness. He wrote extensively in this field, his major works being *The Christian Warfare* (two parts, 1604 and 1611; third enlarged edition, totaling over 1750 quarto pages, in 1612 and 1619) and *A Guide to Godlynesse, or a Treatise of a Christian Life* (folio, 1622). He develops the characteristic Puritan themes: the Christian life as a pilgrimage and a warfare against the world, the flesh, and the devil; the need for self-discipline and for arming oneself against the evil day with preservatives and remedies against sin and morbidity; the way to live by faith in Christ, in the enjoyment of assurance and in eager anticipation of heaven; the way to glorify God in every department of life. Downame is a pedestrian writer, but his practical teaching is clear, sound, scriptural, balanced, and wise.

Bibliography:
B. Brook, *Lives of the Puritans* (London, 1813), II, 496 f.
T. Fuller, *Worthies of England* (Chester, 1663), 191.
G. Goodwin, *DNB*, s.v.
W. Haller, *The Rise of Puritanism* (New York, 1938), 85, 155 ff.

James I. Packer

DOWRY in Scripture may carry its generic meaning of "endowment, gift" (cf. Gen. 30:20, where it describes Leah's God-given son). In marriage contexts, however, it translates מֹהַר (Arabic, *mahr*). This term does not signify presents *from* the bride's father (as in Gen. 29:24; Judges 1:15; I Kings 9:16; cf. Roman dowries, Plautus, *Trinum*, iii, 2; v, 72) but rather a compensation *to* him from the groom (Gen. 34:12; Ex. 22:16). The dowry thus represents a survival of "bride purchasing" (Ruth 4:10; Hos. 3:2; parallel to the Homeric *hedna, Iliad*, xi, 244; xvi, 178; *Odyssey*, xvi, 391; xxi, 160). "Dowries of virgins" were paid at betrothal or upon cases of seduction (even if the marriage did not follow, Ex. 22:

17). A dowry was generally 50 shekels (Deut. 22:28-29), which was twice the value of a slave (Ex. 21:32; Lev. 27:4). Dowries and gifts to the bride (Gen. 24: 53) could be stipulated in advance. They varied according to her rank (Gen. 34: 12; I Sam. 18:18, 23). Specified labor or heroic deeds might constitute equivalents (Gen. 29:18-20, 27-30; Judges 1: 12; I Sam. 18:17, 25).

See MARRIAGE.

BIBLIOGRAPHY:

J. L. Burckhardt, *Travels in Syria and the Holy Land* (London, 1822), 297-298.

S. R. Driver, *The Book of Exodus* (Cambridge, 1929), 228-229.

H. Granqvist, *Marriage Conditions in a Palestinian Village* (Helsinki, 1929), 228-229.

W. P. Paterson, "Marriage," *HDB* II, 270-271.

W. R. Smith, *Kinship and Marriage in Early Arabia* (London, 1903), 68, 78 f.

H. B. Tristram, *Eastern Customs in Bible Lands* (London; 2nd ed., 1894), 92.

J. BARTON PAYNE

DOXOLOGY

I. *Definition.* A doxology is an expression of adoration addressed *to* Deity according to an established pattern. A doxology differs from a benediction in that a benediction is a declaration of a blessing *from* God. A benediction usually comes at the close of a writing (e.g., II Cor. 13:14; Gal. 6:18); a doxology (as an ejaculatory expression) may be found at the beginning (Gal. 1:5), middle (Eph. 3:21), or end (II Pet. 3:18), or anywhere it is needed (Rev. 1:6; 5:13; 7:10).

II. *Parts of a Doxology.* (1) The person addressed. Christ is definitely addressed in three doxologies (II Tim. 4:18; II Pet. 3:18; Rev. 1:6), and probably in two other doxologies (Heb. 13:21; I Pet. 4:11). He is addressed as co-equal with God the Father in two doxologies (Rev. 5:13; 7:10). God the Father is addressed through Christ in two doxologies (Rom. 16:27; Jude 25), and alone in six doxologies (Rom. 11:36; Gal. 1:5; Eph. 3:21; Phil. 4:20; I Tim. 1:17; 6:16). (2) The attributes ascribed. "Glory" alone is found in eight doxologies (Rom. 11:36; 16:27; Gal. 1:5; Eph. 3:21; Phil. 4:20; II Tim. 4:18; Heb. 13:21; II Pet. 3:18). "Dominion" is found in one (I Pet. 5:11, ARV). The other doxologies combine the following number of attributes: two (I Tim. 1:17; 6:16; I Pet. 4:11; Rev. 1:6), four (Jude 25; Rev. 5:13), five (cf. I Chron. 29:11), seven (Rev. 7: 12). (3) The time involved. "For ever" (Gal. 1:5; Rom. 11:36; 16:27), "for ever and ever" (Phil. 4:20; II Tim. 4:18; Heb. 13:21; I Tim. 1:17; I Pet. 4:11; 5:11; Rev. 1:6; 5:13; 7:12), "throughout all ages, world without end" (Eph. 3:21), "everlasting" (I Tim. 6: 16), and "both now and for ever" (II Pet. 3:18, but see ARVm; Jude 25). (4) The connecting verb. The "be" of our English versions is unexpressed in the Greek. However, "is" (ἐστιν) is found in one place (I Pet. 4:11). The "be" of our English probably represents the optative (εἴη) rather than the imperative (ἔστω). (5) The concluding "Amen." This word concludes all the doxologies except one (Rev. 5:13). An instructive parallel is found in the "Amen, and Amen" at the end of all but the last of the five "books" of Psalms (41:13; 72:19; 89:52; 106:48).

III. *The Purposes of a Doxology.* (1) To utter an ejaculatory praise over some important truth (e.g., Rom. 11: 36). (2) To conclude a writing with a note of adoration (e.g., Rom. 16:27; Jude 25; cf. Ps. 41:13; 72:19; 89:52; 106:48). (3) To display the Divine attributes (e.g., I Chron. 29:11; Rev. 7:12). (4) To affirm the co-equality of Jesus Christ with God the Father (Rev. 7:12).

IV. *Concluding Observations.* (1) In their rudimentary forms, as in the very common "Blessed be . . . ," doxologies date from a very early time (Gen. 9:26;

14:20; 24:27). Such doxological expressions abound in the OT (Ex. 18:10; I Kings 8:15; Ps. 28:6). Similar expressions are found in the Gospels (Luke 1:68; 19:38; John 12:13) and in the Epistles (II Cor. 1:3; Eph. 1:3; I Pet. 1:3). All of these have elements in common with the regular doxologies discussed above. (2) Romans 9:5 is not to be taken as a doxology addressed to God (as in RSV), but, rather, as an affirmation of the Deity of Christ (as in AV and ARV). (3) The three ancient doxologies known as "Gloria in Excelsis" (based on Luke 2:14), "Gloria Patri" (based on Mt. 28:19 f.), and "Trisagion" (based on Isa. 6:3), which still find a place in modern liturgical usage, are by no means of apostolic origin or authority. (4) Finally, the doxology at the end of the Lord's Prayer in Mt. 6:13 is supported by all but 10 mss, but these include *B, Aleph, D,* and *S,* so that it is omitted from the modern critical text.

WICK BROOMALL

DRAGON. The dragon occurs frequently as a mythical monster in Mesopotamian culture, particularly in the Sumerian period in the third millennium B.C. The killing of the dragon is a creative activity, performed by gods and heroes. The dragon itself is a monster-power, always in the bad sense.

In the Bible we do not encounter the dragon in connection with creation, nor does it play a significant role anywhere else, since heroes and warring gods are out of place in the thought-world of Holy Scripture. Only occasionally, as, for example, when the Leviathan is mentioned, do we come upon a remote reminiscence of the monsters of Mesopotamian mythology. The term *dragon* does not appear in the Hebrew text, but the LXX often uses the word where the text speaks of a serpent or sea-monster.

We do, however, find the dragon in the Revelation of John (12:3 ff.). Here, the meaning of the monster described is made clear by a reference to the old serpent, Satan.

The dragon appears in Greek mythology (probably borrowed from the older Mesopotamian culture), especially in the lives of heroes such as Hercules and Perseus. However, the monster was seldom pictured, and we cannot say that it played a significant role.

In the Christian world we scarcely ever encounter the dragon, outside of the few places in the Bible which merely suggest it. In primitive Christian art we find it only where the story of Jonah is portrayed. Only later, around A.D. 1000, do we see the dragon more frequently in pictorial art. This is probably due to the fact that in that period artists devoted themselves to illustrating the Apocalypse, where particularly in Rev. 12:3 the dragon is mentioned. The form in which the monster was portrayed was borrowed from ancient written sources, in which it was spoken of as a real animal, a sort of serpent with feet and wings. This was the appearance of the dragon throughout the Middle Ages. We also find the dragon in tales of chivalry, probably inspired by the story of Tristan or the accounts of the heroes of King Arthur's Round Table. In the illustrations, these dragons have the same appearance as those described above.

In Chinese culture the dragon makes its appearance at a very early date. The Chinese dragon is a reptile-like creature, with horns and large, flat ears, a ridge of spines along its back, and feet like those of a bird of prey. Although this dragon is rough and wild, it is a creature friendly to man, and is a sort of half-god that lives in the water. Particularly since the 13th century the dragon has been frequently portrayed because it was a symbol of the emperor.

Since the 15th century this Chinese

dragon exercised a great influence on the image of the dragon which people had in W Europe, and this form of the dragon soon began to replace the older form so that the medieval type disappeared almost entirely. However, except for ornaments of the Chinese type, the dragon has had little significance in pictorial art in more recent times, and even less in phantasy. Only in fairy tales do we still come across it. In our century the dragon is very seldom seen in any form of art.

H. R. ROOKMAAKER

DRAWERS OF WATER, together with "hewers of wood," anciently signified menial laborers or actual slaves, though they did participate in Israel's redemptive covenant (Deut. 29:11-12; Josh. 9:23). Joshua thus made the deceptive Gibeonites to be drawers of water for the house and altar of God (Josh. 9:23, 27); and David conscripted foreign residents for temple service (I Chron. 22:2; II Chron. 2:17-18; Ezra 8:20). Solomon likewise drafted bondservants of the surviving Canaanites (I Kings 9:20-21).

Water-drawing devolved upon young women (Gen. 24:13, 43; I Sam. 9:11) or day laborers (Ruth 2:9). Heavy pitchers were carried on the shoulder to wells (Gen. 24:15, 45), generally near city gates (II Sam. 23:16; Nahum 3:14). Deep wells required ropes, dragged by men or beasts as they walked away from the mouth of the well (John 4:11). Gatherings for such labor (Judges 5:11) normally occurred at evening (Gen. 24:11; contrast John 4:6). To draw out the life-giving water effectively illustrates one's receiving of eternal salvation (Isa. 12:3).

J. BARTON PAYNE

DREAMS. The exact nature of dreaming is still a mystery, but we recognize types of dreams that occur in Scripture:

(1) Dreams commonly arise from events of the past day or from some physical condition (Job 7:14; Eccles. 5:3; Isa. 29:8).

(2) Dreams can become a withdrawal substitute for action (Eccles. 5:7).

(3) Psychiatrists emphasize the symbolism of dreams. Joseph dreamed of himself as the chief sheaf of wheat and of his family as the heavenly bodies bowing down to him (Gen. 37:5-10). A Midianite soldier dreamed of a loaf overturning a tent (Judges 7:13, 14). Nebuchadnezzar dreamed in symbols of the humbling of his self-sufficiency (Dan. 4).

(4) Parapsychologists investigate precognitive dreams. Such dreams are recorded of Gentiles, such as Pharaoh's servants (Gen. 40), Pharaoh himself (Gen. 41), and Nebuchadnezzar (Dan. 2 and 4). And Joseph also dreamed of his future (Gen. 37:5-10).

(5) Dreams sometimes contain a warning. In the NT Joseph was told in a dream not to be afraid that Mary had been unfaithful (Mt. 1:20), and the Wise Men were similarly warned not to return to Herod (Mt. 2:12).

(6) Modern investigators are often skeptical of Divine revelation in dreams, but God sometimes used dreams to speak to prophets, although a false prophet might regard a dream arising from his own subconscious as a genuine revelation from God (Jer. 23:16, 25-32). We may distinguish between revelation in sleep, e.g., to Jacob at Bethel (Gen. 28), to Solomon (I Kings 3:5-15), and to Jeremiah (Jer. 31:26); and a trance or vision which might come at any time. Peter's vision that led to his opening of the door to the Gentiles was a trance, and not a dream (Acts 10:9; 11:5). The Hebrew words translated "vision" are not the same as "dream," but are similar to the two words translated "seer." The detailed predictions in Dan.

7–12 are called "visions," except in Dan. 7:1, where what follows is also said to be a dream.

J. S. WRIGHT

DRELINCOURT, Charles (1595-1669), French Reformed theologian. Born in Sedan, this eminent Calvinist enjoyed very great popularity throughout the 17th century, not only in France but also in much of Europe and English America. His ministry and writings did much to disseminate Reformed doctrine. After studying theology and the humanities in Sedan, and philosophy in Saumur, he became pastor of a church in Langres. But the opposition of the government led to his going to Paris, where in 1620 he accepted the responsibilities of minister in the church in Charenton, serving this church until his death. It was here that his brilliant writings and moving sermons gained for him prestige and popularity, not only with religious leaders but also with powerful political supporters of the Reformed position, such as the Duke of Turenne and the Duchess of Tremouille. His literary works, well written and polished, are characterized by constant reference to Scripture.

Drelincourt left some 50 writings, many of which were translated into English, German, Italian, and Flemish. Among the most popular of these were his *Catechism* (1662), in which a strongly Calvinistic theology is expressed, and *The Christian's Defense against the Fears of Death* (1651). In the latter, sometimes also translated as *Consolations,* the author reveals his pastoral concern for anxious souls. Readers are advised to think often of death and to rest assured in the certainty that God ordains whatever befalls His children. They are also exhorted to free their minds of temporal worries and give themselves to lives of piety and service to God and man. The writer's complete trust in the providence of God is further revealed in his *De la persévérance des saints* (1625) and *Triomphe des Églises sous la croix* (1629). As an active participant in the religious conflicts in France, Drelincourt used his pen with telling effect. Among his polemical writings are *Abridgment of Controversies* (1630) and *Defense of Calvin* (1667). He was married to the daughter of a wealthy merchant, and had 16 children. His death in 1669 deprived the Reformed circles of a most persuasive and influential voice.

BIBLIOGRAPHY:

C. Drelincourt, *The Christian's Defense* (Trenton, 1808).

E. and E. Haag, *La France protestante* (Paris, 1877-86).

Lichtenberger, *Encyclopédie des sciences religieuses*, IV, 81-84.

J. Pannier, *L'église réf. de Paris sous Louis XIII* (Paris, 1922).

PETER J. KLASSEN

DRINK, STRONG. The Hebrew word שֵׁכָר (*shēkar*) and the Greek σίκερα (*sikera*) which is derived from it, denote a drink (sweet in its initial stages) which satiates or intoxicates, depending on its state. It is sometimes designated wine (Num. 28:7), but more often is distinguished as strong drink. It is made from barley, honey, or dates. Wine, in the usual sense, is derived from grapes (cf. Isa. 24:9, where the second reference is probably to palm wine, though the stricter term is not used). Although the modern means of intoxication may be more powerful than those generally available to the ancients, the addition of stimulants to drinks was not unknown. The rebukes of Prov. 23:30 and Isa. 5:22 apparently refer to the practice because of the excesses connected with it.

Among the beverages with which the Jews were acquainted were beer and cider (also called apple wine). The former was introduced into Palestine from Egypt. In many instances the Hebrews would adopt the customs of the peoples with whom they had contact. This undoubtedly included certain processes used to prepare and ferment beverages. On fermentation see Jer. 48:11, 12. The notion that fermentation of alcoholic beverages among the Hebrews was little known or practiced goes completely against all the evidence. Indeed, many of the references to strong drink in the Bible are directed to the problem of intoxication arising out of over-indulgence (cf. Prov. 20:1; Isa. 28:7).

On the other hand, strong drink is not universally condemned in Scripture. At the feast prepared by the one who brought tithes, it was allowed (Deut. 14:26). Note that this was done "before the Lord." In Prov. 31:6 is the exhortation, "Give strong drink unto him that is ready to perish." This was taken to apply, among others, to the criminal about to die (the Mishna). Thus Christ was offered "wine mingled with myrrh" (Mark 15:23). The use of wine here in place of strong drink shows (as above) that the two were, on occasion, identified. In particular, this suggests that ordinary wine could become, in effect, strong drink by the addition of certain elements (here myrrh).

Proverbs 31:6, 7 recommends strong drink as well as wine for those in certain unhappy circumstances. This is put forth in the same context where kings and princes are warned against both wine and strong drink, presumably in the performance of their duty. To the extent that the exhortation would apply beyond this area, it would have to be taken as a warning against over-indulgence, a responsibility of men of every estate. In this same tenor is the prohibition of use by the priest (Lev. 10:9) who is ready to go into the sanctuary. That the intent of these commands was not always heeded is seen from Isa. 28:7, depicting the inebriated condition of prophets and priests.

Strong drink was forbidden the Nazarite, who was set apart to live an abstemious life for a certain specified period. But also included was the prohibition of wine, vinegar, any juice of the grape, and even fresh grapes themselves. This was, however, a special case, as for example John the Baptist (Luke 1:15).

LLOYD F. DEAN

Though it is true that wine and strong drink are recommended for use in particular circumstances, this should in no way be construed as recommending or condoning general use in normal circumstances. Modern study of the effects of alcohol shows that it is an anesthetic, which means that it affects the higher centers of the brain that regulate morals and judgment before it affects perception or motor coordination. Christians should know and be aware that even minimal use has some influence upon these higher centers. Also, alcoholic beverages are generally used in much the same way and for the same reasons as dangerous drugs (see DRUGS AND DRUG ABUSE). Since man has the inherent tendency to excuse himself, these factors should cause Christians to question strongly any claims of liberty with regard to their use.

DRIVER, S. R. (1846-1914), British Hebraist. Driver received his education at Oxford, where in 1870 he was elected Fellow of New College. In 1883 Driver succeeded the conservative Edward B. Pusey and continued until his death as Regius Professor of Hebrew in the University of Oxford. Driver's reputation as a Semitics scholar was established by his *Treatise on the Use of the Tenses in Hebrew* (1874). His *Notes on the Hebrew Text of the Books of Samuel* (1890) set a new standard for textual criticism; and his articles on prepositions, adverbs, and conjunctions constituted the backbone of the Brown, Driver, and Briggs *Hebrew and English Lexicon of the Old Testament* (1891-1905).

Driver's most influential publication was his *Introduction to the Literature of the Old Testament* (1891). It represented a thoroughgoing acceptance of Wellhausen's criticism by its revolt against Biblical authority and its commitment to theories of Israel's religious evolution. Passing through nine editions, it brought respectability to Wellhausenism; "and so English scholarship was set free to participate in the great critical movement" (Emil G. Kraeling, *The Old Testament Since the Reformation*, London, 1955, p. 95). At his death in 1914, Driver's followers asserted, "There is no retreat from his teaching today, nor ever will be" (*HTR* 9 [1916], 252). Half a century later, despite evangelical protest, Driver's positions remain definitive as the *sine qua non* for acceptability in circles of British OT scholarship.

The commentaries and other exegetical works produced by S. R. Driver cover half the books of the OT. They appear in such series as The International Critical Commentary (*Deuteronomy*, 1895; *Job*, completed 1921); Westminster Commentaries (*Genesis*, 1904); The Cambridge Bible for Schools and Colleges (*Exodus*, 1911; *Daniel*, 1900; *Joel-Amos*, 1897); and The Century Bible (*Nahum-Malachi*, 1905). Liberal leaders have criticized their cautiousness, rigorously limited inferences, and even conservatism. Yet these very qualities, which have given lasting value to his studies, have reduced their power to inspire appreciation for the living Biblical Word (*HTR, loc. cit.*). Indeed, the exegete who restricts himself to man's rational judgment must inevitably fall short of God's truth.

See HIGHER CRITICISM.

BIBLIOGRAPHY:

T. K. Cheyne, *Founders of Old Testament Criticism* (London, 1893), 248 f.

G. A. Cooke, "Driver and Wellhausen," *HTR* 9 (1916), 249-257.

S. R. Driver, *The Ideals of the Prophets* (Edinburgh, 1915), 213-234.

E. G. Kraeling, *The Old Testament Since the Reformation* (London, 1955), 95, 293.

W. Sanday, *The Life-Work of Samuel Rolles Driver* (1914).

A. D. White, *A History of the Warfare of Science with Theology* (New York, 1955), I, 20-21; II, 359.

J. BARTON PAYNE

DROSS, a general term for the impurities of metals, especially silver, which resulted from the smelting of ore in the furnaces. It generally occurs in the plural in Hebrew, though the singular is found in Ezek. 22:18. Metals were usually smelted in a pot or crucible in refineries. Dross is generally symbolic of moral decay (Isa. 1:22; Ezek. 22:18-19; cf. Ps. 119:119). The "silver dross" of AV Prov. 26:23 should be read "glaze," with RSV, following the Ugaritic *spsg* ("glaze"). The term does not occur in the NT.

DRUGS AND DRUG ABUSE. During the 1960's an old minor problem became a new problem of major proportions for the W world, namely, the problem of drug abuse. The use of opium, heroin, and marijuana is not a new phenomenon. India and Nigeria, for example, after long experience with the unrestricted use of products manufactured from the *cannabis sativa* (hemp) plant, from which marijuana and hashish are produced, have banned their sale and use. The opium trade of the Orient has been well known for centuries. Even Sigmund Freud was dependent upon the use of cocaine in periods of depression. Yet with the addition of a wide spectrum of new synthetic drugs that have become available, the illegal production, sale, possession, and use of drugs grew

The Drug Problem

almost overnight into a problem with national and even international implications.

The natural curiosity of youth coupled with the search of many young people for an experience and dimension in life that transcends the crass materialism of their culture, and the affluence, rebellion, distrust, and basic disorientation of modern students, gives the various elements of organized crime a strong incentive to exploit this rapidly expanding portion of the population by the organization of an amazingly effective worldwide operation for the manufacture and marketing of illegal drugs at huge profits. Advertising, and particularly television commercials, with which the youth culture grows up, pictures the use of drugs and medications as the sovereign solution to all of life's problems. Parents too, with over-encouragement by many physicians and (especially) psychiatrists, set a forceful example for their children by their widespread acceptance of and dependence on tranquilizers and other mood-enhancing drugs as the prime means of coping with the complex problems of society and the family.

The influence of some early experimenters like Dr. Timothy Leary, who themselves became dependent upon drugs, the widely publicized drug dependence of the Beatles and other rock musician idols, and the general distrust of the "establishment" were also potent factors. The use of pot (marijuana) by American soldiers became widespread. From a sterile husk of Christianity young people have turned in droves to the oriental religions that offer a psychedelic religious experience beyond the coldly rational or insipidly irrational approach of liberal theologians. Oriental mysticism and the transcendent experience go hand in hand with the effects obtained through the "trips" arranged by the use of hallucinogenic drugs, the "highs" of the amphetamines (or pep pills), the dream-like Nirvana of the opiates (heroin) and marijuana.

Classes of Drugs Involved

Drug abuse extends to two classes of drugs: (1) those that are *addictive* and (2) those that are *habituating*. Addictive drugs are those upon which a user may become "hooked" by becoming both physiologically and psychologically dependent on them. The body builds up a tolerance for such drugs and ever-larger doses are required to obtain the same effects. When one "kicks" (withdraws) from use of the drug, withdrawal reactions occur. Habituating drugs are those drugs that as far as is known cause psychological dependence only and do not cause physiological dependence in the user. In any case, there is no withdrawal period upon the cessation of the use of a habituating drug, although as a result the user may become tense, uneasy, depressed, and irritable.

Within these two larger classes are several sorts of drugs:

I. ADDICTIVE

A. OPIATES. Heroin, morphine, codeine, paregoric, demerol (meperidene), methadone (the last two are synthetically produced) are the principal drugs in this category. All opiates are narcotics, drugs that relieve pain (produce analgesia), cause sedation, and depress. The analgesic properties of the opiates distinguish them from other sedatives, depressants, and tranquilizers. Of these, heroin ("horse") is the most popular because of its strong effects. Heroin wipes out fears and anxieties, brings on drowsiness, and causes sexual responses (even to the point of orgasm). Heroin is sometimes sniffed, but more often taken by injection ("shot"). Thus opiate users may often be identified by the needle marks on their legs or arms. Heroin is illegally marketed and therefore can be sold at an enormous profit. It is not unusual for a user soon to have a habit costing $40 to $50 per day. Theft and other associated crimes have increased markedly with the rise of drug abuse since drug addicts who soon exhaust their own resources turn to robbery in desperation in order to obtain needed funds. Many themselves become "pushers" (salesmen) for the drug in order to obtain funds and in this way the number of new users grows. Female addicts often turn to prostitution in order to raise money for drugs.

B. AMPHETAMINES. Benzedrine, dexamyl, dexadrine, and methedrine are the principal stimulants ("ups" or "pep" pills) used by drug addicts. They are stimulants that cause excitement, euphoria, and happiness, and keep one awake. Amphetamines may be taken orally or by injection. Amphetamines impair judgment, make one reckless or heedless of himself and others, and if the user remains awake for two or more days he becomes subject through sleep loss to the same perceptual distortions that are caused by hallucinogens. Amphetamines may produce high blood pressure, accelerated or irregular heartbeat, and even heart attack. Users of methamphetamine or methedrine ("speed") may also suffer from liver infections, abscesses, abdominal cramps, and respiratory disorders. They tend to become hostile, violent, and even destructive toward others. Whereas opiates tend to relax, the amphetamines stimulate the user.

C. BARBITURATES. Amytal, barbital, luminal, nembutal, phenobarbital, seconal, and tuinal are the chief barbiturates on the market. Barbiturates are sedatives that are taken in order to relieve anxiety and may cause sleep. Sometimes they are taken by amphetamine users in order to counteract the effects of "pep" pills. By depressing the central nervous system barbiturates induce sleep; unlike opiates, they do not relieve pain. Overdoses, particularly when used together with alcohol, can cause death. Barbiturates cause impatience and irritability, loss of balance, and slurred speech. Seventy-five percent of all suicides by drugs involve the use of barbiturates. Withdrawal symptoms are severe.

D. TRANQUILIZERS. Equinil, librium, miltown, placidyl, valium are used to help one cope with life by reducing anxiety, and bringing on euphoria and a "who cares" attitude. Tranquilizers filter out and reduce sensory information, keeping the user from being agitated by his environment. Thus judgment is impaired. Tranquilizers may damage white blood cells. Dangerous severe convulsions may occur upon withdrawal. Tranquilizers have been prescribed with abandon by psychiatrists and physicians, as if happiness and the solution to life's problems were contained in a pill. But dependence on tranquilizers in order to cope with life is merely the substitution of one inadequate pattern of problem-solving for another.

II. HABITUATING DRUGS

A. LSD AND OTHER HALLUCINOGENS. LSD (lysergic acid diethylamide) and other hallucinogens (including mescaline, peyote, psilacybin, DMT, MDA, belladonna, and morning-glory seeds) are used. These drugs are taken in order to "turn on" or "tune in" a whole new world of sensory experience. Because of their ability to distort sensory data by impairing perception, users become entranced by the distorted world and think (erroneously) that they are having a deep, transcendent, or even religious experience. Time and space and one's body and mind may seem to float; hallucinations and delusions occur. Depth perception is impaired, and there is a 10 percent chance of suicidal or homicidal attempts. Hallucinogens are deceptive: rather than opening up new worlds by "expanding the mind," they dangerously close the mind to the true world around and distort much of the data that reach the mind. The same perceptual distortions are experienced by users of hallucinogens as in those reported by persons who suffer from acute sleep loss (two or more days), and those who have been labeled "psychotic" or "schizophrenic." LSD "trips" may last as long as eight hours. "Bad trips" can occur to any user of LSD; in these he becomes confused, anxious, depressed, or "panicky." LSD is a very dangerous drug that does not improve but rather distorts perception, lowers intelligence, damages the gene make-up, may bring about malformations in babies and may possibly lead to leukemia, suicide, or violence.

B. MARIJUANA. Marijuana ("grass, pot, tea") users claim that since marijuana is physically non-addictive and does not ordinarily cause such a violent reaction as LSD and other hallucinogens, its sale and use should not be prohibited. What are the effects of "pot"? Usually one becomes drunk. Three or four marijuana cigarettes ("joints") bring about a pleasurable unawareness of time and space and may make colors seem brighter and the hearing keener; ten will lead to hallucinations. Reactions may differ from person to person. Reports include among the effects: depression, euphoria, confusion, hallucination, drunkenness, panic and fear, over-confidence, lack of self-criticism and judgment, loss of concentration, acute sensitivity to sound, dryness of mouth, enlargement of the pupils, and a floating sensation. Most of these reactions are also associated with LSD and the other hallucinogens. In current medical literature there are few defenses of marijuana. Instead one reads about progression from marijuana to other stronger drugs, failures in school, loss of memory, inability to learn, listlessness and lack of initiative, and other undesirable results.

What is the Christian's position toward the use of these several sorts of drugs? Six fundamental replies may be given:

The Christian Attitude Toward Drugs

(1) A Christian may not buy, sell, condone, use, or possess any drug illegally. The principles of Romans 13:1-5 and I Peter 2:13-17 are explicit: in such matters a Christian must submit to the laws of the land.

(2) A Christian may not use any drug that is harmful to the body or is likely to be so (cf. Rom. 14:23). His body is the "temple of the Holy Spirit" (I Cor. 6:19) and should be used in order to "glorify the Lord" (vss. 13, 20). God has not given Christians an option about how they may use their bodies: their bodies, like the rest of themselves, belong to God (vs. 19).

(3) A Christian may not become addicted to or dependent upon a drug (I Cor. 6:12). Although controlled use of drugs for medical purposes is legitimate, habituation and addiction necessarily involve a "mastery" by the drug (vs. 12) over the individual.

(4) A Christian may not make use of drugs that distort his perception and thus lead to wrong and sinful responses by him. In I Cor. 12:23 Paul observes that all things do not edify.

(5) A Christian may not use drugs as a substitute for taking responsible action in solving life's problems. Drugs may not be used to relieve guilt and anxiety stemming from one's failure to handle problems God's way. Paul speaks disparagingly of those who "sear" (i.e., make as insensible to pain as burned flesh) the conscience (I Tim. 4:2) and characterizes those who are "past feeling" as opposed to Christ (Eph. 4:19, 20).

(6) A Christian may not rely upon distorted perceptual experiences and mastery by a chemical as a means of discovering truth or entering into a re-

ligious experience. Such an attitude shows rebellion against God since it substitutes drugs for the study of the Scriptures and the true worship of the Triune God. The principle behind the verse, "be not drunk with wine, but be filled with the Spirit," seems to apply (Eph. 5:18).

Pastors and other Christian leaders need to discover that they have more to offer in helping drug-dependent persons withdraw and find independence from drugs than they might think. The six reasons stated above are not merely reasons for not using dependence-inducing drugs; they are also good reasons for drug abusers to cease. The power of Christ to strengthen (Phil. 4:13) and the ability of the Scriptures to give us all that is necessary to meet every life situation (II Tim. 3:17) are profound factors in helping drug abusers to withdraw. Pastors should undertake the task of helping drug-dependent persons (if necessary, in conjunction with a physician) rather than referring them to a psychiatrist or someone else (see COUNSELING).

COLLOQUIAL AND SLANG NAMES FOR DRUGS

acid—LSD
barbs—barbiturates
bennies—amphetamines (esp. benzedrine)
blues—barbiturates
candy—barbiturates
cocktail—methadone substituted for an opiate
coke—cocaine
copilots—amphetamines
dope—a depressant
drivers—amphetamines
eye openers—amphetamines
footballs—amphetamines
goofballs—barbiturates
grass—marijuana
hard stuff—an addicting drug (usually heroin)
harry—heroin
hash—hashish, marijuana
horse—heroin
joint—marijuana cigarette
jolly beans—amphetamines
junk—any drug causing psychological or physical dependence
Mary Jane—marijuana
monkey—morphine
nimbies—barbiturates (nembutal)
peanuts—barbiturates
pep pills—amphetamines
pink ladies—barbiturates
pot—marijuana
reefer—marijuana cigarette
seggies—barbiturates (seconol)
sleeping pills—barbiturates
snow—cocaine
speed—methedrine
stick—marijuana cigarette
stuff—drugs
sugar—cube of LSD
tea—marijuana
truck drivers—amphetamines
weed—marijuana
yellowjackets—barbiturates

BIBLIOGRAPHY:

A Federal Source Book: Answers to the most frequently asked questions about drug abuse, National Clearinghouse for Drug Abuse Information (Chevy Chase, Md., n.d.).
J. Adams, *Competent to Counsel* (Nutley, N. J., 1970).
R. Blum, *Society and Drugs* (San Francisco, 1970), 2 vols.
O. Byrd, *Medical Readings on Drug Abuse* (Reading, Mass., 1970).
L. Relin, *A Doctor Discusses Narcotics and Drug Addiction* (Chicago, 1968).

JAY E. ADAMS

Though alcoholic beverages, coffee and teas, and tobacco are frequently overlooked in discussions of drug abuse, it must be pointed out that they have many of the same characteristics as the drugs mentioned above. They can and do become addictive or habituating; they contain chemicals that produce similar physiological effects, depending upon the dose; and they are often used for the same reasons as other drugs. Since this is the case, they must come under the same condemnation and Scriptural restrictions given above.

DRUMMOND, Henry (1851-1897), Free Church of Scotland professor, evangelist, and lecturer on science and religion. Drummond was born at Stirling, Scotland. He studied at the University of Edinburgh (1866-1870), at New College, Edinburgh (1870-1873, 1875-1876), and at the University of Tübingen (1873). He participated actively in the revival campaigns of D. L. Moody and Ira D. Sankey (1874-1875), particularly in meetings for young men. He was appointed lecturer in natural science at the Free Church College, Glasgow, in 1877; in 1884 he was made a full professor and ordained to the Free Church ministry. In his short life, crowded with interests and activities, he made several scientific expeditions and explorations. But his greatest work was in the interest of student evangelization. He travelled to European, American, and Australian universities and spoke at numerous conferences, stressing the necessity of personal commitment to Jesus Christ and the importance of Christian service. The Student Volunteer Movement was in large measure indebted to his student mission. Possessing a gift for spiritual diagnosis and counsel, he influenced the lives of thousands. His books were immensely popular for they appeared to many readers to have reconciled the claims of Christianity with those of modern science and Biblical criticism. He was a theistic evolutionist. His book *Natural Law in the Spiritual World* (London, 1883) saw the same Divine laws at work in the physical universe and in religious experience. His 1893 Lowell Institute Lectures in Boston, published under the title *The Ascent of Man* (New York, 1894), presented "evidence" for moral and spiritual order in early stages of evolutionary development. Although he never rejected the evangelical element of Christianity or the necessity for regeneration, his endeavors to reconcile Christianity with modern thought led him to modify or de-emphasize the older orthodoxy. His other writings include *Tropical Africa* (New York, 1888), *The Greatest Thing in the World* and *Pax Vobiscum* (New York, 1890), *The Changed Life* (New York, 1891), *The Programme of Christianity* (New York, 1892), *A Life for a Life, and Other Addresses, With a Tribute by D. L. Moody* and *The Ideal Life; Addresses Hitherto Unpublished* (New York, 1897), *The New Evangelism, and Other Addresses* and *Stones Rolled Away, and Other Addresses to Young Men* (New York, 1899), and *Dwight L. Moody, Impressions and Facts* (New York, 1900).

BIBLIOGRAPHY:

T. H. Boyd, *Henry Drummond: Some Recollections* (London, 1907).

J. W. Kennedy, ed., *Henry Drummond: An Anthology, with the Story of His Life* (New York, 1953).

C. Lennox, *The Practical Life Work of Henry Drummond* (London, 1901).

W. R. Nicoll, *Princes of the Church* (London, 1921), 93-102.

G. A. Smith, *The Life of Henry Drummond* (New York, 1898).

ALBERT H. FREUNDT, JR.

DRUNKENNESS. Drunkenness is a sin because it mocks man, who was made in the image of God. Under its influence man loses his power of self-control, his dignity, and his judgment; and he becomes prey to incitements to his own passions and to temptations of the Devil.

That drunkenness is a heinous sin is seen in the judgments pronounced upon it: a drunkard should be excluded from Christian fellowship (I Cor. 5:11); and he will not inherit the kingdom of God (I Cor. 6:9,10; Gal. 5:21). Moses directed that an incorrigible son, one of whose sins was drunkenness, should be stoned. "So shalt thou put evil away from you; and all Israel shall hear, and fear" (Deut. 21:18-21).

Alcohol in immoderate amounts has an overpowering influence to evil which is analogous to the sovereign power of the Holy Spirit for holiness (Eph. 5:18). Under its power, men lose their dignity and prudence (Prov. 20:

1); they come to poverty and need (Prov. 23:20 f.); they fall prey to contentions, nervousness, and physical ills (Prov. 23:29 f.); and they succumb to temptations to adultery and lying (Prov. 23:33). David counted on this when he sought to deceive Uriah (II Sam. 11:13), but providentially the attempt failed. Noah's drunkenness was the occasion for the Hamite sin and curse (Gen. 9:20 f.). Lot's intoxication led to incest (Gen. 19:32 f.; cf. Hab. 2:15).

Prov. 31:4 f. warns kings against strong drink, "lest they . . . forget the law, and pervert the judgment of any of the afflicted." (See also Eccles. 10: 17.) Where this warning was not heeded, the results were disastrous: Benhadad's stupidity in battle (I Kings 20: 16), Ahasuerus' rashness before his nobles (Esther 1:10 f.), and Belshazzar's folly at the time of the Medo-Persian menace (Dan. 5:1 f.). Indeed, all those in authority, whether political or religious, are particularly warned against the perversions which come with drunkenness (Lev. 10:9; Isa. 5:11, 12, 22, 23; 28:1-8; Ezek. 44:21).

Drunkenness renders men helpless before their enemies (I Kings 16:9; Nahum 1:10). It dulls senses against warnings of impending peril and judgment (Mt. 24:38, 49; Luke 21:34). Man's helplessness from intoxication provides for vivid and vigorous figures of speech (Ps. 109:27; Isa. 19:14). The figurative use of the concept is a favorite device of the prophets to warn of the nation's instability and helplessness in time of Divine judgment (Isa. 24:20; Jer. 13:13; and many others). Similarly, John writes that they who have drunk of Babylon's fornication shall also drink of the wine of God's wrath (Rev. 14:8, 10; 17:2; 18:3).

But care should be used in accusing men of drunkenness. Our Lord was slandered because contact with drunkards whom He came to save was construed as drunkenness (Mt. 11:18 f.; Luke 7:13 f.). The Spirit-filled disciples were also erroneously criticized, but only because their conduct was unusual (Acts 2:15). (See also I Sam. 1:13 f.)

Deliverance from the sin of drunkenness is in the Gospel, and those who struggle with its bondage should be directed to the Savior (Rom. 13:13; I Cor. 6:9-11). It should be part of the church's witness that Christians engage in reclaiming inebriates, and they not leave such social service to secular organizations.

Although the command of Christ (Luke 21:34) and the exhortation of Paul (Eph. 5:18) are clear indications of the will of God in this matter, the people of God have been vulnerable to the temptation to intemperance. Aside from the instances of the saints' inebriation noted above, the drunkenness of the Corinthians is reproved by Paul, a particularly shocking example of intoxication since it took place in connection with the church's celebration of the Lord's supper.

The only safeguard against this temptation is for one to be filled with the Spirit (Eph. 5:18).

See DRINK, STRONG.

JOHN W. SANDERSON, JR.

DRUSILLA, a Jewess and the wife of Felix, the Roman governor of Judea. Together with her husband, she heard Paul discourse "concerning the faith in Christ Jesus" during Paul's imprisonment at Caesarea (Acts 24:24 f.). According to the margin of the Harclean Syriac version, Drusilla made special request to see and hear Paul. The same authority states that it was for Drusilla's sake that Felix left Paul in prison, and this reading is found in at least two Greek mss. This is undoubtedly a gloss arising out of the effort to make the imprisonment of Paul parallel to that of

John the Baptist. Josephus tells us that Drusilla was the youngest daughter of Agrippa I. She was born about A.D. 36 and was married at the age of 14 years to Azizus, king of Emesa. In A.D. 54 she was married to Felix, after he had induced her to leave her husband.

BIBLIOGRAPHY:

A. C. Clark, *The Acts of the Apostles* (Oxford, 1933), 352, 381.

Jackson and Lake, *The Beginnings of Christianity* (London, 1926 ff.), III, 227; IV, 304; V, 487.

DUALISM. The word "dualism" is often used to refer to a doctrine that there are, within a particular frame of reference, two distinct, basic, controlling elements which cannot be reduced to each other or referred back to a deeper principle of unity, and which may even be in conflict with each other. The suffix "ism" strongly suggests, however, that the universe of discourse is of the broadest kind, so that everything that is, is said to be controlled by two separate or even conflicting principles.

Depending upon the point of view, various kinds of dualism may be identified. Thus a position which maintains that there are two diverging sources of moral action has been called "ethical" dualism; the position that man is composed of a substantial soul and a substantial body has been called "anthropological" or "ontological" dualism; and a position holding that there are two fundamental diverging sources of knowledge might be called "epistemological" dualism. Such positions do not require that the duality in question be all-embracing. That is not the case, however, with many so-called "metaphysical" or "religious" dualisms, in which diverging principles are thought to control everything that is.

An ultimately dualistic position combatted in the Scriptures is gnosticism. This sect taught that there are two ultimate powers, that of light and that of darkness. It held that the light could not approach the darkness, which was irreconcilably opposed to it. To bridge the gap there had to be a chain of intermediate beings (eons). Christ was sometimes thought to be one of the eons, which spanned the chasm between the light and the darkness. Under the influence of Gnosticism some teachers in the early church insisted that Christ, the light, could not have come in the flesh, for that would have meant entering into the realm of darkness. In opposition, the Apostle John insists on the concrete, tangible presence of Christ among the disciples (I John 1:1-2).

Because of its confession of the unity of the Godhead, the all-embracing character of God's plan, and His providential rule of the cosmos, the Christian faith should not be called a dualism. Indeed, in arguing for theistic in contrast to pantheistic and other monistic positions, some have used the term "dualism" to describe Christianity. They do this because Christianity asserts that there is a fundamental distinction between God, the Creator, and the creature. In agreement with this, Christianity has been called the most consistent dualism, because it alone avoids confusing the Creator with His creation.

It is more appropriate not to use the term "dualism" of the Creator-creature distinction, but to restrict its use to designate positions which arrive at a dualistic view of the cosmos because they have lost sight of the true source of unity. Only Christianity can attain a standpoint from which to see the true unity of the cosmos in its relationship to God, its Creator. All other positions elevate one or another aspect of the creation to the status of a pretended origin, setting it up therefore, of necessity, in opposition to some other aspect. Thus, any position failing to attain insight into the true origin inevitably must come to hold that there are at least two religiously incompatible and irreconcilable origins.

Failure to attain to the true origin irrevocably leads to "dualism."

That one acknowledges that there is a tremendous variety and complexity in the cosmos does not mean that one is a dualist, for such a recognition need not entail that the variety in question is of the basic, controlling kind taught by dualism. It must be asserted that Christianity offers a principle of unity which can account for the stupendous variety of the creation, while at the same time, it refers this variety back to its ultimate origin and unity in the Creator-God who has revealed Himself in Jesus Christ.

See DOCETISM, EONS, GNOSTICISM, PLATONISM.

BIBLIOGRAPHY:
H. Bavinck, *Philosophy of Revelation* (New York, 1909).
H. Jonas, *The Gnostic Religion* (Boston, 1958).
A. O. Lovejoy, *The Revolt Against Dualism* (New York, 1930).

ROBERT D. KNUDSEN

DU BOURG, Anne (1527?-1559), French Reformation martyr. Counsellor in the Parliament of Paris, Du Bourg was previously professor of law at Orleans, where Calvin had studied; then he moved to Paris. On the last Wednesday of April, 1559, the solemn meeting of the Parliament was held (this was called *Mercuriale* because it was held on Wednesday, Mercury's Day) to deal with the questions raised by the arrest and the execution of those who were called "Lutherans." King Henry II himself attended the meeting on June 10 to press for a severe punishment for the "heretics." Anne Du Bourg pronounced on this occasion a discourse which ended as follows: "It is no small matter to condemn those who in the midst of flames invoke the name of Jesus Christ." The king was extremely angered by this discourse, and he ordered the captain of the guards, Montgomery, to arrest immediately and to dispatch to the Bastille Anne Du Bourg and other counsellors, notably DuFaur, Antoine Fumée, and Paul De Foix. In his rage, he added that he would be present in person to witness the occasion when Anne Du Bourg was burned at the stake. But a few days after, on the occasion of the marriages of his daughter Elizabeth with Philip II of Spain and of his sister Margaret with Philibert of Savoie, Henry II was wounded in the eyes in a tournament and died two days later without seeing the execution that he hoped to witness.

Questioned in his prison, Anne Du Bourg boldly confessed his faith, presenting in detail the Reformed doctrine which the Synod of Paris had just promulgated (May, 1559). He was condemned to be burned at the stake. There were those who encouraged him to recant, but he held on and was strengthened in his faith by his pastor Marlorat, who was to die a martyr himself later on, and by another condemned prisoner, Margaret Le Riche. He walked toward the flames with an admirable prayer. His last words were, "Lord do not forsake me lest I should forsake Thee." His death made a profound impression. Florimond de Raemond, noted Catholic apologist, wrote: "All Paris was amazed at the courage of this man. As we came back from the place of execution to our colleges, we could not hold back the tears, and we were pleading his case even after his death, taking to task the unrighteous judges who had condemned him without proper ground. His address at the stake did more harm than 100 pastors could have done."

JEAN CADIER

DUDITH, Andrew, or DUDICH or DUDITIUS, Andreas (1533-1589), Hungarian churchman and humanist. Born Dudith Sbardellat of Orehowicz, Dudith's father was a Croat, and his mother an Italian. Because his father died when he was still young, he became a ward of his uncle Augustin Sbardellat, a Hungarian bishop (d. 1552). Dudith was a student at Breslau, and in 1550 he went to Italy, coming in contact with Reginald Cardinal Pole and Paulus Manutius at Venice. In September 1553 he went to England as secretary to Pole, who was sent there as papal legate and who became Archbishop of Canterbury in 1554. Dudith also visited Brussels at that time and studied Greek and Hebrew in Paris. Upon his return to Hungary in 1557, he was consecrated as priest and became a recipient of a few prebends. He studied law in Padua from 1558-60 and also showed an interest in astronomy and medicine. After visiting Paris once more, he resumed his task in Hungary in 1561. Through the patronage of Emperor Ferdinand he soon became Bishop of Tininium, or Knin. As a representative of the emperor, Dudith went to the Council of Trent, which was continuing its sessions in 1562. At the same time, with Colosvar, Bishop of Csánad, he represented the Hungarian clergy. On July 16, 1563, even before the Council had concluded its sessions, Dudith left Trent. For, at the death of Colosvar (November 24, 1562), he had succeeded him as Bishop of Csánad. Shortly afterwards, in November, 1563, he became Bishop of Fünfkirchen. Because the see city of this bishopric, Pecs, was in the hands of the Turks at this time, it was transferred to Posony, but Dudith brought it to Szigeth. Emperor Maximilian charged Dudith with diplomatic duties for which, in the early part of 1565, he travelled to the court of King Sigismund at Cracow. In 1567 he married and shortly afterward resigned from his duties. This led to a trial in Rome under Pope Pius V, and on February 6, 1568, he was excommunicated and condemned to be burned in effigy. Meanwhile Dudith remained in Cracow. Because of his breach with Rome he was commended by Beza and Bullinger, who dedicated a publication to him in 1568. Dudith tended to agree with the anti-Trinitarians who had found refuge in Poland at that time. Of great importance in this respect was a letter from Dudith to John a Lasco, dated June 9, 1571. This letter was published in Switzerland without his permission and was later frequently drawn into the discussion about Socinianism. In 1576 Dudith settled in Silesia. In later years he lived mainly in Breslau, although he also stayed in Poland temporarily. After the death of his first wife, he remarried in 1574. He entrusted the education of his oldest son to students of Ursinus. He corresponded with many scholars, e.g., with Lipsius, Ortelius, and Faustus Socinus. Dudith was a humanist in his views with an independent theological position, which showed influences of Melanchthon but which was Arian at the same time. He defended freedom of investigation and of conscience. He rejected the idea of a true church.

Bibliography:

Benrath, *P.R.E.* V (1898, 3rd ed.), 54 f.

P. Costil, *André Dudith humaniste hongrois 1553–1589* (Paris, 1935).

W. Janssen, *Charles Utenhove. Sa vie et son oeuvre 1536–1600* (Maastricht, 1939), 38.

K. Juhasz, "A. Dudith," *HJb* 1 (1935, V), 55-74.

D. Nauta, *Samuel Maresius* (Amsterdam, 1935).

K. Voelker, *Kirchengeschichte Polens* (1930), 255.

D. Nauta

DUFF, Alexander (1806-1878), Scottish Presbyterian missionary. Born at Moulin, Perthshire, Scotland, Duff experienced "the assurance of acceptance through the atoning blood of Jesus Christ" at the age of 12. At 15 he entered the University of St. Andrews and completed his Arts course in record time being powerfully influenced by Thomas Chalmers, professor of moral philosophy. At Chalmers' breakfast table he met such outstanding missionaries as Marshman of India and Morrison of China. At 23 he was ordained as the Church of Scotland's first foreign missionary and was designated to India, being twice shipwrecked on the way.

In Calcutta he concentrated on school work, seeking to influence intelligent young Hindus through the use of the Bible as a textbook. After two years he won his first convert, who was soon followed by three more. "These four men were the firstfruits of Duff's labours in India, and their profession of Christian faith the outcome of those dramatic early years." But Duff as schoolmaster, editor of *The Calcutta Christian Observer*, and pastor of St. Andrew's church, was carrying too heavy a load, and in 1834 he returned to Scotland on sick leave, receiving the degree of D.D. from Aberdeen University. At home he engaged in extensive deputation work and stimulated interest in missions among university students.

Returning to the field in 1839, he again threw himself wholeheartedly into the work. At the disruption of the Church of Scotland in 1843, along with all but one of that church's missionaries, he threw in his lot with the evangelical Free Church of Scotland. The stream of converts from high-caste Hindu and Brahmin circles continued; and in 1848 a congregation was organized. Two years later another extended furlough became necessary for health reasons. Duff was elected Moderator of the Free Church General Assembly in 1851, visited Canada and the United States in the interest of missions, addressed Congress and spent a day with the President, and was awarded the LL.D. degree by the University of New York.

His third tour of duty in India was soon interrupted by the Indian "Mutiny" (1857), in which one of his first converts lost his life. But Duff could not speak too highly of the way in which the church stood firm in the crisis. In 1863 he declined the vice-chancellor's office in the newly formed Calcutta University, health reasons forcing his final retirement from the field the same year. He was promptly elected professor of evangelistic theology in the New College, Edinburgh. Ten years later he was again called to the Moderator's chair. Strongly conservative in theology, he deplored "the mischievous questionings of carnal reason" put forth by men like Robertson Smith.

Duff died at the age of 71. Men remarked on his Pauline austerity, his Calvinistic conviction, his Puritan morality, and yet his remarkable catholicity.

BIBLIOGRAPHY:

G. Smith, *The Life of Alexander Duff D.D., LL.D.* (London, 1879), 2 vols.

W. Paton, *Alexander Duff: Pioneer of Missionary Education* (London, 1923).

R. STRANG MILLER

DUKHOBORS. See DOUKHOBORS.

DUMAH, "dumb":

(1) A son of Ishmael (Gen. 25:14; I Chron. 1:30), the descendants of whom, according to Arabian sources, settled in N Arabia in the oasis area Dumat-el–Jandil, known today as Dumat-el–Dsjof.

(2) A town in the hill country of S Judah, approximately 15 miles SW of Hebron (Josh. 15:52). It is the present-day scene of a ruin heap called ed-Domeh (L. H. Grollenberg, *Atlas of the Bible*, Melbourne, 1957, Map 13, p. 60).

(3) The land of Edom (Isa. 21:11). The exact usage of the term by Isaiah has not been established. Commentators present various views: (a) Edom was in the direction of Dumah, from which the message sounded forth; (b) Dumah of Arabia had in the past been in some alliance with Edom and thus identified

by Isaiah; (c) it was an emblematic designation of Edom as the land of silence and death (Ps. 94:17; 115:17), since Edom had once been a strong and fierce opponent of the Lord's chosen people. This last interpretation has etymological and historical support.

GERARD VAN GRONINGEN

DUMBNESS. Inability to speak appears in Scripture in three primary aspects:

(1) As an attribute of inanimate idols, indicating their impotence (Ps. 135:16; Hab. 2:18, 19).

(2) As a temporary condition imposed by God: on Ezekiel as a sign to and a punishment upon Israel (3:26; 24:27; 33:22); on Zacharias as chastisement for his unbelief (Luke 1:20).

(3) As an affliction, which in the NT frequently was the object of the Messiah's healing ministry in accordance with the prophecy of Isa. 35:6, and was often closely associated with demon possession (Mt. 9:32, 33; 12:22; 15:30, 31; Mark 9:17-29; Luke 11:14) and deafness (see also Mark 7:32-37).

Silence appears also as an expression of awe (Acts 9:7), submission to God (Isa. 52:15; Dan. 10:15), faith under oppression (Ps. 38:13; 39:2, 9), and inability to exonerate oneself (Mt. 22:12). Jesus, silent before the cross, is likened to a sheep dumb before its shearers (Isa. 53:7).

DU MOULIN, Pierre (1568-1658), famous French Reformed theologian. Du Moulin was four years old at the time of Saint Bartholomew's Massacre, from which he was saved by an elderly maid who hid him under some straw and blankets. His youth was marked by poverty. When he was 20, his father died, leaving him alone with twelve coins in his pocket. He went to Cambridge, where he studied theology. Leaving Cambridge in 1592, he was appointed professor of philosophy at Leiden, where he had the renowned Grotius for a pupil. In 1599 he became a pastor in Paris and was chosen to be chaplain by Catherine of Bourbon, duchess of Bar, sister of King Henry IV.

From that moment on, he manifested himself as a vigorous controversialist. First, he debated against the apostate Palma Cayet in conferences that were instituted in a vain attempt to convert Princess Catherine to Romanism. Then, he wrote against a Portuguese Jesuit, *The Waters of Siloam, to Quench the Fire of Purgatory.* This Jesuit, who was none other than Suares, replied through Cayet: *The Fiery Furnace and the Reverberated Oven to Evaporate the So-called Waters of Siloam and to Corroborate Purgatory, against the Heresies, Falsehoods, Calumnies, and Cavils of the so-called Minister Du Moulin* (1603). Du Moulin replied with *Increase of the Waters of Siloam to Quench the Fire of Purgatory* (1604). The third section of this work is devoted to "The Fulfillment of the Prophecies." It is a subject to which Du Moulin often returned, in the conviction that the prophecies of Daniel and the Apocalypse applied to his era. His *Apology for the Holy Supper of the Lord Against the Bodily Presence and Transubstantiation, and Against Masses Without Communicants and Communion under a Single Species* (1607) elicited attacks upon him by Coeffetau. Du Moulin replied to him with his *Anatomy of the Book of Mr. Coeffetau* (1610). Continuing his struggles against Roman doctrines, Du Moulin, with three other ministers of Charenton—Montigny, Durand, and Mestregat—wrote against the Jesuit Mr. Arnoux, who had claimed in a sermon preached before King Louis XIII that the references to Holy Writ contained in the *Confession of Faith of the Reformed Churches of France* were false. This *Défense de La Confession de*

Foi became in its second edition *Le Bouclier de la Foi* (*The Shield of the Faith* [1618]), one of the best works of Reformed controversy, republished several times, even in the 19th century. In the same year he published another basic work: *La vocation des Pasteurs.* Then came the Synod of Dort, which Du Moulin was unable to attend because of an order of King Louis XIII forbidding the Reformed Churches of France to participate in it. However, he defended the synod by a famous treatise and had the Synod of Arlès (1619) adopt its decisions. In 1621 he left Paris for Sedan, where he was appointed professor of theology. From there he wrote *Du Combat chrétien ou des afflictions* (1622). After a stay in England, on the request of King James II, he wrote a book to refute Cardinal Du Perron, entitled, *The Novelty of Papism Opposed to the Antiquity of True Christianity* (1627). A few years later he published his important work *On the Judge of Controversies, a Treatise in which the Authority and the Perfection of the Holy Scriptures are Defended Against the Usurpations and Accusations of the Roman Church.* These two volumes deal with the ever-current problem, Scripture and tradition. His *Anatomy of the Mass* (1636) shows by Scripture and by the witness of the primitive church that the mass is contrary to the Word of God and is removed from the way of salvation. He did not fight only against RC theologians but also against Protestant ones, such as Tilenus on the question of the Divine nature of Christ, Piscator on certain errors concerning redemption, and Amyraut on hypothetical universalism. This theologian was also a great preacher, and his sermons on the preparation for the Lord's supper (1643) were read by a great number of Christians of his time. Occasionally harsh as a controversialist, he was an outstanding shepherd of souls, and his books of sermons (1641-1654) strengthened the faith of persecuted Protestants.

JEAN CADIER

DUNCAN, John "Rabbi" (1796-1870), Scottish Presbyterian, professor of Hebrew. "An eminent scholar and metaphysician, a profound theologian, a man of tender piety and of a lowly, loving spirit," Duncan was converted through the instrumentality of Caesar Malan of Geneva (1826). The searching ministries of Gavin Parker and John Kidd, together with the writings of John Love, Owen, and Witsius, contributed to "his second conversion," in which he discovered painfully the danger of taking for granted the reality of his faith in Christ.

He took part with Black, Keith, McCheyne, and Andrew Bonar in an exploratory mission to the Jews (1839). Duncan's further labors in Hungary were rewarded by the conversion of the Saphir family, Alfred Edersheim, and others. In 1843 he became professor of Hebrew and Oriental languages in New College of the Free Church of Scotland. He published little, but his personal influence was great. *Colloquia Peripatetica* consists of notes of conversations in which Duncan's deepest thoughts came to spontaneous expression. The following is characteristic:

"The Law ordained, 'Thou shalt love'; and love ordained that law. Man could not keep it, and love ordained a gospel; that Gospel is 'God so loved.' Thus, 'Thou shalt love' is the whole of the law; 'God so loved' is the whole of the Gospel. That is so clear that it is at once law and Gospel for children and for savages; but it is so deep in its limpid clearness that no philosopher can fathom it."

See BROWN, DAVID; EDERSHEIM, ALFRED; KIDD, JOHN; LOVE, JOHN; MALAN, CAESAR; SAPHIR, ADOLF.

BIBLIOGRAPHY:
D. Brown, *Life of the late John Duncan, LLD* (Edinburgh, 1872).
D. Brown, *The Late Rev. John Duncan . . . in The Pulpit and at The Communion Table* (Edinburgh, 1874).
W. Knight, *Colloquia Peripatetica, Deep-sea Soundings, being Notes of Conversations with the late John Duncan, LLD* (Edinburgh and London; 6th ed., enlarged, 1907).
J. MacLeod, *Scottish Theology in Relation to Church History since the Reformation* (Edinburgh, 1943), 282-286.
J. S. Sinclair (ed.), *Rich Gleanings after the Vintage from "Rabbi" Duncan* (London, 1925).
A. M. Stuart, *Recollections of the late John Duncan, LLD* (Edinburgh, 1872).

WILLIAM YOUNG

DUNG, DUNGHILL, translates correctly five Biblical roots but renders misguidingly four others.

(1) גֵּל (*gēl*) and גָּלָל (*galal*), meaning *ball* (root, *to roll*), describes human excrement (Ezek. 4:12, 15). Dung thus suggests decomposition (Job 20:7; Zeph. 1:17) and requires removal (I Kings 14:10; Deut. 23:10-14).

(2) חֲרָאִים (*chraîm*) designates human dung (II Kings 18:27; Isa. 36:12, referred to as abhorrent for eating) or guano of birds (II Kings 6:25, consumed under duress; Josephus, *Wars,* v, 13, 7).

(3) צְפִיעַ (*tsaphîa'*) of cattle, when mixed with straw and dried produced fuel cakes (Ezek. 4:15).

(4) דֹּמֶן (*domen*) signifies excrement in a field and is compared with untended corpses (II Kings 9:37; Ps. 83:10; Jer. 8:2; etc.). Its cognate מַדְמֵנָה (*madmēnah*) *dunghill* (Isa. 25:10), identifies manure piles. Correspondingly in the NT, (5) κόπριον (*koprion*) *manure,* served as fertilizer (Luke 13:8), and κοπρίαν (*koprian*) *dunghill,* designates heaps of dung and rubbish (Luke 14:35).

But the following are improperly rendered as *dung* or *dunghill*:

(1) פֶּרֶשׁ (*peresh*) describes the cud or stomach contents of cattle, used by Beduins for covering fires in which meat is roasted (*KB*, 783). It is mentioned in OT ritual contexts (Ex. 29:14; Lev. 4:11; etc.), though it was considered a disgrace for Hebrew contact (Mal. 2:3).

(2) אַשְׁפֹּת (*ashpot*) *dunghill,* means ash pit, where beggars slept or asked alms, thus signifying lowliness (I Sam. 2:8; Ps. 113:7; Lam. 4:5). It identifies Jerusalem's *dung gate* (Neh. 2:13; 3:13-14), the *gate of potsherds* (Jer. 19:2 ARVm), which opened S onto the ash heaps of the Hinnom Valley (Neh. 12:31; II Kings 23:10; Job 2:8).

(3) נְוָלִי (*nevalî*) and נְוָלוּ (*nevalû*) describe ruins (Ezra 6:11; Dan. 2:5 *ICC*, 146-149; 3:29), but probably not a public latrine (II Kings 10:27).

(4) NT σκύβαλον (*skubalon*) depicts refuse left from a feast (Phil. 3:8).

J. BARTON PAYNE

DUNS SCOTUS, John, the "subtle doctor" (*c.* 1266-1308), medieval philosopher. Born at Maxton, Scotland, Duns Scotus became a Franciscan (*c.* 1281), studied at Paris (1293-6), and lectured at Oxford (1297-1301). In 1305 he became doctor in theology at Paris, after having lectured on Lombard's *Sententiae,* and died three years later at Cologne. In addition to the Oxford and Paris Commentaries (*Opus Oxoniense* and *Reportata Parisiensia*), Scotus' authentic writings include works on logic, *Quaestiones Subtilissimae* on Aristotle's *Metaphysics, Quaestiones Quodlibetales* (which express Duns's last word on the points discussed), and the *De Primo Principio,* an important work on natural theology. Unauthentic works include the *De Rerum Principio,* the *Grammatica Speculativa,* and commentaries on Aristotle's *Physics.* The famous *Theoremata* are doubtful and the *De Anima* questioned.

According to Scotus, the proper object of philosophy, i.e., of metaphysics, is being as being, while that of theology is God as infinite Being. The human mind must abstract its knowledge of being from the data of the senses. That we have no direct intuition of pure being in the present life is probably a consequence of original sin. The primary natural object of our intellect is being as being. Hence, every being falls within the scope of the intellect. Thus, God is a natural object of the human intellect, although we do not have an immediate, natural knowledge of God.

The concept of being is univocal, not merely analogical, for Scotus. "I call a concept univocal if it is one in such a manner that its unity suffices to make it contradictory to affirm it and to deny it, at one and the same time, of one and the same thing" (*Op. Ox.*, I, d3, q. 2, a. 4, 5). The univocal concept of being makes metaphysics possible. Aristotle's prime mover, the existence of which physics proves, is but part of the universe, as a keystone in the arch. To know God as the cause of the very being of the world, one must argue not from physical being, but from being as such. The two basic modes of being are the finite and the infinite. This distinction is antecedent to that of finite being separated into the 10 Aristotelian categories. God as infinite Being cannot be included under any category or genus. Consequently, the univocity of being with respect to its modes cannot imply pantheism, much less deism or anthropomorphism. God and the creature are completely different in the real order, although the concept of being is univocally applied to both in the logical order.

Scotus inclined to thoroughgoing realism in his doctrine of universals, distinguishing various *formalitates* in the individual thing corresponding to the logical determinations of thought. The unity of the individual thing with its generic, specific, and individual forms requires the Scotist to make formal distinctions based on the nature of things. Likewise, essence and existence in the creature are neither identical nor really different, but formally distinct.

Duns rejects the Aristotelian theory that matter is the principle of individuation. Prime matter is itself an individual entity, according to its Divine idea. Scotus, however, does not teach that form is the principle of individuation, but identifies the latter with the ultimate reality of the form, the *haecceitas* or *thisness*. The individual, as Heidegger has observed, is an irreducible ultimate.

Much has been written on the Scotist doctrine of the primacy of the will. Scotus allows a priority of the Divine intellect in what is logically necessary but stresses the sovereignty of the Divine will as well as human freedom. Foreknowledge of contingent events depends on the free determination of God's will. Predestination is purely an act of will. God first predestinates the elect to glory and consequently to grace. Reprobation is based on the guilt of the reprobate but is explained in the supralapsarian four-moment theory. In the first moment, God is silent as to Judas when he elects Peter to glory. In the second, grace is willed for Peter, but nothing for Judas. The third permits sin for Peter and Judas alike, while the fourth moment reprobates Judas as a sinner. The speculation that the birth of the reprobate is a consequence of Adam's sin does not enable Scotus to reconcile his indeterministic doctrine of freedom with his emphasis on the Divine sovereignty. Scotist supralapsarianism is associated with the thesis that the Word would have become flesh even if Adam never sinned.

The Scotist system, though incomplete, is extremely complex. No simple characterization of it as nominalism, realism, or voluntarism does justice to the subtle nuances of its concrete individuality. The unstable realism of its logic and its inconsistent presentation of the sovereignty of God contributed to the dissolution of the medieval synthesis. Scotus' acceptilation theory of the atonement was a deviation from orthodoxy, destined to influence Grotius and other modern theologians.

See ARISTOTLE; ATONEMENT; PREDESTINATION; WILL.

BIBLIOGRAPHY:

Duns Scotus, *Opera Omnia* (Paris, 1891-5).

E. Gilson, *Jean Duns Scot, Introduction a ses Positions Fondamentales* (Paris, 1952).

C. R. S. Harris, *Duns Scotus* (Oxford, 1927), 2 vols.

M. Heidegger, *Die Kategorien—und Bedeutungslehre des Duns Scotus* (Tübingen, 1916).

P. Mignes, *Joannis Duns Scoti doctrina philosophica et theologica quod res praecipuas proposita et exposita* (Quaracchi, 1930), 2 vols.

W. Pannenberg, *Die Prädestinationslehre des Duns Skotus* (Göttingen, 1954).

WILLIAM YOUNG

DUNSTAN, SAINT (*c.* 909-988), Archbishop of Canterbury. After serving at King Aethelstan's court, Dunstan became a monk and then abbot at Glastonbury, which he made famous for asceticism and learning. In 959 he was appointed archbishop of Canterbury by Edgar, who had just added Wessex to his kingdom of Mercia and Northumbria. King and archbishop effected a complete reform of church and state, a policy continued under Edward the Martyr. When Edward was murdered (978), Dunstan's star waned. He is remembered chiefly for having revived monastic life and made it an influence in the country's affairs. A versatile man, one of his illuminated mss is in the British Museum.

DU PLESSIS-MORNAY, Philippe (1549-1623), French aristocrat and Huguenot leader. Born in Buhy, Normandy, Du Plessis-Mornay came of a lineage connected with the royal family of France and with the Bourbons. As a younger son of the family, he originally intended to take orders in the RC Church, but on the death of his father, who was a zealous Roman Catholic, he was converted to Protestantism through the influence of his mother. After making this decision, he spent some time traveling throughout Europe studying at various schools. Having gained considerable experience and understanding of European politics in this way, he returned to France, where he urged Henry III to support the Netherlands, which were at this point fighting Spanish domination. In this way he almost immediately began to make a name for himself at court but soon also became known as a very determined Protestant and a strong supporter of Admiral Coligny, the Huguenot leader. Assisted by a RC friend, he escaped the St. Bartholomew's Massacre (*q.v.*) and fled to England.

In 1575 he entered the service of Henry, king of Navarre, the Huguenot leader, who immediately began to employ him on various missions. The most important was that to Elizabeth of England in search of aid for the Huguenots in their struggle against the persecution of the French government. Shortly afterwards, he went to the Netherlands as a gentleman of the chamber to the Duc d'Anjou when the latter attempted to become leader of the RC rebels who were trying to throw off the Spanish yoke. Henry of Navarre obtained this appointment for him. In 1576 the Catholic League was organized to prevent Protestantism from taking France, and in 1584 it opposed Henry of Navarre's being named heir presumptive to the French throne. At that time Mornay became one of Henry's leading administrators, acting as his superintendent-general with the responsibility of maintaining the royal household and administration. When the Guises, who led the League, finally fell by assassination, Mornay advised Navarre to ally himself with Henry III.

This he did, and when this coalition captured Saumur, Mornay became its governor (1589). Here he founded a Protestant university (1593).

When in 1589, on Henry III's assassination, Henry of Navarre became Henry IV, King of France, Mornay continued as his chief councillor. After the Battle of Ivry (1590), which Henry won, Mornay advised him to seize Paris immediately, but he refused to take such drastic action. Instead, he had Mornay negotiate peace with the Duc de Maienne, leader of the League. Subsequently, Mornay divulged some of the negotiations, thus causing a certain amount of trouble. When Henry IV, after besieging Paris for some months, decided that he could not capture the city as long as he remained a Protestant and therefore should become a Roman Catholic, Mornay strongly opposed his plan. But once he realized that he could not dissuade him, he devoted himself to protecting the interests of the Huguenots as far as possible, formulating many of the provisions which Henry included in the Edict of Nantes (1598).

Despite his embarrassing opposition to Henry's conversion, he continued as a trusted royal adviser until 1598, when he published his *Traité de l'Institution de l'Eucharistie*, a vitriolic attack upon the Mass, which contained a number of misstatements of fact owing to wrong information furnished him by his assistants. A court debate resulted in which Mornay suffered defeat, partially because he received no word of the charges against him until the debate commenced. After this he retired from court to Saumur, where he lived most of the time, although he occasionally visited court to advise the king.

On Henry IV's assassination in 1610, Mornay submitted to the regent, Marie dè Medici, but in 1620 he supported King Louis XIII against his mother. He retired to his castle, where he died two years later.

Besides his activities as an administrator and an active leader of the Huguenot party, he wrote a number of works: *Traité de la vie et de la mort* (Geneva, 1575); *Traité de l'Église* (1577); *Traité de la vérité de la religion chrétienne* (Antwerp, 1580); *Discours sur le droit prétendu par ceux de la maison de Guise* (1582); *Le Mystère d'iniquité ou histoire de la papauté* (1607); and *Memoires* (1624-52).

BIBLIOGRAPHY:

H. M. Baird, *The Huguenots and the Revocation of the Edict of Nantes* (New York, 1895), I, 16-186.

A. Du Plessis, "Mornay, Philippe de," *Biographie Universelle* (Paris, 1821), XXX, 194-202.

A. Garnier, *Agrippe d'Aubigné et le parti Protestant* (Paris, 1928).

L. Marlet, "Mornay, Philippe de," *La Grande Encyclopedie* (Paris), XXIV, 358 f.

R. Patry, *Philippe Du Plessis, un huguenot homme d'état* (Paris, 1933).

W. S. REID

DURANDUS OF SAINT-POURÇAIN (*c.* 1270-1332), French scholastic theologian. Durandus became a Dominican and studied and taught in Paris, where in 1313 he received the degree of Doctor Theologiae. From 1313 to 1317 he served at the papal court at Avignon, after which he became bishop successively of Limoux (1317), Le Puy-en-Velay (1318), and Meaux (1326). His main work was the *Commentary on the Sentences* (of Peter of Lombard), which survives in three recensions. In 1333, after his death, eleven articles from his book on the beatific vision were censured by a papal commission. Although a Dominican, he did not slavishly follow Thomas, but criticized him on several points. On the whole he took the nominalist position, without going to the Scotist extreme. Resolutely he rejected the Thomist synthesis of philosophy and theology. Concerning tradition, he sharply distinguished between official theological statements of the church (which he accepted) and opinions derived from them (which he regarded as not binding). He viewed with even more suspicion extra-ecclesiastical authorities: "It is no part of natural philosophy to know what Aristotle or other philosophers thought, but the truth of the matter is the essential thing; wherefore when Aristotle deviates from the truth of the matter it is no science to know what Aristotle thought, but rather error" (Pref. in sent., qu. 1, no. 6). These views explain why Durandus was called "Doctor Modernus" and also "Doctor Resolutissimus." From his doctrine of the sacraments, it is clear that he had difficulty with the prevalent theory of transubstantiation, even though he accepted the dogma as such. He further preferred an occasional to an instrumental operation of the "gratia interna" (internal grace). Being a critical rather than a creative thinker, he did not produce his own theological system. But his *Commentary on the Sentences* was very influential during the Middle Ages. At his own request the following words were put on his tombstone: "Here lies the hard (*durus*) Durandus under the hard marble. Whether he is saved I do not know, nor care."

BIBLIOGRAPHY:

A. d'Amato, "Durandus," in *EC* IV (1950), col. 2006.

S. M. Deutsch, "Durand of Saint-Pourçain," in *SHERK* IV (1952), 34-36.

P. Fournier, "Durand de Saint-Pourçain," in *Histoire littéraire de la France* XXXVII (1938), 1-38.

P. Godet, "Durandus," in *DThC* IV (1911), cols. 1964-66.

KLAAS RUNIA

DÜRER, Albrecht (1471-1528), German painter and engraver. Second of a Nuremberg goldsmith's eighteen children, Albrecht soon forsook his father's trade and was apprenticed to the wood engraver Michael Wohlgemuth. He later spent some time in Italy and as a result introduced new concepts of art to his country. Dürer is also considered by many to have been the inventor of etching. In 1498 he completed his magnificent engravings of the Apocalypse, and in 1514 his memorable copperwork piece, "St. Jerome in his Study," came. Of his many religious paintings, perhaps the best known is "The Adoration of the Magi" (1504). His work still exists in collections throughout the world and is best represented in the Albertine in Vienna and in the British Museum. A man of serene character despite unpromising home circumstances, Dürer remained a Roman Catholic to the end, though he had sympathies for the Reformation and had respect of Luther and other Protestants.

DURHAM, James (1622-1658), leading theologian of the so-called Second Reformation. James Durham was the eldest son of John Durham, a landed proprietor in Forfar, Scotland. He studied at St. Andrews University. He then took up residence in his own country house and married Anna, a daughter of Francis Durham of Duntarvie. Anna's mother was a lady of deep piety, and it was due to her persuasions that Durham, while on a visit to her home, was induced to go to church on the Saturday of the Communion season there. The Spirit of God used the sermon then preached by Ephraim Melvil on I Peter 2:7 for his conversion, and from then on he became marked as a man of prayerful and studious habits.

During the Civil War, Durham served for a time as a captain in the Scots army. It was while he was thus engaged that David Dickson, then professor of divinity in Glasgow, happened to hear him leading his men in prayer. Dickson was so impressed that he urged Durham to enter the Gospel ministry. After the completion of his theological studies in Glasgow, Durham was licensed to preach, and in 1647 he became minister of the Blackfriars Church in Glasgow. In 1650 he was appointed successor to Dickson as professor of divinity in Glasgow University, but, before he could enter upon the duties of that appointment, the General Assembly decided that he should, instead, attend the king as chaplain. This he did in a manner that made the deepest impression upon the court. Later, he became minister of the Inner Kirk of Glasgow. But his ministry there was of short duration, for he died at 36. He had a pacifying influence in the church at a time when division was rife, his treatise on *The Scandal of the Church* being regarded as the Scottish classic on this subject. David Dickson had recognized his gifts as a theologian and had brought him into his scheme for the provision of commentaries on various books of the Bible. Durham's special contribution was his *Commentary on Revelation.* Equally noted was his *Commentary on the Song of Solomon.* His expositions of the *Ten Commandments* and of the *Fifty-third chapter of Isaiah* were also highly esteemed. Several collections of his sermons appeared posthumously.

See DICKSON, DAVID.

G. N. M. COLLINS

DURY, John (1537-1600), Scottish protestant divine. John Dury was suspected of "heresy" when he was a monk at Dunfermline, and so he was condemned to life imprisonment. Escaping when the Reformation triumphed in Scotland, he became minister at Leith and supported John Knox with zeal. After becoming minister at Edinburgh about 1573, he was imprisoned for openly rebuking the sins of men high in the court of King James VI. Later he was ordered to leave Edinburgh (1582). He returned shortly afterward and was met by a great concourse of the citizens who went in procession through the streets singing Psalm 124 "till heaven and earth resounded."

DURY, John, also, **DURIE, DURAEUS** (1596-1680), early ecumenist. A native of Scotland, Dury engaged for more than 50 years, in both personal activities and writing, in an attempt to restore the confessional and ecclesiastical unity of the Protestants of his time. He studied first at Leiden, where his father, Robert Dury, was the minister of the English Presbyterian Church for a few years, and then at Oxford. He himself became a Presbyterian minister in the Polish city of Elbing, where, in 1628, he met the Swedish Lutheran jurist Kasper Godemann. This meeting was to be of decisive significance for the rest of Dury's life. There he became involved in Godemann's attempts to unite Lutherans and Reformed in the matter of the doctrine of the Lord's supper. From then on, he considered it his lifework to devote all his powers to the restoration of the unity between Lutherans and Reformed, as well as among the Reformed themselves.

In the beginning, he enjoyed the support of the Swedish king Gustavus Adolphus, the English statesman Sir Thomas Roe, and George Abbot, archbishop of Canterbury. When the latter died in 1633, Dury changed over to the Anglican church, apparently to assure himself of the support of Abbot's successor, Laud. Afterwards, he continued his efforts in Germany, Sweden, and Denmark. When in 1642 the daughter of the English king, Charles I, left for The Hague as wife of the stadtholder William II, Dury was sent along with her as an Anglican clergyman. Subsequently he was the minister of the English church in Rotterdam for a short while. In 1645 he returned to the presbyterian church and attended the sessions of the Westminster Assembly. During the supremacy of Cromwell, he went over to the Independents and was again sent to the Continent. At this stage his contact with the Lutherans receded into the background, and his objective was restricted to uniting the Reformed. Even at that, however, his labors had practically no results, either in regard to the league of Protestant nations, which Cromwell had envisioned, or the unity of the church, which he himself so fervently desired. Even when he was forced to leave England for good in 1661, after the Restoration, he continued to pursue his lifework.

In evaluating his efforts, it must be noted that he had no firm conviction regarding the way in which unity should be effected. Sometimes he was satisfied with unity in the fundamentals, while secondary matters could remain the object of free discussion. At other times, he placed all his hope in the formulating of a new confession of faith. At times, he tried to decide what was fundamental by using the early church as a standard; then again, he believed that it was necessary only to ask about the degree to which communion with God and Christ was experienced in a certain church. Furthermore, the ease with which he changed over from one side to another did little to promote confidence in his endeavors. This does not alter the fact that we have in Dury a classic example of the homesickness for the unity of Christ's church in this world and of the willingness to exert every effort for the restoration of that unity.

Y. FEENSTRA

DUST. The term "dust" is used of earth in general. The serpent moves his head along at ground level (Gen. 3:14; Isa. 65:25). The poor are raised from the dust (I Sam. 2:8), and the proud abased to it (Isa. 47:1). It is thrown over the head as a sign of grief (Job 2:12). The word also signifies the material compounds which make up the body (Gen. 2:7; 3:19), and which appear again when the body disintegrates (Ps. 104:29; Eccles. 12:7). Resurrection restores the body from the dust (Isa. 26:19).

Metaphorically it signifies vast quantity (Gen. 13:6) and smallness (Deut. 9:21; II Kings 13:7; Isa. 40:15). To shake the dust of a place off one's feet (Mt. 10:14; Acts 13:51) is to demonstrate that one will not carry away the slightest link with it.

DUVERGIER DE HAURANNE, Jean, usually called "Saint-Cyran," from the monastery of that name (1581-1643), one of the founders of Jansenism. After studying in his native country of France, Saint-Cyran went to Louvain, Belgium, to study theology. There he met Jansen, the man whose friendship was to have such a great influence upon him. At the close of their studies around 1611, the two friends went to Bayonne, where together they began to study the Church Fathers, especially Augustine. As a result of this study, Jansen produced his famous *Augustinus*, a summary of Augustinian thought. But this work would have remained unknown if Saint-Cyran had not extracted from this ponderous folio spiritual nourishment for the nuns and *solitaires* of Port-Royal. Saint-Cyran was put in charge of the spiritual direction of this famous monastery, which Mother Angélique Arnaud had just restored. Unfortunately, Cardinal Richelieu became displeased with Saint-Cyran and, on May 15, 1638, ordered him imprisoned in the Dungeon of Vincennes, where he was held captive for five years. Deprived of books, pen, and paper, he secretly read the Bible and the Confessions of Augustine. On the death of Richelieu, Saint-Cyran was released, but he died eight months later in Paris.

He was first and foremost a spiritual counselor, and from his *Lettres chré-*

tiennes et spirituelles (1645, 2 vols.), we know the nature of his counseling. He fashioned the spirit of Port-Royal, the spirit of humility, of a great love for Jesus Christ and of the study of the Holy Scriptures.

The opponents of Jansenism accuse Saint-Cyran, along with Jansen, Arnaud d'Andilly, Camus (Bishop of Bellay), and others, of having fomented a plot against the RC faith, and in particular against the sacraments of penance and the eucharist. Known as the plot of Bourg-Fontaine, it was a pure invention of the Jesuits.

Among the works of Saint-Cyran the following may be mentioned: *Question royale, où il est montré en quelle extrémité, principalement en temps de paix, le sujet pourrait être obligé de conserver la vie du prince au dépens de la sienne* (1609). This work is something of an exercise of wit. *Somme des fautes et faussetés contenues en la Somme théologique du R. P. Garasse* (1626), an attack (against the errors and falsehoods of Garasse) which unleashed against its author the tenacious hatred of the Jesuits; *Oeuvres du théologien Petrus Aurelius* (1631), which Saint-Cyran and his nephew M. de Barcos wrote under the pseudonym of Aurelius. It is a defense of the episcopal hierarchy against usurpation by the religious orders, in particular, the Jesuits. We are compelled to believe that the Jesuits have continued to harbor a strong resentment against him, if we are to judge by the chapter in Henri Brémond's *L'Histoire littéraire du sentiment religieux* (vol. IV; 1925), where he presents Saint-Cyran as a wretched aspirant and a dangerous conspirator. One would do better to read over again what Sainte-Beuve says of him in his *Port-Royal*, and Louis-Frederic Jaccard in his *Saint-Cyran* (Lausanne, 1944).

JEAN CADIER

DWIGHT, Timothy (1752-1817), Congregationalist theologian and educator. Born in Northampton, Massachusetts, Dwight owed much of his early instruction and moral character to his mother, Mary, a daughter of Jonathan Edwards. After graduation from Yale (A.B., 1769; M.A., 1772), he became the principal of Hopkins Grammar School, New Haven (1769-1771) and a tutor at Yale (1771-1777). In 1777 he was licensed to preach and served as a chaplain in the Continental Army (1777-1778). At his father's death he returned home to manage the farm, supply churches, and run a school (1779-1783). In 1781 and 1782 he was a representative in the state legislature. He was then ordained to the pastorate of the Greenfield Congregational Church in Fairfield, Connecticut (1783-1795). There he also opened a coeducational academy which established his fame as an educator. He also published poetry, endeavored with others to establish an American literary tradition, and became an acknowledged leader in Connecticut Congregationalism, using his influence for union between Congregational and Presbyterian denominations. He received the D.D. from the College of New Jersey (1787) and the LL.D. from Harvard (1810).

From 1795 until his death he was president and professor of divinity at Yale College. He also gave instruction in other subjects, such as literature and philosophy. He was a brilliant teacher and a good administrator, with a strong sense of moral responsibility. During his presidency he reformed the government, discipline, and curriculum of the college, and almost tripled the enrollment. The stability of his administration was remarkable for the times. When he went to Yale he found many students professing the popular deism and skepticism of the post-war period. By means of his evangelical preaching a revival of religion took place, and by 1802 a third of the students had professed conversion. His commendation of the claims of personal religion to educated minds was a powerful influence in the New England phase of the Second Great Awakening. His chapel sermons constituted a system of theology, and after his death they were published under the title *Theology, Explained and Defended* (5 vols., New Haven, 1818-1819). He was a moderate Calvinist of the Edwardean School, but denying the doctrine of imputation and advocating the use of means on the part of the unregenerate. He was a man of wide learning, which he always had at his command for systematic presentation. In many respects he was one of the most conspicuous figures and dominating forces in New England in his day, exerting his influence against the rationalistic and democratic tendencies of his age, and supporting the formation of Andover Seminary, the American Bible Society, and the American Board of Commissioners for Foreign Missions. He revised the *Psalms* of Watts with additions of his own and made a selection of hymns which was adopted by the congregationalists and presbyterians. As a poet he is scarcely remembered today, except for his hymn, "I Love Thy Kingdom, Lord."

Among his other principal works are *The Conquest of Canaan; A Poem* (Hartford, 1885); *Triumph of Infidelity* (1788); *A Discourse, on the Genuineness and Authenticity of the New Testament* (New York, 1794); *Greenfield Hill: A Poem* (1794); *The Nature, and Danger, of Infidel Philosophy* (New Haven, 1798); *Hymns Selected from Dr. Watts, Dr. Doddridge, and Various Other Writers* (New Haven, 1803); *Travels in New England and New York* (New Haven, 1821-1822); and *Sermons on Miscellaneous Subjects* (2 vols., 1828).

BIBLIOGRAPHY:

C. E. Cuningham, *Timothy Dwight, 1752–1817* (New York, 1942).

S. E. Dwight, "A Memoir of the Life of the Author," in *Theology, Explained and Defended*, by T. Dwight, I (London, 1843), ix-cvii.

F. H. Foster, *A Genetic History of the New England Theology* (Chicago, 1907).

R. Johnson, ed., *The Twentieth Century Biographical Dictionary of Notable Americans*, III (Boston, 1904).

V. L. Parrington, ed., *The Connecticut Wits* (New York, 1926).

K. Silverman, *Timothy Dwight* (New York, 1968).

W. B. Sprague, *Annals of the American Pulpit*, II (New York, 1857), 152-165).

W. B. Sprague, "Timothy Dwight," *The Library of American Biography*, ed. by Jared Sparks, 2nd series, IV (Boston, 1845), 225-364.

ALBERT H. FREUNDT, JR.

DYE, DYEING. The art and business of dyeing began in antiquity. Phoenicians developed a method of dyeing. They made their dyed products the basis of a rich and far-reaching trade. The expensive production of purple from the small amounts of dye in the dye-fish (*murax trunculus*) made it imperative to find a source of vegetable dye. This source was found in the "Atlantic Islands." It met the needs of the growing dye works of Tyre and Sidon. This vegetable dye was combined with local dyes. It enabled the Phoenicians to produce purple fabric of luminous red. Dyers also found a source of color in dyer's lichen and the dragon tree which were important to the Phoenician industries. Purple was in demand by royalty and the rich. Tyre was at first a supplier but later also a manufacturer, so that it became known as Tyrian purple. It is thought that the guilds of Thyatira used madder-root instead of shell-fish for the production of purple dyestuffs. The color from madder-root is now called Turkish red.

The source of dyed goods used by the Israelites is not known. From archaeology we learn dyed goods were used in Egypt. Israelite colored goods may have come from Phoenicia by way of Egypt. Colors used by the Israelites were carmen, blue (violet), purple, and scarlet. The colors used in the building of the Tabernacle were blue, purple, scarlet, and red (Ex. 25:4, 5). Specifications for the tents were for rams' skins dyed red (Ex. 26:14; 35:7; 36:19; 39:34). Later when Solomon prepared to build the Temple, he asked Hiram, King of Tyre, for cunning workmen to work purple, crimson, and scarlet for him (II Chron. 2:7). Isaiah spoke of sin as scarlet (Is. 1:18). Dyed garments are mentioned in Isaiah 63:1. Blue is mentioned in Ezekiel 23:6. Dyed headgear is spoken of in Ezekiel 23:15 (see COLORS IN THE BIBLE).

Merchandizing in dyed stuffs was an important business. Lydia, a seller of purple, of the city of Thyatira, was a dealer in purple dye (Acts 16:14,15; 40). Lydia was presumably a wealthy woman; her home was large enough to entertain a whole missionary group. A guild of dyers made the celebrated purple dye. Lydia of Thyatira seems to have represented her guild in Philippi (Acts 16:14).

ELMER H. NICHOLAS

DYKE, Daniel (d. 1614), Puritan practical theologian. The son of the vicar of Hempstead, Essex, Dyke was educated at St. John's College, Cambridge. He ministered at Coggeshall until Aylmer, bishop of London, suspended him for nonconformity in 1583; he refused to be ordained priest or to wear the surplice. He moved to St. Albans, but there Aylmer suspended him again, permanently this time, although on the petition of Dyke's parishioners Lord Burghley intervened to ask for his reinstatement.

Dyke's most noted work was *The Mystery of Self-Deceiving* (1614; 7th ed., 1620), a posthumously published anatomy of the "Gospel-hypocrite." Thomas Fuller called it "a book that will be owned for a truth while men have any badness in them, and will be owned as a treasure while they have any goodness in them" (*Worthies of England*, 1811 ed., I, 437). It is a plain, forthright, searching exposition which deserved its popularity.

BIBLIOGRAPHY:

A. C. Bickley, *DNB*, s.v.
B. Brook, *Lives of the Puritans* (London, 1813), II, 235.
D. Dyke, *Works* (1635), 2 vols.
T. Fuller, *Worthies of England* (1811), I, 437.
D. Neal, *History of the Puritans* (2nd ed., London, 1754), I, 292 f.

JAMES I. PACKER

EADIE, John (1810-1876), Scottish Bible scholar. Born at Alva, Eadie studied at Glasgow University, where he attained high distinction in classics. Subsequently, as a student of the Theological College of the United Secession Church, he became deeply interested in exegetical studies. Inducted to Cambridge Street Church, Glasgow, in 1835, he held that charge for 28 years, and then accepted a call to Lansdowne Church in the same city, where he remained until his death. He was appointed professor of Biblical literature in the Secession College in 1843, holding the chair along with his successive pastorates. Meanwhile he became a diligent writer. The merit of his early artcles attracted the attention of Charles Hodge of Princeton. Among his larger works are *The Biblical Cyclopaedia* (1848), Commentaries on the Epistle to the Ephesians (1854), the Epistle to the Colossians (1856), the Epistle to the Philippians (1859), the Epistle to the Galatians (1869), and the Epistles to the Thessalonians, issued posthumously. Bishop Ellicott regarded the exegesis in the first two commentaries published as being superior to the handling of grammatical points, and exegesis was generally acknowledged to be Eadie's forte. More recently, Vincent Taylor paid tribute to Eadie's commentary on Philippians (Taylor, *The Person of Christ*, London, 1958, p. 67). In the year of his death Eadie was a member of the Committee on Revision of the New Testament and dedicated a book on the English Bible to his fellow-members. Glasgow University conferred on him the degree of LL.D. in 1844 and St. Andrews University the degree of D.D. in 1850.

BIBLIOGRAPHY:
DNB XVI (London, 1888), 307.
J. Brown, *Life of John Eadie* (London, 1878).
WILLIAM J. CAMERON

EADMER (*c.* 1060-*c.*1124), English historian and ecclesiastic. When Anselm became Archbishop of Canterbury (1093), Eadmer served as his assistant. In 1120 he was elected to the Scottish diocese of St. Andrews but had to return south when the Scots refused to recognize the authority of Canterbury. His most important works, still of great value to scholars, are the *Historia Novorum*, dealing with English history between 1066 and 1122, and a life of Anselm, to whom he was much attached.

EARTHQUAKES, which characterize the fault running S along the Jordan, through the Arabah, Red Sea, and E Africa, are prominent in both the history and thought of Israel. In Scripture they constitute a major feature of the disruptive intrusion of God into the world, most frequently signaling the shaking of men and human power in judgment (Ps. 60:2; Isa. 2:19, 21; 5:5; 13:13; 24:18 ff.; 29:6; Jer. 4:24; 10:10; 50:46; Ezek. 38:19 f.; Joel 2:10; 3:16; Nahum 1:5; Hab. 3:6,10; Hag. 2:6, 21; Zech. 14:4; Mt. 24:7; Mark 13:8; Luke 21:11; Rev. 6:12; 8:5; 11:13,19; 16:18).

The shaking of the earth also appears as a means of God's manifesting His glory (Job 9:6; Ps. 29:6, 8; 97:4; 104:32) and delivering His people (I Sam. 14:15; II Sam. 22:8; Ps. 18:7; Acts 16:20, 26). Judgment on sin, salvation, and the manifestation of God's glory repeatedly function in and through one another, and it is not surprising that earthquakes contributed substantially to those two events central to Biblical revelation in which these intertwined Divine purposes were so mightily wrought.

Thus, seismic disturbances played a vital role in the exodus and conquest of Canaan as is implied in the historical narratives and as clearly stated in Heb. 12:26 (cf. Ex. 19:18); Num. 16:31 f.; Judges 5:4 f.; and Ps. 68:8,16; 77:18; 114:4, 6-7. In the NT the death of Christ was marked by an earthquake (Mt. 27:51, 54).

JOSEPH P. DUGGAN

EASTER, a church holy day in which the Passover was transformed into a memorial to Christ's Resurrection. Sharp and sometimes bitter division on the correct date plagued the early church, the 14th of Nisan (Passover) being dominant in the E and a Sunday following in the W. Polycarp (*c.* 154), Irenaeus (*c.* 198), and the Quartodecimans opposed efforts by the Roman bishops, Anicetus and Victor, to compel uniformity, but the Council of Nicea (325) decreed a Sunday observance based on the spring equinox. Although the mode of calculation was subject to later debate and revision, E Christendom largely conformed thereafter.

The English word "Easter" is derived from the goddess of spring, Eastre (cognate to Ishtar, Astarte, Ashtoreth), and points to the pagan influences which have from antiquity influenced the celebration. In it the resurrection is often transformed into a vehicle for paying homage to the spring renewal of nature and the concept of fertility symbolized in the eggs and rabbits that still play a large role in Easter folk-custom. The lack of Scriptural precedent and authorization coupled with the belief that the weekly Lord's day sufficiently commemorates Christ's Resurrection has caused only limited dissent from the almost universal practice of Christendom.

BIBLIOGRAPHY:

F. E. Brightman, "The Quartodeciman Question," *JTS* 25 (1924).

E. O. James, *Seasonal Feasts and Festivals* (London, 1961).

E. Schwartz, *Judische und Christliche Ostertafeln* (1905).

V. Staley, *The Seasons, Feasts and Festivals of the Christian Year* (London, 1910).

JOSEPH P. DUGGAN

EASTERN ORTHODOX CHURCH, a major branch of the Christian church whose origins are to be found in the theological and political developments of the first four centuries of the Christian era, both in the church and in the Roman Empire. Yet it would be inaccurate to conclude that the emergence of the Eastern Orthodox Church can be found exclusively in these two developments, important as they are. The Greek and Roman minds were quite different in outlook on many basic questions, and this difference was carried over into their Christian practice. Thus, the E church tended to be speculative and mystical in its approach to theological questions, whereas the Roman mind was much more practical in its approach to these issues. The theologians of the E were more given to disputing questions concerning the nature of the Trinity and the two natures of Christ. The W mind, on the other hand, was more concerned with the question as to how a man may be saved and what the work of Christ means. The speculative tendency in the E was the direct result of the fact that the Greek Christian mind was unduly under the influence of Platonic and Neoplatonic philosophy, and was thus frequently blind to the radical difference between the Gospel and all forms of Greek thought. This assumed an even greater importance since theological leadership of the early church lay in the E, particularly in the schools of Antioch and Alexandria, which were unrivalled in the W before 400. It is important to note that in the history of the E church there was never any period of revival or great theologians like those of the W church.

Historical Development

The history of the Eastern Orthodox Church may be conveniently divided into three eras. The first, or the classical period, was one of great theological activity and came to an end with John of Damascus about 750. His *Fountain of Knowledge* presented in systematic form the whole theology of the Greek Fathers and ecumenical councils to his own day. The second, the Byzantine period, beginning about 750, came to an end with the capture of Constantinople in 1453. This Byzantine period parallels rather closely in chronology the medieval period of the history of the W Roman Church. This second period, because of a sterile dogmatism, was followed by deterioration. It also witnessed the gradual division of the Greek and Roman Churches. During this period the E Roman Empire suffered an almost continuous loss of territory, first to the Arabs and then to the Seljuk Turks. The invasion of this latter group culminated in the fall of Constantinople in 1453.

The Eastern Orthodox Church, originally consisting of the four patriarchates of Antioch, Jerusalem, Alexandria, and Constantinople and their dependencies, developed this pattern of organization from that of the Roman Empire. The ecclesiastical areas of jurisdiction tended to follow those of the empire, particularly the dioceses since they had been divided by the emperor, Constantine. The Council of Nicea in 325 gave to the bishop of Rome the title of patriarch also. The final divisions of the church in two was aided and hastened by the final division of the empire in 395 by Theodosius, which was carried out on the basis of fairly defined linguistic and ethnic differences. By the time of Justinian (527-565) the church in the E had acquired most of its essential characteristics and, unlike the church in the W, was firmly under the control of the E emperors. But these political factors working for a division of the church must be balanced against the long period of theological controversy which engulfed the E church. Both the E and the W had accepted the doctrinal formulations of the Council of Nicea of 325 and of the Council of Constantinople of 381.

The phraseology of part of the creed of 381 was the cause of sharp controversy in the E. Particularly controversial was the clause that affirmed that Christ was consubstantial with the Father and that He was also truly man. The Nestorians, who had accepted the basic affirmations of the first two councils, found this clause to be offensive. They rejected all later doctrinal innovations as unwarranted. Their position was quite extreme in denying a real union of the two natures of Christ in one person. On the other hand, the Monophysites, largely centered in Egypt, accepted the decisions of the first three ecumenical councils (Nicea, Constantinople, and Ephesus), but rejected the union of the two natures in the one person of Christ. Their position was also extreme in insisting on a mixture of the two natures to the point that the human nature of Christ was virtually absorbed into the Divine. The insistence at Ephesus and Chalcedon that the term *theotokos* should be applied to the Virgin Mary caused the Nestorians to withdraw formally from the E church. But controversy continued in the E. It now focused on the will of Christ. Did Christ possess two wills or one? At the sixth ecumenical council, the Council of Constantinople of 680, it was decided that Christ possessed two wills acting in perfect harmony, following the general leading of the Council of Chalcedon. The Monophysites rejected this solution and withdrew to form the Maronite Church, which later entered into communion with Rome in the twelfth century.

From the fifth to the eleventh century there was continuous theological controversy between the E and the W, caused by the doctrinal and ecclesiastical innovations which Rome had introduced and in the constantly expanding claims of the papacy to both spiritual and political supremacy. In the W it became the practice to limit the administration of confirmation to the bishops and to require the use of unleavened bread in the eucharist. The growing insistence on clerical celibacy at all levels in the W was offensive in the E, where the priests were allowed to marry. Even more obnoxious was the action of the W church in adding the *filioque* clause to the Niceno-Constantinopolitan Creed of 381 at the Synod of Toledo in 589. This action was taken without the approval of an ecumenical council and without any consultation with the Greek church. The clause, which affirmed that the Holy Spirit proceeds from the Son as well as from the Father, was regarded as a necessary safeguard against Arianism, but it was viewed with deep suspicion in the E.

Equally important, however, in the growing estrangement between the E and the W was the growth of papal power. In the early church, Rome, Alexandria, and Antioch had all stood out as churches of great pre-eminence, but the division of the empire in 395 had given to Rome a peculiar place of prominence in the W which could not be claimed by any patriarch in the E. This commanding position given to Rome by geography and politics was reinforced by the great ability of some of the early popes, notably Leo I (440-461) and Gregory I (590-604) who gave to Rome a new dignity because of the way in which they administered the papal office. But there was still another factor at work which increased the prestige of the W Roman church. By 400 it was beginning to be clear that the intellectual and theological leadership of the church was also passing to the W with the appearance of Jerome, Ambrose, and Augustine. Thus the E was threatened with the loss of both its political and intellectual leadership. The pattern was sufficiently clear for the E to take note. The final break, however, did not take place until 1054, when Pope Leo IX placed the whole Eastern Orthodox Church under sentence of excommunication. This action, coupled with the flagrant actions of the Norman crusaders and the sack of Constantinople by the Fourth Crusade in 1204, made reconciliation virtually impossible.

Gregory IX (1227-1241) made the first serious effort to heal the breach when he entered into negotiations with Germanus, the Patriarch of Constantinople, but the conditions which he laid down for reunion were impossible for the E to accept. He required the acceptance of papal supremacy and the use of unleavened bread in the eucharist. Gregory was willing to allow the omission of the *filioque* clause in the creed on condition that the E should burn all the books which had been written against Rome. Later in this same century Innocent IV (1243-1254) and then Clement IV (1265-1268) renewed negotiations on terms much like those offered by Gregory IX. The last great effort to secure reunion during the Middle Ages was made during the Council of Florence in 1439. This project was dear to the heart of Eugenius IV. The emperor, John Paleologus, and the patriarch, Joseph of Constantinople, appeared at the council to secure papal aid against the Turks who were threatening Constantinople. The E delegates agreed to the *filioque* clause and an ambiguous statement concerning papal supremacy. This agreement was repudiated as soon as the E delegates returned home. The fall of Constantinople to the Turks in 1450 brought a dramatic change in the life of the E church.

Creeds and Later History

Creeds have never had the same importance in the life of the Eastern Orthodox Church which they have had in both the Roman and Protestant churches. It has continued to hold firmly to the decisions of the first seven councils as expressions of its faith and has added to them the canons of the Trullan Synod of 692. During the Reformation there was some contact between the E church and the Reformers. Melanchthon sent a copy of his Greek translation of the Augsburg Confession to the Patriarch of Constantinople. Somewhat later the Patriarch Jerome officially condemned the distinctive doctrines of Lutheranism in his *Censura Orientalis Ecclesiae*. However, the Reformation continued to have some impact in the E, and then in the early part of the 17th century Cyril Lucaris, Patriarch of Constantinople, made a serious effort to reform the E church by bringing its doctrine and liturgy into harmony with Calvinism. For this purpose he sent young theologians to Geneva, the Netherlands, and England. This attempt met with such vigorous opposition that it ended in failure and in Cyril's martyrdom. As a result, however, the E church issued several confessional statements defining its position in distinction from both the RC and the Protestant positions. In 1640 Peter Mogila, the Metropolitan of Kiev, drew up a confession which was accepted by the four E patriarchs and then by the

Synod of Jerusalem in 1672 as the creed of all Orthodoxy. This synod of 1672 is probably the most important in the modern history of the Eastern Orthodox Church. It published in eighteen articles the Confession of Dositheus, Patriarch of Jerusalem at the time, which was accepted by the Orthodox church in Russia in 1838.

After the fall of Constantinople the concept of Moscow as the Third Rome emerged. This view insisted that Moscow was divinely appointed to succeed both Rome and Constantinople, and that as the Third Rome it would endure to the end of time. This trend was strengthened when Ivan III of Moscow married Sophia of the Byzantine royal family in 1472. In 1589 Moscow achieved new heights when Jeremiah of Constantinople presided over the consecration of an independent patriarch. Nikon, elected patriarch in 1652, engaged in the task of making the czar of Russia the leader of all Orthodox churches. The deep suspicion with which the Greeks and the Russians viewed each other proved a formidable obstacle to the success of such an undertaking. But the attempt also produced a schism within the Russian church in the withdrawal of the "Old Believers."

In the 20th century the Eastern Orthodox, and RC and Protestant churches have moved much closer together, and the E church sent several observers to Vatican II Council in 1963. In 1964, and again in 1965, the Patriarch Athenagoras and Pope Paul VI met in Jerusalem and retracted the anathemas which their respective predecessors had hurled against each other in 1054. E Orthodoxy, in its various branches, has also involved itself in the ecumenical movement through membership in the World Council of Churches.

Bibliography:

W. F. Adeny, *The Greek and Eastern Churches* (Edinburgh, 1908).

E. Benz, *The Eastern Orthodox Church* (Chicago, 1963).

G. P. Feddov, *The Russian Religious Mind* (Cambridge, 1946), 2 vols.

J. Gill, *The Council of Florence* (Cambridge, 1959).

V. Lossky, *The Mystical Theology of the Eastern Church* (London, 1957).

J. M. Neale, *The Holy Eastern Church* (London, 1873), 4 vols.

J. G. Walch, *Historia Controversiae de Processu Spiritus Sancti* (Jena, 1751).

N. Zernov, *Eastern Christendom* (London, 1961).

C. Gregg Singer

EATING. The basic meal in Biblical times was bread with some extras such as milk, cheese, salad, olives, fruit, or honey (Num. 11:5). Flat bread formed either a plate or a rolled sandwich. Meat was eaten at festivals after sacrifices had been offered (Lev. 7:11-18) and at special celebrations (Luke 15:23, 29). The AV translation of "meat" for "food," once standard, is misleading today.

Metaphorically one eats (absorbs and digests) the Word of God (Ps. 119: 103; Jer. 15:16; Heb. 5:11-14) and is sustained by Christ, the Living Bread (John 6:30 ff.). Eating and drinking art the central acts in the Lord's supper.

EBAL, one of the twin mountains which stand on the sides of the valley of Shechem. This one stands at 3080 feet above sea level and forms the N wall of the modern city of Nablus (the ancient Shechem). Its twin, Gerizim, bounds the S portion of the valley city and has a crest reaching to 2890 feet.

It was on the crest and sides of Ebal that the curses for disobedience to God's law were read. Upon Gerizim were read the blessings. Moses had commanded that this be done on Israel's entrance into Palestine (Deut. 27:4-13; 11:29), and Joshua saw to it that this moving ceremony was performed (Josh. 8:30-35). Upon Ebal the tribes of Reuben, Gad, Asher, Zebulun, Dan, and

Naphtali repeated the curses (Deut. 27:13-26; 28:15-68), while the other tribes stood on Gerizim on the opposite side of this natural amphitheater to repeat the blessings (Deut. 27:12; 28:1-14).

"Har Ebal" to the Israelis and "Sitti Salamigah" to the Moslems, with the remains of tombs at its foot, stands today above Nablus in Samaria as a reminder of the Biblical past. Disobedience to God's law brought on the prophesied curses. Today Ebal is a former Jordanian territory, now in Israeli hands.

GARY G. COHEN

EBED:

(1) An Ephraimite whose son, Gaal, rebelled against Abimelech (Judges 9:26 ff.).

(2) An exile who returned with Ezra (Ezra 8:6).

EBED-MELECH, an Ethiopian courtier of the Judean King Zedekiah. His name appropriately means "servant of the king." He made a plea for Jeremiah, who had been thrown into a dungeon to die a miserable death. Ebed-melech asked and received the king's permission to take Jeremiah out of the dungeon. He took great care in pulling the prophet out of the dungeon. For his care he received the promise of the Lord that he would survive the destruction of Jerusalem (Jer. 38:7-13; 39:15-18).

EBENEZER, "stone of help." This name occurs twice in the Bible:

(1) In I Sam. 4:1 it is the name of a place where the Israelites encamped facing the Philistines, who had pitched their tents at Aphek. It is possible that the place may be identified with the present site of Deir Balluth.

(2) In I Sam. 7:12 it is the name of a memorial stone erected by Samuel, who wanted to perpetuate the memory of the victory which the Lord had given to the Israelites over the Philistines between Mizpah and Shen. Because the location of Shen is unknown, the place of this second Ebenezer cannot be determined exactly.

EBER. A descendant of Shem, who is listed in Gen. 10:24, 25 and 11:14-17. His name shows that he was the ancestor of the Hebrews (Gen. 10:21; Num. 24:24). Thus, although the term *Hebrew* may later have been used in inscriptions as a class name, it was originally racial.

See HEBREWS.

EBIASAPH, "father has increased," a division of the Levites descended from Korah, which seems to have been responsible for doorkeeping duties in the Temple. This name is found in I Chron. 6:23, 37, but in Ex. 6:24 an alternative form, Abiasaph, is found, which means "father has gathered." In I Chron. 9:19; 26:1, Ebiasaph should be read for Asaph.

EBIONITES, a name given to Jewish-Christian sects exhibiting certain tendencies of thought in the early history of the Christian church. Historically, they were the product of conflict between rigid Judaism and the simpler, comparatively unstructured character of early Christianity. They were more recognizable for their Jewish than for their Christian attributes, however, and as time progressed they became increasingly detached from orthodox Christianity. At the point of their extinction in the 5th century A.D. they were regarded as heretical.

Name. While it is evident that the sects derived their designation from the Hebrew term meaning "poor," it is far from certain as to why the Ebionites were thus described. Patristic writers such as Origen ridiculed them for their poverty of intellect, faith, and Christology. The Dead Sea Scrolls have shown the existence of a pre-Christian

Jewish sect which in its formularies described itself as "poor" to indicate that its members alone were faithful to the revelation of God through Moses, as opposed to all other priesthoods, which they deemed apostate. Conceivably the early Ebionites were following this general tradition, since all the deviant sects made a point of exalting the Law, even at the expense of diminishing the person of Christ.

Types of Ebionism. It is far from easy to classify the various tendencies of Ebionite thought because the patristic writers, who have preserved so much of the information about the Ebionites, were not particularly clear either about who actually were Ebionites or what their heretical views were. In addition, the sects were dispersed between Syria and Rome, and the doctrines propounded by differing bodies were apt to vary with local influences. Epiphanius and Jerome discussed some 4th century A.D. Nazarene Ebionites who lived in Transjordan, but Epiphanius seemed confused about their tenets. They accepted the supernatural origin of Christ, but they held to a Christology which was otherwise unclear. They desired to remain Jews and accepted the obligations of the Mosaic law.

Irenaeus, Eusebius, and others described a Pharisaic or non-gnostic Ebionism which followed the teachings of Cerinthus. This man held that Jesus was born an ordinary mortal, but that after His baptism the "Christ" descended upon Him, leaving Him again shortly before the crucifixion. Jesus was justified before God by fulfilling the law, and hence the sectarians believed that through keeping the whole law they could become "Christs" also. In general they were monotheists, they were not Trinitarians, and in their rigid exclusion of the Gentiles they exhibited a movement away from Christianity. There were also gnostic elements in their Christology, particularly in the view that a material, and which to them would mean evil, Jesus was unable to unite into one personality with the spiritual, and therefore fundamentally good, Christ.

What may be called Essenic Ebionism was described by Epiphanius and differed from other forms in incorporating non-Jewish elements into its tenets. However, it was decidedly Pharisaic in character, emphasizing the Law, circumcision, and sabbath observance, while repudiating the virgin birth and Pauline Christianity in general. Essenic Ebionite Christology was far from uniform, with some groups maintaining that Christ was a superior spiritual being and others that He was a mere mortal of unusual virtue. Most of these Ebionites thought of Christ as the successor of Moses, so that for them Christianity was actually the fullest expression of historic Mosaism. Their canon of Scripture comprised part of the Pentateuch and St. Matthew's Gospel only, but they were unusual in rejecting the whole sacrificial system. Like others they were vegetarians and ascetics, who renounced wine in their celebration of the Lord's supper in favor of water. At an early stage these Ebionites rejected the institution of marriage, but later groups came to accept it. They regarded matter as evil and tended to withdraw from worldly pursuits to avoid contamination. Their doctrine of the immortality of the soul had prominent gnostic overtones. A type of gnosticism that differed little from Essenic Ebionitism was found in the book of Elkesai and the pseudo-Clementine writings. It sought to promote Mosaism as a world religion.

Conclusion. The degeneration of Ebionism resulted from its breach with Christianity as it developed and from its impoverished Christology. In the end its elements were absorbed either by Jewish factions or heathen speculative groups.

Do Not Take From This Room